RICHARD WAGNER

ROUTLEDGE MUSIC BIBLIOGRAPHIES
Series Editor: Brad Eden

COMPOSERS

Isaac Albéniz (1998)
Walter A. Clark

C. P. E. Bach (2002)
Doris Powers

Samuel Barber (2001)
Wayne C. Wentzel

Béla Bartók (1997)
Second Edition
Elliot Antokoletz

Vincenzo Bellini (2002)
Stephen A. Willier

Alban Berg (1996)
Bryan R. Simms

Leonard Bernstein (2001)
Paul R. Laird

Benjamin Britten (1996)
Peter J. Hodgson

Elliott Carter (2000)
John F. Link

Carlos Chávez (1998)
Robert L. Parker

Frédéric Chopin (1999)
William Smialek

Aaron Copland (2001)
Marta Robertson and Robin Armstrong

Gaetano Donizetti (2000)
James P. Cassaro

Edward Elgar (1993)
Christopher Kent

Gabriel Fauré (1999)
Edward R. Phillips

Charles Ives (2002)
Gayle Sherwood

Scott Joplin (1998)
Nancy R. Ping-Robbins

Zoltán Kodály (1998)
Michael Houlahan and Philip Tacka

Guillaume de Machaut (1995)
Lawrence Earp

Felix Mendelssohn Bartholdy (2001)
John Michael Cooper

Giovanni Battista Pergolesi (2001)
Clara Marvin

Giacomo Puccini (1999)
Linda B. Fairtile

Groachino Rossini (2002)
Denise P. Gallo

Alessandro and Domenico Scarlatti
(1993)
Carole F. Vidali

Jean Sibelius (1998)
Glenda D. Goss

Giuseppe Verdi (1998)
Gregory Harwood

Tomás Luis de Victoria (1998)
Eugene Casjen Cramer

Richard Wagner (2002)
Michael Saffle

GENRES

Central European Folk Music (1996)
Philip V. Bohlman

Choral Music (2001)
Avery T. Sharp and James Michael Floyd

Jazz Research and Performance Materials,
Second Edition (1995)
Eddie S. Meadows

Music in Canada (1997)
Carl Morey

North American Indian Music (1997)
Richard Keeling

Opera, Second edition (2001)
Guy Marco

Serial Music and Serialism (2001)
Johns D. Vander Weg

RICHARD WAGNER
A GUIDE TO RESEARCH

MICHAEL SAFFLE

ROUTLEDGE MUSIC BIBLIOGRAPHIES
ROUTLEDGE
NEW YORK AND LONDON

Published in 2002 by
Routledge
29 West 35th Street
New York, NY 10001

Published in Great Britain by
Routledge
11 New Fetter Lane
London EC4P 4EE

Routledge is an imprint of the Taylor & Francis Group.
Copyright © 2002 by Routledge

Printed in the United States of America on acid-free paper.

10 9 8 7 6 5 4 3 2 1

Library of Congress Cataloging-in-Publication Data

Saffle, Michael, 1946–
    Richard Wagner : a guide to research / Michael Saffle.
        p. cm.—(Routledge music bibliographies)
    Includes index.
    ISBN 0-8240-5695-7
    1. Wagner, Richard, 1813–1883—Bibliography. I. Title. II. Series.

ML134.W1 S24 2002
016.7821'092—dc21

                                                          2001048162

for Thomas, who helped me get started

Contents

Acknowledgments

The present research guide could not have been completed without the assistance of a number of individuals and organizations. I would like to thank Virginia Polytechnic Institute and State University for travel monies that enabled me to pay extended visits to the Library of Congress (1994) and the Harvard University Libraries (1996, 2000) on behalf of researching and writing the guide. The Fulbright Foundation, which awarded me the Bicentennial Fulbright Professorship of American Studies at the University of Helsinki for the 2000–2001 academic year, gave me a chance to compile much of the guide and research portions of its contents.

James Deaville, James R. Heintze, and Günther Fischer—the last an official of the Zentrale Verwaltung, Richard-Wagner-Museum, Bayreuth—sent me photocopies of articles I was unable to locate in American archives. The editors and staff at Routledge (previously Garland Publishing) deserve special thanks for their assistance and almost legendary patience. I am especially grateful to Marie Ellen Larcada for proposing the present project to me, and to Richard Carlin and Henry Bashwiner for their many helpful suggestions. Finally, the faculty and staff of the Renvall Institute of Historical Studies in Helsinki made my work much more efficient and easier; as did the staffs of the Harvard University libraries, the British Library, London, and the libraries of the University of Toronto, the University of Virginia, and Virginia Tech.

I am, as always, grateful to my wife Sue for her innumerable kindnesses and patience. My son's contribution to the present volume is acknowledged in its dedication.

To Users of this Research Guide

In the following chapters, each separately annotated book and article is identified by author(s), title, editor(s) and/or translator(s) if any, publication information (place, publisher, year, and number of pages if a book; periodical title, volume, date, and page range if an article), and ISBN, ISSN, and/or Library of Congress shelf-numbers. Thus the first citation appears as:

1. *The Wagner Compendium: A Guide to Wagner's Life and Music*, ed. Barry Millington. New York: Schirmer, 1992. 431pp. ISBN 0028713591 ML410.W13W122 1992

Relevant items are also identified by edition(s) and/or series title and number(s), if any. Numbered editions are identified as "2nd ed.," "3rd ed.," and so on; unnumbered editions are described as briefly as possible; series titles without numbers or that might be mistaken for item titles are placed in quotation marks. Thus Millington's volume-length Wagner survey study is identified as:

9. Millington, Barry. *Wagner*, corrected rev. ed. "Master Musicians Series." . . .

Because LC numbers vary from library to library,[1] those given below have either been confirmed through the Library's own on-line catalog or appear on CIPs (Copyright Information Pages) in the publications themselves; a few exceptions are identified in relevant annotations. ISBNs pertain whenever relevant to hardcover rather than paperback editions.

Each item separately identified and described is assigned a number; thus "1" refers to the *Wagner Compendium*, "2" to the *Wagner Handbook* edited by Ulrich Müller and Peter Wapnewski (including the German edition of 1986, described in the annotation), and so on. In many cases the sources of chapters and articles are described in terms of these item numbers; thus Millington's synopsis of Wagner's compositional output, published in the *Compendium*, is cited as:

87. Millington, Barry. "The Music." In item 1, pp. 270–324.

Items cross-referenced are identified by asterisks (*) as well as item numbers; item 87, for instance, is cross-referenced as follows:

*   Millington, Barry. "The Music." Described as item 87.

Certain abbreviations and typographical practices are employed *vis-à-vis* works titles. Wagner's operas and music dramas, for example, are identified in annotations by abbreviated titles: thus *Tristan* (instead of *Tristan und Isolde*), *Holländer* (instead of *Der fliegende Holländer* or "The Flying Dutchman"), and "the *Ring*" (instead of *Der Ring des Nibelungen*). In book and article titles, the use of italics—if any—is replaced by double or single quotation marks; thus the title of item 645 is given as *Wagner's "Ring of the Nibelung": A Companion*, that of item 646 as *A Guide to the Ring of the Nibelungs: The Trilogy [sic] of Richard Wagner* (because no italics or quotation marks appear in the original title; "*sic*" here refers to the fact that there are four rather than three parts to the *Ring*), item 661 as "The Structure of the 'Ring' and Its Evolution," and so on.

Square brackets identify modifications to or comments on direct quotations. Parentheses are used throughout to separate item and/or page numbers from other portions of annotations.

Except for Russian words and titles, which are transliterated, and a very few Icelandic and Greek characters, which are given in their original forms, all citations to languages other than English appear below as they do in the sources consulted. In the index, the German "ß" is alphabetized as "ss"; all other foreign-language characters and diacritical marks are ignored in alphabetization.

I

Introduction

WAGNER IN 1,000 WORDS

Born in Leipzig on 22 May 1813, the son of Carl Friedrich Wagner (or Ludwig Geyer) and Johanna Rosine Wagner, Wilhelm Richard Wagner grew up in a Leipzig household filled with enthusiasm for the theater; later Richard developed enthusiasms of his own for music, antiquity, and the opera. Lessons in piano, violin, and the elements of composition anticipated his career as a music-dramatist. By 1833, when he left Leipzig and university studies in law to settle in Würzburg, Wagner had written a symphony and several sonatas, and arranged for piano the Ninth Symphony of his musical idol Beethoven; the following year he began work on *Das Liebesverbot*, based on *Measure for Measure* by his dramatic idol Shakespeare.

Wagner's early career was tumultuous; during the later 1830s and most of the 1840s he held musical-theatrical positions in Magdeburg, Königsberg, Riga, and Dresden; however, his attempt to break into Paris's musical establishment failed dismally. By May 1849, when he participated in the Dresden revolution, he had completed *Rienzi*, *Der fliegede Holländer*, *Tannhäuser*, and *Lohengrin*, published pamphlets, articles, and reviews, and made public his anti-royalist, aesthetically radical sympathies. Condemned to death in absentia by Saxon officials, Wagner fled to Switzerland with the help of his loyal colleague, sometime friend, and (later) father-in-law Franz Liszt. He spent the 1850s writing books and articles—*Opera and Drama*, *Art and Revolution*, and the dreadful *Jewishness in Music* among them—and hoping for a pardon; visits to London and Paris added to his growing reputation as a brilliant innovator and a difficult human being. By 1853 he had completed the poem for what eventually became *Der Ring des Nibelungen*; by 1856 he had written *Das Rheingold* and *Die Walküre* (two of its four parts) and begun work on a third, *Siegfried*; *Tristan und Isolde*, conceived during his love affair with Mathilde Wesendonk (one of several liaisons he conducted during his insatiably self-aggrandizing life), was finished in 1859. In 1862 he received a full amnesty from German officials; the previous year, however, *Tannhäuser* failed spectacularly in Paris and there seemed little hope of a *Tristan* production.

In 1864, rescued from enormous debts and mounting disillusionment by Ludwig II, King of Bavaria, Wagner settled briefly in Munich. *Tristan* received its premiere the following year there, but Wagner's demands upon the Bavarian treasury and disapproval over his liaison with Cosima Liszt von Bülow, then wife of Hans von Bülow (who, in 1868, conducted the premiere of *Die Meistersinger* in Munich), led to Wagner's "dismissal" from that city in December 1865. The following year his long-suffering wife Minna finally died (they had wed in 1836), and the composer settled with Cosima at Tribschen on Lake Lucerne. They were married in 1870, although their daughter, Isolde, had been born five years earlier; their other children, Eva and Siegfried, appeared in 1867 and 1869. The Franco-Prussian War and complex shifts in Wagner's political enthusiasms occurred almost simultaneously with renewed work on *Siegfried*, which he completed in 1871; the fourth and final *Ring* music drama, *Die Götterdämmerung*, dates from 1873 through 1874. Meanwhile the Wagners met and befriended the remarkable, mentally unstable philologist-turned-philosopher Friedrich Nietzsche, whose "pro and contra" Wagner pronouncements rank among the most exciting in music history.

In the Bavarian town of Bayreuth, Wagner built his own home (Haus Wahnfried, completed in 1874), and, in 1872, he laid the cornerstone for his own theater there. Tremendous effort and last-minute financial assistance from Ludwig II enabled the Festspielhaus to open in 1876 for the first complete *Ring* production; a second Festival, presented in 1882, witnessed the premiere of the "stage-consecration play" *Parsifal*, Wagner's last music drama. In 1880, at the urging of his physician, the composer moved with his family to Italy; it was in Venice—apparently after a row with Cosima over his interest in a pretty English singer named Carrie Pringle—that he suffered a heart attack and died on 13 February 1883. Ludwig II followed Wagner to the grave in 1886; so did Liszt, but not before finishing several remarkable piano pieces "about" Venice and his son-in-law's death. Cosima and son Siegfried succeeded Wagner as directors of the Bayreuth Festival, which continues to this day; Cosima died only in 1930, after welcoming Adolf Hitler to the Festspielhaus. Bayreuth's "Nazi legacy" still haunts Wagner's descendents and Germany's international reputation; for decades it was forbidden to perform any of the composer's works in Israel.

Wagner gave the world more than Bayreuth, however; more even than great music and an intoxicating vision of Germany Triumphant. His compositions, which look backward in certain respects to the works of Beethoven, Marschner, Meyerbeer, Spohr, and Carl Maria von Weber, influenced many of his contemporaries and successors, including Berg, Bruckner, Debussy, Elgar, Franck, Edward MacDowell, Mahler, Massanet, Schoenberg, Sibelius, Richard Strauss, and Hugo Wolf. (Wagner's musical interactions with Berlioz, Brahms, and Liszt were more complex; each influenced and was influenced by the other.) "Wagnerism" was perhaps even more influential; movements sprang up in America and almost every part of late-nineteenth- and early-twentieth-century Europe, including Catalonia, Hungary, and Russia. Many artists were influenced by this movement, including French poets, painters, and novelists Baudelaire, Fantin-Latour, Monet, Proust, Renoir, and Valéry; English authors and illustrators Beardsley, Eliot, Joyce, Lawrence, Bernard Shaw, and Oscar Wilde; and German cultural icons Heinrich and Thomas Mann, among a host of others, including Hitler. Wagner helped shape our understanding of the Middle Ages, of the German stage, and of art as business and politics. His impact on Adorno, on Thomas Mann, on Nietzsche, on film music (think of John Williams and the *Star Wars* movies), on conducting, staging, and operatic singing, on musical instruments (the Wagner tuba), and on musicologists and aestheticians from Dahlhaus to Hanslick to Ernest Newman—should not be underestimated. Even Wagner's prose polemics, often dismissed (except by German scholars), seem today both more sensible and more outrageous than they once did; postmodernist critics are turning increasingly to Wagner, and an entire industry has grown up around Wagner's anti-Semitic pronouncements.

CONCERNING THE PRESENT RESEARCH GUIDE

Those familiar with Richard Wagner's career, compositions, and influence know that a great deal has been written about him. The number of books and articles devoted exclusively to Wagner's life and music dramas, for example, may have been exaggerated in the past, but it is safe to say there are thousands of them. If one also takes into account the editions of his compositions, correspondence, and prose works, the total probably reaches the tens of thousands. Add to this figure the reviews of Wagner productions, performances, and recordings published during the last 160 years in hundreds of newspapers and magazines around the world, and the total may reach the hundreds of thousands.

These estimates are by no means inflated. In his survey of German Wagner criticism prior to the end of 1855 (item 954), Helmut Kirchmeyer not only identifies but reprints the texts of some 3,257 periodical publications of the 1840s and 1850s. Many of these were overlooked or ignored by Nicholas Oesterlein, whose "comprehensive" Wagner bibliography (item 67) appeared in 1873 and mentions some 10,200 artifacts. The *National Union Catalog*'s "Pre-1956" series of volumes identifies more than 2,500 editions of individual music-drama texts and scores, and that source is far from complete.[2] In early 2001, on-line and CD-ROM databases provided references to some 10,000 scholarly publications devoted in whole or part to Wagnerian issues.

When editors at Garland Publishing—today, Routledge—asked me to prepare a Wagner research guide, they also asked me to confine myself to four hundred printed pages of text, including front matter, a brief survey of the composer's life and works, and an index of authors, editors, and translators. To meet those goals, or try to, I set out initially to identify and describe no more than one thousand publications in some 350 pages of print. As you can see, the guide you hold in your hands is some 450 pages long and includes 1,175 numbered citations. In no sense, therefore, do I consider my work "complete." It isn't, nor was it ever intended to be. Anyone who wishes can easily locate studies I overlooked, or deliberately chose to ignore, or mention only in passing. And new Wagner publications appear in print virtually every day.[3]

The questions remain, however: What to include? and what to leave out? In a review-article devoted to Tom Sutcliffe's *Believing in Opera* (London: Faber & Faber, 1998), James Treadwell indirectly identifies one of the problems associated with the Wagner literature in general and especially with performance and production studies:

> [The a]rguments . . . have the same kind of wearisome predictability as family squabbles. One enters the debate with resignation rather than trepidation, the much-rehearsed script already known to all parties. Appeals to the historical inevitability of reinterpretation will be countered by citations of the composer's and/or librettist's instructions. What to one person looks like theatrical inventiveness is absurd self-indulgence to another. Directors are brilliant interpreters or arrogant and patronizing buffoons. Tradition and innovation square off against each other, as if the former never had anything to do with the latter. We've heard it all before.[4]

This does not mean, however, that conflicting claims of "tradition and innovation" are of little interest to Wagner researchers. Quite the contrary: *Rezeption* is an acknowledged musicological specialty. On the other hand, Sutcliffe has a point; reviews are legion, and many of them cover the same ground. With the exception of those incorporated or examined in secondary sources, then, reviews of production and performance have been excluded from the present research guide.

Quantity is one issue, quality another. Some experts, John Deathridge among them (see item 152), have argued that there is very little worthwhile Wagner secondary literature. The late Carl Dahlhaus would have agreed. Dahlhaus, in fact, opened the introduction to *Richard Wagner's Music Dramas* (item 566) by stating:

> For decades writing on Wagner was compounded of wide-ranging, historico-philosophical speculation, insatiable delight in the minutiae of his life, however far-fetched or trivial, and a curious complacency when it came to the study of the music, which hardly aspired to anything beyond labeling the leitmotive. Views were stated in one of two tones of voice: emphatic or outraged. And even today, a hundred years after the founding of the theatre in Bayreuth, people who write about Wagner veer to one pole or the other: to polemics or apologetics. (item 566, p. 1)

Unfortunately, Dahlhaus's argument is in large part indefensible. There is and has long been far more to Wagner scholarship than "speculation," "minutiae," and "curious complacency." True, many outstanding studies—including the *New Grove Wagner* volume (item 3), itself a collaboration by Deathridge and Dahlhaus, as well as the *Sämtliche Werke* edition of Wagner's compositions co-edited by Dahlhaus (item 156) and the *Wagner-Werk-Verzeichnis* (or "*WWV*"; item 83) co-written by Deathridge—postdate Dahlhaus's statement above, which appeared in print for the first time in 1971. On the other hand, Dahlhaus had his own "emphatic" agenda—one that, for better or worse, has itself become part of an all-too-often "outraged" Wagner literature.[5] Finally, Dahlhaus was especially interested in defending the aesthetic significance of Wagner's music dramas against critics of certain social-critical persuasions. But the issues those critics have sought to explore, anti-semitism among them, are part and parcel of Wagner's cultural legacy. They cannot and should not be ignored.

To attempt to deal with all this—which is to say, to attempt to meet or at least approach my original goals involving numbers of pages and annotations—I adopted six fundamental strategies. The first five of these involved selecting for annotation those books, monographs, anthologies, editions, and articles that

1. were of outstanding quality or interest;

2. reflected the results of recent researches—i.e., were published prior to 31 December 2000; a few important studies, such as the *"New Grove 2"* Wagner article (item 26), were too recent to be dealt with carefully in the pages that follow;

3. were written in English or had appeared in English-language editions;

4. reported on various topics in Wagner scholarship, not simply biographical or musical ones; and

5. contained the word(s) "Wagner," "Wagnerian," "Wagnerism(s)," or the name of one of Wagner's works in their titles or subtitles.

The sixth involved selecting studies that collectively represented as many phases and aspects of Wagner scholarship as possible.[6]

Sooner or later I had to break every one of my own rules. There simply are no studies "of outstanding quality or importance" devoted, say, to "Wagner and homosexuality." The one study I do cite, Hanns Fuchs's *Richard Wagner und die Homosexualität* (item 426), is merely the most familiar; it does not happen to have appeared in print recently, much less in English.[7] Another lackluster publication is Hermann Barth's *Internationale Wagner-Bibliographie* (item 66), which

I place at the beginning of the subsection on "Bibliographies" in chapter three solely because it is the closest thing to a comprehensive modern reference work. It, too, is in German. So are several of the finest studies dealing with Wagner and medieval legends and literatures, and these were published decades or even a century ago; among them—at least according to Elizabeth Magee, whose *Richard Wagner and the Nibelungs* (item 663) has been proclaimed the finest recent work in the field—is Wolfgang Golther's *Sagensgeschichtliche Grundlagen der Ringdichtung Richard Wagners*, which I was unable to consult at all.

I also had to refer to a very few important works of criticism "about" Wagner that do not mention him or any of his music dramas on their title pages. Joseph Kerman's "Opera as Symphonic Poem" (item 979) is a case in point, although every Wagnerian understands that the title of Kerman's volume—*Opera as Drama*—is a pun on the title of Wagner's own treatise *Opera and Drama*. Another exception is Carolyn Abbate's *Unsung Voices: Opera and Musical Narrative in the Nineteenth Century* (item 990), which deals mostly, but by no means exclusively, with the *Ring*. On the other hand, I omitted publications as important as *Nineteenth-Century Music* by Dahlhaus primarily because it isn't "Wagner-specific." For the same reason I omitted such important volumes as the *Oxford History of Music*, Paul Henry Lang's *Music in Western Civilization*, and Rey M. Longyear's *Nineteenth-Century Romanticism in Music*, as well as important works written in other languages.

This is not to say that I always broke my own rules. Sometimes I merely bent them. I strove, for instance, to include studies by a variety of researchers rather than limit my choices to "reputable" scholars. I did not even try to include all of Dahlhaus's Wagner publications; there simply wasn't room. Nor did Dahlhaus concern himself with a great many Wagnerian topics, especially non-German ones. It seems to be true that there are more books and articles about Wagner in German than other continental European languages. It is indefensible to argue, however, that Karel Wauters's *Wagner en Vlaanderen, 1844–1914* ("Wagner in Flanders, 1844–1914," item 1060) is "unimportant" because it is written in Flemish. I emphasize English-language publications because I am, after all, an American,[8] and because I am writing primarily for English-speaking readers. But I also deal with a great many German publications, as well as with some in French, Italian, and—with regard to certain specialized subjects—Catalan, Hungarian, Latvian, Polish, and Spanish. Sometimes I even cite studies missing from standard reference works simply because they are (or were) missing. Unusual items such as Elaine Padman's *Wagner* for children (item 316), or *Les Rendez-vous Wagnériens* by Henri Perrier (item 433), or Hans von Wolzogen's *Richard Wagner und die Tierwelt* (see item 425)—the last outfitted with photographs of the composer's dogs!—may not be of the greatest scholarly significance, but what enthusiastic Wagnerian would want to be ignorant of them?

Finally, I made one decision with amateur rather than professional researchers in mind: I "keyed" much of my guide to just two reference works: the

Compendium, edited by Barry Millington (item 1), and the *Handbook,* edited by Ulrich Müller and Peter Wapnewski (item 2). These reference works incorporate the results of a great many studies published prior to the early 1990s. A research guide should be more than a bibliography, more even than a selection of organized and annotated bibliographic entries. It should reflect the state—which is to say, the results—of research at the time of its completion. I felt that the best way to do this, and to reach out to beginning Wagner scholars, was to emphasize the information so readily and intelligently available in the *Handbook* and *Compendium.*

A comparison of several bibliographies devoted in whole or part to *Die Meistersinger von Nürnberg,* just one of Wagner's music dramas, should make the scope and character of the present research guide easier to grasp.

The *New Grove Wagner* bibliography (item 76) identifies in the relevant section just 20 books and articles devoted to *Meistersinger* and published before c. 1983, when the bibliography itself—based on the *New Grove Dictionary* "Wagner" article, published in 1980 (see item 3)—was prepared for press. By contrast, the "select bibliography" appended to John Warrack's *Meistersinger* companion (item 755, pp. 168–72) lists 86 studies, including all but one of the *New Grove Wagner* selections. (The missing selection—Egon Voss's "Wagner's 'Meistersinger' als Oper des deutschen Bürgertums," published in the relevant *rororo Opernbuch* edited by Attila Csampai and Dietmar Holland—cannot be considered a major omission, because both the *New Grove Wagner* bibliography and Warrack include other studies by Voss. I omit it too.[9])

On the other hand, Warrack cites only six *Meistersinger* studies published after 1983 but prior to 1994, when his own volume appeared in print. Furthermore, most of the pre-1983 studies cited by Warrack, but overlooked or ignored by the *New Grove Wagner* authors, were published well before 1980; more than a few of them, in fact, predate the twentieth century. Other differences involve which studies—this also means, what kinds of studies—are cited, and where. The *New Grove Wagner* bibliography, for instance, does not specifically identify Ludwig Finscher's discussion of *Meistersinger* counterpoint (item 462), although it does cite the volume (item 447) in which Finscher's discussion appears—a volume, incidentally, edited by Dahlhaus, who also prepared the *New Grove* bibliography. Warrack cites Finscher's discussion separately. Warrack also includes a few "ephemeral" items, albeit by first-rate scholars, such as Deryck Cooke's liner notes for a London LP issued in 1976 and reissued again on CD in 1984. Dahlhaus ignores such material. Finally—this is my interpretation, based on a rather small amount of evidence—Warrack appears to be more interested in English-language publications, the *New Grove Wagner* authors less interested. In fact, throughout the *New Grove Wagner* bibliography there are more than a few references to periodical publications difficult to obtain outside German archives; these include articles published originally or often exclusively in Bayreuth Festival program books between 1924 and 1939 (see item 51).

Compare Warrack's and the *New Grove Wagner*'s bibliographies with the list of sources provided in Millington's *Compendium* (item 1, pp. 412–18). Only six of the 86 *Meistersinger* studies cited by Warrack appear in Millington's list. Two of these—the English National Opera guide book (see item 619), and Alfred Lorenz's classic analytical study (item 482, vol. 3)—are mentioned only in conjunction with the ENO guides as a series and the whole of Lorenz's *Das Geheimnis der Form bei Richard Wagner*. Another volume mentioned in the *Compendium*, Dette and Michael Petzet's *Die Richard Wagner Bühne König Ludwigs II.* (item 840), which Warrack also mentions, is by no means devoted exclusively to *Meistersinger*. Only one study—a paper presented by Warren Darcy at a 1989 Wagner conference in Seattle—is cited only by Millington, who describes it as "forthcoming." We must remember, however, that Millington's is a list of works consulted or mentioned by *Compendium* authors rather than a reference work—which is to say, a bibliography—in its own right. So, too, is the list of publications in the *Handbook* (item 2, pp. 655–80).

All this suggests several things. First, that in spite of their many praiseworthy features, the *Handbook* and *Compendium* are not the best sources of information about publications devoted to *Meistersinger*. Second, that much of the best *Meistersinger* secondary literature appeared in print quite a while ago. Third, that *Meistersinger*—for whatever reason or reasons—may not be as important or interesting as, say, *Tristan und Isolde* or the *Ring*; Millington, for instance, cites ten studies devoted exclusively to *Tristan* and 34 devoted to the *Ring*, as opposed to just seven *Meistersinger* studies. Fourth—and this, unfortunately, is nowhere stated or even implied by Dahlhaus, Millington, Warrack or any of the other authors mentioned above—that because less attention was paid to *Meistersinger* "in the past," less *may* be paid "in the future."

Now consider the *Meistersinger* citations found in chapter ten. In addition to three studies cross-referenced under that work's title—these include Vol. 9 of the *Sämtliche Werke* as well as the studies by Lorenz and Finscher mentioned above—I, too, identify and describe precisely 20 *Meistersinger* books and articles. First, and I feel most important, is Warrack's volume; I list it first in the first—and broadest—category: that of "Guidebooks and Survey Studies." (That it is written in English is fortuitous, but I am more concerned with its quality). I also identify five other studies published during or after 1990, approximately when the *Compendium* and the English-language edition of the *Handbook* were being prepared for press. Of these I want to pause and mention Millington's article "Nuremberg Trial: Is There Anti-Semitism in 'Die Meistersinger'?" (item 773), published in 1991 in the *Cambridge Opera Journal*. Here is a new slant on Wagner's music-drama, and one representative of Wagner studies published during the past ten or fifteen years: a discussion of the composer as anti-semite and a search for possible anti-semitic "encodings" in his stage works. Dahlhaus might have ignored this study, even if it had been available to him. Warrack cites it but was unable, of course, to cite three other studies (items 757 and 769–70) that appeared in print after 1994. On the other hand, I have not ignored earlier publications. Five or six of the books and articles I cite (items 760–61, 764–65, 772, and probably 767) were published before 1914.[10] Two others (items 762, 766) appeared in print for the first time before World War II; it should be noted that one of these, Robert Rayner's *Wagner and "Die Meistersinger"* (item 758), is considered a rare publication by the British Library, London, where I was able to consult a copy.

I cannot claim to have included as many *Meistersinger* citations as has Warrack, although I drew upon his work *and* gave it pride of place in my own. Unlike Warrack, however, I have divided individual *Meistersinger* studies among subcategories ("Document and Source Studies," "Musical Studies," "Performance and Reception Studies," and so on). Finally, I have done my best to identify bibliographies in every one of the books and articles I single out for closer scrutiny. Whenever relevant I also provide information about illustrations, graphs, charts, and musical examples. More than this, it seems to me, I could not have done.

At least a few readers, I am certain, will disagree with this last statement. Perhaps they will someday publish Wagner bibliographies of their own.

Notes

1. Although LC numbers are supposed to be "standard," they are in fact quite variable. Consider *Richard Wagner: ein deutsches Ärgernis*, ed. Klaus Umbach (item 37)—the first volume listed as having "no LC number available" in the present research guide. Brown University's librarians have cataloged it as ML 410 .W2 R523x 1982; Princeton's as ML 410.W2 R523; UCLA's (the University of California, Los Angeles) as ML 410.W12 R53 1982; the University of Pennsylvania's as ML 410.W131 R415 1982; and Williams College's as ML 410.W1 R54 1982. NB: These numbers differ not merely in such details as whether the year of publication is included; they also differ in terms of classification subcategories assigned. Readers of the present guide are advised to consult individual library catalogs before looking for Wagner publications on those institutions' shelves.

2. See the *National Union Catalog: Pre-1956 Imprints*, Vol. 644 (Chicago and London, 1979), especially pp. 467–612. These pages are devoted exclusively to editions ranging from complete scores of *Die Feen* to arrangements of *Tristan* fragments. They do not identify thousands of other Wagner primary and secondary sources.

3. Omitted from the chapters that follow are several studies I was unable to locate for one reason or another. Many of these appeared in print only recently; others are uncommon or were unavailable for examination at various libraries. One example is Bernadette Fantin-Epstein's *Wagner et la Belle Epoque* (Toulouse, 1999); another is *Richard Wagner im Dritten Reich: Ein Schloss Elmau-Symposion*, ed. Saul Friedländer and Jörn Rüsen (Nördlingen, 2000).

4. James Treadwell, "Opera Beyond Belief," *Music & Letters* 80 (1999), p. 595.

5. See James Hepokoski, "The Dahlhaus Project and Its Extra-musicological

Sources," *19th Century Music* 14 (1990–1991), pp. 221–46. See also Arnold Whittall, "Carl Dahlhaus, the Nineteenth Century, and Opera," *Cambridge Opera Journal* 3 (1991), pp. 79–88.

Many contemporary scholars would argue that all of us have agendas; Dahlhaus's agenda is the only one I shall refer to in these pages—besides my own, of course.

6.   Among such "phases and aspects" are Wagner's family, the philosopher Friedrich Nietzsche, and Bayreuth—the last associated especially with Haus Wahnfried, the Festival Theater, and Wagner Festival performances. Scattered throughout the present research guide, therefore, are descriptions of monographs and other works that deal with the composer's wife Cosima (including items 211–12), son Siegfried, grandsons Wieland and Wolfgang, and so on. See chapter V, items 338–44, and chapter XIII, items 1143–75, for information about the composer's ancestors, siblings, spouse Cosima, and descendents. References to Minna [Planer] Wagner, the composer's first wife, are scattered throughout the literature, but little has been written specifically about her and her relationship with husband Richard; exceptions include items 263 and 420.

7.   Certain portions of the Wagner literature are surprisingly large, yet remain obscure (sometimes justifiably so). One of these involves "psychological" studies of the composer's character and works that began appearing in the later nineteenth century and mostly ceased during World War II. In place of most of these studies—Fuchs's is an exception—I cite instead Isolde Vetter's superb article "Wagner in the History of Psychology," published in item 2 (pp. 118–55) and separately identified and described as item 1019. Other portions of the literature, including publications dealing with Wagner and the United States, I mostly ignore; in place of most of them I cite two studies of my own (items 362 and 815), as well as a few publications by other authors (items 598, 1024, and 1052–54).

8.   Throughout the present volume I refer to "the United States" as "America," although the same word is often used in conjunction with "North America" (including Canada and, sometimes, Mexico) and "Latin America" (including Central and South American countries as well as, sometimes, Mexico).

9.   In part because of space considerations, in part because the various ENO handbooks and others in similar series resemble each other quite closely, I cite only one or at most two items in each series. Thus I describe only one of André Le François's guides (that for *Holländer*, item 605), only one of Wakeling Dry's (that for *Lohengrin*, item 637), only two ENO guides (those for *Tannhäuser*, item 619; and *Tristan*, item 721), and so on. Nor do I annotate Csampai's and Holland's *Meistersinger* volume, although I mention it in my comments concerning their *Richard Wagner: Parsifal. Texte, Materialen, Kommentare* (item 780); I also mention the *Opernführer* they published with Irmelin Bürgers and identify its Wagner section (*Opernführer*, pp. 481–551).

10. Two of these—*The Sources and Text of Richard Wagner's "Die Meistersinger von Nürnberg"* by Anna Maude Bowen (item 764), and *Der Meistergesang in Geschichte und Kunst* by Curt Mey (item 772)—were reprinted in the 1970s.

II

Introducing Wagner:
Compendia and Other Survey Studies

Most books and articles devoted to Richard Wagner deal with only one or at most three specific issues: his political opinions, for instance, or his years in Dresden, or harmonic aspects of the Tristan *Prelude. A few publications, however, attempt to deal with* all *of Wagner, or at least with more than a few aspects of his career and accomplishments. This chapter is devoted to identifying and describing these publications; among them are anthologies of studies by one or more scholars, compendia of several kinds, dictionary and encyclopedia entries, handbooks, "readers," and periodicals devoted entirely or primarily to the composer and his world.*

COMPREHENSIVE SURVEY STUDIES

Introductions to Wagner and Wagner Research

Almost every Wagnerian—whether friend or foe, beginning researcher or published scholar—will wish to consult the following compendia:

1. *The Wagner Compendium: A Guide to Wagner's Life and Music*, ed. Barry Millington. New York: Schirmer, 1992. 431pp. ISBN 0028713591 ML410.W13W122 1992

    Not only the best all-around introduction in any language to Wagner's life and character, literary and intellectual activities, prose works, music dramas and other compositions, and a variety of closely related subjects, but the fairest and most up-to-date. Contains items 87, 92, 98, 100, 127, 153, 168, 170, 200, 222, 277, 332, 334–35, 339–40, 378–79, 395, 415, 425, 429, 434–35, 451, 454, 456, 461, 476, 493, 509, 536, 577, 829–31, 833, 838, 926–27, 943, 967, 1008, 1050, 1102, and 1115–16 as well as chapters dealing with Wagner's interest in ancient Greece (pp. 158–61), Wagner's impact on literature (pp. 396–98), German history before and during Wagner's lifetime (pp. 36–49), and philosophical, religious, and literary issues pertaining to Wagner as poet and prose writer (pp. 52–61). Includes a carefully selected bibliography (pp. 412–18) and information about contributors to the volume as a whole (p. 420); see also item 491. Concludes with a useful index. Illustrated with 30 black-and-white reproductions of portraits, caricatures, photographs, and facsimiles of musical manuscripts; among the last are reproductions of autograph pages from *Lohengrin, Meistersinger*, and *Parsifal*, as well as the opening of a draft for the *Faust* overture. Unfortunately, however, no printed musical examples appear in the text itself.

2. *The Wagner Handbook*, ed. Ulrich Müller and Peter Wapnewski; trans. ed. John Deathridge. Cambridge, MA, and London: Harvard University Press, 1992. xv, 711pp. ISBN 0674945301 ML410.W131R41613 1992

   Contains items 99, 126, 152, 199, 347, 394, 399, 449, 459, 491, 533, 576, 578, 828, 834, 909, 996, 1001, 1007, 1019, 1021, 1049, 1101, 1138, and 1145 as well as "The Historical Background" (pp. 36–49), which traces the political evolution of Central Europe before and during Wagner's lifetime. Also contains a translation of the original German foreword by general editors Müller and Wapnewski (pp. ix–x), as well as an introduction by Deathridge (pp. xi–xiv), information on citations (p. xv), and a list of sources useful especially for its citations of secondary studies dealing with psychology and the other arts (pp. 655–80). Concludes with information about contributors (pp. 683–84), as well as indexes identifying references to Wagner's compositions (pp. 685–87), literary works (pp. 689–92), and names and subjects. No plates or other visual images are included, but several essays are illustrated with a variety of handsomely printed musical examples.

   Published originally as the *Richard-Wagner-Handbuch* (Stuttgart, 1986; ISBN 3520824019). Ostensibly the "same" but actually quite different; this edition includes a timeline (pp. 1–5), a family tree (p. 6), and more than a few scattered musical examples. Also includes Manfred Eger's "Richard Wagner in Parodie und Karikatur" (pp. 760–76), with its own illustrations, list of sources, and discography, as well as Dieter Schickling's "Wagner bein Wort genommen: Zur Psychologie seiner Opern" (pp. 792–802); and Dieter Schnebel's "Religiöse Klänge–Klangreligion" (pp. 698–703). In certain respects the English *Handbook* is to be preferred; Josef Rattner's "Richard Wagner im Lichte der Tiefenpsychologie" (pp. 777–91), for instance, is replaced in item 2 with Isolde Vetter's much more fulsome essay (item 1019). On the other hand, the original bibliography (pp. 852–79), compiled by Deathridge, is much more extensive. NB: Portions of both the English and German editions have appeared in print separately; item 1101, for instance, was published for the first time in English in 1985 in *Wagner* magazine (item 49).

Also extremely useful are the following briefer but insightful survey studies:

3. Deathridge, John, and Carl Dahlhaus. *The New Grove Wagner*. London: Macmillan, 1984. xiv, 226pp. ISBN 0393016889 ML410.W1D43 1984 *780.92 W134Yd*

A superb summary of the composer's life and musical-literary legacy, compiled by two of this century's finest Wagner scholars. Contains item 76; includes sixteen illustrations, among them portraits of the composer and his wife Cosima (the daughter of Franz Liszt, her first marriage was to Hans von Bülow) as well as two musical examples, and a number of documentary facsimiles. Also includes a fine works list (pp. 165–93), although one necessarily less complete than the *Wagner-Werk-Verzeichnis* (hereafter *WWV*; item 83) and less informative in terms of compositional circumstances and the stories and production histories associated with various of the music dramas than Millington's ready-reference catalog (item 87). Concludes with an index.

Partially a new work, partially a revision of the article "(Wilhelm) Richard Wagner" published in *The New Grove Dictionary of Music and Musicians*, ed. Stanley Sadie (New York and London, 1980), Vol. 20, pp. 103–45.[1] NB: The author was unable to examine a volume edited by Millington entitled *The New Grove Wagner* published last year by St. Martin's Press (New York, 2000; ISBN 0312233248). Whether this constitutes an edited version of *The New Grove Wagner* or a publication based on the "new" *New Grove* article mentioned below (see item 26), it certainly deserves to be consulted.

4. Magee, Bryan. *Aspects of Wagner*, rev. ed. Oxford and New York: Oxford University Press, 1988. 102pp. ISBN 0192177680 ML410.W13M105 1988 *780.92 W134Yma*

A collection of six concise, convincing essays dealing with "Wagner's Theory of Opera" (pp. 3–16), "Wagnerolary" (pp. 29–44), "Wagner in Performance" (pp. 57–72), and "Wagner as Music" (pp. 73–91), as well as the composer's influence on Western culture—including the presence of Wagnerian elements in T. S. Eliot's *Wasteland*—and his anti-semitism. No illustrations or musical examples. Indexed. Originally published in 1968 by Stein & Day (ML410.W1M24 1969) in a version containing only five essays. The revised edition was reviewed enthusiastically in *Wagner* 10/3 (July, 1989), pp. 121–22.

Finally, those interested in an "easy" introduction to Wagner's life, thought, and works may be amused by:

5. White, Michael, and Kevin Scott with Richard Appignanesi. *Wagner for Beginners*. Cambridge: Icon Books, 1995. 176pp. ISBN 1874166277 ML410.W1W58 1995

A clever and engaging introduction to Wagner's life, works, and thoughts—including his political and racial views—in comic book form.

Includes scattered but "real" musical examples as well as a large number
of quotations from or paraphrases of Wagner's writings, and a one-page
bibliography (p. 174). Similar volumes have appeared in print dealing
with the careers and accomplishments of Karl Marx and Sigmund Freud.
Also published under the title *Introducing Wagner* (New York, 1995) with
the same ISBN.

Another self-consciously light-hearted introductory survey to Wagner's life and works is William Berger's *Wagner Without Fear* (New York:
Vintage, 1998; ISBN 0375700544). Subtitled "Learning to Love—and
Even Enjoy—Opera's Most Demanding Genius," Berger's volume
includes a biographical synopsis, brief discussions of each music drama
from *Holländer* to *Parsifal*, information about Wagner publications,
recordings, and films, a glossary that includes descriptions of "audience
types"—the "we came for 'Kunst' crowd," the "armchair conductors,"
and so on—at Wagner performances (pp. 431–42), two maps, and an
index. No musical examples.

Other Comprehensive Survey Studies

*Most Wagner surveys approach their subject from an historian's perspective: that
is, they work through the composer's life and accomplishments from beginning to
end, pausing frequently, occasionally, or not at all to examine certain issues in
greater detail. Such surveys may be distinguished from biographies by their
greater breadth of scope, and their more technical discussion of the music dramas, instrumental compositions, and/or prose works. Others represent, in effect,
conflations of several semi-independent studies or sections within a single volume. An example of the first kind is described below:*

6. Gregor-Dellin, Martin. *Richard Wagner: His Life, His Work, His Century*,
   trans. J. Maxwell Brownjohn. San Diego, CA: Harcourt, Brace Jovanovich,
   1983. xi, 575pp. ISBN 0151771510 ML410.W1G73413 1983

   Evaluates Wagner's background, career, and personality, and provides at
   least a little information about virtually all of his compositions. Nevertheless, more biographical than comprehensive in focus and scope; Gregor-
   Dellin offers no musical analysis as such. Includes twelve black-and-
   white plates, as well as a brief chronological table of Wagner's career
   (pp. 557–60) and an index. No musical diagrams or examples.

   Originally published in German as *Richard Wagner: Sein Leben—sein
   Werk—sein Jahrhundert* (Munich, 1980); a second edition also exists
   (Munich and Zurich, 1991; ISBN 3492025277), as do other editions
   (Munich and Zurich, 1989; Mainz and Munich, 1983). Reviewed in the

last of these editions—together with items 32, 88, 107, 150, 169, 178, 712, 871, 886, 941, and 954 as well as German editions of items 204 and 893— by Werner Breig in *Die Musikforschung* 40 (1987), pp. 279–84.[2]

Additional examples of both kinds of surveys include the following volumes, evaluated in alphabetical order by authors' surnames:

7. Bauer, Hans-Joachim. *Richard Wagner. Sein Leben und Wirken, oder Die Gefühlwerdung der Vernunft.* Frankfurt a.M.: Propyläen, 1995. 640pp. ISBN 3549054688 ML410.W1B38 1995

Largely biographical; nevertheless, Bauer not only describes a witty and ironic Wagner, but also explains how the man produced many of his musical and literary works. Outfitted with a bibliography (pp. 602–23) that incorporates paragraph-long synopses of various authors' contributions to the literature. Also contains a catalog of works according to *WWV* numbers (pp. 589–602) and a fulsome index (pp. 624–40).

8. Culshaw, John. *Wagner: The Man and his Music.* New York: Metropolitan Opera Guild, 1978. 181pp. ISBN 0525229604 ML410.W1C9

782.1 W134Ycu

A somewhat sanitized introduction to the composer by an expert on his music dramas. Culshaw addresses the average reader and lavishly illustrates his observations with several hundred color and black-and-white plates, most of them depicting scenes from Wagner productions at the Metropolitan Opera, New York City. Concludes with brief sketches by Stephen Wadsworth of the music-dramas from *Die Feen* through *Parsifal* (pp. 149–69); a list of world and Met premieres of Wagner works, complete with cast information (pp. 170–76); and an index.

9. Millington, Barry. *Wagner*, corrected rev. ed. "Master Musicians Series." Oxford and New York: Oxford University Press, 1999. xii, 342pp. ISBN 0198164874 ML410.W1M58 1999

An intelligent introduction to Wagner's life and works, illustrated with more than a dozen black-and-white portraits, caricatures, and other images as well as fifty musical examples. In addition to a bibliography (pp. 314–23), Millington provides a calendar of Wagner's activities (pp. 288–99), a works list (pp. 300–306), and a short glossary of important Wagnerians (pp. 307–13). Concludes with an index.

Incorporates corrections for a previous revised edition published by Princeton University Press in 1992 (ISBN 0691027226). Originally published by J. M. Dent of London in 1984 (ISBN 0460031813).

10. Richter, Karl. *Richard Wagner. Visionen.* Singapore: Arun, 1993. 668pp.
    ISBN 3927940054 ML410.W1R57 1993

    An introduction to "visionary" aspects of the composer's life and works.
    Includes chapters on Wagner's conception of and relationship to the German
    people, his unfinished opera *Wieland der Schmied*, the *Ring*, and *Parsifal*;
    discussions of the last two works and of Bayreuth take up much of the vol-
    ume (pp. 367–623). Illustrated throughout with scattered musical examples;
    concludes with a bibliography (pp. 643–58) and an index of names.

11. Skelton, Geoffrey. *Wagner in Thought and Practice.* London: Lime Tree,
    1991. 212pp. ISBN 0413452719 ML410.W13S44 1991

    A thoughtful, well-written collection of essays on a variety of subjects,
    including Wagner's treatise *Opera and Drama*, the role of the actor-singer
    in the mature music dramas, the Dresden and Paris versions of
    Tannhäuser, Bayreuth and its Festspielhaus, and the history of *Parsifal*.
    Skelton writes well and argues persuasively; still, one wishes he had illus-
    trated at least some of his observations with visual images or musical
    examples—there are none in this volume—and provided footnotes, end-
    notes, or bibliographic citations. Unindexed.

12. Westernhagen, Curt von. *Richard Wagner: sein Werk, sein Wesen, seine
    Welt.* Zurich: Atlantis, 1956. 559pp. ML410.W1W5

    Among the author's finest Wagner studies and much superior to his later
    two-volume biography (item 303). Rather than discussing issues and
    events in chronological order, Westernhagen divides his many shorter
    chapters into three principal sections: "Creation and Work," "Creative
    Conflict," and "The Whole of His Character" (*Die Summe der Persön-
    lichkeit*); an appendix, entitled "The Critic of a Legend," is concerned pri-
    marily with the Wagner-Nietzsche relationship. Other sections are devoted
    to Schopenhauer's influence on Wagner, Luther as an historical figure and
    Wagner's draft for *Luthers Hochzeit*, Bismarck and the consolidation of
    the Second German Empire, and Wagner's ideas about the German people
    and their music. Includes a scattering of musical examples and a very few
    illustrations, among them a facsimile of a letter Prince Otto von Bismarck
    addressed to Wagner in 1871. Also includes several appendices devoted to
    certain of Wagner's letters, as well as one of Richard Strauss's, a timeline
    (pp. 535–41), and a bibliography (pp. 542–50); concludes with an index.

*More than 100 Wagner surveys exist; many of them were published during the
later nineteenth and earlier twentieth centuries, some in Danish, Finnish, Hungarian, Portuguese, Rumanian, Russian, and Swedish editions. Among the best*

earlier surveys available in English, French, or German—the languages most often familiar to Wagner scholars—are:

13. Chamberlain, Houston Stewart. *Richard Wagner*, trans. G. Ainslie Hight. London: J. M. Dent, 1900. xvii, 402pp. ML410.W1C43 1900

    A single-volume introduction to Wagner's life, literary works, and compositions of various kinds. Handsomely illustrated with a large number of engravings (portraits, pictures of places, scenes from various music dramas, and so on) and documentary facsimiles; supplemented with a list of illustrations (pp. xiii–xvii) and scattered musical examples. Chamberlain writes in this volume about Wagner as a composer, but his interest lies especially in Wagner's thoughts about aesthetic and especially nationalist and racial issues. Originally published in Munich in 1895 and reprinted in various editions prior to the outbreak of World War I. Regarding Chamberlain, see item 1073.

14. Finck, Henry T. *Wagner and His Works: The Story of His Life, with Critical Comments*, 7th ed. 2 vols. New York: Charles Scribner's Sons, 1904; reprinted New York: Haskell House, 1968. ML410.W1F3 1968

    782.1 W134Yf

    A substantial survey by an important early twentieth-century American historian and music commentator. Throughout both volumes Finck alternates biographical passages with descriptions and discussions of Wagner's musical and literary works. Includes a chapter on "Wagner and Wagnerism in America" (Vol. 2, pp. 503–15) as well as a few scattered illustrations but no musical examples; the second volume concludes with an index.

15. Jullien, Adolphe. *Richard Wagner: His Life and Works*, trans. Florence Percival Hall. 2 vols. Boston: Knight & Millet, 1900. ML410.W1J91

    An English-language version of *Richard Wagner: sa vie et ses oeuvres* (Paris, 1886) and reprinted several times in various languages and by various firms. The American edition includes an introduction by B. J. Long (Vol. 1, pp. xxi–xxii) as well as fifteen Wagner portraits and 113 miscellaneous illustrations—among them photographs, stage settings, and a number of caricatures not often reproduced in the literature. Concludes with an appendix that identifies Wagner works played in Paris during the composer's lifetime (Vol. 2, pp. 415–22) and an index. Paginated continuously through both volumes.

16. Schuré, Edouard. *Richard Wagner: son oeuvre et son idée = Le Drame musical*, Vol. 2. Paris: Sandoz et Fischbacher, 1875. 426pp. ML1700.S32 t. 2

A survey of Wagner's life and works, especially his music dramas and contemporary productions of them. Includes two illustrations: a frontispiece depicting the interior of the Festspielhaus in Bayreuth, and a final flyleaf floor plan of the same building. Schuré's observations have often been quoted with regard to Wagner's nineteenth-century reception. See also item 272.

Other surveys may be of interest primarily to specialists (including bibliographers), or primarily for portions of their contents. Among such surveys are the following, arranged in alphabetical order by authors' surnames:

17. Drusche, Esther. *Richard Wagner.* Wiesbaden: Breitkopf & Härtel, 1983. 192pp. ISBN 3765101885 ML410.W1D74 1985b

   An abbreviated introduction to Wagner's personal and professional lives, with a bit of supplementary material thrown in. Catering largely to the general reader, Drusche provides a biographical sketch (pp. 7–39); an extensive and handsome collection of plates, some in color (pp. 41–137); a selection of documentary excerpts, including quotations from *My Life* and other autobiographical and literary works (pp. 138–75); a timeline (pp. 176–87); a little advice about the literature (p. 188); and an index. Co-published in what at the time was the German Democratic Republic by the VEB Verlag für Musik, Leipzig (no ISBN available).

18. Fremgen, Leo. *Richard Wagner heute. Wesen—Werk—Verwirklichung: ein Triptychon.* Heusenstamm: Orion-Heimreiter, 1977. 218pp. ISBN 0875880978 ML410.W1F66

   A survey divided into three parts: the first dealing with Wagner's life and influence on such figures as Friedrich Nietzsche and Theodor Adorno; the second with Wagner's musical and literary works; and the third with Wagner's reputation, the "New Bayreuth," the career of Wieland Wagner, and so on. Includes an index, but no illustrations or musical examples.

19. Gal, Hans. *Richard Wagner,* trans. Hans-Hubert Schönzeler. New York: Stein & Day, 1976. 226pp. ISBN 081281942X ML410.W1G143 1976

   A respectable, albeit brief survey of Wagner's activities and compositions, complete with scattered musical examples. Concludes with an index (pp. 219–26). Published in several other versions, including *Richard Wagner: Versuch einer Würdigung* (Frankfurt a.M., 1967).

20. Hight, George Ainslie. *Richard Wagner: A Critical Biography.* 2 vols. London: Arrowsmith, 1925. ML410.W1H68

In spite of its title, a survey of Wagner's musical and literary works as well as of his life and affairs. Hight discusses at some length the form, melodic material, and musical structure of *Tristan*, *Parsifal*, the *Ring*, and so on, illustrating his observations with short, scattered musical examples. As an introduction to his discussions he appends a chapter on *Leitmotive* and a separate section devoted to longer musical examples (Vol. 2, pp. 271–99). Also contains a bibliography (Vol. 2, pp. 299–302) and a portrait of Wagner printed as a frontispiece to the first volume.

21. Mayer, Hans. *Richard Wagner*, ed. Wolfgang Hofer. Frankfurt a.M.: Schurkamp, 1998. 619pp. ISBN 3518410148 ML410.W1M39 1998

An eccentric volume, much of it written some thirty years ago and devoted to such topics as "Richard Wagner's Spiritual Development," " 'Lohengrin,' or Utopia in A Major," and "Wagner's 'Ring' as Bourgeois Novel." Also includes three more recent "supplements": an interview with Pierre Boulez; a discussion by Meyer, Heinz-Klaus Metzger, and Rainer Riehn of moral and legal issues associated in large part with Wagner's anti-semitism (see also item 1099); and the text of a conversation between Mayer and Harry Kupfer entitled "Bayreuther Gespräch über den 'Ring' " (pp. 493–544). Concludes with an afterword by Hofer, a brief bibliography (pp. 609–10), and an index. Much of this volume's contents appeared originally under Mayer's name alone as *Anmerkungen zu Richard Wagner* (Frankfurt a.M., 1966).

22. Müller-Blattau, Joseph. *Richard Wagner. Leben und Werk.* Königstein im Taunus: Hans Köster, 1963. 64pp. ML410.W1M83 1962

Briefly introduces Wagner's activities and works. Contains twelve black-and-white portraits of the composer and important people in his life. No bibliography or musical examples. Cited in a number of general Wagner bibliographies, but readers can find better studies to consult.

23. Tanner, Michael. *Wagner.* Princeton, NJ: Princeton University Press, 1996. x, 236pp. ISBN 0691011621 ML410.W13T36 1996 782.1 W134Ytn2002

Addressed by its author to "people who have some, not necessarily very much, acquaintance with Wagner's operas and who feel that they raise questions which are both urgent and difficult" (p. ix). Includes biographical and a little musical information, plus plot summaries of the operas and music dramas from *Rienzi* to *Parsifal*. Concludes with a chronology of Wagner's career (pp. 215–21), a bibliography (pp. 222–25), and an index. No musical examples.

24. Taylor, Ronald. *Richard Wagner: His Life, Art, and Thought*. London: Paul
    Elek, 1979. 285pp. ISBN 0236400711 ML410.W1T4 1977b

    782.2 W 134 Ybe

    A cursory introduction to Wagner as man and artist. Includes some 30
    illustrations but only a few musical examples. Taylor is a decent popular
    biographer but not much of a musicologist; on the other hand, he provides
    a postscript entitled "Wagner: For and Against," consisting of excerpts
    from the writings of Adorno, Pierre Boulez, Eduard Hanslick, Thomas
    Mann, and other confirmed and concerned Wagnerphiles and -phobes (pp.
    249–65). Also contains a brief bibliography (pp. 271–75) and an index.

25. White, Chappell. *An Introduction to the Life and Works of Richard Wagner*.
    Englewood Cliffs, NJ: Prentice-Hall, 1967. vi, 186pp. ML410.W1A5F67

    782.1 W134 Ywh

    A short survey, illustrated with 72 musical examples and outfitted with an
    appendix devoted to "The Story of the 'Ring' " (pp. 174–78), a bibliogra-
    phy (pp. 179–81), and an index. Now somewhat out-of-date.

DICTIONARY AND ENCYCLOPEDIA ENTRIES AND RELATED PUBLICATIONS

Perhaps the finest article about Wagner ever published in a general reference
work was subsequently revised and published as a volume unto itself (see item 3).
Other valuable Wagner dictionary and encyclopedia entries are identified below
in reverse chronological order of publication:

26. Millington, Barry, et al. "Wilhelm Richard Wagner." In: *The New Grove*
    Dictionary of Music and Musicians, ed. Stanley Sadie; 2nd ed. New York
    and London: Macmillan, 2001; Vol. 26, pp. 931–71. ISBN 0333608003
    ML100.N48 2000

    Quite different from the 1980 *New Grove* Wagner article revised and repub-
    lished as item 3. Like Dahlhaus and Deathridge, Millington and his colleagues
    deal with a variety of biographical and musical subjects—the latter mostly
    covered by Robert Bailey; they illustrate their observations with twelve black-
    and-white portraits, caricatures and cartoons, and documentary facsimiles;
    and they provide detailed works lists (pp. 956–66). NB: the bibliography (pp.
    956–71) includes "pp. 970A–D," which supplement the on-line material
    available for a short time while the present research guide was being com-
    pleted. See also item 76.

27. "Wilhelm Richard Wagner." In: *Brockhaus Riemann Musiklexikon*, ed.
    Carl Dahlhaus and Hans Heinrich Eggebrecht. Mainz: B. Schott's Sons,
    1989; Vol. 4; pp. 329–33. ISBN 3492183042 ML100.B7 1989

Summarizes Wagner's activities and accomplishments, followed by a useful but incompletely documented bibliography. NB: The *Riemann Musiklexikon* exists in many other editions and versions, including a second revised edition of the Dahlhaus-Eggebrecht version published in 1995; the original "modern" edition was published in Munich in 1979.

28. Westernhagen, Curt von. "Wilhelm Richard Wagner." *Die Musik in Geschichte und Gegenwart*, ed. Friedrich Blume, Kassel: Bärenreiter, 1949–1979; Vol. 14 (1968), cols. 88–130. ML100.M42

Devoted to essential aspects of the composer's life and thought. Incorporates a works list, now out-of-date, as well as a bibliography (cols. 128–30). Illustrated with three black-and-white manuscript facsimiles as well as portraits of Wagner's mother Johanna, his step-father Ludwig Geyer (the famous self-portrait) and his uncle Adolf, and two Wagner portraits: that of Ernst Kietz, done in the early 1840s, and—in color, as a separate glossy plate—that of Joseph Bernhardt, done in 1868. No printed musical examples. A few corrections appear in Vol. 16 of the same work (1979), cols. 1514–15.

A new edition of *MGG* is currently being published under the editorship of Ludwig Finscher but has not yet reached the "Personenteil" volume in which either an extensively revised or an altogether new article on Wagner will appear in print.

29. Strobel, Otto. "Richard Wagner." *International Cyclopedia of Music and Musicians*, 10th ed.; ed. Bruce Bohle. New York: Dodd, Mead & Co., 1975; pp. 2397–408. ML100.I642 1985 (both 10th and 11th eds.)

Written by a leading scholar whose terminology for and description of his subject's compositional process is summarized here in English. Includes a timeline and a list of works, but no musical examples. Strobel died in 1953, but his contribution to earlier editions of the *Cyclopedi*a has been reprinted in several times.

In addition to encyclopedia and dictionary entries, a few essay-length surveys have appeared in compendia, readers, and other book-length publications. Among them is:

30. Burbidge, Peter. "Richard Wagner: Man and Artist." In item 31, pp. 15–33.

Claiming that "the facts of Wagner's adult life are too well known to need rehearsing here" (p. 16), Burbidge briefly examines the composer's working methods as well as his musical and literary legacies; he also adds comments about the composer's marriages, love affairs, anti-semitism, and dislike of composing at the piano. Especially useful for its comments on Wagner's personality and character. No illustrations or musical examples (see also item 1100).

COMPANIONS, HANDBOOKS, AND READERS

The two finest Wagner compendia are identified above as items 1–2. Additional handbooks and readers include:

31. *The Wagner Companion*, ed. Peter Burbidge and Richard Sutton. London: Faber & Faber, 1979. 462pp. ISBN 0571104711 ML410.W131W25

    A less comprehensive reader aimed mostly at musical enthusiasts. Contains items 30, 108, 450, 453, 502, 877, 884, 895, 920, 942, and 1126, as well as endnotes, a bibliography (pp. 441–53), and a general index. Burbidge and Sutton ignore iconography, psychology, and anti-semitism; in spite of these limitations, however, their *Companion* remains useful, if only for Bailey's summary of Wagner's compositional methods (item 453) and for Lucy Beckett's discussion of "Wagner and His Critics" (item 942). Most of the essays on musical topics include examples. Criticized for certain errors by Deathridge in *19th Century Music* 5 (1981–1982), pp. 81–89 (see also item 1111).

32. *Richard Wagner: Das Betroffensein der Nachwelt. Beiträge zur Wirkungsgeschichte*, ed. Dietrich Mack. Darmstadt: Wissenschaftliche Buchgesellschaft, 1984. 399pp. ISBN 3534068130 ML410.W131R415 1984

    A "reader" or compilation of observations by various composers, critics, and scholars—among them Theodor W. Adorno, Ernst Bloch, Paul Dukas, Charles Gounod, Eduard Hanslick, Stéphane Mallarmé, Thomas Mann, and Wieland Wagner. Among the most useful of Mack's selections is Alfred Lorenz's article "Über die musikalische Form von Richard Wagners Musikwerken" (pp. 75–87), published originally in the 1924 *Bayreuther Festspielführer* (see item 51); this article includes a few diagrammatic illustrations. Incorporates no Nazi-era texts, with the exception of two excerpts published under the title "Die Vereinnahmung durch den Nationalsozialismus" selected by the editor (pp. 169–71). Lacks musical examples and a bibliography; concludes with a useful index. See item 6 for review information.

*   *The Wagner Companion*, ed. Mander and Mitchenson. Described as item 581.

Less a comprehensive handbook than a rather fulsome *Opernführer* (or guide book). Includes, however, an essay on Bayreuth, excerpts from item 987, a brief bibliography, a glossary of characters' names found in Wagner's operas and music dramas (pp. 230–35), and an index.

CONFERENCE PROCEEDINGS AND OTHER ANTHOLOGIES

Most published collections of conference papers that deal primarily or even exclusively with Wagnerian subjects are organized around specific eras, themes, or works; the same holds true for most essay and article collections. Among the comparatively few anthologies devoted to Wagner "in general" is the following especially important volume:

33. *Wagnerliteratur—Wagnerforschungen. Bericht über das Wagner-Symposium München 1983*, ed. Carl Dahlhaus and Egon Voss. Mainz: B. Schott's Söhne, 1985. 239pp. ISBN 3795722020 ML410.W131W346 1985

An outstanding collection that considers mostly musical and literary issues. Includes introductory comments by Dahlhaus and Voss, as well as a group of essays devoted to staging act I of *Tannhäuser*, the extent and value of existing Wagner studies, and issues associated with preparing complete editions of Wagner's works and letters; see also items 176, 274, 529, and 635. Illustrated with scattered musical examples as well as a few documentary facsimiles. Concludes with an index of names.

34. *Re-Reading Wagner*, ed. Reinhold Grimm and Jost Hermand. Madison, WI: University of Wisconsin Press, 1993. [Published on behalf of *Monatshefte*, a University of Wisconsin periodical.] ML410.W131R3 1993 (no ISBN available)

Includes item 431 as well as studies of the respect paid Wagner by Richard Strauss, Hans Pfitzner, and Thomas Mann, the "social politics" of the musical redemption Wagner both sought and offered to his listeners, Wagner and Swiss society, and so on. Illustrated sporadically with pictures and a few musical examples (see also item 358).

Other essay collections and published conference proceedings include the following, described in reverse chronological order according to date of publication:

35. *Richard Wagner: Mittler zwischen Zeiten. Festvorträge und Diskussionen aus Anlass des 100. Todestages*, ed. Gerhard Heldt. Wort und Musik: Salzburger akademische Beiträge, 3. Anif/Salzburg: Ursula Müller-Speiser, 1990. 220pp. ISBN 3851450035 ML410.W19R48 1990

A collection of papers originally presented at a Schloss Turnau conference celebrating the centenary of Wagner's death. Includes a version of item 1011 as well as an essay about Wagner and Hitler (see item 1138), evaluations of the composer's influence on twentieth-century music, his visits to Venice, and so on. Concludes with information about contributors, including the editor. Illustrated with two photographs and a few line drawings; contains no musical examples.

36. *Wagner in Retrospect: A Centennial Reappraisal*, ed. Leroy R. Shaw et al. Amsterdam: Rodopi, 1987. 241pp. ISBN 9062037097 ML410.W13W123 1987

The proceedings of a conference devoted to Wagner's life, works, and reception from the perspective of late twentieth-century European and North American scholars. Includes item 147, as well as essays by Warren Darcy, Jean-Jacques Nattiez, Andrew Porter, and Alexander Ringer; topics range from reassessments of Wagner's musical and literary legacy to Wagner and "The Jewish Question," Wagner and "The Media" (the last mostly a discussion of stage production in Wagner's day), and "Wagner as Entrepreneur." Concludes with a list of participants. No index or musical examples. Reviewed positively in *Wagner* 10/1 (January 1989), pp. 29–30.

37. *Richard Wagner: ein deutsches Ärgernis*, ed. Klaus Umbach. Spiegel-Buch, 34. Reinbek: Spiegel, 1982. 190pp. ISBN 3499330342 (no LC number available)

Eight essays, followed by a miscellaneous collection of documents concerning the "war of faith" (*Glaubenskrieg*) associated with Wagner and Bayreuth. Includes Eva Rieger's "Szenen zweier Ehen: Minna, Cosima, Richard Wagner—Erlösung im Theater?" (pp. 109–27), one of the few serious studies of the composer's first marriage. No illustrations, musical examples, bibliography, or index, however.

Less wide-ranging or noteworthy collections of articles about Wagnerian subjects include:

38. Kesting, Hanjo. *Das schlechte Gewissen an der Musik: Aufsätze zu Richard Wagner*. Stuttgart: Klett-Cotta, 1991. 175pp. ISBN 3608957499. ML410.W131K47 1991.

Seven essays dealing with aspects of Wagner's life and music, among them " 'Mehr als befreundet—weniger als Freund': Richard Wagner und Franz Liszt" (pp. 53–95), and "Wagner und kein Ende: Musik und Ideologie bei Thomas Mann" (pp. 114–44; see also item 1044). No illustrations or musical examples.

39. *Zu Richard Wagner: Acht* [8] *Bonner Beiträge im Jubiläumsjahr 1983,* ed. Helmut Loos and Günther Massenkeil. Studium Universale, 5. Bonn: Bouvier Verlag Herbert Grundmann, 1984. 159pp. ISBN 3416040058 ML410.W131Z8 1984

A lackluster anthology published in celebration of the centenary of Wagner's death. Includes discussions of the quality of Wagner's libretto for *Meistersinger,* Nietzsche in Bayreuth, and the Wagner reception in Germany. Reviewed with significant qualifications in *Wagner* 8/3 (July 1987), p. 120.

Published conference proceedings occasionally contain semi-independent groups of papers devoted specifically to Wagner and closely related topics. One such group of papers appears in:

40. *Bericht über den internationalen musikwissneschaftlichen Kongress Bayreuth 1981,* ed. Christoph-Hellmut Mahling and Sigrid Wiesmann. Kassel and London: Bärenreiter, 1984. xvi, 642pp. ISBN 3761807503 ML36.I629 1981

Includes contributions by Dahlhaus, Deathridge, Voss, and other leading scholars; most of these deal with musical issues, but Voss's contribution ("Ergebnisse und Aufgaben der Wagnerforschung," pp. 437–39) briefly considers the Wagner literature as a whole. Unfortunately, the papers presented by Vetter and Voss are merely summarized. Also includes item 745. Published originally in the form of several supplements to *Die Musikforschung* 36 (1983); see item 1005. See also items 623 and 641.

Essay collections dealing exclusively with Wagnerian subjects have mostly been written and compiled by individual scholars. Among such collections are the following, arranged alphabetically by author:

41. Abbetmeyer, Theodor. *Richard-Wagner-Studien. Neue Untersuchungen über die Persönlichkeit und das Kulturwerk des Bayreuther Meisters.* Hannover and Leipzig: Hahn, 1916. iv, 276pp. ML410.W13A2

A reverential introduction to Wagner's life and art. Abbetmeyer concerns himself mostly with the composer's personality—topics include "Wagner's Love of Truth" (*Wahrheitsliebe*) and "Wagner and Good Luck"— with various works and aesthetic issues, including the Wagner reception in Germany during World War I. Concludes with a two-page bibliography. No musical examples.

42. Adler, Guido. *Richard Wagner. Vorlesungen gehalten an der Universität zu Wien,* 2nd ed. Munich: Drei Masken, 1923. xi, 382pp. ML410.W13A23 1923

Twenty-three lectures on various aspects of Wagner's life and art, as presented during the 1903–1904 academic year at the University of Vienna by one of the foremost musicologists of late nineteenth-century Europe. Includes an introduction and survey of the collection's contents, essays with titles such as "Wagner als Romantiker," a timetable of Wagner's life and activities (pp. 352–61), and a useful index. Illustrated with a portrait of Wagner as frontispiece and with scattered musical examples. Originally published at Leipzig by Breitkopf & Härtel in 1904.

43. Graf, Max. *Wagner-Probleme und andere Studien*. Vienna: Viener Verlag, c. 1900. 182pp. ML60.G736

A collection of essays, not all of them devolving upon Wagner, devoted to considering such issues as: Wagner as an "authentic" German composer, Wagner's role in the "victories" of Nietzsche and Bülow as heroes of German culture, Wagner's personal and professional relationships to Otto von Bismarck and Germany's Second Reich, and so on. Most of these issues appear in "Wagner-Probleme" (pp. 13–86). Powerfully influenced by Freud, Graf often considers interpersonal and even national issues in terms of intrapersonal emotional conflicts. No illustrations or musical examples. Interesting for students of German culture and the German Wagner reception prior to World War I.

44. Seidl, Arthur. *Wagneriana: Angewandte Aesthetik*. 3 vols. Berlin and Leipzig: Schuster & Loeffler, 1901–1902. ML60.S45

Vol. 1: *Richard Wagner-Credo. Eine Ergänzung zur "Richard Wagner-Schule."*

Vol. 2: *Von Palestrina zu Wagner. Bekenntnisse eines musikalischen "Wagnerianers."*

Vol. 3: *Die Wagner-Nachfolge im Musik-Drama. Skizzen und Studien zur Kritik der "modernen Oper."*

Among the broadest-ranging collections of Wagner essays, and certainly the most comprehensive written by a single individual. In his first volume Seidl surveys or examines specific aspects of individual Wagner works and issues, including *Das Liebesmahl der Apostel*, *Rienzi*, Senta's character in *Holländer*, "Wagner in seinen Schriften," and so on, together with several appendices—among them an essay entitled "Christianity and Germanity" (*Christentum und Germanentum*). In his second volume the author turns to topics not always explicitly Wagnerian, including the *Palestrinastil* of the later nineteenth-century Regensburg Caecilianists, Bach's B-minor Mass, Haydn's *Creation*, and so on, as well as essays on works by Berlioz,

Brahms, Bruckner, Liszt, Marschner, and Robert Schumann, and an account of the career of singer Adelina Patti. The third volume returns to topics associated with Wagner's influence on other composers—among them Eugen d'Albert, Felix Draeseke, Karl Goldmark, Gounod, Engelbert Humperdinck, Ruggiero Leoncavallo, Bedřich Smetana, and so on; the final portion of this volume deals with German Wagner societies and the Bayreuth phenomenon. Musical examples appear in a few essays in Vol. 1.

* *Neue Wagner-Forschungen. Erste Folge (Herbst 1943)*, ed. Otto Strobel. Described as item 104.

Issued by and devolving largely upon the Wagner family and its Bayreuth archives; at the same time a collection of essays by Strobel himself as well as by Max Fehr, Willy Krienitz, and several other scholars.

45. Wolzogen, Hans von. *Aus Richard Wagners Geisteswelt. Neue Wagneriana und Verwandtes*. Berlin and Leipzig: Schuster & Loeffler, 1908. 322pp. ML410.W13W6

A collection of essays, including "Schiller und Wagner" and "Bayreuther Kunst und deutsche Kultur" as well as a series of short articles dealing with four separate aspects of the *Ring*, accounts of Siegfried Wagner's *Bärenhäuter* and Liszt's oratorio *Die Legende von der heiligen Elisabeth* in contemporary productions, a collection of anecdotes about the infamous racist Count Joseph de Gobineau (whom Wagner admired), and so on. Contains no musical examples, illustrations, bibliography, or index. A sequel of sorts to Wolzogen's *Wagneriana. Gesammelte Aufsätze über R. Wagner's Werke vom Ring bis zum Gral* (Leipzig, 1888), itself issued in conjunction with one of the earliest Bayreuth festivals.

PROGRAMS AND PROGRAM BOOKLETS

An enormous amount and variety of information about Wagner and his world can be found in theatrical and concert programs, especially those printed by major European opera houses or for special occasions abroad or in the United States. The most important series of such program publications is:

46. *Programmhefte der Bayreuther Festspiele*. Bayreuth 1952–. ML410.W2B26

The post–World War II Bayreuth house organ. Includes items 79, 197, 276, and so on, as well as a host of other articles and essays, virtually all of them published in each issue in English, French, and German. Most issues also include handsome illustrations and facsimiles of important documents. Indexed through the early 1970s in item 66, and more thoroughly through 1986 in item 79. Unfortunately, complete runs of this periodical can be found in few North American libraries; the Library of Congress is supposed to own one, but the present author has never been able to examine certain issues that seem always to be "not on the shelves."

Discussed, criticized and, in effect, "reviewed" by a number of scholars, including Martin Cooper in "Wagner as Christian Prophet or Jungian Adept" in his *Ideas and Music* (London, 1965), pp. 116–21; in this instance, Cooper tackles *Programmhefte* articles by Johannes Jacobi and Anton Orel.

Individual programs and program booklets of special value include:

47. *Bayreuther Festspielführer, 19.–30. Juli* [and] *18.–31. August 1936*, ed. Otto Strobel. Bayreuth: Georg Niehrenheim, 1936. 306pp. + travel brochures and information. (no LC number available)

   A testimonial to Bayreuth's productions during the Hitler era. Contains "Liszt an Wagner: Zwei unveröffentliche Briefe" (pp. 128–29) as well as a large number of illustrations, fold-out documentary facsimiles, scattered musical examples, and so on. Also contains a frontispiece portrait of Wagner, a map of Bayreuth, and photographs and biographies of every soloist who performed during the 1936 season, arranged in alphabetical order by surname (pp. 219–73). In German throughout. Uncommon; the British Library, London, owns a copy.

48. *Wagner Handbook for the Festival Concerts Given in 1884 under the Direction of Theodore Thomas. Analytic Programmes with English Texts, Biographic and Critical Essays by Henry T. Finck.* Cambridge: John Wilson & Son, 1884. 112pp. ML410.W13F48

   A pocket guide to Wagner and his works, compiled in honor of American conductor Theodore Thomas's assault on London during April 1884. Includes essays by Finck in defense of Wagner and his music. Also includes the complete text of *Götterdämmerung*, act III, and portions of the libretti for *Walküre, Meistersinger, Holländer*, and so on—all in English as well as German—together with program notes for Beethoven's Fifth Symphony, a brief biography of Thomas himself (pp. 43–44), a portrait of Thomas printed as a frontispiece, and a few unpaginated illustrations of scenes and the artists who presented them.

SPECIALIZED PERIODICALS, PERIODICAL ISSUES, AND RELATED STUDIES

Perhaps the most wide-ranging Wagner "surveys" are those periodicals devoted primarily or even exclusively to the composer's activities, works, and cultural influence. Many of these periodicals—there are dozens of them, and more than a few enjoy or have enjoyed extremely small readerships as well as rather low standards of scholarship—are issued by Wagner societies.[3] *Most of the more important Wagner periodicals have appeared or continue to appear at least twice each year. These include:*

49. *Wagner*, ed. Barry Millington. London 1980–. ML410.W1A585

The source of a number of articles (e.g., items 151, 274, 286) and reviews (e.g., of items 4, 35, 38) cited throughout the present research guide. Modest in appearance and physical production standards, this magazine has gained respect around the world for its intelligent and well-balanced commentary on a wealth of issues, Wagner's anti-semitism among them. Includes advertisements and illustrations of various kinds; after 1990 the quality of the latter began to improve rapidly. Unfortunately less common in North American libraries than one might expect. For several years published quarterly; recently only three issues have appeared annually.

50. *Richard Wagner Blätter*. Bayreuth and Tutzing 1977–1988 (?). ML410.W1A558

Issued by the Aktionskreis für das Werk Richard Wagners of Bayreuth; after the early 1980s published in Tutzing by Hans Schneider. Issues published by Schneider are handsomely printed and include illustrations, documentary facsimiles, and musical examples. The number of issues per year varies, and the present author was unable to determine whether this magazine is still in print. Available in at least partial runs in many American libraries.

51. *Offizieller Bayreuther Festspielführer*. c. 16 vols. Bayreuth: Georg Niehrenheim, 1924–1939. (no LC number available)

Contains a number of valuable articles, several of which are cited in item 76 but omitted in the present volume. Rare in American libraries, probably because—especially in its earlier issues—it was discarded as an ephemeral publication devoted to encouraging tourism. See item 47 for a description of and information about a sample issue, one that contains maps and other travel information; see also item 32.

In spite of its provenance and the occasional value of its contents—Wagner himself contributed to it, and for decades it remained Bayreuth's "house organ"—the following periodical is too full of propaganda on behalf of Wagner and his circle to be taken at face value:

52. *Bayreuther Blätter: Deutsche Zeitschrift im Geiste Richard Wagners*, ed. Hans von Wolzogen et al. Bayreuth 1878–1938. ML5.B35

The Wagner family's "house organ" throughout the later nineteenth and earlier twentieth centuries. Important for students of the Wagner reception, even though much of its "factual" content cannot be trusted; certain issues, however, do contain articles by reputable and relatively unbiased scholars, while others include worthwhile musical supplements. Early issues are subtitled "Monatschrift des Bayreuther Patronatvereines." Available in reprint editions or on microfilm. Information about the magazine's origins appears in Martin Vogel, "Nietzsche und die Bayreuther Blätter," published in the *Beiträge zur Geschichte der Musikkritik*, ed. Heinz Becker (Regnesburg, 1965), pp. 55–68. See also items 201, 620, 788, and 1005.

Other, older periodicals are primarily of interest to students of Wagnerisms in various nations and of the Wagner reception during the nineteenth and twentieth centuries in Europe:

53. *Tribschener Blätter: Mitteilungen der Gesellschaft Richard-Wagner-Museum Tribschen.* Lucerne 1956–?1989. (no LC number available)

Published under several slightly different subtitles, one of which reads "Zeitschrift der Schweizerische Richard-Wagner-Gesellschaft." Issue No. 48 (July 1983), for example, includes an interview with Wolfgang Wagner called "Bayreuth heute" (pp. 1–9) as well as reports on performances and recording reviews; issue No. 30 includes item 397. A few articles that appeared in this magazine have been translated and reprinted in item 49. Uncommon in American libraries, at least in complete runs.

54. *Revue Wagnérienne*, ed. Edouard Dujardin. Paris 1885–1888. ML410.W1A

A valuable source of information for the Wagner reception in France. For information about its history and contents, see item 63. See also items 1030 and 1050.

55. *The Meister: The Quarterly Journal of the London Branch of the Wagner Society.* London 1885–1895 (8 vols.). (no LC number available)

A handsome but somewhat amateurish nineteenth-century fanzine. Its eight volumes include reprints of Wagner's essays on Bellini and Weber's *Freischütz*, excerpts from *Art and Revolution* and other prose works, articles about Wagner and various composers, "reminiscences" of Wagner by Gounod and Liszt, poems in Wagner's honor, and so on. Of research value primarily to students of the nineteenth-century British Wagner reception. See also item 1050.

Among Wagner periodicals have been several yearbooks. The most important of these are:

56. *Richard-Wagner-Jahrbuch*, ed. Ludwig Frankenstein. Leipzig: Deutsche Verlagsactiven-Gesellschaft, 1906–1908, 1912–1913. ML410.W1A57

A valuable periodical publication, one that unfortunately appeared only in five installments prior to World War I. Includes items 600, 632, 639, 740, 760, 765, 782, 794, 808, and 913 as well as other studies worth consulting today.

57. *Richard-Wagner-Jahrbuch*, ed. Wolfgang Perschmann. Irregular: 1988–. ML410.W1A58

A "home-made" miscellany of studies devolving upon Wagner, his circle, and performances of his works, published by the Richard-Wagner-Verein of Graz, Austria. Includes contributions by the likes of Joachim Bergfeld, Julius Braun, and several other accomplished Wagner scholars, although most of the articles are by Perschmann himself and other members of the Graz Wagner Society. Among the contents of the two volumes published to date are a brief article by Braun on "Richard Wagner in Wien" (1988, pp. 247–52) and the complete reprinted libretto of Hans Pfitzner's *Palestrina* (1994, pp. 377–416).

Other, less specialized periodicals have devoted individual issues to Wagnerian topics. Among such issues are the following, arranged in reverse chronological order by date of publication:

58. *The Richard Wagner Centenary in Australia*, ed. Peter Dennison = *Miscellanea Musicologica: Adelaide Studies in Musicology* 14 (1985). vi, 202pp. ML410.W12A85 1985 (no ISBN available)

A collection of essays about Wagner, several by scholars such as Deathridge and Andrew McCredie. Also includes a version of item 86, as well as Jennifer Marshall's "Richard Wagner's Letters to Australia" (pp. 149–66), Gerhard Schulz's "Liebestod: The Literary Background of Wagner's 'Tristan und Isolde' " (pp. 117–30), and Silke Beinssen-Hesse's "Ideological Implication of Wagner's Changes to Wolfram's 'Parzival' " (pp. 131–48).

Reviewed at some length in *Wagner* 7/2 (April 1986), pp. 65–70. The LC number for *Miscellanea Musicologica* as a periodical is ML5.M34.

59. *Wagner: la lingua, la musica*, ed. Ferruccio Masini and Luigi Pestalozza = *Musica/Realtà* No. 9 (1984). 206pp. ISBN 8870618935 ML5.M739

Most of the papers presented in this issue of Pestalozza's music magazine were presented at a conference held in Ravenna during November of 1983. Most of them, too, have to do with Wagner as composer and poet, but a few deal with other issues, including the Wagner-Nietzsche relationship, Wagner's influence on Baudelaire, and revolutionary aspects of Wagner's life and thought. Includes an Italian version of item 889. The volume as a whole contains no illustrations or musical examples.

60. *Richard Wagner* 1 = *Nouvelle Ecole* No. 30 (Fall–Winter 1978). 2 vols. AS161.N65

A Wagner survey of sorts: the first volume presents information about the composer's career and works, and is mostly written by Giorgio Locchi; the second deals with the Wagner reception in France. The first volume also includes a Wagner "bibliographie Française" by Locchi, and a "Discographie les 'integrales de la Tetralogie' " (i.e., a survey of *Ring* recordings) by one "N. E.," as well as a list of books about Wagner in French (p. 49); the second volume includes reprinted articles by Dujardin and Schuré. Illustrated throughout with a variety of photographs and drawings in a "slick" postmodern style. Handsome, opinionated, and possibly something of a collector's item in years to come.

61. *Richard Wagner.* "Collection Génies et Réalités." Paris: Hachette, 1962. 302pp. ML410.W1R5

One of a number of similar volumes about great composers in Hachette's series. The bulk of this volume consists of nine essays about Wagner's character, love affairs, philosophical enthusiasms, death in Venice, and so on, written by the likes of Marcel Brion, Bernard Gavoty, Jean Mistler, and Walter Panofsky. Also includes a works list and discography compiled by Jean Witold (pp. 279–99) and a list of illustrations that identifies all 137 color and black-and-white images—portraits, paintings, drawings, and photographs of various places, stage sets, a plan of the Bayreuth Festspielhaus, and so on—distributed in the form of five fascicles throughout the volume.

62. *Die Musik* 1–IV (1901–1902). ML5.M9

Includes items 587, 627, and 761, as well as an article by Lorenz entitled "Parsifal als Übermensch," a review of Arthur Seidl's *Wagneriana*, Vols. 2–3 (item 44 above), and a number of other essays and observations.
       Several issues of *Die Musik* were devoted to Wagner, and a great many others contain at least one article or review concerning his life, works, or influence; see item 64 below for information about additional Wagner issues of this and other German-language music magazines. More recent periodical publications devoted to Wagner studies include the "3. Quartal" of the *Archiv für Musikwissenschaft* 40 (1983), which contains item 774, a

version of item 590, an essay closely related to item 742, and "Tonalität und Form in Wagners 'Ring des Nibelungen' " by Dahlhaus (pp. 165–73)—the last illustrated with a few hand-copied musical examples.

* *La Revue musicale* "Wagner" issue. Described as item 1064.

Published originally in October 1923 and reprinted in 1977 because of the value of some of its articles and essays.

Finally, studies related to individual Wagner periodicals and special Wagner issues are identified below in alphabetical order by author:

63. Wyzewska, Isabelle [also Isabella de Wyzewa]. *La Revue Wagnérienne. Essai sur l'interprétation esthétique de Wagner en France.* Paris: Librairie Académique Perrin, 1934. 220pp. ML410.W12F78

   A study of item 54. Includes a chapter on the *Revue*'s history (pp. 43–104) as well as observations concerning Maurice Barrès, Villiers d'Isle Adam, Stéphane Mallarmé, and Téodor Wyzéwa. Also includes a bibliography (pp. 203–17) that lists, among other things, every item published in the *Revue* itself (pp. 203–07); concludes with a table of contents instead of an index.

   Wyzewska, who attended Smith College in the United States and later taught at Barnard College in New York City, may have been responsible for the second full-title page published in some copies; this reports in English that the volume was accepted as her doctoral thesis at Columbia University. See also Dujardin's article " 'La Revue Wagnérienne,' " published in item 1064, pp. 141–60.

64. Roberge, Marc-André. "Focusing Attention: Special Issues in German-Language Music Periodicals of the First Half of the 20th Century." *RMA Research Chronicle* 27 (1994), pp. 71–100. ML5.R14

   Identifies and partially describes the contents of 41 special Wagner issues of *Die Musik* (see item 62), the *Neue Zeitschrift für Musik*, *Melos*, the *Allgemeine Musik-Zeitung*, and other prominent German music magazines published prior to 1950. Tables provide bibliographic particulars about the issues themselves.

65. Wahnes, Gunther H. *Heinrich von Stein und sein Verhältnis zu Richard Wagner und Friedrich Nietzsche.* Leipzig: Schwabia, 1926. 167pp. (no LC number available)

   Among his many activities, von Stein edited a short-lived nineteenth-century *Richard Wagner-Jahrbuch* (not to be confused with item 56) and thus influenced the Wagner reception in a variety of ways. Originally presented as a dissertation at the University of Jena.

Notes

1. Westernhagen's biographical contributions to the *New Grove* article may have been jettisoned after British musicologists—John Deathridge among them, in his review of item 303 [*19th Century Music* 5 (1981–1982), pp. 81–89]—reacted sharply to their German colleague's attempts to "sanitize" the composer's personality, especially his anti-semitic biases. In a review of the original *New Grove* article, John Boulton pointed out that "Wagner was a supremely great artist. He was also a self-confessed racist, and it is serving [*sic*] no purpose for *The New Grove* [i.e., Westernhagen] to urge otherwise—except, of course, that of lowering the standard of the *Dictionary* in the esteem of serious Wagnerians" [*Music Review* 42 (1981), p. 278].
2. The review in question also evaluates three volumes excluded from the present research guide: the Deutscher Taschenbuch-Verlag guide to Wagner's music dramas, 2nd ed. (Munich, 1981); Friedrich Oberkogler's guide to *Parsifal* (Stuttgart, 1983); and Peter Wapnewski's *Richard Wagner: Die Szene und ihr Meister*, 2nd rev. ed. (Munich, 1983).
3. See the article on such societies in *The New Grove Dictionary of Music and Musicians*, 2nd ed. (London and New York, 2001), Vol. 26, pp. 978–79; see also items 49–50, 55, and 57.

III

Researching Wagner:
Reference Works of Various Kinds

No scholar has ever produced a comprehensive Wagner bibliography, and only one—Nikolaus Oesterlein (see item 67)—has even tried. The Wagner literature is much too large to be systematically identified and described in anything short of an encyclopedic publication, and much of it is interesting only to a handful of specialists. On the other hand, many published Wagner reference works are of great value. For these reasons most of the more familiar bibliographies, exhibition catalogs, iconographies, discographies, and other Wagner research tools are identified and discussed below. Specialists, however, may often wish to turn instead to books and articles that contain bibliographies of their own. In every possible instance, these tools are identified throughout the present volume.

BIBLIOGRAPHIES AND RELATED STUDIES

Although useful, the series of volumes described below is by no means definitive:

66. *Internationale Wagner-Bibliographie*, ed. Herbert Barth. 4 vols. Bayreuth: Edition Musica, 1956–1968; Bayreuth: "Mühl'scher Universitätsverlag," 1979. ISBN 3921733081 (Vol. 4) ML134.W1B37 (series)

Identifies most of the important Wagner studies that appeared in print between the end of World War II and the late 1970s. Issued in four volumes: "1945–1955" (published 1956), "1956–1960" (1961), "1961–1966" (1968), and "1967–1978" (1979). The first volume is accompanied by facsimiles of letters written by Thomas Mann and Romain Rolland, as well as by three appendices: a brief Wagner discography, statistics concerning Wagner performances from 1945–1955, and information about four collections of Wagneriana in Bayreuth, Eisenach, Lucerne, and the Burrell Collection (see item 102); the second includes item 843; the third is illustrated with portraits of Wagner and his son Siegfried; and the fourth lists Polish, Czech, Slovak, and Hungarian publications from 1945 and the 1970s (pp. 145–64). Indexed.

Although useful, especially for information about articles published in the Bayreuth *Programmhefte* (item 46) between the early 1950s and the 1970s, Barth's bibliography is incomplete and does not always discriminate between studies dealing exclusively or primarily with Wagner and those that merely refer to him or to members of his circle; furthermore, its annotations seem to have been added almost at random. In his survey of the literature, Dieter Borchmeyer calls Barth's volumes "an unprofessional muddle-headed undertaking . . . virtually useless in scholarly terms" (item 151 below, p. 61). The authors of item 2 ignore it altogether.

More comprehensive are two ground-breaking nineteenth-century studies, both reprinted several decades ago:

67. Oesterlein, Nikolaus. *Katalog einer Richard-Wagner-Bibliothek. Nach den vollegenden Originalien systematisch-chronoloigsch geordnetes und mit Citaten und Anmerkungen versehens authentisches Nachschlagebuch durch die gesammte Wagner-Literatur.* 4 vols. Leipzig: Breitkopf & Härtel, 1882–1895; reprinted Wiesbaden: M. Sändig, 1970. ML134.W1O2 1970

    Identifies and often describes more than 10,170 books, scores, manuscripts, sources for Wagner's own works (literary and musical), studies of Wagner's life and music, and contemporary accounts of the composer as well as portraits and caricatures, telegrams, and so on. NB: much of what Oesterlein deals with is rare and/or no longer of interest. Includes neither illustrations nor musical examples.

68. Kastner, Emerich. *Wagner-Catalog. Chronologisches Verzeichniss der von und über Richard Wagner erschienenen Schriften, Musikwerke, etc., etc. nebst biographischen Notizen.* Offenbach a.M.: Johannes André, 1878; reprinted Hilbertshum: Frits Knuf, 1966. x, 131pp. ML134.W1K24 1966

    Notorious among Wagner scholars, in part because Wagner himself described it as "exacting work, carelessly done" (quoted in item 2, p. 207). Entries are arranged by year; performance information is given for relevant compositions. Concludes with an detailed index.

More useful to scholars today, perhaps, are the following specialized reference works, described in alphabetical order by author and/or title:

69. Klein, Horst F. G. *Erstdrucke der musikalischen Werke von Richard Wagner. Bibliographie.* Musikbibliographische Arbeiten, 5. Tutzing: Hans Schneider, 1983. 236pp. ISBN 3795203988 ML134.W1 K63 1983

    Describes first editions for each of Wagner's published compositions (e.g., most of what he actually composed). Includes facsimiles of title pages as well as a chronological catalog of musical works from 1828–1882 (pp. 221–27), and a *Bildanhang* (illustrative supplement; pp. 205–20); concludes with an index of names. Reviewed in *Notes* 41 (1984–1985), pp. 284–85, where it is sharply criticized for "inadequate research" (p. 285); among other lapses cited in this review is Klein's failure to cite item 166.

70. Klein, Horst F. G. *Erst- und Frühdrucke der Textbücher von Richard Wagner: Bibliographie.* Musikbibliographische Arbeiten, 4. Tutzing: Hans Schneider, 1979. 63pp. ISBN 3795202701 ML134.W1K6

Identifies and describes first editions for each of Wagner's published librettos. Klein also provides information about many later (but early) editions. Like item 69, includes facsimiles of first-edition title pages, as well as additional illustrations appended to the end of the volume.

71. Pleßke, Hans-Martin. *Richard Wagner in der Dichtung. Bibliographie deutschsprachiger Veröffentlichungen.* Bayreuth: Edition Musica, 1971. 84pp. ML134.W3P6 (no ISBN available)

Provides references to Wagner and Wagnerian subjects in German poetry from their beginnings to 1970. Includes as a supplement entitled "Wagneriana. Opere di e su Richard Wagner pubblicate in Italia dal 1958–1970" by Maria Adelaide Bertoli Bacherini (pp. 70–77; see also item 197). Concludes with an index.

French-language Wagner publications, although less numerous than those in English and German, are nevertheless extensive. One useful guide to these often neglected sources is:

72. Silège, Henri. *Bibliographie wagnérienne française, donnant la nomenclature de tous les livres français intéressant directement le Wagnérisme parus en France et à l'étranger depuis 1851 jusqu'à 1902.* Paris: Fisch-Pbacher, 1902. 35pp. ML134.W1S5

Covers the last half of the nineteenth century in an incomplete but nevertheless informative manner. Entries are listed alphabetically by author in pp. 8–26 (i.e., "par ordre alphabétique de noms d'auteurs et de traducteurs," as summarized on the full title page), and by title in pp. 28–35 (i.e., "par order alphabétique des titres"). No illustrations or musical examples.

The most recent and reliable reference guide to Wagner's massive correspondence is:

73. Breig, Werner, with Martin Dürrer and Andreas Mielke. *Wagner-Briefe-Verzeichnis (WBV). Chronologisches Verzeichnis der Briefe von Richard*

Wagner. Wiesbaden: Breitkopf & Härtel, 1998. 845pp. ISBN 3765103306 ML410.W1A53

Identifies 9,030 dated and undated letters written by Wagner; also identifies 694 published letters by year and, insofar as possible, by month and date of composition. Includes a concordance with Altmann's catalog (pp. 836–45; see item 74 below). Indexed by recipients (pp. 747–74) and incipits (pp. 775–835). Also includes as a cover illustration a facsimile of a letter Wagner addressed on 6 April 1870 to Breitkopf & Härtel, his own publisher as well as the publisher of this catalog.

Older but still of interest are:

74. Altmann, Wilhelm. *Richard Wagners Briefe nach Zeitfolge und Inhalt.* Leipzig: Breitkopf & Härtel, 1905; reprinted Wiesbaden: Breitkopf & Härtel, 1971. viii, 560pp. ISBN 3500237002 ML410.W1A45 1971

For each of 3,143 letters written by Wagner, Altmann provides recipient, date, place(s) of composition and/or publication, and at least one representative quotation; he also provides an index of recipients (pp. 553–60). Less comprehensive than item 73.

75. Kastner, Emerich. *Briefe von Richard Wagner an seine Zeitgenossen, 1830–1883.* Berlin: Leo Liepmannssohn, 1897. x, 138pp. (no LC number available)

In effect a "bibliography" of Wagner's published letters to his contemporaries. Identifies by recipient, date, and place of publication some 1,470 missives; includes indexes of addressees (pp. 115–27) and of opening words or phrases (pp. 129–38); sources are cited at the beginning of the volume (pp. xii–x). The book is bound with blank pages of lined paper between the printed leaves to facilitate note-taking! Especially useful for locating nineteenth-century publications containing Wagner's correspondence. Uncommon in American libraries; the Loeb Music Library at Harvard University owns a copy.

Four specialized bibliographies of great interest to Wagnerians are:

76. Dahlhaus, Carl. Bibliography: *The New Grove Wagner.* In item 3, pp. 194–220.

An excellent guide to many important works of Wagner scholarship that had appeared in print prior to c. 1985. Unfortunately, although Dahlhaus provides places and dates for book-length publications, his bibliography omits the first names of many authors, complete pagination for most periodical articles, and fascicle numbers for certain periodicals (e.g., *Die Musik*) paginated by issue instead of year. Especially good, however, as a guide to printed matter dealing with Wagner's music dramas, letters, prose works, and political-aesthetic ideas. Closely related (Deathridge, its author, co-wrote item 3 with Dahlhaus) but less well-organized is the bibliography in the German edition of item 2, pp. 852–79.

77. Bibliography: *Wagner-Werk-Verzeichnis.* In item 83, pp. 32–62.

Without question the finest bibliography ever assembled of works providing information about the compositional histories of Wagner's compositions. Specialists may be irritated using it, however, because only the initials of authors' first names are given, and because in many cases information about periodical fascicles and pagination is incomplete. A bit out-of-date but still invaluable.

78. Bibliography: *Wagner en Vlaanderen, 1844–1914.* In item 1060, pp. 506–26.

A valuable source of material about the European Wagner reception in Lowlands Europe prior to World War I. Unfortunately omitted even from many of the most comprehensive and recently published Wagner bibliographies, including those found in items 1, 2, and 76.

79. Vogt, Matthias Theodor. "Index der Bayreuther Programmhefte 1951–1986." *Programmhefte der Bayreuther Festspiele* III–VI (1986). ML410.W2B26

Identifies the contents of Bayreuth Festival program booklets (*Programmhefte*) published between World War II and the mid-1980s. In this bibliography Vogt alphabetizes articles by authors' last names: thus "A–F" appear in III ("Rheingold"), pp. 25–42; "G–O" in IV ("Walküre"), pp. 37–62; "P–T" in V ("Siegfried"), pp. 25–46; and "V–Z" in VI ("Götterdämmerung"), pp. 29–52. Several installments contain illustrations not always immediately pertinent to the entries themselves; furthermore, articles are identified by "volumes" (i.e., "H" for "Programmheft *Der fliegende Holländer*," "S" for *Siegfried*," and so on) rather than numbered fascicles (i.e., I, II, etc.) and page numbers. Like other *Programmhefte* publications, this one can be difficult to locate in American libraries.

Related to these and other Wagner bibliographies are:

80. Limberg, Eva-Maria. *Richard Wagner-Bibliographie. Problemanalyse und Vorstudien zu einer neu zu erstellenden Personalbibliographie.* Arbeiten

und Bibliographien zum Buch- und Bibliothekwesen, 7. Frankfurt a.M.: Peter Lang, 1989. 115pp. ISBN 3631417268 ML134.W3L5 1989

In large part a study of the problems of compiling Wagner bibliographies, based primarily on familiar reference works already in print. Limberg concentrates on German-language publications, which she examines and compares in part using four tables, the last two of which are printed as back-to-back foldouts illustrating essential features of the works she considers most important. Includes a source list of its own (pp. 101–109) and a catalog of principal published Wagner bibliographies (pp. 95–100); concludes with an index.

* Gallia, Francesco. "Contributo alla bibliografia wageriana." Described as item 197.

Includes bibliographic information about various Italian translations of Wagner's prose works and a brief bibliography of Wagner prose editions in Italian.

* Hopkinson, Cecil. *Tannhäuser. An Examination of 36 Editions.* Described as item 166.

A bibliographic study as well as an examination of the contents and significance of various musical editions.

In addition to these sources, there exist other, less familiar, but occasionally useful and intriguing Wagner bibliographies. Some of these, like the long-defunct catalogs of publications issued by individual firms like Breitkopf & Härtel, have been entirely taken over into more recent studies (i.e., item 83). Others may be of greater interest to specialists; among these are auction catalogs that lie beyond the purview of the present volume. Identified below are two miscellaneous works that may be of interest:

81. Manly, Martha. "Bibliography of biographical material on Richard Wagner, 1900–1933." Columbia University: typescript, 1933. (no LC number available)

   Not seen; cited in item 95, p. 183. According to this source, a copy belongs to the New York Public Library. If this item still exists, it may be of considerable value to students of Wagner literature in American library collections.

82. *The Wagner Collection.* Antiquarian Listing, 8. Chicago: The Roundelay Book & Music Shop, 1964. 73pp. ML134.W3R6

   A sales catalog that identifies some 1,025 publications, including accounts of Wagner's life, activities, and musical and literary works; editions of the composer's writings, including his letters; scores of compositions; studies of art works, costume designs, stage designs, and photographs. Also includes a handful of playbills, posters, theater programs, and other ephemera. Illustrated with a cover photograph of a bust of the composer.

MUSICAL CATALOGS AND RELATED STUDIES

Perhaps the single finest and most useful of all Wagner reference works, and one that supercedes previous efforts along similar lines, is:

83. Deathridge, John, with Martin Geck, Egon Voss, and Isolde Vetter. *Wagner-Werk-Verzeichnis (WWV). Verzeichnis der musikalischen Werke Richard Wagners und ihre Quellen.* Mainz: B. Schott's Sons, 1986. 607pp. ISBN 3795722012 ML134.W1A15 1986

Identifies each and every one of Wagner's known compositions—finished or unfinished, extant or lost—first by title and *WWV* number in chronological order of composition, then by performing forces, versions, principal themes or incipit(s), date(s) of drafts, revisions, and completed scores, date(s) of first performances, manuscript source(s), published editions, references in autobiographical documents and reminiscences, appropriate secondary sources of information, and so on. Also includes information about doubtful and "phony" works. An essential research tool, and one that replaces the few previous and, by comparison, pitiful catalogs of Wagner's instrumental and vocal works. Reviewed enthusiastically and at length in a variety of periodicals, including *Music & Letters* 69 (1988), pp. 396–98.

Additional non-thematic catalogs of Wagner's compositions include:

84. *Verzeichnis sämmtlicher* [*sic*] *Werke von Palestrina, Schütz, Bach . . .* [*and*] *Wagner.* Leipzig: Breitkopf & Härtel, c. 1895. Unpaginated. (no LC number available)

Contains a number of pages that identify various editions of Wagner's music dramas and other compositions; among these are excerpts from longer works, piano-vocal scores, and arrangements of certain numbers for other vocal and/or instrumental forces—the last including most of Liszt's Wagner transcriptions and paraphrases—as well as information about editions of Wagner's literary works. The title page of the section in question, dated 1886, bears a black-and-white portrait of the composer. Especially useful for individuals seeking information about turn-of-the-last-century arrangements and transcriptions. Uncommon; the British Library, London, owns a copy.

Many "catalogs" of Wagner's compositions are actually guides to the musical contents of his mature music dramas, as the following example illustrates:

85. Windsperger, Lothar. *Das Buch der Motive und Themen aus sämtlichen Opern und Musikdramen Richard Wagner's. Für Klavier zu 2 Händen mit übergelegtem Text.* 2 vols. Mainz and Leipzig: B. Schott's Sons, 1921; plate nos. 300–301. MT100.W2W56

   A collection of 491 themes and motives from *Rienzi* to *Parsifal,* arranged first in rough chronological order (Vol. 2 contains motives from *Parsifal* and the *Ring*), then in order of their appearance in each music drama. Windsperger cites manuscript sources as well as piano-vocal scores. Useful especially for pianists. Apparently reprinted several times; various copies contain more or less "modern" title pages.

Studies related to the origins and contents of Wagner thematic and compositional catalogs include:

86. Deathridge, John. "Cataloguing Wagner." *The Musical Times* 124 (1983), pp. 92–96. ML5.M85

   Briefly explains the need for a reliable Wagner catalog (subsequently published as item 83), and discusses aspects of several Wagner documents, including changes in the *Holländer* score that shift the location of that opera from Scotland to Norway, as well as the non-existent "Starnberg Quartet." Illustrated with two facsimiles of documentary details. More accessible, perhaps, in this magazine than as a somewhat longer version of the same study published in item 58, pp. 193–97. See, too, Egon Voss's comments on "Notwendigkeit und Nutzen" [about Wagner catalogs and editions] in the *Programmhefte der Bayreuther Festspiele* I (1987), 16–41.

87. Millington, Barry. "The Music." In item 1, pp. 270–324.

   Much briefer than item 83, but useful for English and American readers because it presents so much information in their own language. Millington divides Wagner's works into categories such as "operas," orchestral music, choral music, and so on, then identifies and describes individual compositions according to their full or "official" titles, English titles, *WWV* numbers, dates of composition and/or first performances (if known), stories (if relevant), and so on. Lacks thematic incipits as well as information about certain compositions, manuscript sources, and secondary sources of information. Nevertheless, a useful ready-reference work.

DICTIONARIES, LEXICONS, GLOSSARIES, AND CHECKLISTS

Perhaps the best guide to Wagner terminology—whether biographical, historical, dramatic, or musical—is:

88. Gregor-Dellin, Martin, and Michael von Soden. *Richard Wagner. Leben—Werk—Wirkung.* "Hermes Handlexikon." Düsseldorf and Vienna: Econ, 1983. 288pp. ISBN 3430134102 ML410.W1G718 1983

    Defines names, terms, and roles pertaining to Wagner's life and especially to his music dramas. Illustrated with portraits, photographs, and documentary facsimiles, a few of them in color; no musical examples, however, except for scattered reproductions of handwritten score pages. Includes a rather brief timeline (pp. 280–83) and a bibliography (pp. 283–88). No index. See item 6 for review information.

In spite of their age, the best reference guides to Wagnerian concepts, extra-musical references, and terms remain:

89. Glasenapp, Carl Friedrich. *Wagner-Encyklöpadie. Haupterscheinungen der Kunst- und Kulturgeschichte im Lichte der Anschauung Richard Wagners.* 2 vols. Leipzig: E. W. Fritzsch, 1891. ML410.W1A145

    A monumental publication, unfortunately uncommon today and inevitably somewhat outdated insofar as the results of recent researches are concerned. Vol. 1 covers "Achilleus bis Lykurgos", Vol. 2 the rest of the alphabet. The titles of the entries themselves suggest the breadth of the work, which identifies and summarizes Wagner's involvement with a galaxy of literary, musical, philosophical, historical, and artistic phenomena. Among the entries are studies of Wagner's relationships with various individuals and/or references to them in his writings (e.g., Beethoven, Liszt, Weber, etc.). The indexes (Vol. 1, pp. 445–502; Vol. 2, pp. 385–423) are mini-encyclopedias in their own right.

90. Glasenapp, Carl Friedrich, and Heinrich von Stein. *Wagner-lexikon. Hauptbegriffe der Kunst- und Weltanschauung Richard Wagner's.* Stuttgart: J. G. Cotta, 1883. x, 984pp. ML410.W1A147

    Similar to item 89 but devoted to "central concepts" in Wagner's artistic endeavors and "world view"; among the titles of individual entries are "Geld," "Künstler," and "tempo." A valuable source of information about the history and development of attitudes toward Wagner's music and philosophy. Contains a few scattered musical examples as well as a comprehensive index, which is itself worth consulting (pp. 935–84).

More recent and in certain senses more complete, although not always more useful or reliable, are the following glossaries and lexicons, described in alphabetical order by author:

91. Bauer, Hans-Joachim. *Richard Wagner Lexikon.* Bergish Gladbach: Gustav Lübbe, 1988. 608p. ISBN 378570495X ML410.W1B32 1988

Provides information about persons, places, and characters in Wagner's operas and music dramas, and Wagnerian terminology; some articles are relatively fulsome (e.g., "Liszt," pp. 241–46). Illustrated with numerous smaller black-and-white pictures of various kinds (portraits, photographs of places, etc.), as well as a few full-sized plates; concludes with an index of names prepared by Uwe Steffen. Reviewed in *Wagner* 10/1 (January 1989), pp. 33–35, where it is sharply criticized.

92. Grey, Thomas S. "A Wagnerian Glossary." In item 1, pp. 230–41.

Provides comparatively fulsome definitions for such technical Wagnerian terms as "anticipation motif," "Bar form," "Gesamtkunstwerk," "quadratic melody," and "Stabreim." With the exception of the last topic and a very few others associated with Wagner's verse, Grey limits himself to terms employed primarily by music analysts. Includes a few quotations from various literary works, but no musical examples.

93. Lewsey, Jonathan. *Who's Who and What's What in Wagner.* Aldershot: Ashgate, 1997. xiii, 350pp. ISBN 1859282806 ML410.W19L48

Defines characters, scene locations, and certain technical terms found in Wagner's music dramas; representative entries include "Beckmesser," "Seil" (the latter the Rope of Destiny mentioned in *Götterdämmerung*), and "Valhalla." No biographical entries. Includes a Wagner discography (pp. 336–47) as well as a glossary of translations from portions of Wagner's libretti (pp. 278–335); concludes with a short bibliography. More up-to-date in certain respects than items 89–90, but scholars may wish to refer to those older publications for more complete information.

Less comprehensive, intelligent, and/or accurate are the following English-language reference works:

94. Hodson, Phillip. *Who's Who in Wagner: An A-to-Z Look at His Life and Work.* New York: Macmillan, 1984. xviii, 182pp. ISBN 002552030X ML410.W19H64 1984

A pocket dictionary devoted to individual music-drama characters and the stage works themselves in their completion. Intended for non-specialists; a reviewer for the *Opera Quarterly* [3/1 (Spring 1985), p. 112] calls Hodson's volume "entertaining." Includes a family tree (p. vi) and timeline (pp. xiv–xviii), as well as lists of the composer's non-operatic compositions (pp. 179–81) and literary works (pp. 181–82). NB: The English edition (London: Weidenfeld & Nicholson, 1984) is not subtitled.

95. Terry, Edward M. *A Richard Wagner Dictionary*. New York: Wilson, 1939; reprinted Westport, CT; Greenwood, 1971. 186pp. ISBN 083714356X ML410.W1A15 1971

The first and most familiar English-language Wagner reference work. Identifies and describes works and dramatic characters as well as places the composer lived; also contains entries dealing with a few additional composers. An appendix presents motifs from many of the operas and music dramas. Concludes with a bibliography of pre–World War I, mostly English-language Wagner books and articles; many of these are not described in the present volume. See, too, item 81.

Two outstanding specialized dictionaries deal, respectively, with Wagner's vocabulary and that of his critics:

96. Ott, Felix. *Richard Wagners poetisches Wortschatz*. Biala [Austro-Hungarian Galicia]: "Felddruckerei der Burgarmee," 1916. 107pp. ML410.W19O88

Essentially a dictionary of new words Wagner himself constructed from existing German particles and roots; an index of these roots appears on pp. 95–103. Organized alphabetically; for each word he cites Ott gives its source, quotes the line or lines from the libretto(s) in which it appears, and explains its meaning(s). A unique publication. Apparently presented as a doctoral dissertation, although the printed version lacks precise information about where the author received his degree.

97. Tappert, Wilhelm. *Richard Wagner im Spiegel der Kritik. Wörterbuch der Unhöflichkeit, enthaltend grobe, höhnende, gehässige und verleumderische Ausdrücke, die gegen den Meister Richard Wagner, seine Werke und seine Anhänger von den Feinden und Spöttern gebraucht wurden*. 2nd ed. Leipzig: C. F. W. Siegel, 1903. vii, 106pp. ML410.W19T17

A dictionary of negative and offensive terms employed by Wagner's opponents during the latter half of the nineteenth century. Each term is not only identified and defined, but at least one published source is cited to illustrate its use; certain entries, such as that for *Zukunftsmusik* ("Music of the Future"; pp. 101–105), are essays in their own right.

Originally published in 1876 in a substantially shorter version entitled *Ein Wagner-Lexicon* [*Wörterbuch der Unhöflichkeit* . . .]; the second edition contains the first-edition foreword. Either this edition or that described above may have been reprinted at Munich in 1967 under the simpler title *Wörterbuch der Unhöflichkeit*, but the present author has never seen a copy of this edition.

Many Wagner glossaries are devoted primarily or even entirely to terminology or characters in the music dramas. One work devoted entirely to Wagner's family members, friends, and acquaintances is:

98. Millington, Barry. "Who's Who of Wagner's Contemporaries." In item 1, pp. 22–34.

Provides birth and death dates, brief biographical and professional summaries, and additional information for dozens of persons, including a few individuals like the anarchist Mikhail Bakunin. Omits some older and influential contemporaries like Beethoven, but includes most of Wagner's immediate family.

Checklists of several kinds may be found scattered throughout the Wagnerian literature. Among the finest of these are two ready-reference guides to the composer's prose publications:

99. Kühnel, Jürgen. "Checklist of Writings." In item 2, pp. 638–51.

Identifies in roughly chronological order 214 prose works by Wagner. For each work, book or essay, Kühnel gives its original German title or identifies it with a brief description (a few newspaper squibs appeared without titles); he also provides its date(s) of authorship, if known; date and place of first publication, if known (some works have been lost); alternate title(s) and/or designation(s) of authorship, if appropriate (Wagner sometimes employed pseudonyms or published his observations anonymously); and volume and page number(s) of republication in the *Sämtliche Schriften und Dichtungen* (item 173)—the last an outgrowth of the *Gesammelte Schriften und Dichtungen* assembled under Wagner's direction between 1871 and 1883 (item 172). Invaluable as a ready reference, especially since most of the other lists of Wagner's prose publications are inaccurate, incomplete, or difficult to use.

100. Millington, Barry. "The Prose Works: A List of Wagner's Writings, Speeches, Open Letters and Reviews." In item 1, pp. 326–32.

A less complete list of the same documents. Millington provides the original title and date of authorship for each work as well as the volume of its republication, if any, in the *Gesammelte Schriften / Sämtliche Schriften* and Ellis's English-language edition (item 175). Concludes with a bibliography of additional prose-works publications (p. 332).

Finally, many books and articles about Wagner include lists of performances and performers. One of the studies devoted exclusively to these subjects is:

101. Kastner, Emerich. *Chronologisches Verzeichnis der ersten Aufführungen von Richard Wagners dramatischen Werken*, 2nd ed. Leipzig: Breitkopf & Härtel, 1899. 52pp. ML410.W1K2

A checklist of Wagner premiere performances; accompanied by a frontispiece portrait of the composer. Scholars today, however, are advised to consult item 83 above or several of the specialized "local histories" dealing with the Wagner reception in various cities and countries rather than Kastner's study.

COLLECTION AND EXHIBITION CATALOGS

General or Broader-Based Catalogs

Wagner documents survive today in a large number of museums and libraries scattered around the world. There is no guide to such documents, although WWV *provides a great deal of information about musical autographs and editions. In addition to on-line sources, researchers may wish to consult the following descriptions of especially important collections preserved in Dresden and Philadelphia:*

102. *Catalogue of the Burrell Collection of Wagner Documents, Letters, and Other Biographical Material*. London: Nonpareil, 1929. xi, 99pp. (no LC number available)

Identifies 518 artifacts, including letters, manuscripts, and published volumes. Includes as a frontispiece a facsimile of a two-page letter signed "Peter E. Wright," dated 21 August 1929. An appendix (p. 99) identifies lost Wagner documents. Uncommon, although both the British Library, London, and Harvard University's Loeb Music Library own copies. NB: Portions of the Burrell Collection have belonged at various times to the Curtis Institute of Music, Philadelphia, and the Bayreuth Wagner archives (see item 108).

103. Westernhagen, Curt von. *Richard Wagners Dresdener Bibliothek 1842–1849. Neue Dokumente zur Geschichte seines Schaffens*. Wiesbaden: F. A. Brockhaus, 1966. 116p. ML410.W19W35 1966

A catalog of 169 books (pp. 84–110) owned by Wagner prior to his participation in the Dresden uprising. Among the books mentioned are *Parcival* by Wolfram von Eschenbach, some of the *Eddas*, and four editions of the *Nibelungenlied*, as well as works by Dante, Herodotus, Homer, Schiller, Shakespeare, and so on. Includes a portrait of Wagner painted in the early 1840s by E. B. Kietz as well as four addition pages of black-and-white plates, an appendix (pp. 111–13) that supplies supplementary information about the authors and subjects of the books Wagner owned, and a general index.

Several publications draw exclusively or largely upon Bayreuth Wagner collections. Among them is:

104. *Neue Wagner-Forschungen. Erste Folge (Herbst, 1943)*, ed. Otto Strobel. Karlsruhe: G. Braun, 1943. 255pp. ML410.W1B24

The first and only volume in a series interrupted by Germany's downfall in World War II. Contains items 286, 356, and 370, as well as other articles dealing with Wagneriana and an introductory essay by Strobel himself— "Ziele und Wege der Wagnerforschung" (pp. 15–32)—intended to improve Wagner's image by reevaluating items in the Burrell collection. Also contains an essay by Westernhagen, "Wagner und das Reich" (pp. 43–73), of a markedly political character that also deals with Bismarck and German unification. Illustrated throughout with documentary facsimiles in black-and-white, and carefully indexed.

Although valuable, other—and more emphatically "Bayreuth"—studies by Strobel can be difficult to locate. See, for example, his *Genie am Werk: Richard Wagners Schaffen und Wirken im Spiegel eigenthandschriftlicher Urkunden. Führer durch die einmalige Ausstellung einer umfassenden Auswahl von Schätzen aus dem Archiv des Hauses Wahnfried* (Bayreuth 1933; revised 1934); and "Richard-Wagner-Forschungsstättee und Archiv des Hauses Wahnfried" published in *Bayreuth: die Stadt Richard Wagners*, ed. Strobel and Ludwig Deubner (Munich, 1943). Both are cited in item 76 and other important Wagner bibliographies.

Two additional catalogs document Wagner's German biases and their impact on twentieth-century musical and social history:

105. Zelinsky, Hartmut. *Richard Wagner—ein deutsches Thema. Eine Dokumentation zur Wirkungsgeschichte Richard Wagners, 1876–1976.* Berlin and Vienna: Medusa, 1983. 292pp. ISBN 3886020665 ML410.W131Z45 1983

A massive collection of materials touching on Wagner's German heritage and ideological leanings, especially on the Wagner reception in Germany since the first production of the *Ring* in 1876. Large, crowded, densely printed and somewhat difficult—as well as fascinating—to peruse. Zelinsky is critical of Wagner scholarship in general, and keenly aware of links between the composer's music ideas and more than one disreputable political cause. The materials themselves—portraits, caricatures, facsimiles of title pages and other publications, excerpts from a variety of books, pamphlets, magazines, newspapers, cartoons, and a few musical examples as well as a lot of Nazi stuff—are set off by an introduction (pp. 4–5) and "surrounded" by paired essays (pp. 6–22, 278–84). Also includes a list of sources (pp. 287–89) and an index.

106. Eger, Manfred. *Wagner und die Juden. Fakten und Hintergründe.* Bayreuth: Druckhaus Bayreuth, 1985. 80pp. ML410.W19E45 1985 (no ISBN available)

Associated with an exhibition held at the Richard-Wagner-Museum during the 1980s. Among the exhibits reproduced in the catalog is a complete facsimile of Wagner's *Jewishness in Music* (pp. 9–19) as it appeared in September 1850 issues of the *Neue Zeitschrift für Musik*. Illustrated with a number of black-and-white plates, including portraits of Giacomo Meyerbeer, Houston Stewart Chamberlain, Cosima Wagner, and so on. Contains a few scattered musical examples. Handsome and well-documented.

Catalogs of Individual Exhibitions and Collections

Most exhibition catalogs are concerned with artifacts relating to, or at least displayed in, particular cities. Although quite useful—many of them provide information about issues of local history unavailable elsewhere—such catalogs may be considered ephemera even by their publishers and often lack publication information or ISBNs; furthermore, many of them are scarce in American libraries. The following selection, by no means complete, is arranged first in alphabetical order by city (all of them German, unless otherwise indicated), then in alphabetical order by author or title:

Bayreuth: see also items 1133 and 1172.

107. *Bayreuth im Dritten Reich. Richard Wagners politische Erben: eine Dokumentation,* ed. Berndt W. Wessling. Weinheim and Basel: Beltz, 1983. 336pp. ISBN 3407390068 ML410.W2B288 1983

Catalogs an exhibition, presented by the City of Bayreuth and its several Wagner organizations, celebrating the centenary of Wagner's death. The volume itself, a "reader" full of sources ranging from Wagner's essay *Jew-*

ishness in Music to Nazi proclamations and publications of the 1930s; it is extensively illustrated with portraits of Wagner, Hitler, and other individuals, as well as with facsimiles of Bayreuth Festival program covers, photographs of local places, a few caricatures, and the like. Includes an essay by the editor on "Richard Wagners Antisemitismus und die Folgen" (pp. 306–27). Indexed.

*   Habermann, Sylvia. *Der Auftritt des Publikums.* Described as item 1133.

Documents a 1991 exhibition devoted to Bayreuth Festival visitors prior to the outbreak of World War I.

108. Kraft, Zdenko von. Appendix on "The Wahnfried Archive," trans. Cedric Williams. In item 31, pp. 429–32.

Describes the establishment by Wagner's son Siegfried of an invaluable documentary collection incorporated in 1973 into Bayreuth's Richard-Wagner-Stiftung. Kraft summarizes the original holdings at Wahnfried; he also mentions the assimilation in October 1978 into the Stiftung's collections of "chief items from the great Burrell Collection, formerly in the possession of the Curtis Institute of Music at Philadelphia" (p. 432). With regard to the latter collection's original holdings, see item 102 above; see also item 1126.

*   *Mit ihm: Musiktheatergeschichte. Wolfgang Wagner zum 75. Geburtstag: eine Ausstellung.* Described as item 1172.

Documents a 1995 Bayreuth exhibit devoted to Wolfgang Wagner's career and accomplishments.

109. *Richard-Wagner-Museum Bayreuth.* Braunschweig: Westermann, 1982. 128pp. ML141.B283W34 1982 (no ISBN available)

An illustrated guide to the museum's collections as of the early 1980s. Includes a number of illustrations, some in color; among these are diagrams of the museum's rooms with information about the location of particular exhibits as well as portraits of Wagner and his family, photographs of places and production scenes, a few documentary facsimiles, and a few musical examples. The anonymous authors also provide information about Wagner's Wahnfried library and the composer's relationship with his sometime friend and father-in-law, Franz Liszt (pp. 96–99). Concludes with a brief timeline (pp. 124–26) rather than a bibliography or index.

Eichstätt: see item 1172.

Graupa near Dresden: see item 901.

Graz, Austria
110. *Richard Wagner und Graz.* Graz: H. Schmerzeck & Co., ?1980. 48pp. (no ISBN or LC numbers available)

Commemorates an exhibition held at the Stadtmuseum (Palais Khuenburg from 21 May–13 June 1980) dealing with Wagner's relationship with Graz and surrounding villages. Descriptions of some 79 artifacts—publications, pictures, musical scores, and so on—comprise the bulk of the publication, and are arranged by the rooms in which they were displayed. Accompanied by 98 black-and-white illustrations; the last are especially useful for students of Wagneriana and Austrian local history. The Harvard University libraries own a copy of this volume.

Hobart, Tasmania
111. Borchardt, Dietrich Hans. *Catalog of a Collection of Books Relating to Richard Wagner and His Circle Used by Henry Handel Richardson as Sources for "The Young Cosima" (1939) and Housed in the University of Tasmania Library.* Monash University English Department Bibliographic Checklists, 2. Melbourne: (typescript), 1973. 14pp. ML134.W3B67

Identifies precisely what its lengthy title says. Contains no illustrations or musical examples. NB: Richardson's novel is omitted from the present research guide.

Karlsruhe
112. *Richard Wagner und Karlsruhe.* Karlsruher Beiträge, 4. Karlsruhe: G. Braun, 1987. 132pp. ISBN 3765004030 (no LC number available)

A collection of essays and documents published in conjunction with an exhibition held in Karlsruhe from 17 February–7 May 1983. Includes an account of that event by Werner Schulz, "Ruckblick auf die Ausstellung 'Richard Wagner und Karlsruhe' " (pp. 109–32), as well as three articles on exclusively or primarily Wagnerian topics—Werner Breig's "Eduard Devrient und Richard Wagners 'Ring des Nibelungen': Eine kommentierte Dokumentation" (pp. 9–34); Kurt Pietschmann's "Richard Wagners Werke auf Karlsruher Bühnen 1919–1985" (pp. 75–108); and Schulz's "Das Karlsruher Hoftheater, Felix Mottl und Bayreuth" (pp. 35–74). Pietschmann's essay is accompanied by a number of black-and-white illustrations dealing with Karlsruhe productions of Wagner's works.

Koblenz

113. *Richard Wagner und die politischen Bewegnungen seiner Zeit.* Koblenz: SZ-Druck, 1983. 51pp. (no ISBN or LC numbers available)

Identifies and describes some 195 artifacts exhibited in the Bundesarchiv, Koblenz, during the 1983 "Wagner year," and provides black-and-white illustrations of some of them. Among the artifacts in question are a few dealing with anti-semitism, vegetarianism, and other peripheral Wagner issues, as well as with the composer's music dramas and more important life events. Also contains a timeline (pp. 14–16).

Leipzig

114. *Leipzig. Die Geburtstadt Richard Wagners feiert den 125. Geburtstag des Meisters.* Leipzig: Max Beck, 1938. 110pp. (no LC number available)

An oblong volume commemorating an exhibition held from 13 February–6 June 1938 in the city where Wagner was born. A number of illustrations document the history of the city and reproduce portraits of the composer and members of his family, photographs and portraits of other celebrated Leipzig performers and citizens, and the like. Includes illustrations associated with productions given in Leipzig of every Wagner stage work from *Die Hochzeit* to *Parsifal*, as well as complete cast lists for many nineteenth- and early-twentieth-century productions. Also includes a few documentary facsimiles. As one might expect of a Nazi-era publication, Felix Mendelssohn in not mentioned. Harvard University's Loeb Music Library owns copies of this volume and item 113.

Lucerne, Switzerland

The most up-to-date of several publications is:

115. *Richard Wagner: His Lucerne Period. The Museum in Tribschen.* Lucerne: Keller & Co., 1983. 100pp. ISBN 3857660066 ML410.W11R5313 1983

A general catalog of the Wagner museum collections outside Lucerne in the form of a room-by-room guidebook. Includes hundreds of photographs, documentary facsimiles, and other illustrative materials, some in color, as well as Michael Riedler's "Richard Wagner and Lucerne" (pp. 7–33). Concludes with a one-page index of names. Also available in German as *Richard Wagner. Seine Zeit in Luzern. Das Museum in Tribschen* (ISBN 3857660038).

Previous catalogs include:

116. Schmid, Anton. *Das Richard Wagner-Museum in Tribschen*, 2nd ed. Lucerne: Richard Wagner-Museum, 1938. 32pp. ML410.W12S98 1938

Provides information about portions of its collections and exhibits, as well as scattered illustrations, mostly of familiar local Wagner "places." Outdated and in any case less comprehensive than item 115 above. NB: an earlier, slightly shorter edition of the same work appeared in print in 1933. Other guides to the Wagner collections in Tribschen outside Lucerne also exist: see, for instance, the catalog published in at least five editions and available in its fifth edition, published in 1963, on microform copy at the Library of Congress, Washington, D.C. (shelf-number MLCS 92/16370).

117. Zinssag, Adolf. *Die Briefsammlungen des Richard Wagner-Museums in Tribschen bei Luzern (Originale und Fotokopien)*. Basel: "selbstverlag" [published by the author], n.d. (c. 1960). 85pp. (no LC number available)

Identifies 91 letters written by various individuals, including Wagner, between 1831–1933. Also contains a table of contents (pp. 5–8) and an index of names. Useful for students of Swiss history and culture, as well as for Wagnerians interested in knowing more about this significant documentary collection.

Milan, Italy
* *Il caso Wagner al Teatro alla Scala, 1873–1991*. Described as item 844.

Nuremberg
118. *"Die Meistersinger" und Richard Wagner. Die Rezeptionsgeschichte einer Oper von 1868 bis heute*. Nuremberg: Germanisches Nationalmuseum, 1981. 339pp. ML410.W1A286 1981 (no ISBN available)

A lavishly illustrated commemorative volume-*cum*-exhibition catalog, associated with the exhibition held at the German National Museum from 10 July–11 October 1981. The volume includes essays by Manfred Eger, Reinhard Ermen, Rita Fischer ("Hans Sachs und die Meistersinger in der Oper des 19. Jahrhunderts"; pp. 69–78), Hans Mayer, Michael Petzel ("Die Münchner Uraufführung der 'Meistersinger' [21. Juni 1868]"; pp. 23–34), and so on. Concludes with a collection of press clippings and other reception materials assembled by Ermen (pp. 317–30), and with an index. The plates include color reproductions of sets and costume designs as well as Wagner portraits, program covers, documentary facsimiles of various kinds, and photographs.

Paris, France

119. *Exposition Richard Wagner*. Paris: Grandes Imprimeries, c. 1966. 51pp. (no LC number available)

The substantial catalog of an exhibit held in Paris at the Musée Galliera from 24 June–17 July 1966. Some 650 artifacts are identified and described; unfortunately, only a few are illustrated. Harvard University's Loeb Music Library owns a copy of this scarce volume.

120. Kahane, Martine, and Nicole Wild. *Wagner et la France*. Paris: Bibliothèque Nationale [and] Opéra, 1983. 175pp. ISBN 2733500597 ML410.W12F742 1983

Identifies and describes in considerable detail 389 artifacts exhibited from October 1983–January 1984 at the Bibliothèque Nationale, Paris, dealing with Wagner's visits to and relationship with France and the French capital, and especially with Wagner's music dramas in French productions during the later nineteenth and twentieth centuries. Includes a French-oriented Wagner timeline (pp. 150–57); a catalog of Wagner productions in Paris, 1891–1914 (pp. 158–65); and an essay on Wagner and the Paris Opéra, 1861–1983 (pp. 165–73). Concludes with a bibliography. The illustrations, some of them printed in color, include portraits, photographs, sketches and polished illustrations for production and costume designs, caricatures, documentary facsimiles, and even facsimiles of advertisements inspired by Wagner and his music.

Strasbourg, France

121. *Richard Wagner et le wagnérisme: centennaire du Festival de Bayreuth (1876–1976)*, ed. H. Strauss. Typescript; 73pp. ML141.S77W37

Describes 238 artifacts, largely French in origin and orientation—portraits, photographs and engravings and places and productions, copies of books and periodicals, etc.—exhibited at the Bibliothèque Nationale et Univérsitaire de Strasbourg in June 1976. Includes excerpts from Schuré's *Richard Wagner* (item 16) are included; also included is a brief essay on "Wagner et Strasbourg" (pp. 35–37). Unlike many catalogs, this one provides shelf-numbers for many little-known items borrowed from relevant libraries. No illustrations.

Venice, Italy

122. Batacchi, Franco, and Paolo Costantini. *Itinerari Veneziani di Richard Wagner / Venezianische Wege Richard Wagners*. Venice: Bubola & Naibo, 1995. 118pp. ML410.W12I83525 1995 (no ISBN available)

A beautiful picture book devoted to the city of Venice and its musical traditions, and especially to Wagner's Venetian sojourns during the later years of his life, and his death in Venice in February 1883. Published in conjunction with an exhibition presented first at Spazio Olivetti, Venice, then at the Richard-Wagner-Museum, Eisenach, between June and September 1995. Includes an introduction by Giuseppe Pugliese, and important historical photographs by Mario Vidor, as well as a wide variety of portraits and other illustrations, many printed in color and some in mezzotint, interspersed with historical information and reminiscences in both German and Italian. Concludes with a one-page bibliography; the table of contents at the beginning of the volume serves as its index.

* *Wagner e la caricatura / Wagner e la fotografia.* Described as item 133 below.

Documents an exhibit of items held in Venice in 1983, the centenary of the composer's death.

Wiesbaden

123. *Richard Wagner in Wiesbaden. Begleitheft und Katalog zur Ausstellung der Hessischen Landesbibliothek Wiesbaden 14. Dezember 1983–15. Februar 1984.* Wiesbaden: Karlheinz Holz, 1984. 45pp. ML410.W11R4 1984 (no ISBN available)

Identifies 66 exhibits documenting Wagner's visits to Weisbaden in 1835 and 1862 as well as performances of his music dramas there. In addition to unpaginated plates, the volume contains a facsimile and a transcription of Wagner's letter to Louis Schindelmeisser of 12 November 1852 (pp. 24–27), and other illustrations. Accompanying the catalog is an essay by Helmut Schwitzgabel, "Richard Wagner in Wiesbaden: Der Beitrag des Wiesbadener Theaters zur Wagner Rezeption im 19. Jh." [*sic*] (pp. 5–23).

ICONOGRAPHIES AND RELATED STUDIES

Most collections of Wagner "images" are either illustrated biographies or specialized studies dealing with stage sets, costume designs, individual performers, and so on. Only a few identify and evaluate systematically portraits of the composer or discuss illustrations depicting more than one aspect of his career or cultural influence.

The only monograph devoted exclusively and systematically to images of Wagner himself is:

124. Geck, Martin. *Die Bildnisse Richard Wagners.* Studien zur Kunst des neun-
     zehnten Jahrhunderts, 9. Munich: Prestel, 1970. 164pp. ML410.W196G4

     Devoted primarily to identifying, describing, and reproducing 43 portraits or
     groups of related portrait images of the composer: paintings or drawings
     done in oils, pastels, and pencil, printed engravings; photographs; medal-
     lions; busts; cast statues; and death masks. Original versions of all images
     dealt with by Geck date from 1833 to 1883, although reproductions of some
     artifacts appeared after Wagner's death; a small number of additional images
     are described and reproduced in smaller format in an appendix (pp. 160–61).
     Geck also discusses the significance of Wagner portraiture in an introduction
     (pp. 13–60), itself illustrated with eight tipped-in color reproductions of art
     by Joseph Bernhardt, Paul von Joukowsky, Franz von Lenbach, Auguste
     Renoir, and so on. Includes a one-page bibliography of sources cited in
     descriptions of the portraits (p. 128) and extensive notes (pp. 129–59); con-
     cludes with indexes of the names and works of the artists themselves.

*A second study identifies, reproduces, and describes images associated with Wag-
ner as well as portraits of him:*

125. Weber, Solveig. *Das Bild Richard Wagners. Ikonographische Bestandsauf-
     nahme eines Künstlerkults.* 2 vols. Mainz: B. Schott's Sons, 1993. ISBN
     (both volumes): 3795702631 ML410.W196W4 1993

     A study of the Wagner reception in visual terms. Vol. 1 contains the text of
     Weber's arguments, Vol. 2 the illustrations themselves, including a group of
     Beethoven portraits. More a catalog than a social study; Weber reproduces
     very few caricatures. Outfitted with an outstanding bibliography (Vol. 1, pp.
     285–310) and an index (Vol. 1, pp. 311–19). A valuable and most unusual
     contribution to the Wagner literature. Reviewed positively in *Imago Musi-
     cae: International Yearbook of Musical Iconography* 13 (1996), p. 191.

*Two brief studies—the former more fulsome—summarize Wagner's impact on the
visual arts and various individual artists; these are not iconographies per se, but
they discuss subjects that have been or may become material for iconographers
and art historians:*

126. Metken, Günter. "Wagner and the Visual Arts," trans. Simon Nye. In item
     2, pp. 354–72.

     Epitomizes Wagner's attitude toward painting, sculpture, and the like; then
     goes on to identify and briefly evaluate Wagner's influence on and Wag-
     nerian aspects of painters such as Aubrey Beardsley, Henri Fantin-Latour,
     Pablo Gargallo, Gustav Klimt, Oscar Kokoschka, Hans Makart, Claude
     Monet, Odilon Redon, and James Whistler, as well as the decorations

ordered by Ludwig II for Neuschwanstein, Salvador Dalí's set designs for the *Bacchanal* ballet produced during the 1939–1940 season at the Metropolitan Opera in New York, the politically provocative *Volksempfänger* tableaux of Edward Kienholz, and—especially—the various Wagner memorials erected in Berlin, Leipzig, Munich, and other parts of Germany since the turn of the last century. See also items 618 and 678.

127. Hall, Michael. "Wagner's Impact on the Visual Arts." In item 1, pp. 398–400.

Briefer and less comprehensive than item 126 above. Among other tie-ins between Wagner and various painters, Hall mentions Paul Gauguin's *Texte Wagner* scrapbook, now owned by the Bibliothèque Nationale, Paris, the composer's influence on Wassily Kandinsky during his *Blauer Reiter* period, and purported resemblances between Albert Ryder's 1880s visual depiction of the Dutchman's ship and Jackson Pollock's *Seascape* of 1934.

Other reference works devoted to Wagnerian visual imagery are somewhat more specialized:

128. *Das Werk Richard Wagners im Spiegel der Kunst*, ed. Jordi Mota and Mária Infiesta. Tübingen: Graebert, 1995. 306pp. ISBN 3878471505 (no LC number available)

An unsystematic but nevertheless wide-ranging "catalog" of Wagnerian artists—among them Beardsley, Arnold Böchlin, Dalí, Fantin-Latour, Wilhelm von Kaulbach, William Morris, and others—handsomely illustrated with 424 reproductions of paintings, statues, pieces of stained glass, stamps, and so on, many in color; omits portraits of the composer, however. Supplemented with a catalog of the illustrations (pp. 289–306) and brief biographies of the more important artists (pp. 271–88). A preface by Walter Schertz-Parey in German (pp. 5–14) and English (pp. 15–27) explains the scope and purpose of this beautiful volume.

129. *Richard Wagners photographische Bildnisse*, with a foreword by A. Vanselow. Munich: F. Bruckmann, 1908. 10 pp. (numbered i-x) + 34 numbered plates. No LC number available.

A collection of 34 photographs, all of them Wagner portraits (although one also includes his son Siegfried), taken between 1860–1882 in Brussels, Munich, Paris, St. Petersburg, Vienna, and several other cities. Some of the photos are reprinted on thick white paper and bound as regular "plates"; others are mounted on thick, textured paper. Except for Vanselow's brief introduction, the names of the photographers, and the years in which the

pictures were taken, no commentary or iconographical information is provided. Less than satisfactory as a study of its subject; item 133 below, for
instance, includes 47 Wagner photos and provides more information about
them. Unindexed.

Among the most lavishly and comprehensively illustrated of the classic Wagner
biographies and survey studies is:

130. Engel, Erich W. *Richard Wagners Leben und Werk im Bilde*, 2nd ed.
     Leipzig: C. F. W. Siegel, 1922. xxiv, 691pp. ML410.W196R72

     A biographical survey supplemented by a full-color reproduction of
     Lenbach's famous Wagner portrait (frontispiece), a bibliography (pp.
     681–84), an index of the hundreds of additional illustrations it contains
     (pp. 687–91), and a one-page timeline that doubles as a table of contents.
     Portraits, caricatures, silhouettes, photographs, documentary facsimiles—
     all are here. A handsome publication. See also items 1144 and 1168.

Three studies of Wagner caricatures—works not only of considerable value, but
entertaining to peruse—are described below in descending order of breadth:

131. Kreowski, Ernst, and Eduard Fuchs. *Richard Wagner in der Karikatur.*
     Berlin: B. Behr, 1907. v, 208pp. ML410.W19K92

     Features 223 black-and-white illustrations of various kinds, some full-
     page. Emphasizes German-language and -published caricatures, as well as
     caricatures of famous German Wagnerians, among them Hans von Bülow,
     Franz Dingelstedt, Liszt, Wagner's wife Cosima, and others. A valuable
     contribution to the literature, and one somewhat broader-based in the vari-
     ety of its images than Grand-Carteret's volume (item 132).

132. Grand-Carteret, John. *Richard Wagner en caricatures.* Paris: Larousse,
     1892. 336pp. ML410.W19G8

     A collection of caricatures and cartoons supplemented by running commen-
     tary on Wagner's reputation and reception in nineteenth-century Europe,
     mostly in France and mostly between about 1860 and 1880. In addition to a
     few documentary facsimiles, including one of a Wagner letter dated 25 Octo-
     ber 1876 (pp. 25–30), Grand-Carteret's volume contains 130 black-and-
     white illustrations, some printed as full-page plates. An index of sorts, "pour
     l'iconographie de Wagner" (pp. 299–324), groups these by country of origin
     before identifying them. Includes such familiar images as Gil's hilarious
     cover illustrations for *L'Eclipse* (pp. 91, 93) as well as little-known items.
     Unfortunately omitted from many Wagner bibliographies, possibly because
     of the pro-German and/or anti-French biases of certain bibliographers.

133. *Wagner e la caricatura. 76 tavole del Richard Wagner Museum* [and] *Wagner e la fotografia. 47 ritratti fotografici del Richard Wagner Museum.* Venice: Teatro la Fenice, 1983. 119pp. ML410. W196W34 1983 (no ISBN available)

Consists for the most part of black-and-white reproductions of the items described in the title as well as two short essays: Italo Mussa's "Wagner e lo specchio della caricatura" (pp. 9–10) and Michele Falzone del Barbarò's "Annotazioni per una iconografia fotografica di Richard Wagner, 1860–1881" (pp. 69–71). Most of the images are familiar; the photographs, however, are more interesting than the caricatures and include several family portraits as well as pictures taken at Wagner's entombment in Bayreuth and 5 versions of a Wagner portrait photo produced by Elliott & Freys, London, in 1877 (the last pp. 104–108). The cover bears the title *Wagner / Caricatura e fotografia.* Includes no musical examples per se, bibliography, or index.

* *Richard der Einzige*, ed. Hermann Hakel. Described as item 299.

Includes caricatures and cartoons but neither identifies them precisely nor evaluates their contents.

Among the most attractive studies devoted to visual aspects of Wagner's music dramas is:

134. Tubeuf, André. *Wagner. L'Opéra des images.* Paris: Chêne, 1993. 199pp. ISBN 2851087933 ML410.W13T82 1993

A gorgeous picture book covering virtually every aspect of Wagner's operas and music dramas, either "on stage" or in illustrations of various kinds. Includes reproductions of oil paintings and drawings as well as photographs of stage sets, photographs of performers, a few caricatures, and other images associated with the composer and his best-known compositions. Also includes a list of sources for the illustrations themselves (pp. 196–99) but contains no bibliography or index per se.

A few less familiar, possibly more eccentric Wagner publications also deal with iconographical issues. Among them is:

135. Leeke, Ferdinand. *Pictorial Wagner*, with an introduction by Henry T. Finck. New York: Franz Hanfstaengl, n.d. Unpaginated throughout. (no LC number available)

A collection of full-page illustrations, each protected by tissue paper, of scenes from *Holländer*, the *Ring*, and other works. A collector's item, handsomely bound. Finck, an important American music critic and the author of books and articles about Edward MacDowell, discusses Wagner as a dramatic composer (pp. 1–12). Rare: the Loeb Music Library at Harvard owns a copy.

Finally, studies related to Wagner and visual imagery include:

136. Gratl, Franz. *Iconographies of Music, 1976–1995* = *Imago Musicae: International Yearbook of Musical Iconography* 14–15 (1997–1998). ISBN 88709622466 ML85.I5

Identifies and briefly characterizes some forty publications that touch upon images of, or images inspired by, the composer, including many omitted from the present volume. Indexed by subject, which greatly facilitates locating Wagner references.

DISCOGRAPHIES AND RELATED STUDIES

Sound recordings of musical performances are invaluable sources of information to singers, instrumentalists, conductors, and scholars alike. Many bibliographies and lists of sources, however, overlook or exclude them, perhaps because recordings have often been taken less seriously than "published" materials, and have been preserved neither as carefully nor as well as books and periodicals.

The most comprehensive Wagner discography remains:

137. "Clym." *Wagner: La discographie idéale des oeuvres de jeunesse à Parsifal.* Paris: Ramsay, 1982. 284pp. ISBN 2859562842 ML156.5.W2C6 1982

A collection of essays rather than a catalog per se, and one devoted to individual Wagner genres, works, performers, and performances, including discussions of *Rienzi*, "Les Wesendoncklieder et le Siegfried-Idyll," "Wolfgang Wagner: la stéréophonie est née à Bayreuth," "Karajan et Wagner," and so on. Of considerable interest to students of the Wagner reception in late twentieth-century France as well as discographers and music lovers everywhere. Concludes with an index that also functions as a table of contents.

Somewhat more limited but nevertheless extensive Wagner discographies include the following, described in reverse chronological order of publication:

138. Favre, Georges. *Richard Wagner par le Disque [sic].* Paris: Durand & Cie., 1958. 90pp. ML156.5.W2F39 1958

More—some might say "less," because less factual information per se is provided—than a simple discography. Favre reviews Wagner's entire life and career, albeit briefly, pausing to discuss recordings of various works and the artists who perform them in approximately the order in which the works themselves were composed; he even provides a few musical examples to illustrate his observations. Includes fourteen plates that reproduce portraits of celebrated Wagner performers, pictures of the Bayreuth Theater, and so on.

139. Bagar, Robert C. *Wagner on Record*, with a foreword by Fritz Reiner. New York: Four Corners, 1942. 95pp. (no LC number available)

Published at a time when only *Tannhäuser* and *Tristan* were available "almost complete" on 78rpm disks. Concludes with a catalog of Wagner works recorded by Columbia Records, mostly overtures and highlights conducted by the likes of Reiner, Bruno Walter, Felix Weingartner, Leopold Stokowski, and Thomas Beecham. Other discographical Wagner publications by Bagar include the "Complete List of [Wagner] Recordings by the Philharmonic-Symphony Society of New York" in that author's *Wagner and His Music-Dramas* (New York, 1950), pp. 49–52.

Several of the finest Wagner discographies have been devoted to recordings of individual music dramas:

140. Brown, Jonathan. *"Parsifal" on Record: A Discography of Complete Recordings, Selections, and Excerpts of Wagner's Music Drama.* Discographies, 48. Westport, CT: Greenwood, 1992. 152pp. ISBN 0313285411 ML156.5.W2B76 1992

Evaluates 420 recorded selections, prepared by an Australian lawyer and diplomat turned discographer. Brown's discussions of complete performances are especially fulsome. Employs a few musical examples to indicate where excerpts begin in the full score; concludes with a helpful index of conductors and singers. A useful reference work and one that's unusually enjoyable to read.

141. Brown, Jonathan. *"Tristan und Isolde" on Record: A Comprehensive Discography of Wagner's Music Drama with a Critical Introduction to the Recordings.* Discographies, 85. Westport, CT: Greenwood, 2000. xvii, 267pp. ISBN 0313314896 ML156.5.W2B75 2000X

The second in a series of volumes by the author who has also given us item 140. The present volume is accompanied by sixteen illustrations, most of them portraits of Wagner conductors and singers, although facsimiles of a few *Tristan* record jackets are also included. An introduction (pp. 1–74) deals with the literature on Wagner recordings and performances in general. Concludes with an index.

Other useful Wagner discographies can be found in more comprehensive publications; the following examples are described in reverse chronological order of publication:

142. "Wagner." In: *The Metropolitan Guide to Recorded Opera*, ed. Paul Gruber. New York: Metropolitan Music Drama Guild and Norton, 1993; pp. 670–739. ISBN 0393034445 ML156.4.O46M5 1993

A collection of discographical essays with recommendations of recordings concerning Wagner's "mature" music dramas. Among the contributors (and essay topics) are: Barry Millington (*Holländer, Tannhäuser*, and *Lohengrin*); David Hamilton (*Tristan*); Kenneth Furie (*Meistersinger* and *Parsifal*); and Jon Alan Conrad (the *Ring*). The essays as a whole are arranged chronologically—first by music drama, then by date of recording. Already a bit outdated.

143. "Wagner." In: *Music Drama on Record*, ed. Alan Blyth. New York: Harper & Row, 1981; pp. 338–451. ISBN 0092499807 ML156.4.O46O55

The relevant pages include seven essays on complete recordings and excerpts from Wagner's "mature" stage works. Among the contributors (and essay topics) are: William Mann (*Holländer*), John Steane (*Tannhäuser*), Charles Osborne (*Lohengrin*), Robin Holloway (*Tristan*), Richard Law (*Meistersinger*), and Alan Blyth (the *Ring*). Each essay concludes with a list of complete recordings and excerpts, arranged in chronological order, with information about casts, conductors, and stamper or album numbers.

144. Anderson, John. *Wagner: A Biography, with a Survey of Books, Editions, and Recordings*. Hamden, CT: Linnet, 1980. 154pp. ISBN 0208016775 ML410.W1A599

Provides a brief survey of Wagner recordings to 1980 (pp. 126–43). Helpful for discussions of non-dramatic works as well as for information about "Outstanding Wagner Singers" and "Outstanding Wagner Conductors." Also published in England by Clive Bingley of London.

Three additional surveys of Wagner recordings—many others have appeared in High Fidelity *and a variety of other popular magazines—are described below in alphabetical order by author:*

145. Furie, Kenneth. "Wagner Recordings." *High Fidelity* (May 1983), pp. 52–57 and 88–89 ["The Early Music Dramas"]; (July 1983), pp. 62–68 ["The Love Stories"]; and (October 1983), pp. 86–89 and 112–115 ["Passing the Torch"]. ML1.H45

Describes in depth—role by role, singer by singer—the complete Wagner music-drama recordings through the early 1980s, excluding those of the *Ring*, as well as noteworthy excerpts from them. Furie rarely chooses one recording over others, except in the case of Knappertsbusch's 1962 Philips recording of *Parsifal*; instead, he points out the strengths and weaknesses of each conductor and singer.

146. Glass, Herbert. "The Wagner Music Dramas on Microgroove." *High Fidelity* (November 1961), pp. 57–60 and 132–38. ML1.H45

An introduction to "recent" recordings of Wagner on 33rpm phonorecords, including such performances as Furtwängler's *Tristan* on the Angel label and Knappertsbusch's *Parsifal* on London. Supplements but does not altogether supercede James Hinton, Jr.'s, "Wagner on Microgroove, Part I: 1831–1859," *High Fidelity* (April 1955), pp. 73–85; and "Part II: 1867–1882," *High Fidelity* (August 1955), pp. 64–69. Hinton, incidentally, comments not only on dramatic works, but also on recordings of such instrumental compositions as the composer's Piano Sonata in B-flat major and Symphony in C major.

147. Schreiber, Ulrich. "Die Mysterien und die Bits: Wagners Musikdramen auf Schallplatte—eine Auswahldiskographie." In item 36, pp. 148–60.

Includes information about recordings of *Die Feen* and *Rienzi* and orchestral excerpts by Toscanini and the NBC Symphony Orchestra, as well as Karajan's and Solti's *Ring* recordings and other classics. Unfortunately, Schreiber provides neither musical examples nor hard information about labels, catalog numbers, and stamper numbers.

Finally, studies of individual Wagner conductors often include discographical information:

148. Ardoin, John. *The Furtwängler Record.* Portland, OR: Amadeus, 1994. 376pp. ISBN 0931340691 ML422.F92A85 1994

Examines all of Furtwängler's recordings of Wagner's music dramas, chiefly in terms of the conductor's own artistry, but also in terms of singers and casting (see pp. 193–222). Similar kinds of comments appear in discussions of other famous conductors and their recorded legacies. See, for instance, the annotated discography of Arturo Toscanini's recorded legacy in B. H. Haggin's *Conversations with Toscanini* (Garden City, NY, 1959).

* Breckbill, David. "Conducting." Described as item 830.

Includes remarks about ways in which the birth of modern recording techniques shifted the emphasis from "total art-work" performances to recordings that preserved only—and thus, wittingly or unwittingly, exaggerated the significance of—the musical portions of Wagner's music dramas. Especially intelligent on the origins and influence of what Breckbill calls "the Mahler/Toscanini legacy of symphonic intentionality" (p. 371), as well as the significance of Furtwängler as a conductor who synthesized many styles of music-making.

FILMOGRAPHIES AND VIDEOGRAPHIES

Studies of Wagner films, whether biographical, documentary, or quasi-fictional in character, remain scarce. The only detailed catalog of such items, whether on 16mm, 35mm, or 70mm celluloid or videotape, is:

149. Bauer, Ostwald Georg. "Richard Wagner im Film." *Bayreuther Festspielprogramme* (1985): II, pp. 12–21; III, pp. 11–21; IV, pp. 11–20; V, pp. 3–13; VI, pp. 6–14; and VII, pp. 19–30. ML410.W2B26

Beginning with the first biopic (i.e., biographical film or "picture") devoted to Wagner in 1913, Bauer surveys in chronological order those movies in which "this extraordinary composer's life [was] either dramatically monumentalized or the genius [himself] . . . presented as an ordinary, everyday person" (II, p. 12). Stills from the films themselves fill the first installment, published in the 1985 Bayreuth *Parsifal* program; the five remaining portions of this valuable reference tool are devoted to identifying and discussing the films in greater detail. Full of largely otherwise unavailable illustrations. Includes introductory remarks in English, French, and German.

*   Müller, Ulrich. "Wagner in Literature and Film." Described as item 1021.

Includes information about Wagner as a movie character, film music by Wagner—as well as music reminiscent of his; the latter category includes works by Jerry Goldsmith and John Williams—employed in Hollywood film scores, and especially film versions of Wagner's music dramas; the last category includes Thomas A. Edison's silent *Parsifal* films of 1904 and 1910, *Pandora and the Flying Dutchman* of 1951, and Herbert von Karajan's 1975 television film of *Rheingold*.

TIMELINES

Timelines—also known as Zeittafeln *(the singular is* Zeittafel*)—are compilations of facts organized and identified chronologically by date and/or month as well as* *by year. One of the finest and certainly the most readily available Wagner time-lines is described below; others incorporating illustrations or additional forms of commentary are described in chapter V:*

150. Gregor-Dellin, Martin. *Wagner Chronik: Daten zu Leben und Werk.* Reihe Hanser Chroniken, 97. Munich: Carl Hanser, 1972. 188pp. ISBN 3446116400 ML410.W1G74

Provides a wealth of information about the whens, wheres, and whats of Wagner's complex life. Many activities are identified by date as well as month and year. Gregor-Dellin also includes a few quotations from such Wagnerians as Adorno, Thomas Mann, and Romain Rolland (pp. 5–7). Also includes an excellent biographical bibliography (pp. 173–80); concludes with an index (see item 6 for review information).

RESEARCH REPORTS AND RELATED STUDIES

Among recent surveys of publications about Wagner are these outstanding and provocative essays, described in alphabetical order by author:

151. Borchmeyer, Dieter. "Wagner Literature (1): A German Embarrassment" and "Wagner Literature (2)." *Wagner* 12/2–3 (May and September 1991), pp. 51–74 and 116–37. ML410.W1A585

Deals mostly with publications about Wagner and German culture, including those touching on anti-semitism (pp. 123–27). Also evaluates publications concerning Wagner's relationship with Nietzsche and the "mortal injury" issue (pp. 67–74). Referring to "the madhouse of Wagner literature" (p. 116), Borchmeyer attacks the complacency many German scholars have displayed toward their subject; he also identifies high-quality studies of various kinds.

152. Deathridge, John. "A Brief History of Wagner Research." In item 2, pp. 202–23.

Among the best surveys of the enormous literature on Wagner. Confessing that an outline of his subject "is almost impossible to write" (p. 202), Deathridge goes on to consider Wagner's personal attitudes toward scholarship, the "authenticity bonus" notion that has "prevented many scholars from challenging what we claim to know . . . simply because . . . it comes from the master's pen" (p. 203), interdisciplinary issues, the value of the *Bayreuther Blätter*—Deathridge calls it a "dreadful" publication (p. 204)—and such specialized areas as source studies and biographies.

An earlier version of this report appeared in *Wagner* 8/3 (July 1987), pp. 92–114; the latter includes a postscript on "Wagner, the Jews, and Jakob Katz" (pp. 220–23).

153. Spencer, Stewart. "Miscellaneous." In item 1, pp. 408–10.

Brief but insightful comments on the evolution of Wagner scholarship from its earliest days until the 1980s. Among other topics Spencer addresses: the general superiority of certain older publications, especially those dealing with Medieval literary sources; problems faced by those scholars who have written about the composer's nationalism and anti-semitism; the "Bayreuth Circle" and its mythologizing tendencies; and studies by students of the *Ring*, libretto history, and the enormously complex Wagner reception throughout Europe and the United States.

Somewhat older but nevertheless valuable is:

154. Serauky, Walter. "Richard Wagner in Vergangenheit und Gegenwart." *Deutsches Jahrbuch der Musikwissenschaft für 1958*, Vol. 3 = Jahrbuch der Musikbibliothek Peters, 50 (Leipzig, 1959); pp. 7–54. ML1.D486

A review of Wagner research from the later nineteenth century to the years immediately following World War II, with special emphasis on key issues associated with Wagner's place in musical, dramatic, and intellectual history; among these are the composer's use of *Stabreim*; his place in the writings of Thomas Mann and Adorno; questions surrounding the nature and even the existence of a *Wagnerstil* (i.e., individual compositional style); the purportedly "romantic" character of Wagner's works and their relationship to ancient drama and Baroque music; and so on. Illustrated with scattered musical examples. In spite of the intelligence it displays, Serauky's study is cited only occasionally in the literature.

Finally, the following falls loosely within the purview of research-related Wagner publications:

155. Kloss, Erich. *Wagner-Anekdoten, aus den besten Quellen geschöpft.* Berlin: Schuster & Loeffler, 1908. 128pp. ML410.W19K65

A reference work in the sense that it constitutes an organized collection of anecdotes by and about the composer, prepared by a recognized early twentieth-century Wagner scholar.

IV

The Documentary Legacy

Wagner left behind him so enormous a legacy of primary source materials, musical and otherwise, that scholars are still identifying and describing its various parts and their individual and overall significance. In addition to published and unpublished sources for the music dramas and instrumental compositions, there are autobiographical statements, diaries, collections of correspondence, and a variety of other artifacts to be considered. Furthermore, other individuals have left us memoirs and reminiscences of Wagner. The following pages cannot possibly mention every published or unpublished Wagner source; in the case of reminiscences and letters published in periodicals, they do not even identify very many. On the other hand, most of the collections of correspondence and a good selection of prose publications are described, as are most of the principal musical editions.

MUSICAL EDITIONS AND RELATED STUDIES

Collected Editions

No complete and completely reliable edition of Wagner's compositions has yet appeared in print. Literally thousands of "miscellaneous" editions exist, however: full scores, abbreviated and pocket scores, piano-vocal scores, scores of songs and other shorter works, facsimile editions, and arrangements for various combinations of voices and instruments—including, among the last, Liszt's monumental keyboard transcriptions.

Furthermore, the following superb series of volumes may be finished in the near future:

156. *Richard Wagner. Sämtliche Werke*, ed. Carl Dahlhaus et al. Mainz: B. Schott's Sons, 1970–. In progress. M3.W23

   Vol. 3: *Rienzi: der letzte der Tribunen* (5 facsicles), ed. Reinhard Strohm and Egon Voss.

Vol. 4: *Der fliegende Holländer* (2 facsicles), ed. Isolde Vetter.

Vols. 5–6: *Tannhäuser* (4 fascicles), ed. Reinhard Strohm (Vol. 5, 3 fascicles) and Peter Jost (Vol. 6).

Vol. 7: *Lohengrin*, ed. John Deathridge and Klaus Döge.

Vol. 8: *Tristan und Isolde* (3 fascicles), ed. Isolde Vetter.

Vol. 9: *Die Meistersinger von Nürnberg* (3 fascicles), ed. Egon Voss.

Vol. 10: *Der Ring des Nibelungen: Das Rheingold* (2 fascicles), ed. Egon Voss.

Vol. 13: *Der Ring des Nibelungen: Die Götterdämmerung* (3 fascicles), ed. Hartmut Fladt.

Vol. 14: *Parsifal* (3 fascicles), ed. Egon Voss and Martin Geck.

Vol. 15: "Compositions for the Theater," ed. Egon Voss.

Vol. 16: "Choral Works," ed. Reinhard Kapp.

Vol. 17: "Songs for Voice and Piano," ed. Egon Voss.

Vol. 18: "Orchestral Works" (3 fascicles), ed. Egon Voss and Peter Jost.

Vol. 19: "Works for Piano," ed. Carl Dahlhaus.

Vol. 20: "Arrangements for Piano" (3 fascicles), ed. Christa Just, Egon Voss, etc.

Vol. 23: *Dokumente und Texte zu "Rienzi, der Letzte der Tribunen,"* ed. Reinhard Strohm.

Vol. 29/1: *Dokumente zur Entstehungsgeschichte des Bühnenfestspiels Der Ring des Nibelungen*, ed. Werner Breig and Hartmut Fladt.

Vol. 30: *Dokumentation zur Entstehung und erster Aufführung des Bühnenweihfestspiels Parsifal*, ed. Martin Geck and Egon Voss.

As of January 2001 this purportedly definitive edition remained a work-in-progress. Several installments constitute collections of shorter pieces; thus Vol. 15 contains Wagner's "supplements" to Marschner's *Vampyr* and Carl Blum's *Mary, Max und Michel* (respectively *WWV* 33 and 43); Vol. 19 the sonatas and *Albumblätter*, among other works; and Vol. 20 Wagner's arrangement of Beethoven's Ninth Symphony and other operatic arrangements, including the composer's piano-vocal arrangement of his *Tannhäuser*; and so on. Three remaining volumes (23, 29/1, and 30) document the history and reception of *Rienzi*, the *Ring*, and *Parsifal*.

A previous attempt at a complete edition of Wagner's musical works was never finished:

157. *Richard Wagners musikalische Werke. Erste kritisch revidierte Gesamtausgabe*, ed. Michael Balling. 10 vols. Leipzig: Breitkopf & Härtel, 1912–1929; reprinted New York: Da Capo, 1971. M3.W13 1971

Vol. 1: *Die Hochzeit*
Vol. 2: *Die Feen*
Vol. 3: *Tannhäuser*
Vol. 4: *Lohengrin*
Vol. 5: *Tristan und Isolde*
Series XIV/III: *Das Liebesverbot*
Series XV/I: *Lieder und Gesänge*
Series XVI/II: *Chorgesänge*
Series XVIII/IV: *Orchesterwerke* (1st part)
Series XX/VI: *Orchesterwerke* (3rd part)

Among the various volumes of this fragmentary publication may be found the Introduction, Chorus, and Septet—all that's left, in fact—of *Die Hochzeit*, the *Faust* overture, and *Siegfried-Idyll* ("Orchesterwerke," 1st part), as well as the Symphony in C, the "Adagio" for clarinet and string quintet, and other minor ensemble works ("Orchesterwerke," 3rd part), the *Wesendonck-Lieder* ("Lieder und Gesänge"), and so on. Each volume includes introductory comments and critical apparatus, including references to questionable passages in certain editions. Full-title and facing series pages identify some volumes simply with numbers (e.g., *Tristan*); others seem to be identified in terms of series as well as parts (e.g., *Das Liebesverbot*). Uncommon; the British Library owns a complete set in its original bindings.

The Da Capo reprint edition of 1971 reprinted the original ten volumes as seven. Bibliographers, beware: both the original series and the reprint edition are inconsistently identified in a variety of sources; furthermore, the original volumes themselves are divided inconsistently into "series" and "volumes" or fascicles.

Individual Editions

Certain of Wagner's works have been published in editions of especially high quality and/or low price. Among these are:

158. [Wagner, Richard. *The Music-Dramas and Orchestral Excerpts.*] Dover paperback reprint editions. New York: Dover, 1973–. M1500.W13

   Tristan und Isolde. 1973. 655pp.
   Die Meistersinger von Nürnberg. 1976. 823pp.
   Die Walküre. 1978. 710pp.
   Die Götterdämmerung. 1982. 615pp.
   Lohengrin. 1982. 395pp.
   Siegfried. 1983. 447pp.
   Das Rheingold. 1985. 320pp.

Parsifal. 1986. 592pp.
The Flying Dutchman. 1988. 432pp.
Overtures and Preludes. 1996. 288pp.
The Ride of the Valkyries and Other Highlights from the Ring in Full Score. 1997. 272pp.

Orchestral scores of the most important music dramas and some of the concert works and excerpts, published originally in Germany during the second half of the nineteenth century. The *Overtures* volume includes the various preludes to *Tannhäuser* and *Lohengrin*, the *Faust* overture, and so on; the *Highlights* volume "Wotan's Farewell and Magic Fire Music" (*Walküre*), "Forest Murmurs" (*Siegfried*), and the like. A boon to libraries, professional scholars, and students, because Wagner scores can be expensive to buy and difficult to find. Paperbound; each volume includes a "classic" Wagner image on its cover.

159. *Richard Wagner: Prelude and Transfiguration from "Tristan und Isolde,"* ed. Robert Bailey. "Norton Critical Scores" series. New York: W. W. Norton, 1985. x, 307pp. ISBN 0393022072 M1505.W13T83 1985

Includes discussions of the work's origins, compositional history, and early performances as well as comments on *Liebestod* (love-death) as a designation for the concluding measures of the music drama as a whole. Also includes the music itself, essay-length observations by Deryck Cooke, Ernest Newman, Roger Sessions, and Donald Francis Tovey as well as lengthy quotations—and, in a few cases, entire articles—by the likes of Milton Babbitt, Edward T. Cone, Ernst Kurth (from item 465), Leonard B. Meyer, and Arnold Schoenberg; William J. Mitchell's essay is described separately as item 744. Concludes with a bibliography.

Facsimile Editions

Reproductions of a few Wagner musical manuscripts have also appeared in print:

160. Wagner, Richard. *Siegfried Idyll*. 2 vols. Lucerne, Switzerland: Edition René Coeckelberghs, 1983. ML96.5.W26 (no ISBN available)

A scholarly edition of Wagner's holograph score. Vol. 1 includes the score itself, introduced by Wolfgang Wagner and supplemented with a scholarly description of the artifact by Ernst-Hans Beer. Vol. 2 consists of commentary by Carl Dahlhaus, Michael Riedler, and Peter Wapnewski. Those seeking a simpler introduction to this lovely piece of music may wish to consult the "Penguin Critical Scores" edition outfitted with Dyneley Hussey's biographical notes and Gordon Jacob's introduction (Harmondsworth, Middlesex, 1951).

161. *Richard Wagner. Lohengrin: Vorspiel zur Oper und Einleitung zum dritter Aufzug*, ed. Heinz Krause-Graumnitz. Leipzig: VEB Deutscher Verlag für Musik, 1974. 5pp. of text + facsimile. (no ISBN or LC number available)

A satisfactory facsimile of a manuscript owned today by the Bayreuth Wagner archives but presented originally by Wagner to Liszt and bearing Wagner's heartfelt dedication "Seinem 'alter Ego' " on its title page. Apparently uncommon; the University of Toronto Music Library owns a copy, however.

162. Wagner, Richard. *Schusterlied: aus der Oper "Die Meistersinger von Nürnberg. Faksimile nach dem Autograph in der Wiener Stadt-und Landesbibliothek*, ed. Ernst Hilmar. Tutzing: Hans Schneider, 1988. 20pp. ISBN 3795205204 ML96.5.W26

Reproduces in facsimiles Wagner's sketch for baritone voice and instrumental accompaniment of "Die Schuster gratulieren zum Geburtstag" prepared for Joseph Standthartner, dated 3 February 1963 and signed by the composer.

EDITIONS OF LIBRETTOS AND TEXTS

One cannot finally altogether separate the words and music that Wagner wrote for his dramatic creations. Consequently, editions of the composer's poems—the present author prefers "librettos" or "texts"—may be of interest to individuals otherwise concerned exclusively with musical issues. Among such editions are:

163. Wagner, Richard. *The Ring of the Nibelung*, trans. Andrew Porter. New York: W. W. Norton, 1976. xli, 362pp. ISBN 0393021920 ML50.W14R32 1976

The complete *Ring* poem in two-column text presenting the German original and Porter's translation—the latter prepared for performances at Sadler's Wells Opera and the English National Opera between 1970–1973 (see also item 721). Also includes Porter's essay "Translating the Ring" (pp. vii–xviii) as well as "Wagner as Poet" by Peter Branscombe (pp. xxix–xl), and "The Ring: Its Musical Language" by Jeremy Noble (pp. xix–xxvii). NB: In his essay Porter identifies and writes about a number of previous English *Ring* translations, including those prepared by Peggie

Cochrane, Alfred Forman, Oliver Huckel, Reginald Rankin, and so on. Illustrated with a beautiful set of woodcuts prepared especially for this volume by Eric Fraser. No bibliography, however—although detailed notes follow each of the essays—and no musical examples.

164. Wagner, Richard. *The Flying Dutchman, Tannhäuser, The Mastersingers of Nuremberg, The Rheingold*, and *The Valkyries*, trans. Ernest Newman; rev. Wolfgang Golther. 5 vols. Leipzig: Breitkopf & Härtel, 1912. (no LC number available)

Unpaginated translations of five important librettos by one of England's most important Wagner scholars, revised by one of Germany's ranking Wagnerians. Each translation also includes Wagner's original German. No illustrations or musical examples. The British Library, London, owns copies of these pamphlets.

165. *Siegfried and The Twilight of the Gods by Richard Wagner*, trans. Margaret Armour. New York: Garden City Publishers, n.d. 180pp. ML410.W1A292F39

A handsome English-language edition of two of the four *Ring* texts, accompanied by twelve color reproductions of Arthur Rackham's celebrated illustrations and one black-and-white illustration on the full title page. One of many Wagner volumes intended as much or more for collectors than performers or scholars.

*   *Guide des opéras de Wagner*, ed. Michel Pazdro. Described as item 574.

Includes on two-column pages the complete texts of all libretti from *Holländer* to *Parsifal* both in Wagner's German and in French translations.

Several studies deal primarily with various editions of the music-dramas and/or their librettos:

166. Hopkinson, Cecil. *Tannhäuser. An Examination of 36 Editions*. Musikbibliographische Arbeiten, 1. Tutzing: Hans Schneider, 1973. 48pp. ISBN 3795201225 ML410.W135H66 1973

A close study of the textual differences among editions of *Tannhäuser*, including changes Wagner himself neglected to mention in *My Life*. Includes a catalog of the published editions in question (pp. 42–43), of which some copies also contain Wagner's handwritten corrections, and illustrated with facsimiles of a few cover pages.

*   Klein, Horst F. *Erstdrucke der musikalischen Werke von Richard Wagner.* Described as item 69.

*   Klein, Horst F. *Erst- und Frühdrucke der Textbücher von Richard Wagner.* Described as item 70.

Both works by Klein provide bibliographic information about first and/or early editions of Wagner's compositions and music-drama texts.

Finally, a few studies related to editions of Wagner's music dramas have appeared in print:

167. Annen, Josef. *Le versioni italiane rappresentate delle opere di Riccardo Wagner.* Modena: Muralto-Locarno, 1943. 159pp. ML410.W1A63

Especially useful as a guide to Italian translations of Wagner's librettos, from *Rienzi* to *Parsifal,* as prepared for performance by the likes of Guido Manacorda, Angelo Zanardini, and so on. Presented originally as a doctoral dissertation in 1943 at the University of Fribourg, Switzerland; supplemented in the published version with a useful bibliography (pp. 151–57) and a one-page index.

168. Darcy, Warren. "Printed Editions." In item 1, pp. 221–27.

Describes the scope, contents, and something of the editorial methods for items 156–57; Darcy also comments on other publications of Wagner's compositions, including Dover reprint editions (item 158) and Eulenberg pocket scores. Several volumes of the *Sämtliche Werke* have appeared in print since Darcy's essay appeared in 1992; as a consequence, his observations are no longer entirely accurate.

MUSICAL MANUSCRIPTS AND RELATED STUDIES

Because even the Sämtliche Werke *is not yet complete, certain Wagner compositions have yet to appear in print, at least in definitive form. Furthermore, manuscript copies even of published scores may still have much to tell us about the composer's working methods and certain characteristics of his musical works. Among the finest Wagner music-manuscript studies is:*

169. Heidgen, Norbert. *Textvarianten in Richard Wagners "Rheingold" und "Walküre."* Berliner musikwissenschaftliche Arbeiten, 22. Munich and Salzburg: Emil Katzbichler, 1982. 276pp. ISBN 3873970627 (no LC number available)

A close textual study of differences between and among: (1) the version of the *Ring* libretto printed privately in 1853; (2) Wagner's handwritten corrections for that edition and one published in 1863; (3) the version published in Vols. 5–6 of the *Gesammelte Schriften*, 4th ed. (see items 172 and 174); and (4) the Schott libretto editions published in 1869 and 1870. Heidgen illustrates his study with a large number of short, hand-copied musical examples. Concludes with a four-page bibliography. Omitted from a number of Wagner bibliographies, including those found in items 1–2 and 76. See item 6 for review information.

Related studies include:

170. Darcy, Warren. "Autograph Manuscripts." In item 1, pp. 196–206 and 217–21.

    Describes Wagner's working methods, drawing mostly upon the prose sketches, prose drafts, verse drafts, and fair copies of his librettos, as well as upon individual sketches, complete drafts, and scores of the *Ring*, including the unique draft score and fair copy of *Rheingold*. No illustrations or musical examples, but the essay is interrupted by brief comments and a fascicle of documentary facsimiles entitled "Wagner's Hand" (pp. 207–16) devoted to examples of his calligraphy.

171. Deathridge, John. "The Nomenclature of Wagner's Sketches." *Proceedings of the Royal Musical Association* 101 (1974–1975), pp. 75–83. ML28.L8M8

    Defends modifying terminology used to describe the various kinds of musical documents Wagner employed to compose his mature music dramas. Deathridge dislikes the term "draft," preferring "sketch" and "score" because of the way he perceives Wagner as having worked; he admires Strobel's description of Wagner's compositional processes (see item 29) but describes Istel's synopsis of them (item 457) as "greatly flawed" (item 171, p. 75).

EDITIONS OF LITERARY WORKS AND RELATED STUDIES

Collected Editions

Although incomplete, the older editions identified below do include the German-language texts of almost all of Wagner's books, essays, reviews, and other prose writings; they are identified in chronological order of publication:

172. *Richard Wagner. Gesammelte Schriften und Dichtungen.* 10 vols. Leizpig: E. F. Fritzsch, 1871–1883. ML410.W1A1

The first and largely "authorized" collected edition of Wagner's prose works. Begun under the composer's supervision; by the time of his death in February 1883 nine volumes had appeared in print; a tenth followed before the end of that year. For detailed information about its contents, see item 99; for information about the history of the edition as a whole, see item 249. See, too, the superb tabular summary of this edition and items 173–75 in item 25, pages 964–66.

173. *Richard Wagner: Sämtliche Schriften und Dictungen*, ed. Richard Stern-feld (Vols. 12–16). 16 vols. Leipzig: Breitkopf & Härtel, 1912–1914. ML410.W1A1 1912

Still the closest thing to a complete scholarly edition of Wagner's prose works. Based on item 172, but expanded to include four additional volumes (Vols. 13–16) omitted from the revised Breitkopf edition of 1911. Vol. 16 contains an index of names and subjects, originally prepared by Hans von Wolzogen, but subsequently revised and enlarged by E. Schwebsch.

174. *Richard Wagners gesammelte Schriften*, ed. Julius Kapp. 14 vols. Leipzig: Hesse & Becker, 1914. ML410.W1A1 1914

Includes two volumes of autobiographical writings, the texts of virtually all Wagner's choral works, operas, and music dramas (Vols. 3–5), and a chronological register of the series' contents (Vol. 14), as well as such familiar works as *Art and Revolution*, *Opera and Drama*, and *The Art-Work of the Future*. Also includes scattered plates, several bound as frontispieces for Vols. 1, 4, 7, and 10, as well as a few additional portraits, documentary facsimiles, and other illustrations. Not to be confused with item 172.

The most complete and certainly the most familiar English-language editions of the prose works appeared in print almost a century ago:

175. *Richard Wagner's Prose Works*, trans. William Ashton Ellis. 8 vols. London: Routledge & Kegan Paul, 1893–1899; reprinted New York: Broude Bros., 1966. ML410.W1A127 1966

Still the "standard" English-language edition of Wagner's prose writings. Volume 8 contains articles and reviews published only after their author's death; the remaining volumes present the bulk of Wagner's prose in no altogether logical, although generally chronological, order. Each volume is separately indexed and contains useful synopses of its contents; Volume 8 concludes with an unpaginated "General Chronological Table of the Contents of the Eight Volumes," identifying each work by title, date of authorship or original publication, and volume in the series.

Portions of this multi-volume anthology have appeared recently in paperback reprints; see, for example, *Art and Politics* and *Actors and Singers* (Lincoln and London: University of Nebraska Press, 1995), which represent Vols. 4–5 of Ellis's series. Both reprint volumes feature cover illustrations by Rackham, one of nineteenth-century England's most "Wagnerian" illustrators. The original "Actors and Singers" essay is the subject of Thomas Grey's article "Eduard Hanslick on Wagner's 'Actors and Singers,' " published in *Wagner News* 19/1 (January 1998), pp. 34–40.

176. *Wagner on Music and Drama: A Compendium of Richard Wagner's Prose Works*, ed. Albert Goldman and Evert Sprinchorn. New York: E. P. Dutton, 1964; reprinted New York: Da Capo, 1981. 447pp. ISBN 0306761092 ML410.W1A128 1981

A collection of Ellis's translations (see item 175), including all or parts of such celebrated treatises as *Opera and Drama*, *The Art-Work of the Future*, and *Art and Revolution*. Supplemented with a list of sources (pp. 445–47) in place of an index. Illustrated with a single frontispiece portrait of the composer. NB: Every edition to date of Wagner's prose works has adopted its own organizational schema, either—and often only in part—chronological or categorical, or both. For a discussion of such organizational issues, see Dahlhaus's essay "Chronologie oder Systematik? Probleme einer Edition von Wagner's Schriften," in item 33, pp. 127–30.

Anthologies

A few anthologies offer Wagner scholars more reliable texts, better annotations, and more useful indexes than the "complete" editions described above; they may also be easier to consult. Those described below are listed in reverse chronological order of publication:

177. *Richard Wagner: Dichtungen und Schriften*, ed. Dieter Borchmeyer. 10 vols. Frankfurt a.M.: Insel, 1983. ISBN ML410.W1A1 1983

A *Jubiläumsausgabe* (anniversary edition) published in conjunction with the centenary of Wagner's death. Includes among its many prose selections—*Opera and Drama, A Communication to My Friends, A Visit to Beethoven*, and so on—a few scattered musical examples.

178. *Richard Wagner: Ausgewählte Schriften*, ed. Esther Drusche. Leizpig: Philipp Reclam jun., 1982. 383pp. ML410.W1A113 1982 (no ISBN available)

Includes, among other selections, the texts of *Art and Revolution*, Wagner's essay on vivisection, and *What is German?* Also includes a useful timeline (pp. 341–77) as well as a short bibliography (pp. 378–80) and six musical examples. Concludes with an index. See item 6 for review information.

179. *Richard Wagner: Schriften. Ein Schlüssel zu Leben, Werk und Zeit*, ed. Egon Voss. Frankfurt a.M.: Fischer, 1978. 218pp. ISBN 3596220750 ML410.W1A1225

A collection of the composer's writings outfitted with commentaries and an introduction by an important Wagner scholar. Includes, among other items, Wagner's early essays on Bellini and Weber's *Freischütz*, the *Neue Zeitschrift* article on the Goethe-Stiftung, the complete text of *Art and Revolution*, and others. Also includes a short timeline (pp. 216–18), as well as an abbreviated catalog of Wagner's literary works (pp. 214–15). Unindexed.

180. *Richard Wagner: Ausgewählte Schriften*, ed. Dieter Mack. Frankfurt a.M.: Insel, 1974. 281pp. ISBN 3458017666 ML410.W1A12 1974

Not to be confused with item 178. Includes an introductory essay by composer Ernst Bloch, as well as a number of the well-known book excerpts and essays mentioned in conjunction with other editions.

181. *Richard Wagner: Die Hauptschriften*, ed. Ernst Bücken; 2nd ed. rev. Erich Rappl. Stuttgart: Alfred Kröner, 1956. (vii), 431pp. ML410.W1A122 1956

A collection of Wagner's most important writings, including *Art and Revolution*, *The Art-Work of the Future*, and *A Communication to My Friends*, among others. Bücken's collection was originally published in Leipzig in 1937; Rappl reworked it for post–World War II republication. Illustrated with a frontispiece facsimile of Veit Bauern's Wagner portrait. No bibliography or index.

182. *Art Life and Theories of Richard Wagner* [*sic*], ed. Edward L. Burlingame; 2nd ed. New York: Henry Holt & Co., 1904. xiii, 305pp. ML410.W1A143

Primarily a collection of the prose writings, including *A Pilgrimage to Beethoven*, both essays on *Freischütz*, *The Music of the Future*, and so on.

Burlingame also provides introductory observations (pp. v–xiii). Concludes with an incomplete catalog of the composer's published books and articles (pp. 291–302), and an index of "names, places, and important works mentioned in this volume." Originally published in 1875.

Most of the anthologies described above consist primarily of more familiar prose works by Wagner; the following volumes, on the other hand, are composed for the most part of unfamiliar books, articles, essays, and reviews, as well as some of the librettos and poems:

183. *Nachgelassene Schriften und Dichtungen von Richard Wagner*, 2nd ed. Leipzig: Breitkopf & Härtel, 1902. 216pp. ML410.W1A112

A miscellany of Wagner's less familiar poems and prose writings, including the librettos for such unfinished music dramas as *Die Sarazenin* and *Jesus von Nazareth*, drafts for portions of *The Art-Work of the Future*, and comments on metaphysical issues, morals, Christianity, and so on. Like item 184, includes a table of contents (pp. 185–216) that also functions as a concordance to portions of the *Gesammelte Schriften* selected by the unidentified editor.

184. *Richard Wagner. Entwürfe. Gedanken. Fragmente. Aus nachgelassenen Papieren zusammengestellt.* Leipzig: Breitkopf & Härtel, 1885. 170pp. ML410.W1A11

A collection of Wagner's prose sketches and fragments of unfinished or otherwise revised literary works, published shortly after his death and without editorial attribution; thus it supplements, rather than replaces, the *Gesammelte Schriften* Wagner himself helped prepare for publication. Includes a detailed table of contents (pp. 133–70) that not only identifies individual selections, but comprises a concordance to the collected edition; for the sketch entitled *Zum Princip des Kommunismus* we find cross-references on p. 133 to relevant passages in *The Art-Work of the Future*, *A Communication to My Friends*, and *Religion and Art*.

Many anthologies contain smaller numbers of prose works; they, too, are often organized around a particular place or theme. Perhaps the best of these is:

185. *Richard Wagner. Schriften eines revolutionären Genies*, ed. Egon Voss. Munich and Vienna: Langen Muller, 1976. 325pp. ISBN 3784416462 ML410.W1A1233

An anthology of "revolutionary" literary works—including *A Pilgrimage to Beethoven* and *Art and Revolution*—outfitted with a useful introductory foreword (pp. 7–23), detailed notes (pp. 295–315), a list of sources (pp. 316–27), a chronological catalog of Wagner's writings as a whole (pp. 318–20), and a timeline (pp. 321–25). One work, an essay on Weber's *Freischütz* (pp. 117–36), appears in print here for the first time; another, an open letter dealing with animal cruelty (pp. 273–94), may be of special interest to students of Wagner's interest in vivisection. No illustrations, musical examples, or index.

Other collections are described below, first in reverse chronological order of publication, then in alphabetical order by title:

186. *Three Wagner Essays*, trans. Robert L. Jacobs. London: Eulenburg, 1979. x, 127pp. ISBN 09038873559 ML410.W1A1282

   A handsome cased edition of *The Art-Work of the Future, On Conducting,* and *On Performing Beethoven's Ninth Symphony* (1873). Included in the translations of the last two prose works are some 108 musical examples. No illustrations, however, and no bibliography or index. The *Music Review* 43 (1982), p. 272, praised Jacobs for his "lucid English," but complained about missing passages in at least one of the essays.

187. *Richard Wagner: Die Kunst und die Revolution, Das Judentum in der Musik, Was ist deutsch?*, ed. Tibor Kneif. Munich: Rogner & Bernhard, 1975. 133pp. ISBN 380770034X ML410.W1A122 1975

   Presents, in addition to the texts of these mostly well-known essays, a lengthy afterword by the editor. *What is German?*, begun as early as 1865 and published in 1878, is perhaps less familiar to English readers. Supplemented by a few illustrations and scattered musical examples in Wagner's texts, but without bibliography or index.

188. *Richard Wagner: Stories and Essays*, ed. Charles Osborne. London: Peter Owen, 1973. 187pp. ISBN 0720601223 ML410.W1A135

   Contains some of the composer's lighter-hearted prose works, including *A Pilgrimage to Beethoven*, as well as the charmless *Jewishness in Music* and a less familiar offering: *The Wiebelungs*, a prose sketch for what eventually became the *Ring* libretto (pp. 150–87). Illustrated with a frontispiece Wagner portrait.

189. *Wagner Writes from Paris . . . Stories, Essays and Articles by the Young Composer*, ed. Robert L. Jacobs and Geoffrey Skelton. New York: John Day, 1973. 198pp. ML410.W1A1283 1973b (no ISBN available)

Includes *A Pilgrimage to Beethoven*, Wagner's 1841 review of Weber's *Freischütz* as performed by the Paris Opéra, as well as articles about Berlioz, Liszt, and others. Jacobs and Skelton include a catalog of Wagner's Paris writings (pp. 196–98); notes and an index to the volume as a whole are presented together in pp. 189–95. Also includes as a frontispiece a facsimile reproduction of Ernst Kietz's "young Wagner" portrait.

190. Kapp, Julius. *Der junge Wagner: Dichtung, Aufsätze, Entwürfe, 1832–1849.* Berlin and Leipzig: Schuster & Loeffler, 1910. viii, 495pp. (no LC number available)

    Deals with Wagner's earlier prose and poetry from the sketch for the *Hochzeit* libretto to *Die Revolution*. Among other texts Kapp includes the composer's reports from Paris published in the *Dresdner Abendzeitung* between 1840 and 1842. Lacks critical apparatus, and in other ways has been supplanted by better and more recent publications.

*   *Wagner on Conducting*, trans. Edward Dannreuther. Described as item 832.

    A collection of Wagner's writings on that subject.

Editions of Individual Prose Works

The following are described in reverse chronological order of publication:

191. Wagner, Richard. *Bericht an Seine Majestät den König Ludwig II. von Bayern über eine in München zu errichtende deutsche Musikschule.* Facsimile edition, ed. Christa Jost. Tutzing: Hans Schneider, 1998. 60pp. ISBN 3795209528 ML410.W1A208 1998

    A reprint of the 1865 edition published by Christian Kaiser of Munich. Includes the original pamphlet itself (pp. 1–50), historical and textual information by the editor (pp. 51–60), and a single documentary facsimile (p. 55). No other illustrations or musical examples.

192. *Richard Wagner: Der Liebesmahl des Apostel*, ed. Karl Wilhelm Geck. Patriomonia, 114. Dresden: Sächsische Landesbibliothek / Staats- und Universitätsbibliothek, 1996. 40pp. ISSN 0941-7036 (no ISBN or LC number available)

    A slender volume containing the text of the choral-orchestral cantata (*WWV* 69) Wagner completed in Dresden in 1843. Illustrated with six beautiful colored facsimile reproductions from the manuscript, as well as a few portraits and other images. Also contains two articles: Hans John's "Richard Wagners Wirken in Dresden" (pp. 13–21), and Geck's own "Männerchöre in der Frauenkirche: Richard Wagner und 'Der Liebesmahl des Apostel' " (pp. 23–33).

193. Wagner, Richard. *Judaism in Music (Das Judenthum in der Musik). Being the Original Essay Together with the Later Supplement,* trans. Edwin Evans. London: William Reeves, 1910. xvi, 95pp. ML410.W1A22 1910

Contains translations of both the 1850 article (pp. 1–50) and the 1869 supplements to it (pp. 51–92), with notes and a rather fulsome introduction. Useful to students of Wagner's anti-semitism and British reactions to it. No illustrations. More recent editions and translations of this treatise include one published in *Wagner* 9/1 (January 1988), pp. 20–33. A critical edition by Jens Malte Fischer was also published recently by Insel-Verlag (Frankfurt a.M. 2000; ISBN 3458343172). NB: Throughout the present research guide Wagner's essay is otherwise identified in English as "Jewishness in Music." See also item 1107.

Scholars may still wish to consult early prose-works editions, especially if they are uncommon or printed in languages other than English and German. Examples of such early editions include:

194. Wagner, Richard. *Die Wibelungen [sic]. Weltgeschichte aus der Sage.* Leipzig: Otto Wigand, 1850. 75pp. ML410.W1A258

Wagner's prose draft for what finally became the *Ring* poem; portions of the pamphlet's text may date from 1848. Both Harvard University's Loeb Music Library (shelf-number Mus. 5660.755) and the Library of Congress own copies. Other editions of this material include Otto Strobel's *Skizzen und Entwürfe zur Ring-Dichtung* (Munich, 1930).

195. Wagner, Richard. *Art et politique,* "1re Partie." Brussels: J. Sannes, 1868. 73pp. ML410.W1A2144 v. 1

The first half of Wagner's essay in an early French edition. Early editions of other individual essays also exist in a variety of languages.

The texts of certain prose works also appear in specialized Wagner periodicals (see item 193, for instance) and program volumes. Again, one example must suffice:

196. Wagner, Richard. Prose drafts for the various parts and versions of the *Ring*. In: *Programmhefte der Bayreuther Festspiele* (1984). ML410.W2B26

Includes the complete text of Wagner's draft for *Der junge Siegfried*, dated 24 May 1851, in English, French, and German, as well as the prose drafts for *Rheingold, Walküre, Siegfried*, and *Götterdämmerung*, all in the same three languages. NB: Other writings by Wagner himself appear in other Bayreuth program booklets; thus *A Pilgrimage to Beethoven* appeared in German, French, and English in the *Programmhefte der Bayreuther Festspiele* IX (1951).

Related Studies

Studies devoted to the character and contents of Wagner's various prose publications and editions include:

197. Gallia, Francesco. "Contributo alla bibliografia wagneriana: le traduzioni in italiano delle 'Gesammelte Schriften.' " *Nuova Rivista Musicologia Italiana* 22 (1988), pp. 40–56. ML5.N93

A discussion of the history and reception of Wagner's prose works in Italy, followed by a volume-by-volume catalog of the *Schriften*'s contents with notes about Italian translations and editions (pp. 45–53). Includes a bibliography of Italian sources (pp. 54–55) and a table that identifies Italian translations of the poems from *Rienzi* to *Parsifal* by translators' names and the dates of editions published by Lucca, Ricordi, Sansoni, and other houses. Also includes a silhouette of Wagner cut by Otto Böhler.

Gallia is one of many authors whose Wagner studies cannot altogether be considered in the present research guide; among others, he is the author, editor, and translator of *Wagner nell'officina dei Nibelunghi: "Il Mito del Nibelunghi" e Abbozzi in prosa per "l'Anello del Nibelungo"* (Torino, 1996).

198. Kühnel, Jürgen. "The Prose Writings," trans. Simon Nye. In item 2, pp. 565–638.

An extremely useful work-by-work summary of virtually every book, article, and essay written and mostly published by Wagner during his long and complex literary career. For each item Kühnel provides: a brief synopsis of its arguments or character; comments, if relevant, on the work's significance and its relationship, if any, to other of the composer's prose publications; and observations on its relationship to appropriate aspects of the Wagner reception. See also item 99: the "checklist" that follows Kühnel's essay.

199. Spencer, Stewart. "Collected Writings." In item 1, pp. 193–96.

Describes the progress of Wagner's prose works in print, from early plans for a four-volume collected edition through the ten-volume *Gesammelte Schriften* (item 172), reprints of that collection, the sixteen-volume *Sämtliche Schriften*, Ellis's eight-volume English-language edition (item 175), recent anthologies, and so on. Among other topics Spencer takes pains to distinguish between the advantages and disadvantages of Wagner's original chronological scheme and the thematic organizational schemes of Wolzogen, Sternfeld, Ellis, and more recent editors.

Related studies published in periodicals are described below in alphabetical order by authors' surnames:

200. Dahlhaus, Carl. "Wagner's 'A Communication to My Friends': Reminiscence and Adaptation." *The Musical Times* 124 (1983), pp. 89–92. ML5.M85

Considers and forcibly rejects Wagner's observations concerning the "complete, unbroken web" of musical associations in *Holländer* associated with the composition of Senta's Ballad in act II. As Dahlhaus points out, the *Communication* was written in 1851, when Wagner was already thinking about the *Ring* and new musical methods; thus, "what appears to be reminiscence is in reality anticipation" (p. 91) of the *Leitmotiv* technique the composer was already formulating for use in *Rheingold*.

201. Einstein, Alfred. "Wagners letztes Thema." In: Einstein, *Von Schütz bis Hindemith: Essays über Musik und Musiker*. Zurich and Stuttgart: Pan, 1957; pp. 117–20. ML60.E39

After *Parsifal* Wagner may have written no music, but his final essay— "Über das Weiblichen im Menschlichen," published in the *Bayreuther Blätter*—postdates that music drama; it deals with the "tragedy of love," capitalism, and other obsessions of its author's literary-political career. Einstein's volume also contains essays on *Meistersinger* and the Wagner-Nietzsche relationship.

202. Lippmann, Friedrich. "Ein neuentdecktes Autograph Richard Wagners: Rezension der Königsberger 'Norma'-Aufführung von 1837." In: *Musicae*

scientiae collectanea. Festschrift Karl Gustav Fellerer zum. siebzigsten Geburtstag am 7. Juli 1972, ed. Heinrich Hüschen. Cologne: Arno Volk, 1973; pp. 373–79. ML55.F35 1972

Includes a facsimile of Wagner's little-known report as an unpaginated full-page plate; also includes a complete transcription in the original German of the review itself (pp. 374–77). No other illustrations and no musical examples.

203. Münnich, Richard. "Haydn in Wagners Schriften." *Musikalisches Wochenblatt* 40 (1909–1910), pp. 147–49. ML5.M92

Briefly identifies and explains Wagner's respect for Haydn as Beethoven's predecessor and refers to comments in Wagner's prose works and letters about Haydn's motivic ingenuity, his expansion of the symphony as an expressive form, his orchestration, his use of variation procedures, and so on. Unfortunately includes no bibliographic citations.

AUTOBIOGRAPHIES, CURRICULA VITAE, DIARIES, AND RELATED STUDIES

Autobiographies and Confessional Writings

Wagner's "official" full-length autobiography appeared originally in a four-volume edition printed privately in Basel and Bayreuth in 1869. A copy of that edition was purchased by Mary Burrell shortly before her death, and knowledge of its existence prompted the publication of "corrected" early-twentieth century editions in both English and German. A reliable English translation, however, appeared for the first time only in 1983:

204. Wagner, Richard. *My Life*, ed. Mary Whittall; trans. Andrew Gray. Cambridge and New York: University Press, 1983; reprinted New York: Da Capo, 1992. ix, 801pp. ISBN 0306804816 ML410.W1W146 1992

The definitive English edition of Wagner's longest, most complex, and most controversial autobiographical document. Outfitted in the Da Capo reprint edition with a map of Central Europe (pp. vi–vii) and an index (pp. 789–801) as well as an afterword by Martin Gregor-Dellin (pp. 741–59) devoted to the history, editions, and contents of this erratic but informative and often reliable work, including differences between Wagner's privately printed edition and that of 1911. The 1983 edition is unindexed.

Available in German as *Mein Leben*, ed. Gregor-Dellin (2nd ed.; Munich, 1976); reviewed in this edition in *Die Musikforschung* 40 (1987), pp. 279–84. The 1983 Whittall-Gray edition was reviewed enthusiastically in *Wagner* 5/3 (July 1984). It replaces the "Authorized Translation from the German" published as *My Life* in New York in 1911, and was itself reprinted in London in 1994 (ISBN 0094738602) with a new index.

205. Wagner, Richard. *Mein Leben*, ed. Wilhelm Altmann. 2 vols. Leipzig: Bibliographisches Institut, 1923. ML410.W1W14 1923.

According to the title page, "kritisch durchgesehen, eingeleitet, und erläutet" by Altmann. Apparently somewhat abridged from Wagner's original. Includes two facsimiles as illustrations. Only one of several German editions published between the end of the nineteenth century and 1976.

Other autobiographical writings include:

206. *Richard Wagner's Lehr- und Wanderjahre. Autobiographisches.* Leipzig: Franz Wagner, 1871. 30pp.

A pamphlet, the contents of which appeared originally in the pages of the *Zeitung für die elegante Welt*. Superceded by more recent publications. Rare. The Loeb Music Library at Harvard owns a copy (shelf-number 5661.45).

207. Wagner, Richard. "Autobiographical Sketch." In item 222, Vol. 1, pp. 93–114.

A much shorter, less controversial essay. The *Sämtliche Briefe* edition includes documentation in the form of endnotes (pp. 112–14). Other editions also exist.

208. Wagner, Richard. "The Work and Mission of My Life." *North American Review* 129 (August 1879), pp. 107–24 and 238–58.

The composer's last attempt to describe in print something of his career and accomplishments, his artistic theories, and his attitudes toward music, society, and the Jews. Published posthumously in German as *Richard Wagners Lebens-Bericht* in several editions (e.g., Leipzig, 1884; Hannover, 1912) in a translation by E. Schloemp.

Diaries

Wagner was no systematic or life-long diarist, but sometimes he jotted down notes about his activities and accomplishments. The following documents preserve some of those jottings:

209. Wagner, Richard. *"Das braune Buch": Tagebuchaufzeichungen 1865–1882*, ed. Joachim Bergfeld. Zurich: Atlantis, 1975. 251pp. ISBN 3761104731 ML410.W1W13

    A transcription with linking text of one of Wagner's most important autobiographical documents. Outfitted with a detailed introduction (pp. 9–21) that gives information on the history and contents of the document itself, as well as with a color facsimile of the book's cover as a frontispiece, four musical examples, four additional documentary facsimiles, and an index (pp. 249–51).

    Translated by George Bird, published as *The Diary of Richard Wagner, 1865–1882: The Brown Book* (Cambridge University Press, 1981), and reviewed in this version by Paul Lawrence Rose (see item 303). Those able to read German, however, will want to study Wagner's words in his native language.

210. Wagner, Richard. *Die rote Brieftasche*. In item 222, Vol. 1 (1967), pp. 81–92.

    A fragmentary document, published as a sort of preliminary supplement to the most recent collected edition of the composer's letters. Includes notes (pp. 85–92) as well as the text of the sketchbook itself.

More important, perhaps, than Wagner's jottings are the diaries his wife Cosima kept from 1869 to the day of her husband's death in 1883. This massive documentary legacy appeared only recently in print, albeit in several editions; these include:

211. *Cosima Wagner's Diaries*, ed. Martin Gregor-Dellin and Dieter Mack; trans. Geoffrey Skelton. 2 vols. New York: Harcourt, Brace Jovanovich, 1978–1980. ISBNs 0151126350 and 0151226369 ML429.W133A373 1978

    One of the most remarkable music-related documents of the nineteenth century. In hundreds of diary entries Cosima reveals—and conceals—a wealth of information about her husband's opinions on subjects ranging from Beethoven and the Jews to vegetarianism and religion. Published originally as *Cosima Wagner: Die Tagebücher, 1869–1883* (Munich, 1976–1977). Reviewed in Skelton's English-language translation (see item 303).

212. *Cosima Wagner's Diaries: An Abridgement*, ed. Geoffrey Skelton. London: Pimlico, 1994. xiv, 524pp. ISBN 0712659528 ML410.W11A38213 1994

A fulsome selection of Cosima's remarkable jottings. Includes an introduction by Skelton, who prepared the English-language translation of the unabridged *Diaries* (item 211), as well as a small number of illustrations and an excellent and much-needed index to this dense and often confusing material.

An American edition of the same volume, published in 1997 by Yale University Press, is also available (ISBN 0300069049); the latter was reviewed not altogether positively in *The Opera Quarterly* 15 (1999), pp. 106–109.

The diaries of other individuals also contain valuable observations on Wagner's life and activities. These include:

213. *Richard Wagner an Mathilde und Otto Wesendonck. Tagebuchblätter und Briefe.* Berlin: Schreiter, c. 1930. 375pp. ML410.W1A428

   Covers the years 1852 to 1865. Texts from Wagner's hand are reprinted, but without benefit of modern editorial techniques; in fact, no editor is named on the title page. Contains a brief introduction by one G. Will (pp. 5–11) but no other commentary, notes, or index. NB: The couple's name is also spelled "Wesendonk"; except in the titles of books, articles, and musical compositions, the latter spelling is used throughout the present research guide.

214. *Richard Wagner an Mathilde Wesendonk: Tagebuchblätter und Briefe, 1853–1871*, ed. Wolfgang Golther. Leipzig: Breitkopf & Härtel, 1922. 424pp. ML410.W1A39 1922

   A much more reliable volume. Includes diary entries as well as the complete texts of fourteen letters addressed by Mathilde to Wagner between 1861 and 1865 (pp. 373–95); also includes a frontispiece portrait of Mathilde herself as well as detailed notes (pp. 397–416); concludes with a general index. As a special supplement an additional 31 pages at the end of the volume present Wagner's complete five songs on texts by Mathilde: the so-called *Wesendonck-Lieder* (*WWV* 91).

*   Kobbé, Gustav. *Wagner and His Isolde.* Described as item 421.

   A collection of correspondence from 1858 to 1869 outfitted with linking text and based on item 214.

215. *Der Kampf zweier Welten um das Bayreuther Erbe: Julius Knieses Tagebuchblätter aus dem Jahre 1883*, ed. Julie Kniese. Leipzig: Theodor Weicher, 1931. 135pp. ML410.W2K7

Memoirs in the form of diary entries, written by that "stalwart of the Bayreuth festival" (item 301, Vol. 4, p. 622) who also, from 1892 to 1912 and with Cosima's approval, trained Wagnerian performers in what Jens Fischer has called a "wildly exaggerated" version of the composer's *Sprechgesang* or "speech-singing" (item 1, p. 528). Illustrated with several handsome portrait photographs.

Related Studies

Studies of the histories, contents, and significance of Wagner's autobiographical writings, together with evaluations of Cosima's diaries and other eyewitness documents, are described below in alphabetical order by authors' surnames:

216. Hollinrake, Roger. "The Title-Page of Wagner's 'Mein Leben.' " *Music & Letters* 51 (1970), pp. 415–22. ML5.M64

Examines the possible significance behind Nietzsche's suggestion that Wagner include the image of a vulture (or *Geier*) in the privately printed copies of *My Life* he circulated only among his closest friends. As Hollinrake points out, Nietzsche's oft-quoted observation that "a vulture [*Geier*] is much like an eagle [*Adler*]"—the latter, of course, symbolic not only of Germany but also of nobility—has been used to "prove" Wagner was or believed himself to be the son of Ludwig Geyer (see items 339–42) and therefore "Jewish."

217. Irvine, David. "Wagner's Bad Luck." In: Irvine, *Two Essays on Wagner: 1. Wagner's Bad Luck, an Exposure of 800 Errors in the Authorized Translation of Wagner's Autobiography. 2. The Badness of Wagner's Bad Luck, a First Exposure of Anti-Wagnerian Journalism.* London: Watts & Co., 1912. 128pp. ML410.W1I172 1912

Rabid, pro-Wagner rants: the first part consists primarily of a line-by-line "correction" of the "grotesque blunders" (p. 1) the author feels litter the 1911 English translation of *My Life*; the second attacks Ernest Newman as well as the anti-Wagnerians for their "general shallowness of mind" (p. 9) and the "evil of anti-Wagnerism" (p. 11). An eccentric publication by a celebrated English Wagnerian.

218. Istel, Edgar. "Heinrich Marschner beim Pariser Tannhäuser-Skandal: Mitteilungen aus Marschners ungedrucktem Tagebuch." *Die Musik* 10/1 (1910–1911), pp. 42–52. ML5.M9

Presents excerpts from Marschner's then-unpublished diary associated with the disasterous 1861 Paris performances of *Tannhäuser*, connected and complemented by linking text. Istel also quotes Wagner's rather unflattering opinions of Marschner's music. No musical examples.

219. Rehder, Helmut. "Wagner's Last Vita." In: *Paul A. Pisk: Essays in His Honor*, ed. John Glowacki. Austin, TX: "University of Texas" [*sic*], 1966; pp. 181–91. ML55.P6G6

Discusses the origins and contents of the autobiographical article published originally as item 208. Rehder speculates that Allen T. Rice, editor of the *Review*, may have translated it from Wagner's German; he also reminds us that this *vita*, unlike previous autobiographical publications, "offered the opportunity [to Wagner] to assemble, as it were, in one focal point—or one grand finale—all the themes and observations he had formerly belaboured in separate involved and ponderous treatises" (p. 182). The *vita* itself contains intriguing passages about several topics, including race; unfortunately, its text is not incorporated into Rehder's essay.

220. Reindl, Ludwig Emanuel. *Cosima Wagners Tagebücher, 1869–1883: Ein Essay*. Konstanz, Verlag des "Südkurier," 1979. 30pp. ML410.W11A3837 (ISBN "cancelled")

One of a number of scholarly reactions to the diaries' character and contents, this one sponsored by one of southern Germany's most prestigious newspapers. In a few pages Reindl attempts to explain to readers of his own day how this new Wagner source would transform—today we would say, "has transformed"—our understanding of Wagner as man and artist. Illustrated with a photograph of the author (p. 30). Other reactions also exist in the form of review articles; see, for instance, Eric Salzman's "On Reading Cosima Wagner's 'Diaries' " published in *The Musical Quarterly* 68 (1982), pp. 337–52.

221. Spencer, Stewart. "Autobiographical Writings" and "Diaries." In item 1, pp. 182–90.

Says something about the origins of *My Life* and that work's relationship to such sources as the "Brown Book" and "Red Pocketbook" (items 209–10). Spencer also summarizes the histories and characters of the *Autobiographical Sketch* of 1843, the *Communication to My Friends* of 1851, and printing errors associated with German and English editions of *My Life*; with regard to the last subject, he also evaluates the rather dubious contributions of Hurn and Root (item 337) to the controversy over that autobiography's contents, and the significance of suppressed passages published in *Die Musik* 22 (1929–1930).

PUBLISHED CORRESPONDENCE AND RELATED STUDIES

Collected Editions and Anthologies

The Wagner literature is littered with letters publications; most of them are less than fully satisfactory in one way or another, and more than a few contain deliberate omissions. Scholars, for instance, should tread warily when consulting the latest "definitive" edition of the composer's correspondence:

222. *Richard Wagner. Sämtliche Briefe*, ed. Gertrud Strobel et al. Leipzig: VEB Deutsche Verlag für Musik, 1967–c. 1989; Wiesbaden: Breitkopf & Härtel, c. 1990–. In progress. ML410.W1A32F67

Purportedly a comprehensive critical edition of Wagner's extensive correspondence; in fact a somewhat disappointing and still-incomplete series of publications. By 1999 eleven volumes had been published, the last of which brings the collection's contents to the end of 1859; future volumes will be devoted to the years 1860 to 1883. Each volume is equipped with scholarly apparatus, including indexes, glossaries, notes, and (after Vol. 2) timelines; scattered musical examples also appear in the texts of a few letters. Many volumes also include Wagner portraits and documentary facsimiles; the former appear as frontispieces, the latter mostly tipped in as foldouts at the ends of volumes; finally, Vol. 1 also contains items 207 and 210. Nevertheless, much is missing, especially from the earlier volumes, and much may also have been overlooked or ignored.

A damning review by Voss of Vols. 1–5 appeared in the *Neue Zeitschrift für Musik* in 1978. Improvements have been made in editorial practices since German reunification, but it may take decades for the rest of the letters to appear in print (see also item 274).

An earlier "collected edition" was interrupted after only two substantial installments:

223. *Richard Wagners Gesammelte Briefe*, ed. Julius Kapp and Emerich Kastner. 2 vols. Leipzig: Hesse & Becker, 1914. ML410.W1A302

Incomplete. Presents the texts of 486 letters addressed by Wagner to various recipients and arranged in chronological order: Vol. 1 covers the years 1830 to 1843 and includes the first 187 letters, Vol. 2 covers 1843 to 1850 and includes the rest. Also contains an introductory essay on "Richard Wagner als Briefschreiber (Vol. 1., pp. x–xiv), as well as *Adressatentafeln* (glossaries of addressees) that incorporate useful biographical data (Vol. 1, pp. 331–37; Vol. 2, pp. 470–73) and indexes. Some letters appear in this collection in rather different versions than they do elsewhere; for example, the Vol. 2 text of the letter Wagner addressed to Liszt on 2 July 1850 concerning Liszt's forthcoming production of *Lohengrin* includes sketches and diagrams of stage sets missing from several other collections.

Much more useful is the following invaluable English-language anthology:

224. *Selected Letters of Richard Wagner, With Original Texts of Passages Omitted from Existing Printed Editions*, ed. Stewart Spencer and Barry Millington. New York: Norton, 1988. ix, 1,030pp. ISBN 0393025004 ML410.W1A319 1987

The finest collection of Wagner correspondence in English and one even larger, more carefully compiled, and more comprehensively indexed than items 225–26. Spencer and Millington provide complete texts of 500 letters written between 1830 and 1883, as well as two appendices: the first contains the texts of three letters written by Wagner's first wife Minna, his close friend and later father-in-law Liszt, and his sponsor and friend Ludwig II of Bavaria (pp. 935–38); the second reprints the German-language passages omitted from previous editions, as the full-title page states (pp. 939–52). Brief introductory essays preface each of six chapters, divided according to the composer's "Youth and Early Career, 1813–1839," "Indigence in Paris; Recognition in Dresden, 1839–1849," and so on. Also contains a bibliography (pp. 953–58) and glossary of correspondents (pp. 959–85); concludes with a general index.

Reviewed with praise in *Wagner* 9/3 (July 1988), pp. 116–20, where it is described as "a major publishing event" (p. 120). Also reviewed by George Steiner in *The New Yorker* (3 October 1988), pp. 102–10, where musicological publications are seldom mentioned. Published for the first time in 1987 by J. M. Dent & Sons of London (ISBN 0460046438). See also items 227–28.

Important German-language collections of Wagner's letters include:

225. *Richard Wagner. Briefe 1830–1883*, ed. Werner Otto. Berlin: Henschel, 1986. 512p. ML410.W1A33 1986 (no ISBN available)

Provides the texts of 402 letters spanning most of Wagner's career, as well as notes (pp. 453–88), a list of addressees (pp. 490–505), and a catalog of sources (pp. 506–12). A fine anthology of Wagnerian correspondence, but neither as comprehensive nor as heavily annotated as several other publications.

226. *Richard Wagner. Briefe*, ed. Hanjo Kesting. Munich and Zurich: R. Piper, 1983. 677pp. ISBN 3492028291 ML410.W1A31 1983

A collection of 206 Wagner letters spanning the years 1832 to 1883. In addition to a lengthy introduction (pp. 5–43), Kesting provides endnotes and editorial comments for each letter (pp. 627–59), as well as a list of sources for the letters themselves (pp. 660–63), a bibliography of secondary sources (pp. 664–67), and several indexes.

Other important correspondence collections are identified below in reverse chronological order of publication:

227. *Letters of Richard Wagner: The Burrell Collection*, ed. John N. Burk. New York: Macmillan, 1950; reprinted New York: Vienna House, 1972. xi, 665pp. ML410.W1A3125 1972

Presents the texts of 435 letters written by Wagner between the 1830s and his death in 1883; a few of these were addressed to Mrs. Burrell, who put the collection together. Includes excerpts from the 1875 to 1876 diary of Susanne Weinert, governess to the composer and his wife Cosima from August 1875 to May 1876 (pp. 430–38)—a document that, according to Ernest Newman, "positively cries out for publication" (item 301, Vol. 4, p. 303n)—as well as three appendices: a catalog of the collection itself (pp. 438–603), an essay entitled "Cosima's Blue Pencil: The Uhlig Letters, As Written" (pp. 605–41), and the texts of 25 additional letters from 1852 to 1882 (pp. 645–57). Subsequently translated into German and published as *Briefe: Die Sammlung Burrell* (Frankfurt a.M. 1953).

228. *Letters of Richard Wagner*, ed. Wilhelm Altmann, trans. M. M. Bozman. 2 vols. London: J. M. Dent, 1927. ML410.W1A32F25

Together, these two volumes reproduce the texts of 738 letters, with Vol. 1 covering the years 1830 to 1858 and Vol. 2 covering 1858 to 1882. Each volume contains nine plates and other illustrations, including fold-out facsimiles of individual letters, as well as chronologies of Wagner's life and associated activities (Vol. 1, pp. 356–58; Vol. 2, pp. 397–409); Vol. 2 also contains an index to both volumes (pp. 311–33). Published originally as *Richard Wagners Briefe* (Leipzig, 1925).

229. *Richard Wagner: Sein Leben in Briefen. Eine Auswahl aus den Briefen des Meisters mit biographischen Einleitungen*, ed. Carl Siegmund Benedict. Leipzig: Breitkopf & Härtel, 1913. viii, 471pp. ML410.W1A4 1913

Virtually an epistolary biography outfitted with running commentary and an index of names (pp. 453–59). Benedict includes the complete texts of

112 letters written between 1832 and 1882, but the documents he selects are important, representative, and fulsome. Includes a catalog of the letters themselves (pp. v–viii), but no general index and no illustrations other than a frontispiece portrait of the composer.

230. *Richard Wagner an Freunde und Zeitgenossen*, ed. Erich Kloss, 2nd ed. Berlin and Leipzig: Schuster & Loeffler, 1909. xxvii, 616pp. ML 410.W1 A355

Contains the texts of 336 letters addressed to various of the composer's relatives, friends, and acquaintances between 1834 and 1883. Not to be confused with Kastner's *Briefe von Richard Wagner an seine Zeitgenossen, 1830–1883* (item 75), which is itself a catalog rather than a collection of correspondence. See also item 840.

Other older anthologies are available only in foreign languages:

231. *Lettres françaises de Richard Wagner "recueillies et présentées par Julien Tiersot"* [i.e., ed. Tiersot]. Paris: Bernhard Grasset, 1935. 415pp. ML410.W1A334

A miscellany of several hundred letters written by and to Wagner in French between 1838 and 1882. Includes indexes of Wagner's correspondents (pp. 413–14) and names mentioned in Wagner's letters (pp. 409–12), as well as a single letter facsimile, scattered footnotes, and two illustrations—one of them a portrait sketch of the composer, reproduced here as a frontispiece. Anything but a scholarly edition, Tiersot's collection nevertheless remains valuable if only because it documents Wagner's French correspondence in some detail.

Specialized Anthologies and Collections

Many collections of Wagner's correspondence have been devoted to letters addressed either to certain individuals or groups of people associated with particular places or projects. Among the most important of these are volumes of "Bayreuth," "Munich," and "family" letters, as well as collections of letters Wagner exchanged with Liszt, Ludwig II of Bavaria, and Friedrich Nietzsche. Examples of these volumes are subdivided below by headings, then described—unless otherwise noted—in reverse chronological order of publication by date of most recent original or reprint edition:

"Bayreuth Letters"

232. *The Story of Bayreuth, As Told in The Bayreuth Letters of Richard Wagner*, ed. and trans. Caroline V. Kerr. Boston: Small, Maynard & Co., 1912;

reprinted New York: Vienna House, 1972. 364pp. ISBN 0844300152
ML410.W1A325 1972

A collection of letters written between 1848 and the 1880s that, together
with running commentary, traces the evolution and accomplishment of
Wagner's plans to build a festival theater for performances of his own
works. Includes a considerable amount of information about the Festivals
of 1876 and 1882. Illustrated with six portraits and pictures of Bayreuth
places. An unpaginated index was added to the end of the reprint edition.
Published originally as *Bayreuther Briefe von Richard Wagner
(1871–1883)*, ed. Carl Friedrich Glasenapp (Berlin and Leipzig, 1907).

233. *Richard Wagner an seine Künstler: Zweiter Band der "Bayreuther Briefe"
(1872–1883)*, ed. Erich Kloss. Berlin and Leipzig: Schuster & Loeffler,
1908. xxiv, 414pp. ML410.W1A322

Not to be confused with item 232, which was edited originally by Glasenapp; note the LC numbers above. The first volume includes the texts of
233 letters addressed by Wagner to Carl Brandt, Friedrich Feustal, Emil
Heckel, and other individuals associated with the Bayreuth Theater and
related undertakings; the second includes the texts of 333 letters addressed
to Edward Dannreuther, Richard Fricke, Lill Lehmann, Hermann Levi, and
so on. Both volumes include lists of the letters they contain as well as
indexes; item 232 above also includes an introduction by Glasenapp (pp.
v–ix) and notes (pp. 315–28).

"Munich Letters"

234. Röckl, Sebastian. *Richard Wagner in München: ein Bericht in Briefen.*
Regensburg: Gustav Bosse, 1938. 99pp. ML410.W1A3673

A miscellany of some 75 documents concerning the composer's activities
in and around Munich especially during the 1860s; among the volume's
contents are the texts of letters from Ludwig II to his mistress (!), from
architect Gottfried Semper to the King, and so on. Also includes excerpts
from the diaries of Peter Cornelius. No linking text, table of contents, or
index.

"Family Letters"

235. *Family Letters of Richard Wagner*, trans. William Ashton Ellis; ed. John
Deathridge. Ann Arbor, MI: University of Michigan Press, 1991. lvi,
432pp. ISBN 0472102923 ML410.W1A31285 1991

Contains 191 letters addressed by Wagner to members of his immediate
family, including his several sisters; 124 of these were included in Ellis's

1911 volume (see below); the rest were edited by eminent Wagnerian John Deathridge, whose introduction (pp. xix–xlvii) brings this collection up to date. Concludes with an index (pp. 421–32).

Ellis's translation of these letters was published originally in 1911 by Macmillan of London; this edition, not the one containing Deathridge's introduction, was reprinted by Vienna House of New York in 1971 (ISBN 0844300144). The letters in Ellis's collection also appeared in two volumes as *Familienbriefe von Richard Wagner, 1832–1874*, ed. Glasenapp (Berlin, 1907).

Collections Addressed to Individual Recipients

Franz Liszt

236. *Franz Liszt—Richard Wagner: Briefwechsel*, ed. Hanjo Kesting. Frankfurt a.M.: Insel, 1988. 758pp. ISBN 3485143696 ML410.L7A4 1988

Includes the texts of 351 letters exchanged by two of nineteenth-century Europe's leading musician figures. Announced as a thoroughly reliable edition of a correspondence previously issued only in expurgated versions (see items 237–38) but neither entirely accurate nor complete. Reviewed by Stewart Spencer in *Wagner* 10/1 (January 1989), pp. 35–36, who gives the correct dates for some of the "new" letters Kesting includes in his collection.

237. *Correspondence of Wagner and Liszt*, trans. Francis Hueffer; rev. ed. 2 vols. New York: Charles Scribner's Sons, 1897; reprinted New York: Vienna House, 1973. ML410.W1A365 1973

Essentially an English-language translation of item 238; includes an index prepared by William Ashton Ellis. Vol. 1 covers 1841 to 1853, Vol. 2 1854 to 1882. The 1897 edition of these volumes did not include the supplementary letter and telegram texts found in item 238. A somewhat earlier reprint edition was published in New York in 1969 under the imprint of Haskell House.

238. *Briefwechsel zwischen Wagner und Liszt*, ed. Erich Kloss; 3rd rev. ed. "Zwei Teile in einem Bande" (i.e., 2 vols. in one). Leipzig: Breitkopf & Härtel, 1910. ML410.W1A362 1910

Comprises the texts of 330 letters written by both composers between 1841 and 1882, as well as two supplements (Vol. 1, pp. 294–343; Vol. 2, pp. 313–34) to the third edition that, between them, contain the texts of an additional 45 letters and telegrams. A few musical examples, written into the letters themselves, are scattered throughout this publication.

A somewhat different edition appeared in two volumes in 1900 as *Briefwechsel zwischen Wagner und Liszt*, 2nd ed. (Leipzig: Breitkopf & Härtel, 1900). It contains only 316 letters; its Vol. 1 covers 1841 to 1853 (letters 1–142), while its Vol. 2 covers 1854 to 1861 (letters 143–316). An appendix to the second volume includes additional complete and fragmentary letter texts, including some written in French by the Princess Carolyne zu Sayn-Wittgenstein, for many years Liszt's lover and Wagner's confidante (pp. 293–332).

Ludwig II of Bavaria

239. *Richard Wagner und König Ludwig II. von Bayern: Briefwechsel*, ed. Kurt Wölfe. "Korrespondenzen," 1. Stuttgart: Gerd Hatje, 1993. 183pp. ISBN 3775704140 ML410.W1A36 1993

A selection of 74 of Liszt's letters to Ludwig, accompanied by notes (pp. 159–68) and an afterword by the editor (pp. 171–83). No illustrations or musical examples.

240. *König Ludwig II. und Richard Wagner: Briefwechsel*, ed. Otto Strobel. 5 vols. Karlsruhe: G. Braun, 1936–1939. ML410.W1A366

The first four volumes present the texts of 597 letters exchanged by Wagner and Bavaria's controversial and tragic Wittelsbach ruler, together with lengthy quotations from diary entries and other sources. These are indexed in Vol. 4, pp. 267–84; notes and "second thoughts" for the first three volumes also appear in Vol. 4, pp. 257–64; portraits, photographs, and documentary facsimiles are scattered throughout this superb multi-volume series.

The fifth volume, published later than the others (Vols. 1–4 appeared together in print in 1936), bears a somewhat different title: *König Ludwig II. und Richard Wagner. Briefwechsel. Neue Urkunden zur Lebensgeschichte Richard Wagners, 1864–1882*, and was co-edited by Strobel and Winifred Wagner; it presents the texts of another 157 letters, many of them exchanged by Wagner and Ludwig, and the rest by other individuals. A *Vorbericht* (introductory report) entitled "Richard Wagner and Malvina Schnorr von Carolsfeld (Vol. 5, pp. xvii–l) appears as a kind of supplement. This volume also contains a timetable of Wagner's "Munich and Triebschen years"—10 March 1864 to 22 May 1872, the latter the composer's fifty-ninth birthday (pp. 179–221)—and an index (pp. 235–43), as well as excerpts from Hans Richter's diary, a portrait of Wagner, and information about his ancestors and relatives.

Reviewed at some length by Einstein in the *Monthly Musical Record* No. 668 (March–April 1938)—a review later reprinted as "Wagner and

Ludwig II" in Einstein's *Essays on Music* (London 1958); pp. 256–63. According to Einstein, Strobel's edition constitutes "the most sobering and damaging picture of Wagner's character that anyone could present" (*Essays*, p. 256).

Friedrich Nietzsche

241. *Friedrich Nietzsche. Briefwechsel: kritische Gesamtausgabe*, ed. Giorgio Colli and Mazzino Montinati. Berlin and New York 1975–. B3316.A253 1975

The most reliable, although not yet complete, edition of Nietzsche's complete correspondence to date. Includes volumes of critical commentary as well as annotated texts of the letters themselves; among the latter are, of course, the philosopher's letters to Wagner; the last fascicle of Vol. 3 includes a *Register* of the entire correspondence. See also item 398.

* *Nietzsche und Wagner: Stationen einer epochalen Begegnung.* Described as item 398.

Incorporates the texts of all Nietzsche's letters to Wagner and his wife Cosima (Vol. 1, pp. 9–302), as well as the complete texts of his various "Wagnerian" books and articles.

242. *The Nietzsche-Wagner Correspondence*, ed. Elisabeth Förster-Nietzsche; trans. Caroline V. Kerr. London: Duckworth, 1923; reprinted New York: Liveright, 1970. xvii, 312pp. ISBN 0871400235 B3316.A47 1970

The well-known English-language version of *Wagner und Nietzsche zur Zeit ihrer Freundschaft: Erinnerungsgabe zu Friedrich Nietzsches 70. Geburtstag den 15. Oktober 1914* (Munich, 1915). In the 1923 edition appeared H. L. Mencken's lively preface, which exalts Nietzsche at the expense of Wagner—"But when he plunged into the great exhortations and expostulations of his maturity . . . Wagner was far below and behind him, and could be no more imagined guiding him than Rossini could be imagined guiding Wagner" (p. xvi)—is thoroughly in line with Förster-Nietzsche's wishes to defend her brother against posthumous attacks. The Liveright reprint was itself reprinted in paperback in 1983 (ISBN 0871402300).

243. *Wagner-Nietzsche Briefwechsel während des Tribschener Idylls*, ed. Wilhelm Jerger. Bern: Alfred Scherz, 1951. 61pp. ML410.W1A3683

Deals almost exclusively with letters exchanged during the first and happiest years of the tempestuous Wagner-Nietzsche relationship. Includes, as a kind of postscript, a lengthy quotation from a letter Cosima Wagner addressed to the young philosopher on 1 January 1872; also includes as an introduction by Jerger (pp. 3–7) and a table of Nietzsche's visits to Tribschen between May 1869 to April 1872 (p. 61). Intended for general readers.

Other Individuals

Each collection is identified and described below in alphabetical order by correspondents' (married) surnames or, in one case—that of item 248—by the name of the city associated with a group of correspondents:

244. *Richard Wagner an Theodor Apel*, ed. Theodor Apel. Leipzig: Breitkopf & Härtel, 1910. xii, 95pp. ML410.W1A35

Consists of the texts of 42 letters, all addressed by the composer to the older Apel (1811–1867) between 1832 and 1835, as well as notes (pp. 90–95). A childhood friend of Wagner's, Apel was the author of a play about Columbus for which Wagner composed the music (*WWV* 37).

245. *Richard Wagner: Briefe an Wilhelm Baumgartner, 1860–1861*, ed. Walter Keller. Zurich: Zurich Wagner-Verein, 1976. 68pp. ML410.W1A30155 1976 (no ISBN available)

Contains the complete texts of sixteen letters from Wagner to Baumgartner, as well as facsimiles of some of them. Also contains a portrait of Baumgartner, printed as a frontispiece; comments by Wagner about Baumgartner's songs, published originally on 7 February 1852 in the *Eidgenössische Zeitung* (pp. 55–57); a catalog of Baumgartner's compositions (pp. 58–59); and an index of names (pp. 67–68). Newman described Baumgartner as "a composer of no outstanding ability but of an agreeable disposition" (item 301, Vol. 2, pp. 164–65) who befriended Wagner during the latter's years in Zurich during the early 1850s.

246. *Letters of Hans von Bülow to Richard Wagner and Others*, ed. Richard Du Moulin-Eckart; trans. Hannah Walter. New York: Alfred A. Knopf, 1931; reprinted New York: Da Capo, 1979. xxx, 434pp. ISBN 0306795396 ML422.B9B963 1979

Comprises 462 letters in all, some 20 of which were addressed to Wagner between 1858 and 1869 (pp. 185–239) and another 21 to Cosima by Bülow after their divorce and between 1869 and 1881 (pp. 241–86); the rest of the volume is taken up with letters Bülow addressed to his daughter Daniela, Karl Klindworth, Carl Bechstein, and so on. Several of the Bülow-Wagner letters include musical examples. An index at the end of the volume is paginated separately (pp. i–vi). The 1979 edition also includes a six-page preface and notes by Scott Goddard. See also item 247 and the edition of Bülow's papers edited by Marie Bülow (item 977).

Also reprinted in 1972 by New York's Vienna House (ISBN 0844300519) under a slightly different title—*Letters of Hans von Bülow to Richard Wagner, Cosima Wagner, his Daughter Daniela* [etc.]—and with notes by Goddard.

More fulsome but suspect, if only because it was published without editorial attribution, is:

247. *Richard Wagner: Briefe an Hans von Bülow.* Jena: Eugen Diederichs, 1916. xlii, 278pp. ML410.W1A35

Comprises the texts of several hundred unnumbered letters Wagner addressed to his long-suffering colleague between 1847 and 1869. Includes a lengthy, unsigned introduction; some of the letters include musical examples. No illustrations of other kinds, however, and no bibliography or index. NB: the LC shelf-number given above comes from a copy owned by Emory University, Atlanta.

248. *Richard Wagner's Letters to His Dresden Friends Theodor Uhlig, Wilhelm Fischer, and Ferdinand Heine*, trans. J. S. Shedlock. New York: Scribner & Welford, 1890; reprinted New York: Vienna House, 1972. xi, 512pp. ISBN 0844300063 ML410.W1A378

Presents the texts of 92 letters addressed between 1849 and 1853 to Uhlig, a court violinist in Dresden, as well as 59 letters addressed between 1841 and 1859 to Fischer, who served as stage director for the premiere performance of *Rienzi*, and 26 letters addressed between 1841 and 1868 to Heine, costume designer for the same performance. Valuable in spite of its editorial shortcomings; a testimonial to Wagner as friend and fellow artist during the earlier years of his mature musical development. Includes a portrait of Wagner painted in 1853 and reproduced as a frontispiece. Published originally in German as *Richard Wagner's Briefe an Theodor Uhlig, Wilhelm Fischer und Ferdinand Heine* (Leipzig, 1888).

249. Jost, Christa and Peter. *Richard Wagner und sein Verleger Ernst Wilhelm Fritzsch.* Tutzing: Hans Schneider, 1997. 213pp. ISBN 3795209021 ML410.W1A31288 1997X

Describes Wagner's relationship with the man who worked closely with him to organize and print the *Gesammelte Schriften* (pp. 11–76). The Josts also deal with such closely related topics as Wagner's finances during the 1870s. Most of the volume, however, consists of the texts of 165 letters from Wagner to Fritzsch between 1870 and 1877 (pp. 80–192), as well as three letters from Fritzsch to Wagner and three additional documents. Illustrated with six photographs and a larger number of facsimiles. Includes a list of the *Schriften*'s contents (pp. 198–202) as well as a general index (pp. 203–13). No bibliography, however, and no musical examples.

250. *Richard et Cosima Wagner: Lettres à Judith Gautier*, ed. Léon Guichard. Paris: Gallimard, 1964. 382pp. ML410.W1A3385

A revised and more comprehensive edition of item 251 below that presents original French-language texts of Cosima's letters to Gautier as well as those written by her husband. Also includes several portraits and documentary facsimiles as illustrations.

251. *Die Briefe Richard Wagners an Judith Gautier*, ed. Willi Schuh. Leipzig and Erlenbach-Zurich: Rotapfel, 1936. 196pp. ML410.W1A338

Reproduces the texts of some three dozen letters Wagner addressed to Gautier between 1865 and 1878. Includes one or two short musical examples, as well as a fold-out facsimile of Wagner's *Albumblatt*, other facsimiles, a frontispiece portrait of Gautier, and a half-dozen additional plates of illustrations. A lengthy introduction ("Die Freundschaft Richard Wagners mit Judith Gautier," pp. 5–97) deals with the complex and controversial Wagner-Gautier relationship.

252. *Richard Wagner und die Putzmacherin, oder: Die Macht der Verleumdung*, ed. Ludwig Kusche. Wilhelmshaven: Heinrichsofen, 1967. 140pp. ML410.W1A3672

Presents the texts of some forty letters Wagner sent his seamstress and confidante Berthe (or Bertha) Goldwag, the *Putzmacherin* (seamstress) of the title, between 1864 and 1871. Supplemented by two plates of Wagner caricatures, and several facsimiles of the letters themselves. An introductory essay presents background information about this remarkable correspondence, in which Wagner orders and occasionally fantasizes about a considerable number of lavishly decorated dressing gowns and other apparel made by Goldwag of satin and silk.

Supercedes *Richard Wagner and the Seamstress*, ed. Daniel Spitzer (New York, n.d.) as well as *Zu den Briefen Richard Wagners an eine Putzmacherin*, ed. Ludwig Karpath (Berlin, 1906), both of which reprint the texts of fewer Wagner-Goldwag letters. See also item 444.

253. *Briefe Richard Wagners an Emil Heckel. Zur Entstehungsgeschichte der Bühnenfestspiele in Bayreuth*, ed. Karl Heckel; 3rd ed. Berlin: S. Fischer, 1912. 170pp. ML410.W1A34

A collection of letters covering the years 1871 to 1883, and connected by linking text that explains Wagner's relationship with the Mannheim music dealer who did so much to raise money for the 1876 and 1882 Bayreuth Festivals. No illustrations or musical examples. Another edition of the original German text appeared under the Breitkopf & Härtel imprint (Leipzig, 1912). An English translation is reputed to exist, but the present author has never seen a copy.

254. *Zwei unveröffentlichte Briefe Richard Wagners an Robert von Hornstein. Zur Erklärung der auf Robert von Hornstein bezuglichen Stellen in Wagners "Mein Leben,"* ed. Ferdinand von Hornstein. Munich: E. W. Bonsels, 1911. 27pp. ML410.W1A344

A pamphlet published to set Robert von Hornstein's reputation to rights *vis-à-vis* comments in Wagner's autobiography and in two of his letters dated 16 and 27 December 1861. Includes comments on Hornstein published in the contemporary press (pp. 23–27), as well as an unpaginated four-page catalog of his songs appended to the end of the volume.

255. Scholz, Hans. *Richard Wagner und Mathilde Maier (1862–1878)*, 2nd ed. Leipzig: Theodor Weicher, 1930. x, 286pp. (no LC number available)

A collection of 129 letters, supplemented by an appendix containing the texts of additional letters, including one from Nietzsche. Also includes a colored frontispiece portrait of Maier herself, several documentary facsimiles, a number of black-and-white photographs, a second color portrait of Maier at age 68, and so on; concludes with an index. Like many collections of Wagner documents, this one is tainted: portions of the autograph documents themselves were deliberately defaced more than a century ago and can no longer be read. Consequently, we may never understand fully Wagner's relationship with the woman he met at the home of one of his publishers, and with whom he may have carried on a prolonged affair.

256. *Richard Wagner an Ferdinand Praeger*, ed. Houston Stewart Chamberlain; 2nd. rev. ed. Berlin and Leipzig: Schuster & Loeffler, 1908. 188pp. ML410.W1A43 1908

Incorporates the texts of 21 letters, addressed by Wagner to Praeger between 1855 and 1876 (pp. 13–47), as well as two critiques by Chamberlain of Praeger's unreliable Wagner reminiscences. No illustrations or index.

257. *The Letters of Richard Wagner to Anton Pusinelli*, trans. and ed. Elbert Lenrow. New York: Knopf, 1932; reprinted New York: Vienna House, 1972. xxvii, 293pp. ISBN 0844301043 ML410.W1A4 1972

Presents the texts of 84 letters, some of them previously unpublished, dating from 1843 to 1877 and addressed to Wagner's family physician and trusted friend. Several dozen additional documents, numbered 85 to 109, were addressed by Pusinelli to Wagner, by Pusinelli to Minna, by Cosima to Marie Pusinelli, and so on. Includes a brief introduction (pp. xiii–xxviii), a table of the letters themselves (pp. ix–xii), and an index paginated (i–x) at the end of the volume.

According to its editor, the Pusinelli volume was published in part to amplify a much more limited gathering of the same documents that appeared in 1902 in the *Bayreuther Blätter* under Wolzogen's editorship (p. xv).

258. *Richard Wagner: Briefe an Hans Richter*, ed. Ludwig Karpath. Berlin: Paul Zsolnay, 1924. xvi, 177pp. ML410.W1A37

A collection of 100 letters addressed by Wagner between 1868 and 1883 to the man who not only conducted the first complete *Ring* cycle at Bayreuth, but served Wagner during the 1860s as a copyist and musical factotum. Also contains a few annotations in the form of footnotes, as well as an index of names (the latter pp. 173–77).

259. *Richard Wagners Briefe an Frau Julie Ritter*, ed. Siegmund von Hausegger. Munich: F. Bruckmann, 1920. 158pp. (no LC number available)

Reproduces the complete texts of 36 letters addressed by Wagner to Ritter between 1850 and 1860. Includes an introduction by Hausegger (pp. 7–13); a portrait of Ritter herself, added as a frontispiece; a fold-out facsimile printed on blue paper of Wagner's first letter to Ritter, dated 22 March 1850; and an index of names on two additional unnumbered pages at the end of the volume.

260. *Richard Wagner's Letters to August Roeckel*, trans. Eleanor C. Sellar. Bristol: J. W. Arrowsmith, 1897. 178pp. ML410.W1A376

Reproduces the texts of twelve letters addressed by Wagner to his Dresden friend and co-revolutionary August Röckel between 1851 and 1865; also includes an introduction by Chamberlain. Largely a translation of *Briefe an August Röckel von Richard Wagner*, ed. "La Mara" [pseud. of Marie Lipsius] (Leipzig, 1894), although differences do exist between the two volumes. La Mara, for instance, gives the date of the first letter, whereas

Sellar doesn't; furthermore, Sellar's translation includes a lengthy preface entitled "Wagner" by Chamberlain (pp. 5–40).

261. Konrad, Ulrich. "Robert Schumann und Richard Wagner: Studien und Dokumente." *Augsburger Jahrbuch für Musikwissenschaft* 4 (1987), pp. 211–320. ML5.A682

An important examination of the Wagner-Schumann relationship, based in part on 33 documents written between 1835 and 1848—some by Schumann, some by Wagner—transcribed and annotated in detail (pp. 280–320). Konrad also discusses "Die Korrespondenz zwischen Robert Schumann und Richard Wagner" (pp. 269–77), which itself contains a facsimile of a Wagner letter dated 5 February 1842. No other illustrations, however, and no musical examples.

* Semper, Manfred. *Das Münchener Festspielhaus. Gottfried Semper und Richard Wagner.* Described as item 411.

Mostly a collection of letters, including missives Wagner addressed to one of nineteenth-century Germany's leading architects and city planners.

262. *Richard Wagner's Briefwechsel mit seinen Verlegern*, ed. Wilhelm Altmann. 2 vols. Leipzig: Breitkopf & Härtel, 1911; reprinted Wiesbaden: Breitkopf & Härtel, 1971. ML410.W1A397 1971

In spite of its title, Altmann's collection deals with just two publishers: Breitkopf & Härtel, represented by 254 letters exchanged by Wagner and this prestigious Leipzig firm between 1831 and 1874 (Vol. 1); and B. Schott's Sons, represented by 274 letters exchanged by Wagner and the most important of Mainz's music-publishing firms between 1830 and 1882 (Vol. 2). Both volumes are indexed (Vol. 1, pp. 235–38; Vol. 2, pp. 246–52). Invaluable for insights into the history of Wagner's publications and the composer's business practices.

263. *Richard to Minna Wagner: Letters to his First Wife*, trans. William Ashton Ellis. 2 vols. London: H. Grevel, 1909. xviii, 812pp. (2 vols. paginated as one). ML410.W1A32F09

A fascinating collection of letters addressed by the composer to an irritable as well as long-suffering spouse. Vol. 1 covers the years 1842 to 1858 and includes letters 1–151; Vol. 2 covers the years 1858 to 1863 and includes letters 152–270. Vol. 2 is also equipped with an index (pp. 789–812) and Vol. 1 with a translator's preface (pp. v–xviii); a few illustrations are scattered through both volumes.

Based on *Richard Wagner an Minna Wagner*, edited in two volumes by Wolzogen (Berlin and Leipzig, 1908), but not merely a translation of it; Ellis, for example, includes one more letter than does the anonymous editor of the German edition and rearranges the illustrations. Other editions of Ellis's translation also exist; one was published in New York in 1902 by Charles Scribner's Sons.

264. *Richard Wagner to Mathilde Wesendonck*, trans. William Ashton Ellis. New York: Charles Scribner's Sons, 1905. lxii, 386pp. ML410.W1A32F05

Contains the texts of 147 letters Wagner addressed to his lover and confidante between 1852 and 1875, as well as those of fourteen letters from Mathilde to Wagner. Also includes a portrait of Mathilde as a frontispiece, a substantial introductory essay (pp. vii–lxii), a "valedictory" (pp. 369–75), and an index (pp. 376–86). Other editions of the Wagner-Mathilde Wesendonk correspondence exist; see, for example, items 213–214 above as well as *Richard Wagner à Mathilde Wesendonk: Journal et letters (1853–1871)*, trans. G. Khnopff and Stanislaus Mazur (Paris, 1986). See also Werner Breig, "Zur Überlieferung des Briefwechsels zwischen Richard Wagner und Mathilde Wesendonck," published in *Die Musikforschung* 51 (1998), pp. 57–63.

265. *Briefe Richard Wagners an Otto Wesendonk, 1852–1870*, ed. Wolfgang Golther; rev. ed. Berlin: Alexander Duncker, 1905. xiv, 170pp. ML410.W1A395 1905

Wagner's correspondence with the retired businessman-turned-arts patron who also happened to be married to the beautiful Mathilde. Related to item 213 above, but includes an introduction by Golther, an important early twentieth-century Wagner scholar (pp. v–xiv), as well as a short index and several illustrations of Otto, including a frontispiece facsimile of an 1860 portrait painted by Julius Roeting. Another edition appeared in Paris in 1924.

266. *Fünfzehn Briefe Richard Wagners mit Erinnerungen und Erläuterungen von Eliza Wille, geb. Slowan*, ed. Ulrich Wille. Munich and Berlin: R. Oldenbourg, 1935. 116pp. ML410.W1A396 1935

A collection of letters from Wagner to the woman, herself a novelist, who befriended him during his Zurich exile, and who helped and supported him financially during his darkest hours of the early 1860s. Also contains an introduction (pp. 5–7) by Wille's son, a frontispiece portrait of Wille, reminiscences of Wagner during the years 1852 to 1870 (pp. 9–27), and several documentary facsimiles. Like other "miscellaneous" collections of

Wagner's correspondence, this one was published originally in a magazine: the *Deutsche Rundschau* of February–March 1887.

Other editions also exist. Among these is *Richard Wagner an Eliza Wille: Fünfzehn Briefe des Meisters nebst Erinnerungen und Erläuterungen von Eliza Wille* (Leipzig and Berlin, 1908), with an introduction by Golther.

Letters in Periodical Publications

Dozens, perhaps hundreds, of periodical publications have been devoted to Wagner's correspondence. The following few examples are identified and described in chronological order of publication:

267. Altmann, Wilhelm. "Richard Wagner und die Berliner General-Intendantur: Verhandlungen über den 'Fliegenden Holländer' und 'Tannhäuser.' " *Die Musik* 2–VI (1902), pp. 331–45. ML5.M9

     Provides background information about Wagner letters held in the Dresden archives and overlooked or ignored by Glasenapp in his Wagner biography (item 305), as well as the text of twelve of the letters addressed by the composer to Count Hochberg, a director of the Berlin Opera. No musical examples.

268. Prod'homme, J. G. "Wagner and the Paris Opéra: Unpublished Letters (February–March, 1861)." *The Musical Quarterly* 1 (1915), pp. 216–31. ML1.M725

     Introduces a previously little-known collection of documents associated with the sensational Parisian premiere of *Tannhäuser* (and omitted from the account of its rehearsals and performances) published originally in *Bayreuther Festblätter in Wort und Bild* (Munich, 1884). Prod'homme provides the original French texts and English translations for six letters Wagner sent to various individuals, including a letter dictated to him by "Nuitter" (pseud. of Charles Truinet), dated 7 March 1861 and addressed to Count Walewski. No facsimiles or other illustrations.

269. "Lettres inédites de Wagner à Léon Leroy et Gaspérini," ed. Maxime Leroy. In item 1064, pp. 43–52.

     Includes the French texts of eleven letters addressed by Wagner to Leroy and Gaspérini between 1859 and 1961.

270. Strobel, Otto. "Wagners Münchener Zeit, im Lichte unveröffentlicher Briefe des Meisters." *Nationalsozialistische Monatshefte* 40 (July 1933). DD253.A1N38

Not seen; cited as a source in Newman's *Life of Richard Wagner* (item 301, Vol. 3, p. xiv). NB: Nazi publications of whatever kind are scarce in American archives, although they continue to be bought and sold worldwide. The Library of Congress is supposed to own two runs of this periodical, one available only on microfilm.

271. Holde, Arthur. "Four Unknown Letters of Richard Wagner, Translated with Commentary." *The Musical Quarterly* 27 (1941), pp. 220–34. ML1.M725

In addition to Holde's comments on each letter—the translation was done by Arthur Mendel—Holde's article contains the texts of four missives: one addressed on 15 June 1861 to Heinrich Esser (at that time conductor of the Vienna Opera) and reproduced complete on four pages of facsimile illustration, one possibly addressed to Eduard Lassen in 1863, and two addressed to unknown recipients or "admirers." Of these last documents, that dated 6 October 1852 to someone in Dresden makes it quite clear how eager Wagner is to avoid "political controversy" (p. 220). The letter to Esser includes a musical example.

272. Mercier, Alain. "Douze lettres inédits de R. Wagner à E. Schuré (23 janvier 1869—6 Février 1878)." *Revue de musicologie* 64 (1968), pp. 206–21. ML5.R32

Provides introductory comments (pp. 206–208) about Schuré, a leading figure in the Wagnerian movement in later nineteenth-century France (see item 1000), as well as the texts of the letters in their original French. No illustrations.

273. Spencer, Stewart. "Wagner Autographs in London." *Wagner* 3/4 (October 1982), pp. 98–123; 4/4 (October 1983), pp. 98–114; and 5/1–2 (January 1984), pp. 2–20 and 40–45. ML410.W1A585

Part 1—entitled "Wagner in London (1)"—provides the texts of forty letters and other documents dating from 1854 to 1855, together with facsimiles of all eight Philharmonic Society programs on which Wagner took part during his visit to the British capital. Part 2 presents the texts of nine additional letters written between 1833 and 1872, while Part 3 provides the texts of another fourteen letters and drafts—among them, an incomplete fair copy of a letter addressed by Wagner to Friedrich Heine (see item 248 above). All texts are presented in their original languages and in English translations; Part 2 also includes three facsimiles as full-page plates.

Related Studies

Representative discussions of the provenance, character, and contents of certain editions or examples of Wagner's correspondence are described below in alphabetical order by author(s):

274. Breig, Werner. "Editing Wagner's Letters: The Problems of a Complete Edition." *Wagner* 18/1 (January 1997), pp. 31–52. ML410.W1A585

Discusses problems and possibilities associated with the *Sämtliche Briefe* edition described above, including those pointed out by Voss in the *Neue Zeitschrift*. Breig pays special attention to Vols. 6–8, published from 1986 to 1991, and includes an appendix on difficulties associated with the Uhlig letters (pp. 48–52). Originally published in German in *Der Brief in Klassik und Romantik: Aktuelle Probleme der Briefedition*, ed. Lothar Bluhm and Andreas Meier (Würzburg, 1993), pp. 121–53. See also Breig's "Probleme und Perspektiven der Richard-Wagner-Briefausgabe" in item 33, pp. 139–42; as well as his "Richard Wagner an Ferdinand Heine: Der Brief vom 18. January 1842 als Problem der Wagner-Briefedition," published in the *Archiv für Musikwissenschaft* 51 (1994), pp. 190–212. In the latter essay Breig points out that the document in question was mistakenly printed in two parts in Vol. 1 of the *Sämtliche Briefe*.

* Breig, Werner, with Martin Dürrer and Andreas Mielke. *Wagner-Briefe-Verzeichnis (WBV)*. Described as item 73.

Identifies almost 10,000 letters. Also contains a concordance with item 74.

275. Eger, Manfred. "The Letters of Richard and Cosima Wagner: The History and Relics of a Destroyed Correspondence." *Programmhefte der Bayreuther Festspiele* V–VI (1979), pp. 25–47 and 25–55. ML410.W2B26

At once a careful and an imaginative "recreation" of the lost Wagner-Cosima correspondence, based on a painstaking examination of its remaining relics and associated documents. Among other sources Eger deals with the first (and only surviving) page of a letter Wagner addressed to his wife on 9 December 1871, several calling cards and rather cryptic notes in both Wagner's and Cosima's hands, and sketches Wagner made of the layout of various rooms and their furnishings at Tribschen. The last are among the facsimiles reproduced as illustrations to this two-part article. Also published in French and German in the same *Programmhefte* volumes.

276. Spencer, Stewart. "Letters." In item 1, pp. 190–93.

A useful summary of the character and extent of Wagner's letter-writing activities and especially of the composer's correspondence as it has appeared in various editions from 1877, when the "Letters to a Seamstress" (item 252) first appeared in 1877 in Vienna's *Neue freie Presse* to the *Sämtliche Briefe* still being published today. As Spencer observes, "With the exception of Strobel's edition of the Ludwig-Wagner correspondence" (item 240), all of the editions published between the 1880s and the 1970s— even editions sponsored by the Burrell Collection's owners (item 227)— were "compromised by omissions, inadequate annotation and uncertain editorial practices" (p. 192). Spencer longs for "a fresh start" in Wagner correspondence studies, as well as for an edition that would include the "letters *to* Wagner"; according to him, the new collected edition is "notable only for its incompleteness and unreliability" (pp. 192–93).

MEMOIRS AND REMINISCENCES

Collections

Hundreds of published and unpublished volumes of memoirs and reminiscences refer to Wagner in greater or lesser detail. No one has yet attempted to locate and describe them all, but the following collection brings together valuable excerpts from a great many of them:

277. Spencer, Stewart. *Wagner Remembered*. London and New York: Faber & Faber, 2000. xii, 308pp. ISBN 0571196535 ML410.W1S65 2000

A fine collection of reminiscences and memoirs concerning Wagner, his family, and more than a few productions of his works. Spencer's volume is divided into sections, each covering a particular period of the composer's life and activities, and each introduced by its own timeline. Among the individuals whose impressions are recorded herein are Judith Gautier, Charles Hallé, Mathilde Wesendonk, and Eliza Wille. Supplemented by twenty-two illustrations, among them several famous Wagner portraits as well as images of Ludwig Geyer and other members of Wagner's immediate and extended family and a few documentary facsimiles. Includes an excellent list of primary sources (pp. 277–90). Enthusiastically reviewed in *Wagner* 21/2 (July 2000), pp. 110–13.

Individual Reminiscences and Memoirs

Examples, most of them cited frequently in the Wagner literature, are described below in alphabetical order by author, then by title:

278. Davison, Henry. *From Mendelssohn to Wagner, Being the Memoirs of J. W. Davison, Forty Years Music Critic of "The Times."* London: William Reeves, 1912. xviii, 539pp. ML423.D18

Includes the text of James William Davison's reports on the Bayreuth Festival of 1876 as they appeared in the *London Times* (pp. 503–29), as well as scattered observations about and reminiscences of Wagner, preserved in the writings of one of Victorian England's most celebrated critics. The volume as a whole is illustrated with a frontispiece pencil portrait of the critic himself, with facsimiles of eight letters written by Berlioz, Mendelssohn, Sterndale Bennett, and so on, and with several dozen additional portraits—among them, one of Wagner (facing p. 512). Edited by the critic's son.

279. *A Memoir of Bayreuth, 1876, Related by Carl Emil Doepler*, ed. Peter Cook. London: Staples, 1979. 75pp. ISBN 0950436011 ML410.W2C65 1979

Contains reminiscences of the first Bayreuth Festival, as well as the texts of letters Wagner addressed to Professor Doepler between 1874 and 1876 (pp. 22–52); these are followed by handsome plates of costume designs drawn by Doepler and originally published c. 1885—at least according to Ernest Newman (item 301, Vol. 4, p. 431n)—in a volume entitled *Der Ring des Nibelungen: Figuren erfunden und gezeichnet von Prof. Carl Emil Doepler, mit Text von Clara Steinitz*. Concludes with a one-page bibliography.

280. Fricke, Richard. *Wagner in Rehearsal, 1875–1876: The Diaries of Richard Fricke*, trans. George R. Fricke; ed. James Deaville, with Evan Baker. Franz Liszt Studies Series, 7. Stuyvesant, NY: Pendragon, 1998. xviii, 124pp. ISBN 0945193868 ML410.W2F713 1998

One of the finest surviving accounts of Wagner as man, musician, and conductor. Illustrated in this edition with 43 beautifully printed, unpaginated pages of black-and-white plates, as well as a few other illustrations. Several earlier German editions of the diaries have appeared in print, including *Bayreuth vor dreissig Jahren. Erinnerungen an Wahnfried und aus dem Festspielhause* (Dresden, 1906).

Reviewed in George Fricke's translation in *The Opera Quarterly* 16 (2000), pp. 101–103. Another English-language translation with notes appeared in several issues of *Wagner* 11–12 (1990–1991); Deaville's notes, however, are superior in extent and detail.

281. Gautier, Judith. *Après de Richard Wagner. Souvenirs (1861–1882)*. Paris: Mercure de France, 1943. 248pp. ML410.W11G3

Reminiscences by the brilliant and beautiful daughter of Théophile Gautier—herself the husband of critic and poet Catulle Mendès, and both of them friends of poet Villiers de l'Isle'Adam, with whom they several times visited Tribschen in 1869–1870. Wagner and Judith may have been lovers, and unquestionably carried on a secret correspondence for more than a decade. This volume, one of several by Gautier, includes a frontispiece photograph of the author taken in 1868 and several documentary facsimiles, including one from *Parsifal*: an opera Gautier "helped" Wagner compose. Also includes a preface by Gustave Samezeuilh (pp. 7–17) and a list of Gautier's publications.

282. Gautier, Judith. *Wagner at Home*, trans. Effie Denreith Massie. New York: John Lane, 1911. 257pp. ML410.W1G28

Another volume of reminiscences by Gautier, illustrated with nine images, including a frontispiece portrait of Wagner himself, photographs of Wagner and Gautier in certain of the residences they inhabited separately, pictures of rooms Gautier inhabited in Brittany, and three facsimiles of musical manuscripts printed as plates and bound at the end of the volume.

Gautier's reminiscences are also available in several French editions, including *Visites à Richard Wagner*, ed. Christophe Looten ("Mayenne," 1992; ISBN 285920203X). Looten's edition includes quotations from Wagner's correspondence, notes, and several illustrations, including a caricature.

283. Kietz, Gustav Adolph. *Richard Wagner aus den Jahren 1842–1849 und 1873–1875. Erinnerungen*, ed. Marie Kietz. Dresden: Carl Reissner, 1905. 225pp. ML410.W11K5

"Interesting and valuable" reminiscences (item 301, Vol. 1, p. 432) of Wagner in Paris and especially in Dresden, written by the sculptor-brother of Ernst Benedikt Kietz, himself a painter and producer of some well-known Wagner portraits as well as one of the composer's few lifelong Paris friends. Includes a chapter on the Dresden uprising of 1849 (pp. 75–107), as well as a letter addressed from Gustav Kietz to his wife about the summer he spent in Bayreuth in 1873. Unindexed; no bibliography, notes, or musical examples.

A translation of Kietz's memoirs into English may be found in *Wagner* 15–16 (1994–1995), complete with several illustrations and copious annotations in the form of footnotes.

284. Krienitz, Willy. "Felix Mottls Tagebuchaufzeichungen aus den Jahren 1873–1876." In item 104, pp. 167–234.

Includes a portrait of Mottl, several facsimiles, one of them a reproduction of the poster advertising the 2 March 1876 Viennese performance of *Lohengrin*, as well as an appendix containing the text of 32 documents pertaining to Mottl's background and family, among them a family tree (pp. 209–34).

285. Lindau, Paul. *Nüchterne Briefe aus Bayreuth. Vergeblicher Versuch im Jahre 1876, Zeit und Geister Richard Wagners zu bannen*, ed. Hellmut Kotschenreuther. Berliner Beiträge zum Vergnügen des Witzes und Verstandes, 5. Berlin: "Das Arsenal," 1989. 95pp. ISBN 3921810833 ML3860.W13 1989

Includes the texts of five "letters"—in fact, rather detailed and often amusing reports—describing rehearsals and performances of the *Ring* dramas at the first Bayreuth Festival. Kotschenreuther's edition includes an introduction (pp. 3–22), scattered caricatures, a portrait of Lindau (p. 18), and a facsimile of the title page for the original edition published in Breslau in 1876. Concludes with notes rather than an index.

Also translated into English as "Letters from Bayreuth," and published with copious notes in several issues of *Wagner* 17 (1996). The Breslau edition, printed by S. Schottlaender, is uncommon today; Harvard University's Loeb Music Library owns a copy.

286. Michotte, Edmond. *Richard Wagner's Visit to Rossini (Paris 1860) and An Evening at Rossini's in Beau-Sejour (Passy) 1858*, trans. and ed. Herbert Weinstock. Chicago and London: University of Chicago Press, 1968. 144pp. ML410.W11M42

Includes complete English translations of Wagner's and Michotte's reminiscences, the latter devoted largely to a conversation between Rossini and Wagner about Carl Maria von Weber and his operas. Supplemented by additional Rossini reminiscences written by Eduard Hanslick and Emil Naumann. Also includes a detailed and well-documented preface, in which Weinstock evaluates the contents, purposes, and relative merits of the two authors' essays, as well as three illustrations, among them a facsimile of the title page for an edition of Wagner's essay published in 1906. Concludes with a useful index.

Reviewed in *Notes* 25 (1968–1969), pp. 727–28. Michotte's reminiscences are also available in a different English translation in *Wagner* 13/3–4 (January–April 1992).

287. Neumann, Angelo. *Personal Recollections of Wagner*, trans. Edith Livermore. New York: Henry Holt, 1908; reprinted New York: Da Capo, 1976. 329pp. ISBN 0306708434 ML410.W1N42 1976

Wagner reminiscences of 1862 to 1882 (as well as recollections of post-Wagner years) by the Austrian singer and stage-director who produced the *Ring* in its entirety in Leipzig in 1878, and later took the work on tour throughout Europe. Illustrated with five plates of portraits and other images, including the facsimile of a letter addressed to Neumann by Wagner on 11 February 1883, only a few days before the composer's death. Indexed.

Originally published in German as *Erinnerungen an Richard Wagner* (3rd ed.; Leipzig 1907).

288. Nietzsche, Friedrich. *Richard Wagner in Bayreuth*, ed. Kurt Hildebrandt. Reclams Universal-Bibliothek, 7126. Leipzig: P. Reclam Jun., 1937. 107pp. ML410.W11N5

The philosopher's only Wagner "reminiscence"; among other things, it deals with his impressions of the 1876 Bayreuth Festival. Hildebrandt's edition includes observations by Nietzsche unpublished during his life-time. See also item 398. English editions include Walter Kaufmann's con-troversial translations of this and other Nietzsche volumes.

*   Förster-Nietzsche, Elisabeth. *Wagner und Nietzsche zur Zeit ihrer Freund-schaft*. Described as item 401.

Includes "reminiscences" assembled posthumously in the form of excerpts from the philosopher's letters, books, and essays.

289. Porges, Heinrich. *Wagner Rehearsing the "Ring": An Eye-Witness Account of the Stage Rehearsals of the First Bayreuth Festival*, trans. Robert L. Jacobs. Cambridge and New York: Cambridge University Press, 1983. xiii, 145pp. ISBN 052123722X ML410.W2P853 1983

Not merely a memoir or collection of miscellaneous reflections, but a mea-sure-by-measure account of what Wagner actually did at the 1875 and 1876 Bayreuth *Ring* rehearsals, illustrated with literally hundreds of short musical examples. Invaluable for conductors. Includes a translator's pref-ace (pp. vii–xiii). Published originally as *Die Bühnenproben zu den Bayreuther Festspielen des Jahres 1876* (Leipzig, 1877 and 1896). Other Wagner reminiscences by Porges include *Die Aufführung von Beethovens 9. Symphonie unter Richard Wagner in Bayreuth* (Leipzig, 1872).

290. Praeger, Ferdinand. *Wagner as I Knew Him*. New York: Longmans, Green & Co., 1892. xxiii, 334pp. ML410.W1P9

A memoir full of fabrications, written by a minor German author and com-poser who did in fact know Wagner but distorted his description of this relationship. Famous primarily for the texts of a number of letters Wagner purportedly addressed to the author between 1861 and 1865, together with quotations from additional documents (the latter pp. 309–16). Also includes a brief Wagner biography and a chapter on Jews in music (pp. 205–17).

291. Serova, Valentina. "Richard Wagner: An Extract from my Memoirs." *Wagner* 12/1 (January 1991), pp. 13–24. ML410.W1A595

Comprised mostly of Wagner reminiscences from 1863 to 1864 and 1868 to 1869, available previously only in Russian and published originally in 1891 in the magazine *Teatral'nij I muzikal'nij zurnal artist*. Among other incidents, Serova recalls her husband Alexander Serov's visit to Tribschen in August 1859.

* Wagner, Siegfried. *Erinnerungen*. See item 1161.

Includes reminiscences of the younger composer's father, as well as of Bayreuth and the Wagner Festivals of the late-nineteenth and early-twentieth centuries.

292. [Wölfel, Karl.] *Richard Wagner in Bayreuth. Erinnerungen*, ed. Heinrich Schmidt and Ulrich Hartmann. Leipzig: Carl Klinner, 1909. 139pp. ML410.W253

A collection of poems, letters, and anecdotes about Wagner and Bayreuth during the 1870s and mostly devolving upon Wölfel (1833–1893), an architect Wagner consulted about Haus Wahnfried. Illustrated with fourteen plates of building designs and construction photographs. Concludes with a collection of letters dealing with the construction of Wagner's home (pp. 131–39). See also item 1125.

In addition to these eyewitness sources, many nineteenth-century memoirs at least mention Wagner and his undertakings. Among the most familiar and fascinating of such reminiscences is:

293. Berlioz, Hector. *Memoirs of Hector Berlioz from 1803–1865, Comprising his Travels in Germany, Italy, Russia, and England*, trans. Rachel and Eleanor Holmes; rev. Ernest Newman. New York: Alfred A. Knopf, 1932; reprinted New York: Dover, 1960. xxviii, 533pp. ML410.B5A243 1960

Includes an account of a partial performance of *Rienzi* Berlioz heard in 1843 (pp. 289–90), as well as a great deal of information about German musical life during the 1840s and 1850s, observations on Wagner's character and compositions, and a lengthy note by Newman (p. 509) explaining much about the troubled Berlioz-Wagner relationship. Also available in a translation prepared by David Cairns (London, 1970) that includes illustrations, maps, musical examples, portraits, and a bibliography (pp. 769–72).

OTHER DOCUMENTARY COLLECTIONS

Among general or broad-based collections of Wagner documents is the following publication:

294. Barth, Herbert, with Dietrich Mack and Egon Voss. *Wagner—A Documentary Study*, trans. P. R. J. Ford and Mary Whittall. London: Thames & Hudson, 1975. 256pp. ISBN 0500011380 ML410.W1B1853 1975

A survey of Wagner's life, works, and influence—based almost entirely upon and consisting of primary sources—that can also be read as a documentary biography. Accompanied by 169 plates containing some 281 illustrations, many of them in color; these include a large number of documentary facsimiles as well as portraits, pictures of places, and scenes from the composer's various music-dramas. Barth and his colleagues also provide substantial quotations about Wagner by the likes of Bismarck, Bruckner, Hebbel, Liszt, Meyerbeer, Malvina von Meysenbug, the Schumanns, and Tchaikovsky, as well as a family tree (pp. 10–11) and a detailed timeline (pp. 13–30).

Subsequently published in German and in a revised edition as *Richard Wagner: Sein Leben und Sein Werk in zeitgenössischen Bildern und Dokumenten*, ed. Voss (Mainz, 1982). A previous German edition (Vienna, 1975) is shorter and less useful.

Another important anthology is devoted to Wagner's philosophical, literary, and religious pronouncements:

295. *Richard Wagner. Mein Denken*, ed. Martin Gregor-Dellin. Munich and Zurich: R. Piper & Co., 1982. 416pp. ISBN 3492005640 ML410.W1R52 1982

A selection from Wagner's correspondence and published prose chosen, as an advertisement by its publisher states, to demonstrate "what Richard Wagner thought, how he thought, what he thought about, and with what result" (p. ii). Among Gregor-Dellin's selections are portions of *The Art-Work of the Future, Jewishness in Music*, selections from the composer's diary entries for 1865, and so on. Introduced by a foreword (pp. 7–28) that establishes intellectual perspectives on many of the issues associated with Wagner, his music dramas, and certain of his friends and acquaintances.

Still other anthologies include the following, described in alphabetical order by author, editor, or title:

296. Beck, Walter. *Richard Wagner: Neue Dokumente zur Biographie. Die Spiritualität im Drama seines Lebens.* Tutzing: Hans Schneider, 1988. 339pp. ISBN 3795205328 ML410.W1B28 1988

   A documentary biography of sorts. The documents themselves cover 1833 to 1886 (i.e., to Liszt's death) and are accompanied by linking text. Concludes with lists of the documents themselves (pp. 335–37) and of some thirty facsimiles and portraits (p. 339). Unfortunately, no information is provided either about where individual documents may be found or whether they are new to Wagner research; more than a few of them, including a facsimile of the title page of *Art and Revolution* (Leipzig, 1850; here p. 56) either contain no new information or have been reproduced on a number of previous occasions. Reviewed in *Notes* 47 (1992–93), pp. 718–22.

*   *Der Ring am Rhein*, ed. Wolfgang Storch. Described as item 656.

   Composed almost entirely of drafts of Wagner's poem, as well as of excerpts from books and articles by Claudel, Liszt, Nattiez, Spengler, Wapnewski, and others.

*   Kirchmeyer, Helmut. *Das zeitgenössische Wagner-Bild* in 5 volumes. Described as item 954.

   Includes literally thousands of documents, most of them newspaper and magazine pieces, published between the 1830s and the end of 1852.

*   *Nietzsche und Wagner: Stationen einer epochalen Begegnung.* Described as item 398.

   Comprises virtually the entire Wagner-Nietzsche textual legacy; in effect (like the item cross-referenced immediately below) the "documentary biography" of a relationship.

*   *Richard Wagner: Dokumentarbiographie.* Described as item 322.

297. Schweizer, Gottfried. *Richard Wagner und seine Getreuen: Erinnerungen und Briefe aus der rhein-mainischen Landschaft.* Veröffentlichungen des Manskopfschen Museums für Musik- und Theatergeschichte, 4. Frankfurt a.M.: Waldemar Kramer, 1940. 228pp. ML410.W1A377

   A miscellany of letters, reminiscences, and scattered portraits and documentary facsimiles. Includes the texts of letters from Wagner to several Frankfurt citizens, as well as missives written by the composer's wives

Minna and Cosima, his sister Johanna Wagner-Jachmann (see item 344), Bülow, Liszt, etc. The texts of other letters, together with plates reproducing paintings, drawings, and photographs of a number of figures and a few facsimiles, are supplemented by information about the 1862 Frankfurt performance of *Lohengrin* (together with a reproduction of a poster advertising the event), an account of Liszt's Mainz concerts of the early 1840s, and so on. Supplemented by detailed endnotes (pp. 213–225); concludes with an index.

298. Strecker, Ludwig. *Richard Wagner als Verlagsgefährte: eine Darstellung mit Briefen und Dokumenten*. Mainz: B. Schott's Sons, 1951. 340pp. ML410.W1S77

Essentially a collection of Wagner's correspondence with his publishers Breitkopf & Härtel, B. Schott's Sons (various versions of the firm's name exist in publications), and Franz Schott's Nachfolger as well as documents associated with Wagner's self-publishing efforts. Handsomely illustrated with a large number of black-and-white documentary facsimiles and more than a few portraits. Includes after p. 340 several unpaginated tables, among them one providing information about various European currencies in use during Wagner's lifetime. Also includes a catalog of illustrations (pp. 334–35); concludes with an index of proper names.

Finally, several anthologies concentrate on parodies and put-downs of Wagner and his works. One such collection is:

299. *Richard der Einzige: Satire, Parodie, Karikatur*, ed. Hermann Hakel. Vienna and Hannover: Forum, 1963. 320pp. (no LC number available)

A fascinating collection of Wagner "put-downs," a few of them from the composer's own (unwitting) hand. Hakel reprints cartoons as well as the texts of Johann Nestroy's *Tannhäuser* parody (pp. 61–98), Alexander Mozkowski's *Aus "Der Ring der nie gelungen"* (pp. 177–91), "Ein jüdischer Wagnerianer" and other essays by Daniel Spitzer, excerpts from Lindau's *Nüchterne Briefe aus Bayreuth* (item 285), and a variety of newspaper critiques, poems, and other lampoons, as well as several of the "Putzmacherin" letters. Unfortunately contains no table of contents, information about sources, or bibliography. Include an index of authors. Limited to German-language sources, thereby necessarily ignoring parodies in other languages. See also item 1075.

Finally, see *Richard Wagner und Bayreuth in Karikatur und Anekdote*, ed. Herbert Barth (2nd ed.; Bayreuth, 1970). An earlier edition, published simply as *Bayreuth in der Karikatur* (Bayreuth 1957), includes a variety of newspaper and magazine cartoons.

ADDITIONAL SOURCES

300. *Das Nibelungenlied.* "Richard-Wagner Gedächtnis-Ausgabe." Berlin: Carl Albert Kindle, 1940. xxvi, 138 + 426pp. (no LC number available)

A limited-edition commemorative volume, bound in vellum embossed with black-and-gold lettering, honoring Wagner's knowledge of and borrowings from this medieval poem. Incorporates item 1090 as well as introductory material paginated separately from the bulk of the volume, which itself contains the poem, printed in *Fraktur* and translated into modern German by Karl Simrock; and an essay by Golther entitled "Richard Wagners Ringdichtung" (pp. i–xxvi), originally written in 1932. The introductory material contains illustrations both tipped-in and printed on the pages themselves; in Golther's essay these include photographs of celebrated Wagnerian performers as well as artists' realizations of scenes from the poem and Wagner's music dramas. No critical apparatus, bibliography, or index, however.

Originally published by the same firm in 1933. The British Library, London, owns a copy of the 1933 edition; the only copy of the 1940 edition seen by the present author is in private hands.

V

Wagner's Life and Character

Few individuals have had their life story told as many times or from as many perspectives as has Wagner. This chapter identifies and describes a mere handful of Wagner biographies; it deals somewhat more carefully with specialized studies devoted to particular periods of the composer's life and activities, or to particular places where he lived and worked, or to relationships with particular individuals or groups of persons.

AUTOBIOGRAPHIES

*   Wagner, Richard. *My Life*. Described as item 204.

Famous for its omissions, errors, and outright falsehoods, but nevertheless invaluable as a guide to the composer's career and accomplishments. Items 207–10 contain more of Wagner's autobiographical writings.

BIOGRAPHIES AND RELATED STUDIES

Traditional Biographies

By "traditional biography" I mean a more or less straightforward, book-length account of the life of a man or woman. Although completed more than a half-century ago, the following study remains among the best of Wagner life-histories:

301. Newman, Ernest. *The Life of Richard Wagner*. 4 vols. London: Cassell; and New York: Alfred A. Knopf, both 1933–1947; reprinted New York: Alfred A. Knopf, 1960. ML410.W1N53

Vol. 1 covers the years 1813 to 1848, Vol. 2 covers 1848 to 1860, Vol. 3 1859 to 1866, and Vol. 4 1866 to 1883. Each volume is indexed separately and includes its own list of sources and *sigla*; a few volumes contain short, scattered musical examples. Vol. 2 also contains appendices entitled "Wag-

ner and Meyerbeer" (pp. 603–7) and "Wagner's Origins" (pp. 608–19)—
the latter itself containing item 342 below as well as a discussion of the
"Prince Constantin" question; Vol. 3 contains "Johanna Wagner and
Geyer" (pp. 558–62) as well as "The 'Madness' of King Ludwig" and
"The Putzmacherin Letters" (pp. 567–69); and Vol. 4 contains "New Light
on the 'Siegfried Idyll' " and "Bombastes Furioso"—the last a reply to
Carl Engel's 1941 review of Newman's third volume in *The Musical Quarterly*. Illustrated in each volume with black-and-white plates, as well as
copious quotations from a host of sources, including those Mary Burrell
unearthed around the turn of the century (see item 345). Still considered
one of the finest Wagner studies ever written; in one of his own Wagner
biographies, Curt von Westernhagen wrote that "the importance of Newman's *Life* as the standard work has in no way been diminished" (item 303,
Vol. 1, p. ix) by more recent publications in the field.

Another reprint edition, this time of the Knopf edition, appeared in
1976 from Cambridge University Press (ISBN 0521291496). NB: The
New York and London editions of the 1930s and 1940s are paginated
somewhat differently; throughout the present research guide, references
are to the London edition.

*Other influential and relatively recent Wagner biographies include the following,
arranged in alphabetical order by author:*

302. Gutman, Robert W. *Richard Wagner: The Man, His Mind, and His Music*,
      rev. ed. San Diego: Harcourt Brace Jovanovich, 1990. xxiv, 492pp. ISBN
      0156776154 ML410.W1G83 1990

      Written prior to the publication of the *Brown Book* (item 209) and
      Cosima's diaries (item 211), this volume describes a man who enriched or
      enjoyed himself at the expense of others, a bigoted voluptuary who lolled
      about in fancy-dress and took pleasure, real or imagined, in other men's
      wives. As Stewart Spencer puts it, Gutman's volume—although "itself not
      free from prejudice"—nevertheless "brought a welcome blast of fresh air
      to the incense-laden sanctum of the Bayreuth Circle, as ministered by
      Westernhagen, Kraft, and others" (item 334, p. 403). Includes a variety of
      illustrations bound as two unpaginated fascicles (identified on pp. viii–x);
      also includes a bibliography (pp. 457–69) and index. Reviewed by Egon
      Voss in "Vom guten und bösen Wagner," in *Die Musikforschung* 26 (1973),
      pp. 245–47; Voss objects strongly to Gutman's interest in Wagner's sexual
      proclivities and self-indulgences.

      Originally published in 1968; reprinted in paperback in 1971 and sub-
      sequently revised. In addition to the "standard" first edition, a handsome

large-format *Time-Life Records* special edition (New York, 1968) is outfitted with a great many more illustrations, some in color.

303. Westernhagen, Curt von. *Wagner: A Biography*, 2 vols.; trans. Mary Whittall. Cambridge and New York: Cambridge University Press, 1978. ISBNs
05212193002 and 0521219329 ML410.W1W55

A disappointing work, especially in light of other publications by Westernhagen, as well as those of Newman (item 301), Gutman (item 302), and
Bekker (item 317). Vol. 1 covers 1813 to 1864, Vol. 2 the rest of Wagner's
life to 1883. Each volume contains sixteen pages of plates featuring portraits of Eduard Devrient, Anton Pusinelli, the Wesendonks, and other
important figures, as well as pictures of Wagner family members and occasional facsimile illustrations. Vol. 2 concludes with a short chronological
table (pp. 604–10; no such title is found in Vol. 1, despite a statement to the
contrary in the table of contents), a list of Wagner's works, a bibliography,
and an index to both volumes.

   Revised extensively from item 320. Reviewed harshly, together with
items 31, 1025, and 1058, by John Deathridge in *19th Century Music* 5
(1981–1982), pp. 81–89. In "The Noble Anti-Semitism of Richard Wagner," another review published in the *Historical Journal* 25 (1982), pp.
751–63, Paul Lawrence Rose refers to a little-known Nazi-era pamphlet by
Westernhagen—*Richard Wagners Kampf gegen seelische Fremdherrschaft*
(Munich, 1935; see also item 104)—and calls Westernhagen's 1978
description of Wagner's relationships with Jewish musicians "dishonest
special pleading" (review, p. 759).

Older influential Wagner biographies include:

304. Ellis, William Ashton. *Life of Richard Wagner: Being an Authorized Eng-
lish Version of C. F. Glasenapp's "Das Leben Richard Wagners."* 6 vols.
London: Kegan Paul, Trench, Trübner & Co., 1900–1908; reprinted New
York: Da Capo, 1977. ISBN 0306708876 ML410.W1G533 1977

Based largely—but by no means entirely—on *Das Leben* (item 305), one
of the most controversial Wagner biographies in print. Having begun translating Glasenapp's work and finding it unsatisfactory, Ellis branched out
on his own and completed six volumes—the first three largely as Glasenapp wrote them, the last three almost entirely Ellis's own—of a study its
author-translator considered far from satisfactory, if only because the
"Bayreuth strong box" prevented scholars from consulting invaluable primary sources then under Cosima's control. Vol. 1 of Ellis's work covers
Wagner's life to 1843, Vol. 2 the years 1843 to 1849 (whereas Glasenapp's

Vol. 2 covers 1843 to 1853), and so on; Ellis's Vol. 6 brings Wagner's life up only to 1859. The Da Capo reprint edition includes an introduction by George Buelow (Vol. 1, pp. v–xiv).

305. Glasenapp, Carl Friedrich. *Das Leben Richard Wagners*, 4th ed. 6 volumes. Leipzig: Breitkopf & Härtel, 1904–1911. ML410.W1G52

The basis of Ellis's partial "translation" (item 304). Covers all of Wagner's life; Vols. 1–2 and 4–6 include frontispiece portraits as well as other illustrations, including scattered documentary facsimiles and musical examples. The first two editions appeared under the title *Richard Wagner's Leben und Wirken*; the title changed only with the third edition (Breitkopf & Härtel, 1894–1911). Ninth and tenth editions were published in Munich in 1936 and 1940, respectively.

306. Marcuse, Ludwig. *Das denkwürdige Leben des Richard Wagner*. Diogenes Taschenbuch 21/4. Zurich: Diogenes, 1973. 303pp. ISBN 325720079X ML410.W1M26 1973

A lively, elegantly written life story by the polymath and philosopher who also wrote Freud's, Heine's, and Strindberg's biographies. Cited in virtually every authoritative German-language Wagner bibliography (e.g., items 2, 6, 27–28, 76, etc.) but apparently consulted infrequently, if at all, by scholars of other nations. The edition published in 1963 by Szczesny Verlag of Munich contains no source references, bibliography, or index. According to OCLC (Accession No. 31911470) the 1973 edition, one the present author has never seen, may also have appeared, with an index, under the title *Richard Wagner: ein denkwürdiges Leben*; only the New York Public Library, however, is identified as owning such a copy.

307. Newman, Ernest. *Wagner as Man and Artist*, rev. ed. New York: Alfred A. Knopf, 1924. xvii, 399pp. ML410.W1A5F24

A lively but less carefully considered or reliable study of Wagner's activities and creative accomplishments than item 301. Illustrated with ten black-and-white plates of portraits and Wagner "places." Includes a rather detailed "Synthetic table [timeline] of Wagner's life and works and synchronous events" (pp. 373–94), as well as scattered musical examples; concludes with a perfunctory index. Originally published in somewhat different form in 1914; the revised edition was reprinted in 1963.

Briefer but nevertheless useful English-language biographies include:

308. Osborne, Charles. *Wagner and His World*. New York: Charles Scribner's Sons, 1977. 128pp. ISBN 0684148927 ML410.W1O8

A biography—not a comprehensive survey, as its title might be taken to suggest—outfitted with some 142 black-and-white illustrations; among these are several of Paul von Joukowsky's designs for the 1882 premiere performance of *Parsifal*, as well as a variety of Wagner family photographs. Also contains a timeline (pp. 120–21), a very brief bibliography (p. 121), and a list of illustration sources (pp. 122–26). Concludes with a three-page index. Published the same year in London by Thames & Hudson (ISBN 0500130604).

309. Watson, Derek. *Richard Wagner: A Biography*. New York: Schirmer, 1981. 352pp. ISBN 0028727702 ML410.W1W13 1981

A straightforward, readable life story. Because Watson offers few surprises, his work appeals to general readers even as it offers specialists little in the way of new discoveries or insights. Illustrated with 61 black-and-white portraits, photographs, and other pictures of Wahnfried, the Bayreuth Festspielhaus, and others. Also outfitted with a useful glossary of people important to the composer's career and activities (pp. 321–34) and a short bibliography (pp. 335–39); concludes with an index. Available in a similar edition published in London in 1979 (ISBN 046003166X). Reviewed in *Notes* 37 (1980–1981), pp. 57–58, where it is compared unfavorably with Carl Dahlhaus's "dazzling, virtuoso" performance in item 566.

Wagner biographies are available in Albanian, Arabic, Bulgarian, Catalan, Chinese, Czech, Dutch, Estonian, Finnish, Georgian, Greek, Hungarian, Japanese, Latvian, Lithuanian, Pali, Portuguese, Russian, Spanish, and Swedish as well as in other languages. In their place a single modern French-language biography is identified and described below:

310. Hofmann, (Michel) Rostislav. *Richard Wagner*. Paris: Pierre Waleffe, 1966. 215pp. ML410.W1H68

A generally satisfactory survey of the composer's life and activities. Includes boxed quotations from some of Wagner's prose works, as well as a number of small illustrations—portraits, documentary facsimiles, caricatures, and the like—but no musical examples as such. Also includes a chronological table of Wagner's activities (pp. 213–14). Unindexed.

More than a few Wagner biographies bear deceptive titles—which is to say, they do not appear at first glance to be biographies at all. These include:

311. Gasperini, A[uguste] de. [*Richard Wagner.*] *La nouvelle allemagne musicale.* Paris: Heugel & Cie., 1866. 173pp. ML410.W1G2

Covers Wagner's life to the mid-1860s. Written by a young physician who met and befriended Wagner during the later 1850s and 1860s and who, in this volume, pays special attention to the "New German School" of composition and the impact of Wagner's music on French audiences. Includes two facsimiles: the first of a letter Wagner addressed to the author on 4 June 1860 concerning the "Paris" *Tannhäuser*, the second a two-sided foldout of *Tannhäuser*'s concluding measures in Wagner's hand. Also includes comments on most of the important works from *Rienzi* to *Tristan*.

   Underwritten as a book-length publication by the French music magazine *Le Ménestrel*. Sometimes identified in bibliographies as "*Richard Wagner: La nouvelle . . .*"; hence the bracketed material above.

312. Hueffer, Francis. *Richard Wagner and the Music of the Future: History and Aesthetics.* London: Chapman & Hall, 1874; reprinted Freeport, NY: Books for Libraries, 1971. v, 333pp. ISBN 0836925084 ML390.H88 1971

Sometimes identified in bibliographies as a "life" of Wagner, this volume is perhaps more important as a study of the composer's impact on dramatic music; Hueffer, its author, was an admirer of the composer's who also reviewed Wagner's 1877 London concerts for the *Times*. Only the first part of the book (pp. 1–122) concerns Wagner; the rest devolves upon other individuals. Includes an appendix devoted to the 1876 Festival at Bayreuth, as well as a lengthy discussion of the songs of Liszt, Schubert, Robert Schumann, and Robert Franz.

Other biographies, although of comparatively little interest as a whole, may nevertheless contain information of value. Here are three examples, described below in alphabetical order by author:

313. Anderson, Robert. *Wagner: A Biography, with a Survey of Books, Editions, and Recordings.* London and Hamden, CT: Clive Bingley and Linnet Books, 1980. 154pp. ISBN 0208016775 ML410.W1A599

Consists of a biographical sketch (pp. 9–75) followed by a bibliographical essay (pp. 76–109) and an essay about Wagner recordings (pp. 126–43). Of interest primarily to discographers, there being little unusual about the rest of Anderson's volume. Indexed.

314. Kienzel, Wilhelm. *Richard Wagner*, 2nd ed. "Weltgeschichte in Karakterbildern." Munich: Kirchheim, 1908. 147pp. ML410.W1K54

Provides, among other things, a good deal of material about a number of the composer's colleagues and collaborators in various stage productions. Includes 91 illustrations, many of them portraits. Hundreds of educational publications like this one appeared in print in Germany prior to World War I, this one in a series devoted to "world history through character portraits."

315. Marbach, Paul Alfred. *Richard Wagner*. Berlin: Buchverlag der Gesellschaft zur Verbreitung Klassischer Kunst, 1925. 96pp. (no LC number available)

   A brief account of Wagner's activities and interests, supplemented with material on Bayreuth as a city, the Festival Theater as a musical-architectural monument, Festival performances of the music dramas during the late-nineteenth and early-twentieth centuries, and so on. Illustrated with a variety of portraits, family photographs, documentary facsimiles, and—perhaps of greatest usefulness today—detailed diagrams of the Festival Theater's layout and design. No bibliography or index. Uncommon; Harvard University's Loeb Music Library owns a copy.

Finally, consider this biography that addresses itself to younger readers:

316. Padman, Elaine. *Wagner*. New York: Thomas Y. Crowell, 1971. 100pp. ISBN 0690865112 ML410.W1P23 1972

   In many respects a lackluster publication, but among its musical examples is the complete text of Wagner's *Albumblatt* in C Major (pp. 64–67). Also includes a few portraits and other familiar views; concludes with an index. Wagner remains, at least in the opinion of the present author, an unlikely figure of interest for today's young people and by no means a moral example to set before them; fortunately, the *Albumblatt* is easy enough for many children to play.

Thematic Biographies

All biographies are at least implicitly thematic: they present their subject in light of a particular topic, or as seen from a particular perspective; thus Newman's four-volume biography is "objective," Gutman's monograph "debunking," and so on. Arranged and described below in alphabetical order by author are several explicitly thematic Wagner biographies:

317. Bekker, Paul. *Richard Wagner: His Life in His Work*, trans. M. M. Bozman. London: J. M. Dent & Sons, 1931; reprinted Westport, CT: Greenwood, 1971. vii, 522pp. ISBN 0837134439 ML410.W13B243 1971

Perhaps the best earlier Wagner biography, especially in terms of its author's insistence on examining the composer's music as the primary and often exclusive goal and purpose of his other activities and affairs. Thus, rather than "explaining" *Tristan* in terms of Wagner's relationship with Mathilde Wesendonk, Bekker assumes that art was what mattered most to Wagner, and that the love affair was of subordinate importance to, and possibly even inspired by, the music drama.

Published originally as *Wagner. Das Leben im Werke* (Berlin, Stuttgart, and Leipzig, 1924).

318. Kröplin, Eckhart. *Richard Wagner: Theatralisches Leben und lebendiges Theater*. Leipzig: VEB Deutscher Verlag für Musik, 1989. 194pp. ISBN 3370002922 ML410.W1K896 1989

A discussion of Wagner's life and contributions to music, literature, and theater from a socialist perspective. Incorporates 54 black-and-white illustrations, some of them of interest to students of the composer's revolutionary activities and attitudes. Contains no musical examples; concludes with an index.

319. Sabor, Rudolph. *The Real Wagner*. London: Cardinal, 1989. 382pp. ISBN 0233976704 ML410.W1S12 1989

Wagner's life in a version officially authorized by 1980s Bayreuth but nevertheless "realistic." Sabor provides a detailed chronological table of the composer's activities (pp. 3–23), a glossary of "Principal Characters" in his life-story (pp. 24–34), a family tree (p. 35), a few musical examples, and several illustrations. Introduced by Wolfgang Wagner; rounded off with a bibliography (pp. 365–67) and index. Reviewed enthusiastically in *Wagner* 9/4 (October 1988), pp. 163–64.

Published originally as *Der wahre Wagner: Dokumente beantworten die Frage "Wer war Richard Wagner wirklich?"* (Vienna, 1987). Another English-language edition exists (London, 1987).

320. Westernhagen, Curt von. *Wagner*. Zurich: Atlantis, 1968. 571pp. ML410.W1W47

In the opinion of most critics the poorest of Westernhagen's several Wagner monographs; Spencer calls the 1956 study (item 12) "superior in every way" to this one, which, he asserts, "represents a reversion to the purblind adulation and uncritical acceptance of the Master's word that typified the old Bayreuthians" (item 1, p. 403). The theme, in other words, is "reverence." Includes a few portraits and photographs, among them a color frontispiece reproduction of an early likeness, as well as a timeline (pp. 545–50), a bibliography (pp. 558–61), and an index of names. Reviewed in *Die Musikforschung* 26 (1973), pp. 245–47.

321. Williams, Simon. *Richard Wagner and Festival Theatre.* Westport, CT: Praeger, 1994. xv, 181pp. ISBN 0313274355 MLW410.W13W32 1994

Emphasizes Wagner's associations with, activities on behalf of, and love for, the stage. In part because of his specialized approach, Williams avoids some of the pitfalls into which other biographers have fallen. Includes thirteen illustrations, a timeline (pp. 163–69), and a bibliography (pp. 171–75).

Documentary Biographies

Documentary biographies are composed entirely or almost entirely of primary source materials. Wagner documentary biographies include studies which, like the following, emphasize written documentation:

322. *Richard Wagner. Dokumentarbiographie,* ed. Egon Voss. Mainz: B. Schott's Sons, 1982. 582pp. ISBN 3442330815 ML410.W1R54 1983

Includes an extensive selection of various letters, testimonials, excerpts from literary works, and so on—all reprinted in whole or part—as well as a variety of illustrations. Similar to items 294–95 described in the previous chapter. Also includes a bibliography (pp. 567–70) and index.

* *Richard Wagner: Sein Leben in Briefen.* Described as item 229.

An epistolary biography. Includes the texts of 112 letters written between 1832 and 1882, as well as running text and commentary.

Other documentary biographies emphasize the visual and verbal equally, or give greater weight to images; several of these are described below in alphabetical order by author:

323. Kretschmar, Eberhard. *Richard Wagner. Sein Leben in Selbstzeugnissen, Briefen und Berichten.* Berlin: Propyläen, 1939. 387pp. ML410.W1A138

Employs linking text to expand upon the chronology and significance of letters, excerpts from literary works, and other primary sources deemed "suitable" by the Nazi propaganda ministers who oversaw books and magazines published during the Third Reich. Illustrated with 55 portraits, photographs, and documentary facsimiles, as well as a fold-out genealogical table.

324. Mayer, Hans. *Portrait of Wagner: An Illustrated Biography*, trans. Robert Nowell. New York: Herder & Herder, 1972. 175pp. ML410.W1M28 1972

Consists mostly of familiar texts, among them letters and excerpts from some of Wagner's literary works. Illustrated with a number of portraits, photographs, documentary facsimiles, and so on, all reproduced in black-and-white. Concludes with a brief but nevertheless useful bibliography, now somewhat out of date. A pocket synopsis of Wagner's character and activities. Originally published as *Richard Wagner in Selbstzeugnissen und Bilddokumenten* (Hamburg, 1959).

More than a few Wagner documentary biographies are primarily visual. Examples are described below in reverse chronological order of publication or republication:

325. *Das Leben von Richard Wagner. Eine chronologische Dokumentation*, ed. Doris Kopf. Baden-Baden: Verlag "Klimas+Panten," 1996. Unpaginated. ISBN 3928813064 ML410.W1L42 1996

Essentially a picture book outfitted with captions, printed throughout in English and German and arranged in double columns; also includes an introduction by the editor. The illustrations, some in full color, include documentary facsimiles as well as Renoir's Wagner portrait as cover art. The copy examined by the present author had no full inside title page; instead, title page and CIP appear to have been combined.

326. Gregor-Dellin, Martin. *Richard Wagner. Eine Biographie in Bildern*. Munich and Zurich: R. Piper, 1982. 220pp. ISBN 3492026931 ML410.W195G65 1982

Long on pictures: Gregor-Dellin includes some 325 illustrations, more than a few of them in color. Much shorter on text. Among the plates are several facsimiles, as well as a timeline (pp. 217–20).

327. Bücken, Ernst. *Richard Wagner*, 2nd ed. "Die grossen Meister der Musik." Laaber: Laaber-Verlag, 1980. 160pp. + unpaginated plates. ISBN 3921318493 ML410.W1B68

A black-and-white picture book supplemented by a single color portrait of the composer. Also includes musical examples; concludes with a short index. The first edition was published in Potsdam in 1933; a revised edition appeared ten years later, during the height of World War II—and, in that sense, represents a testimonial to continuing German enthusiasm for Wagner and his compositions.

328. Batka, Richard. *Richard Wagner*, 2nd ed. Berlin: Schlesische Verlagsanstalt, 1919. 128pp. ML410.W1B2 1919

An illustrated biography of interest today principally for its handsome
fold-out documentary facsimiles, tipped-in portraits mounted on colored
paper, and cleanly printed caricatures. Also includes a few short musical
examples. Originally published in 1912. See also items 129–30 as well as
item 1118 and other illustrative Bayreuth and Wagner-family volumes.

Biographical Timelines and Other Concise Publications

Some Wagner "chronologies" (also known as "timelines" or Zeittafeln*) are more
or less readable; others, like item 150, serve primarily as reference works. Among
the more readable Wagner timelines are the following publications, described in
reverse chronological order of publication:*

329. Kröplin, Karl-Heinz. *Richard Wagner, 1813–1883: Eine Chronik*. Leipzig:
VEB Deutscher Verlag für Musik, 1987. 184pp. ISBN 3370000822
ML410.W1K9 1987

An unusually detailed timeline (pp. 13–138). Supplemented by a summary
of the composer's ancestors and relatives (pp. 9–12); a table of information
about the sketches, librettos, score preparation, and first performances of
the principal dramatic works from *Die Feen* to *Parsifal* (pp. 140–41); and
indexes of Wagner's compositions, literary works, places, and people. Also
includes three blank pages (pp. 182–84) useful for note-taking! No illustrations or musical examples.

330. Mack, Dieter, and Egon Voss. *Richard Wagner: Life and Works in Dates
and Pictures*, trans. Patricia Crampton. Frankfurt a.M.: Insel, 1978. 126
pp. (no ISBN or LC number available)

A book-length timeline (pp. 87–113) that includes a catalog of Wagner's
"major compositions" (pp. 115–23) and the dates of their first performances, as well as 74 illustrations and a bibliography (pp. 124–26).
Draws upon materials utilized in Barth, Mack, and Voss in item 294 and
its revised German-language editions. Item 330 is also available in
German from the same publisher under the title *Richard Wagner: Leben
und Werk in Daten und Bildern* as "Insel Taschenbuch," 334 (ISBN
3458320342); the German version is considerably longer.

331. Strobel, Otto. *Richard Wagner: Leben und Schaffen: eine Zeittafel*.
Bayreuth: Verlag der Festspielleitung, 1952. 142pp. ML410.W1S885

A detailed timetable of Wagner's activities and affairs, illustrated with a single frontispiece portrait and accompanied by several indexes (pp. 133–42).

A much shorter but nevertheless useful reference work is:

332. Millington, Barry. "Calendar of Wagner's Life, Works and Related Events." In item 1, pp. 12–19.

Identifies events in Wagner's life, with comments about such other individuals as his two wives, Liszt, Berlioz, Bruckner, Ludwig II, and so on. The data Millington provides is reliable; unlike other timeline compilers, however, he ignores such contemporaneous non-musical events as the unification of Italy, the Philadelphia Exposition of 1876—for which Wagner composed the *Grosser Festmarsch* (*WWV* 110), and which Millington mentions elsewhere—and the deaths of Beethoven (1827) and Berlioz (1869).

Finally, a few respectable and even outstanding Wagner biographies intended for adult readers are unusually short; these include items 308, 313, and 315 above, as well as the following publication by an internationally respected Wagner researcher:

333. Gregor-Dellin, Martin. *Das kleine Wagnerbuch.* Salzburg: Residenz, 1975. 127pp. ISBN 3701700788 ML410.W1G7

Contains a few observations about musical issues, music-drama productions, and so on. Includes a list of works, among them Wagner's most important books and essays (pp. 122–24) and a one-page bibliography (p. 126); also includes some forty portraits, photographs, facsimiles of playbills, and other images. First published in 1969.

Related Studies

Many scholars have commented on the contents, character, and reliability of individual biographies, but the following article tackles Wagner biography as a whole:

334. Spencer, Stewart. "Wagner Literature: Biographies." In item 1, pp. 402–404.

Identifies and summarizes the characters and impacts of major Wagner biographies, general and specialized, beginning with works by Glasenapp and Chamberlain, "two members of the Bayreuth Praetorian Guard" (p. 402), and proceeding to the monographs and survey studies of Newman,

Gutman, Gregor-Dellin (item 6), Taylor (item 24), and Millington (item 9). Among the issues Spencer considers is the need for Wagner biographies at all; he also mentions "inadequately documented" (p. 403) phases of the composer's life, such as his visits to England (see item 273).

Misapprehensions, rumors, and untruths are scattered throughout the Wagner literature. The catalog described below identifies some of them:

335. Millington, Barry. "Myths and Legends." In item 1, pp. 132–38.

Corrects a dozen rumors about Wagner's life and works, including some the composer himself—deliberately or unwittingly—was responsible for. Among the falsehoods found in *My Life* is that of the impression Wilhelmine Schröder-Devrient is supposed to have made on the young Wagner during a performance of Beethoven's *Fidelio* in Leipzig; the opera in question was almost certainly Bellini's *I Capuleti ed I Montecchi*. Other stories that have crept into the literature concern the notion that the Valkyries depicted in the *Ring* are the daughters of Erda, that there really was a Starnberg Quartet (see item 807), that the "La Spezia" explanation of the *Rheingold* Prelude is true (but see items 702 and 705), and so on.

Finally, among other studies of Wagner biography as a whole are these two interrelated monographs:

336. Newman, Ernest. *Fact and Fiction About Wagner.* London: Cassell, 1931. xvii, 318pp. ML410.W1N32

A series of essays that address problematic aspects of the composer's ancestry, activities, and relationships. Among the topics Newman considers are the reception accorded *Tannhäuser* in Paris, Wagner's business dealings with several of his publishers, Geyer as Wagner's "father," the "Nietzsche problem," and Liszt's relationship with the Comtesse Marie d'Agoult—the last a bone of contention for Liszt scholars, who for decades have had to deal with Newman's outlandish criticisms of their hero in *The Man Liszt* (London, 1935). In *Fact and Fiction* Newman also criticizes Hurn and Root's *Truth About Wagner* (item 337). Concludes with an index.

337. Hurn, Philip Dutton, and Waverley Lewis Root. *The Truth About Wagner.* New York: Frederick A. Stekes, 1930. 313pp. ML410.W1H93

A lively, unreliable, often unfair study that attempted to debunk myths about Wagner and ended by perpetrating some of its own. The authors criticize Cosima for almost everything she ever did, including her attempts to control the existence and contents of the Burrell Collection (see item 102); they also proclaim Minna Planer the composer's only "true wife" (p. 297). In their attempt to correct errors in early editions of *My Life*, however, Hurn and Root themselves misread a passage and declared Geyer Wagner's biological father (see items 339–40). Not all of Hurn and Root's volume is worthless, however; it contains, for instance, eleven plates, one of which reproduces in facsimile the souvenir handkerchief given to guests when Wagner married Minna in 1836. Concludes with a bibliography (pp. 299–304) and an index.

SPECIALIZED BIOGRAPHICAL STUDIES

Among a host of specialized studies are those touching upon Wagner's ancestry and family, various periods of his life, places where he lived and worked, relationships with various individuals or groups of people, and such topics as his fondness for animals and his late-life interest in vegetarianism. The following studies are arranged according to categories, then—unless otherwise indicated— described in alphabetical order by author and/or title:

Ancestors, Parents, and Siblings

One of the best surveys of Wagner's lineage appeared in print shortly before the beginning of World War II:

338. Lange, Walter. *Richard Wagners Sippe*. Leipzig: Max Beck, 1938. 109pp. ML410.W1L18

Precisely identifies Wagner's ancestors. Illustrated with 72 images of people, places, buildings, and documents; among the latter are facsimiles of parish registers and other proofs of the composer's lineage between the seventeenth and nineteenth centuries. Includes a catalog of illustrations (pp. 108–109) as well as several indexes (pp. 103–108).

Additional genealogical studies appeared in Germany during the 1930s and 1940s, mostly in specialized periodicals. See, for example, W. K. von Arnswaldt's *Ahnentafel des Komponisten Richard Wagner* (Leipzig, 1930) as well as W. Reihlen's "Die Stammtafel Richard Wagners" and "Die Eltern Richard Wagners," and W. Rauschenberger's "Die Abstammung Richard Wagners"—the last three published (respectively) in issues of the *Familiengeschichtliche Blätter* for 1940, 1943, and 1944. Today the *Blätter* is an uncommon publication; the British Library, London, however, owns a complete run. Many bibliographies omit some or all of these articles. See also item 1166.

339. Millington, Barry. "Family." In item 1, pp. 95–97.

A summary based on the most reliable researches available as of the early 1990s. Among other subjects Millington refers briefly to the various legends associated with Johanna Wagner, the composer's mother—including one that asserted she was actually the illegitimate child of Constantin, Prince of Saxe-Weimar-Eisenach (see also item 301, Vol. 2, pp. 613–19); we know now, however, that Johanna "was not the prince's daughter, but his mistress" (p. 95). Also provides essential information about the complete names and gives the birthdates of Wagner's several siblings.

340. Millington, Barry. "Paternity." In item 1, pp. 94–95.

Reviews what we know about Carl Friedrich Wagner and Ludwig Heinrich Geyer, either of whom may have been the composer's biological father. Among other incidents, Millington summarizes and evaluates the significance of the "Tieplitz episode," an excursion Johanna Wagner undertook in difficult circumstances to visit with Geyer shortly after Richard was born (one that actually proves nothing in itself of the composer's origins); and Friedrich Nietzsche's suggestions that the composer was Geyer's son, and that Geyer himself was a Jew. See also item 301, Vol. 3, 558–62; and items 216, 341–42, and 380.

Who Wagner's biological father really was remains uncertain; the possibility that it might have been Geyer—and that Geyer may himself have been Jewish—haunted Wagnerians for decades. The following studies provide the best information available on these issues:

341. Bournot, Otto. *Ludwig Heinr. Chr. Geyer [sic] der Stiefvater Richard Wagners.* Leipzig: C. W. F. Siegel, 1913. 74pp. PN2658.G4B6

Describes the origins, family, activities, and character of the actor and playwright who became Wagner's stepfather and whose name Wagner bore for several years during his childhood. Includes four portraits of Wagner and Geyer illustrating purported physical similarities (Bournot accepted the theory that Geyer was Wagner's real father), as well as a two-page bibliography printed on unnumbered pages at the end of the volume.

342. "The Geyer Question." In item 301, Vol. 2, pp. 608–13.

Defends the theory that Geyer may have been Wagner's real father. Newman bases his assertions in part of Nietzsche's belief that Wagner was descended from the "Jew Geyer" and, consequently, that Wagner himself was—or believed himself to be—Jewish. (We know now, however, that

Geyer was himself Protestant both by birth and conviction.) Well-argued but no longer accepted by scholars as the last word on Wagner's paternity.

Aside from her involvement with Prince Constantin, little has been written about Johanna Wagner, the composer's mother. One exception to this rule is:

343. Gillespie, Iris. "Wagner's Mother." *Wagner* 13/2 (May 1992), pp. 51–60. ML410.W1A585

An interpretive essay, based largely on Wagner's comments about his mother and illustrated with a portrait of her. Much of Gillespie's study, however, focuses on the significance of mother figures in the composer's music dramas; she also discusses "the cultural conventions of motherhood at the time of [Wagner's] youth . . . [and] the debatable but once fashionable question of the importance of their mothers' character in the making of 'great men' " (p. 51).

Wagner boasted almost a dozen brothers and sisters, of whom several died in infancy or childhood. Of those who survived to adulthood, three—Albert, Clara, and Johanna—became singers; two others—Rosalie and Luise—became actresses. It was Johanna, however, better-known as Johanna Jachmann-Wagner, who made a real name for herself as a performing artist. The most thorough account of her career remains:

344. Jachmann, Hans. *Wagner and His First Elisabeth*. London: Novello, 1944. viii, 63pp. (no LC number available)

Devoted to the composer's sister who, herself, sang the parts of Elisabeth in 1845 and 1856 performances of *Tannhäuser*, Ortrud in the 1859 Berlin performance of *Lohengrin*, and both Schwertleite and the First Norn in the 1876 Bayreuth *Ring*. Illustrated with seven plates bound at the end of the volume, as well as with a portrait of Johanna reproduced as a frontispiece. Harvard University's Loeb Music Library owns a copy.

A longer, somewhat more careful study by Jachmann, prepared with Julius Kapp, was published originally as *Richard Wagner und seine erste "Elisabeth," Johanna Jachmann-Wagner* (Berlin, 1927); this contains sixteen pages of illustrations and nine documentary facsimiles, as well as previously unpublished letters by Wagner. See also Elizabeth Forbes's article on "Johanna Wagner" in *The New Grove Dictionary of Music and Musicians* (New York and London, 1980), Vol. 20, p. 1084. See, too, Friedrich Dieckmann's "Rosalie oder Das Liebesverbot: Wagners Schwester in Wagners Werken," published in *Der Merkur* 48/2 (1994), pp. 124–39; the latter deals with issues of incest in the composer's early works and his relationship with his sister Rosalie (1803–1837), herself a celebrated actress. Finally, also with regard to Rosalie, see Emil Müller's scarce pamphlet *Das Verhältnis Richard Wagners zu seiner Schwester Rosalie* (Bayreuth 1921), excerpted from the author's University of Rostock dissertation.

Childhood and Youth (1813–1840)

Wagner's early years are thought to have lasted until 1834, when he took up his first professional position at Magdeburg, or even until 1843, when he was appointed Kapellmeister to the Royal Saxon Court in Dresden. The best study of these years is also one of the classics of Wagner scholarship:

345. Burrell, Mary. *Richard Wagner: His Life and Works from 1813–1834, Compiled from Original Letters, Manuscripts & Other Documents.* London: privately printed, 1898. 129pp. ML410.W1B82

Unquestionably one of the most physically beautiful of Wagner studies. Published by her husband shortly after his wife's death (see p. 129), Burrell's is among the first documentary biographies of any composer. Included in its contents are facsimiles of the composer's birth certificate; his *Hochzeit* fragment; a poster advertising the 16 March 1832 production in Leipzig of Ernst Raupach's play *König Enzio*, complete with Wagner's incidental music; an article published on 29 October 1821 in the *Dresdner Abend-Zeitung* about Wagner's stepfather Geyer (himself a playwright of some consequence); and the texts of several of Geyer's plays, including *Der Parnass*. Also includes linking text, as well as transcriptions of its documentary contents and a variety of beautiful portraits and other illustrations, many in color.

Printed on specially laid paper and published as the work of "The Honorable Mrs. Burrell née Banks." Issued in 100 numbered copies, each bound in white leather embossed with gold lettering. The British Library, London, owns two of these, only one of which (shelf-mark Hirsch 5219) was examined by the present author.

Among other studies of the composer's earlier life are these, all of them oriented largely or even exclusively around his first compositions:

* Daube, Otto. *Richard Wagner: "Ich schriebe keine Symphonien mehr."* Described as item 802.

Devoted primarily to the young composer's first musical creations, although Daube also comments on what else Wagner was doing when he wrote them. See too Nattiez's *Wagner Androgyne* (item 991), containing valuable discussions of the composer's early years.

346. Schilling, A. *Aus Richard Wagners Jugendzeit*, 2nd. ed. Berlin: E. Globig, 1902. 127pp. (no LC number available)

Describes Wagner's life and activities from his birth in 1813 to 1840, and some of his experiences in Paris. An eccentric and unreliable work concerned in large part with superstitious "anticipations" in the composer's youth of events in his later life; Schilling even includes a chapter on Wagner and the "number 13"! (pp. 115–27). Includes a frontispiece depicting the young musician and his sister Cäcilie. Uncommon; Harvard University's Loeb Music Library owns a copy.

* Segnitz, Eugen. *Richard Wagner und Leipzig (1813–1833)*. Described as item 355.

Discusses the composer's birth, childhood, and earliest compositions, all in association with his childhood home. Includes a large number of musical examples.

The "May Revolution" (1849)

347. Ellis, William Ashton. *1849. A Vindication*. London: Kegan Paul, Trench, Trubner & Co., 1892. 72pp. (no LC number available)

A study of Wagner in Dresden and his role in the uprising there. Ellis argues that the composer acted not on behalf of "the advancement of his own artistic projects" (p. 71), but out of sincere political and social convictions. Includes lengthy quotes from *A Communication to My Friends* and other prose works, especially Wagner's speech "To Intendant von Lüttichau at the Assembly of the Vaterlandsverein, presented on 18 June 1848" (see pp. 30–35). The title of Ellis's pamphlet is a pun on the title of Wagner's *A Capitulation*, which deals with the fall of Paris during the Franco-Prussian War of 1870–1871.

Originally published in German as *1849. Der Aufstand in Dresden— Ein geschichtlicher Rückblick zur Rechtfertigung Richard Wagner's* (Leipzig, n.d.). Uncommon in both editions; the Library of Congress, however, owns a copy of the latter (ML410.W11E5). See, too, Ernest Newman's account in item 301, pp. 462–509.

348. Krohn, Rüdiger. "The Revolutionary of 1848–49," trans. Paul Knight. In item 2, 156–65.

A useful introduction to the composer's brief but crucial involvement in revolutionary politics. Krohn discusses the events of the "May Revolution," especially in terms of passages from *My Life*. For Krohn, "Wagner's convictions during his turbulent Dresden years continued to make their

mark on his creative work long after the events of 1848–49, albeit in frag-
mented and indirect form," if only because, for Wagner, "more than with
other artists, all thought and action [was] directed toward the furtherance
of his artistic creativity and realization of his artistic concepts" (p. 165).
See also item 349, as well as such other publications as Georg Hermann
Müller's pamphlet *Richard Wagner in der Mai-Revolution 1849* (Dresden,
1919), which includes the text of the *Steckbrief* (arrest warrant) issued by
Sachsen authorities as well as other source materials and several portraits.

Exile (1849–1862)

*For more than a decade Wagner lived in Switzerland and France because German
authorities had condemned him to death for his revolutionary activities. The only
book-length study devoted primarily to this period of his life is:*

349. Lippert, Woldemar. *Wagner in Exile, 1849–1862*, trans. Paul England.
London: George G. Harrap & Co., 1930. 217pp. ML410.W11L43

Describes the Dresden revolution that led to Wagner's exile for more than
a decade from German soil, as well as his activities during the 1850s and
early 1860s in Zurich, Paris, and other parts of Europe. Lippert, a director
of Saxony's "national" archives during the 1920s, drew upon documents at
his disposal to correct previous misstatements and misinterpretations.
Illustrated with a frontispiece reproduction of Caesar Willich's 1862 Wagner portrait; outfitted with notes (pp. 191–205) and a bibliography (pp.
207–208), as well as four documentary appendices and an index.

Originally published as *Richard Wagners Verbannung und Rückkehr,
1849–1862* (Dresden, 1927) and, in this edition, handsomely illustrated
with seventeen plates of portraits and pictures of the Dresden theater
where Wagner worked until he fled for his life in 1849, as well as with five
documentary facsimiles, several of them printed on special paper and
bound as fold-outs. Among other sources cited by Lippert in both German
and English editions of his work are the texts of several otherwise unpublished letters.

Death (February 1883)

350. Conrad, Herbert. "Absturz aus Klingsors Zaubergarten: Ein biographischer
Beitrag zu den letzten Lebensjahren Richard Wagners." *Fränkische
Heimatbote* = Supplement to the *Nordbayerischer Kurier* 11 (1978): No. 8.

Not seen, but cited in the bibliography of item 1 and dealt with in item 351.
See references to other studies in items 3, 26, and so on.

351. Westernhagen, Curt von. "Wagner's Last Day." *The Musical Times* 120 (1979), pp. 395–97. ML5.M85

Explains that Wagner probably died from a heart attack suffered after an altercation with Cosima concerning Carrie Pringle, an English singer engaged as solo Flower Maiden for the 1882 Bayreuth premiere of *Parsifal*, and Pringle's proposed visit to the Palazzo Vendramin. Westernhagen defends Conrad's contentions about Pringle (see item 350) by referring to previously obscure primary sources.

Wagner's Activities in Various Places

Wagner traveled less than some of his contemporaries; think of Liszt's tours of Iberia, Russia, and Turkey, or Berlioz's German concert tours. Nevertheless, Wagner lived in or visited England, France, Italy, and Switzerland, as well as many parts of "greater" Germany—including Riga (the capital of present-day Latvia)—and he contemplated visiting South America and the United States. That he visited or even lived in certain cities more than once means that his relationship with them cannot be treated in a straightforward chronological fashion; hence the division in the present research guide between "Wagner periods" (childhood, old age, etc.) and "Wagner places" (Berlin, Paris, Tribschen, etc.).

Unless otherwise noted, studies in each section or subsection below are described in reverse chronological order of publication:

Wagner and Germany

352. Nicolai, Wilhelm. *Richard Wagner und die Anfänge seiner Kunst in Thüringen*. Eisenach: Vereinigung Eisenacher Bibliophilen, 1928. 46pp. ML410.W12G464

A pamphlet, illustrated with mezzotints of people and places associated with southeastern Germany, that describes Wagner's visits to Liszt and Weimar, his interest in the Wartburg (home of the contest he depicts in *Tannhäuser*), his relationship with Rose von Milde, and associated topics. In other words, this is a study that ranges over much of Wagner's life. Contains no musical examples, bibliography, or index.

Studies devoted to Wagner and Bavaria include articles by Martin Geck. See also items 356–57 below concerning Wagner's relationship with Munich, and with musical life in that city during the 1860s.

Berlin

353. Kapp, Julius. *Richard Wagner und die Berliner Oper: Die Berliner Staatsoper dem Gedächtnis Richard Wagners*. Berlin-Schoeneberg: M. Hesse, 1933. 62pp. ML410.W12G42

Describes Wagner's relationship with the Berliner Staatsoper, especially in terms of the latter's earliest productions of *Holländer*, *Rienzi*, *Tannhäuser*, and *Meistersinger*. Includes portraits of Count Redern, Pauline Marx, Johanna Wagner (the composer's sister; see also item 344), and other administrators and performers associated with Berlin productions; also includes facsimiles of posters and a few musical manuscript pages. In addition to all this, Kapp provides statistics concerning Wagner performances at the Staatsoper from 1836 to 13 February 1933 (pp. 61–62), as well as the texts of a number of letters.

Leipzig

354. Lange, Walter. *Richard Wagner und seine Vaterstadt Leipzig*. Leipzig: Friedrich Kistner & F. W. Siegel, 1933. (ix), 300pp. ML410.W1L16

Examines Wagner's relationship with the "home town" of Bach, Mendelssohn, and one of Europe's most influential music schools. In addition to the composer's birth and childhood in Leipzig, Lange identifies and discusses works by Wagner composed and/or performed in Leipzig (pp. 283–90); with regard to the performances, especially those that took place at the Gewandhaus (pp. 289–90). Lange also provides information about Leipzig artists, and the city's Wagner funeral celebrations in 1883. Includes the texts of four letters Wagner addressed to the city's Historical Museum between 1855 and 1877 (pp. 269–73), as well as the text of a letter Goethe sent Adolf Wagner, the composer's uncle, in 1827 (pp. 273–74). Illustrated with a scattering of portraits, a time-line (pp. 187–88), and a handsome facsimile of an 1819 map of Wagner's "home town"—the last folded and tipped into the end of the volume. See also items 1108–09 and other studies dealing with Leipzig, Mendelssohn, the Jews, and so on.

The author was unable to compare carefully the text of this Hitler-era edition with a copy of the original edition published in 1921.

355. Segnitz, Eugen. *Richard Wagner und Leipzig, 1813–1833*. Musikalische Studien, 5. Leipzig: Breitkopf & Härtel, 1901; reprinted Nedeln/Lichtenstein: Kraus-Thomson, 1976. 80pp. ML410.W1S3 1976 (no ISBN available)

As much a musical as a biographical study; Segnitz discusses his subject's birth, childhood, and early educational experiences, as well as some of his first instrumental and vocal works. Includes about 24 musical examples, as well as a collection of endnotes (pp. 77–80) in place of a bibliography. Unindexed.

Meiningen: see item 386.

Munich
*   Röckl, Sebastian. *Richard Wagner in München: ein Bericht in Briefen.*
     Described as item 234.

356. Strobel, Otto. "Richard Wagner und die Königlich Bayerische Kabinetts-
     kasse." In item 104, pp. 101–66.

     A detailed examination of Wagner's relationships with Ludwig II's minis-
     ters and their political undertakings. Includes the texts of 29 documents,
     among them letters, bills, and financial statements of various kinds. Less a
     description of personal relationships than a documentary history of official
     dealings in terms of the "public record."

357. Stemplinger, Eduard. *Richard Wagner in München (1864–1870): Legende
     und Wirklichkeit.* Munich: Knorr & Hirth, 1933. 158pp. ML410.W11S8

     In addition to describing the composer's personal and professional activi-
     ties in the Bavarian capital, Stemplinger devotes whole chapters to Wag-
     ner's relationships with Bülow, Peter Cornelius, Ludwig Nohl, and other
     of his contemporaries, and to Cosima's relationship with the "mad king."
     Includes a timetable of events from 1864 to 1870 (pp. 7–11); also includes
     a short bibliography (pp. 12–14).

Nuremberg
358. Spencer, Stewart. "Wagner's Nuremberg." *Wagner* 14/1 (January 1993),
     pp. 2–29. ML410.W1A585

     Describes the composer's various visits to the "Meistersinger city." Illus-
     trated with 24 antique views of Nuremberg and maps of the city in pre-
     vious centuries, as well as Wagner's, stage sets for *Meistersinger*
     productions, and so on. A somewhat different article by Spencer, contain-
     ing only nine city views and *Meistersinger* scenes, appeared under the
     same title in the *Cambridge Opera Journal* 4 (1992), pp. 21–41. See also
     Peter Hohendahl's "Reworking History: Wagner's German Myth of
     Nuremberg" in item 34, pp. 39–60.

359. Stock, Richard Wilhelm. *Richard Wagner und die Stadt der Meistersinger.*
     Nuremberg and Berlin: Karl Ulrich & Co., 1938. 229pp. ML410.W16S86
     1938

     Issued to commemorate the 125th anniversary of Wagner's birth and the
     centenary of Cosima's. In many ways a piece of Nazi propaganda, full
     of photographs of Wagner's descendents posing with Hitler and other
     German political leaders, but nevertheless valuable for the background

information it provides on Nuremberg's musical legacy, and for the facsimile reproductions of important sixteenth-century documents and maps it contains.

Riga
360. Arro, von Elmar [*sic*]. "Richard Wagners Rigaer Wanderjahre: Über einige baltische Züge im Schaffen Wagners." *Musik des Ostens* 3 (1965), pp. 123–68. ML240.M88

Describes Wagner's years in Riga and his activities there as composer and opera conductor, as well as a pointed dissection of autobiographical observations about these issues in *My Life*. Handsomely illustrated with four plates that include photographs of the "Rienzi-Haus," and a miscellany of documentary facsimiles as well as a complete, double-sided, four-page foldout facsimile of the autograph score of the *Nicolai-Hymne* (*WWV* 44), an anniversary offering Wagner composed in 1837 for the birthday of the Russian tsar.

Other studies of Wagner's Riga years exist, some of them written in Latvian. Among these is Vita Lindenburgera's "Riharda Vagnera Rigas gadi," published in *Gadsimtu skanuloka* ["Music Through the Centuries"], ed. Lindenburgera et al. (Riga, 1997), pp. 100–117.

Würzburg
361. Ritter, Hermann. "Das Richard Wagner-Haus in Würzburg." *Die Musik* 1–IV (1901–1902), pp. 1830–32. ML5.M9

Identifies the existence and describes the significance of the house in which Wagner lived from January or early February 1833 to January 1834. During his sojourn in Würzburg, where his brother Albert was also living at the time, the young composer heard the first performance of excerpts from his unfinished opera *Die Hochzeit*, worked on *Die Feen*, and became briefly involved with a soprano named Therese Ringelmann. Unfortunately, Ritter provides neither visual images nor detailed information about the building itself.

Wagner and Other Countries

America
362. Saffle, Michael. "Wagner and America, 1840–1861." *Programmhefte der Bayreuther Festspiele* III (1989), pp.17–37. ML410.W2B26

Explores Wagner's interest in visiting America, primarily for purposes of making money. Illustrated rather whimsically with illustrations of various kinds chosen for the *Programmhefte* by Matthias Theodor Vogt to illustrate the theme *reines Gold/falsches Gold* ("true gold and false gold," alluding to issues associated with the Rhine Gold of the *Ring*). Also printed in German and French in the same volume.

Wagner's interest in America is more extensively documented than many scholars realize. See, for example, Viola E. Knoche's extensive article "The Early Influence of Richard Wagner in America," published in the *Deutsch-Amerikanische Geschichtsblätter* (1892), pp. 623–73. See also items 1052–54.

Austria
The most fulsome account of Wagner's relationship with the "other Germany" is:

363. Millenkovich-Morold [or Morold], Max (von). *Richard Wagner in Wien.* Leipzig: P. Reclam jun., 1938. 76pp. ML410.W11M5

> Describes the composer's several visits to the capital of the Austrian Empire, and provides information about performances (or near-performances) there of several music dramas, including plans concerning and rehearsals for a Viennese production of *Tristan* abandoned in the early 1860s. Another, two-volume edition of the same work, or at least covering the same material—*Wagners Kampf und Sieg, dargestellt in seinen Beziehungen zu Wien* (Vienna, 1930)—is purported to exist, but the author has never seen a copy.

Additional studies include:

364. Bauer, Oswald Georg. "Richard Wagner und Wien." *Österreichische Musikzeitschrift* 41 (12986), pp. 617–28. ML5.O1983

> Briefly summarizes all of Wagner's visits to the Austrian capital, including those of 1832 and 1848, as well as those of the 1860s and 1870s. Includes two illustrations: a photograph of Oesterlein's "Wagner Museum" in Vienna (see item 67), and a silhouette of the composer conducting in what may have been the Prater. No musical examples.

365. Seydlitz, R. von. "Richard Wagner und das K. K. Hof-Operntheater in Wien. Mit Benutzung bisher unveröffentlichter Briefe Wagners aus den Jahren 1858–1870." *Die Musik* 11 (1912), pp. 1–18 and 67–90. ML5.M9

> Primarily a collection of documents reprinted in whole or part, including a lengthy letter from Wagner to B. Schott's firm, dated 21 August 1866, concerning the piano score of *Tristan.* Illustrated with a single musical exam-

ple in a letter of Wagner's dealing with the use of the alpenhorn in the same music drama.

England

* Spencer, Stewart. "Wagner Autographs in London." Described as item 273.

Includes documents associated with Wagner's visit to London in the mid-1850s.

France

366. Prod'homme, J. G. "Les Maisons de Wagner à Paris." In item 1064, pp. 166–74.

Mostly given over to pinpointing and describing the places Wagner lived during his Paris sojourn at the beginning of the 1840s. Unfortunately unillustrated, but the details about neighborhoods and individual lodgings Prod'homme provides—no other biographer gives so many of them—make this a useful article. See also item 1065.

Italy

367. Dieckmann, Friedrich. *Richard Wagner in Venedig. Eine Collage.* Leipzig: Reclam, 1983. 236pp. ISBN 3472614994 ML410.W12I825

Largely a collection of documents, observations, and miscellaneous information associated with Wagner's visits to Venice between 1858 and his death there in 1883, although Dieckmann includes quotations from a variety of reminiscences as well as comments on the composition of *Parsifal* and the composer's anti-semitism. Among its 57 illustrations are several portraits, photographs of places Wagner visited, facsimiles of Venetian playbills, manuscripts, and other primary sources, and so on. Contains a one-page bibliography (p. 235). Other studies of approximately the same material include Erwin Koppen's essay "Wagner und Venedig," published in item 39, pp. 101–20.

Switzerland

Among a variety of publications devoted to Wagner's Swiss years and visits are the following survey studies:

368. Fehr, Max. *Richard Wagners Schweitzer Zeit.* 2 vols. Arrau and Leipzig: H. R. Sauerländer, 1934, 1954. ML410.W11F195

A detailed account of Wagner's years in Switzerland, supplemented by the texts of almost 200 documents—among them, a number of the composer's letters. Vol. 1 covers 1849 to 1855, and includes documents 1–85 (pp.

353–414); Vol. 2 covers 1855 to 1872 and 1883, and includes documents 86–190 (pp. 341–502). Among the scattered illustrations is a photograph, printed as a frontispiece to Vol. 2, of Wagner standing in front of Triebschen (also spelled "Tribschen") and holding his infant daughter Eva. A review of Fehr's first volume, written by Alfred Einstein ("Wagner in der Schweiz"), appeared in Einstein's *Nationale und universale Musik: Neue Essays* (Zurich and Stuttgart, 1958), pp. 96–98.

369. Gysi, Fritz. *Richard Wagner und die Schweiz*. Frauenfeld and Leipzig: Huber & Co., 1929. 129pp. ML410.W12S82

A concise but reasonably detailed account of Wagner's sojourns in and visits to Switzerland during the 1850s, 1860s, and 1870s. Popular rather than scholarly in character, Gysi's work incorporates no apparatus or musical examples.

Several studies concentrate on Wagner's sojourns in Lucerne and Tribschen (or Triebschen):

370. Fehr, Max. "Richard Wagners Einzug und erster Sommer in Tribschen (mit einem Nachtrag 'Tribschen 1867')." In item 104; pp. 75–100.

Supplements Fehr's other publications (especially item 368) concerning this important interlude in Wagner's life. Contains the texts of eight letters and newspaper articles, plus two sets of plans for the house Wagner occupied with Cosima, photographs of the house and environs, and facsimiles of the beginning and end of the orchestral sketch for *Meistersinger*, act II, made by the composer during the summer of 1866.

371. Fries, Othmar. *Richard Wagner und Luzern: Vortrag anlässlich der Generalversammlung des Schweizerischen Bühnenverbandes vom 16. April 1983 in Luzern*. Schriftenreihe des Schweizerischen Bühnenverbandes [unnumbered]. Lucerne: Raeber, 1983. ML410.W12S954 1983 (no ISBN available)

The printed text of a lecture honoring Wagner's association with Fries's own home, delivered during the 1983 "Wagner year." Includes a timeline (pp. 5–9) and notes (pp. 28–29) as well as a good deal of information about the composer's "Tribschen-Idyll" and related topics. No illustrations.

372. Zimmermann, L. *Richard Wagner in Luzern*, ed. Gustave Kanth. Berlin and Leipzig: Schuster & Loeffler, 1916. 148pp. ML410.W11Z4

A rather odd collection of historical observations, reminiscences, and memorabilia associated with Wagner's sojourn in this Swiss city during

1859. Includes eight plates printed on blue paper, some of them documentary facsimiles; also includes a few other illustrations and one or two musical examples. Omitted from many Wagner bibliographies, including those found in item 301. No bibliography or index. Another edition appeared in 1919, this one apparently without Kanth's editorial assistance.

The best studies of Wagner's Zurich sojourns include:

373. *Richard Wagner in Zürich. Materialien zu Aufenthalt und Wirken, 1.–2. Folge*, ed. Werner G. Zimmermann. 2 vols. Neujahrsblätter der Allgemeinen Musikgesellschaft Zürich. Zurich: Hug & Co., 1986–1988. ML410.W12S998 (no ISBNs available)

A detailed study of topics relating to Wagner and Zurich. Vol. 1 includes reminiscences by Bertha Roner-Lipka, "Richard Wagner in der Zürcher Presse, 1849–1853," and a poem about and dedicated to Wagner written by Johanna Spyri; Vol. 2, subtitled "Richard Wagner in der Zürcher Presse, 1854–1858," deals with journalistic coverage of Wagner's Zurich years. Both volumes contain facsimiles of concert programs, caricatures, and—as one would expect—the texts of dozens of advertisements, announcements, reviews, and articles taken from the *Tageblatt der Stadt Zürich*, the *Neue Zürcher Zeitung*, and other newspapers. Vol. 2 also contains several facsimiles, as well as an appendix reproducing the text of a letter Wagner addressed to Heinrich Szadrowsky dealing with a performance of *Tannhäuser* in St. Gallen in 1859.

374. *Richard Wagner in Zürich. Eine Chronik.* Zurich 1983; no publisher indicated. Unpaginated. ML410.W12S997 1983 (no ISBN available)

A handsome and rather lengthy pamphlet devoted to a variety of topics, some of which are identified on the full-title page (i.e., "Die Villa Wesendonck zur Zeit ihrer Erbauer," "Das 'Asyl' Richard Wagners," and "Mathilde Wesendonck 'Zum 18. Februar 1883' "). Illustrated with a variety of portraits and documentary facsimiles and outfitted with a timeline covering the years 1849 to 1858. Printed throughout in red ink.

375. Bélart, Hans. *Richard Wagner in Zürich (1849–1858)*. Musikalische Studien, 3. Leipzig: H. Seamans Nachfolger, 1901; reprinted Nendeln (Liechtenstein): Kraus, 1976. 2 vols. in one. 78pp. ML410.W12S92 1976 (no ISBN available)

A three-part survey of Wagner's relationship with the Swiss city. Includes chapters on Wagner's relationships with the theater administration in Zurich, as well as with Emilie Heim and Mathilde Wesendonk, and on

Wagner's Zurich concerts. Concludes with a brief index of Zurich residents (p. 71) and a combined essay and chronological table devoted to the composer's activities between 1849 and 1858 (pp. 72–78).

Less scholarly accounts of Wagner's Zurich sojourns also exist:

376. Erismann, Hans. *Richard Wagner in Zürich.* Zurich: Verlag "Neue Zürcher Zeitung," 1987. 253pp. ISBN 3858231657 ML410.W11E7 1987

A popular history of Wagner's Zurich years, published by one of the world's foremost newspapers: the *Neue Zürcher Zeitung*—in which, incidentally, important documents concerning those same years appeared in print in the 1850s. Erismann's volume is illustrated handsomely with portraits, photographs of various "Wagner places," documentary facsimiles, and the like. Includes a brief bibliography (pp. 246–47).

Wagner's Relationships with Groups and Couples

Aside from political institutions and the Patrons' Associations that helped sponsor the construction of the Festspielhaus in Bayreuth, Wagner had surprisingly little to do with "groups" during his life; he was no "joiner," held no academic appointments, and—in spite of the fact that he worked with any number of theatrical organizations and companies—was never a "company man." Consequently, the only non-traditional biographical studies of Wagner and groups of people, like-minded or not, have tended to concentrate either on the composer's "friends" or "enemies." One example is described below:

377. Ehrenfels, Christian von. *Richard Wagner und seine Apostaten. Ein Beitrag zur Jahrhundertfeier.* Vienna and Leipzig: Hugo Zeller, 1913. 59pp. (no LC number available)

A rant against those who opposed or deserted Wagner and his cause, published in conjunction with the centenary of the composer's birth. Among the individuals criticized by Ehrenfels, himself a philosopher and sometime advocate of interpreting Wagner's music in terms of its sexual content, are Nietzsche and Brahms. Illustrated with four brief musical examples. Worth consulting for students of Wagner's German reception.

Publishers and Critics
With his publishers Wagner acted in different ways to suit different circumstances—and, of course, to suit himself; with critics he mostly responded energetically. More than a few studies deal with Wagner and a particular publishing house (e.g., Breitkopf & Härtel) or a particular critic (e.g., Eduard Hanslick); several exceptions are described below:

*   Jost, Christa and Peter. *Richard Wagner und sein Verleger Ernst Wilhelm Fritzsch.* Described as item 249.

Evaluates Wagner's relationship with the publisher who helped him organize and print the *Gesammelte Schriften*, and reprints their correspondence.

*   *Richard Wagner's Briefwechsel mit seinen Verlegern*, ed. Wilhelm Altmann. Described as item 262.

Contains Wagner's correspondence with two firms, Breitkopf & Härtel and B. Schott's Sons.

378. Taylor, Ronald. "Dealings with Critics." In item 1, pp. 126–28.

Briefly considers Wagner's responses to a few of his principal critics, especially Eduard Hanslick. Taylor identifies some of Wagner's characteristic responses, rational and otherwise, of handling criticism (among the latter, ascribing negative responses to the influence of Meyerbeer, or another of Wagner's particular enemies). Taylor also points out that the Wagner-Hanslick dispute "nevertheless rested on a solid foundation": that of the "moral responsibility of art, the eternal antithesis of Classic and Romantic . . . [and] that demand for total emotional submission which has made Wagnerians of some and anti-Wagnerians of others" (p. 127). Includes a few quotations from relevant documents.

    More specialized studies of Wagner's relationships to criticism include Dahlhaus's article "Wagners Berlioz-Kritik und die Ästhetik des Hasslichen," published in *Festschrift für Arno Volk*, ed. Hüschen (Cologne, 1974), pp. 107–23; Dahlhaus, however, examines Wagner's contentions that Berlioz's music was "obscurantist" in its excessively decorative quality, and thus represented only a transitional stage in the evolution of music toward its redemption in Wagnerian music drama.

379. Taylor, Ronald. "Dealings with Publishers." In item 1, pp. 124–26.

A brief summary of Wagner's relationships with B. Schott's Sons, Breitkopf & Härtel, and C. F. Peters, and synopses of some of the good and bad deals the composer made with those firms. Among other topics Taylor asserts that lack of copyright protection cost Wagner a great deal during his purportedly "greedy" business career. See also items 1097 and 1107 for information about Wagner and Maurice Schlesinger.

Married Couples
A number of couples figured prominently in Wagner's life and activities; studies of two such couples include:

380. Bélart, Hans. *Richard Wagners Beziehungen zu François und Eliza Wille in Mariafeld bei Zürich (1852–1872) und sein Asyl auf Mariafeld (1864)* . . . Dresden: Carl Reissner, 1914. 88pp. ML410.W11B3

A valuable source of information about the composer's Swiss years, especially his relationship with novelist Eliza Wille, one of his confidantes during his years in exile. Includes passages dealing with Wagner's interest in Schopenhauer's philosophy; the "asylum" Wagner sought at Mariafelt during March and April 1864, one of the lowest moments of his life; and his relationship with Henriette von Bißing, Wille's wealthy sister, whom Wagner briefly considered marrying. Also includes as an appendix an essay entitled "Ludwig Geyer, der Schauspieler und Maler, als lieblicher Vater Richard Wagners" (pp. 67–88).

381. Bergfeld, Joachim. *Otto und Mathilde Wesendoncks Bedeutung für das Leben und Schaffen Richard Wagners*. Bayreuth: Emil Mühl, 1968. 23pp. ML410.W19B53

A pamphlet by a leading Wagner scholar describing one of the most important paired relationships in his life and one closely associated with his Swiss sojourns of the 1850s (see item 368 and other studies described above) and, of course, with the composition of *Tristan*. Bergfeld includes portraits of each of the Wesendonks as well as a brief bibliography (pp. 21–22) and an appendix dealing with the various spellings of the couple's name (p. 23).

Wagner's Relationships with Individual Men

Wagner had few friends but many acquaintances of both sexes; the men he knew especially well and worked closely with included Berlioz, Liszt, King Ludwig II, architect Gottfried Semper, and of course Nietzsche. Unless otherwise noted, the studies described below are dealt with in alphabetical order, first by subject, then by author:

Hector Berlioz
Perhaps the best synopsis of the Berlioz-Wagner relationship remains:

382. Tiersot, Julien. "Hector Berlioz and Richard Wagner," trans. Theodore Baker. *The Musical Quarterly* 3 (1917), pp. 453–92. ML1.M725

A compact review of an often stormy relationship characterized by increasing suspicion on the part of both composers. Tiersot makes special reference to nationalist issues—and no wonder, considering the publication date of this essay; among his bold statements is his assertion that the

two men "could not live in amity for the reason that they were born enemies" (p. 489). Includes short musical examples from *Roméo* and *Tristan,*
but more biographical than musical in its overall emphasis.

Other Wagner-Berlioz studies are described below in alphabetical order by
author:

383. Bouyer, Raymond. "Petites Notes sans portée: Berlioz jugé par Wagner."
Le Ménestrel 69 (20 September 1903), pp. 300–301. (no LC number available)

A brief summary of early contacts and growing enmity between the two
composers, culminating in 1841 in Wagner's first attacks on Berlioz in the
pages of the *Revue et Gazette Musicale de Paris.* Published, as were other
studies of the Berlioz-Wagner relationship, in conjunction with the centenary of the older composer's birth in 1903. Not seen; see item 384.

384. Macdonald, Hugh. "Berlioz and the 1861 "Tannhäuser.' " *Berlioz Society*
Bulletin No. 34 (April 1961), pp. 2–6. (no LC number available)

Describes the French composer's opposition to the Paris Opéra production
of Wagner's work and explains his indirect role in its failure. This article,
item 383, and several others are identified and summarized in Jeffrey Langford's and Jane Denker Graner's *Hector Berlioz: A Guide to Research* (New
York, 1989), pp. 126–29. NB: Students of Wagner's relationships with other
composers are advised to consult this and other volumes in the Routledge
Musical Bibliography series.

385. Newman, Ernest. "The Relations of Wagner and Berlioz." In: *Berlioz,*
Romantic and Classic, ed. Peter Heyworth. London: Victor Gollancz,
1972; pp. 97–101. ISBN 0575013656 ML410.B5N49

Explains that Wagner knew little about Berlioz's music even though he
often criticized it; Newman also reminds us that many Wagnerians have
glossed over this important fact. A supplement of sorts—although published originally at the very beginning of the twentieth century—to the
comments Newman makes about Berlioz and Wagner in item 301.

Johannes Brahms

386. Einstein, Alfred. "Wagner, Brahms und wir. Eine Neujahrs-Betrachtung."
In: Einstein, *Nationale und universale Musik: Neue Essays.* Zurich and
Stuttgart: Pan, 1958; pp. 110–15. ML60.E385

Written to celebrate the Wagner and Brahms anniversaries of 1933, Einstein's essay discusses the lack of Wagner-Brahms researches and consid-

ers the reputations of both composers: Wagner as a cult figure, Brahms as a "mere musician" (p. 114). Like similar studies, this one slights personal contacts in favor of professional and artistic issues.

387. Muller, Herta. "Richard Wagner und Johannes Brahms in Meiningen." *Musik und Gesellschaft* 33 (1983), pp. 282–85. ML5.M9033

Briefly reviews Wagner's and Cosima's relationships with Georg II of Saxe-Meiningen, who befriended the composer, corresponded with his wife, and in 1875 loaned a number of instruments to members of the first Bayreuth Festival orchestra; some twenty-one musicians who performed in that ensemble also belonged to Meiningen's. Includes a photograph of the Meiningen Hoftheater, which burned to the ground in 1908.

Franz Liszt

The best summary of Wagner's relationship with his colleague, friend, father-in-law, and unfailing supporter is:

388. Gleaves, Ian Beresford. "Liszt and Wagner." *Wagner* 6/3 (July 1985), pp. 77–99. ML410.W1A585

An intelligent account not only of a relationship that flourished throughout most of both composers' lives, but of their mutual musical influences on each other. On the other hand, Gleaves—like most Wagnerians—cannot resist putting Liszt down. In his concluding remarks, he observes that it may have been the Hungarian composer's "very versatility, both in his own artistic activity and in its influence . . . that is ultimately responsible for restricting and limiting" his achievements (p. 98). Which achievements those may be Gleaves does not say. Illustrated with a variety of musical examples.

Additional Wagner-Liszt studies include the following, evaluated in alphabetical order by author:

389. Eősze, László. "Liszt und Wagner: neue Aspekte eines Künstlerbundes." *Studia Musicologia* 28 (1986), pp. 195–200.

Explains that *Am Grabe Richard Wagners*, one of several musical tributes dedicated by Liszt to Wagner after the latter's death in Venice, incorporates material from Liszt's *Orpheus* because Wagner especially admired that composition. Eősze also very briefly summarizes important aspects of the Wagner-Liszt personal relationship. Illustrated with two musical examples from Liszt's late piano works. Also published in Hungarian in *Magyar zene* 28 (1987), pp. 131–40.

390. Kapp, Julius. *Richard Wagner und Franz Liszt. Eine Freundschaft.* Berlin and Leipzig: Schuster & Loeffler, 1906. 204pp. ML410.W19K295

For the most part a history of the complex and often turbulent relationship shared by Liszt and Wagner between the early 1840s and Wagner's death in 1883. Kapp also includes quotations from Liszt's letters and prose writings dealing with Wagner and his music (pp. 147–78) and vice versa (pp. 179–99). Useful observations about the Wagner-Liszt relationship may be found scattered in Alan Walker's *Franz Liszt: The Weimar Years, 1848–1861* (New York and London, 1989), especially pp. 112–19 and 236–42; these last pages deal with Wagner's flight to Weimar, the celebrated premiere performance there of his *Lohengrin*, and Liszt's comments on and thoughts about the man who later became his son-in-law. Additional observations appear in Walker's *Franz Liszt: The Final Years, 1861–1886* (New York, 1995). See also item 934.

Ludwig II of Bavaria

Perhaps the finest recent study of the circumstances associated with Wagner and Bavaria's "mad king" is:

391. Naegeli, Verena. *Parsifals Mission. Der Einfluß Richard Wagners auf Ludwig II. und seine Politik.* Cologne: Dittrich, 1995. 414pp. ISBN 3920862090 ML410.W11N34 1995

A study not so much of the Wagner-Ludwig personal relationship as of the composer's influence on the Bavarian king's political thought and career. Illustrated with portraits of Wagner, Ludwig himself, architect Gottfried Semper, statesman and Cabinet Secretary Franz von Pfistermeister, onetime Minister of the Interior Max von Neumayr, and other figures associated with Bavarian politics of the 1860s and 1870s, as well as with several documentary facsimiles. Concludes with a specialized bibliography (pp. 401–408) and an index of names.

Other valuable studies of this tumultuous personal and professional friendship include:

392. Herzfeld, Friedrich. *Königsfreundschaft: Ludwig II. und Richard Wagner.* Leipzig: Wilhelm Goldman, 1939. 354pp. DD801.B387H4

A "relationship biography" that also concerns itself with Bavarian political and military history. Includes a scattering of portraits and depictions of important places and scenes from Wagner's music-dramas as well as a brief bibliography (pp. 351–52), a list of the illustrations themselves (p. 353), and a timeline of events between 1813 (Wagner's birth) and 1886

(Ludwig's death). NB: A book with the same title, published in Bayreuth between 1988 and 1993, was unavailable for examination; it may be a reprint of Herzfeld's work.

393. Röckl, Sebastian. *Ludwig II. und Richard Wagner*, 2nd ed. 2 vols. Munich: C. H. Beck, 1913–1920. ML410.W11R62

Vol. 1 covers the years 1864 to 1865, Vol. 2 Wagner's life following his expulsion from Munich. Concentrates on the composer's tumultuous relationship with Bavaria's "mad king," himself a remarkable historical figure and the subject of several dozen biographies and books of reminiscences. Illustrated with portraits of Wagner and Ludwig, as well as documentary facsimiles of letters, concert programs, and other documents associated with Wagner's sojourn in Bavaria's capital city.

Two much briefer summaries of the Wagner-Ludwig relationship exist:

394. Eger, Manfred. "The Patronage of King Ludwig II," trans. Stewart Spencer. In item 2, pp. 317–26.

Summarizes the tumultuous relationship between Wagner and the Bavarian king as it evolved primarily from 1864 (when the two men met one another for the first time), to the period between 1868 and 1870 (when *Meistersinger*, *Rheingold*, and *Walküre* were given their premiere performances in Munich). Eger, who takes pains to point out Ludwig's and Wagner's individual strengths and weaknesses, also explains the precise extent and character of the financial support the king provided Wagner on behalf of his personal life, professional career, and Bayreuth building projects.

395. Millington, Barry. "Relationship with King Ludwig II." In item 1, pp. 121–24.

Covers the years 1864–1876, emphasizing Ludwig's shyness and occasional changes of heart, Wagner's attempts to keep his affair with Cosima private, and Ludwig's support for the 1876 Bayreuth Festival. Also describes some of the incidents associated with the monarch's death in June 1886, more than three years after Wagner's own.

Giacomo Meyerbeer

396. Einstein, Alfred. "Meyerbeer und Wagner." In: Einstein, *Nationale und universale Musik: Neue Essays*. Zurich and Stuttgart: Pan, 1958; pp. 91–95. ML60.E385

Takes Wagner's side as an artist against Meyerbeer, but protests against the German composer's ill-treatment of his Jewish contemporary and especially his anti-semitic remarks. As Einstein points out, without Meyer-beer's help *Rienzi* might never have been produced in Dresden.

397. Kröplin, Eckart. "Aspekte der ästhetisch-künstlerischen Auseinander-setzung Wagners mit Meyerbeer und der Grossen Oper." *Tribschener Blätter* No. 30 (1971), pp. 1–6 (no LC number available)

Asserts that Wagner's hatred of Meyerbeer stemmed primarily from aes-thetic and artistic differences rather than personal considerations, a posi-tion often discounted in recent years by students of Wagner's anti-semitism. Drawing upon a variety of sources, Kröplin correctly points out that the Meyerbeer-Wagner relationship profoundly influenced the his-tory of nineteenth-century opera.

Friedrich Nietzsche
Nothing about Wagner seems more difficult fully to grasp than his relationship with and influence on one of the nineteenth century's most brilliant and contro-versial philosophers. The best source of information about this complex subject is the two-volume documentary anthology:

398. *Nietzsche und Wagner: Stationen einer epochalen Begegnung*, ed. Dieter Borchmeyer and Jörg Salaquarda. 2 vols. Frankfurt a.M.: Insel, 1994. ISBN 3458166092 (set) B3316.N57 1994

A massive collection of letters and other primary sources that comprises virtually the whole of the Wagner-Nietzsche documentary legacy; in other words, a "documentary biography" that employs very little linking text. Borchmeyer and Salaquarda reproduce Nietzsche's correspondence with Wagner and his wife Cosima, all of the philosopher's books and articles about the composer and his works, and all of the references in Cosima's diaries to Nietzsche. Also includes bibliographic references (pp. 1263–70) and a lengthy "afterword" (pp. 1271–1386). Concludes with an index. Boxed as a set.

Other celebrated Nietzsche-Wagner studies include the items described below in reverse chronological order of publication:

399. Borchmeyer, Dieter. "Wagner and Nietzsche," trans. Michael Tanner. In item 2, pp. 327–42.

Comparing Nietzsche and Wagner (respectively) to Schiller and Goethe, Borchmeyer points out that the composer found in the philosopher ["the most astute analyst of the kind of artistic personality he embodied"], and that Nietzsche's "critical analysis of Wagner has still not been surpassed"

(p. 328). He also reminds us that many of Nietzsche's most penetrating observations—as well as much of the information we need to understand more fully the evolution of the philosopher's admiration for, and disgust with, his musical mentor—can be found only in Nietzsche's posthumously published literary fragments. Finally, Borchmeyer observes that Nietzsche's Wagner observations have been "misunderstood" by the Germans, and that the idea "it is not life in the 'ascendent' but life in 'decline' that finds its legitimate expression in Wagner's art" (p. 341) was borne out when "decadence" and *Wagnérisme* seized the French in the closing decades of the nineteenth century.

400. Abraham, Gerald. "Nietzsche's Attitude to Wagner: A Fresh View." *Music & Letters* 13 (1932), pp. 64–74. ML5.M64

Discusses Nietzsche's "Wagnerism" as an episode rather than something more representative in his life and philosophical work. According to Abraham, "Nietzsche was not so much a Wagner worshipper as a 'Tristan' worshipper" (p. 64); he also points out that, in the rewritten version of *The Birth of Tragedy*, Nietzsche extols act III of *Tristan* "as a vast symphonic period" (p. 71) rather than as a work of drama, and that the philosopher "was powerfully excited by Wagner's music and . . . profoundly disappointed and disgusted when he found that the excitement was not musical but emotional" (p. 74). Reprinted in Abraham's *Slavonic and Romantic Music* (London, 1968), pp. 313–22. See also item 52.

401. Förster-Nietzsche, Elisabeth. *Wagner und Nietzsche zur Zeit ihrer Freundschaft. Erinnerungen zu Friedrich Nietzsches 70. Geburtstag den 15. Oktober 1914.* Munich: Georg Müller, 1915. v, 289pp. B3316.F76

Twenty-four chapters of Nietzsche reminiscences by the philosopher's sister, including lengthy excerpts from Nietzsche's letters and other writings; only the last chapter deals explicitly with the break between Nietzsche and Wagner. The author, Nietzsche's sister and editor of several other posthumous publications, has been criticized by Wagnerians for her "willful distortions" and "interference in his unpublished papers" (item 2, p. 383). Illustrated with two or three portraits, including a frontispiece depicting Nietzsche himself as he looked in 1873. Concludes with an index.

Excerpts from this volume appeared for the first time in English as "Wagner and Nietzsche: The Beginning and End of Their Friendship" in *The Musical Quarterly* 4 (1918), pp. 466–89, as translated by Caroline V. Kerr.

402. Bélart, Hans (Z.) *Friedrich Nietzsches Freundschafts-Tragödie mit*

Richard Wagner und Cosima Wagner-Liszt. Dresden: C. Reissner, 1912. 182pp. ML410.W19B4

Not seen. Harvard University's Widener Library purportedly owns a copy (shelf-number "Widener Depository Phil 3640.190.20"), but it was unavailable for examination by the author, as was the copy identified in the Library of Congress on-line catalog. The high quality of Bélart's other Wagner publications suggests, however, that this one deserves to be consulted. Another study worth consulting is Mazzino Montinari's "Nietzsche-Wagner im Sommer 1878," published in *Nietzsche-Studien* 14 (1985), pp. 13–21.

A great deal exists in print about Nietzsche and Wagner, much of it intelligent. Unfortunately, less intelligent and—especially from the perspective of serious researchers—less useful studies also exist. One of these boasts a famous performer as its author:

403. Fischer-Dieskau, Dietrich. *Wagner and Nietzsche*, trans. Joachim Neugroschel. New York: Seabury, 1976. 232pp. ISBN 0816492808 ML410.W19F53

    A superficial account of the composer's relationship with the philosopher who began his career as an ardent advocate and ended it as a sworn opponent, written by a celebrated singer-turned-cultural historian. Outfitted with some endnotes (pp. 217–27), many of which identify individuals mentioned in the text itself; lacks visual illustrations, musical examples, or a useful bibliography. Originally published in German under the title *Wagner und Nietzsche: der Mystagoge und sein Abtrunniger* (Stuttgart, 1974).

Robert Schumann
Like most other groups of closely related studies, these are described below in alphabetical order by author:

404. Kapp, Julius. "Richard Wagner und Robert Schumann." *Die Musik* 11/4 (July 1912), pp. 42–49 and 100–108. ML5.M9

    Summarizes the Wagner-Schumann relationship, especially during the years 1836 to 1848. Kapp reprints the complete texts of several documents, including Wagner's letter to Schumann of 21 January 1843; he also quotes from Schumann's correspondence. One of many intelligent Wagner articles published in German musical magazines prior to the outbreak of World War I.

*   Konrad, Ulrich. "Robert Schumann und Richard Wagner." Described as item 261.

In addition to the documents he presents and annotates, Konrad discusses Wagner's and Schumann's relationship between 1830 and 1848, as well as Wagner's contributions to Schumann's *Neue Zeitschrift für Musik* during 1835 and 1836.

Other Men

Studies of Wagner's relationships, real and hypothetical, with a variety of other individuals are described in alphabetical order by subjects' surnames:

405. Scharlitt, Bernard. "Chopin und Wagner." *Die Musik* 8/1 (1908–1909), pp. 58–60. ML5.M9

     Muses upon, rather than explains the details of, any relationship—personal, professional, or intellectual—that might have existed (but did not; only in his later years did Wagner encounter so well-known a collection of pieces as Chopin's *Preludes*, which he professed to enjoy) between these very different masters of nineteenth-century melody and harmony. No musical examples. Still, one of the only studies in print devoted to this speculative subject.

406. Loos, Helmut. "Heinrich Dorn in seinem Verhältnis zu Robert Schumann und Richard Wagner." in: *Musica Baltica: Interregionale musikkulturelle Beziehungen im Ostseeraum. Kongressbericht Greifswald-Gdansk, 28. November bis 3. Dezember 1993*, ed. Ekkehard Ochs et al. Sankt Augustin: Academia, 1996; pp. 365–86. ISBN 3883457248 ML240.M837 1996

     Deals in part with Dorn as a minor nineteenth-century German composer, his growing enmity with Wagner, and references to Dorn in *My Life*. Schumann, incidentally, studied composition briefly with Dorn and also enjoyed a less-than-pleasant relationship with his former teacher. Also of interest is Adelyn Peck Leverett's "Liszt, Wagner and Heinrich Dorn's 'Die Nibelungen,' " published in the *Cambridge Opera Journal* 2 (1990), pp. 121–44; Leverett points out that, in supporting Dorn's Nibelung opera, Liszt may have exposed a hidden desire to compete with Wagner.

407. Sietz, Reinhold. "Dr. Hermann Franck, ein Freund Wagners, Hillers und Heines: Beiträge zu seiner Biographie." In: *Musicae scientiae collectanea. Festschrift Karl Gustav Fellerer zum. siebzigsten Geburtstag am 7. Juli 1972*, ed. Heinrich Hüschen. Cologne: Arno Volk, 1973; pp. 532–560 + unpaginated portrait. ML55.F35 1972

     Describes Franck's career as traveler and reporter of concert activities in early- and mid-nineteenth-century Europe. Primarily of interest to Wagner researchers for its lengthy quotations concerning the Dresden premiere of

Tannhäuser in 1845 (pp. 545–49) and Wagner's *Nibelungen* poem (pp. 558–59); also contains part of a letter from Franck to Wagner written on 9 April 1846. Includes a portrait of Franck but no musical examples.

408. Humperdinck, Eva, with Sr. M. Evamaris. *Engelbert Humperdinck in seinen persönlichen Beziehungen zu Richard Wagner, Cosima Wagner [und] Siegfried Wagner, dargestellt am Briefwechsel und anderen Aufzeichnungen.* Koblenz: Görres, 1996. 339pp. ISBN 392038850X ML410.H9A42 1996

Essentially a collection of letters—from Wagner to Humperdinck, from Humperdinck to Wagner and his son Siegfried, from Humperdinck to Cosima, and so on—supplemented with running text, some two dozen black-and-white illustrations of various kinds—among them family portraits, facisimiles of various documents. and a photograph of the Alhambra in Spain—and extensive endnotes (pp. 271–330). Also includes a list of printing errors (p. 7) and two "family trees" (pp. 13–14) detailing Humperdinck's personal and professional—rather than biological or marital—relationships with the Wagners. Concludes with an index of names (pp. 331–335), a one-page bibliography (p. 337), and a list of archival and illustration sources (p. 339). Uncommon in American libraries; the LC number cited above belongs to a copy owned by the University of Chicago.

409. *Richard Wagner und Albert Niemann. Ein Gedenkbuch, mit bisher unveröffentlichten Briefen, besonders Wagners, Bildern und einem Faksimile,* ed. Wilhelm Altmann. Berlin: Georg Stilke, 1924. 264pp. ML420.W12

A study of the tenor's life, character, and relationship with Wagner, especially insofar as the 1876 Bayreuth Festival performances are concerned. Includes an essay by Gottfried Niemann entitled "Zur Charakteristik Albert Niemanns" (pp. 13–25), the texts of a number of letters, an index of names (pp. 257–64), and sixteen numbered black-and-white illustrations—among the latter a frontispiece depicting Niemann's place of birth; also contains a few documentary facsimiles.

410. Prod'homme, J. G. "Wagner, Berlioz and Monsieur Scribe: Two Collaborations that Miscarried." *The Musical Quarterly* 12 (1926), pp. 359–75. ML1.M725

Touches on Wagner's youthful years in Paris and especially on the early history of *Holländer.* Prod'homme includes the complete original scenario for that opera (pp. 359–68), as well as the text of a letter Wagner addressed

to Scribe on 8 May 1840 dealing with related issues (pp. 365–68). The rest
of the article is devoted to other topics.

411. Semper, Manfred. *Das Münchener Festspielhaus. Gottfried Semper und
Richard Wagner.* Hamburg: Conrad Kloß, 1906. xvi, 116pp. ML410.W11S4

A detailed history of the festival theater Semper hoped to build in conjunction with Wagner performances in the Bavarian capital, and of Semper's
relationship with the composer during the mid-1860s. Consists largely of
letters written by Wagner, Ludwig II, and other individuals concerned with
the project.

412. Riesemann, O. von. "Alexander Seroff and His Relations to Wagner and
Liszt," trans. Theodore Baker. *The Musical Quarterly* 9 (1923), pp.
450–68. ML1.M725

Summarizes Seroff's (or Serov's) careers as musician and music critic,
especially his leadership of the Imperial Theater in St. Petersburg. Rise-
mann also discusses Wagner's relationship with his Russian colleague
between 1858 and 1871, his correspondence with him, and his visits to
Russia in early 1863 to give concerts of his own—Wagner's—music (pp.
450–64). Includes lengthy quotations from Seroff's letters to his wife
Valentina (see also item 291). No musical examples.

*   Engel, Hans. "Wagner und Spontini." Described as item 526.

Includes information about Wagner's early indebtedness to a composer
almost forty years older than himself.

413. Klimov, Pavel. "Richarda Vagnera i Pavel Zukovskij" [Richard Wagner
and Pavel Zukovski]. *Zurnal ljubitelej iskusstva* 2–3 (1997), pp. 71–78.
(no LC number available)

One of several Russian-language Wagner studies to appear in recent years.
Among other subjects Klimov describes the composer's relationship with
Zukovski (1845–1912); a friend and painter and one of the stage decorators
and costume designers for the 1882 Bayreuth production of *Parsifal*. Not
seen; cited in RILM on-line, where a reference to illustrations also appears.

*Finally, studies related to Wagner's male friends and acquaintances include the
following interesting article:*

414. Einstein, Alfred. "Der 'Antipode' Wagners." In: Einstein, *Von Schütz bis
Hindemith: Essays über Musik und Musiker.* Zurich and Stuttgart: Pan,
1956; pp. 105–111. ML60.E32

Deals with Peter Gast, a friend of Nietzsche's set up by Nietzsche as Wagner's "antithesis." Among other topics Einstein draws upon six musical examples from Gast's *Lion of Venice* in order to cast doubt on the philosopher's artistic judgment; he also considers Nietzsche's own failures as a composer.

Wagner's Relationships with Women

Among Wagner's female family members, friends, lovers, and wives were his sister, singer Johanna Wagner (see item 344), Mathilde Wesendonk, and of course the redoubtable Cosima. Unless otherwise noted, studies of relationships with these and other women are identified below in alphabetical order by subject, then described in alphabetical order by author.

Perhaps the best synopsis of Wagner's relationship with women is:

415. Millington, Barry. "Wagner and Women." In item 1, pp. 118–21.

Ridiculing charges that Wagner was a Lothario, Millington briefly discusses the composer's attitudes toward marriage and the reasons why he may have married his first wife Minna; he also describes Wagner's extramarital affairs with Mathilda Wesendonk, Judith Gautier and, possibly, Carrie Pringle. With regard to Pringle, see items 350–51. With regard to Wagner and "the feminine," see item 991 (Nattiex, *Wagner Androgyne*) and other postmodern studies devolving upon gender.

Other studies concentrate exclusively on the composer's amorous involvements; these include the following volumes, described in reverse chronological order of publication:

416. Kapp, Julius. *The Loves of Richard Wagner.* "Authorized Translation." London: W. H. Allen, 1951. 280pp. ML410.W19K292 1951

Examines in turn each of the important relationships Wagner sustained with women throughout his lengthy and chequered career. Assisted (?) by his unidentified translator, Kapp carefully documents most of his claims and discoveries with quotations from Wagner's letters printed in smaller type wherever they appear. Outfitted with a useful index as well as with two appendices: the first consists of a brief discussion of the Burrell collection (pp. 261–65), the second a series of observations about Ludwig Geyer, Hans von Bülow, Malwine von Schnorr, and others. A better book than its somewhat sleazy title suggests.

Also better than *The Women in Wagner's Life*, trans. Hannah Walter (New York, 1931; ML410.W19K292); the latter is based on Kapp's *Richard Wagner und die Frauen* (Berlin, 1929).

417. Barthou, Louis. *La vie amoureuse de Richard Wagner*. Paris (?): Ernest Flammarion, 1925. 203pp. ML410.W19B18

A popular account of Wagner's relationships, real and at least partially imagined, with his first wife Minna, with Mathilde Wesendonk, with his second wife Cosima, and so on. Published in a series entitled "Leurs amours"; not to be taken too seriously by scholars, and probably not meant to be. Includes a brief bibliography (p. 202). Other descriptions of Wagner's amours include portions of Basil Howitt's *Love Lives of the Great Composers: From Gesualdo to Wagner* (Toronto, 1995).

418. Materna, Hedwig H. *Richard Wagners Frauengestalten*. Berlin and Leipzig: Frauen-Rundschau, 1903? 138pp. (no LC number available)

Primarily a study of the female roles in Wagner's music dramas, with biographies of singers who portrayed them in early performances. Captions that accompany photographs of many of these performers provide additional biographical information; the frontispiece reproduces a portrait of the author. Apparently reprinted or adapted from a popular women's magazine and of interest largely to historians of the stage and the Wagner reception in Germany. Uncommon in American libraries; Harvard University's Loeb Music Library owns a copy.

Studies of Wagner's relationships with a number of individual women—his wives Cosima (Liszt von Bülow) Wagner and Minna (Planer) Wagner, Mathilde Maier, and so on—are identified below under subheadings and/or described in alphabetical order by authors' and/or subjects' (married) surnames:

Mathilde Maier
*   Scholz, Hans. *Richard Wagner und Mathilde Maier (1862–1878)*. Described as item 255.

Comprises the published correspondence exchanged by Maier and the composer.

Cosima [Liszt von Bülow] Wagner
*   Moulin-Eckart, Richard du. *Cosima Wagner: Ein Lebens- und Charakterbild*. Described as item 1149.

In part a careful examination of Cosima's relationship with Wagner. Unlike poor Minna, Cosima was quite capable of living her own life after Richard died.

419. Skelton, Geoffrey. *Richard and Cosima Wagner: Biography of a Marriage*. London: Victor Gollancz, 1982. 319pp. ISBN 0575030178 ML410.W15S5

Drawing upon sources such as Cosima's diaries and the *Brown Book*—unavailable to earlier biographers, including Newman and Gutman—Skelton examines the complex relationship between Wagner (as man and composer) and the woman who was Liszt's daughter, Bülow's wife, and for years the "keeper of the flame" at Bayreuth. Illustrated with 24 portraits, pictures of places, photographs of family scenes, and the like. Includes a good bibliography (pp. 307–310); concludes with an index. Reviewed in *Wagner* 3/2 (May 1982), pp. 58–61.

Minna [Planer] Wagner
420. Herzfeld, Friedrich. *Minna Planer und ihre Ehe mit Richard Wagner.* Leipzig: Wilhelm Goldmann, 1938. 369pp. (no LC number available)

The biography of a marriage, rather than an individual, and one written to cast the most favorable possible light on Wagner's character. Contains a few facsimiles (cataloged on p. 368), including one of a letter addressed by Minna to Pusinelli on 16 June 1862. Also contains other illustrations, a timeline spanning 1809 to 1883 (pp. 357–59), the texts of a number of other letters, miscellaneous documents, and excerpts from Wagner's prose works. No bibliography; concludes with an index. See also item 37, pp. 109–27.

Mathilde Wesendonk (also "Wesendonck")
421. Kobbé, Gustav. *Wagner and His Isolde.* New York: Dodd, Mead, 1905. xv, 255pp. ML410.W1A395 1905

A collection of correspondence from 1858 to 1869, outfitted with linking text. Based on Wagner's letters to the Wesendonks (item 214); a recent publication from Kobbé's perspective. Accompanied by seven illustrations, including a frontispiece portrait of Mathilde herself.

Other volumes devoted to the Wagner-Mathilde Wesendonk relationship exist; see, for instance, Bélart's *Richard Wagners Leibestragödie mit Mathilde Wesendonk* (Dresden, 1912). The title is given as it appears in the Library of Congress on-line catalog; the present author has never seen a copy.

Other Women
422. Sabor, Rudolph. "Judith Gautier." *Wagner* 11/4 (October 1990), pp. 119–34. ML410.W1A585

A useful summary of the Wagner-Gautier relationship, together with information about some of Gautier's associates: Catulle Mendès, Victor Hugo, and so on. Includes portraits of Gautier and Mendès, among others, as well as a facsimile reproduction of an *Albumblatt* Wagner probably composed for Judith in 1877.

423. Wallace, William. *Liszt, Wagner, and the Princess.* London: Kegan Paul, Trench, Trübner & Co., 1927. xiv, 196pp. ML410.L7W5

A pioneering but inadequate study of Princess Carolyne zu Sayn-Wittgenstein's influence upon the lives of two of the nineteenth century's most important musical figures. Wallace pays more attention to Liszt, with whom the princess lived for more than a decade, than to Wagner. Includes several portraits, a brief bibliography (189–91), and an index. Also published in New York City the same year.

Other Specialized Biographical Studies

These are identified below under subheadings, then described in alphabetical order by author:

Animals
424. Rather, L. J. "Wagner on the Human Use of Animal Beings." In Rather, *Reading Wagner: A Study in the History of Ideas* (Baton Rouge, LA and London, 1990), pp. 78–113. ISBN 0807115576 ML410.W19R25 1990

Examines—as Thomas Grey states in his review of Rather's otherwise disappointing volume [*Notes* 49 (1992–1993), pp. 558–60]—"19th-century anti-vivisectionist movements in the context of medical and scientific ethics and related issues," including vegetarianism and "attitudes toward kosher ritual slaughtering" (review, p. 559). Rather, who made his reputation as an historian of medicine, was also the author of *The Dream of Self-Destruction: Wagner's Ring and the Modern World* (Baton Rouge, LA, 1979).

425. Thiery, Joachim, and Ulrich Tröhler. "Wagner, Animals and Modern Scientific Medicine," trans. Stewart Spencer. In item 1, pp. 174–77.

For the most part a discussion of the composer's reactions to animal cruelty in general and *Die Folterkammern der Wissenschaft* ("The Torture Chambers of Science"), an anti-vivisectionist tract written by Ernst von Weber, and a book that upset the composer so much he addressed an "open letter" to Weber inveighing against the animal experiments the pamphleteer had described; this letter appeared, among other places, in the *Bayreuther Blätter* (see item 52). Thiery and Tröhler point out that, for Wagner, the issues involved not merely cruelty but also questions regarding "the abandonment of ethical values" on behalf of the spread of knowledge (p. 177).

Other studies touching on Wagner and the animal kingdom tend toward the sentimental. See, for instance, Wolzogen's *Richard Wagner und die Tierwelt. Auch eine Biographie.* 3rd enlarged ed. (Berlin and Leipzig, 1910)—a highly sympathetic account of the composer's love of animals, illustrated with four photographs of his dogs Ruß, Marke, Fafner, and Fasolt. See also items 434 and 436.

Homosexuality

426. Fuchs, Hanns. *Richard Wagner und die Homosexualität. Unter besonderer Berüchsichtigung der sexuellen Anomalien seines Gestalten.* Berlin: H. Barsdorf, 1903. viii, 278pp. ML410.W19F95

Drawing upon lengthy quotations from the libretto to *Rheingold* and other literary works, as well as upon Wagner's relationship with Ludwig II and the eccentricities reported in the infamous "Letters to a Seamstress" (item 252), Fuchs does his best to prove Wagner's "mental homosexuality"; no evidence survives for any actual homosexual affairs. Fuchs's volume contains no illustrations, musical examples, bibliography, or index. One of many unusual publications dealing with Wagner's life and character summarized by Vetter in her superb essay on Wagner and psychology (item 1019).

Medicine

427. Thiery, Joachim, and Dietrich Seidel. " 'I Feel only Discontent': Wagner and his Doctors." *Wagner* 16/1 (January 1995), pp. 3–22. ML410.W1A585

Describes the composer's relationship with Josef Standhartner, perhaps the only physician ever to examine him, and with a few other individuals. In spite of its title, this article does not attack the medical profession in general or any of the individual practitioners Wagner knew. Includes a facsimile of a letter Wagner addressed to Standhartner in February 1863, together with the text of a much longer letter to the same man, dated 1 November 1867, and several other illustrations. Also includes references to the heart condition that probably caused the composer's death in February 1883. Translated from the *Münchener medizinisches Wochenblatt* 136 (1994), pp. 491–502. See also item 798.

Money Matters

428. Kesting, Hanjo. *Das Pump-Genie. Richard Wagner und das Geld, nach gedruckten und ungedruckten Quellen.* Frankfurt a.M.: Eichborn, 1993. 512pp. ISBN 3821805099 ML410.W1A144 1993

Comprises 471 documents associated with Wagner's personal and public business dealings and spanning the years 1829 to 1883 (pp. 25–475), together with a catalog of these fascinating artifacts (pp. 503–12), a glossary of individuals mentioned in the documents themselves (pp. 491–502), a brief time-line (pp. 488–90), a few caricatures as illustrations, and a list of sources (pp. 479–82). A just-the-facts introduction to the man who was able to obtain money under the most diverse and, often, discouraging circumstances.

429. Millington, Barry. "Finances and Attitude To Money." In item 1, pp. 116–18.

Defends Wagner against those who claim he was a moocher and con man. Millington refers especially to copyright laws that made Wagner himself the dupe of unscrupulous publishers and producers; he also explains the several ways Otto Wesendonk "befriended" the composer, even as Wagner himself garnered rental fees and prestige as a friend of the arts.

Politics
430. Paillard, Bertita, and Emile Haraszti. "Franz Liszt and Richard Wagner in the Franco-German War of 1870," trans. Willis Wager. *The Musical Quarterly* 35 (1949), pp. 386–411. ML1.M725

Among other topics, authors Haraszti and Paillard consider Wagner's role in establishing and maintaining an alliance between Prussia and Bavaria prior to the outbreak of war, as well as issues of post-war German hegemony as they pertained to the composer's plans for a festival theater in Bayreuth (pp. 398–410). A rather lackluster performance, especially in light of the brilliant political sleuthing documented in *Franz Liszt and Agnes Street-Klindworth: A Correspondence, 1854–1886*, ed. and trans. Pauline Pocknell (Hillsdale, NY, 2000). Pocknell's volume also touches on Wagner's political opinions and positions.

Vegetarianism
431. Hermand, Jost. "Wagner's Last Supper: The Vegetarian Gospel of His 'Parsifal.' " In item 34, pp. 103–18.

Explains that, just as Wagner incorporated other of his intellectual and emotional enthusiasms in his music dramas, so in *Parsifal* he drew upon the vegetarianism that he himself temporarily adopted during his later years, and that became increasingly popular throughout Europe during the 1850s and 1860s, as well as upon his own anti-semitic prejudices. See also item 434.

Additional Specialized Studies
Described below in alphabetical order by author:

432. Braun, Joachim. "Ein Gerichtsverfahren in Sachen des Königsberger Kaufmanns Schirach Sternberg wider Musikdirektor Richard Wagner." *Musik des Ostens* 8 (1982), pp. 113–27. ML240.M88

Describes the lawsuit filed in September 1838 against Wagner by Sternberg, who was awarded the following May some 179 rubles in monies owed. Braun draws in this article upon documents formerly in the possession of the Central Historical Archive, Latvian Soviet Socialist Republic. Illustrated with documentary facsimiles. Also identified in some sources as having been published in the "Feldman Festschrift," which *is* Vol. 8 of *Musik des Ostens*.

Other studies deal more peripherally with Wagner's friendships and financial activities. Among them is Ottfried Hafner's "Ferdinand Raimund, Gustav Albert Lortzing, Richard Wagner: Verborgene Beziehungen und Spuren," published in *Studia Musicologica* 37 (1990), pp. 235–40, which describes Wagner's relationships with and/or opinions of Raimund and Lortzing as composers and/or colleagues. See the bibliographies in items 3–4, 26, 76–79, etc., for other relationship studies.

433. Perrier, Henri. *Les Rendez-vous Wagnériens*. Lausanne: "La Tramontane," 1981. 278pp. ML410.W1P38 1981 (no ISBN available)

An unusual and quite interesting work dealing with Wagner "places": countries, cities, towns, concert halls, houses, and other locations where the composer lived, worked, visited, and performed. Complete with annotated "walks" that enable readers to stroll about as they familiarize themselves with Wagner's Bayreuth, Dresden, Leipzig, Lucerne, Munich, Vienna, Venice, Zurich, and so on. Quotations from Wagner letters, literary works, and reminiscences provide documentation and detail; an introduction by Wolfgang Wagner serves as Bayreuth's imprimatur. Includes a bibliography (pp. 275–78), unfortunately, no maps are included.

434. Thiery, Joachim, and Ulrich Tröhler. "Wagner's Critique of Science and Technology," trans. Stewart Spencer. In item 1, pp. 177–79.

In addition to such subjects as vivisection, vegetarianism, and the Industrial Revolution, the authors consider briefly Wagner's negative reactions to most technological innovations and his fears concerning the "degeneration" of the human race (p. 177). With regard to the last point, however, Thierry and Tröhler steer clear of invoking the composer's anti-semitic statements, including those recorded in his wife Cosima's diaries.

CHARACTER STUDIES

Few composers have inspired more respect and *disgust than has Wagner. He was a mass of contradictions, real or perceived: his professional integrity, for example, was offset by personal insincerity and outright dishonesty; his extraordinary industry by his equally extraordinary self-indulgence; and the nobility of his artistic and cultural interests and enthusiasms by his penchant in old age for fads like vegetarianism, and especially by his virulent, lifelong anti-semitism.*

Because "character" cannot be separated altogether from "activity" or "accomplishment," it goes without saying that Wagner's personality and attitudes are treated almost everywhere in the literature. Especially insightful, however, are the following character studies—beginning with an excellent synopsis:

435. Millington, Barry. "Appearance and Character." In item 1, pp. 97–99.

    Describes Wagner physically as he aged, and refers briefly to his two marriages, his fabulous sense of his own importance, and his penchant for self-indulgence—the last including the "silks and satins" episode involving seamstress Goldwag. Like other Wagner character studies, this one slights or ignores certain aspects of the composer's behavior and beliefs in order to emphasize others. Equally important is Millington's assertion that "one's view of Wagner's character is inevitably colored by one's attitude to the 19th-century notion of a genius and the social expectations such a category engendered" (p. 98).

A longer, more completely documented discussion of some of Wagner's traits and interests also exists:

436. Buderath, Bernhard. *Richard Wagner allzu menschlich: der Meister, die Frauen und das Geld—unter Verwendung von Selbstzeugnissen, Lebensberichten, Briefen und Dokumenten.* Munich: Knaur, 1983. 184pp. ISBN 3426010666 ML410.W19R37 1983

    Includes comparatively lengthy chapters not only concerning Wagner's enthusiasms for money and women, but also tracing his enthusiasm for animals ("Richard Wagner und die Tiere," pp. 149–174). Buderath provides copious but mostly familiar quotations from primary sources, especially the composer's prose works and published letters. Illustrated with a scattering of caricatures, most of them well-known (among these the 1867 *Münchener Punsch* cover cartoon of Wagner calling on Ludwig II to request more cash); concludes with a list of sources and *sigla* (p. 175), a brief timeline (pp. 177–80), and an index of names.

437. Weissmann, Adolf. "Richard Wagner: Constructive and Destructive." *The Musical Quarterly* 11 (1925), pp. 138–56. ML1.M725

Purportedly an evaluation of Wagner's "achievement" (p. 138); in fact an attack mostly on his character and influence on music history. Weissmann suggests that Wagner is "never sincere" (p. 139), that his music is unnatural, that he—and it—were far too sensual, and so on. "By the creation of his seductive, gigantic work, and forcing its success by a ruthlessly uncompromising propaganda, [Wagner] brought about disintegration, started controversies, and sowed the seed of all dissensions regarding the later music down to the present" (p. 139).

* Burbidge, Richard. "Richard Wagner: Man and Artist." Described as item 30.

Especially useful for its observations about the composer's preference for feminine companionship, his recklessness and "forgetfulness" where money was concerned, his enormous capacity for work, his lack of interest in the musical works of his contemporaries, and other distinctive characteristics.

Longer, more complex, but not uniformly more successful character studies include the following volumes, described in reverse chronological order of publication:

438. Lee, M. Owen. *Wagner: The Terrible Man and His Truthful Art.* "The 1998 Larkin-Stuart Lectures." Toronto and Buffalo, NY: University of Toronto Press, 1999. x, 102pp. ISBN 0802047211 ML410.W13L47 1999

A three-part survey study that emphasizes issues of character and influence. Lee praises Wagner's accomplishments as a creator of extraordinary ability and influence, even as he attacks the composer's woeful morals and sense of self-importance, and especially his anti-semitism. In Lee's opinion, "Wagner probably wrecked more havoc on himself with his essay 'Judaism in Music' than with anything else he wrote"; on the other hand, the works of this "arrogant Teuton whom Hitler had made his own and who, three-quarters of a century before [the end of World War II] had appropriated art, politics, philosophy, and almost everything else in sight to fashion his gigantic *Gesamtkunstwerke*," live on, if only because "Wagner was not quite the monster our propaganda and his made him out to be" (p. 38). Includes, as a cover illustration, a reproduction of Wassily Kandinsky's *Night* as well as a bibliography (pp. 95–98); concludes with an index.

Reviewed by Christopher Hatch in *The Opera Quarterly* 16 (2000), pp. 659–60, who praises it aptly by pointing out that "readers may be surprised how many big ideas have found a place in this little volume" (p. 660).

439. Abbetmeyer, Theodor. *Richard-Wagner-Studien. Neue Untersuchungen über die Persönlichkeit und das Kulturwerk des Bayreuther Meisters.* Hannover and Leipzig: Hahnsche Buchhandlung, 1916. iv, 276pp. ML410.W13A2

Includes "Wagners Persönlichkeit" (pp. 1–60): an all-out hymn of praise to the composer and precisely the kind of thing so many of Wagner's critics consider objectionable. Essays like Abbetmeyer's, in which only positive anecdotes are recounted and anything that might be considered objectionable is kept under wraps, prevent readers from learning much about Wagner's emotional life and personal relationships. The volume as a whole includes a short bibliography (pp. 275–76).

The possibility that Wagner was mad, peculiar, or at least "distinctive" in his mental makeup has inspired a flurry of publications ignored for the most part in the present research guide. One volume, however, deserves to be mentioned, if only because it has itself been the subject of examination by a leading Wagner scholar:

440. Puschmann, Dr. Th. [*sic*]. *Richard Wagner. Eine psychiatrische Studie*, 3rd rev. ed. Berlin: B. Behr, 1873. 67pp. (no LC number available)

Asserting his credentials as a medical authority, Puschmann accuses Wagner of practically every imaginable mental and moral disorder; Ernest Newman, writing of Puschmann's pamphlet in the last of his biographical volumes, calmly—indeed, altogether ironically—describes it merely as "notorious" (item 301, Vol. 4, p. 388). The pamphlet itself includes quotations from the composer's prose works and the poems of his music dramas; Puschmann cites no other sources, however, and provides neither bibliography nor index. Uncommon in American libraries.

441. Vetter, Isolde. "Richard Wagner and Theodor Puschmann." *Wagner* 10/3 (July 1989), pp. 96–110. ML410.W1A585

Explores in greater detail the significance—or lack of same—of Puschmann's ideas about and attitudes toward Wagner. Translated from Vetter's "Das Kunstwerk der Zukunft aus der Perspektive psychiatrischer Vergangenheit: Richard Wagner und Theodor Puschmann," published in *Das musikalische Kunstwerk: Geschichte—Ästhetik—Theorie. Festschrift Carl Dahlhaus zum 60. Geburtstag*, ed. Hermann Danuser et al. (Laaber, 1988), pp. 269–84.

Other studies of Wagner's character have probed into what we know of his dreams, his sexual life, and interactions between his character and his musical-dramatic creations; these include the following, described in alphabetical order by author:

442. Muller, Philippe. *Wagner par ses rêves.* Brussels: Pierre Margada, 1981. 234pp. ISBN 2870091559 ML410.W1M82 1981

Identifies by date, organizes into some 41 categories, describes, and examines some 421 dreams drawn from Cosima's diaries and attributed to Wagner himself. Also includes an introductory essay, comments on the dream analyses of other authors insofar as they apply to Wagner, and bibliographical references. A remarkable piece of fact-finding by a noted psychologist; Muller cites the work of Calvin Hall, as well as a schema proposed for the Thematic Apperception Test. In Vetter's opinion, however, all this work leads to little "clearly recognizable goal or result" (item 2, p. 145). Of interest, nevertheless, to students of dreams, as well as to historians of psychological methodology.

443. Noll, Justus. "'Es wollte ihn wecken'—oder, Bach auf gehacktem Fleisch spielen. Ein Versuch über Träume Richard Wagners." *Neue Zeitschrift für Musik* 144/2 (February 1983), pp. 4–8; and 144/3 (March 1983), pp. 12–15. ML5.M183

Quotes books and essays by Adorno, Sigmund Freud, and Erwin Koppen (item 1023), as well as Cosima's diaries and other primary sources, to comment on our knowledge of Wagner's dream-life and what it may tell us about the composer's character and musical-dramatic accomplishments. Illustrated with a caricature and three other images, one of them a facsimile of a page of Cosima's handwriting on which her daughter Eva heavily crossed out a tell-tale dream passage.

444. Saffle, Michael. "Wagner's 'Letters to a Seamstress': Crossdressing, Egoism, and Polymorphous Perversity." In: *Gender Blending*, ed. Vern and Bonnie Bulough and James Elias. Proceedings of the I. International Congress on Gender, Cross-dressing, and Sex Issues. Amherst, NY: Prometheus, 1997; pp. 256–66. ISBN 1573921246 HQ77.G46 1997

Considers issues associated with the "Seamstress Letters," and the possibility that Wagner was a transvestite. Saffle suggests that the composer's sensitive skin, love of finery, and lifelong appetite for luxuries of all kinds call to mind Freud's notion of "polymorphous perversity": a largely undifferentiated desire for pleasures both sensual and sexual. Includes quotations from Cosima's diaries as well as from lampoons of Wagner written by some of his Jewish detractors.

445. Wintle, Christopher. "Analysis and Psychoanalysis: Wagner's Musical Metaphors." In: *Companion to Contemporary Musical Thought*, ed. John Paynter et al. 2 vols. London and New York: Routledge, 1992; Vol. 2, pp. 651–691. ISBN 0415030927 ML55.C74 1992

A psychoanalytic study of Wagner's music dramas—and, by extension, of Wagner himself—with special reference to the *Ring, Tristan,* and *Parsifal.* Includes twelve musical examples as well as a diagram of the underlying harmonic patterns associated with the "Kiss" in *Parsifal,* act II.

VI

Wagner as Composer: Studies in Techniques, Styles, and Influences

SURVEYS OF WAGNER'S COMPOSITIONS AND STYLISTIC ISSUES

*Almost all of the books and articles written about Wagner as composer, rather than Wagner as music-dramatist, have been devoted either to individual compositional elements and procedures—form, harmony, and so on—or to individual works—*Lohengrin, *the* Faust *overture, and so on—or to both; for example, the use of* Leitmotive *in* Rheingold. *Three exceptions to this rule include the following studies, which are described in alphabetical order by title and/or author's surname:*

446. Bauer, Jans-Joachim. *Richard Wagner.* "Reclams Musikführer" [series]. Stuttgart: Philipp Reclam jun., 1992. 426pp. ISBN 3150103746 MT92.W14B4 1992

    A useful survey of Wagner's vocal *and* instrumental compositions, illustrated with some 358 musical examples and 33 visual illustrations; the last include several facsimiles and, as frontispiece, a reproduction of a well-known 1860 Wagner photograph. Also includes a well-rounded discography that, insofar as possible, identifies at least one recording of each composition (pp. 393–404) and a synopsis of the composer's life and career (pp. 7–40). Concludes with a bibliography (pp. 405–21) and an index of works identified by *WWV* numbers as well as titles.

447. *Das Drama Richard Wagners als musikalisches Kunstwerk,* ed. Carl Dahlhaus. Studien zur Musikgeschichte des 19. Jahrhunderts, 23. Regensburg: Gustav Bosse, 1970. 315pp. ML410.W131D3

    In spite of its title, one of the best introductions to Wagner's musical-dramatic procedures and influences in general, rather than to individual music dramas as completed works of art. Includes items 462–63, 472, 475, and 716, as well as discussions by Werner Breig of the "Fate" motive and associated harmonic issues in the *Ring* ("Das Schicksalskunde-Motiv im Ring des Nibelungen: Versuch einer harmonischen Analyse," pp. 223–33); by Klaus Hortschansky of Wagner and the "marvellous" ("Das Wunder und das Wunderbare im Werk Richard Wagners," pp. 41–61); and by Egon Voss of instrumentation and drama ("Über die Anwendung der Instrumentation auf das Drama bei Wagner," pp. 169–75). See also items 508, 599, and 631. Certain articles are followed by the texts of discussions that took place at the unidentified conference where these papers were originally presented. Illustrated throughout with musical examples, as well as a few analytical diagrams; concludes with an index of names.

448. Schmid, Manfred Hermann. *Musik als Abbild. Studien zum Werk von Weber, Schumann und Wagner.* Münchner Veröffentlichungen zur Musikgeschichte, 33. Tutzing: Hans Schneider, 1981. ISBN 3795203325 ML90.S293 1981

Deals mostly with Wagner's place in nineteenth-century music. Schmid pays special attention to *Tristan*, act II, and to the "Liebestod"; he also discusses aspects of Wagner's harmonic language. Includes an outstanding bibliography of analytical studies (pp. 333–52) and facsimiles of musical manuscripts (pp. 353–68), as well as a selection of hand-copied sketches Wagner prepared for portions of *Tristan* (pp. 293–329). Reviewed by Arnfried Edler in *Die Musikforschung* 40 (1987), pp. 179–80.

A number of briefer introductory or survey studies are described below in alphabetical order by author and/or title:

449. Breig, Werner. "The Musical Works," trans. Paul Knight and Horst Loeschmann. In item 2, pp. 397–482.

Devoted to Wagner's early instrumental works (pp. 397–400) and songs (pp. 400–403), as well as to his operas and music dramas, among them the *Liebesmahl der Apostel.* Breig interrupts this scheme with a brief essay entitled "The Creative Process in Wagner's Music" (pp. 427–31), as well as with discussions of the composer's instrumental works after 1850 (pp. 453–57) and the *Wesendonck-Lieder* (pp. 457–58). Illustrated with quotations from a few of Wagner's librettos as well as with six tables devoted to structural aspects of musical and literary elements in various of the music dramas, and with 30 often multi-partite musical examples. Breig's discussions of the *Ring* and *Parsifal* are especially detailed.

450. Cooke, Deryck. "Wagner's Musical Language." In item 31, pp. 225–68.

A concise and well-argued introduction to the kind of music Wagner produced for his music-dramas. Emphasizing that what "really matters" about Wagner is his stage works, and what "really matters" about those works is their music (p. 225); Cook asserts that "no true understanding of Wagner's music is possible without the realization that he was not simply a composer but a musical dramatist" (p. 242). Also tackles issues of harmony, musical texture, and the role various *Leitmotive* and other devices play in *Tannhäuser*, the *Ring*, and *Parsifal*, among others. Includes 45 musical examples. This essay incorporates aspects of Cooke's controversial monograph *The Language of Music* (London, 1959), a volume that, like some of Wagner's pronouncements, has more often been disparaged than intelligently evaluated.

*   *Wagner-Werk-Verzeichnis (WWV)*. Described as item 83.

The definitive catalog of Wagner's compositions. Includes a splendid but highly specialized bibliography described separately as item 77.

451. Whittall, Arnold. "Musical Language." In item 1, pp. 248–61.

Emphasizes Wagner's youthful borrowings from predecessors such as Marschner and Weber and certain of his compositional practices, including his replacing "numbers-opera" organizational schemes with "an extraordinary variety of periodic designs in which the continuity or discontinuity of motivic and harmonic processes is the crucial component" (p. 261). Limited to the operas and music dramas; furthermore, the absence of musical examples forces Whittall to fall back on verbal descriptions of such concepts as "cadential evasion" (p. 259)—the last employed as soon as Brünnhilde's final words have been sung near the very end of *Götterdämmerung*.

WAGNER'S COMPOSITIONAL DEVELOPMENT, METHODS, AND PROCEDURES

Wagner's Development as a Composer

The sheer scope and complexity of this subject has probably prevented many scholars from tackling the whole of it. Among the issues associated with it, however, are the differences between Wagner as opera composer and as mature music-dramatist. The following article deals precisely with this last subject:

452. Whittall, Arnold. "Wagner's Great Transition? From 'Lohengrin' to 'Das Rheingold.' " *Music Analysis* 2 (1983), pp. 269–80. ML1.M2125

Among other things, Whittall considers a passage from act I, scene iii, of *Lohengrin*, and compares it to aspects of *Rheingold*—the latter work containing no one comparable passage, because Wagner's style had grown so much more flexible and better integrated; he concludes that *Rheingold* "most purely fulfills" (p. 279) the composer's own mature musical-dramatic goals. Includes two musical examples. See also Gerald Abraham's observations in *A Hundred Years of Music* (New York, 1938), especially those in "Wagner the Musician" (pp. 132–53), which examines in part evolutionary issues involving *Rheingold* and *Lohengrin*.

Wagner's Working Methods

453. Bailey, Robert. "The Method of Composition." In item 31, pp. 269–338.

A compact description of compositional processes, based on Bailey's own researches, as well as the terminology other scholars have employed for the various kinds of sketches and drafts Wagner prepared for some of his music dramas. Bailey distinguishes carefully between Wagner's earlier and later compositional methods, and illustrates his discussion with 63 musical examples drawn from published and unpublished musical sources, as well as two valuable tables, the second of which (pp. 336–37) summarizes Wagner's working methods from *Die Feen* and *Rienzi* through various portions of the *Ring*, *Tristan*, and *Parsifal*.

454. Darcy, Warren. "Compositional Process." In item 1, pp. 244–48.

A satisfactory summary of Wagner's working methods but less brilliant than Bailey's effort (item 453), and weakened by a complete lack of musical examples. Nevertheless, Darcy does a fine job of explaining the differences between Wagner's approaches to composition before and "after" *Siegfried*; among other things, the latter era was distinguished by the composer's sketching "a passage in the first [pencil] draft and almost immediately elaborat[ing] it in the second [in ink]" (p. 247). Another study that touches on some of these issues is Abraham's article "Wagner's Second Thoughts," published in that author's *Slavonic and Romantic Music* (London, 1968), pp. 294–312, and illustrated with nineteen musical examples.

Other studies of the same or related issues, including precisely how and when Wagner liked to compose, include the following essays and articles, again described in alphabetical order by author:

455. Bailey, Robert. "The Evolution of Wagner's Compositional Procedures after 'Lohengrin.' " In: *Report of the Eleventh Congress: Copenhagen*

1972 [International Musicological Society], ed. Henrik Glahn et al. Copenhagen: Wilhelm Hansen (and other firms), 1974; Vol. 1, pp. 240–46. ISBN 8774550268 (no LC number available)

Considers issues of terminology vis-à-vis Wagner's sketches, drafts, copies, and other kinds of holographic musical documents. Like Deathridge (see item 171), Bailey bases much of his discussion on Otto Strobel's terms and categories of classification. Includes two musical examples as well as a diagram devoted to "Stages in the Composition of the Later Operas" (p. 245). See also item 492.

456. Grey, Thomas S. "Wagner's Working Routine." In item 1, pp. 102 and 113–114.

Explains when and under what physical circumstances Wagner liked to compose, including his use of pianos during the early and middle stages of work on each of his mature music dramas. More biographical, however, than a technical study of specific compositional practices.

457. Istel, Edgar. "How Wagner Worked: A Glance into the Master's Workshop," trans. Theodore Baker. *The Musical Quarterly* 19 (1933), pp. 38–44. ML1.M725

Outlines Wagner's compositional procedures and routines, complete with references to his love of luxury and daily schedule of activities. Istel categorizes the composer's methods as "midway between Beethoven's (most apparent in an impassioned striving after finality on the music-sheet) and Mozart's (which could offer a well-nigh mechanical script," because Wagner's "unexampled memory permitted him to retain the most complicated schemes in mind" (p. 38). Lacks musical examples. Originally published under the title "Wie Wagner am 'Ring' arbeitete: Mitteilungen über die Instrumentationsskizze des 'Rheingold' und andere Manuskripte" in *Die Musik* 10/4 (1910–1911), pp. 67–75. See also item 701.

458. Peyser, Herbert F. " 'Tristan,' First-Hand." *The Musical Quarterly* 11 (1925), pp. 418–26. ML1.M725

Discusses Wagner's penchant for fine handwriting, especially in light of the "blemishes, erasures, angry corrections and a variety of miscalculations and slips that for him, at least, amount to positive disorder" (p. 418) preserved in the original complete manuscript copy of *Tristan*. Includes three facsimiles of score pages.

Wagner and Compositional Techniques

General Studies

Evaluating Wagner's compositional decisions almost inevitably involves invoking various analytical concepts developed during the later nineteenth and twentieth centuries. Three introductions to the most important of these concepts are described below in alphabetical order by author:

459. Dahlhaus, Carl. "The Music," trans. Alfred Clayton. In item 2, pp. 297–314.

     More concerned with aesthetic and analytical issues than specific practices. Dahlhaus considers especially the "intractable difficulties" associated in the composer's prose writings with the terms "music" and "drama" (p. 297), "problematic" aspects of Ernst Kurth's treatise on Wagnerian harmony (p. 302; see item 465), Alfred Lorenz's analyses of Wagnerian form (item 481 below), the expressive functions of *Leitmotive* considered in terms of Schopenhauer's influence on Wagner's thought and works, and so on. No musical examples.

460. Murray, David R. "Major Analytical Approaches to Wagner's Musical Style: A Critique." *The Music Review* 39 (1978), pp. 211–22. ML5.M657

     Begins by proclaiming the existence of a "large gap"—NB: this in 1978—in English-language scholarship concerning the "investigation of Wagner's musical style" (p. 212). Murray then identifies and examines Wagnerian concepts associated with three prominent German musicologists: Lorenz and the *dichterlich-musikalische Periode* (poetic-musical phrase or period), Dahlhaus's reactions against periodicity, and Kurth's concept of *Alterationsstil* (the notion that the introduction of chromaticism of any kind necessarily alters the tonality of otherwise diatonic passages). Murray concludes that the greatest problem confronted by all three scholars is their "inability to reconcile the composer's motivic technique and linear polyphony with the elements of tonal order . . . within his style" (p. 222). No musical examples.

461. Wintle, Christopher. "Analysis and Criticism." In item 1, pp. 404–408.

     Offers a brief synopsis of influential analytical approaches to formal, harmonic, motivic, and evolutionary aspects of the music dramas. Among the approaches Wintle mentions are Lorenz's dissections of "secret form" in Wagner's works, Dahlhaus's arguments in favor of the "centrality of dialogue as a determinant of form" in the music dramas (p. 405), Kurth's sophisticated approach to both functional and non-functional aspects of Wagner's harmonic practices, certain theoretical positions of Milton Babbitt, Adele Katz, and Heinrich Schenker, and information gleaned by the careful documentary studies of Bailey (items 453 and 455), Patrick McCreless (item 712), and Anthony Newcomb (items 488–89), among others. Unfortunately includes no musical examples.

Studies of Individual Compositional Procedures
Unless otherwise specified, studies of each procedure are described in alphabetical order by author under each subheading below:

Counterpoint
462. Finscher, Ludwig. "Über den Kontrapunkt der Meistersinger." In item 447, pp. 303–13 (including discussion).

Considers the several uses of Bach-like counterpoint in Wagner's music drama, noting that some are merely craftsmanlike (i.e., they suggest "craftsmanly" or bourgeois values), some are employed for purposes of musical parody, and some are "meditative" in character. Includes several short musical examples, including two devoted to the evolution from sketch to finished product of a line of music found in the *Meistersinger* prelude. See also Istel's "Doppelfuge" article under item 807.

Dynamics
463. Fellinger, Imogen. "Bemerkungen zur Dynamik Wagners." In item 447, pp. 149–60.

One of the few discussions on Wagner's dynamic markings. Includes examples from *Rheingold*, *Walküre*, and *Siegfried*, some of them based on the testimony of Heinrich Porges (see item 289), who attended rehearsals for the 1876 *Ring* performances at the first Bayreuth Festival.

Harmony
Wagner's harmonic practices transformed Western music forever; so did his "endless melodies" and other thematic techniques. One work examines both subjects at length:

464. Ergo, Emil. *Ueber Richard Wagner's Harmonik und Melodik. Ein Beitrag zur Wagnerischen Harmonik.* Leipzig: Breitkopf & Härtel, 1914. xxxiv, 156pp. ML410.W19E8

Employing 169 well-chosen musical examples as well as an outmoded system of symbols for chords and intervals, Ergo discusses a number of fine points concerning Wagner's melodic lines, use of leading tones, modulations, dissonances, and so on. Examples drawn from other composers—but not, it seems, from Liszt—make comparisons clearer, and Wagner's place in the evolution of nineteenth-century musical practices more easily understood. Includes a list of subjects that doubles as both a table of contents and an index (pp. v–x).

Reprinted from issues of the *Bayreuther Blätter* (1907–1912); omitted from many standard bibliographies.

No study of Wagnerian harmony has exerted more influence than the following volume:

465. Kurth, Ernst. *Romantische Harmonik und ihre Krise in Wagners "Tristan,"* 2nd ed. Berlin: Max Hesse, 1923; reprinted Hildesheim: Georg Olms, 1968. x, 573pp. ML444.K9 1968

A groundbreaking study of functional harmony and its limitations published during the twentieth century. Kurth's argument—that in the famous "dissonance" that appears in the opening measures of the Prelude to *Tristan*, as well as in other features of this revolutionary music drama, Wagner in effect challenged the whole notion of tonality—is presented systematically and in great detail. Illustrated with some 345 musical examples of various kinds. Originally published by Paul Haupt (Berlin, 1920).

The following volume evaluates Kurth's discussion of Wagnerian harmony in light of the general history of Western musical theory:

466. Vogel, Martin. *Der Tristan-Akkord und die Krise der modernen Harmonie-Lehre.* Orpheus: Schriftenreihe zu Grundfragen der Musik, 2. Düsseldorf: Gesellschaft zur Förderung der systematischen Musikwissenschaft, 1962. 163pp. ML410.W19V6

Taking up where Kurth, Lorenz, and other important analysts of Wagner's harmonic innovations left off, Vogel considers much of the history of music theory in terms of the celebrated chord and ways of approaching its contents, resolutions, and key implications. Extensively illustrated with diagrams and musical examples of various kinds; concludes with a useful bibliography (pp. 153–59) and an index of names.

Three additional studies, described below in reverse chronological order of publication, deal with Wagner's use of individual keys in large-scale harmonic structures:

467. Petty, Jonathan Christian, and Marshall Tuttle. "The Genealogy of Chaos: Multiple Coherence in Wagnerian Music Drama." *Music & Letters* 79 (1998), pp. 72–98. ML5.M64

Considers key areas as significant in Wagner's psychomusical organizational scheme, together with such factors as Norse mythology, Greco-Roman influences, alchemical symbolism, and others in the *Ring,* and especially in terms of Alberic and the theft of the Rhinegold. "Through the complex network of mutually coherent imagery commanded by its central protagonist [i.e., Alberic], the associated keys of B-flat major, B-flat minor and G minor become characterized by means of a host of poetic entailments deriving from fire, Mars, Hades, spring and sulphur" (p. 98). Two musical examples.

468. Josephson, Nors S. "Tonale Strukturen im musikdramatischen Schaffen Richard Wagners." *Die Musikforschung* 32 (1979), pp. 141–49. ML5.M9437

Examines Wagner's music dramas from *Holländer* to *Tristan* in order to explain how the composer's use of keys helps hold large-scale musical structures together without interrupting dramatic actions. Josephson also demonstrates that Wagner assigned each character or "region" (geographical or ideological) in *Rheingold* a key in keeping with that work's overall harmonic form; in *Götterdämmerung,* on the other hand, Wagner assigned different keys to some of the same characters and "regions." Concludes by observing that these practices anticipate harmonic procedures in works by Debussy and Bartók, and in Stravinsky's *Sacre du printemps.* Includes two harmonic diagrams.

469. Blümer, Hans. *Über den Tonarten-Charakter bei Richard Wagner.* Dissertation: University of Munich, 1958. 25pp. ML410.W19B6

A pamphlet-length consideration of the circumstances in which Wagner employed various keys as principal tonality, temporary tonality, in modulatory passages, and so on, from *Holländer* to *Parsifal.* Detailed in its arguments, but outfitted with only 30 hand-copied and unnumbered music examples appended to its conclusion.

Instrumentation

470. Voss, Egon. *Studien zur Instrumentation Richard Wagners.* Studien zur Musikgeschichte des 19. Jahrhunderts, 24. Regensburg: Gustav Bosse, 1970. 343pp. ML410.W19V7

Less a study of particular passages—although many are mentioned—than of Wagner's use of individual instruments (flute, trumpet, harp, percussion, etc.), and of the roles they play in establishing or reinforcing musical structures. Voss also comments on books and articles that refer to Wagner as orchestrator, deals briefly with history of pre-Wagnerian orchestration, and explains Wagner's contributions to the modern symphonic ensemble. Also includes a brief bibliography (pp. 337–39); concludes with an index. Unfortunately, this volume contains no musical examples whatever; all musical passages and effects are described in prose.

Intervals

471. Brandhofe, Thomas. *Studien zu Intervallstruktur und Personalstil bei R. Wagner. Interdependenzen zwischen Wort- und Tonfeldern im "Ring des Nibelungen."* Dissertation: Wilhelms-University, Münster; 1987. 315pp. (no ISBN or LC numbers available)

A detailed discussion of Wagner's music dramas, and especially the *Ring,* in terms first of links between particular intervals and the scenes in which they are used, then of interval classes and longer passages of music. Brandhofe also discusses ways in which Wagner uses various intervals to set to music particular portions of the *Stabreim* he employs in his *Ring* librettos. Illustrated with a variety of diagrams and tables, several of them folded and bound into the volume itself, as well as with 21 musical examples (the latter pp. 303–15). No bibliography or index.

Leitmotive or "leading motives"

472. Dahlhaus, Carl. "Zur Geschichte der Leitmotivtechnik bei Wagner." In item 447, pp. 17–40 (including discussion).

A solid introduction to the origins and functions of *Leitmotive* in the composer's works. Beginning with *Holländer,* Dahlhaus demonstrates how Wagner gradually built up a system for employing "leading motifs" especially in the *Ring* but also—employing such motifs in different musical and dramatic manners—in *Lohengrin* and *Tristan.* Includes nine musical examples, as well as references to and quotations from several prose works dealing with the composer's musical-dramatic methodologies.

473. Rümenapp, Peter. "Hans von Wolzogen und Gottlieb Federlein—zwei Leitmotivexegeten der 'Ring des Nibelungen.' " *Acta Musicologica* 59/2 (July–December 1997), pp. 120–33. ML5.I6

Examines the analyses of *Leitmotive* by Wolzogen and Federlein published mostly in German periodicals of the 1870s, as well as in Wolgozen's influential books. Although long believed to have shared virtually the same outlook, Federlein and Wolzogen were—as Rümenapp concludes—rather different in their theoretical perspectives. Includes five short musical examples.

474. Stoll, Albrecht. "Richard Wagners Leitmotivtechnik im Lichte seiner Phonologie." In: *Studien zur Musikgeschichte: Eine Festschrift für Ludwig Finscher*, ed. Annegrit Laubenthal and Kara Kusan-Windweh. Kassel and New York: Bärenreiter, 1995; pp. 602–13. ISBN 3761812221 ML55.F49 1995

Evaluates Wagner's use of *Leitmotive* in light of the *Figurenlehre* practiced by eighteenth-century composers; Stoll also considers the construction of certain motifs in terms of the sounds of individual words and phrases. Includes eight musical examples drawn from *Tristan*, the *Ring*, and other music dramas.

Melody
475. Reckow, Fritz. "Zu Wagners Begriff der 'unendlichen Melodie.'" In item 447, pp. 81–110 (including discussion).

Less an analysis of individual tunes than a discussion of what Wagner wrote about the role and character of melody in his music dramas. Among other works and subjects, Reckow refers to *The Art-Work of the Future*, contemporary critical responses to Wagner performances, German-language studies of eighteenth- and nineteenth-century aesthetic issues, and quotations from the composer's letters. No musical examples.

Orchestral and Vocal Scoring: see also "Instrumentation"
Most studies of Wagner as orchestrator deal primarily or exclusively with one or at most two compositions; the following is an exception:

476. Burton, Jonathan. "Orchestration." In item 1, pp. 334–47.

Describes Wagner as "an extremely practical musician brought up in a tradition of serviceable if unexciting operatic instrumentation" (p. 334), before going on to consider his handling of bowed string instruments, harps, woodwinds, horns, "Wagner tubas," other brass instruments, and percussion as well as the Stierhörner (cow horns) used in *Walküre* and other music dramas, and the bells used in *Parsifal*. Concludes with brief comments on the influence of Wagner's orchestra for such "composers of later generations" (p. 346) as Bruckner, Debussy, Mahler, Ravel, Schoenberg, and Stravinsky. No musical examples. See also item 447.

A very few studies have been devoted to Wagner's writing for vocal ensembles; among them is:

477. Breig, Werner. "On the History of the Chorus in Wagner's Music-Dramas." *Programmhefte der Bayreuther Festspiele* VI (1989), pp. 33–45. ML410.W2B26

    Discusses aspects of Wagner's scoring for vocal ensembles, as well as his repudiation of the chorus in *Opera and Drama* and the consequent absence of choral music from the *Ring*. No musical examples. Another study that touches on the same issues is P. A. Galliard's "Le role du choeur dans l'oeuvre de Wagner," published in the *Schweizerische Musikzeitung* 99 (15 July 1959), pp. 263–66.

Programmism

478. Dahlhaus, Carl. "Wagner and Program Music," trans. Paul A. MacKenzie et al. *Studies in Romanticism* 9 (1970), pp. 3–20. PN751.S8

    Explains why Wagner disapproved of instrumental program music in general and Liszt's *Symphonic Poems* in particular, based on the composer's conviction, "to which he held all the more stubbornly because it was imaginary . . . [that,] since instrumental music in 'orchestral form' attained the goal of music drama for which its history strove, symphonic poetry was superfluous in a historico-philosophical sense" (p. 18). More a discussion of a romantic concept than an exercise in styles analysis; contains no musical examples. A similar article by Dahlhaus appeared in German in 1974 under the title "Wagner und die Programmusik" in the *Jahrbuch des Staatlichen Instituts für Musikforschung*.

Recitative

479. Nathan, Hans. *Das Rezitativ der Frühopern Richard Wagners (Ein Beitrag zur Stilistik des Opernrezitativs in der ersten Hälfte des 19. Jahrhunderts)*. Berlin: H. M. Dobrin, 1934. 79pp. ML410.W2N3

    Evaluates Wagner as a composer of more or less traditional operatic recitative in such works as *Die Feen*, *Rienzi*, and *Holländer*. Illustrated with 91 short musical examples; concludes with synopsis (pp. 76–8) and a one-page bibliography, but contains no other critical apparatus or visual illustrations. A published doctoral dissertation. Uncommon; the British Library owns a copy on microfilm. The LC number above comes from a University of Chicago copy.

Rhythm

480. Sommer, Antonius. *Die Komplikationen des musikalischen Rhythmus in den Bühnenwerken Richard Wagners.* Schriften zur Musik, 10. Giebing (Bavaria): Emil Katzbichler, 1971. 150pp. ML410.W19S55

Describes rhythmic complications at every level of Wagner's music dramas, from particular motifs and phrases to entire scenes. Illustrated lavishly with a variety of musical examples, some of them providing rhythmic information only; a list identifying the longer examples may be found at the very end of the volume. Also includes a brief bibliography (pp. 148–49).

"Symphonic" Organization and Style

481. Abbate, Carolyn. "Opera as Symphony: A Wagnerian Myth." In item 528, pp. 92–124.

Considers and ultimately rejects Wagner's many assertions, especially those made in *The Art-Work of the Future*, that his music dramas were musical fabrics woven of continuously spun-out melodic material. Abbate examines with special care the "Conspiracy Scene" in *Götterdämmerung*, act II, scene v, and demonstrates that its sectional structure, use of refrains, and repetition of textual statements are more characteristic of operatic than instrumental music. Includes facsimiles and musical examples.

* Kerman, Joseph. "Opera as Symphonic Poem." Described as item 979.

Structure and Form
No study of Wagner's musical methods has inspired more controversy than the multivolume work:

482. Lorenz, Alfred Ottokar. *Das Geheimnis der Form bei Richard Wagner*, 2nd "unaltered" ed. 4 vols. Berlin: Max Hesse, 1924–1933; reprinted Tutzing: Hans Scheider, 1966. ML410.W22L82 1966

Vol. 1: *Der musikalische Aufbau des Bühnenfestspieles Der Ring des Nibelungen*; x, 320pp.

Vol. 2: *Der musikalische Aufbau von Richard Wagners "Tristan und Isolde"*; viii, 203pp.

Vol. 3: *Der musikalische Aufbau von Richard Wagners "Die Meistersinger von Nürnberg"*; 195pp.

Vol. 4: *Der musikalische Aufbau von Richard Wagners "Parsifal"*; 211pp.

One of the most carefully argued, detailed, and remarkable dissections of Wagner's musical methodology. Lorenz's contention that the composer's music-dramas were organized systematically, symmetrically, and hierarchically into poetic-musical periods governed by such principles of design as poetic scansion, balanced melodic phrase pairs, bar forms, arch forms, rondo forms, and underlying harmonic relationships would seem to solve all problems—but by no means necessarily solves any of them. On the other hand, it is easier to ridicule Lorenz's analysis as a whole than altogether to refute certain of his contentions. Illustrated throughout with analytic diagrams and musical examples; Vols. 3–4 conclude with indexes.

See also Lorenz, "Über die musikalische Form von Richard Wagners Musikwerken," described under item 32.

Lorenz's ideas have called forth responses from a number of critics, including the following studies:

483. McClatchie, Stephen. *Analyzing Wagner's Operas: Alfred Lorenz and German Nationalist Ideology.* Rochester, NY: University of Rochester Press, 1998. xiii, 262pp. ISBN 1580460232 ML423.L637M33 1998

Deals not only with Lorenz's analytical paradigms, but also with their origins in his aesthetics, and especially in German nationalism. Considers systematically many of Lorenz's notions about simple, portential, and composite forms, including *Bogen* (arch), rondo/refrain, and *Bar* (i.e., AAB) forms, as well as the development of Lorenz's analytical methods. Two appendices summarize Lorenz's formal types (pp. 213–14), as well as the whole of his *Ring* analyses (pp. 215–32). Includes a first-rate bibliography (pp. 233–56) but no musical examples.

484. McClatchie, Stephen. "The Warrior Foil'd: Alfred Lorenz's Wagner Analyses." *Wagner* 11/1 (January 1990), pp. 3–12. ML410.W1A585

Advocates adopting a balanced historical perspective on Lorenz's work rather than merely praising him for his remarkable accomplishment or blaming him, as have most of his critics, for overlooking or ignoring so much in Wagner's complex scores. NB: McClatchie's books and articles are far from the only assessments of Lorenz's work available in print. Another is Egon Voss's "Once Again: The Secret of Form in Wagner's Works," published originally in *Theaterarbeit an Wagners Ring*, ed. Dietrich Mack (Munich, 1978), pp. 251–67, and reprinted in 1983 in *Wagner* (item 49) in English translation.

Other studies of Wagner's formal procedures are dealt with below in alphabetical order by author and/or title:

485. Brinkmann, Reinhold. ". . . einen Schluß machen!' Über externe Schlüße bei Wagner." In: *Festschrift Heinz Becker zum 60. Geburtstag am 26. Juni 1982*, ed. Jürgen Schläder and Reinhold Quandt. Laaber: Laaber Verlag, 1982; pp. 179–90. ISBN 3921518709 ML55.B32M

Devoted to problems associated with the conclusions of certain works, including *Lohengrin* and *Meistersinger*, especially in light of German nationalist issues. Brinkmann draws upon Wagner's prose drafts for both works to make his points.

486. Grey, Thomas S. "Wagner, the Overture, and the Aesthetics of Musical Form." *19th Century Music* 12 (1988–1989), pp. 3–22. ML1.N77

Traces Wagner's notions concerning instrumental music as recorded in his prose works of the 1840s to 1870s. Grey pays special attention to the composer's observations on overtures by Beethoven, Gluck, Mozart, and Weber; he also observes that some of Wagner's early instrumental compositions reflect a heterogeneous aesthetic tradition that predates the creation of conservative and New German musical parties. Illustrated with musical examples drawn from Beethoven's third *Leonora* overture and Wagner's overtures to *Holländer* and *Tannhäuser,* as well as two charts outlining the contents of the last two works in terms of passages identified by measure numbers, keys, and quotations from program notes Wagner wrote in March through April of 1852 for performances in Zurich.

Derived in part from item 883, as well as from Grey's dissertation, *Richard Wagner and the Aesthetics of Musical Form in the Mid-19th Century (1840–1860)* (University of California, Berkeley, 1988); the latter includes a useful bibliography (pp. 433–45).

487. Lewin, David. "Some Notes on Analyzing Wagner: The 'Ring' and 'Parsifal.' " *19th Century Music* 16 (1992–1993), pp. 49–58. ML1.N77

Approaches thematic aspects of Wagner's work—especially the "Valhalla" and "Tarnhelm" motives first presented in *Rheingold*, and the "Communion" and "Grail" motifs from *Parsifal*—from the perspective of Lewin's own *Generalized Musical Intervals and Transformations* (New Haven, 1987). Illustrated with five musical examples drawn from *Rheingold*, *Walküre*, and *Parsifal,* as well as with four diagrammatic tables.

488. Newcomb, Anthony. "The Birth of Music out of the Spirit of Drama: An Essay in Wagnerian Formal Analysis." *19th Century Music* 5 (1981–1982), pp. 38–66. ML1.N77

Considers the complex issues of form, key, and dramatic significance in three scenes from Wagner's mature music dramas, including act II, scene i, of *Walküre*. Seeking to go beyond the accomplishments of Dahlhaus, who chose "to ignore the tonal build of Wagner's [musical-dramatic] units" (p. 40), Newcomb examines various kinds of "shapes" as well as the "form-defining function of tonality" (p. 48) in the composer's works. Includes a useful list of sources cited (pp. 65–66), as well as four musical examples taken from act II, scene ii, of *Tristan* and act III, scene I, of *Siegfried*.

489. Newcomb, Anthony. "Ritornello Ritornato: A Variety of Wagnerian Refrain Form." In item 528, pp. 202–21.

Examines act II, scene i, of *Tristan* and act I, scene ii, of *Siegfried* in light of eighteenth-century ritornello form. Among other, closely related subjects, Newcomb considers Wagner's use of a baroque musical device in terms of the composer's attitudes toward Bach. Includes musical examples.

490. Prox, Lothar. *Structurale Komposition und Strukturanalyse: Ein Beitrag zur Wagnerforschung*. Kölner Beiträge zur Musikforschung, 112. Regensburg: Gustav Bosse, 1986. 218pp. ISBN 3764922273 ML410.W19P84 1986

Addresses general issues associated with analyzing formal elements in Wagner's music-dramas, together with a detailed study of Senta's ballad from *Holländer* (pp. 67–132); the last is supplemented with a few musical examples, as well as a diagram of pitch distributions in the ballad itself. Includes a superb bibliography of analytical source materials (pp. 183–218) but no index.

MUSICAL RELATIONSHIPS AND INFLUENCES

Survey Studies

Most of the books and articles devoted to Wagner's place in musical history deal primarily either with other composers that shaped his musical style, or with ways in which he influenced certain of his contemporaries and followers. Several broader-based studies are described below:

491. Dahlhaus, Carl. "Wagner's Place in the History of Music," trans. Alfred Clayton. In item 2, 99–117.

Considers Wagner's relationships to Brahms and the New German School, to Beethoven and the so-called symphonic style, to Lisztian thematic transformation and the evolution of Wagner's musical language, and to other nineteenth-century operatic and symphonic traditions. No musical examples. More comprehensive but less precise than Thomas Grey's "Musical Background and Influences" (item 1, pp. 64–92), which considers the formation of Wagner's "Earlier Style" as well as "The Music Drama and Its Antecedents" and "Patronage, Commissions and Royalties in Wagner's Day"—the last devoted to describing the music business in Germany between the Congress of Vienna and the composer's death in 1883. Grey also provides a useful list of the operas Wagner conducted in Würzburg, Leipzig, Nuremberg, Magdeburg, Berlin, Königsberg, Dresden, and Riga between 1833 and 1839 (pp. 69–70).

492. Lippman, Edward A. "The Formation of Wagner's Style." In *Music and Civilization: Essays in Honor of Paul Henry Lang*, ed. Edmond Strainchamps and Maria Rika Maniates, with Christopher Hatch. New York: W. W. Norton, 1984; pp. 102–116. ISBN 0393016773 ML55.L213 1984

Traces the composer's evolution as a composer from his earliest instrumental works to *Rheingold* and *Walküre*. Lippman emphasizes both the "community of style" (p. 116), which defined the basis of earlier nineteenth-century European music, and Wagner's individuality, which produced "an apparently endless series of radical innovations with a creative power that has rarely been equalled" in musical history (p. 102). Includes eleven musical examples, some of them multi-partite, drawn from Wagner's early music dramas, A-major Sonata, *Rienzi* overture, and "Dors, mon enfant," and from Beethoven's Sixth Symphony, Marschner's *Hans Heiling* and *Der Vampyr*, and Spohr's *Jessonda*.

Of interest to many researchers have been Wagner's "working relationships" with the compositions and careers of his contemporaries. Evaluations of these relationships include:

493. Grey, Thomas S. "Contemporary Composers." In item 1, pp. 170–73.

Summarizes Wagner's attitudes toward Bruckner, Marschner, Mendelssohn, Meyerbeer, Spohr, and especially Robert Schumann—the last "perhaps the least appreciated" Wagner contemporary (p. 172). Includes brief synopses of what is known concerning the composer's negative reactions to Bizet's *Carmen*, Gounod's *Roméo et Juliette*, and almost all of Brahms's works; Grey also refers to Wagner's preference for the "quieter, more reflective side" of Berlioz's and Liszt's output. No musical examples.

494. Klein, J. W. "Wagner and His Operatic Contemporaries." *Music & Letters* 9 (1928), pp. 59–66. ML5.M64

Epitomizes Wagner's attitudes toward a host of figures, including composers he once admired and later came to detest (Bellini, Halévy, Meyerbeer) and those he always detested (especially Gounod). Klein points out that Wagner did admire aspects of Bizet's *Carmen* and Auber's *Muette di Portici*. Lacks documentation as well as musical examples.

Of special interest has been the complex issue of Wagner's impact on Brahms and vice versa. Three studies of this subject are evaluated below in reverse chronological order of publication:

495. Wirth, Helmut. "Richard Wagner und Johannes Brahms." In: *Brahms und seine Zeit: Symposion Hamburg 1983,* ed. Peter Petersen = *Hamburger Jahrbuch für Musikwissenschaft* 7 (Laaber: Laaber-Verlag, 1984); pp. 147–57. ISBN 3890070183 ML5.H16 [=*Hamburger Jahrbücher* as a series]

Considers ways in which the two composers may have mutually influenced each other's works and styles. Wirth proposes that Wagner's *Faust* overture may have been a reaction to Brahms's *Tragic* overture; that thematic similarities can be detected between Brahms's Op. 5 Piano Sonata and Op. 100 Violin Sonata on the one hand, and Wagner's *Meistersinger* on the other; and that the *Wesendonck-Lieder* of Wagner and *Magelone-Lieder* of Brahms reflect their composers' respective reluctance to experiment with dramatic form and their desire for symphonic dialogue. Includes a half-dozen hand-copied musical examples drawn from most of these works, as well as Bruckner's Ninth Symphony.

496. Einstein, Alfred. "Brahms und Wagner auf gleichen Pfaden." In: Einstein, *Von Schütz bis Hindemith: Essays über Musik und Musiker*. Zurich and Stuttgart: Pan, 1957; pp. 99–104. ML60.E39

In large part a comparison of Wagner's "Marinari" Rossini arrangement with Brahms's arrangements of Schubert's "Geheimnis," "Memnon," and "An Schwager Kronos." Includes a single musical example, taken from Wagner's score. See also item 823.

497. Aldrich, Richard. "Wagner and Brahms on Each Other." In: *Musical Discourse from the "New York Times."* London: Oxford University Press, 1928; pp. 85–102. ML60.A4

A brief comparison of the two composers drawn largely from their own writings and reminiscences of them by their contemporaries, and assembled by one of America's foremost early twentieth-century music critics. Among Wagner's negative assessments of his Viennese contemporary is this one, on Brahms's First Symphony: "What had previously been dressed as quintets and the like, was now served up as symphony; little chips of melody, like an infusion of hay and old tea-leaves, with nothing to tell you what you are swallowing but the label 'best,' and all for the acquired taste of world-ache" (p. 92). No musical examples.

Another complex subject is Wagner's relationship with the so-called Neudeutsche Schule *(New German School), generally considered to have included Liszt and Berlioz, as well as Wagner himself and such less familiar figures as composers Peter Cornelius and Joachim Raff, and critic Franz Brendel.*
   Among discussions of Wagner and the New Germans are the following:

498. Gut, Serge. "Berlioz, Liszt und Wagner: Die französischen Komponisten der Neudeutschen Schule." In item 518, pp. 48–55.

An intelligent attempt to define New German music of the 1850s in terms of admiration for Beethoven's work, attitudes derived from French romanticism, a fascination with "advanced" harmonic practices, a fondness for musical programmism in instrumental compositions, and so on. Gut considers all three composers as having mutually influenced each other. Includes quotations from Wagner's correspondence but no musical examples.

499. Ramroth, Peter. *Robert Schumann und Richard Wagner im geschichtsphilosophischen Urteil von Franz Brendel.* Forschungen zur Musikgeschichte der Neuzeit, 1. Bern: Peter Lang, 1991. ii, 255pp. ISBN 3631438427 ML423.B76R3 1991

Another attempt to "define" Wagner *vis-à-vis* the New Germans. Ramroth's study emphasizes Wagner's place in the writings of Brendel, who succeeded Schumann as editor of the *Neue Zeitschrift* and is generally credited—not altogether accurately—with supporting the activities of Liszt, Wagner, and their contemporaries; Ramroth also discusses the influence of Hegel on Wagner and, more especially, on Brendel. A published dissertation.
   Reviewed with care by James Deaville in *Notes* 52 (1995–1996), pp. 441–44, who—in comparing Ramroth's work with Robert Determann's *Begriff und Ästhetik der "Neudeutschen Schule"* (Baden-Baden, 1989)—observes that the latter author does a better job of establishing Brendel's "sociopolitical motives" (review, p. 442) for supporting the New Germans; on the other hand, Ramroth's "may be a more valuable resource

because of its listings of Brendel's writings and letters and the insights of its aesthetic analysis" (review, p. 444).

Influences Exerted by Other Composers on Wagner

General Studies

Perhaps the best introductions to this considerable subject are the following surveys:

500. Laudon, Robert T. *Sources of the Wagnerian Synthesis: A Study of the Franco-German Tradition in 19th-Century Opera.* Musikwissenschaftliche Schriften, 2. Munich and Salzburg: Emil Katzbichler, 1979. 207pp. ISBN 3873971011 ML410.W13L35

Sets out to determine which "non- or pre-Wagnerian elements became integral parts of the Wagnerian musical synthesis" (p. 10), especially during the years 1830 to 1855. Laudon considers various stylistic components employed in various of his subject's music dramas—among them associations between motives and individual characters or situations, the primacy of harmony over melody in French dramatic music, and certain aspects of French and German orchestral scoring. Besides Wagner's works, Laudon refers to compositions by Cherubini, Gluck, Grétry, Rameau, Spontini, and others. Includes a large number of prose quotations as well as 135 hand-copied musical examples, an epilogue entitled "Wagner in France" (pp. 161–92) that considers *Wagnérisme* as a literary-cultural movement and Wagnerian aspects of Debussy's compositional output, and a bibliography (pp. 193–207).

501. *Richard Wagner und seine "Lehrmeister": Bericht der Tagung am Musikwissenschaftlichen Institut der Johannes-Gutenberg-Universität Mainz, 6./7. Juni 1997. Egon Voss zum 60. Geburtstag,* ed. Christoph-Hellmut Mahling and Kristina Pfarr. Schriften zur Musikwissenschaft, 2. Mainz: "Are," 1999. vii, 268pp. ISBN 3924522030 ML410.W13R47 1999

As the quotation marks in the title suggest, a collection of conference papers devoted to a variety of influences rather than discussions of Christian Gottlieb Müller and Theodor Weinlig, Wagner's real-life early music teachers. Includes "Wagner-and" essays about Bellini, Marschner, Rossini, Spontini, and Weber, as well as Klaus Hortschansky's "Wagner und Donizetti" (pp. 119–27), Reiner Nägele's "Der Wagner'sche Schwindel wird vorüberrauschen': Lindpaintners und Wagners Opernschaffen im Vergleich" (pp. 233–48), and Mathias Spohr's "Spuren des 'Fidelio' in

Wagners Opern" (pp. 81–93). Also includes scattered musical examples, as well as facsimiles of March to June 1855 concert programs (pp. 165–72), the last illustrating Christa Jost's "Wagner und Mendelssohn— Anmerkungen zu einem Zerrbild" (pp. 155–72). Concludes with an index. NB: Mahling's and Pfarr's volume should not be confused with an essay written by Deathridge and published in a Bayerische Staatsoper program in 1979.

502. Warrack, John. "The Musical Background." In item 31, pp. 85–112.

An introduction to musical influences on Wagner, including Beethoven's *Coriolan* overture, as well as such operas as Auber's *La Muette de Portici*, Lortzing's *Undine*, Spontini's *Fernand Cortez* and *La Vestale*, and Weber's *Der Freischütz* and *Oberon*. Warrack also mentions Liszt's influence and Berlioz's *Roméo et Juliette*. Includes fifteen short musical examples.

Other scholars have dealt exclusively with the influence of earlier operatic music on Wagner:

503. Redlich, Hans F. "Wagnerian Elements in pre-Wagnerian Opera." In: *Essays Presented to Egon Wellesz*, ed. Jack Westrup. Oxford: Clarendon, 1966; pp. 145–56. ML55.F662

Discusses Wagner's interest in and borrowings from Auber and other contemporary composers. Illustrated with nine mostly multi-partite musical examples drawn from *La Muette di Portici*, Marschner's *Hans Heiling*, Wagner's own *Tannhäuser*, and so on. According to Redlich, it was borrowings from *Hans Heiling* in *Tannhäuser* that "make it fairly obvious why Wagner preferred to be silent about Marschner's greatest work, while at the same time mentioning it critically in his autobiography" (p. 156). See also item 521.

504. Warrack, John. "The Influence of French Grand Opera on Wagner." In: *Music in Paris in the Eighteen-Thirties / La Musique à Paris dans les années mil huit cent trente*, ed. Peter Bloom. Musical Life in 19th-Century France, 4. Stuyvesant, NY: Pendragon, 1987; pp. 575–87. ISBN 0918728711 ML270.8.P2M76 1987

More on Wagner and Auber, Marschner, Scribe, and other important figures of early nineteenth-century Parisian musical life. According to Warrack, Wagner's "miserable years in the city served to disillusion him with the commerce of operatic intrigue, and to accelerate the process of growing away from French Grand Opera; it [*sic*] also helped to provide him with ideas and examples that were to bear fruit in his art till the end of his life" (p. 575). No musical examples.

At least one expert has tackled questions associated with the influence of "old music" in general on Wagner's works:

505. Geck, Martin. "Richard Wagner und die ältere Musik." In: *Die Ausbreitung des Historismus über die Musik*, ed. Walter Wiora. Regensburg: Emil Katzbichler, 1969; pp. 123–40. ML3797.1.F67A9

Less concerned with "older" compositional influences than Wagner's knowledge of and opinions about music history, German composers before Beethoven, Bach's "Well-Tempered Clavier," the works of Antonio Vivaldi, and concerts of "historical" music. No musical examples.

Specialized Studies
Unless otherwise specified, more general and/or newer studies are described before more specialized and/or older ones under each of the sub-headings below:

Johann Sebastian Bach
506. Dahlhaus, Carl. "Wagner and Bach." *Programmhefte der Bayreuther Festspiele* VII (1985), pp. 51–65. ML410.W2B26

Describes Wagner's early encounters with Bach, his opinions of certain Bach works—among them some of the preludes and fugues found in the *Wohltemperirtes Clavier*, as played to him by Liszt—and his use of counterpoint in *Meistersinger* (on this topic, see also item 462). According to Dahlhaus, Bach's influence on Wagner may have been considerable, especially when we remember that the *Leitmotive* in Wagner's orchestral writing " 'accrue' to the vocal line as an additional melodic element, even if the vocal line in question happens to be declamatory" (p. 51).

507. Geck, Martin. "Bach und Tristan: Musik aus dem Geist der Utopie." In: *Bach-Interpretationen. Walter Blankenburg zum 65. Geburtstag*, ed. Geck. Göttingen: Vandenhoeck & Ruprecht, 1979; pp. 190–96. MT90.B22G4

Considers similarities in Bach's and Wagner's musical works, including "endless melody," as well as differences in philosophical outlook—Wagner's Schopenhauerian pessimism, for example (exemplified in *Tristan*), as compared with Bach's Christian optimism (exemplified in the *St. Matthew Passion*, among other works)—and emotional orientation. Also published in English and French, as well as German in the *Programmhefte der Bayreuther Festspiele* I (1970), pp. 13–17 (English-language version).

NB: The phrase *Geist der Utopie* (spirit of Utopia) comes from the writings of composer Ernst Bloch, himself in certain respects an enthusiastic Wagnerian; see Dahlhaus's article "Ernst Blochs Philosophie der Musik Wagners," published in 1972 in the *Jahrbuch des Staatlichen Instituts für Musikforschung.*

Ludwig van Beethoven: see also item 583.
By far the most fulsome exploration of Beethoven's influence on Wagner is:

508. Kropfinger, Klaus. *Wagner and Beethoven: Richard Wagner's Reception of Beethoven*, trans. Peter Palmer. Cambridge and New York: Cambridge University Press, 1991. xi, 288pp. ISBN 0521342015 ML410.W19K9313 1991

     Considers Beethoven's influence on Wagner's compositions, literary works, conducting activities, and personal philosophy. Kropfinger employs 66 musical examples, many of them multi-partite, to illustrate his discussions of various musical works; he also provides an excellent bibliography (pp. 259–81), as well as indexes of names and subjects. Among the points for which Kropfinger has been praised are his identification of "textural and rhythmic correspondences" between the opening measures of Beethoven's Quartet, Op. 127, and the love scene in act II of *Tristan*, "O sink' hernieder, Nacht der Liebe."

     Reviewed by Thomas Grey in *Current Musicology* No. 52 (1993), pp. 89–99. Published originally as *Wagner und Beethoven: Untersuchungen zur Beethoven-Rezeption Richard Wagners* (Regensburg, 1975). Kropfinger's other Beethoven-Wagner studies include "Wagners Tristan und Beethovens Streichquartett op. 130. Funktion und Structuren der Einleitungswiederholung," in item 447, pp. 259–76.

Other studies of Wagner and Beethoven include the following articles, described in alphabetical order by author:

509. Grey, Thomas S. "The Beethoven Legacy." In item 1, pp. 151–53.

     Evaluates Wagner's "desire to be seen as the legitimate musical offspring" (p. 151) of an older and more venerated composer. Grey refers to Beethoven's purported early influence on Wagner, the role of the Ninth Symphony in Wagner's writings and career, the contents and character of Wagner's novella *A Pilgrimage to Beethoven*, and claims put forth in certain of the composer's prose works that Beethoven had served as "the progenitor of Wagner's motivic-melodic technique and thus a model for the concept of 'infinite melody' " (p. 153).

510. Knittel, Kristen Marta. "Wagner, Deafness, and the Reception of Beethoven's Late Style." *Journal of the American Musicological Society* 51 (1998), pp. 49–82. ML27.U5A83363

Analyzes Wagner's contribution to the widespread and "romanticized" belief that Beethoven's "late" works are his greatest, a belief not generally accepted prior to the middle of the nineteenth century. Knittel's conclusions are based in part on a discussion of Wagner's 1870 *Beethoven* essay, and notions that deafness itself "was in fact the source of Beethoven's creativity and genius" (p. 82). Illustrated with two musical examples taken from Beethoven's Quartets Opp. 132 and 135.

511. Schmid, Manfred Hermann. "Wagner und Beethoven—eine Blasphemie?" *Hudební veda* [Prague] 25 (1988), pp. 238–49. ML5.H845

Contradicts the notion that Wagner was inspired in the opening of *Tristan*, act II, by the "Nachtgesang" movement from Beethoven's Op. 127 String Quartet. On the other hand, according to Schmid, Wagner often invoked Beethoven as an authority. Includes Czech- and English-language summaries. Not seen; cited on-line.

Another study deals primarily with Beethoven's presence in Wagner's Bayreuth:

512. Ipser, Karl. *Beethoven—Wagner—Bayreuth.* Bayreuth: Lorenz Ellwanger, n.d. 115pp. (no LC number available)

A three-part survey of this fascinating subject: Part 1 examines Beethoven's influence on Wagner's music and thought; Part 2 deals with "Beethoven in Bayreuth," including performances of symphonic works during the nineteenth and twentieth centuries; Part 3 comprises the original text of Wagner's celebrated novella, *A Pilgrimage to Beethoven.* Illustrated with portraits of the two composers, facsimiles of pages from Wagner's works (including the title page of *Pilgrimage* in its first edition), Bayreuth concert and theatrical programs, and so on. No musical examples, however.

Hector Berlioz

513. Abraham, Gerald. "The Influence of Berlioz on Richard Wagner." *Music & Letters* 5 (1924), pp. 239–46. ML5.M64

A brief discussion of the personal and professional relationships that existed between these two composers, but primarily a consideration of elements—among them the use of *Leitmotive*, a very large orchestra, and *divisi* string parts—adapted from *Roméo et Juliette* by Wagner and used in *Tristan*. "Not even Beethoven himself exercised a deeper and more lasting influence on the development of musical aesthetics [than Berlioz] . . . one may say safely that without Berlioz there would have been no Wagner" (p. 239). Illustrated with five musical examples.

514. Cresti, Renzo. "Berlioz e Liszt guidano Wagner." *Ricerche musicale* 5 (March 1981), pp. 26–43. (no LC number available)

Examines Berlioz's influence on Wagner in terms of *Leitmotive*, orchestral color, and "architectural scope"; Cresti also differentiates between Wagner and Liszt in terms of their psychological relationships to poetic ideas and varieties of musical programmism. Not seen; cited in Langford's and Jane Graner's Berlioz research guide (see item 384).

One of many studies that touch, albeit in a cursory fashion, on issues of Wagner and his relationships to several of his predecessors and contemporaries; another, more fulsome study is Hans Gál's *Brahms, Wagner, Verdi: drei Meister, drei Welten* (Frankfurt a.M., 1975).

Johannes Brahms: see items 495–97.

Frederic Chopin
515. Breig, Werner. "Wagner und Chopin." In: *Deutsch-polnische Musik-beziehungen: Bericht über das wissenschaftliche Symposion im Rahmen der Internationalen Orgelwoche Nürnberg 1982*, ed. Wulf Konold. Munich and Salzburg: Emil Katzbichler, 1987; pp. 54–70. ISBN 3873972212 ML275.1.D5 1987

Indirectly contradicts Lazarov's thesis (see item 516) that Chopin may have influenced Wagner directly, even though Liszt may have been served as a stylistic intermediary. Breig also discusses similarities between Wagner and Chopin in terms of their harmonic innovations, as well as Wagner's respect during his latter years for Chopin's music.

516. Lazarov, Stefan. "Chopin-Wagner-Mahler." *Rocznik Chopinowski* [Warsaw] 7 (1965–1968), pp. 100–108. (no LC number available)

Traces melodic parallels in the works of the three composers and thus implies Chopin's possible influence on Wagner's style. Among the compositions considered in some detail are Chopin's Sonatas, Opp. 35 and 58, the Prelude to *Tristan*, and act II of *Walküre*. Includes musical examples.

Gäetano Donizetti: see item 501.

Christoph Willibald von Gluck: see also item 500.
517. Nohl, Ludwig. *Gluck und Wagner. Ueber die Entwicklung des Musikdramas.* Munich: Louis Finsterlin, 1870. viii, 368pp. ML1729.4.N8

Considers the evolution of opera and music drama in Europe during the later eighteenth and nineteenth centuries, with special reference to Beethoven (the volume is dedicated to his memory; see p. iii) and Wagner (see especially pp. 227–328). Gluck's influence on Berlioz, Wagner, and several other figures, however, is also discussed in some detail.

Franz Joseph Haydn: see item 203.

Franz Liszt
518. *Franz Liszt und Richard Wagner: Musikalische und geistesgeschichtliche Grundlagen der neudeutschen Schule* [Proceedings of the III. European Liszt Symposium], ed. Serge Gut. Liszt-Studien, 3. Munich and Salzburg: Emil Katzbichler, 1986. 210pp. ISBN 3873971933 ML410.L7E95 1986

Consists of item 498 above, as well as studies of Brendel's relationship to Wagner and Liszt (James Deaville, pp. 36–47), aspects of Liszt's oratorio *Die Legende von der heiligen Elisabeth* as compared with Wagner's *Tannhäuser* and *Lohengrin* (Frank Reinisch, pp. 128–51), the relationship of both composers to certain works of visual art (Walter Salmen, pp. 152–61), and so on. Includes scattered musical examples, both hand-copied and printed, as well as some impressive analytical charts and diagrams; unfortunately, Salmen's essay incorporates no visual images. As one might expect from the series in which it appeared, the bias is in favor of Liszt. Also includes endnotes instead of a single bibliography.

519. Winkler, Gerhard J. "Liszt und Wagner: Notizen zu einer problematischen Beziehung." *Österreichische Musikzeitschrift* 41 (1986), pp. 83–89. ML5.O1983

Evaluates problems associated with Liszt's artistic influence on Wagner and vice versa, including similarities between portions of Wagner's music dramas and Liszt's *Unstern* and *Am Grabe Richard Wagners.* Illustrated with several short musical examples, as well as a reproduction of Wilhelm Backmann's painting of Wagner "at home" at Wahnfried with Liszt, Cosima, and Wolzogen. The Liszt-Wagner relationship, musical and otherwise, is so complex that it has generated its own literature. Among the most famous celebrated contributions to it is Ernest Newman's *The Man Liszt: The Tragi-Comedy of a Soul Divided Against Itself* (London, FILL). See, too, much of item 301–303, 307, etc.

520. Gut, Serge. "De Liszt à Wagner en passant par "Parsifal'." *Revue musicale de Suisse Romande* 30 (1977), pp. 152–155. ML5.R64

Describes particular similarities between passages in *Parsifal* and Liszt's *Excelsior!* and *Am Grabe Richard Wagners*. One of several studies dealing with this subject; another is Arthur W. Marget's "Liszt and 'Parsifal,' " published in *The Music Review* 14 (1953), pp. 107–24.

Heinrich Marschner: see also item 501.
521. Abraham, Gerald. "Marschner and Wagner." In: Abraham, *Slavonic and Romantic Music: Essays and Studies*. London: Faber & Faber, 1968; pp. 251–55. ML300.A16S6

Summarizes Marschner's contributions to early nineteenth-century opera; also describes similarities between passages in his *Templer* and *Adolph von Nassau* and Wagner's *Holländer*, *Tannhäuser*, and *Lohengrin*. Abraham observes that "Marschner's harmony, with its chromaticism and free use of appoggiaturas, sometimes sounds what we are accustomed to call 'Wagnerian' " (p. 254). Includes three short musical examples from Marschner's scores. Originally published in the *Monthly Musical Record*.

Giaccomo Meyerbeer
522. Dahlhaus, Carl. "Wagner, Meyerbeer und der Fortschritt zur Opernästhetik des Vormärz." In *Festschrift Rudolf Elvers zum 60. Geburtstag*, ed. Ernst Herttrich and Hans Schneider. Tutzing: Hans Schneider, 1985; pp. 103–16. ISBN 3795204429 ML55.E48 1985

More than a review of Meyerbeer's influence on Wagner's music dramas; Dahlhaus also discusses ways in which the two composers dealt with melody, harmony, and counterpoint, and points out ways in which Wagner's obsession with certain elements in Germanic mythology paralleled European political issues especially of the late 1840s.

523. Keller, Walter. "From Meyerbeer's 'Robert le diable' to Act II of 'Parsifal.' " *Wagner* 13/2 (May 1992), pp. 83–90. ML410.W1A585

Deals with similarities between portions of Meyerbeer's opera and the storyline and musical events of Wagner's music drama. No examples, but Keller provides tables of similarities in plot and key schemes that link the two works. Published originally in German in the *Tribschener Blätter* No. 30 (December, 1971), pp. 6–12 (see item 53).

*   *Meyerbeer, Wagner: eine Begegnung.* Described as item 1107.

Wolfgang Amadeus Mozart
The best survey is:

524. Engel, Hans. "Richard Wagners Stellung zu Mozart." In: *Festschrift Wilhelm Fischer zum 70. Geburtstag überreicht im Mozartjahr 1956*, ed. Hans Zingerle. Innsbruck: Universität Innsbruck, 1956; pp. 39–48. ML55.F5Z5

Reviews Wagner's opinions of Mozart as composer and dramatist, drawn from Wagner's letters and theoretical writings. Engel briefly considers the attitudes of other nineteenth-century musicians, among them Berlioz, toward their eighteenth-century colleague; he also refers to Glasenapp's biography (item 305) and other secondary sources. One of many studies published in celebration of the bicentenary of Mozart's birth. No musical examples. See also items 793–94.

Gioacchino Rossini: see also item 501.
525. Voss, Egon. "Wagner and Rossini." *Programmhefte der Bayreuther Festspiele* II (1993), pp. 51–61. ML410.W2B26

Considers Rossini's possible influences on Wagner, a subject about which comparatively little has been written, and for which little evidence exists. Instead of dealing with general stylistic issues or specific borrowings from particular Rossini operas, however, Voss "document[s] and describe[s] Wagner's direct encounters with Rossini's works and person and his attempt to come to terms with them" (p. 51)—the latter especially in terms of *Tannhäuser* and *Lohengrin*. Available in the same volume in French and German.

Heinrich Schütz
526. Breig, Werner. "Schütz und Wagner. Musik und deutsche Sprache." *Jahrbuch Peters 1986/87* [*sic*] (Leipzig: C. F. Peters, 1988), pp. 67–79. ML1.D486

Compares two figures rarely considered in conjunction by musicologists. According to Breig, Wagner and Schütz shared an understanding of "the relationship between the sense of language and its sound (*Sprachklang und Sprachsinn*) fundamental to their music" (p. 75), and thus were careful to match the meanings behind the works they set to music with the sounds of the words themselves. No musical examples. Another study by Breig with the same title may be found in *Heinrich Schütz im Spannungsfeld seines und unseres Jahrhunderts*, Vol. 2 (Leipzig, 1987), pp. 67–79.

Gaspare Spontini: see also items 500–501.

527. Engel, Hans. "Wagner und Spontini." *Archiv für Musikwissenschaft* 12 (1950), pp. 167–177. ML5.A63

Summarizes Wagner's knowledge of Spontini's operas and evaluates his early indebtedness to a composer almost forty years older than himself. Illustrated with five multi-partite examples; using these, Engel compares aspects of such works as *Fernando Cortez* and *Rienzi*.

Giuseppe Verdi

528. *Analyzing Opera: Verdi and Wagner*, ed. Carolyn Abbate and Roger Parker. California Studies in 19th Century Music, 6. Berkeley and Los Angeles: University of California Press, 1989. ix, 304pp. ISBN 0520061578 MT95.A59 1989

A collection of essays that inevitably "pits" the two composers against each other, if only through discussions by various scholars of Wagner's and Verdi's individual compositional procedures and accomplishments. Includes items 481, 489, 640, and 738, as well as Patrick McCreless's article "Shenker and the Norns" (pp. 276–97), and studies of *Aïda*, *Ernani*, *Otello*, and *Rigoletto*. Especially enlightening is Abbate and Parker's introductory essay on analytical approaches to opera (pp. 1–24). Indexed; bibliographic references appear in the form of footnotes; concludes with an index. The proceedings of a conference held at Cornell University in 1984.

529. Dieckmann, Friedrich. *Wagner—Verdi. Geschichte einer Unbeziehung.* Berlin: Siedler, 1989. 95pp. ISBN 3886803465 ML410.W1O54 1989

Concerned with the Verdi-Wagner "relationship," but has comparatively little to say about particular musical passages or issues of stylistic influence. Other studies dealing with ways Verdi may have influenced Wagner or vice versa include Ursula Günther, "Wagnerismen in Verdis Don Carlos von 1867," published in item 33, pp. 101–8. Christian Springer's useful "Verdi und Wagner: Gegenseitige Einschätzungen," published in the *Österreichische Musikzeitschrift* 56 (2001), pp. 16–27, appeared too late to be described separately in the present research guide. See also item 568.

Carl Maria von Weber
530. Radice, Mark A. "Carl Maria von Weber: Forefather of Wagner." *The Music Review* 37 (1976), pp. 165–70. ML5.R657

Summarizes Weber's position as Wagner's predecessor in Dresden, and the influence of *Euryanthe* on Wagner's early operas. Most of the article, however, is devoted to a discussion of Weber's use of *Leitmotive*, which Radice claims anticipated Wagner's "easily recognizable yet versatile collection of intervals" (p. 169) in such works as the *Ring*. Illustrated with three musical examples taken from *Der Freischütz*, *Holländer*, and Flotow's *Martha*.

531. Kufferath, Maurice. "Weber et Wagner." *Société novelle* 7/1 (1891), pp. 322–30. (no LC number available)

Apparently an analysis of Weber's *Euryanthe* as the prototype of Wagner's *Lohengrin,* and a comparison of musical and dramatic elements in both works. Not seen; cited in Donald G. Henderson's *Carl Maria von Weber: A Guide to Research* (New York, 1990), p. 290.

Influences Exerted by Wagner on Other Composers

General Studies
Among introductions to and surveys of issues associated with Wagner and his "followers" is:

532. Weinland, Helmuth. *Richard Wagner zwischen Beethoven und Schönberg.* Musik-Konzepte, 59. Munich: "text+kritik," 1988. 113pp. ISBN 3883772801 ML410.W1W45 1988

A collection of three more or less interrelated essays, of which "Wagner zwischen Beethoven und Schoenberg" (pp. 73–113) deals with *Tristan*, Beethoven's Ninth Symphony, Schoenberg's *Kammersymphonie*, Op. 9, and other works in light of the "Thema-Leitmotiv-Grundreihe," a complex of musical methods and principles; also considers issues surrounding Wagner's "musical prose." In "Wagner und Meyerbeer" (pp. 31–72); on the other hand, Weinland discusses issues associated with *Rienzi*, *Holländer*, and Meyerbeer's *Les Huguenots*. The Schoenberg essay includes 27 musical examples, the Meyerbeer essay eleven. No illustrations, bibliography, or index. The volume as a whole opens with a discussion of "Wagner zwischen Hegel und Hitler" (pp. 3–30).

Additional surveys of this subject include the books and essays described below in alphabetical order by author and/or title:

533. Dahlhaus, Carl. "Wagner's Musical Influence," trans. Alfred Clayton. In item 2, pp. 547–62.

Among other composers influenced by Wagner, Dahlhaus refers to d'Albert (see item 546), Richard Strauss (see item 559), and Hugo Wolf (see items 562–64), as well as Emmanuel Chabrier, Friedrich Klose, Edouard Lalo, Hans Pfitzner, Alexander Scriabin, Stravinsky, and Bernd Alois Zimmermann. No musical examples, but Dahlhaus does discuss the work of music theorists, especially that of Kurth, as part of the twentieth-century Wagner reception.

534. *Ryszard Wagner a polska kultura muzyczna / Richard Wagner und die polnische Musikkultur.* Panstwowa Wyzsza Szkoła Muzyczna w Katowicach, 5. Katowice: "Bibliothek der Hochschule für Musik," 1964. 148pp. (no LC number available)

Includes articles by Karl Musioł on Wagner and Polish resistance to Russian forces in November 1831 (see also items 999 and 1080), as well as discussions of Chopin's possible influence on Wagner's harmonic language, Szymanowski's musical indebtedness to Wagner (see item 560), and important Polish Wagner performers, as well as a summary by M. Szewczyk-Skoczylas of the Polish Wagner literature (pp. 133–43). Includes scattered musical examples. In Polish and German with German-language abstracts. The proceedings of a conference held in November 1963 at Katowice's Conservatory of Music.

535. Vlad, Roman. "Wagner e la cultura musicale moderna." In item 999, pp. 1–30.

A useful survey of Wagner's influence on the likes of Debussy, Elgar, Stravinsky, and other prominent late nineteenth- and twentieth-century composers. Illustrated with 23 musical examples drawn from a variety of musical masterpieces.

536. Whittall, Arnold. "Wagner's Impact on the History of Music." In item 1, pp. 393–96.

Discusses Wagner's influence in general on "the birth of modernism" as well as Berg, Debussy (especially in *Pelléas et Mélisande*), Dvořák, Humperdinck (in *Hänsel und Gretel*), Schoenberg (especially in *Erwartung*), and Stravinsky (in *Le Sacre du printemps*); Whittall also refers to the Wagnerian enthusiasms of Luciano Berio (in *Un re in ascolto*), Benjamin Britten, Peter Maxwell Davies, Heinz Werner Henze (in Henze's *Tristan* for piano, tape recordings, and orchestra), and Robin

Holloway (in *Wagner Nights*). No musical examples. See also items 1000 and 1063.

Other studies of Wagner's influence are also described below in alphabetical order by author:

537. Budden, Julian. "Wagnerian Tendencies in Italian Opera." In: *Music and Theatre: Essays in Honour of Winton Dean*, ed. Nigel Fortune. Cambridge and New York: Cambridge University Press, 1987; pp. 299–332. ISBN 0521323487 ML55.D36 1987

Evaluates Wagner's influences on such figures as Alberto Franchetti, Ruggiero Leoncavallo, and Giaccomo Puccini. Singling out the last of these composers, Budden asserts that the composer of *La Bohème* and *Turandot* was "Wagner's best Italian pupil" (p. 332). Includes ten musical examples.

538. Hirsbrunner, Theo. "Richard Wagner's Influence on French Opera: Towards an Invisible Theatre." *Report of the Twelfth [International Musicological Society] Congress: Berkeley, 1977*, ed. Daniel Heartz and Bonnie Wade. Kassel and London: Bärenreiter (with the American Musicological Society), 1981; pp. 492–97. ISBN 33761806493 (no LC number available)

Considers "to what extent the French composers of the 'fin de siècle' copied the scenic aspects of Wagner's musical drama and to what degree they were able to grasp the intentions behind" those works (p. 493). Among the works Hirsbrunner discusses are: Chabrier's *Gwendoline*, Chausson's *Le Roi Artus*, d'Indy's *L'Etranger*, and Debussy's *Pelléas*. Includes a synopsis (p. 497) but no illustrations or musical examples.

539. Hirsbrunner, Theo. "Richard Wagners Musikdramen und ihr Fortwirken bei Debussy, Strauss, Schoenberg und Berg." In: *Gattungen der Musik und ihre Klassiker*, ed. Hermann Danuser. Laaber: Laaber-Verlag, 1988; pp. 271–85. ISBN 3890071147 ML55.G25 1988

Refers specifically to Wagnerian influences on Berg's *Wozzeck* and *Lulu*, Debussy's *Pelléas*, Schoenberg's *Erwartung* and *Die glückliche Hand*, and Strauss's *Salome* and *Elektra*. Hirsbrunner considers textual (i.e., declamatory) as well as harmonic and orchestrational similarities. He seeks in part to establish a "secular mythos" (p. 284) associated with dramatic music during and after Wagner's lifetime. No musical examples.

540. Indy, Vincent d'. *R. Wagner et son influences sur l'art musical français.* "Les grandes musicians par les maitres d'aujourd'hui," 1. Paris: Delagrave, 1930. 92pp. ML410.W12F695

In a series of chapters d'Indy examines the phenomenon of *Wagnérisme,* the Société nationale de musique, César Franck as a Wagnerian composer, and Wagner's influence on "modern" French music; d'Indy illustrates his observations with scattered musical examples, many of them melodies and motifs from *Lohengrin, Meistersinger,* and *Siegfried,* as well as works by Chabrier, Donizetti, Dukas, and especially Debussy's *Pelléas.* Includes a frontispiece woodblock portrait of Wagner, as well as ornamental woodblock chapter headings. No bibliography or index. See also item 1000.

541. Mosusova, Nadazda. "Richard Wagner und die russische Romantik." *Bericht über den internationalen musikwissenschaftlichen Kongress Berlin 1974,* ed. Hellmut Kühn and Peter Nitsche. Kassel and London: Bärenreiter, 1980; pp. 392–94. ISBN 3761805926 ML36.I629 1974

Refers to Wagner's influence on Rimsky-Korsakov, Skriabin, and other Russian composers, as well as critics such as Stasov and musical performances at St. Petersburg's Marionette Theater. Unfortunately, too brief to be of more than passing interest. No musical examples.

Specialized Studies
Again, unless otherwise specified, more general and/or more recent studies are described before more specialized and/or older ones under each of the following subheadings:

Eugen d'Albert
542. Williamson, John. "Eugen d'Albert: Wagner and 'Verismo.'" *Music Review* 45 (1984), pp. 26–46. ML5.M657

Describes "the precise extent of d'Albert's attempt to wed contemporary Italian trends especially in libretto content to post-Wagnerian music drama" (p. 26). Employs twelve musical examples, most of them from such operas as *Tiefland* and *Kain,* illustrating d'Albert's enthusiasm both for Wagner's dramatic works and *verismo* storytelling; for Williamson, *Kain* constitutes a veritable "Wagnerian survey from King Henry to Klingsor" (p. 33).

Béla Bartók
543. Bónis, Ferenc. "Bartók und Wagner. Paul Sacher zum 75. Geburtstag." *Österreichische Musikzeitschrift* 36 (1981), pp. 134–47. ML5.O1983

A study of Wagner's influence on Bartók as a student composer, especially between the summer of 1907 and early 1908, as well as Wagnerian elements in the Hungarian composer's First Violin Concerto, *Bluebeard's Castle*, and—to a lesser extent—*The Wooden Prince*. Includes twelve musical examples, a photograph of Bartók taken in 1930, and a facsimile page of motives from *Walküre* Bartók prepared for his own use.

Similar articles by Bónis appeared in the 1979 *Programmhefte der Bayreuther Festspiele*; and the *New Hungarian Quarterly* 10/34 (Summer 1969), pp. 201–9. The latter, in English, covers Bartók's lifelong involvement with Wagner—an involvement that began when Bartók heard some of Wagner's works in 1891, and that seems to have ended in 1936 with comments the Hungarian composer made in an article on Wagner's father-in-law Liszt. Includes four musical examples, two of them full-page, from *Lohengrin, Rheingold, Bluebeard's Castle,* and *The Wooden Prince.*

Alban Berg

544. Baragwanath, Nicholas. "Alban Berg, Richard Wagner, and Leitmotifs of Symmetry." *19th-Century Music* 23 (1999–2000), pp. 62–83. ML1.N77

Explains that Berg, who revered Wagner throughout his life, may have derived some of his innovative compositional procedures from *Tristan* and the *Ring*, including procedures involving symmetrical properties of some intervallic cycles. Includes sixteen musical examples drawn from Wagner's music dramas, especially *Tristan* and *Götterdämmerung*, as well as Berg's *Lulu*.

Georges Bizet

545. Klein, John W. "Bizet and Wagner." *The Musical Quarterly* 28 (1947), pp. 50–62. ML5.M725

Considers why Bizet—whom Klein calls "the simplest, the most melodious, surely the least Teutonic" of Wagner's French contemporaries—should have "won the epithet of 'fanatical Wagnerite' very early in his career" (p. 50). Klein also demonstrates certain affinities between the two composers. No musical examples.

Anton Bruckner

546. *Bruckner Symposion. Bruckner, Wagner und die Neudeutschen in Österreich, im Rahmen des Internationalen Brucknerfestes Linz 1984*, ed. Othmar Wessely. Linz: Anton Bruckner-Institut, 1986. 224pp. ISBN 3900270198 ML36.B78 1988

Among the contents of this volume—itself the proceedings of a symposium held in 1984 at Linz, Austria—are Theophil Antonicek's "Wagner,

Bruckner und die Wiener Musikwissenschaft" (pp. 71–80), Rudolf Flotzinger's "Bruckner—Hausegger—Wagner" (pp. 201–10), Gerda Lechleitner's "Bruckner—Wagner: ein meßbarer Unterschied: Betrachtungen zur Instrumentation in Melodie und Begleitung" (pp. 123–48), and Rudolf Stephan's "Bruckner—Wagner" (pp. 59–66). Also contains essays touching on the *Neudeutsche Schule*, Liszt, and Wolf. Scattered musical examples accompany several of the articles, and Lechleitner's also contains diagrams of sound patterns recorded during performances of both Wagner's and Bruckner's works. Concludes with an index.

Claude Debussy

547. Holloway, Robin. *Debussy and Wagner*. London: Eulenberg Books, 1979. 235pp. ISBN 0903873257 ML410.D28H6

Examines the younger French composer's ambiguous reaction to the older German's influence on late nineteenth-century music. For Debussy, Holloway asserts, Wagner was "the old" in terms of musical tradition and "the old in him [Debussy] . . . his Wagnerian content" (p. 235). Includes several dozen musical examples drawn primarily from *Tristan, Parsifal, Pelléas*, and *Jeux*—the last possibly Debussy's most Wagnerian composition.

Reviewed positively in *Notes* 38 (1980–1981), pp. 587–88, as well as by William F. Austin at length ("Viewpoint: Debussy, Wagner, and Some Others") in *19th Century Music* 6 (1982–1983), pp. 82–91; Austin considers especially Wagner's and Debussy's influence on Holloway's own compositions.

548. Hirsbrunner, Theo. "Wagner and Debussy." *Programmhefte der Bayreuther Festspiele* III (1985), pp. 47–54, 63; and IV (1985), pp. 48–54 and 61–63. ML410.W2B26

Tackles Wagner's influence on a composer unwilling always to acknowledge that influence, yet also unable—and, often, unwilling—to shake it off. Among other subjects Hirsburnner deals with Wagnerian elements in Debussy's only opera, *Pelléas et Mélisande*, and with the years (1885–1887) Debussy spent in Rome, during which he succumbed "so completely" to Wagner's spell "that he was able to compose very little" (III, p. 47). Also available in the same Programmhefte in German and French.

549. Abbate, Carolyn. " 'Tristan' in the Composition of 'Pelléas.' " *19th Century Music* 5 (1981), pp. 117–41. ML1.N77

Mostly devoted to an examination of certain Debussy manuscripts and what their contents tell us about the evolution of that composer's only completed opera. Abbate also comments on Wagner quotations in *Pelléas* in general, as well as on that opera's act IV, scene iv; it is in that scene, she observes, "where no great overt mimicry of Wagner is discernible on the surface," that Debussy's music "is most nearly parallel to Wagner's *Tristan* on other levels" (p. 136). Includes nine examples, most of them drawn from Debussy's sketches and drafts, as well as four tables and a documentary facsimile.

Antonín Dvořák

550. Vysloužil, Jiří. "Dvořák and Wagner." *Programmhefte der Bayreuther Festspiele* II (1989), pp. 48–54 and 61. ML410.W2B26

Identifies and briefly evaluates Wagner's influence on the musical style of later-nineteenth-century Bohemia's foremost composer. Vysloužil mentions that, after 1865, Dvořák's "sonata-like works, symphonies and chamber music" came to display "features of Wagnerian and Lisztian 'tonality' " (p. 49), and that Dvořák was also influenced by Czech Wagnerianism, a movement launched by the first performance of Bedřich Smetana's heroic opera *Dalibor* in 1868. Also available in German and French in the same volume.

Among Vysloužil's Wagner-Dvořák publications is "Zwischen 'Wagnerianismus' and 'Smetanianismus'?"; see also Markéta Hallová's "Wagner-Smetana-Dvořák," and Eliska Holubová's "Der Einfluss des Wagnerischen Musikdramas auf die Oper 'Rusalka' von Dvořák." All three articles appear in *Musical Dramatic Works by Antonín Dvořák*, ed. Hallová et al (Prague, 1989), pp. 124–28, 13–20, and 109–13 (respectively).

Edward Elgar

551. Dennison, Peter. "Elgar and Wagner." *Music & Letters* 66 (1985), pp. 93–109. ML5.M64

Describes the enthusiasm on Elgar's part that inspired him to conduct a Wagner memorial concert in London in 1883, and to pay several visits to Bayreuth. Drawing upon eleven mostly multi-partite musical examples, Dennison also discusses portions of *The Dream of Gerontius, Caractacus,* and *The Black Knight,* as well as *Tristan, Meistersinger,* and other of Wagner's music dramas. Includes an appendix listing all of Wagner's works performed by Elgar (pp. 108–9).

Franz Liszt

552. Hirschmann, Ursula. "Die Wagner-Bearbeitungen Franz Liszts." In item 871, pp. 103–22.

Mostly concerned with what Liszt did in keyboard terms to those portions of Wagner's music dramas he arranged in inimitable style for piano. Illustrated with musical examples. See also Sigfrid Schibli's "Richard Wagner/Franz Liszt: Isolde's Liebestod" in the *Neue Zeitschrift für Musik* 146/9 (September 1985), pp. 28–30, which treats of Wagner's "Love-Death" music and Liszt's keyboard transcription of it.

Gustav Mahler: see items 476 and 556.

Jules Massanet

553. Huebner, Steven. "Massanet and Wagner: Bridling the Influence." *Cambridge Opera Journal* 5 (1993), pp. 223–38. (no LC number available)

Compares Wagner's musical methods in *Walküre* and other works, among them his use of *Leitmotive*, with certain aspects of Massanet's *Werther* and *Esclarmonde* in order to defend the thesis that the French composer and his contemporaries often "sacrificed native qualities in vain, sterile imitations" of their German contemporary (p. 223). Huebner also discusses Goethe's *Werther* as a fitting operatic subject. Includes seven musical examples drawn from both composers' works.

Mihalovich Ödön

554. Szerző, Katalin. "Mihalovich Ödön: 'Wieland der Schmied.' Der Versuch einen ungarischen Typus des Wagnerischen Musikdramas zu Schaffen." In: *Musica Conservata: Günter Brosche zum 60. Geburtstag*, ed. Josef Gmeiner et al. Tutzing: Hans Schneider, 1999; pp. 407–31. ISBN 3795209714 ML55.B78 1999

A study of similarities between Wagner's aborted *Wieland* and the opera Ödön composed from 1876 to 1878. Szerző pays special attention to aspects of Ödön's manuscript, preserved today in the collections of the Liszt Ferenc Memorial Museum and Research Centre, Budapest. Illustrated with thirteen musical examples.

Arnold Schoenberg

555. Brown, Julie. "Schoenberg's Early Wagnerisms: Atonality and the Redemption of Ahasuerus." *Cambridge Opera Journal* 6 (1994), pp. 51–80. ISSN 0954-5867 (no LC number available)

A study of Wagner's influence on the young Schoenberg, and especially his *Book of the Hanging Gardens*. Brown seasons her study with references to that composer's semitic origins—hence the phrase "redemption of Ahaseurus," one Wagner himself employed in his anti-semitic writings to suggest Jews "purging" themselves of their Jewish characters—as well as observations on the evolution of Schoenberg's musical style. Illustrated with a single musical example as well as five reproductions of Schoenberg self-portraits.

556. Breig, Werner. "Schönberg und Wagner: Die Krise um 1910." In: *Die Wiener Schule in der Musikgeschichte des 20. Jahrhunderts*, ed. Rudolf Stephan and Sigrid Wiesmann. Publicationen der Internationalen Schönberg-Gesellschaft, 2. Vienna: Lafite, 1986; pp. 42–48. ISBN 3851510356 ML410.S283I57 1984

Deals with Schoenberg's changing attitudes toward his predecessor, which seem to have coincided with changes in the younger man's compositional style. In 1910, as Breig explains, Schoenberg temporarily rejected Wagner because of the latter's assertions about preparing, modifying, and thus "softening" dissonances. Other studies also mention Wagner's influence on both Schoenberg and Mahler; see, for instance, Hermann Danuser's intriguing "Musical Manifestations of the End in Wagner and in Post-Wagnerian 'Weltanschauungsmusik,' " published in *19th-Century Music* 18 (1994–1995), pp. 64–82, which includes references to the *Guerrelieder* and *Das Lied von der Erde*. See also item 941.

Jean Sibelius

557. Tarasti, Eero, "Sibelius and Wagner." In: *The Wagner Companion*, ed. Glenda Dawn Goss. Westport, CT: Greenwood, 1996; pp. 61–75. ISBN 0313283931 ML410.S54S53

Evaluates biographical and stylistic links between Wagner and Sibelius, especially in terms of the latter's *Kullervo* and Fourth Symphony, and reviews more briefly the Wagner reception in Finland. According to Tarasti, Sibelius reveals his debt to Wagner in certain aspects of his harmonic language, orchestration, and sense of musical timing; for a variety of reasons these facts have been played down by most Finnish students of Sibelius's music. Includes eight musical examples, as well as a facsimile of a letter Sibelius addressed to his father Aino Sibelius on 19 July 1894. Revised and expanded from the author's "Sibelius et Wagner," published in *Boréales: Revue du center de recherches inter-nordiques* 54/57 (1993), pp. 89–102.

558. Tarasti, Eero. Chapter 8 of *Music and Myth: A Semiotic Approach to the Aesthetics of Myth in Music, Especially That of Wagner, Sibelius and Stravinsky*. Acta Musicologica Fennica, 11. Helsinki: Suomen Musiikkitieteellinen Seura, 1978; pp. 178–222. ISBN 9027979189 ML3849.T37

Entitled "Wagner's 'Siegfried,' " the chapter in question deals instead with mythic elements in the *Ring* as a whole, as well as other of the composer's music dramas, including *Tristan*. In subsequent chapters Tarasti goes on to apply similar analytical techniques (references to *topoi*, *Leitmotive*, etc.) to works by Sibelius—especially *Kullervo*—and, eventually, to those of Stravinsky (*Oedipus Rex*) and Prokofieff; implied but not always elucidated is Tarasti's assumption that Wagner and Liszt both influenced Sibelius and other later composers through their use of topics, motifs, and methods of musical narration. Includes unnumbered musical examples of various kinds, some of them difficult to read in this photo-offset volume, as well as a few tables, diagrams, and other guides to Tarasti's semiotic vocabulary and working methods.

Richard Strauss

559. Wajemann, Heiner. "Die Einflüsse: Brahms, Liszt, Wagner, Mozart, und andere." *Richard Strauss-Blätter* No. 43 (June 2000), pp. 149–78. ML410.S93R46

Considers, among other subjects, Wagner's influence on Strauss's harmonies, orchestral effects, and operas. Includes a variety of musical examples as well as analytical charts and diagrams. Others concentrate on individual works; consider, for instance, Charles Dowell Youmans's dissertation *Richard Strauss's "Guntram" and the Dismantling of Wagnerian Musical Metaphysics* (Duke University, 1996), which reveals Wagnerian aspects of Strauss's first opera—and Strauss's implicit criticism of some Wagnerian procedures—as well as the working out in *Guntram* of philosophical premises derived from Schopenhauer's *World as Will and Idea*.

Igor Stravinsky: see items 468, 476, 533, 535–36, and 558.

Karol Szymanowski

560. Downes, Stephen C. *Szymanowski as Post-Wagnerian: The "Love Songs of Hafiz," Op. 24.* New York and London: Garland, 1994. ix, 364pp. ISBN 0815316348 ML410.S99O7

"Blending ideas drawn from Schenker, Schoenberg, and Kurth" (p. vii), Downes examines various musical and philosophical influences—Nietzsche's, Schopenhauer's, and Mahler's as well as Wagner's—on Szymanowski's music in general, and the *Love Songs* in particular. Outfitted with analytical diagrams, a few facsimiles of concert programs and manuscript pages, and dozens of additional musical examples. Includes notes at the end of each chapter, as well as an extensive and specialized bibliography (pp. 327–56); concludes with an index. Revised from a dissertation completed at Goldsmiths College, London, in 1992.

Peter Ilich Tchaikovsky
561. "Cajkovskijs Wagner-Rezeption—Daten und Texte," ed. Thomas Kohlhase. *Tschaikowsky-Gesellschaft* [Bulletin] No. 4 (March 1997), pp. 70–96. (no LC number available)

Not seen; briefly summarized in several on-line catalogs. According to these sources, Kohlhase's collection of documents also constitutes a review of the works of the two composers in relation to each other, as well as Wagner references in Tchaikovsky's correspondence. May not be in German throughout.

Hugo Wolf
562. Glauert, Amanda. *Hugo Wolf and the Wagnerian Inheritance.* Cambridge and New York: Cambridge University Press, 1998. vii, 161pp. ISBN 0521496373 ML410.W8G53

Evaluates Wolf's music criticism and many of his compositions in light of his mixed reaction to Wagner and Wagnerism; Glauert writes that Wolf was "both drawn [to] and repelled [by]" (p. 3) his predecessor's compositions and theories, as well as works of Mahler and Richard Strauss. Supplemented with quotations from a variety of sources, including Wagner's librettos, as well as a large number of whole-page musical examples. Concludes with a brief bibliography (pp. 157–59) and index.

See also Frank Walker, "Hugo Wolf's Vienna Diary, 1875–76," in *Music & Letters* 28 (1947), pp. 12–24, which considers Wagnerian aspects of a manuscript owned by the Wiener Stadtbibliothek and includes the texts of three notices copied by Wolf from the *Neue freie Presse.*

563. Heckel, Karl. *Hugo Wolf in seinen Verhältnis zu Richard Wagner.* Munich and Leipzig: G. Müller, 1905. 19pp. ML410.W8H26

Suggests that Wolf's nature as a composer was antagonistic to Wagner's; also suggests that the younger composer's charm, wit, and irony were unique, but his ability to convey pathos was inferior to Wagner's. Includes quotations from Wolf's correspondence with the author and a frontispiece photograph of Wolf but no musical examples. Heckel, incidentally, was a close associate of Wolf's, and later published *Corregidor* and other works. Reprinted from a June 1905 issue of the *Süddeutsche Monatshefte.*

564. Mennuti, Luisa. "Due atteggiamenti verso la parola: la declamazione da Wagner a Wolf." *Rivista Italiana de musicologia* 18 (1982), pp. 285–302. (no LC number available)

Describes Wagner's musical declamation as an expression of dramatic ideas rather than metric phenomena, then compares Wagner's methods with those of Wolf, who used music to emphasize poetic characteristics that could not adequately be expressed through spoken words. Includes musical examples from and/or descriptions of passages pertaining to Schubert's *Winterreise*, "Gretchen am Spinnrade," and "Mignon."

Related Studies
The following examination of Wagner's influence on movie music is merely one of several studies devoted to "Wagner and Film"; additional studies are dealt with at the end of chapter IX:

565. Huckvale, David. "Wagner and the Mythology of Film Music." *Wagner* 9/2 (April 1988), pp. 46–67. ML410.W1A585

Primarily a discussion of film as ritual, and of film music employed in support of "images and texts" (p. 46). Huckvale comments on the theories of Tarasti, Cooke, and other aestheticians willing to consider extra-musical or "semiotic" aspects of music; unfortunately, he makes little effort to take a variety of cultural circumstances into account in his search for a morphology of musical "meaning." Among other works mentioned are "Siegfried's Funeral Music" from *Götterdämmerung,* and John Williams's score for *Close Encounters of the Third Kind*; unfortunately, Huckvale does not attempt a catalog of Wagnerian moments in other movies. Includes 21 musical examples.

VII

Wagner as Music Dramatist

SURVEY STUDIES

No composer, not even Mozart, has won more acclaim for his musical dramatic creations than Wagner. In these works—ranging from the more traditionally operatic Rienzi *and* Der fliegende Holländer *through the innovative* Tannhäuser *and* Lohengrin *to such mature masterpieces as* Die Meistersinger, Parsifal, Tristan und Isolde, *and the massive four-part* Ring des Nibelungen—*Wagner displayed his genius as both composer and dramatist; it is finally impossible (and mostly unwise) to consider his words apart from his music.*

Two collections of overwhelming importance present most of Wagner's musical legacy:

*   *Richard Wagner. Sämtliche Werke*; and *Richard Wagners musikalische Werke*. Described as items 156–57.

    Although these editions remain incomplete, they contain virtually everything ever composed or arranged by Wagner.

The studies described below deal with Wagner's musical-dramatic output as a whole. Among them are two comprehensive surveys:

566. Dahlhaus, Carl. *Richard Wagner's Music Dramas*, trans. Mary Whittall. Cambridge and New York: Cambridge University Press, 1979. 161pp. ISBN 0521223970 ML410.W13D153

    Perhaps the best short introduction to Wagner's stage works from *Holländer* to *Parsifal*. Taking his lead from Paul Bekker, whose 1924 Wagner biography (item 317) proposed to "illuminate the life [in terms of] the work" rather than the other way round (item 317, p. 2), Dahlhaus shows how each music drama functions as a composition, and how certain aspects of it may better be understood in terms of Wagner's polemical books and articles. Illustrated, with quotations in German and English from Wagner's libretti, as well as other of his literary works; most chapters also include musical examples. Concludes with "The Works in the Theatre" (pp. 156–61), which considers the impact of Bayreuth traditions on Wagner performances and reception. No bibliography or index.

Originally published as *Richard Wagners Musikdramen* (Hildesheim 1971). A paperback edition of the English translation appeared in 1992. See also chapter I of the present research guide.

567. *Wagner and His Operas*, ed. Stanley Sadie. New York and London: St. Martin's and Macmillan, 2000. xv, 219pp. ISBN 0333790219 ML410.W1W34 2000

Primarily an anthology devoted to Wagner's works from *Die Feen* to *Parsifal*, and one that includes contributions by Barry Millington, Geoffrey Skelton, John Warrack, and Arnold Whittall, although Sadie's volume also contains chapters devoted to Bayreuth, *Leitmotive*, and so on, as well as a chronology of Wagner's life and activities (pp. xiii–xv), an introductory essay, and sketches of the lives of a host of early Wagnerian interpreters including Hans von Bülow, Hermann Levi, and Albert Niemann. Illustrated in part with short musical examples, mostly motivic, and with eight plates of pictures; concludes with a glossary and an index of role names (pp. 213–14).

Additional surveys of Wagner's operas and music dramas include the volumes described below in alphabetical order by author:

568. Gilman, Lawrence. *Wagner's Operas*. New York: Farrar & Rinehart, 1937. xix, 268pp. ML410.W1G3

Discusses the stage works from *Holländer* to *Parsifal*. Includes an introductory chapter entitled "Wagner and the Present Day" (pp. 3–21), written from Gilman's perspective as an American music critic; also includes an appendix devoted to "A Note on Wagner's Motives" (i.e., *Leitmotive*, pp. 257–68). Especially interesting, perhaps, for students of the American Wagner reception. Includes a frontispiece photograph of Wagner, taken in London in 1877, but no musical examples or bibliography. Unindexed. *Phases of Modern Music*, another of Gilman's volumes (New York and London, 1904), contains essays entitled "Verdi and Wagner: An Inquiry" and " 'Parsifal' and Its Significance."

569. Newman, Ernest. *The Wagner Operas*. New York: Alfred A. Knopf, 1949; reprinted Princeton, NJ: Princeton University Press, 1991. xii, 729pp. ISBN 0691027161 MT100.W2N53 1991

Deals with Wagner's dramatic works from *Holländer* to *Parsifal*. In discussing each work in turn Newman quotes from Wagner's poetry and prose, as well as a host of supplementary sources; he also employs a large number of musical examples to make his points. Includes as a frontispiece the familiar photograph of Wagner taken by von Gran in 1883, as well as footnotes and an index.

Published in England under the title *Wagner Nights* (London, 1949). Also available as *The Wagner Operas* in a two-volume paperback edition printed by Harper & Row (New York, 1983).

570. Osborne, Charles. *The Complete Operas of Richard Wagner.* London: Michael O'Mara, 1990; reprinted North Pomfret, VT: "Trafalgar Square," 1991; reprinted again New York: Da Capo, 1993. 288pp. ISBN 1854790110 [original edition] ML410.W13O8 1993

Another survey, this one spanning *Die Feen* to *Parsifal*. Each chapter includes background material on one work's origins, its place in Wagner's output, its plot, and so on. In all includes 37 musical examples, but none accompanies Osborne's discussions of *Die Feen* and *Liebesverbot*, and only one appears in his chapter on *Rienzi*. Also includes a scattering of Wagner family portraits and photographs, as well as stage sets or scenes from the 1842 Dresden *Rienzi* premiere, the 1982 Covent Garden *Meistersinger*, Josef Hoffmann's 1876 design for *Walküre*, act I, and so on. No bibliography; concludes with an index. Similar in many respects to Osborne's more lavishly illustrated *World Theatre of Wagner: A Celebration of 150 Years of Wagner Productions* (Oxford, 1982), which includes an introduction by Sir Colin Davis as well as a "Biographical Dictionary" (pp. 193–220) and index.

571. Rappl, Erich. *Wagner-Opernführer.* Regensburg: Gustav Bosse, 1967. 179pp. MT100.W2R4

One of a number of guide books devoted to the "whole" of Wagner's musical-dramatic output (i.e., *Holländer* to *Parsifal*) and illustrated with a large number of short musical examples, most of them motivic in character. Useful to beginners, perhaps, but too cursory for more experienced researchers.

*   Stein, Jack M. *Richard Wagner and the Synthesis of the Arts.* Described as item 894.

Includes chapters on each of the operas and music dramas from *Rienzi* to *Parsifal*, most of them outfitted with musical examples.

Older but nevertheless valuable studies of the music dramas include:

572. Krehbiel, Henry Edward. *Studies in the Wagnerian Drama*, rev. ed. London: James R. Osgood, McIlvaine & Co., 1893; reprinted Brooklyn, NY: Haskell House, 1977. viii, 197pp. ISBN 0838321371 ML410.W13K8 1977

Largely a guide to *Tristan*, *Meistersinger*, *Parsifal*, and the *Ring*, equipped with scattered musical examples and frequent references to Wagner's librettos. In his first chapter, however, Krehbiel also considers the composer's place "in the history of dramatic music from the Greeks and Monteverdi to now," as well as Wagner's use of *Leitmotive*, something of his verse, and so on. No illustrations, bibliography, or index, although the table of contents reviews in some detail the contents of individual chapters. Also published in New York City in 1893.

573. Neitzel, Otto. *Richard Wagners Opern in Text, Musik und Szene*, 4th ed. Stuttgart and Berlin: J. G. Cotta, 1908. (v), 332pp. ML410.W21R53 1908

A respectable survey of the stage works from *Rienzi* to *Parsifal*, illustrated with a large number of familiar musical "motives" from the mature music dramas. Worth consulting even today. Many other, similar surveys also exist; consider Wolfgang Perschmann's *Zeitlose Aktualität. 6 Wagner-Essays* (Bayreuth, 1982), which consists of a two-page foreword followed by discussions of *Holländer*, *Tannhäuser*, *Lohengrin*, *Tristan*, *Meistersinger*, and *Parsifal*.

Among the many older guides to Wagner's music dramas is Albert Lavignac's *The Music Dramas of Richard Wagner and His Festival Theater in Bayreuth*, trans. Esther Singleton (New York 1904; reprinted New York 1970). Published originally as *Le Voyage artistique à Bayreuth* (4th ed. Paris 1900; reprinted 1950). With regard to Lavignac's ideas, see item 741.

Studies in other languages of Wagner's operas and music dramas include:

574. *Guide des opéras de Wagner*, ed. Michel Pazdro. Paris: Fayard, 1988. 894pp. ISBN 2213020760 MT100.W2G93 1988

A survey mostly of the mature music dramas, with introductory chapters and individual discussions of every work from *Die Feen* to *Parsifal*. Pazdro provides discographical information for each music drama he discusses, as well as the complete texts of all libretti from *Holländer* to *Parsifal*, printed in facing columns in Wagner's original German and his own (?) French translations. Scattered musical examples include the principal motifs associated with each work.

Certain survey studies emphasize dramatic or theatrical elements in Wagner's output:

575. Garten, H. F. *Wagner the Dramatist*. London: John Calder, 1977. 159pp. ISBN 0714536202 ML410.W1G195

    Devoted to Wagner as a teller of tales and presenter of characters and situations. Garten also gives some attention to works Wagner planned or left unfinished, including *Die Hochzeit* and *Wieland der Schmied*. Illustrated with some fifteen plates, including a frontispiece portrait of the composer and scenes from several of his stage works; outfitted with a short bibliography (pp. 151–55); concludes with an index.

Shorter surveys of "the dramatic" Wagner are described below in alphabetical order by author:

576. Branscombe, Peter. "The Dramatic Texts," trans. Stewart Spencer. In item 2, pp. 269–86.

    Summarizes Wagner's attitudes toward his own librettos, ways in which he constructed them, and aspects of his evolution as a "poet" from *Die Feen* to *Parsifal*. Includes passages from the composer's letters and prose works, as well as a few libretto excerpts in German and English and a single musical example used to clarify a tricky point concerning poetic and musical meters. Branscombe confesses that "however admirably Wagner's texts may serve his musical-dramatic purposes, he showed little real talent as a lyric poet," and that in the composer's few sonnets and—"most depressing of all"—his patriotic hymns, "there is . . . an absence of the qualities that make the sung texts unique" (p. 285).

577. Spencer, Stewart. "Wagner as Librettist." In item 1, pp. 264–68.

    Briefly assesses the texts of Wagner's dramatic works, with special attention paid to his use of *Stabreim* in the *Ring* and to the analytical system of "lifts" (*Hebungen*) and "dips" (*Senkungen*) invented by Ludwig Ettmüller, a scholar who exerted an enormous influence on Wagner's later librettos. Includes an Ettmüller-like analysis of a passage from act II of *Siegfried,* as well as a few quotations from the composer's letters and prose works. No musical examples.

578. Wapnewski, Peter. "The Operas as Literary Works." In item 2, pp. 3–95.

    Surveys virtually all of Wagner's musical-dramatic works, completed and unfinished, from the standpoint of stories, plots, characters, literary style, and so on. Wapnewski comments on the evolution of individual works, beginning with *Die Feen*, as well as Wagner's attitudes toward them and certain relationships between various works and Wagner's personal and professional lives. Illustrated with quotations from the *Tristan* and *Ring* librettos.

Two authors have dealt with ways in which words and music fit together in all or most of Wagner's musical-dramatic output:

579. Stein, Herbert von. *Dichtung und Musik im Werk Richard Wagners*. Berlin: Walter de Gruyter & Co., 1962. 323pp. ML410.W1S827

Examines how Wagner employed both language (*Sprache*) and musical materials to reach his expressive and dramatic ends in *Holländer*, *Tannhäuser*, the *Ring*, *Parsifal*, and so on. Illustrated with 169 useful musical examples. Concludes with an index of names.

580. Wolzogen, Hans von. *Musikalisch-dramatische Parallelen. Beiträge zur Erkenntnis von der Musik als Ausdruck*. Leipzig: Breitkopf & Härtel, 1906. 237pp. (no LC number available)

A survey of Wagner's compositional strategies and style that emphasizes how the conjoining of music and words is to achieve particular musical-dramatic goals. Illustrated with 100 musical examples; unfortunately, Wolzogen's monograh includes no precise bibliographic information, no table of contents, and no index.

Anthologies and "companions" also summarize Wagner's musical-dramatic accomplishments. Among such publications are the following, arranged in order of increasing specialization:

581. *The Wagner Companion*, ed. Raymond Mander and Joe Mitchenson. London: W. H. Allen, 1977. x, 246pp. ISBN 0491018568 ML410.W13M14

Mostly a guide to Wagner's operas and music dramas from *Die Hochzeit* to *Parsifal* and, in this sense, an *Opernführer* (opera guidebook). Mander and Mitchenson include a "musical appreciation" and an essay on the Bayreuth Festival centenary celebrations by Millington (pp. 3–21 and 216–27, respectively), however, as well as lists of Wagner's dramatic works and first performances of them in England and the United States (pp. 1–2). Also includes excerpts from Shaw's Bayreuth chapter in *The Perfect Wagnerite* (see item 987), a brief bibliography, a glossary of characters' names (pp. 230–35), and an index.

582. *Richard Wagner—Von der Oper zum Musikdrama. Füuf Vorträge*, ed. Stefan Kunze. Bern and Munich: Francke, 1978. 96pp. ISBN 3772013716 ML410.W131R417

Includes Ludwig Finscher's useful article "Wagner der Opernkomponist: von der 'Feen' zum 'Rienzi' " (pp. 25–46), as well as its editor's survey article "Über den Kunstcharakter des Wagnerischen Musikdramas" (pp. 9–24) and essays by Reinhold Brinkmann, Klaus Günther Just, and Peter Wapnewski. Concludes with information about all five contributors.

583. *Wagner-Interpretationen*, ed. Roswitha Vera Karpf. Beiträge zur Aufführungspraxis, 5. Munich and Salzburg: Emil Katzbichler, 1982. 155pp. ISBN 3873973316 ML410.W13W2 1982

A series of essays that comprise the proceedings of a conference held at Graz during November 1979, including an essay on Wagner and Beethoven by Karpf, as well as speculations upon possible performances today of Wagner's youthful operas by Peter Pachl, and an introduction to the "Bayreuth style" by Egon Voss. Two essays include musical examples.

584. McGlathery, James M. *Wagner's Operas and Desire*. North American Studies in 19th-Century German Literature, 22. New York and Frankfurt a.M.: Peter Lang, 1998. viii, 297pp. ISBN 0820436933 ML410.W13M3

Examines erotic aspects of Wagner's stage works from *Holländer* to *Parsifal*. McGlathery provides quotations in both English and German from Wagner's letters and prose writings, but he employs no musical examples. Concludes with a list of sources cited (pp. 277–85) and an index.

Many survey studies of Wagner's stage works devolve of necessity upon the composer's attitudes toward politics, history, mythology, and a host of other subjects, as well as music and drama per se. One general study that emphasizes the philosophical, religious, and social as well as the dramatic and music is:

585. Candoni, Jean-François. *La Genèse du drame musical Wagnérien: Mythe, politique et histoire dans les oeuvres dramatiques de Richard Wagner entre 1833–1850*. "Collection 'Contacts' " III: Etudes et documents, 44. Frankfurt a.M. and New York: Peter Lang, 1998. xvii, 422pp. ISBN 3906760189 ML410.W13C36 1998

An attempt to grapple with the emergence of Wagner's mature musical-dramatic works and style in terms of the composer's attitudes toward romantic German and French grand opera, his relationship with the "Young Germany" movement, and his attempt "to pick up the thread of ancient myth" (from the "Summary," p. v). Concludes with a bibliography (pp. 383–407) and two indexes, as well as unpaginated information about the two-book series/sponsors in which Candoni's work appears: the Centre de recherches germaniques de Paris IV, and Lang's "Collections 'Contacts.' " Includes no visual illustrations or musical examples.

THE EARLIER (AND UNFINISHED) OPERAS AND MUSIC DRAMAS

Thousands of specialized documentary, interpretive, literary, musical, and performance-oriented studies exist of Wagner's operas and music dramas, especially of the mature works from Tannhäuser *through* Parsifal.

In the pages below, studies of the earlier and unfinished works have been divided into categories (e.g., "Unfinished Operas and Music Dramas" in alphabetical order by title; and "Early Completed Operas" in chronological order of composition). Under "Completed Operas: are two categories: "General Studies: and "Studies of Individual Operas"—i.e., of Die Feen, Das Liebesverbot, *and* Rienzi.

The present research guide cannot begin to identify and describe every important study of a Wagner opera or music drama. See the bibliographies in items 1–3, 26, 301, and a host of reference works for authors, titles, and publication information of other important studies.

Unfinished Operas and Music Dramas

*   Segnitz, Eugen. *Richard Wagner und Leipzig, 1813–1833.* Described as item 355.

Includes observations on the composer's very first attempts at opera.

Die Bergwerke von Falun, WWV 67: see items 901 and 1006.

Erec und Enide (no *WWV* number)
586. Müller, Ulrich. "Wagner's Unwritten Opera *Erec und Enide*." *Wagner* 18/3 (September 1997), pp. 142–51. ML410.W1A585

Discusses issues associated with a reference in one of Wagner's letters to Mathilde Wesendonk that he was interested as a dramatist in Hartmann von Aue's adaptation of Chrétien's *Erec et Enide*. Müller's article was evidently reprinted in translation from Vol. 6 of the *Zeitschrift für Germanistik*. See also item 1006.

Die Hochzeit, WWV 31
587. Muncker, Franz. "Richard Wagners Operntext 'Die Hochzeit.' " *Die Musik* 1–IV (1901–1902), pp. 1824–29. ML5.M9

Examines the origins of Wagner's text for his unfinished opera, with special attention to observations in the composer's *Autobiographical Sketch* concerning the text itself and the years 1832 to 1834. Wagner's claim not to know "where this Medieval stuff came from" is undercut by Muncker, who describes the composer's debt to poet Karl von Immermann, as well as to works by other authors. Accompanied by quotations from a number of sources.

* *Die Hochzeit* = Vol. 1 of *Richard Wagners musikalische Werke.* Described under item 157.

A critical edition containing all that survives of this early work.

Jesus von Nazareth, WWV 80: see especially items 873–74.

Leubald, WWV 1

588. Vetter, Isolde. "Leubald: A Tragedy. Richard Wagner's First Surviving Work." *Programmhefte der Bayreuther Festspiele* VII (1988), pp. 53–68. ML410.W2B26

Discusses the youthful drama Wagner wrote during his infatuation with Shakespeare—a drama he stated in the introduction to Vol. 1 of his *Gesammelte Schriften* was "a great tragedy, one which consisted more or less of *Hamlet* and *King Lear* rolled into one" (p. 53). No music survives for *Leubald,* but the complete text of the play is published in German in the same *Programmheft* (pp. 95–205). Illustrated with two facsimiles of musical examples. Vetter's essay also appears in French and German.

Männerlist größer als Frauenlist, WWV 48

589. Friedrich, Sven. *Richard Wagners unvollendete Jugendoper "Männerlist grösser als Frauenlist oder Die glückliche Bärenfamilie."* Berlin: Kulturstiftung der Länder, c. 1999. 47pp. ML410.W132F75 1999 (no ISBN available)

Not seen; described as a new acquisition on the Library of Congress web page. Apparently includes a facsimile of Wagner's manuscript, owned today by the Richard-Wagner-Museum, Bayreuth, as well as observations by Egon Voss and Friedrich himself.

Die Sieger, WWV 89

590. Osthoff, Wolfgang. *Richard Wagner's Buddha-Project "Die Sieger": Its Traces in the Ideas and Structures of "The Ring" and "Parsifal."* Zurich: Museum Reitberg, 1996. 36pp. ISBN 3907070682 ML410.W175O78 1996

Discusses one of several music dramas Wagner planned but never completed. Osthoff bases many of his conclusions on a sketch for *Die Sieger* surviving from 1856. Accompanied by a variety of musical examples—including some from later works the author believes were anticipated in these sketches, especially in terms of the use of *Leitmotive*—together with detailed notes (pp. 31–36). Revised from Osthoff's article published in the *Archiv für Musikwissenschaft* 40 (1983), pp. 189–211.

Early Completed Operas

GENERAL STUDIES
The following surveys are among the few, and by far the best, devoted to the composer's less-familiar and more youthful compositions—those spanning the years from Die Hochzeit *to* Rienzi. *NB: Many scholars group* Der fliegende Holländer *with* Tannhäuser *and* Lohengrin.

591. Mehler, Eugen. "Beiträge zur Wagner-Forschung: unveröffentlichte Stücke aus 'Rienzi,' 'Holländer' und 'Tannhäuser.' " *Die Musik* 12/1 (1912–1913), pp. 197–206. ML5.M9

   An examination of unpublished fragments from three of Wagner's early but by no means immature operas, based in part upon a careful reading of *My Life* for clues as to the composer's working methods as well as performance and publication histories. Illustrated with musical examples.

*   Finscher, Ludwig. "Wagner der Opernkomponist: von der 'Feen' zum 'Rienzi.' " In item 582.

   Incorporates 6 full-page, partially multipartite musical examples from little-known piano-vocal scores. Described by John Deathridge as "a welcome attempt to see Wagner in a historical context still unknown to, or only vaguely perceived by, the musical world at large" [*Music & Letters* 60 (1979), p. 97].

*   Nathan, Hans. *Das Rezitativ der Frühopern Richard Wagners.* Described as item 479.

STUDIES OF INDIVIDUAL OPERAS
Between 1833 and 1842 Wagner completed three "early operas": in chronological order of "completion" (Wagner often revised his works after their first performances), they are Die Feen, Das Liebesverbot, *and* Rienzi. *Studies devoted exclusively or primarily to each of them are described below:*

Die Feen, WWV 32

* *Die Feen* = Vol. 2 of *Richard Wagners musikalische Werke*. Described under item 157.

A complete score of the opera in the only critical edition available to date.

592. *Richard Wagner: Die Feen*, ed. Michael von Soden and Andreas Loesch. Insel Taschenbuch, 580. Frankfurt a.M.: Insel, 1983. 307pp. ISBN 3458322809 ML50.W14F3 1983

An *Opernführer* or "guide" that includes the complete libretto of this little-known work, as well as a brief unpaginated bibliography printed at the very end of the volume. A similar volume by Soden, devoted to *Lohengrin*, was published in 1980 by the same firm.

593. Riemann, Hugo. "Die Feen." In: Riemann, *Musikalische Rückblicke*, Vol. 2. Berlin: Harmonie, 1900; pp. 7–24. (no LC number available)

A useful discussion of the work as a whole, illustrated with three musical examples.

Das Liebesverbot, WWV 38

* *Das Liebesverbot* = Series XIV/III of *Richard Wagners musikalische Werke*. Described under item 157.

The only complete critical edition in print of this early Wagner opera.

The following studies are arranged in alphabetical order by author:

594. Einstein, Alfred. "Richard Wagners 'Liebesverbot.' " In: Einstein, *Nationale und universale Musik. Neue Essays*. Zurich and Stuttgart: Pan, 1958; pp. 81–87. ML60.E3385

Summarizes the origin of Wagner's opera and provides a brief synopsis of its story. Einstein also discusses similarities between Wagner's music in this score and works by Bellini and Offenbach, as well as anticipations of musical-dramatic gestures found in *Tannhäuser* and *Parsifal*. Includes short musical examples.

595. Engel, Hans. "Über Richard Wagners Oper 'Das Liebesverbot.' " In: *Festschrift Friedrich Blume zum 70. Geburtstag*, ed. Anna Amalie Abert and Wilhelm Pfannkuch. Kassel and Basel: Bärenreiter, 1963; pp. 80–91. ML55.F632

An outstanding synopsis of musical character and influence. Among other things, Engel compares the *Liebesverbot* finale with the finales of Meyerbeer's *Robert le diable*, Auber's *Stummen von Portici*, Bellini's *Norma*, and several other works—comparisons assisted by both the presence of musical examples and the inclusion of two useful diagrams (pp. 87–89).

596. Istel, Edgar. "Richard Wagners Oper 'Die Liebesverbot' auf Grund der handschriftlichen Originalpartitur dargestellt." *Die Musik* 8/4 (1908–1909), pp. 5–47. ML5.M9

Describes extant sources for Wagner's "Shakespeare opera," including the manuscript score owned by the Bayerische Staatsbibliothek, Munich. Illustrated with a large number of musical examples. Like many early studies of Wagner sketches, drafts, manuscripts, and editions, this one retains its place in the literature. See also item 1028.

597. Williams, Simon. "Wagner's 'Das Liebesverbot': From Shakespeare to the Well-Made Play." *Opera Quarterly* 3/4 (Winter 1985–1986), pp. 56–69. ML1699.O65

Identifies precisely what Wagner adapted from *Measure for Measure*. Williams maintains that, although *Liebesverbot* may not deserve a place in the regular operatic repertory, it "should not be cast aside as a mere curio or youthful aberration" either (p. 68). Includes four musical examples.

A single important study devoted to American issues associated with Wagner's Liebesverbot *has appeared in print:*

598. Riggs, Geoffrey S. "The American Premiere of Wagner's 'Das Liebesverbot.' " *Opera Journal* 16/3 (1983), pp. 28–34. ML1.O46

A detailed account of the first *Liebesverbot* performance ever in the United States, which took place in the early 1980s. NB: This is the only "review" (i.e., description of an individual performance) included in the present volume; it appears here because of its detailed summary of Wagner's youthful opera in terms of its musical and dramatic characteristics.

Other accounts of early *Liebesverbot* performances also exist. One of them, occasionally cited in the literature—Julius Kapp's *Das Liebesverbot von Richard Wagner: zur Erstaufführung an der Berliner Staatsoper* (Berlin, 1933)—once belonged to the British Library, London, but was destroyed at some time in the past, possibly during World War II; the present author has never seen a copy.

Rienzi, der Letzte der Tribunen, *WWV* 49
*   *Rienzi = Vol. 3 (5 fascicles) of Richard Wagner. Sämtliche Werke*, Described under item 156.

A critical edition, edited by Reinhard Strohm and Egon Voss.

Perhaps the most influential study of Rienzi *ever to appear in print is:*

599. Deathridge, John. *Wagner's "Rienzi": A Reappraisal Based on a Study of the Sketches and Drafts.* Oxford: Clarendon, 1977. xvii, 199pp. ISBN 019816131X ML410.W132

A careful examination of evidence associated with the composition of *Rienzi* in its original version, now lost in manuscript form and apparently never performed uncut. Among the sources Deathridge discusses are the prose draft of the opera's text prepared in Riga between 1837 and 1838, the composition draft belonging to the Burrell Collection, and the vocal score prepared by Carl Gustav Klink (Dresden, 1844). Illustrated with three facsimile plates and four mostly multi-partite music examples, the latter incorporating the contents of entire surviving sketches. Also includes a valuable bibliography (pp. 191–93) and an index.

Revised from the author's doctoral dissertation. See also Deathridge's article "Rienzi . . . A Few of the Facts," published in *The Musical Times* 124 (1983), pp. 546–49; as well as Martin Geck's article "Rienzi-Philologie" in item 447, pp. 183–96.

* *Dokumente und Texte zu 'Rienzi, der Letzte der Tribunen,' "* ed. Reinhard Strohm. Described under item 156.

Virtually the last word on documentary sources for this opera.

600. Dinger, Hans. "Zu Richard Wagners 'Rienzi.' " *Richard-Wagner-Jahrbuch* 3 (1908), pp. 88–132. ML410.A1W57

A critique of Wagner's successes and failures concerning what, for most listeners, remains his first "real" opera. Dinger also compares aspects of *Rienzi* with aspects of the composer's later music dramas. No musical examples.

HOLLÄNDER, LOHENGRIN, AND TANNHÄUSER

Studies are described first by work (the works themselves are identified in chronological order); then by kind of study ("Document and Source Studies," "Interpretive Studies," and so on); and finally—at least for the most part, because certain studies are singled out for special recognition—in alphabetical order by author and/or title.

Der fliegende Holländer, *WWV* 63

* *Der fliegende Holländer* = Vol. 4 (2 fascicles) of *Richard Wagner. Sämtliche Werke*. Described under item 156.

A critical edition prepared by Isolde Vetter.

Guidebooks and Survey Studies

601. *Der fliegende Holländer. Programmheft*, ed. Edgar Baitzel. Munich: Bavarian State Opera, 1981. 128pp. ML410.W132R5 1981 (no ISBN available)

A superb introduction to Wagner's first "mature" opera, beautifully illustrated with reproductions of art works by Gustave Doré and Edvard Munch, stage sets and scenes from Herbert Wernicke's Munich production of 1981, and a complete facsimile of the article Wagner published on 7 October 1843 in Leipzig's *Illustrirte Zeitung* (pp. 45–60). Includes comments by Wernicke, as well as articles by Dieter Borchmeyer, Carl Dahlhaus, John Deathridge, and Vetter on the background, story, and musical contents of *Holländer*; also includes quotations from relevant or related literary sources—among them, German translations of Coleridge's *Rime of the Ancient Mariner*—and a brief discography (p. 127), as well as scattered musical examples.

Additional survey studies include:

602. Barker, Frank Granville. *The Flying Dutchman: A Guide to the Opera*. London: Barrie & Jenkins, 1979. 159pp. ISBN 0214206556 ML410.W132B4

A respectable overview. Includes the complete libretto in both German and English (pp. 110–46) as well as a timeline (pp. 149–55), introductory observations by Norman Bailey, and a variety of illustrations, most of them depicting Wagner performers and performances, and a few documents in facsimile reproduction.

603. *Der fliegende Holländer: Wirkung und Wandlung eines Motivs*, ed. Bernd Laroche. Europäische Hochschulschriften, 36. Frankfrut a.M. and New York: Peter Lang, 1993. 208pp. ISBN 3631458916 ML410.W132L3 1993

A *Holländer* "reader." Consists of an introduction by Laroche and the texts of Wagner's own prose sketch "Le hollandaise Volant" in French, with a German translation by the editor, as well as Edward Fitzball's story *The Flying Dutchman* in German, Heinrich Heine's *Fabel von dem "fliegenden Holländer,"* and the Paul Foucher/Pierre-Louis Dietch *Vaisseau fantôme*.

Also includes scattered illustrations, among them a few documentary facsimiles, but no musical examples per se; concludes with a bibliography (pp. 203–6) and list of illustrations.

604. Le François, André. *Le Vaisseau fantôme / Der fliegende Holländer (Le Hollandais Volant). Etude thématique et analyse.* Paris: Lafontaine, 1983. vii, 73pp. ISBN 2900318122 (no LC number available)

An introduction to the history and contents of the opera, as well as a discussion and brief analysis of its musical character. Contains a catalog of *Holländer* motifs (pp. v–vii), a brief discography (pp. 71–2), and a one-page bibliography. One in a series of Le François volumes, each devoted to a different Wagner opera or music drama.

605. Oberkogler, Friedrich. *Der fliegende Holländer. Eine musikalisch-geisteswissenschaftliche Werkbesprechung.* Dornbach, Switzerland: Novalis, 1983. 187pp. ISBN 3721405153 ML410.W132D34 1983

A collection of interrelated essays devoted to intersections between the legend of the Dutchman and the composer's own life and intellectual development, as well as literary, mythic, and musical sources Wagner drew upon to complete his opera. Includes a guide to the plot and music as well as dozens of musical examples and four full-color illustrations of scenes from the work painted by Daniel Boillat (between pp. 96–97). Concludes with a short bibliography. Oberkogler also published a guide to *Parsifal*; see the footnote appended to item 6. See also items 490 and 608.

Document and Source Studies

606. Abraham, Gerald. " 'The Flying Dutchman': Original Version." *Music & Letters* 20 (1939), pp. 412–19. ML5.M64

Compares a piano-vocal score of the early version with later, better-known versions of the opera. Among other things Abraham concludes that, during revision, Wagner rewrote many of the brass passages to make them more transparent and effective, and that the familiar version is "indisputably finer than anything" in its model (p. 419). Includes eight musical examples, among them two in full score: one from the early version of Senta's ballad, the other from the revised overture.

607. Breig, Werner. "Das 'verdichtete Bild des ganzen Dramas': Die Ursprunge von Wagners Holländer-Musik und die Senta-Ballade." In: *Festschrift Heinz Becker zum 60. Geburtstag am 26. Juni 1982*, ed. Jürgen Schläder

and Reinhold Quandt. Laaber: Laaber Verlag, 1982; pp. 162–78. ISBN 3921518709 ML55.B32M

Investigates the origins of the music for Wagner's opera in general, and Senta's famous ballad in particular, based on sketches dating from the summer of 1840. Breig contradicts certain claims Wagner himself made in his *Autobiographical Sketch*, *My Life*, and other writings. Illustrated with about a dozen short musical examples, and supplemented with the contents of the complete first sketch for the ballad (pp. 164–65) and critical apparatus concerning it (p. 166).

608. Istel, Edgar. "Autographische Regiebemerkungen Wagners zum 'Fliegenden Holländer,' zum ersten Male veröffentlicht." *Die Musik* 12/2 (1912–1913), pp. 214–19. ML5.M9

Describes and discusses the significance of Wagner's handwritten instructions for *Holländer* performances—as well as similar instructions written into a printed score of *Rheingold*. Includes two musical examples. Published as an afterword of sorts to Istel's study of sketches for the instrumentations of the latter music drama (see item 457).

609. Machlin, Paul Stuart. "A Sketch for the 'Dutchman.' " *The Musical Times* 117 (1976), pp. 727–29. ML5.M85

Deals with a document belonging to Princeton University's libraries; based on its contents, Machlin suggests that Wagner had begun work on portions of *Holländer* before the end of 1841, even before finishing *Rienzi*. Includes several musical examples. Both this study and item 610 are derived from the author's researches for his doctoral dissertation (University of California, Berkeley, 1975).

610. Machlin, Paul S. "Wagner, Durand, and 'The Flying Dutchman': The 1852 Revisions of the Overture." *Music & Letters* 55 (1974), pp. 410–28. ML5.M64

A documentary study of the so-called Dresden theater score, into which Wagner copied *Holländer* orchestral revisions in 1846; comparisons of this source with scores from 1841 and 1852 make it possible to determine precisely which changes Wagner made when. Machlin considers orchestrational changes with special care. Includes eight or nine examples, as well as an appendix (pp. 427–28) that identifies certain stage directions found in the four scores Machlin examines.

A series of studies has concentrated on a single Holländer *issue: that of Wagner's relationship with Philippe Dietsch, to whom he was long thought—and is now known—to have told the story of the Dutchman. The studies in question are described below in chronological order of publication:*

611. LePrince, G. " 'The Flying Dutchman' in the Setting by Philippe Dietsch," trans. Daniel Heartz. *The Musical Quarterly* 50 (1964), pp. 307–20. ML1.M725

    What, precisely, is the historical relationship between Dietsch's *Vaisseau fantôme* and Wagner's *Holländer*? This question, argued over for decades, is introduced here in terms of the content and characteristics of the French composer's work. Includes six musical examples, some of them used as illustrations in LePrince's synopsis of *Fantôme* (pp. 312–20).

612. Millington, Barry. "Did Wagner Really Sell His 'Dutchman' Story? A Reexamination of the Paris Transaction." *Wagner* 4/4 (October 1983), pp. 114–27. ML410.W1A585

    Maintains that, based on available documentary evidence, the "complete truth . . . cannot be ascertained" (p. 126) about Wagner's purported transaction with Dietsch. Includes two documentary facsimiles. See also Millington's article " 'The Flying Dutchman,' 'Le vaisseau fantôme' and Other Nautical Yarns" in *The Musical Times* 127 (1986), pp. 131–35.

613. Vetter, Isolde. "For the Last Time: Wagner *Did* Sell his 'Dutchman' Story." *Wagner* 7/1 (January 1986), pp. 16–22. ML410.W1A585

    Offers documentary proof, based on a ledger uncovered in the archives of the Paris Opéra—and illustrated in three facsimiles—that Wagner sold the story to Dietsch. Millington acknowledges Vetter's discovery and comments on its significance on p. 22 of the same *Wagner* issue. Other articles by Vetter concerning *Holländer* also exist; see, for example, her "Holländer-Metamorphosen," published in 1978 in a joint issue of *Melos* and the *Neue Zeitschrift*.

614. Bloom, Peter. "The Fortunes of the Flying Dutchman in France: Wagner's 'Hollandais volant' and Dietsch's 'Vaisseau fantôme.' " *Wagner* 8/2 (April 1987), pp. 42–66. ML410.W1A585

    An attempt to cast new light on the debate described in items 612–13 without necessarily contradicting either party. Among other issues raised by Bloom is the existence of an *Andante* for organ, published in 1841 in a volume edited by Dietsch, that may be Wagner's work and, in any event, suggests the two men may have known each other a little earlier than generally supposed. Includes a facsimile of the organ piece.

Musical Studies

*   Abbate, Carolyn. "Erik's Dream and Tannhäuser's Voyage." Described as item 635.

Interpretive Studies

*   Cicora, Mary A. *Modern Myths and Wagnerian Deconstructions.* Described as item 1012.

See the discussion devoted to Wagner and postmodern criticism in chapter XI of the present research guide, as well as a reference there to Arthur Groos, "Back to the Future: Hermeneutic Fantasies in 'Der fliegende Holländer,'" *19th Century Music* 19 (1995–1996), pp. 191–211.

615.   Graf, Max. *Richard Wagner im "Fliegenden Holländer." Ein Beitrag zur Psychologie künstlerischen Schaffens.* Leipzig and Vienna: Franz Deuticke, 1911. 46pp. ML410.W132G7

A psychoanalytic study based on the assumption that " 'typical motifs in an artist's work . . . always' . . . represent the artist's attempt to find the 'solution to some emotional problem' " (p. 23; trans. in item 1019, p. 133). In this case, Graf proposes that Wagner's conflicting feelings for his wife Cosima and Mathilde Wesendonk had to do with unresolved Oedipal feelings for his mother. Published as part of a series on "Freudian subjects" (*Freudschen Lehren*) that include Freud's own *Three Contributions to the Psychology of Sex.* Includes quotations from Wagner's libretto but no musical examples.

616.   Seelig, Lutz Eberhardt. *Wagners Sehnsucht nach Kongenialität. Sentas Emanzipation im "Fliedenden Holländer."* Vienna and Cologne: Hermann Böhlaus, 1984. 170pp. ISBN 3205072375 ML410.W132S4 1984

Based on assertions that Wagner worked through personal issues in depicting Senta as a woman who "gave all for love." Illustrated with fifteen black-and-white pictures, mostly photographs of stage sets, as well as a few portraits and a few musical examples. Also includes a discography of *Holländer* recordings from the 1930s to the 1970s (pp. 160–61), and a bibliography (pp. 166–69).

617.   Vill, Susanne. "On Wild Huntsmen, Vampires, and The Flying Dutchman." *Programmhefte der Bayreuther Festspiele* I (1990), pp. 48–50 and 55–62. ML410.W2B26

A diverting account of the composer's interest in the supernatural and its manifestations in dramatic music, including Weber's *Freischütz* and *Oberon*. Vill discusses the legends of the Wandering Jew and the Dutchman that served as inspiration for what many critics consider Wagner's first mature stage work. Available in the same volume in German and French translation.

In addition to these examinations of Wagner's interests in women and the supernatural, the following somewhat eccentric publication presents the Dutchman himself in a new light:

618. *Der fliegende Holländer: Kurt Schmischkes gezeichnete Parodien*, ed. Kurt Grobecker. Hamburg: Busse-Seewald, 1996. 112pp. ISBN 3844122363 ML410.W132S36 1996

A full-color picture book of satiric illustrations and images, mostly of Wagner's *Holländer,* but also of scenes from Herman Melville's *Moby Dick*, Poe's grotesque tales, and so on. A portrait of Schmischke, the artist and a reasonably well-known German illustrator, also appears as an illustration; commentary is provided by Grobecker.

Tannhäuser und der Sängerkrieg auf Wartburg, *WWV* 70

* *Tannhäuser* = Vols. 5–6 (four fascicles in all) of *Richard Wagner. Sämtliche Werke*. Described under item 156.

A complete critical edition of the various *Tannhäuser* versions, edited by Reinhard Strohm and Peter Jost. See also item 824.

* *Tannhäuser* = Vol. 3 of *Richard Wagners musikalische Werke*. Described under item 157.

A critical edition, replaced by the item cross-listed immediately above.

Guidebooks and Survey Studies
619. *Tannhäuser*. English National Opera Guide, 39. London: John Calder, 1988. 96pp. ISBN 0714541478 ML50.W14T22

Contains Carolyn Abbate's essay "Orpheus and the Underworld: The Music of Wagner's 'Tannhäuser' " (pp. 33–50)—itself illustrated with five musical examples—as well as the entire text of Wagner's early music drama, on facing pages, in both German and a new English translation by Rodney Blumer; a thematic guide incorporating 32 motifs and other musical fragments; a brief discography and bibliography; and additional essays by Mike Ashman, Timothy McFarland, and Stewart Spencer. Illustrated throughout with portraits and photographs, mostly of famous singers and representative stage designs.

Similar guides for several other Wagner music dramas, including *Walküre* (ISBN 0714540196), *Meistersinger* (ISBN 0714539619) and *Götterdämmerung* (ISBN 0714540633), have appeared in the same series; the *Götterdämmerung* volume, reviewed in *Wagner* 6/4 (October 1985), pp. 141–44, was pronounced "excellent." See also item 721, as well as *Richard Wagner: Tannhäuser* (Bayreuth, 1989), a pamphlet-length publication that contains essays by Helmut Kirchmeyer and Friedrich Kittler.

Two Tannhäuser *readers have also appeared in print:*

620. Lindner, Edwin. *Richard Wagner über "Tannhäuser": Aussprüche des Meisters über sein Werk.* Leipzig: Breitkopf & Härtel, 1914. 572pp. ML410.W1A188

A substantial collection of documentary evidence about *Tannhäuser.* Draws upon some thirty sources, most of them written by Wagner himself; among them are the composer's letters and prose publications, as well as articles in the *Bayreuther Blätter, Die Musik,* and portions of Gustav Kietz's *Richard Wagner aus den Jahren 1842–1849 und 1873–1875.*

Additional collections of *Tannhäuser* documents also exist. See, for instance, Wolfgang Golther's "Briefe Richard Wagners zum Pariser 'Tannhäuser,' " published in *Die Musik* 3-XI (1903–1904), pp. 308–13, which examines the composer's epistolary comments on the origins and character of the revision that resulted in perhaps the greatest fracas of his remarkable career.

621. *Richard Wagner: Tannhäuser,* ed. Dietrich Mack. Frankfurt a.M.: Insel, 1979. 154pp. ISBN 3458320784 ML410.W135R5

A "reader" comprising information about the work's history, excerpts from Wagner's prose works, a timeline (pp. 73–83), and quotations from Cosima's diaries, as well as the complete texts of Heine's *Tannhäuser: eine Legende* and Baudelaire's celebrated essay of 1861 (item 976). Also includes a one-page bibliography, as well as a group of illustrations (between pp. 80–83) devoted to costumes, stage sets, and a few documentary facsimiles. No musical examples.

Document and Source Studies

622. *Individuum versus Institution: Zur Urfassung (1845) von Richard Wagners "Tannhäuser,"* ed. Udo Bermbach, Ulrich Müller, and Matthias Theodor Vogt. "Kulturelle Infrastruktur," 7. Leipzig: Universitätsverlag, 1996. 91pp. ISBN 3931922254 ML410.W135I35 1996

Proceedings of a conference held in conjunction with a performance of the original version of *Tannhäuser*, presented in Usti nad Labem, Czech Republic (?), in October 1995. Includes the texts of eight essays by Bernbach and Müller, as well as Jiři Fukač, Franz Jochen Herfert, Volkmar Leimert, and Oswald Panagl, devoted to questions of the individual versus musical and cultural institutions, as well as medieval textual and musical sources for Wagner's opera. Also includes illustrations of various kinds—among them facsimiles of medieval manuscripts, production photographs, and the program for the 1995 performance—and scattered musical examples.

623. Abbate, Carolyn. "The Parisian 'Venus' and the 'Paris' Tannhäuser." *Journal of the American Musicological Society* 36 (1983), pp. 73–123. ML27.U5A83363

Examines the evolution of act I, scene ii, which Wagner revised for the notorious Paris performance of his opera in the early 1860s. Abbate also discusses Wagner's role in preparing a French translation of his *Tannhäuser* text and his evolving notion of Venus as a musical-dramatic character. Includes eight mostly multi-partite examples, as well as three facsimiles and an appendix of quotations from the composer's correspondence, and other documents pertaining to "Wagner's French Collaborators" (pp. 118–23). Draws upon research for Abbate's 1985 Princeton University dissertation. A synopsis of Abbate's paper "Richard Wagners Skizzen zur neuen Venus-Szene" appears in item 40, p. 504.

624. Bauer, Ostwald Georg. "Wagner's Previously Unpublished Prose Draft for 'Tannhäuser.' " *Programmhefte der Bayreuther Festspiele* I (1985), pp. 105–7. ML410.W2B26

Traces the history of the *Tannhäuser* story sketch Wagner wrote out during his visit to Teplitz-Schönau in June 1842, and evaluates comments about that opera's origins found in *My Life*. The draft itself appears in print for the first time on pp. 1–14 of the same program; translations of the draft into English and French, and of Bauer's essay into French and German, also appear in the same volume.

625. Golther, Wolfgang. "Die französische und die deutsche Tannhäuser-Dichtung." *Die Musik* 2–VII (1903), pp. 271–82. ML5.M9

Compares French- and German-language versions of and sketches for what the *Wagner-Werk-Verzeichnis* identifies as versions two, three, and four of the *Tannhäuser* libretto. Golther employs tables of parallel text versions to make his points; he also illustrates some of his arguments with musical examples.

*   Hopkinson, Cecil. *Tannhäuser. An Examination of 36 Editions.* Described as item 166.

626. Panzer, Friedrich. "Richard Wagners Tannhäuser: Sein Aufbau und seine Quellen." *Die Musik* 7/3 (1907–1908), pp. 11–27. ML5.M9

Explains how Wagner constructed his *Tannhäuser* and out of what materials: mythical, historical, and musical. A bit more "impressionistic" than similar but more rigorous and document-oriented studies.

627. Tappert, Wilhelm. "Die drei verschiedenen Schlüsse des Tannhäuser vor der jetzigen endgültigen Fassungen." *Die Musik* 1–IV (1901–1902), pp. 1844–66. ML5.M9

Deals primarily with a third, previously unknown ending, discovered in the archives of a Dresden library. Tappert also provides the complete text of this third ending (pp. 1845–47). Illustrated with musical examples.

Textual and Literary Studies

628. Cicora, Mary A. *From History to Myth: Wagner's "Tannhäuser" and its Literary Sources.* Germanic Studies in America, 63. Frankfurt a.M. and New York: Peter Lang, 1992. 217pp. ISBN 326104408X ML410.W135C53 1992

Examines the Tannhäuser story before Wagner encountered it and as he incorporated it especially into the libretto of the 1845 version. Among other sources Cicora reviews Johann Ludwig Tieck's *Der getreue Eckart und der Tannenhäuser* (1799), E. T. A. Hoffmann's *Der Kampf der Sänger* (1819), and Ferdinand Heine's *Der Tannhäuser* (1836); she also considers medieval sources for and versions of both the Tannhäuser and song-contest stories. Includes a bibliography (pp. 207–17) but no illustrations or musical examples. Reviewed in *Music & Letters* 75 (1994), pp. 98–100.

629. Scheinitz, Alexandra von. *Wagner's Tannhäuser und Sängerkrieg auf der Warthburg. Sage, Dichtung und Geschichte.* Meran: F. W. Ellmenreich, 1891. 235pp. ML410.W135S35 1891

A thorough discussion of literary and historical sources underlying the two originally independent stories that went into the making of Wagner's work: the first is the exploits of the knight Tannhäuser, the second the song contest at Wartburg Castle outside Eisenach. Among other sources, Scheinitz discusses the stories by Joseph Eichendorff, E. T. A. Hoffmann, and Tieck (see also item 628). Includes extensive quotations.

630. Steinbeck, Dietrich. "Zur Textkritik der Venus-Szenen im 'Tannhäuser.' " *Die Musikforschung* 19 (1966), pp. 412–21. ML5.M9437

Analyzes various versions of the 212-line libretto for act I, scene ii of Wagner's early music drama. Steinbeck also provides the complete text of the Paris version as an appendix (pp. 415–22), and employs footnotes to comment, line by line, on this and other versions. No illustrations or musical examples.

Musical Studies

631. Rosenblum, Mathew. "Sound, Structure and Signification in Wagner's 'Evening Star' Aria." *Music Analysis* 16/1 (March 1997), pp. 77–103. ML1.M2125

Examines the sound structure of Wagner's text as a basis for the musical structure of the recitative "Wie Todesahnung" and the aria "O du mein holder Abendstern," the latter unquestionably the most famous of the composer's "tunes." Illustrated with diagrams and charts as well as several musical examples. See also Reinhold Brinkmann's closely related, much more thoroughly documented article "Tannhäusers Lied" in item 447, pp. 199–211.

Performance and Reception Studies

632. Nicolai, W. "Die erste Tannhäuseraufführung in Wien." *Richard-Wagner-Jahrbuch* 1 (1906), pp. 3–37. ML410.W1A57

Summarizes the events and presents portions of the correspondence associated with the *Tannhäuser* performance directed by Johann Hoffmann and presented at the Thaliatheater on 28 August 1857. Nicolai includes the texts of thirteen letters addressed by Wagner to Hoffmann, Julius Milius, and others associated with the affair, and written between March 1857 and February 1858. Includes a facsimile of an undated poster printed for the performance in question. A shorter article on roughly the same topic also exists: P. Lorenz's "Der erste Tannhäuser in Wien," published in the November 1959 issue of the *Österreichische Musikzeitschrift*.

* *Richard Wagner et "Tannhäuser" à Paris.* Described as item 976.

633. Steinbeck, Dietrich. *Inszenierungsformen des "Tannhäuser" (1845–1904). Untersuchungen zur Systematik der Opernregie.* Forschungsbeiträge zur Musikwissenschaft, 14. Regensburg: Gustav Bosse, 1964. 290pp. ML410.W135S74

Evaluates the evolution and character of *Tannhäuser* performances from the premiere of that work to the beginning of the twentieth century. Steinbeck also discusses Wagner's theories of drama and music, his conducting techniques, his attitudes toward his work, and plans for its public presentation. Concludes with a bibliography (pp. 239–42) and an index of names.

Another study, this one edited by Steinbeck, appeared as *Richard Wagners Tannhäuser-Szenarium: das Vorbild der Erstaufführungen mit der Kostümbeschreibung und den Dekorationsplänen* (Berlin, 1968). See, too, Charles Suttoni's article "Liszt and Wagner's 'Tannhäuser,' " in *New Light on Liszt and His Music*, ed. Michael Saffle and James Deaville (Stuyvesant, NY: Pendragon, 1997), pp. 17–51, which discusses Liszt's role in performances of 1850, 1856, and 1861.

634. *Tannhäuser. Stagione d'opera e balletto 1983–84*. Milan: "Teatro alla scala" and Oscar Mondadori, 1984. 132pp. (no ISBN or LC number available)

A program book commemorating the Gustav Kuhn production of Wagner's opera. Includes beautiful color plates, as well as historical photographs and a few documentary facsimiles. Like many similar publications, the author(s) of this volume are not clearly identified.

Interpretive Studies

635. Abbate, Carolyn. "Erik's Dream and Tannhäuser's Voyage." In *Reading Opera*, ed. Arthur Groos and Roger Parker. Princeton, NJ: Princeton University Press, 1988; pp. 129–67. ISBN 0691091323 ML2120.R4 1988

Compares Tannhäuser's "Rome narrative" in act III with "Erik's dream" in *Holländer* to explain how narrative can undermine musical coherence in terms both of periodicity and tonality. Includes facsimiles and musical examples as illustrations for Abbate's arguments. Another of this author's *Tannhäuser* studies appears as "Der junge Wagner malgré lui: die frühen Tannhäuser-Entwürfe und Wagners 'übliche Nummer' " in item 33, pp. 59–68.

636. Bless, Marion. *Richard Wagners Oper "Tannhäuser" im Spiegel seiner geistigen Entwicklung*. Hamburger Beiträge zur Musikwissenschaft, 44. Eisenach: Karl Dieter Wagner, 1997. 174pp. ISBN 3889790763 ML410.W135B54 1997X

Considers *Tannhäuser* in light of Wagner's development as musician, poet, polemicist, and culture figure. Among other subjects Bless discusses the influence and inspiration of Weber's stage works and of E. T. A. Hoffmann on Wagner, as well as the notion of "absolute melody." Includes a few musical examples and a couple of documentary facsimiles; concludes with a one-page bibliography. Unindexed.

*   Lee, M. Owen. *Wagner: The Terrible Man and His Truthful Art*. Described as item 438.

Consists of three essays, the third devoted to *Tannhäuser.* Lee asks whether Wagner himself may be considered a Tannhäuser figure.

Lohengrin, *WWV* 75

*   *Lohengrin* = Vol. 7 of *Richard Wagner. Sämtliche Werke.* Described under item 156.

A critical edition prepared by Deathridge and Klaus Döge.

*   *Lohengrin* = Vol. 4 of *Richard Wagners musikalische Werke.* Described under item 157.

Largely replaced by the item cross-referenced immediately above.

Guidebooks and Survey Studies

637. Dry, Wakeling. *Wagner's Lohengrin.* New York: Brentano's, n.d. 60pp. ML410.W137D7

A competent introduction, illustrated with short hand-copied music examples. Volumes on *Tannhäuser* and *Tristan* by the same author, published in London by the De La More Press, as well as by Brentano's of New York, appeared in the same "Nights at the Opera" series. See also Dry's *Wagner's Flying Dutchman* (London, 1906).

638. Himonet, André. *Lohengrin de R. Wagner. Étude historique et critique. Analyse musicale.* "Les Chefs-d'oeuvre de la musique." Paris: Librairie Delaplane, n.d. 174pp. ML410.W137H5

Summarizes the plot and discussions of certain of *Lohengrin*'s musical aspects, together with a brief biographical summary of Wagner's life and career. Illustrated with 95 musical examples.

"Readers" devoted to Lohengrin *and its origins, contents, and impact include:*

639. "Richard Wagner über Lohengrin: Aussprüche des Meisters über sein Werk," ed. Erich Kloss. *Richard-Wagner-Jahrbuch* 3 (1908), pp. 132–88. ML410.W1A57

A collection of Wagner's own comments about the origins, contents, character, and significance of the work in question. Illustrated with scattered musical examples. Similar to several other publications—for example, *Richard Wagner über die "Meistersinger von Nürnberg": Aussprüche des Meisters über sein Werk in Schriften und Briefen* (Leipzig, 1910)—either attributed to Kloss or other authors and cited in reliable Wagner bibliographies, but not seen by the present author. See also item 620.

Document and Source Studies

640. Deathridge, John. "Through the Looking Glass: Some Remarks on the First Complete Draft of 'Lohengrin.' " In item 528, pp. 56–91.

Examines surviving fragments of a draft Wagner made between May and July of 1846; a document that reflects "the creative fantasies and the often paradoxical relation between theory and practice that are part and parcel of this key work and its complex history" (p. 57). Illustrated with six full-page facsimiles of manuscript pages as well as musical examples transcribed from them and several tables comparing the contents of speeches in various versions of *Lohengrin* and Weber's *Euryanthe* (the tables, pp. 82–83). A "greatly expanded version" (p. 56) of item 641.

641. Deathridge, John. "Zur Kompositionsskizze des Lohengrin" In item 40, pp. 420–24.

Carefully examines Wagner's sketches by drawing upon some twelve pages of manuscript material—the "compositional sketch" also described in item 640—that survives for *Lohengrin*.

642. Schmid, Manfred Hermann. "Metamorphose der Themen: Beobachtungen an der Skizzen zum 'Lohengrin'-Vorspiel." *Die Musikforschung* 41 (1988), pp. 105–26. ML5.M9437

Examines *Lohengrin* sketches dating from 1846 to 1848, in order to explore interconnections between motives that also appear in the opera's Prelude—the last a work that, in spite of its alleged monothematic conception, makes good use of thematic transformation. Includes eight musical examples as well as the complete text of "sketch 7," prepared by Wagner in the summer of 1847, together with notes and commentary (pp. 119–26).

Textual and Literary Studies

643. Palm, Helga-Maria. *Richard Wagners "Lohengrin." Studien zur Sprachbehandlung.* Münchner Universitäts-Schriften: Studien zur Musik, 6. Munich: Wilhelm Fink, 1987. 267pp. ISBN 3770523369 ML410.W137P36 1987

Devoted primarily to the intersection of music and words—with an emphasis on the words in terms of their meanings, rhythmic and melodic treatment, dramatic significance, and so on—in *Die Feen, Tannhäuser, Götterdämmerung, Parsifal,* and *Lohengrin*. Palm also considers aspects of Weber's *Euryanthe* and Marschner's *Templer und die Jüdin* that may have influenced Wagner's literary and musical development and styles. Illustrated with diagrams and dozens of musical examples and equipped with a brief but useful bibliography (pp. 265–67).

Performance and Reception Studies

644. Kreim, Isabella. *Richard Wagners "Lohengrin" auf der deutschen Bühne und in der Kritik. Studien zur Aufführungs- und Rezeptionsgeschichte*. Printed from a typescript in 1983? 232pp. (no LC number available)

One of hundreds of oddities in the Wagner literature: a detailed but apparently unpublished study of Wagner's opera in terms of many of its German performances and reviews. Uncommon in America; Harvard University's Loeb Music Library owns a copy, however.

MEISTERSINGER, PARSIFAL, TRISTAN, AND THE RING

Studies are described first by work (the works themselves are identified in chronological order of when each was begun); then—in the case of the Ring—*by individual music drama (including the unfinished drama* Siegfrieds Tod*); then by category ("Document and Source Studies," "Interpretive Studies," and so on); and finally—at least mostly, because certain studies are singled out in a few categories—in alphabetical order by author and/or title.*

Der Ring des Nibelungen, *WWV* 86A–D

General Studies

Among a host of introductory and survey studies, the following may be of special interest to English and American readers:

645. *Wagner's "Ring of the Nibelung": A Companion*, ed. Stewart Spencer. London: Thames & Hudson, 1993. 383pp. ISBN 0500015678 ML50.W14R32 1993

A *Ring* handbook, consisting of an introductory essay, a timeline covering the whole of Wagner's life, essays by Warren Darcy, Roger Hollinrake, Elizabeth Magee, and Millington, an appendix dealing with rejected versions of the *Ring* poem, a glossary of characters (pp. 373–75), a fine bibliography (pp. 376–81), and "The Ring on Compact Disc and Video" (pp. 382–83). The bulk of the volume, however, is taken up with a translation by Spencer of Wagner's poems, identified on the full-title page as "The Full German Text with a New Translation"; Spencer provides a synopsis for each, followed by two-column text in English and German; 67 motives, identified numerically at appropriate places in the translation, appear in another part of the volume. Also illustrated with sixteen black-and-white illustrations, most of them photographs of stage sets and scenes, but a few of them documentary facsimiles. No index or other musical examples. See, too, items 424, 471–472, 866, and 987.

Other surveys devoted to the Ring *as a whole include the following volumes:*

646. Aldrich, Richard. *A Guide to the Ring of the Nibelungs: The Trilogy* [*sic*] *of Richard Wagner. Its Origins, Story, and Music.* Boston: Oliver Ditson, 1905. 125pp. MT100.W25A4

A better-than-average introduction to Wagner's tetralogy—which, by the way, Aldrich always calls a "trilogy" because of the relationship he perceives between its overall structure and that of Greek-tragic trilogies. Illustrated with 78 motivic musical examples and keyed throughout by page and system to the G. Schirmer piano-vocal *Ring* scores edited by Karl Klindworth. Also includes a bibliography (pp. 121–22); concludes with an index of motifs. Aldrich, an important late nineteenth- and early twentieth-century American music critic, published a similar guide to *Parsifal* as well as a variety of books and essays on other musical subjects.

647. Blyth, Alan. *Wagner's Ring: An Introduction.* London and Melbourne: Hutchinson, 1980. 146pp. ISBN 0091420113 MT100.W25B5 1980

A chatty, accessible examination of all four music dramas, illustrated with stage designs for scenes from the cycle's first complete performance at Bayreuth in 1876. Two appendices contain mostly familiar musical examples (pp. 118–27) and comments about complete *Ring* performances on phonorecords (pp. 128–46). Unindexed.

*   Cooke, Deryck. *I Saw the World End: A Study of Wagner's "Ring."* Described as item 1013.

In large part a critique of Donington's volume (item 649), as well as a study of mythic images, legendary figures, and modern critical concepts.

648. Cord, William O. *An Introduction to Richard Wagner's "Der Ring des Nibelungen": A Handbook,* 2nd enlarged ed. Athens, OH: Ohio University Press, 1995. xviii, 212pp. ISBN 0821411128 ML410.W22C67 1995

A satisfactory introduction to Wagner's work. Includes a chapter devoted to "The 'Ring' in Recordings" (pp. 145–51), as well as a list of characters identified according to the acts and scenes in which they appear (p. 32); Cord also provides an extensive but nevertheless "selective" bibliography (pp. 173–94) and an index. Illustrated with a few black-and-white production scenes and documentary facsimiles.

649. Donington, Robert. *Wagner's "Ring" and Its Symbols: The Music and the Myth*, 3rd. ed. New York: St. Martin's, 1974. 342pp. ML410.W15D6 1974b (no ISBN available)

Interprets the entire story of Wagner's tetralogy and certain aspects, especially musical interrelationships between many of its *Leitmotive*, in terms of Jungian symbolism and the reconciliation of opposites inherent in representations of archetypal situations. Includes 91 motifs (pp. 275–306) but no other musical examples; the appendix concludes with an index of the motives. Also includes a depiction of "family trees in the *Ring*" (p. 13) and a bibliography (316–28), as well as an index.

Originally published in 1963. A second edition appeared in 1969, and a third edition was published in 1974 by Faber & Faber of London (ISBN 0571048250). See also item 912.

Among Donington's followers (cynics might prefer the term "copycats") is Jean Shinoda Bolen, whose *Ring of Power: The Abandoned Child, the Authoritarian Father, and the Disempowered Feminine* (San Francisco 1992; ISBN 0062500864) bears the tertiary title "A Jungian Understanding of Wagner's Ring Cycle" and an acknowledgment (p. 232) that its author "did not read any other psychological interpretations" of Wagner's work than Donington's. Bolen's volume includes (pp. 235–36), but her bibliography (pp. 230–34) contains no other references whatsoever to musicological studies or issues!

650. Gaillard, Paul-André. *L'Anneau du Nibelung de Richard Wagner*. Paris: "Editions E. G. P.," 1977. 141pp. (no LC or ISBN available)

A textbook for a course offered by the Université populaire de Lausanne on Wagner and his music dramas. Much of Gaillard's volume is devoted to Wieland Wagner's *Ring* productions and other performances of the 1950s to 1970s. Includes some 50 black-and-white illustrations, among them photographs and other pictures of past and present stage sets and scenes, as well as a portrait of the composer; concludes with a two-page illustrations catalog. No bibliography or musical examples.

651. Holman, J. K. *Wagner's Ring: A Listener's Companion & Concordance*. Portland, OR: Amadeus, 1996. 440pp. ISBN 157467014X ML410.W22H65 1996 ⁊82.1 W134 rYh

A guidebook illustrated with 145 musical examples, as well as a table of motifs and the names under which they appear in Holman's volume (pp.

107–9). Also includes a few illustrations—among them, a frontispiece reproduction of the Peter Cornelius engraving of scenes from the *Nibelung-enlied* that hung above the composer's desk in Dresden during the 1840s— as well as a chronological table of Wagner's activities on behalf of his tetralogy (pp. 31–37), a better-than-average discography (pp. 403–19), notes, and a bibliography of English-language *Ring* publications (pp. 426–34); concludes with an index.

652. Hutcheson, Ernest. *A Musical Guide to the Ring of the Nibelungs*. New York: Simon & Schuster, 1940; reprinted New York: AMS Press, 1972. xvi, 216pp. ISBN 0404034624 MT100.W25H8 1972

A running commentary on Wagner's story and the music to which it is set. Keyed throughout to a glossary of motifs (pp. 201–15) identified by such names as "Bondage," "Flight," and "Smithy"; many of these, as well as other short musical passages, are sprinkled throughout the rest of the volume. Also includes a brief bibliography (pp. 197–99); concludes with the motivic glossary mentioned above instead of a general index.

653. Lee, M. Owen. *Wagner's Ring: Turning the Sky Round*. New York: Summit, 1990. 120pp. ISBN 0671707736 ML410.W13L3 1990

A straightforward discussion of the composer's story and the most elementary aspects of his musical discourse, accompanied by a kind of appendix containing 24 musical motives (pp. 113–20). Also includes a bibliography entitled "Further Reading" (pp. 99–112).

654. Sabor, Rudolph. *Richard Wagner: "Der Ring des Nibelungen"—A Companion Volume*. London: Phaidon, 1997. 254pp. ISBN 0714836508 ML410.W22S22 1997

An excellent guide to Wagner's tetralogy, accompanied by a large number of illustrations and musical examples. Sabor summarizes the story, identifies the charaters, explains how the composer employed various musical devices throughout his scores, and describes the *Ring* orchestra; he also discusses the work's evolution as well as its debt to a variety of literary and mythological sources, and he encapsulates some of the principal critical responses to its contents and to several of its productions. Also includes a brief bibliography, discography, and "videography," as well as a gathering of *Leitmotive* (the last pp. 240–48); concludes with an index.

Anthologies and "readers" devoted to the Ring *as a whole include:*

655. *Bayreuther Dramaturgie: Der Ring des Nibelungen,* ed. Herbert Barth. Stuttgart and Zurich: Belser, 1980. 445pp. ISBN 3763990398 ML410.W15B38

A "New Bayreuth *Ring* reader" rather than a study of stage direction and production per se. Consists primarily of essays, many of them familiar, by Theodor Adorno, Kurt Blaukopf, Ernst Bloch, and Ernest Newman, as well as Dahlhaus, Dietrich Mack, Westernhagen, and Wieland Wagner; these are divided into sections that are themselves organized chronologically: thus the essays by Newman and Westernhagen appear under "Die Jahre 1951–1958," those by Blaukopf and Bloch under "Die Jahre 1960–1964," and so on. The fifth section, entitled "Die Jahre 1976–1980 von Patrice Chéreaus Ring-Inszenierung," includes the text of a lengthy interview with the controversial director (pp. 375–402). Also contains a scattering of musical examples and a list of contributors (pp. 439–41). Closely related selections appear in *Theaterarbeit an Wagners Ring,* ed. Mack (Munich, 1978; ISBN 3492023754).

656. *Der Ring am Rhein,* ed. Wolfgang Storch. Berlin: Hentrich, 1991. 215pp. ISBN 392617594X ML410.W15R57 1991

A collection of texts pertaining to the background and character of Wagner's story, its relationship to certain nineteenth- and twentieth-century cultural issues, and its reception by a variety of critics. Published as a literary "accompaniment" to a production overseen by Kurt Horres. Among the authors represented are medieval poets Snorri Sturluson and Hildegard of Bingen, as well as Wagner himself (*Die Wibelungen* and *Die Nibelungensage,* both complete), his granddaughter Nike Wagner, Paul Claudel, Vincent van Gogh, Carl Gustav Jung, Theodor Lessing, and historian Oswald Spengler. Includes a large number of black-and-white production photographs, as well as color facsimiles of two pastel drawings made in 1906 by Marianne Werefkin. No bibliography or musical examples.

657. *In den Trümmern der eignen Welt: Richard Wagners "Der Ring des Nibelungen,"* ed. Udo Bermbach. Hamburger Beiträge zur offentlichen Wissenschaft, 7. Berlin and Hamburg: Dietrich Reimer, 1989. 275pp. ISBN 3496004525 ML410.W15I5 1989

A collection of essays, among them the editor's own "Die Destruktion der Institutionen: Zum politischen Gehalt des 'Ring,' " which appeared originally under a somewhat different title in the *Programmhefte der Bayreuther Festspiele* III (1988), pp. 13–66. Also includes Werner Breig's "Zur musikalischen Struktur von Wagner's 'Ring des Nibelungen' " (pp. 39–62), and several essays concerning performance and production problems. Illustrated throughout with scattered documentary facsimiles; concludes with a bibliography; Breig's essay contains a few musical examples.

658. *Penetrating Wagner's "Ring": An Anthology*, ed. John DiGaetani. Cranbury, NJ, and London: University Press of America, 1978; reprinted New York: Da Capo, 1991. 456pp. ISBN 0306804379 ML410.W13P46 1991

A miscellany of articles on theoretical issues, passages from celebrated interpretive essays by Donington, Mayer, Ernest Newman, and Bernard Shaw, studies of historical influences, and so on. Many of DiGaetani's selections have appeared in print before: John Culshaw's "New Directions for the 'Ring,' " for example, in *High Fidelity* (November, 1966); Bryan Magee's "Wagner's Theory of Opera," in his *Aspects of Wagner* (item 4); and George Windell's "Hitler, National Socialism, and Richard Wagner" in the *Journal of Central European Affairs*. Also includes a *Ring* chronology—actually a chronology of Wagner's life (pp. 441–42)—and a useful annotated discography by DiGaetani himself, updated for the 1991 edition (pp. 443–46), as well as scattered black-and-white illustrations, most of them performance photographs, and musical examples. Concludes with a rather quirky "annotated" bibliography and an index. Received a mixed review from Deathridge in *19th Century Music* 5 (1981–1982), pp. 81–89.

Document and Source Studies

659. Westernhagen, Curt von. *The Forging of the "Ring": Richard Wagner's Composition Sketches for "Der Ring des Nibelungen,"* trans. Arnold and Mary Whittall. Cambridge and London: Cambridge University Press, 1976. viii, 248pp. ISBN 0521212936 ML410.W15W1853

Beginning with *Siegfrieds Tod*, Westernhagen examines surviving sketches for the entire *Ring* cycle. Outfitted with—and largely based on—75 mostly multi-partite musical examples; also includes a few facsimiles, as well as a chapter entitled "The Significance of Composition Sketches" (pp. 1–12); intended both as an introduction to the entire subject and to the volume in question. Concludes with a bibliography (pp. 244–46) and an index.

Published originally under the title *Die Entstehung des "Ring," dargestellt an den Kompositionsskizzen Richard Wagners* (Zurich, 1973). Evaluated in some detail by Deathridge in "Wagner's Sketches for the 'Ring,' " published in *The Musical Times* 118 (1977), pp. 383–89.

*   *Dokumente zur . . . Ring des Nibelungen,* ed. Werner Breig and Hartmut Fladt. Described under item 156.

The first of several projected volumes of documents associated with the *Ring*'s origins, background, and compositional history. Includes handsome facsimiles and scattered musical examples.

660. *Richard Wagner: Skizzen und Entwürfe zur Ring-Dichtung, mit der Dichtung "Der junge Siegfried,"* ed. Otto Strobel. Munich: F. Bruckmann, 1930. 263pp. (no LC number available)

Contains the complete text of *Der junge Siegfried* (pp. 99–198), Wagner's original draft for what later grew into the *Ring des Nibelungen* libretto, together with other sketches and drafts for portions of the *Ring* libretto and Strobel's own historical and textual observations (pp. 13–22). Handsomely outfitted with some 25 documentary facsimiles, most of them printed in both red and black, folded, and tipped into appropriate places in the volume. Also contains a brief bibliography (p. 10), several musical examples, and a list of facsimile sources (p. 263).

Other studies of sources for the Ring *as a musical-dramatic work include:*

661. Bailey, Robert. "The Structure of the 'Ring' and Its Evolution." *19th Century Music* 1 (1977–1978), pp. 48–61. ML1.N77

Considers Wagner's early sketches and drafts for various portions of the *Ring*, especially *Walküre*, act II, scene iv (the "Todesverkündigung"), and *Götterdämmerung*, act I, to illustrate how the entire tetralogy is organized in terms of tonal congruences. Includes seven musical examples as well as three diagrams devoted to harmonic relationships.

662. Ellis, William Ashton. "Die verschiedenen Fassungen von 'Siegfrieds Tod': Ein Beitrag zur Wagner-Forschung," trans. Rudolf Schlösser. *Die Musik* 3–X (1903–1904), pp. 239–51 and 315–31. ML5.M9

A study of several prose drafts and other preliminary materials, most of them dating from the late 1840s, for what—after extensive alteration and years later—were transformed first into drafts for the librettos of *Siegfried* (*Der junge Siegfried*) and *Götterdämmerung* (*Siegfrieds Tod*), and finally into the basis of the entire *Ring* poem. No musical examples.

Textual and Literary Studies
Of special interest is the following outstanding study:

663. Magee, Elizabeth. *Richard Wagner and the Nibelungs*. Oxford: Clarendon, 1990. 230pp. ISBN 0198161905 ML41.0W15M3 1991

Evaluates the sources upon which Wagner drew for his readings pursuant to drafting and completing his *Ring* poems, *Siegfrieds Tod* among them. Part I (pp. 25–61) concentrates on Wagner's use of the Royal Dresden Library and other sources prior to 1849; Part II (pp. 59–205) is devoted to the composer's own texts, and contains numerous quotations and translations in German and English. Also contains in the form of three appendices a precise chronology of Wagner's *Ring* writings between 1848 and 1863 (p. 212), new information about what he read and when he read it (pp. 213–15), and a synopsis of what he drew from the various *Eddas* (pp. 216–17). Finally, Magee provides a catalog of "Wagner's Personal Library at Dresden" (pp. 25–46). Includes several illustrations, including a frontispiece that reproduces a page from Pfizer's, Simrock's, and Vollmer's edition of the medieval *Nibelungenlied*—one of many sources upon which Wagner is now known to have drawn. Concludes with a bibliography (pp. 218–23) and index.

Reviewed enthusiastically by Millington in *The Musical Times* 134 (1993), p. 177. NB: Magee's study incorporates the results of many others, among them turn-of-the-last-century masterpieces like Golther's *Sagengeschichtliche Grundlagen der Ringdichtung Richard Wagners* (Berlin, 1902), which Magee calls "the most useful work all round to date" (p. 18; see also item 875).

Other textual and literary studies of the Ring *as a whole include:*

664. Hauer, Stanley R. "Wagner and the 'Völospá.' " *19th Century Music* 15 (1991–1992), pp. 52–63. ML1.N77

Explains why this medieval source, rather than the *Völsunga saga*, the *Nibelungenlied*, and various of the *Eddas* "provided Wagner with the essential world-myth which distinguishes the *Ring* from all other Nibelung dramas" (p. 62)—and this in spite of the fact that Wagner wrote nothing about the *Völospá* in a list of ten sources he consulted during the 1850s.

* Koch, Ernst. *Wagners . . . "Der Ring des Nibelungen," in seinem Verhältniss zur alten Sage*. Described as item 1010.

More a mythological than a musical-dramatic study of the *Ring* and its medieval sources.

665. *Wagner's "Ring" and Its Icelandic Sources: A Symposium at the Reykjavík Arts Festival, 29 May 1994*, ed. Úlfar Bragason. Reykjavík: Stornum Sigurðar Nordals, 1995. 88pp. ISBN 9979911123 (no LC number available)

In addition to discussions and pictures of the Reykjavík *Ring* productions, this rather obscure volume contains articles by Millington ("The 'Ring' and its Times: The Social and Political Background to the Tetralogy," pp. 17–30) and Spencer ("Engi má við sköpum vinna: Wagner's Use of His Icelanic Sources," pp. 55–76) as well as Þorsteinn Gylfason's "Richard Wagner as a Poet" (pp. 77–86). Spencer refers to the *Nibelungenlied* and other more familiar sources, including *Þiðreks Saga*, the *Poetic Edda*, Sturluson's *Heimskringla*, and the *Völsunga saga*; his article concludes with a timeline that identifies the composer's readings as well as unfinished works—*Achilleus, Jesus von Nazareth*, and *Der junge Siegfried*— that also incorporate mythological materials (pp. 74–76).

666. Weston, Jessie L. "Legends of the Wagner Trilogy [*sic*]." In: *The Volsunga Saga*, trans. Eiríkr Magnússon and William M. Morris. London and New York: Norroena Society, 1906; pp. 161–340. PT7287.V7E55 1906

Evaluates literary and mythological antecedents of Wagner's *Ring,* especially that work's relationship to the Icelandic sagas. In spite of the title of her essay, Weston addresses all four music dramas (she must have considered *Rheingold,* as did Wagner, a kind of "Introduction"); for each she summarizes the origins of its story and characters, explains the differences between Germanic, Icelandic, and Old Norse sources of the legends themselves, considers the story of *Siegfried* in relationship to the Grail legends of medieval France, and so on. Includes scattered illustrations by nineteenth- and early twentieth-century illustrators, but neither musical examples nor index.

Magnússon's and Morris's translation was originally published in 1870 in London and reprinted in 1888 in New York, without Weston's essay.

Other studies of the literary models for and character of Wagner's Ring include these books and articles, several of them devoted to mythological issues:

667. Benvenga, Nancy. *Kingdom on the Rhine: History, Myth, and Legend in Wagner's Ring.* Harwich, Essex: Anton, 1982. 180pp. ISBN 0946380007 ML410.W15B5 1983

Another study of the *Ring* as story, one that concentrates on historical underpinnings and various medieval sources. Benvenga provides illustrations of old Germanic and Icelanic votive stones and other relics, including reconstructed musical instruments, as well as a hand-drawn map of the Frankish kingdom under Guntram, a few photographs of Wagnerian characters portrayed by famous singers, and scattered musical examples. Unfortunately, her extensive quotations from the *Eddas,* the *Nibelungen-*

lied, and other sources appear only in English. Includes a bibliography (pp. 173–75); concludes with an index.

668. Cicora, Mary A. *Wagner's "Ring" and German Drama: Comparative Studies in Mythology and History in Drama*. Contributions to the Study of Music and Dance, 52. Westport, CT: Greenwood, 1999. viii, 186pp. ISBN 0313305293 ML410.W15C54 1999

A discussion not only of the influence of Goethe and Schiller on Wagner's *Ring*, but of Wagner's knowledge of Hebbel's *Ring* dramas, and his influence on Hugo von Hofmannsthal's libretto for Richard Strauss's *Ariadne auf Naxos*. Includes a useful bibliography (pp. 171–84); concludes with an index. A second, somewhat earlier study by Cicora—*Mythology as Metaphor: Romantic Irony, Critical Theory, and Wagner's "Ring"* (Westport, CT, 1989; ISBN 0313305285), also published by Greenwood—contains another fine bibliography (pp. 161–70).

669. Cord, William O. *The Teutonic Mythology of Richard Wagner's "The Ring of the Nibelung."* Studies in the History and Interpretation of Music, 18. 5 vols. Lewiston, MA: Edwin Mellen, 1989–1991. Vols. 1–2: ISBN 0889464413; Vols. 3–5: ISBN 088946443X (no LC numbers available)

A massive, somewhat oversimplified synopsis of interconnections between ancient Northern European mythology—which is to say, primary sources—and Wagner's music dramas. Each volume is indexed and paginated separately; Vol. 3 is subdivided into "The Natural and Supernatural Worlds," Parts 1 and 2. Reviewed by Elizabeth Magee [*Music & Letters* 75 (1994), pp. 98–100], who criticizes Cord for factual errors as well as his failure to cite secondary sources that influenced Wagner's understanding of Germanic myth. A closely related study also by Cord, "On Dwarves and Giants and Wagner's Ring," appeared in *New Studies in Richard Wagner's The Ring of the Nibelung*, ed. Herbert Richardson (Lewiston, NY, 1991), pp. 1–18, together with essays by John Daverio, Robert Martin, and other contributors.

670. *Richard Wagner—"Der Ring des Nibelungen": Ansichten des Mythos*, ed. Udo Bermbach and Dieter Borchmeyer. Stuttgart and Weimar: J. B. Metzler, 1995. 195pp. ISBN347601326X ML410.W15R45 1995

Incorporates thirteen essays by expert Wagnerians—among them Carolyn Abbate, Ludwig Finscher (see item 1016), and Borchmeyer himself—devoted to mythology and the *Ring* in terms of musical structure, staging problems, performances of and attitudes toward the *Ring* during Germany's "Weimar Republic" (c. 1920–1933), and so on. Includes an introduction by Wolfgang Wagner, 40 color sketches by "Rosalie" for the 1994–1995 Bayreuth *Ring* production, and three photographs; no musical examples, however, and the sketches are bound as an unpaginated fascicle at the end of the volume.

671. Sørensen, Villy. "Greek and Norse Mythology in the 'Ring': Wagner's Sources of Inspiration." *Programmhefte der Bayreuther Festspiele* V (1991), pp. 35–47. ML410.W2B26

Examines various autobiographical sources—including *A Communication to My Friends*, *The Wibelungs*, and the draft of a drama entitled *The Nibelung Myth*—related to Wagner's interests in Aeschylus, the *Eddas*, and so on, especially in terms of "the death of the hero" (p. 37), around which many of his works revolve. Contains representative quotations from literary sources. Also available in French and German in the same volume.

672. *Wege des Mythos in der Moderne: Richard Wagner, "Der Ring des Nibelungen,"* ed. Dieter Borchmeyer. Munich: Deutscher Taschenbuch Verlag, 1987. 264pp. ISBN 3423044683 ML410.W15W18 1987

A sophisticated anthology devolving primarily upon mythology and post-modern criticism. Includes essays by Carl Friedrich von Weizsäcker on the nature of myth as an object of scientific study, and by Klaus Kanzog on Franz Lang's *Ring* films (see item 865) as "alternatives" to Wagner's and Hebbel's dramatic productions; also includes more specifically Wagnerian studies by Borchmeyer himself, Dieter Bremer, Dahlhaus (see item 673), and so on. Supplemented with a foreword by conductor Wolfgang Sawallisch; outfitted with notes instead of a bibliography.

Musical Studies

673. Dahlhaus, Carl. "Formprinzipien in Wagners 'Ring des Nibelungen.' " In: *Beiträge zur Geschichte der Oper*, ed. Heinz Becker. Studien zur Musikgeschichte des neunzehnten Jahrhunderts, 15. Regensburg: Gustav Bosse, 1969; pp. 95–129. ML1700.1.B43

Criticizes Lorenz's concept of evolving form. As in other of his Wagner studies, Dahlhaus strives to illustrate the close relationships that exist between the composer's melodic periods and speech patterns, as well as the interdependence of musical and dramatic—which is to say, musical and mythic—elements in Wagner's most important works. See also "Musik als strukturale Analyse des Mythos: Claude Lévi-Strauss und 'Der Ring des Nibelungen,' " published in item 672. See, too, Dahlhaus's article "Tonalität und Form in Wagners 'Ring des Nibelungen,' " described briefly under item 62.

*   Lorenz, Alfred. *Der musikalische Aufbau . . . "Der Ring des Nibelungen."*
    Described as item 482, Vol. 1.

674. Riedlbauer, Jörg. " 'Erinnerungsmotive' in Wagner's 'Der Ring des
     Nibelungen.' " *The Musical Quarterly* 74 (1990), pp. 18–30. ML1.M725

     Attempts not only to explain how and why certain of Wagner's motifs
     function as "reminders" within the *Ring*, but more accurately to define the
     character and function of such motifs overall. For Riedlbauer, Wolzogen's
     notion of *Leitmotive* is problematic; for him, too, Wagner's references in
     certain of his prose works to *Erinnerungsmotive* "must be looked at in
     light of his [Wagner's] symphonic ambitions" (p. 30). Includes short musi-
     cal examples scattered throughout both the text and footnotes.

675. Schäfer, Wolf-Dieter. "Syntaktische und semantische Bedienungen der
     Motivinstrumentation in Wagners 'Ring.' " In: *Festschrift Heinz Becker
     zum 60. Geburtstag am 26. Juni 1982*, ed. Jürgen Schläder and Reinhold
     Quandt. Laaber: Laaber Verlag, 1982; pp. 191–204. ISBN 3921518709
     ML55.B32M

     Examines Wagner's instrumentation for certain *Leitmotive*, especially the
     "Tarnhelm" and "Fate" motifs, throughout the *Ring* and especially in act
     II, scene iv, of *Walküre*. Schäfer also discusses transitions between scenes
     to point out more effectively how orchestrational changes reflect changes
     in overall meaning; this, then, is an interpretive as well as a stylistic study.

More than a few publications devolve entirely upon motives as a guide to the
Ring*'s story and musical contents:*

676. Heintz, Albert. *Wegweiser durch die Motivenwelt der Musik zu Richard
     Wagner's Bühnenfestspiel Der Ring des Nibelungen, in besonderer Rück-
     sicht auf ihren organischen Zusammenhang mit dem dichterischen Gehalte
     des Dramas.* Berlin-Charlottenburg: Verlag der "Allgemeinen Musik-
     Zeitung," 1893. 135pp. (no LC number available)

     A "musical map" based primarily on 245 musical *Leitmotive* identified by
     Heintz in a catalog appended to the end of his volume (pp. i–v). Quite
     detailed; unindexed, however, and equipped with neither bibliography nor
     other scholarly apparatus. But one of several nineteenth-century motivic
     guides to the *Ring*.

677. Wolzogen, Hans von. *Guide Through the Music of R. Wagner's "The Ring
     of the Nibelung,"* trans. Ernst von Wolzogen; 3rd ed. Boston: Arthur P.
     Schmidt, c. 1898. 80pp. MT100.W25W7 1898

An English-language version of Wolzogen's motivic guidebook, illustrated throughout with musical examples of individual *Motive*. Originally written and published in German as *Thematischer Leitfaden durch die Musik zu Richard Wagners Festspiel "Der Ring des Nibelungen"* (Leipzig, 1876; London, 1882); the 3rd edition was also published in 1896 in Leipzig. See also items 472–74 and 649.

Performance and Reception Studies: see also items 847–49 and 860.

678. Fay, Stephen. *The Ring: Anatomy of an Opera*. Dover, NH: Longwood, 1985. 218pp. ISBN 0893415324 ML410.W1F4 1985

Essentially a log of the 1983 Bayreuth *Ring* conducted by Sir Georg Solti. Ray's observations are documented visually in unusual detail; the author himself writes about the "remarkable photographs" (p. 174) taken by Roger Wood during dozens of administrative and business meetings, rehearsals, and performances. Almost as much an iconography, therefore, as an historical and technical study of a Bayreuth production and a reception study. Includes a synopsis of the *Ring* story (pp. 214–15) and a list of cast members involved in the performances (p. 215); concludes with an index. Reviewed in greater detail in *Opera Quarterly* 3/2 (Summer 1985), pp. 173–74.

679. *Histoire d'un "Ring": Der Ring des Nibelungen (l'Anneau du Nibelung) de Richard Wagner, Bayreuth 1976–1980*, with Sylvie de Nussac and François Regnault. Paris: Robert Laffont, 1980. 255pp. ISBN 2221500741 (no LC number available)

A lavishly illustrated history of the Chéreau *Ring* at Bayreuth. Includes rehearsal and performance photographs, many of them in color, as well as introductory comments by Wolfgang Wagner and co-editor Nussac, essays by conductor Pierre Boulez, Chéreau himself, stage designer Richard Peduzzi, and costume designer Jacques Schmidt, and short articles by co-editor Regnault on Chéreau's neo-Marxist "reading." Also includes cast lists for the 1976 to 1980 productions (pp. 254–55). No bibliography, however, and no index. In French throughout.

680. Kolland, Hubert. *Die kontroverse Rezeption von Wagners Nibelungen-Ring, 1850–1870*. Berliner Musik-Studien, 5. Cologne: Studio, 1995. vi, 193pp. ISBN 3895640077 ML410.W1K64 1995

Describes the reception accorded Wagner's massive work even before it was finished and performed complete for the first time. Kolland examines with special care Wagner performances of 1863 to 1865 (a table of them appears on pp. 92–93), as well as performances of *Rheingold* and *Walküre* presented during the late 1860s. Illustrated with scattered pictures and documentary facsimiles; concludes with a bibliography (pp. 183–93). Adapted from the author's 1992 doctoral dissertation.

681. Kügler, Ilka-Maria. *"Der Ring des Nibelungen": Studie zur Entwicklungs-geschichte seiner Wiedergabe auf der deutschsprachigen Bühne.* Dissertation: University of Cologne typescript copy, 1967. iv, 361pp. (no LC number available)

An "evolutionary history" of the *Ring* in German-language performances from 1876 to the 1960s, with chapters devoted especially to post–World War II productions. Concludes with a useful bibliography.

682. Lewin, Michael. *Der Ring. Bayreuth 1988–1992.* Hamburg: Europäische Verlagsanstalt, 1991. 367pp. ISBN 3434500057 (no LC number available)

A good-sized, beautifully printed volume consisting of an introduction to Bayreuth performances of the late 1980s and early 1990s, comments on the *Ring* by several literary "greats," and interviews with performers—including conductor Daniel Barenboim—as well as essays by Barenboim, Harry Kupfer, Hans Mayer, and others, photographs and information about virtually everyone associated with the various productions, almost fifty pages of newspaper reviews of the Bayreuth performances, a "Ring-Bibliographie," a "Ring-Diskographie," and indexes. Especially impressive are the numerous color illustrations of sets, rehearsals, performances, and singing stars. Also includes a few scattered musical examples.

A single study has been devoted exclusively to stage and set designs for a celebrated Ring *production:*

683. *Der Ring des Nibelungen von Richard Wagner: Dekorationsentwürfe von Prof. Max Brückner in Coburg.* Bayreuth: Heinrich Heuschmann, 1896. Unpaginated. (no LC number available)

A small oblong volume comprising thirteen stage and set designs for the 1896 Bayreuth Festival *Ring* production. Of special interest to students of Wagner performances is the high degree of realism evident in the designs themselves; whether they were in fact designed by Brückner or merely adapted from designs of Joseph Hoffmann (as was the case with the 1876 *Ring*) is not clear. Includes a one-page introduction. Uncommon: Harvard University's Loeb Music Library owns a copy.

Interpretive Studies

One especially important study deals with the Ring *as a whole and the Greek dramatist Aeschylus:*

684. Ewans, Michael. *Wagner and Aeschylus: The "Ring" and the "Oresteia."* London: Faber & Faber, 1992. ISBN 0571118089 ML410.W15

Attempts to show "that the examples of Aeschylus' great trilogy is present in the procedures of the *Ring* at several major levels, from the overall concept of a cycle of three closely interrelated dramas—disguised for consecutive performance and solely for festival occasions—right through to profound aspects of subject-matter and form" (p. 10). Ewans draws upon Denys Page's translation of the *Oresteia*, as well as his own translations of Wagner's texts; in an appendix (pp. 256–60), Ewans also considers whether Wagner was influenced in the *Ring* more by Aeschylus' *Prometheus Bound*, and concludes he was not. Contains scattered quotations and musical examples, most of them brief, as well as a "select bibliography" (pp. 261–65); concludes with an index.

Reviewed in *Wagner* 4/3 (June, 1983), pp. 90–93; and the *Music Review* 43 (1982), p. 271.

NB: Pearl C. Wilson, in *Wagner's Dramas and Greek Tragedy* (Dissertation: Columbia University, 1919) was apparently the first person to suggest the *Ring-Oresteia* connection. Other authors have also discussed Wagner and Aeschylus; see, for example, Mische Meier's "Das Gericht der Eumeniden und der Götterdämmerung" in *Die Musikforschung* 51 (1998), pp. 409–19. In his "Droysens und Wagner: Zum Konzept des musikalischen Dramas," published in *Neue Musik und Tradition: Festschrift Rudolf Stephan zum 65. Geburtstag*, ed. Josef Kuckertz et al. (Laaber, 1990), pp. 251–57, Arno Forchert evaluates the influence on Wagner of historian J. G. Droysen's Aeschylus translation during 1847, Wagner's "Greek year."

Several studies have also been devoted to notions of might, justice, and vengeance in the Ring, *especially in terms of Germanic moral and legal traditions:*

685. White, David A. *The Turning Wheel: A Study of Contracts and Oaths in Wagner's "Ring."* London: Associated University Presses, 1988. 135pp. ISBN 0941664899 ML410.W15W19 1988

Considers the *Ring* as a network of interlocking contracts and promises, with reference to Shaw's *Perfect Wagnerite*, Donington's *Ring and Its Symbols*, and other important secondary studies. Reviewed by Donington in *The Musical Times* 130 (1989), pp. 283–84, who notes the significance of "pre-conscious" choices, as well as fully conscious legalistic decisions in grappling with Wagner's psychologically complex work.

Also published in the United States (Selinsgrove, PA, 1988). Earlier studies of the *Ring* and legal issues more often tend to justify the composer; among such studies is Mary E. Lewis's *Ethics of Wagner's "The Ring of the Nibelungs"* (New York, 1906), which proposes that the tetralogy demonstrates "the advancement of the thought of the world" (p. v).

Other studies of Wagner's Ring, justice, and "the law" include:

686. Koch, Thomas. *Recht, Macht und Liebe in Richard Wagner's "Der Ring des Nibelungen."* Nomos Universitätsschriften: Recht [law], 222. Baden-Baden: Nomos, 1996. 110pp. ISBN 3789044210 ML410.W15K76 1996

Deals with justice, retribution, punishment, and forgiveness—all of them considered from "more" and "less" primitive vantage points—in Wagner's tetralogy, together with issues involving German legal history, the *Oresteia* (item 684), and the myth of Oedipus. Concludes with a bibliography (pp. 101–10) rather than an index.

687. Kopnick, Lutz. *Nothungs Modernität: Wagner's "Ring" und die Poesis der Macht im neunzehnten Jahrhundert.* Munich: Wilhelm Fink, 1994. 270pp. ISBN 3770529848 ML410.W15K75 1994

A study of "the sword" as power symbol and Wagner's grasp of power politics in nineteenth-century Europe. Among other culture heroes Kopenick considers relevant to Wagner's circle of influence are Freud, Marx, and partisans of German nationalism, Hitler among them. Includes a few black-and-white illustrations of *Ring* scenes, as well as two musical examples and a useful bibliography (pp. 259–66).

688. Pidde, Bernst von. *Wagners Musikdramen "Der Ring des Nibelungen" im Lichte des deutschen Strafrechts,* 4th ed. Hamburg: Hoffman & Campe, 1987. 78pp. ISBN 3455059252 ML410.W15P5 1987

A rather amusing discussion of the *Ring* in terms of its compacts, broken and unbroken, and of its various felonies, including the theft of the gold itself, the kidnapping of Freia by Fafner and Fasolt, the murder of Hunding, Siegfried's "cruelty" to the dragon (!), and so on. For each Pidde discusses punishments under German law; near the end of his work (pp. 74–75) he identifies the name of each criminal, identifies his/her crime(s) by name and precise reference to the post-World War II German Criminal Code, and explains what its punishment would be today. Also includes eight black-and-white plates of scenes from the *Ring* story and an index (pp. 76–77); concludes with a one-page bibliography. Originally published at Frankfurt a.M. in 1968.

689. Seiler, Stefan. *Das Delikt als Handlungselement in Richard Wagners "Der Ring des Nibelungen."* Juristische Schriftenreihe, 150. Vienna: "Verlag Österreich," 1998. 194pp. ISBN 370461257X ML410.W22S4 1998

Discusses issues associated with such legal concepts as "might" and "power" and outfitted with a bibliography of mostly legal sources (pp. 185–88), as well as a brief discography of *Ring* recordings (pp. 189–92) and an index. Illustrated with a few cartoons contributed by Peter Schwarzbauer. Apparently revised from a dissertation of the same name completed at the University of Salzburg in 1993 (ISBN 3853699138).

Additional interpretive studies devoted to the Ring *as a whole include the following books and articles:*

* Abbate, Carolyn. *Unsung Voices*. Described as item 990.

A sophisticated postmodern study primarily of the *Ring* as narrative. Includes musical examples.

690. Ackermann, Peter. *Richard Wagners "Ring des Nibelungen" und die Dialektik der Aufklärung*. Frankfurter Beiträge zur Musikwissenschaft, 9. Tutzing: Hans Schneider, 1981. 167pp. ISBN 3795203104 ML410.W15A3 1981

Should Wagner's *Ring* be "read" in terms of hope, evolution, and progress, or in terms of nihilism and despair? Ackermann adopts the latter perspective, especially in light of Enlightenment political and social theory. Includes a few musical examples; concludes with a brief bibliography.

691. Benz, Bernhard. *Zeitstrukturen in Richard Wagners "Ring"-Tetrologie*. Europäische Hochschulschriften: Musikwissenschaft, 112. Frankfurt a.M.: Peter Lang, 1994. 418pp. ISBN 3631468202. ML410.W15B56 1994

A theoretical study devoted to Schopenhauer's and Nietzsche's influence on Wagner's thought and artistic practice, notions of "endless melody," and "the end of things" in the *Ring*. Illustrated with 31 musical examples; also includes a bibliography (pp. 411–18).

692. Darcy, Warren G. "The Metaphysics of Annihilation: Wagner, Schopenhauer, and the Ending of the 'Ring.' " *Music Theory Spectrum* 16/1 (Spring 1994), pp. 1–40. MT6.M9622

Attempts to dispel the widely accepted notion that the *Ring* ends "happily" by referring to Schopenhauer's influence on Wagner's music and, specifically, by certain harmonic aspects, especially of the conclusion of *Götterdämmerung*. Darcy claims that a misreading by Wolzogen of a passage Wagner himself repudiated led to mistaken theories about "the redemption of the world through love and the rebirth of the world in innocence," and that "it is perhaps best to agree with Deryck Cooke that 'the story told in *The Ring*,' undeniably, is the history of a whole world, from its origins to its dissolution, since nothing is imagined . . . as capable of happening after its last event" (p. 40). Illustrated with fifteen musical examples and Schenkerian reductions as well as three charts.

693. Jacobs, Robert L. "A Freudian View of 'The Ring.' " *Music Review* 26 (1965), pp. 201–19. ML5.M657

Considers the completed *Ring* as Wagner's unwitting but nevertheless serious attempt to "psychoanalyze" *Siegfrieds Tod*, the composer's original sketch for the libretto that eventually was expanded to encompass the events of all four music dramas (p. 205). Includes extensive quotations from a variety of sources, as well as four musical examples. Unfortunately, Jacobs's analysis of Wagner's hidden intentions is limited for the most part—as he himself confesses—to "obvious aspects of the Oedipus Complex" (p. 201).

694. Lindlar, Heinrich. " 'Weißt du, wie das wird?' 100 Jahre Wagners 'Ring des Nibelungen' im Zentenar, Bayreuth 1876–1976. Rezeption und Konzeption." In: *Heinrich Lindlar: Leben mit Musik. Aufsätze und Vorträge, Köln 1960–1992*. Beiträge zur rheinischen Musikgeschichte, 145. Berlin: Merseburger, 1993; pp. 57–67. ISBN 3875555372506 ML55.L51 1993

Musings on the ideas Lindlar perceives behind and within the *Ring*, as well as a sketchy survey of some of the literature associated with the music dramas themselves. Includes a single musical example and a single illustration, the latter a facsimile of Mendel's drawing *Richard Wagner auf der Probe, 1875*.

695. McDonald, William E. "What Does Wotan Know? Autobiography and Moral Vision in Wagner's 'Ring.' " *19th-Century Music* 15 (1991–1992), pp. 36–51. ML1.N77

Examines relationships between love, power, musical elements, and aspects of Wagner's own life and that of his character, especially in terms of Wotan's act II monologue in *Walküre*. Instead of a scheming "capitalist"

Wotan who mysteriously becomes an otherworldly and spiritual figure, McDonald suggests that a more complex, psychologically interesting figure was what the composer had in mind. Includes two musical examples, both from the monologue.

696. Schroeder, Leopold von. *Die Vollendung des arischen Mysteriums in Bayreuth.* Munich: J. F. Lehmann, 1911. 258pp. ML410.W2S4

A blend of quotations from and allusions to the *Rig-Veda* and other Hindu texts, combined with discussions of erotic and racial issues, intended apparently to clarify the meaning of the *Ring* as a work of "Ayran mystery." Anything but a traditional *Opernführer*. Indexed (pp. 244–55), but lacking illustrations or musical examples of any kind.

* Shaw, George Bernard. *The Perfect Wagnerite: A Commentary on Wagner's Ring.* Described as item 987.

Related Studies

697. Treadwell, James. "The 'Ring' and the Conditions of Interpretation: Wagner's Writings, 1848 to 1852." *Cambridge Opera Journal* 7 (1995), pp. 207–31. ISSN 0954-5867 (no LC number available)

A study of the *Ring*'s origins and significance based on the premise that "it may be worthwhile to adopt a purely literary approach to Wagner's texts [i.e., *Art and Revolution*, *Opera and Drama*, and other "Zurich writings" as well as the librettos themselves], if only because such criticism may direct attention away from their content towards a broader interpretation of their preoccupations, strategies and attitudes" (p. 207). No illustrations or musical examples.

STUDIES OF INDIVIDUAL RING DRAMAS AND FRAGMENTS

Siegfrieds Tod (no *WWV* number): see also items 659–60 and 662.

698. Bailey, Robert. "Wagner's Musical Structures for 'Siegfrieds Tod.' " *Studies in Music History: Essays for Oliver Strunk*, ed. Harold Powers. Princeton, NJ and London: Princeton University Press, 1968; pp. 459–94. ML3791.1.S88 1968

Describes and evaluates the significance of the *Gesamtentwurf* ("complete sketch," combining words and music) made by Wagner on 12 August 1850 for *Siegfrieds Tod*, and later made use of, "after careful revision" (p. 459), in various portions of the *Ring* as a whole. Bailey provides a transcription of the celebrated sketch (pp. 485–84) as well as nine musical examples of other kinds.

699. Westernhagen, Curt von. "Die Kompositions-Skizze zu 'Siegfrieds Tods' aus dem Jahre 1850." *Neue Zeitschrift für Musik* 124 (1963), pp. 178–82. ML5.M183

A brief description of the same sketch (see item 698), as well as a facsimile (pp. 180–81) of it and two additional musical examples that illustrate certain similarities and differences between the music Wagner gave to Brünnhilde in 1850 and 1870.

Das Rheingold, WWV 86A

* *Das Rheingold* = Vol. 10 (2 fascicles) of *Richard Wagner. Sämtliche Werke*. Described under item 156.

A critical edition prepared by Egon Voss.

Guidebooks and Survey Studies
700. Darcy, Warren. *Wagner's "Das Rheingold."* Studies in Musical Genesis and Structure, (7). Oxford: Clarendon, 1993. xv, 259pp. ISBN 0198162669 MT100.W26D33 1993

A superb "introduction" to the first of the four *Ring* dramas, although Darcy does not cover many of the theoretical issues raised by such other specialists as Lorenz and Dahlhaus. Among the illustrations are Schenkerian-style analytic musical diagrams. Outfitted with an outline of *Rheingold* by scene, key, motif, and so on (pp. xiv–xv), and a transcription of Wagner's *Gesamtentwurf* as an appendix (pp. 220–47), as well as a bibliography (pp. 248–54), and index. Reviewed at length by William Kinderman in *Music Theory Spectrum* 19/1 (Spring 1997), pp. 81–86; and by Patrick McCreless in *19th Century Music* 18 (1994–1995), pp. 277–90.

Document and Source Studies
701. Knapp, J. Merrill. "The Instrumentation Draft of Wagner's 'Das Rheingold.' " *Journal of the American Musicological Society* 30 (1977), pp. 272–95. ML27.U5A83363

Examines a manuscript belonging to the Scheide Collection at Princeton University, as well as supplementary materials belonging to the Wagner archives in Bayreuth, in order to consider Wagner's concern for such minutiae as pagination and format in laying out orchestral music in full score. Illustrated with three facsimiles of pages taken from the Scheide document.

702. Wiesend, Reinhard. "Vision and Calculation: The La Spezia Episode and

its Underlying Significance." *Programmhefte der Bayreuther Festspiele* II (1992), pp. 45–59. ML410.W2B26

Discusses and evaluates Wagner's claim in *My Life* that he fell asleep at La Spezia in September 1853 and, upon awakening, realized that he had dreamed the *Rheingold* prelude. Among other sources Wiesend cites the so-called *Gesamtentwurf* of *Rheingold*, which provides evidence—but does not prove—that "essential elements of the prelude were not conceived until the end of 1853 and beginning of 1854" (p. 47). Illustrated with five brief musical examples. An appendix (pp. 53–59) reproduces passages from Wagner's writings concerning the episode.

Textual and Literary Studies

703. Hagen, Edmund von. *Richard Wagner als Dichter in der zweiten Scene des "Rheingolds."* Munich: Christian Kaiser, 1879. xix, 266pp. (no LC number available)

An extremely close reading of Wagner's poem in terms of its vocabulary, grammar, syntactical constructions, and other philological aspects. Introductory comments explain the author's method. Uncommon in American libraries.

*   Heidgen, Norbert. *Textvarianten in Richard Wagners "Rheingold" and "Walküre."* Described as item 169.

Musical Studies

704. Breig, Werner. "Der 'Rheintöchtergesang' in Wagners 'Rheingold.' " *Archiv für Musikwissenschaft* 37 (1980), pp. 241–63. ML5.A63

Analyzes measures 534–68 of *Rheingold*, scene i. Among other subjects Breig refers rather briefly both to symmetrical aspects of the section in question and Wagner's ideas about the origins of human speech. Includes musical examples. See also item 447.

705. Darcy, Warren. " 'Creatio ex nihilo': The Genesis, Structure, and Meaning of the 'Rheingold' Prelude." *19th Century Music* 13 (1989–1990), pp. 79–100. ML1.N77

Mostly devoted to surviving manuscript sources, especially insofar as they cast light on the La Spezia episode, and on the role the prelude plays in the *Ring* as a whole. Darcy concludes by asserting that, while the evidence in no way confirms Wagner's story in *My Life* concerning his Italian "vision" of the prelude, it does not contradict it. Includes more than a dozen musical examples as well as four charts and other visual aids; also includes two appendices: the first a chronological summary of the *Ring* poem and *Rhein-gold* music, the second a list of documentary sources consulted—most of the latter, incidentally, found in Bayreuth archives. See also item 702.

706. Nitsche, Peter. "Klangfarbe und Form: das Walhallthema in Rheingold und Walküre." *Melos/Neue Zeitschrift für Musik* 1/2 (March-April 1975), pp. 83–88. ML5.M183

Discusses timbre not merely in terms of the "Valhalla" motif but as a uni-fying factor that creates both small- and large-scale congruences and helps "forge" the entire *Ring* into a unified artistic whole. Includes two full-page musical examples and one melodic excerpt. See also item 487.

Interpretive Studies
707. Darcy, Warren G. " 'Everything that Is, Ends!': The Genesis and Meaning of the Erda Episode in Das Rheingold." *The Musical Times* 129 (1988), pp. 443–47. ML5.M85

Considers the significance of the line "Alles, was ist, endet!" ("Everything that is, ends!") in the text of Erda's monologue in *Rheingold*, especially in terms of changes Wagner made to the original drafts of both his text and music. Among other subjects Darcy discusses links between Wagner's text and portions of the *Poetic Edda* and the Battle of Ragnarök the ancient Northmen believed would bring the world to an end. Includes a costume-design sketch as illustration.

708. Dyson, J. Peter. "Ironic Dualities in 'Das Rheingold.' " *Current Musicol-ogy* No. 43 (1987), pp. 33–50. ML1.C98

A study of "opposites" and, thus, of "irony"—especially "ironic reversals begotten by the now-satisfied, now frustrated ambition of Wotan" (p. 33)—in the first of the *Ring* music dramas. Includes Wagner's treat-ment of his Rhinemaidens, Alberich, and the *Ring* from the beginning of *Rheingold* to its final scene. Illustrated with seven musical examples, some multi-partite.

Die Walküre, WWV 86B

Guidebooks and Survey Studies: see items 645–54.

Musical and Interpretive Studies
   *   Burzawa, Ewa. " 'Die Walküre' von Sergei Eisenstein: Versuch der Rekon-struktion." Described as item 850.

709. Serauky, Walter. "Die Todesverkündigungsszene in Richard Wagners 'Walküre' als musikalisch-geistige Achse des Werkes." *Die Musik-forschung* 12 (1959), pp. 143–51. ML5.M9437

Examines the crucial role played by act II, scene iv, in the music drama's overall organization and impact; Serauky also argues against Lorenz's analysis of the same scene and in favor of its "open form." Includes four musical examples. See also items 488–89.

710. Voss, Egon. "Wagner konzertant, oder 'Die Walkürenritt' im Zirkus als Rettung vor der Oper." In *Festschrift für Walter Wiora zum 30. Dezember 1966*, ed. Ludwig Finscher and Christoph-Hellmut Mahling. Kassel and New York: Bärenreiter, 1967; pp. 547–54. ML55.W46F5

A brief survey of Wagner's opinions concerning the performance of excerpts from his operas and music dramas, followed by a case study: a request by one E. Renz, presented in a letter to Wagner dated 2 July 1878, to perform the "Ride of the Valkyries" as circus music! Also includes Wagner's reply the following day, together with entries in Cosima's diaries (pp. 552–53). As Voss observes, Wagner often sought the "unconventional" (p. 553). No musical examples.

Siegfried, WWV 86C

Guidebooks and Survey Studies

711. *Richard Wagner: Siegfried*, trans. Rudolph Sabor. London: Phaidon, 1997. 230pp. ISBN 0714836552 (no LC number available)

A handsome volume consisting of Wagner's libretto in English, together with a translator's introduction, a synopsis of the *Ring* story up to the end of *Walküre*, a list of characters in *Siegfried*, a bibliography, a discography (three recordings only), and even a videography (four performances, including Chéreau's). Concludes with a list of *Leitmotive* by name; the translation contains numbered references to the motifs. Illustrated with photographs of famous performers and performances and a few caricatures. Not indexed.

Additional studies of Siegfried *as a musical-dramatic whole include:*

712. McCreless, Patrick. *Wagner's "Siegfried": Its Drama, History, and Music.* Studies in Musicology, 59. Ann Arbor, MI: UMI Research Press, 1982. xiv, 248pp. ISBN 083571361X ML410.W15M35 1982

Examines Wagner's third *Ring* music drama, its interrupted compositional history, and its overall character and style. McCreless pays closest attention to issues of musical structure and coherence (pp. 81–219). Illustrated with 34 figures and tables as well as 31 musical examples, many of them quite long. Also includes extensive endnotes (pp. 221–39), a bibliography (pp. 241–43), and an index. Reviewed in *Wagner* 7/2 (April 1986), pp. 70–72; see also item 6.

713. Wolzogen, Hans von. "Wagners Siegfried." In: *Sammlung musikalischer Vorträge*, 1st series, No. 5. Leipzig: Breitkopf & Härtel, 1879; pp. 59–80. ML44.W16

A defense of Wagner's drama, especially its story; on the other hand, Wolgozen believes the work could continue to be loved "as music" (p. 74) even if it were to be rejected as mythologizing or moralizing. No musical examples. The *Musikalische Vorträge* may have been reprinted in 1975, but the present author has never seen a copy of the reprint edition.

Musical and Interpretive Studies

714. Brinkmann, Reinhold. " 'Drei der Fragen stell' ich mir frei.' Zur Wanderer-Szene im 1. Akt von Wagner's 'Siegfried.' " *Jahrbuch des Staatlichen Instituts für Musikforschung Preussischer Kulturbesitz 1972* (Berlin, 1973), pp. 120–62. ML5.S74

Argues on behalf of a flexible attitude toward Wagner's music dramas insofar as they incorporate structural principles of various kinds, not merely those identified by Lorenz and other theorists. Among other subjects Brinkmann discusses in detail is the interplay of poetic and musical events as characteristic of his subject's approach to music and drama. Includes ten musical examples, as well as several tables and quotations from a variety of verbal and musical documents; concludes with a two-page list of secondary sources.

715. Coren, Daniel. "Inspiration and Calculation in the Genesis of Wagner's 'Siegfried.' " In: *Studies in Musicology in Honor of Otto E. Albrecht*, ed. John Walter Hill. Kassel: Bärenreiter, 1980; pp. 266–87. ISBN 3761804334 ML55.A375 1980

Rejects "one of the most durable Wagner myths": that the composer foresaw the details of the *Ring* dramas' musical contents even as he was writing their librettos (p. 266). Coren considers the length, character, and purported origins (e.g., the La Spezia episode) of the *Rheingold* prelude; concerning the prelude to *Siegfried* he asserts that "even Wagner could not have projected a purely instrumental overture long enough to satisfy the formal conditions he establishes" earlier in the tetralogy (p. 275).

Illustrated with several diagrams and eleven musical examples. Related to the author's doctoral dissertation (University of California, Berkeley, 1971); see also Coren's article "The Texts of Wagner's 'Der junge Siegfried' and 'Siegfried,'" published in *19th Century Music* 6 (1981–1982), pp. 17–30.

716. Dahlhaus, Carl. "Das unterbrochene Hauptwerk. Zu Wagners Siegfried." In item 447, pp. 235–38.

Proposes that Wagner stopped work on *Siegfried* in 1857, primarily because he had come to disagree with certain attitudes presented in Schopenhauer's famous treatise *The World as Will and Representation*. Includes important quotations from Wagner's correspondence but no musical examples.

717. Petty, Jonathan Christian. "Sieglinde's 'Long Day's Journey into Night.'" *Opera Journal* 30/2 (June 1997), pp. 11–35. ML1.O46

Examines Sieglinde's "tonal language" in act I, scene i, in terms of "complexes of poetic images [that] control the flow of keys according to principles typical of the associative processes of dreams" (p. 11). In other words, a study of harmony as dramatic subtext. Illustrated with diagrams illustrating harmonic relationships and their association with literary and ideological aspects of the scene in question.

Other studies involving night and day in Wagner's music dramas include Constantin Floros's "Tag und Nacht in Wagners 'Tristan' und in Mahlers Siebenter Symphonie," *Österreichische Musikzeitschrift* 49 (1994), pp. 9–17. See also Petty's "Sieglinde and the Moon" in *Opera Quarterly* 14/2 (Winter 1997–1998), pp. 41–56.

718. Voss, Egon. "Siegfrieds Musik." In: *Das musikalische Kunstwerk: Geschichte—Ästhetik—Theorie. Festschrift Carl Dahlhaus zum 60. Geburtstag*, ed. Hermann Danuser et al. Laaber: Laaber-Verlag, 1988; pp. 259–268. ISBN 3890071449 ML55.D185 1988

A discussion of the evolution of Siegfried as a character who pervades the *Ring* as a whole and "stars" in his "own" music drama. Voss's particular concern is the transformation of the so-called Siegfried motif, sung for the first time by Brünnhilde in *Walküre*, act III. Illustrated mostly with short motivic musical examples. On a closely related subject, see Klaus Kropfinger's article "Wagners 'Entsagungs'-Motif [Renunciation motif]," published in the same *Festschrift* (pp. 241–58).

Die Götterdämmerung, *WWV* 86D

*   *Die Götterdämmerung* = Vol. 13 (3 fascicles) of *Richard Wagner.*
     Sämtliche Werke. Described under item 156.

Another complete critical edition prepared by Voss.

Guidebooks and Survey Studies: see items 645–54, especially item 619.

Musical and Interpretive Studies
719. Darcy, Warren. "The Pessimism of the Ring," *Opera Quarterly* 4/2 (Summer 1986), pp. 24–48. ML1699.O65

Considers the *Ring* as a whole, and the "Immolation Scene" in *Götterdämmerung* in particular, in terms of Schopenhauer's influence on Wagner's "message": that of "transforming society" which, as Darcy claims, "is today more relevant than ever" (p. 43). Darcy also explains that excised lines originally belonging to Brünnhilde's final monologue employed Buddhist imagery involving Nirvana and the renunciation of the material world. Copiously documented with more than four full pages of endnotes and citations, as well as a single musical example that outlines the harmonic structure of the "Immolation Scene" (the last p. 41).

720. Kinderman, William. "Dramatic Recapitulation in Wagner's 'Götterdämmerung.'" *19th Century Music* 4 (1980–1981), pp. 101–12. ML1.N77

Examines large-scale "interrelationships in the tonal structure" in *Siegfried,* and especially in *Götterdämmerung*, that are "regulated by a musical hierarchy" that "coincides with and reinforces a hierarchy in dramatic values" (p. 112). Includes four musical examples and three charts of harmonic relationships.
     Performance studies of *Götterdämmerung* also exist. See, for instance, *Götterdämmerung: der neue Bayreuther Ring*, ed. Udo Bermbach and Hermann Schreiber (Berlin, 2000), with splendid photographs by Hermann and Clärchen Baus.

Tristan und Isolde, *WWV* 90

*   *Tristan und Isolde* = Vol. 8 (3 fascicles) of *Richard Wagner. Sämtliche Werke*. Described under item 156.

A critical edition prepared by Isolde Vetter.

*   *Tristan und Isolde* = Vol. 5 of *Richard Wagners musikalische Werke.* Described under item 157.

Another critical edition, now replaced by item 156.

Guidebooks and Survey Studies

721. *Tristan und Isolde.* English National Opera Guides, 6. London: Calder, 1981. 96pp. ISBN 0714538493 ML410.W14

Includes an essay by John Luke Rose on the music drama as a landmark in musical history, musical commentary by Anthony Negus, comments on productions by Patrick Carnegy, a thematic guide incorporating 47 musical examples of varying lengths, and the complete poem in English translation by Andrew Porter (see also item 163), together with a variety of illustrations—most of them photographs of stage sets and performers—as well as a brief bibliography (p. 94), and a discography that gives information about a small number of performances recorded on compact disks.

Other Tristan *guidebooks and surveys include:*

722. Chailley, Jacques. *Tristan et Isolde de Richard Wagner.* "Au-dela des notes: Collection d'explication de texts musicaux dirigée par Jacques Chailley," 3. Paris: Alphonse Leduc et Cie., 1972. 107pp. ISBN 2856890067 MT100.W24C5

A "companion," consisting of background information about the Tristan legend and its sources in Gottfried von Strasbourg's poem, the *Chanson d'Aube,* and so on; the evolution of the music drama itself; a discussion of musical elements, together with an analysis of the prelude's harmonic structure (the last pp. 34–36); and a guide to the music drama as a whole. Chailley identifies some 62 "love-themes" in the work (pp. 39–55), but provides musical examples for only a few of them; his analysis of the prelude is extremely concise. Includes quotations from a variety of sources and scattered musical examples of various kinds but no illustrations, bibliography, or index. Another volume by Chailley with the same title was published in Paris in 1963.

723. Wolzogen, Hans von. *Guide to the Legend, Poem, and Music of Richard Wagner's "Tristan und Isolde."* Leipzig: Breitkopf & Härtel, 1884. 52pp. (no LC number available)

One in a series of similar publications by Wolzogen; this one introduces readers to the origins of the lovers' story, Wagner's libretto for his music drama, and something of the music itself. Illustrated with many short musical examples identifying highlights in the score. Originally published as *Richard Wagners Tristan und Isolde: ein Leitfaden durch Sage, Dichtung und Musik* (Leipzig, 1880; ML410.W14W8).

Among Tristan *anthologies and "readers" are the following volumes:*

724. *100 Jahre Tristan. Neunzehn Essays,* ed. Wieland Wagner. Emsdetten: Lechte, 1965. 204pp. ML410.W14H95

    One of the most frequently consulted *Tristan* secondary sources, in part because it incorporates excerpts from earlier studies. Among the nineteen essays edited by the composer's grandson are musical studies, including a portion of item 465 (pp. 77–80); performance and reception studies, including Kurt Blaukopf on conductors of *Tristan* (pp. 13–26); and studies of the music drama's place in literature dealing with love, including Denis de Rougemont, "Wagner oder die Vollendung" (pp. 159–64). Illustrated with a variety of portraits, photographs, and documentary facsimiles, as well as a number of musical examples and a table of motifs interleaved between pp. 66–67.

725. Lindner, Edwin. *Richard Wagner über Tristan und Isolde: Aussprüche des Meisters über sein Werk.* Leipzig: Breitkopf & Härtel, 1912. xxxii, 387pp. ML410.W1A19

    A collection of primary sources. Most of the volume is taken up with excerpts from letters Wagner addressed to colleagues and friends between 1854 and 1883 (pp. 1–298) that are indexed separately (pp. vi–xviii); the balance consists of excerpts from the composer's literary works (pp. 299–377). An appendix identifies a list of musical self-citations taken from *Tristan* that appear in *Meistersinger* (pp. 278–79). Concludes with an index.

726. *Richard Wagner. Tristan und Isolde.* Musik-Konzepte, 57/58. Munich: "text+kritik," 1987. 153pp. ISBN 3883772690 (no LC number available)

    A somewhat eccentric set of reflections on *Tristan,* outfitted with illustrations, diagrams, and musical examples. Among the contents of this volume are two essays, both devoted to "sorrow" and "death" as musical, literary, and structural motifs: Sebastian Urmoneit's "Untersuchungen zur den beiden 'Todesmotiven' aus 'Tristan und Isolde' " (pp. 104–17); and Christian Thorau's "Untersuchungen zur 'traurigen Weise' im III. Akt von 'Tristan und Isolde' " (pp. 118–28). Contains scattered musical examples.

Document and Source Studies

727. Bailey, Robert. *The Genesis of "Tristan und Isolde" and a Study of Wagner's Sketches and Drafts for the First Act.* Ann Arbor, MI: UMI Research Press, 1969. xi, 266pp. (no LC number available)

Investigates documents associated with the first act of *Tristan*, music Wagner drafted and sent to his publishers prior to beginning work on the rest of the music drama. Illustrated with 36 hand-copied music examples as well as several facsimiles. Contains a bibliography no longer up-to-date but nevertheless useful for students of the composer's manuscripts (pp. 265–66). A revision of Bailey's Princeton dissertation (1969).

728. Bartels, Ulrich. *Analytisch-entstehungsgeschichtliche Studien zu Wagners Tristan und Isolde, anhand der Kompositionsskizze des zweiten und dritten Aktes.* 2 vols. Musik und Musikanschauung im 19. Jahrhundert, 2, Teils 1–2. Cologne: Studio, 1995. ISBN 3895649903 ML410.W14B37 1995

Another masterful study and one that, in effect, takes up where Bailey left off. Vol. 1 presents Bartels's arguments and contains a few short musical examples; Vol. 2 consists almost entirely of manuscript facsimiles. Also includes a bibliography (Vol. 1, pp. 150–52) and notes (Vol. 2, pp. 222–36). Like Bailey's work, Bartels's study is derived from his doctoral dissertation (University of Göttingen, 1991).

* Peyser, Herbert F. " 'Tristan,' First Hand." Described as item 458.

729. Voss, Egon. "Die 'schwarze und die weiße Flagge': Zur Entstehung von Wagners Tristan." *Archiv für Musikwissenschaft* 54 (1997), pp. 210–27. ML5.A63

Deals with the earliest sketches for *Tristan* and the evolution of Wagner's thoughts concerning his musical-dramatic lovers. Among other subjects Voss explains that the idea of bringing Parzifal into act III belongs to Wagner's plans of August 1857. Includes several musical examples.

Textual and Literary Studies

730. Golther, Wolfgang. "Tristan und Isolde von Richard Wagner." In: Golther, *Tristan und Isolde in den Dichtungen des Mittelalters und der neuen Zeit.* Leipzig: S. Hirzel, 1907; pp. 421–60. PT685.T8G6

The ninth and last of a collection of essays devoted overall to the Tristan story in European, and especially German, history and literature. Golther's Wagner essay deals primarily with the contents of the composer's poem and its borrowings or adaptations from earlier sources; it also includes the text of the letter Wagner addressed on 22 May 1862 to Mathilde Wesendonk (pp. 452–53). No illustrations or musical examples; the volume as a whole concludes with an index.

731. Riemann, Hugo. "Altprovenzalisches in Wagner's 'Tristan.' " In Riemann, *Musikalische Rückblicke*, Vol. 2. Berlin: Harmonie, 1900; pp. 41–47. (no LC number available)

A brief discussion of Wagner and the medieval legend of Tristan in Old Provençal poetry. No musical examples.

732. Rosenband, Doris. *Das Liebesmotif in Gottfrieds "Tristan" und Wagners "Tristan und Isolde."* Goppinger Arbeiten zur Germanistik, 94. Göttingen: Alfred Kummerle, 1973. (v), 87pp. ISBN 3874521877 PT1526.R6 1973

A close textual study of "love motives"—concepts or notions, not musical *Leitmotive*—in Gottfried von Strassburg's medieval poem and Wagner's libretto. Includes a bibliography (pp. 83–87). But one of several similar studies devolving upon the Tristan legend and Wagner's adaptation of it.

Musical Studies

*   Lorenz, Alfred. *Der musikalische Aufbau von . . . "Tristan und Isolde."* Described as item 482, Vol. 2.

733. North, Roger. *Wagner's Most Subtle Art: An Analytic Study of "Tristan und Isolde."* London: "Book Factory" [i.e., published by the author], 1996. xvi, 699pp. ISBN 095279750X MT100.W24N67 1996

Defends the theory that *Tristan* reflects Wagner's infatuation with Schopenhauer's philosophy. Outfitted with several fold-out charts, as well as what seem to be almost innumerable diagrams and musical examples. Readers may wish to consult the detailed table of contents (pp. vii–xvi) and one-page catalog of North's idiosyncratic analytical symbols (p. iv) before reading further.

734. Overhoff, Kurt. *Richard Wagners Tristan Partitur. Eine musikalisch-philosophische Deutung.* Bayreuth: Julius Steeger, 1948. 88pp. MT100.W24O8

Musical analysis couched in philosophical terms and dedicated to Karl Jaspers. Illustrated with 98 musical examples. An intriguing study omitted from many Wagner bibliographies.

735. Rößler, Susanne. *Die inhaltliche und musikalische Funktion der Motive in Richard Wagners "Tristan und Isolde."* Dissertation, University of Munich; Munich: CD Copy & Druck, 1989. 337pp. (no ISBN or LC number available)

Analyzes the musical form and significance of *Tristan* based on 51 motives. Illustrated with hundreds of musical examples; outfitted with a specialized bibliography devoted to musical studies of the work many consider Wagner's masterpiece (pp. 333–37). Apparently not commercially available.

736. Scharschuch, Horst. *Gesamtanalyse der Harmonik von Richard Wagners Musikdrama "Tristan und Isolde."* Forschungsbeiträge zur Musikwissenschaft, 12. Regensburg: Gustav Bosse, 1963. 236pp. MT100.W24S3

A measure-by-measure, chord-by-chord analysis of *Tristan*, using symbols such as "I," "V_7," and so on, rather than verbal statements and brief musical examples; the whole analysis is superimposed, where appropriate, over or under Wagner's libretto. Scharschuch pays special attention to sequential passages of various kinds. Printed directly from a typescript, this volume can be difficult to read, containing as it does a great many characters added by hand. No additional illustrations and no bibliography or index, although a *Beiband* (accompanying volume), subtitled "Die Festlegung der harmonischen Vorgänge in der Klangschrift und Leitmotivtabelle" (77pp.), provides additional analytical argument as well as a two-page table of motifs.

Other musical studies of Tristan*, many of them dealing with harmonic issues, include:*

737. Abbate, Carolyn. "Wagner, 'On Modulation,' and 'Tristan.' " *Cambridge Opera Journal* 1 (1989), pp. 33–58. ISSN 0954-5867 (no LC number available)

Based in part on a few sentences Wagner wrote down in his *Tristan* sketchbook concerning the roles modulation can play both in purely instrumental music and in music drama; in part, too, an attack on Joseph Kerman's discussion of *Tristan* as "symphonic music" (item 979). Abbate reminds us that "even the critical position that takes the composer's voice as guide does not create a secure ground for interpretation" (p. 34), and that we must convince ourselves of what actually goes on in Wagner's scores. Includes four fulsome musical examples.

738. Brown, Matthew. "Isolde's Narrative: From Hauptmotiv to Tonal Model." In item 528, pp. 180–201.

Examines act I, scene iii, "as a test case," based on the assumption that Wagner somehow solved "the compositional problem of constructing episodes that are internally unified yet still promote the continuity and coherence of the whole" (p. 180). Brown considers not only the opinions of Lorenz and Bailey, but also those of Karl Grunsky (item 740) and Heinrich Porges—the last in an article published in 1902 in the *Bayreuther Blätter*; Brown concludes that, in part, Wagner is "able to preserve the overall continuity of Scene 3" only by weakening part of its tonal framework (p. 201). Includes two charts and seven sophisticated musical examples, several of them incorporating Schenkerian analytical principles.

739. Enix, Margery. "Formal Expansion Through Fusion of Major and Minor: A Study of Tonal Structure in 'Tristan und Isolde,' Act I." *Indiana Theory Review* 1/2 (1978), pp. 28–34. MT6.I52

Devoted to discussing "tonality design in one act of an opera which is important not only in the history of the genre but also in the evolution of the major-minor tonal system" (p. 28). Includes three musical examples, as well as several rather confusing diagrams of key schemes and "dramatic structures." Derived from the author's dissertation *The Dissolution of the Functional Harmonic Tonal System, 1850–1910* (Indiana University, 1977).

740. Grunsky, Karl. "Das Vorspiel und der erste Akt von 'Tristan und Isolde.' " *Richard-Wagner-Jahrbuch* 2 (1907), pp. 207–84. ML410.W1A57

A detailed evaluation of the way Wagner's music actually works, with references to—and corrections of mistakes in—various guidebooks published prior to Grunsky's article. Includes twenty musical examples. See also item 738.

741. Jackson, Roland. "Leitmotive and the Form of the 'Tristan' Prelude." *Music Review* 36 (1975), pp. 42–53. ML5.M657

Suggests not only that *Leitmotive* are central to the organization of the prelude, but that Wagner drew upon the works of other composers—Spohr's *Alchymist*, Beethoven's Sonata, Op. 31, No. 3, and portions of Berlioz's *Roméo et Juliette*—in organizing many musical elements and gestures into a single coherent whole. Among other theorists Jackson refers to include Lorenz, William Mitchell (item 744), and Albert Lavignac—the last the author of *The Music Dramas of Richard Wagner* (see item 573), and one of many individuals to propose motivic analyses of the composer's music dramas. Includes ten musical examples, some diagrammatic in character.

742. Kinderman, William. "Dramatic Recapitulation and Tonal Pairing in Wagner's 'Tristan und Isolde' and 'Parsifal.' " In: *The Second Practice of 19th-Century Tonality*, ed. Kinderman and Harald Krebs. Lincoln: University of Nebraska Press, 1996; pp. 178–214. ISBN 0803227248 ML3811.S43 1996

Examines certain passages that Wagner repeats in both music dramas: in *Tristan* these constitute a gigantic "modulation" from A minor to B major between the prelude and "Liebestod," in *Parsifal* from C major to A-flat major employing the Grail and Communion motives (see also item 785). Includes musical examples. See also Kinderman's article "Das 'Geheimnis der Form' in Wagners 'Tristan und Isolde,' " *Archiv für Musikwissenschaft* 40 (1983), pp. 174–88.

743. Knapp, Raymond. "The Tonal Structure of 'Tristan und Isolde': A Sketch." *Music Review* 45 (1984), pp. 11–25. ML5.M657

Proposes that the overall plan of Wagner's music drama is related both to chromatic harmony (i.e., the music), including diminished-seventh chords and modulations by minor thirds, and the story (i.e., the drama), especially in terms of a shift "from" Isolde in the first half of the action "to" Tristan in the second half. Knapp also searches for a "central key" (p. 11)—a notion important to students of Mozart's operas—in a work with acts ending in D major, D minor, and B major (see item 742). Includes twelve partially diagrammatic musical examples.

744. Mitchell, William J. "The 'Tristan' Prelude: Techniques and Structure." *The Music Forum*, ed. Mitchell and Felix Salzar. [The first in a series of volumes.] New York and London: Columbia University Press, 1967; pp. 162–203. ML55.F672, v. 1

An harmonic analysis of Wagner's prelude according to the techniques laid down by Heinrich Schenker and beloved by so many American theorists of the 1960s, 1970s, and early 1980s. Includes analyses of the work's "inclusive plan," as well as of individual sections and overall form. Illustrated with 18 multi-partite musical examples. Reprinted in item 159.

745. Steinbeck, Wolfram. "Die Idee des Symphonischen bei Richard Wagner. Zur Leitmotivtechnik in 'Tristan und Isolde.' " In item 40, pp. 424–36.

A sophisticated study of a problem familiar to Wagner analysts: the issue of the "symphonic" elements or lack of same in the mature music dramas.

Steinbeck explores this issue and illustrates his arguments in favor of a developmental use of *Leitmotive* with four musical examples.

Performance and Reception Studies

*   Ashbrook, William. "The First Singers of 'Tristan und Isolde.' " Described as item 835.

746. Heldt, Brigitte. *Richard Wagner—Tristan und Isolde. Das Werk und seine Inszenierung.* Laaber: Laaber-Verlag, 1994. viii, 343pp. ISBN 3890073077 ML410.W1A395 1994

Deals with Wagner's masterpiece in performance. Includes a catalog of 21 productions presented between 1865 and 1981, the last at Bayreuth (pp. 316–18), as well as a table of *Leitmotive* (pp. 298–99), a timetable of *Tristan*'s evolution as a musical-literary work of art, beginning with the work's conception in 1854, and ending with its premiere on 10 June 1865 (pp. 300–301), and excerpts from prose sketches for the libretto (pp. 303–11). Lavishly illustrated with portraits, drawings, photographs, facsimiles of a few playbills, and other pictures, as well as with musical examples. Also contains a specialized bibliography (pp. 319–34); concludes with several indexes.

Interpretive Studies

747. Bahr-Mildenburg, Anna. *Darstellung der Werke Richard Wagners aus dem Geiste der Dichtung und Musik. Tristan und Isolde: vollständige Regiebearbeitung sämtlicher Partien mit Notenbeispielen.* Leipzig and Vienna: Musikwissenschaftlicher Verlag, 1936. 115pp. MT100.W24B3

A tabular analysis of the six principal characters depicted in Wagner's *Tristan*, organized in double columns and devoted to their actions, statements, and intellectual-dramatic significance as well as their musical representation. On each page the left-hand column presents quotations from Wagner's score and poem, while the right-hand column is devoted to explanations, interpretations, and textual annotations. Brief musical examples are interspersed among the quotations.

748. Dettmar, Hans. " 'Tristan und Isolde' in Paris." *Zürcher Diskussionen* 3/25–26 (1900), pp. 1–14. (no LC number available)

A sort of stream-of-consciousness "meditation" on Wagner's conception of the *Tristan* story, his relationship with Mathilde Wesendonk, his visits to and years living in Paris, and so on. Apparently Dettmar's essay, only sixteen pages long, comprises almost the entire issue of the obscure periodical in which it appears. No illustrations or musical examples. Harvard's Loeb Music Library owns a copy of this little-known publication.

749. Griesser, Luitpold. *Richard Wagner's Tristan und Isolde. Ein Interpretationsversuch.* Vienna and Leipzig: Karl Harbauer, 1917? 291pp. (no LC number available)

A scene-by-scene discussion of Wagner's music drama, with special emphasis on textual details and relationships between the composer's ideas and those of Plato, Feuerbach, Schopenhauer, and other culture heroes. Includes a chapter on Wagner's relationship with Mathilde Wesendonk as well as an index (pp. 290–91).

750. Urban, Petra. *Liebesdämmerung. Ein psychoanalytischer Versuch über Richard Wagners "Tristan und Isolde."* Frankfurt a.M.: Dietmar Klotz, 1991. 142pp. ISBN 3880742413 ML410.W1A295 1991

A Freudian analysis, mostly of Wagner's *Tristan* story, with extensive quotations from the psychoanalytical literature. Includes a useful specialized bibliography (pp. 138–42). Published too late to be cited in item 1019.

751. Wapnewski, Peter. *Tristan der Held Richard Wagners.* Berlin: Severin & Siedler, 1981. 224pp. ISBN 3886800210 ML410.W14W3

A sort of running commentary on Wagner's sources and ideas, the contents of his libretto, and the significance of observations—or lack thereof—made by many of the composer's admirers and critics. Wapnewski draws upon such diverse sources as Gottfried's poem, Calderón's plays, Hanslick's musical journalism, and Wagner's own literary works. Includes extensive quotations from the libretto as well as a "Tristan timeline" spanning the years 1853 to 1879 (pp. 193–98), and extensive notes (pp. 199–216); concludes with an index.

752. Wirth, Moritz. *Die König-Marke Frage. Eine Abwehr für das Kunstwerk, wider den Meister.* Leipzig: Feodor Reinboth, 1886. iv, 47pp. (no LC available)

Takes issue with the image of Mark adopted by Wagner in *Tristan* and presented at performances of that music drama in Bayreuth. Published as a pamphlet as well as in the single issue of the *Wagner-Jahrbuch* edited by J. Kurschner. Rare. Harvard University's Loeb Music Library owns a copy (shelf-number: Mus. 5662.04).

Two additional interpretative studies of Tristan *deal specifically with its influence on twentieth-century artists, authors, and composers:*

753. Truscott, Harold. "Wagner's 'Tristan' and the 20th Century." *Music Review* 24 (1963), pp. 75–85. ML5.M657

Orienting his discussion of *Tristan*'s musical influence on his assertion that "it is not possible to break up tonality any more than it is possible to break up gravity" (p. 75), Truscott demonstrates that each act of Wagner's music drama constitutes a coherent series of key statements, a "perfectly logical tonal scheme" (p. 84) of its own. Illustrated with ten musical examples.

754. Zuckerman, Elliott. *The First Hundred Years of Wagner's Tristan.* New York and London: Columbia University Press, 1964. xiv, 235pp. ML410.W14Z8

Considers subjects ranging from the conception of the composer's music drama during the 1850s and through its early performances to its influence on D'Annunzio, Lorenz, Thomas Mann, Nietzsche, and a number of other important scholars, authors, and philosophers. Zuckerman also provides three appendices: a list of *Tristan* first-performance dates "in the Major Operatic Cities" (pp. 179–80); "A Note on Swinburne and the Sea," which also comments on William Payne's cycle of Wagnerian sonnets (pp. 181–85); and "A Note on Joyce and Eliot" (pp. 186–88). Contains a single musical example. No bibliography; concludes instead with extensive notes (pp. 189–225) and an index.

Die Meistersinger von Nürnberg, *WWV* 96: see also chapter I of the present research guide.

*   *Die Meistersinger* = Vol. 9 (3 fascicles) of *Richard Wagner. Sämtliche Werke.* Described under item 156.

Another critical edition supervised by Voss.

Guidebooks and Survey Studies
The best introduction to Meistersinger *is:*

755. Warrack, John. *Richard Wagner: "Die Meistersinger von Nürnberg."* Cambridge Opera Handbooks. Cambridge and New York: Cambridge University Press, 1994. x, 175pp. ISBN 0521444446 ML410.W1A286 1994

One of the finest guidebooks in any language. Includes information on sources and origins of the libretto, a synopsis of the story, discussions of Sachs, Beckmesser, and historical Meistersinger tunes, "Sachs and Schopenhauer" by Lucy Beckett (pp. 66–82), and a history of productions by Patrick Carnegy (pp. 135–150), as well as a "Select Bibliography" (pp. 168–72; see also chapter I of the present research guide). Also contains three appendices on aspects of Wagner's work, scattered musical examples, and eight pages of plates; concludes with an index.

A similar volume devoted to *Holländer* and edited by Thomas Grey (Cambridge University Press 2000; ISBN 0521582857) appeared too late to be described independently in the present research guide. See also item 775 below: Beckett's "Cambridge Opera Handbook" to *Parsifal.*

Other Meistersinger *surveys and guidebooks include:*

756. Buck, Paul. *Richard Wagners "Meistersinger." Eine Führung durch das Werk.* Quellen und Studien zur Musikgeschichte von der Antike bis in die Gegenwart, 22. Frankfurt a.M.: Peter Lang, 1990. 301pp. ISBN 3631408811 ML410.W16B85 1990

Especially useful to music lovers because it includes 413 musical examples that, together with Buck's prose, introduce readers to almost every aspect of the story, melody, and "meaning" of *Meistersinger*—the whole organized by acts and scenes for easier reading. Includes a brief bibliography (p. 301), as well as diagrams and other visual aids.

757. Perschmann, Wolfgang. *Kunst—Wahn—Liebe. Richard Wagner's "Die Meistersinger."* Judenburg: Offset- und Buchdruckerei, 1996. 229pp. ISBN 3901149082 MT100.W3P47 1996

A homemade *Opernführer* devoted to important aspects of Wagner's music drama. Illustrated with a frontispiece portrait of Wagner and some 105 musical examples. Like other volumes by Perschmann (see items 57 and 778), sponsored by Austria's Richard Wagner Society.

758. Rayner, Robert M. *Wagner and "Die Meistersinger."* Oxford: Oxford University Press, 1940. 263pp. ML410.W16R29

Examines the history, background, text, and music of Wagner's comic masterpiece. Included among its illustrations are two documentary facsimiles (one of Wagner's changes for the "Prize Song" text) and a frontispiece photograph of the Dürer house that served as a model for the composer's original act II décor plans. Also includes dozens of musical examples and a large number of quotations from Wagner's letters and prose works, as well as his *Meistersinger* libretto. The discussion of the joint evolution of text and music (pp. 183–248) is especially interesting. Concludes with two appendices concerning Wagner's borrowings from E. T. A. Hoffmann, Wagenseil, Lortzing, and a number of other figures, and secondary sources. Indexed. Apparently an uncommon publication; the British Library keeps its copy in its Rare Books Room (shelf-number Hirsch 4969).

759. *Richard Wagner. "Die Meistersinger von Nürnberg." Programmheft zur Neuinszenierung 1979.* 2 vols. (issued as a boxed set). Munich: Prestel, 1979. (no ISBN or LC number available)

A lavishly illustrated history of Wagner's music drama and its various productions. Published in conjunction with Klaus Schultz's production at the Bavarian State Opera in 1979. Especially interesting as a picture book, given that other studies cover much of the historical material with equal or greater thoroughness, reliability, and elegance; the exception to this statement is Voss's article "Gedanken über 'Meistersinger'-Dokumente," which deserves close attention.

Document and Source Studies

760. Altmann, Wilhelm. "Zur Geschichte der Entstehung und Veröffentlichung von Richard Wagners 'Die Meistersinger von Nürnberg.' " *Richard-Wagner-Jahrbuch* 5 (1913), pp. 87–137. ML410.W1A57

A detailed account of the work's origins in Wagner's own life and plans, as well as of its eventual publication. Contains a large number of quotations from letters and literary sources but no musical examples.

761. "Richard Wagners erster Entwurf zu den 'Meistersingern von Nürnberg.' " *Die Musik* 1–IV (1901–1902), pp. 1799–809. ML5.M9

Presents the first complete prose draft of this music drama. Followed in the same issue of *Die Musik* by additional comments on early *Meistersinger* sources written by Richard Sternfeld (pp. 1810–14).

762. Thompson, Herbert. *Wagner and Wagenseil: A Source of Wagner's Opera "Die Meistersinger."* London: Humphrey Milford and Oxford University Press, 1927. 39pp. + illustrations. ML410.W16T39

Explores Wagner's knowledge of Johann Christoph Wagenseil's seventeenth-century treatise on the medieval Mastersingers. Includes as illustrations a portrait of Wagenseil and musical examples that demonstrate his knowledge of prize songs (pp. 32–35), as well as facsimiles of his title page, a page of his musical examples, and a fold-out map of "old Nuremberg" tipped into the back of the volume. Deliberately "old-fashioned" in typography and style. Unindexed.

763. Turner, R. " 'Die Meistersinger von Nürnberg': The Conceptual Growth of an Opera." *Wagner* 3/1 (January 1982), pp. 2–16. ML410.W1A595

Examines the composer's three prose sketches and final libretto primarily in terms of Sachs and Beckmesser as characters to show how "the basic ideas of the work changed and conversely to show some light on a more general change in Wagner's aesthetic" (p. 2). No musical examples.

Textual and Literary Studies

764. Bowen, Anna Maude. *The Sources and Text of Richard Wagner's "Die Meistersinger von Nürnberg."* Munich: H. Lüneburg, 1897; reprinted New York: AMS Press, 1977. 96pp. ISBN 040412870X ML410.W16B6 1977

Demonstrates that, in his libretto, Wagner attempted to approximate "archaic" language, yet was "master enough not to overload his text with peculiarities merely . . . to show that he was familiar with his subject" (p. 94). Illustrated with a few short musical examples and outfitted with a bibliography (pp. 95–96), but primarily a line-by-line and word-by-word study of linguistic traditions and usages.

765. Mehler, Eugen. "Die Textvariaten der Meistersinger-Dichtung: Beiträge zur Textkritik des Werkes." *Richard Wagner-Jahrbuch* 5 (1913), pp. 187–233. ML410.W1A57

Identifies and discusses differences between Wagner's drafts and manuscript scores and various published editions of his music drama. Much of Mehler's argument is summarized in tables identifying the variations in question. Contains no musical examples.

766. Roedder, Edwin C. "Richard Wagner's 'Die Meistersinger von Nürnberg' and its Literary Precursors." *Transactions of the Wisconsin Academy of Sciences, Arts, and Letters* 20 (February 1922), pp. 87–129. (no LC number available)

Investigates the origins of the *Meistersinger* poem in terms of Wagner's life and writings, including *My Life*, and of its relationship to both medieval literature and such publications as Gervinus's *Geschichte der deutschen Dichtung* (Leipzig, 1853); from the last work Roedder reprints a substantial passage (pp. 120–29). Offprints of this article were issued as pamphlets. See also Ottfried Hafner, "Von Krähwinkel nach Nürnberg: Neues zur Vorgeschichte von Wagner's 'Meistersinger,' " published in 1994 in the *Österreichische Musikzeitschrift*, which touches on the influences of August von Kotzebue and other figures on Wagner's only comic masterpiece.

Musical Studies

* Finscher, Ludwig. "Über den Kontrapunkt der Meistersinger." Described as item 462.

*   Lorenz, Alfred. *Der musikalische Aufbau von . . . "Die Meistersinger von Nürnberg."* Described as item 482, Vol. 3.

767. Thomas, Eugen. *Die Instrumentation der Meistersinger von Nürnberg von Richard Wagner: ein Beitrag zur Instrumentationslehre*, 2nd ed. Leipzig: C. C. Röder, n.d. [c. 1907]. In two parts: 142pp. + 42pp. (Beispiele). ML410.W16T37

Examines both Wagner's orchestrational practices and *Meistersinger* performances during the late nineteenth century by the orchestra of the Vienna Hofoper. An introductory essay (pp. 5–21) deals with scoring, seating arrangements for orchestral performers, stylistic issues, and so on; the bulk of Thomas's commentary, however, is devoted to details of some 70 musical examples—the plate number "2814" appears at the bottom of many of them—all taken from the music drama, paginated separately and comprising Part II of his study. Includes an appendix identifying cuts made in Hofoper *Meistersinger* performances (pp. 130–33). Illustrated throughout Part I with additional musical examples and seating diagrams of the Hofoper ensemble; Part I also concludes with an index (pp. 135–42) and with four numbered pages of praise for Thomas's study.

768. Wildgruber, Jens. "Das Geheimnis der 'Barform' in R. Wagners 'Die Meistersinger von Nürnberg.' Plädoyer für eine neue Art des Formbetrachtung." In: *Festschrift Heinz Becker zum 60. Geburtstag am 26. Juni 1982*, ed. Jürgen Schläder and Reinhold Quandt. Laaber: Laaber Verlag, 1982; pp. 205–13. ISBN 3921518709 ML55.B32M

Discusses Wagner's use of sixteenth-century bar form, a musical construction generally associated in the literature with Lorenz's analysis of the *Ring* dramas in terms of this and other musical structures; also considers loosely associated, highly "Germanic" issues involving Hegelian dialectic, Adorno's and Dahlhaus's readings of Wagner's music and cultural significance, and so on.

Performance and Reception Studies

769. *Achtet mir die Meister nur! "Die Meistersinger von Nürnberg" im Brennpunkt*, ed. Matthias Viertel. Hofgeismarer Protokolle, 314. Hofgeismar: Evangelische Akademie, 1997. 151pp. ISBN 3892812225 ML410.W16A35 1997

A *Meistersinger* "reader" of sorts, although most of its articles deal with staging in general—Christiane Busch's "Zur Inszenierungsgeschichte der 'Meistersinger' " (pp. 9–30)—and Kassel performances in particular—

Busch's "Anmerkungen zur Kasseler Inszenierung Elmar Fuldas" (pp. 143–46); and Frank Piontek's "Tiefsinn, Komik und Erschütterung: Zur 'Meistersinger'-Aufführung in Kassel" (pp. 147–50). Most or all of the papers were presented at a conference in Germany in January 1997. Illustrated with five or six black-and-white plates; contains no musical examples.

Interpretive Studies

770. Huckvale, David. "Ibsen and Wagner." *Wagner* 17/1 (January 1996), pp. 55–64. ML410.W1A595

Especially interesting for the parallels the author draws between *The Master Builders* and portions of Wagner's music drama. Includes quotations from both works but no musical examples. See also item 981.

771. McDonald, William E. "Words, Music, and Dramatic Development in 'Die Meistersinger.' " *19th Century Music* 1 (1977–1978), pp. 246–60. ML1.N77

Examines various relationships between words and music, especially in terms of three male characters: David, who grows into a capable journeyman; Walther, who achieves the status of a true Mastersinger; and Sachs, who is finally forced to renounce his love of Eva. Deals primarily with issues of character; contains extensive quotations from Wagner's libretto but no musical examples

772. Mey, Curt. *Der Meistergesang in Geschichte und Kunst. Ausführliche Erklärung der Tabulaturen, Schulregeln, Sitten und Gebräuche der Meistersinger, sowie deren Anwendung in Richard Wagners "Die Meistersinger von Nürnberg,"* rev. ed. Leipzig: H. Seemann, 1901; reprinted Walluf: Sändig, 1973. xvi, 392pp. ISBN 3500273505 ML183.M61 1973

A detailed scholarly study of authentic sixteenth-century Meistersinger music and comparisons between the documentary legacy and aspects of Wagner's music drama. Mey illustrates his argument with illustrations, musical examples, and several facsimiles of manuscript pages. Useful for students of secular monody as well as Wagnerians and specialists in the reception of early music in nineteenth-century Europe.

773. Millington, Barry. "Nuremberg Trial: Is There Anti-Semitism in 'Die Meistersinger'?" *Cambridge Opera Journal* 3 (1991), pp. 247–60. ISSN 0954-5867 (no LC number available)

Defends Adorno's often-quoted but rarely-examined claim that "all the rejects of Wagner's works are caricatures of Jews" (quoted p. 247) through a detailed examination of elements of Jewish cantoral style in Beckmesser's melodies; among those elements are the "high trills on 'neuen Schuh' . . . that according to Wagner emanated from every synagogue" (p. 257). Millington asserts that *Meistersinger* represents "the artistic component in Wagner's ideological crusade of the 1860s": namely, to "revive the German spirit" (p. 260) in part through a "purgation" of Jewish elements. Includes four musical examples. See also chapter I and item 1103.

774. Schubert, Bernhard. "Wagners 'Sachs' und die Tradition des romantischen Künstlerselbstverständnisses." *Archiv für Musikwissenschaft* 40 (1983), pp. 212–53. ML5.A63

Proposes that the figure of Sachs represents the development of a theatrical tradition that makes him, in effect, a figure of "acceptable" middle-class artistic manners. Includes excerpts from such writers and composers as E. T. A. Hoffmann, Lortzing, Max Reger, and Tieck. Includes as an illustration Jost Amman's 1576 portrait of Hans Sachs. Painstakingly documented but contains no musical examples.

Parsifal, *WWV* 111

* *Parsifal* = Vol. 14 (3 fascicles) of *Richard Wagner. Sämtliche Werke.* Described under item 156.

A critical edition prepared by Voss and Martin Geck.

Guidebooks and Survey Studies
Without question the finest introduction to Parsifal *in print is:*

775. Beckett, Lucy. *Parsifal.* Cambridge Opera Handbooks. Cambridge and London: Cambridge University Press, 1981. viii, 160pp. ISBN 0521228255 ML410.W17B37

Considers sources, the libretto, issues involving performance, and the work's reception in Europe and North America. Illustrated with six black-and-white photographs and seven short musical examples, as well as with a chapter on the music written by Arnold Whittall (pp. 61–86) that incorporates additional examples drawn from Wagner's score. Concludes with a specialized bibliography (pp. 156–57) and a discography by Malcolm Walker. Reviewed in *Wagner* 3/1 (January 1982), pp. 31–32.

776. Keller, Walter. *Parsifal-Variationen. 15 Aufsätze über Richard Wagner.* Tutzing: Hans Schneider, 1979. 167pp. ISBN 3795202876 ML410.W1A287 1979

A collection of essays dealing mostly with Wagner's last music drama, but also with such topics as his *Kaisermarsch, WWV* 104, and *Großer Festmarsch, WWV* 110, the "Paris" *Tannhäuser*, uses of "forest music" in several of his dramatic compositions, and so on. Illustrated with a few musical examples and a diagram of the *Großer Festmarsh* that identifies its barform elements (p. 28; see item 815).

777. Pahlen, Kurt, and Rosemarie König. *Richard Wagner: Parsifal*, rev. ed. Mainz: B. Schott's Sons, 1986. 302pp. ISBN 3442330572 ML410.W1P352 1986

Includes the complete libretto accompanied by brief musical examples; also includes a history of Wagner's music drama from conception to late twentieth-century performances, a detailed *Parsifal* timeline (pp. 266–90), a brief discography (pp. 300–302), and a large number of illustrations and documentary facsimiles. Pahlen also edited a guide to *Meistersinger* (Mainz, 1986).

778. Perschmann, Wolfgang. *Richard Wagner. Parsifal. Schwanenschuß—Wissenskuß—glühende Befreiung*. Graz: Austrian "Richard Wagner-Gesellschaft," 1991. 196pp. ISBN 3901149007 MT100.W2P47 1991

Summarizes the origins, story, musical contents and character, and—to some extent—reception of Wagner's last music drama; outfitted with a large number of musical examples. A slightly eccentric publication, similar in layout and typography to Perschmann's other volumes and more appropriate to general readers than scholars. No index or bibliography.

779. *Richard Wagner: Parsifal*. Musik-Konzepte, 25. Munich: "text+kritik," 1982. 116pp. ISBN 3883771015 (no LC number available)

A collection of artices devoted to the conception, composition, performance, and reception of Wagner's last music drama. Among its contents are Constantin Floros's "Studien zur 'Parsifal'-Rezeption" (pp. 14–57) and Siegfried Mauser's "Leitmotiv und musikalischer Satz in Richard Wagner's 'Parsifal' " (pp. 58–73), as well as a brief discography (p. 116), comments by Hartmut Zelinsky on Martin Gregor-Dellin's Wagner biography (see item 326), and several other essays. Includes scattered musical examples.

780. *Richard Wagner: Parsifal. Texte, Materialen, Kommentare*, ed. Attila Csampai and Dietmar Holland. "rororo opernbuch," 7809. Reinbek: rororo, 1984. 284pp. ISBN 3499178095 (no LC number available)

A *Parsifal* companion. Contains the complete text of the libretto as well as an introductory essay by Voss, documents concerning the origins and character of Wagner's music drama, texts associated with the 1882 world-premiere performance at Bayreuth (including Hanslick's review and excerpts from Weingartner's reminiscences), and contemporary essays by Dahlhaus, Robert Gutman, Joachim Kaiser, and Zelinsky—the last of whom concerns himself with Wagner's anti-semitism. Also includes a variety of black-and-white illustrations, scattered musical examples, a time-line, a bibliography (pp. 275–77), and information about contributors. No index. Available in Japanese.

Guides by Csampai and Holland to *Holländer, Tristan,* and *Meistersinger* have also appeared in print. In addition, see Csampai's, Holland's, and Irmelin Bürgers's *Opernführer* (Hamburg, 1989), which contain comments on Wagner's music dramas from *Rienzi* to *Parsifal* (*Opernführer*, pp. 481–551; see chapter I, note 9).

Document and Source Studies

*   *Dokumentation zur . . . Parsifal,* ed. Martin Geck and Egon Voss. Described under item 156.

Contains a great deal of information about the origins, growth, first performance, and reception of Wagner's last music drama. Includes handsome documentary facsimiles, musical examples, and a beautiful tipped-in reproduction of Joseph Albert's photograph of the composer, taken at Bayreuth on 1 May 1882. Reviewed in *Notes* 28 (1971–1972), pp. 685–87, in which the strengths and weaknesses of Geck's and Voss's selection of documents are discussed.

781. Kinderman, William. "Die Entstehung der 'Parsifal'-Musik." *Archiv für Musikwissenschaft* 52 (1995), pp. 66–97 and 145–65. ML5.A63

Examines the evolution of Wagner's last music drama between late summer 1877 and January 1882, especially in terms of the "Transformation music" from act I as a representative portion of the whole. Includes a total of fourteen musical examples as well as a variety of figures and documentary facsimiles.

782. Sakolowski, Paul. "Wagners erste Parsifal-Entwürfe." *Richard-Wagner-Jahrbuch* 1 (1906), pp. 317–26. ML410.W1A57

Attempts to disprove the notion that *Parsifal* was Wagner's "swan song" by demonstrating that the composer planned and drafted portions of its text and music as early as 1858 and possibly earlier. Includes as a musical example the "Wo find ich dich" motif from the completed opera, which incorporates the "Dresden Amen" that also appears in a letter Wagner addressed to Mathilde Wesendonk decades before his death in 1883.

Textual and Literary Studies

783. Unger, Max. "The Cradle of the Parsifal Legend," trans. Theodore Baker. *The Musical Quarterly* 18 (1932), pp. 428–42. ML1.M725

Examines the Parsifal story in light of Persian sources "which not only parallel" it in conception, but "in which the very names are quite or almost literally repeated" (pp. 428–29), and which, in 1932, had only recently been unearthed by Fridrich von Suhtscheck. Not exclusively a Wagner study. Accompanied by two photographs.

Musical Studies

784. Bauer, Hans-Joachim. *Wagners "Parsifal." Kriterien der Kompositions-technik.* Berliner musikwissenschaftliche Arbeiten, 15. Munich: Emil Katzbichler, 1977. 338pp. ISBN 3873970457 ML410.W17B35

Devoted to musical aspects of *Parsifal*—and, given the scope and histori-cal significance of Wagner's score, as well as the length of Bauer's study, somewhat perfunctory in its consideration of such issues as large-scale structures, orchestration, and performance-practice issues. The chapter entitled "Die Leitmotivtechnik" (pp. 9–96) is accompanied by 145 musical examples, all photocopied from published scores; the rest of the volume lacks explicit musical citations, although analytical symbols are used to identify certain harmonic features of the work. Concludes with a useful bibliography. See also items 487 and 523.

785. Kinderman, William. "Wagner's Parsifal: Musical Form and the Drama of Redemption." *Journal of Musicology* 4 (1985–1986), pp. 431–46. ML1.J693

Considers the main organizational principle behind Wagner's last music drama not in terms of *Leitmotive*, but of large-scale harmonic structures. Kinderman considers especially the "tonal pairing" of A-flat and C as the basis for the development and resolution of tensions in *Parsifal* as a whole (see also item 742). Includes several musical examples.

786. Lewin, David. "Amfortas's Prayer to Titurel and the Role of D in 'Parsi-fal': The Tonal Spaces of the Drama and the Enharmonic C-flat/B." *Essays for Joseph Kerman = 19th Century Music* 7/3 ("3 April 1984"), pp. 336–49. ML1.N77

A complex argument involving various chromatically "displaced" key centers, including "substitute plagal" events occurring near the end of Wagner's last music drama, especially in the bar-form passages comprising mm. 933–93 of act III. Illustrated with seven figures composed of clustered short musical examples illustrating various motivic and harmonic aspects of the work.

*   Lorenz, Alfred. *Der musikalische Aufbau von . . . "Parsifal."* Described as item 482, Vol. 4.

787.   Maehder, Jürgen. "Formal and Intervallic Structures in the Score of 'Parsifal.' " *Programmhefte der Bayreuther Festspiele* II (1991), pp. 33–48. ML410.W2B26

Begins with Lorenz's bar-form theory of Wagnerian musical organization and proceeds to notions more often associated with serial music and set theory. The German version of this article (pp. 1–24) includes seven musical examples, some by Anton von Webern.

Performance and Reception Studies

788.   Cicora, Mary A. *"Parsifal" Reception in the "Bayreuther Blätter."* American University Studies: Germanic Languages and Literature, 55. New York and Frankfurt a.M.: Peter Lang, 1987. ix, 179pp. ISBN 0820403857 ML410.W17C55 1987

Devolves upon articles and other references to Wagner's final music drama that appeared in the *Bayreuther Blätter* (item 52), the magazine employed by Cosima and her followers after the composer's death to defend his reputation during the late nineteenth and early twentieth centuries. Among other sources, Cicora discusses essays by Robert Bosshart, Otto Mensendieck, and Ludwig Schemann not otherwise described in the present research guide. Includes extensive quotations in German from the *Blätter* and other early German-language Wagner publications; also includes an excellent but highly specialized bibliography (pp. 161–76) and an index.

*   Großmann-Vendrey, Susanne. *Bayreuth in der deutschen Presse.* Described as item 954.

Vol. 2 (*Die Uraufführung des Parsifal*) of this four-volume anthology documents the second Festival of 1882 and the first performance of *Parsifal*; other volumes cover the years 1876–1944.

789.   *Der Hamburger "Parsifal"—eine Provokation?*, ed. Annedore Cordes and Konrad Wulf. Program for a performance of Wagner's music drama pre-

sented on 24 March 1991 and directed by Robert Wisan. Unpaginated. ISBN 3767211661 (no LC number available)

A large-format, trendy program book handsomely illustrated with pictures and texts taken from a variety of magazines and newspapers reporting reactions to the production. The present author was able to examine a private copy of this publication only once, briefly, several years ago; it seems to be uncommon in American libraries.

790. Macedo, Catherine. "Between Opera and Reality: The Barcelona 'Parsifal.' " *Cambridge Opera Journal* 10 (1998), pp. 97–109. ISSN 0954-5867 (no LC number available)

Explores the circumstances leading up to the first performance of *Parsifal* in Catalonia: that of 31 December 1913, at the Teatre Liceu. As Macedo explains, Wagnerism—launched in 1901 by Joaquim Pena, Barcelona's foremost music critic—was for many Catalan nationalists "at first largely synonymous with Catalanism" (p. 98) and the "illusory world of Modernism" (p. 97). A useful study of the Wagner reception outside "central Europe." No illustrations or musical examples.

Interpretive Studies
A number of books and articles have dealt specifically with Parsifal *as a devotional work:*

791. Duffield, Howard. *Parsifal: The Guileless Fool.* New York: Dodd, Mead & Co., 1904. 86pp. ML410.W17D85

A sermon on the religious qualities of Wagner's music drama and its moral benefit to Americans. "Here is no attempt to delve in mediaeval lore, but an effort to catch whatever fresh gleam the re-telling of this old-time tale may shed upon that vision of a Deliverer from mortal ill" (p. 7). Includes an "Afterword" by Fiona Macleod (pp. 85–86) as well as two musical motives affixed as mottoes to chapter headings.

Similar, roughly contemporary studies include Alfred Heinrich Ehrlich's *Wagnersche Kunst und wahres Christenthum. Offenes Brief an den Hofprediger und Garrisonpfarrer Dr. theol. Emil Frommel* (Berlin, 1888); and Albert Ross Parsons's *Parsifal: The Finding of Christ through Art, or: Richard Wagner as Theologian* (New York, 1890).

792. Mark, James. "Wagner, 'Parsifal,' and Christian Faith." *Wagner* 9/3 (July 1988), pp. 99–106. ML410.W1A585

A cautious assessment of Christian elements in Wagner's last music drama, although Mark suggests that an element of compassion in its story may be considered authentically Christian. Also reviews pronouncements about *Parsifal*'s religious significance by such authorities as Dahlhaus and Thomas Mann. Reprinted from the March 1987 issue of *Theology*.

Other interpretive studies examine similarities between Mozart's Magic Flute *and Wagner's final music drama:*

793. Chailley, Jacques. *De la flûte enchantée à Parsifal*. Paris: Firmin-Didot & Cie., 1978. 19pp. ML410.M9C35 (no ISBN available)

    The text of a lecture delivered in February 1978 comparing Mozart's *Singspiel* and Wagner's music drama. Includes four musical examples as well as a cleverly arranged synopsis of the "story" of both works, with paired names of Mozart's and Wagner's characters (Tamino and Parsifal, Pamina and Kundry), locations ("realm of Sarastro" and "realm of the Grail"), and so on, arranged so that parallels between the two works can be perceived at a glance. A handsome publication.

794. Drews, Arthur. "Mozarts 'Zauberflöte' und Wagners 'Parsifal': eine Parallele." *Richard-Wagner-Jahrbuch* 1 (1906), pp. 326–61. ML410.W1A57

    Points out that both works, otherworldly and silly though at first they may appear to be, were not only their creators' last dramatic compositions, but exemplify devotion to dramatic reform—this in terms of Mozart's choice of Masonic and "enlightened" subject matter as well as Wagner's debt to Schopenhauer's philosophy. Furthermore, both musical dramas tell stories of redemption achieved through tribulation and suffering, and both represent the victory of light over darkness. Includes a few quotations from Wagner's and Da Ponte's librettos but no musical examples. See also item 1070.

Additional Parsifal *interpretive studies include:*

795. Barone, Anthony. "Richard Wagner's 'Parsifal' and the Theory of Late Style." *Cambridge Opera Journal* 7 (1995), pp. 37–54. ISSN 0954-5867 (no LC number available)

    Addresses the problem of *Parsifal* as "unique," a word employed by Adorno and Mann among others, in terms of the "apocalyptic significance" (p. 54) of "late style"—a concept invented to set Beethoven's last works apart not only from that composer's other pieces, but from the rest of music history. Among other sources Barone quotes from Goethe's *Faust* and Cosima's diaries. No musical examples. Based on researches under-taken on behalf of the author's dissertation (Columbia University, 1996).

796. Brode, Anna Christine. *Kundry und Stella. Offenbach contra Wagner.* Bielefeld: Aisthesis, 1997. 158pp. ISBN 3895281689 (no LC number available)

Examines what might at first strike Wagnerians as surprising similarities between the *Contes d'Hoffmann*, performed for the first time in Paris in 1882, and Wagner's final music drama, performed for the first time in Bayreuth the following year. Brode employs a considerable number of musical examples to make her points; she also offers insightful observa-tions about Wagner's and Offenbach's presentations of women in their dra-matic works. Includes nineteen plates of illustrations; concludes with an excellent bibliography. Other studies of Kundry include Hermann Gün-tert's *Kundry* (Heidelberg, 1928), which describes the significance of Wag-ner's heroine in terms of German legend, literature, and the visual arts.

797. Dreyfus, Laurence. "Hermann Levi's Shame and Parsifal's Guilt: A Cri-tique of Essentialism in Biography and Criticism." *Cambridge Opera Journal* 6 (1994), pp. 125–45. ISSN 0954-5867 (no LC number available)

Questions whether Levi was a Jewish "self-hater" and *Parsifal* a work of profound anti-semitism, in order to point out that critical accounts incor-porating those attitudes "need to be revalued by a musicology that traffics in both an aesthetic understanding of art works and a critical assessment of the cultural framework in which this understanding is produced" (p. 125). Dreyfus also considers both the role of Jewish issues in Wagner's life and activities, c. 1881, and the account of the first *Parsifal* performance pub-lished in 1901—but only in an expurgated version—in an issue of the *Bayreuther Blätter*. Illustrated with five musical examples and two por-traits of Levi.

* Hermand, Jost. "Wagner's Last Supper: The Vegetarian Gospel of His 'Parsifal.' " Described as item 431.

798. Hutcheon, Linda, and Michael Hutcheon. "Syphilis, Sin and the Social Order: Richard Wagner's 'Parsifal.' " *Cambridge Opera Journal* 7 (1995), pp. 261–75. ISSN 0954-5867 (no LC number available)

A study of "suffering and social decline in the context of sexually trans-mitted disease" (p. 261) that invokes the impact on Europe of syphilis dur-ing the several centuries that preceded the creation of Wagner's last music drama. Also a comparison of the Fisher-King story, especially as told by

Chrétien de Troyes and Wolfram von Eschenbach, with the "soldier's disease" (p. 271) in a complex essay written by "a literary theorist and a physician" (p. 261). Also published as chapter 3 of *Opera: Desire, Disease, Death* (University of Nebraska Press, 1996). But one of several Wagner articles by these authors; another is "Death Drive: Eros and Thanatos in Wagner's 'Tristan und Isolde,' " *Cambridge Opera Journal* 11 (1999), pp. 267–94.

799. Kienzle, Ulrike. *Das Weltüberwindungswerk. Wagners "Parsifal"—ein szenisch-musikalisches Gleichnis der Philosophie Arthur Schopenhauers.* Thurnauer Schriften zum Musiktheater, 12. Laaber: Laaber-Verlag, 1992. 236pp. ISBN 3890072763 ML410.W17K52 1992

A measure-by-measure, scene-by-scene evaluation of *Parsifal* in terms of Wagner's enthusiasm for Schopenhauer's pessimistic world view. Includes 22 musical examples, as well as extensive quotations that bring similarities and associations between composer and philosopher into sharper focus; concludes with a bibliography (pp. 231–36).

800. Stewart, Suzanne R. "The Theft of the Operatic Voice: Masochistic Seduction in Wagner's 'Parsifal.' " *The Musical Quarterly* 80 (1996), pp. 597–628. ML1.M725

A "late psychoanalytic" study of Wagner's hero and story. In Stewart's own words: "Parsifal in his victoriously failed seduction becomes feminized—and thus self-begotten—in order to have access to a form of enjoyment that is not phallically organized in any overt fashion. . . . Such a construction is at once demystifying and fantasmatic: it is demystifying insofar as it subverts 'the ideology of *femininity as masquerade* according to which man is 'man as such'. . . . And yet this demystification remains always fantasmatic insofar as it creates Parsifal's subjectivity both as self-possession (as imaginary identification) and as a form of self-objectivization, as an instrument of enjoyment for the law (as symbolic identification)" (p. 620; italics and parentheses in the original). No musical examples or textual quotations.

VIII

Wagner as Instrumental and Vocal Composer and Arranger

Wagner's reputation rests more firmly upon his prose works and the influence he exerted over a number of painters and poets than upon his instrumental and choral compositions, songs, and arrangements of other composers' works. As a consequence, comparatively few studies of the symphonies, piano pieces, and miscellaneous vocal compositions have appeared in print; many of those that exist were published prior to the outbreak of World War I, when enthusiasm for anything both "Wagnerian" and unfamiliar was at its height.

Unless otherwise noted, studies in each category below are described in alphabetical order by author and/or title.

WAGNER AS INSTRUMENTAL COMPOSER

General Studies

The following volumes represent the best introductions to Wagner's instrumental compositions:

801. Voss, Egon. *Richard Wagner und die Instrumentalmusik. Wagners symphonischer Ehrgeiz.* Taschenbücher zur Musikwissenschaft, 12. Wilhelmshaven: Heinrichshofen, 1977. 205pp. ISBN 3795900891 ML410.W13V7

In three principal chapters Voss examines the history of Wagner's instrumental corpus, issues involving relationships between instrumental music and literary or dramatic "understanding," and instrumental aspects of the composer's music dramas. Accompanied by a scant three musical examples (pp. 182–84), as well as by a fine bibliography (pp. 185–91), a list of editions (pp. 192–96), and a phonorecord discography that identifies performances of such unfamiliar works as the *Columbus* overture, *WWV* 37, the piano sonatas and *Albumblätter*, and the C-major Symphony, *WWV* 29 (together pp. 192–201).

*   Voss, Egon. *Studien zur Instrumentation Richard Wagners*. Described as item 470.

Contains information about the composer's use of individual instruments in a variety of contexts.

Also useful, especially for information about the early works, is:

802. Daube, Otto. *"Ich schreibe keine Symphonien mehr": Richard Wagners Lehrjahre nach den erhaltenen Dokumenten*. Cologne: Hans Gerig, 1960. xii, 278pp. ML410.W11W13

Examines Wagner's earliest pieces, all of them instrumental. An appendix (pp. 225–74) presents the complete text of one of the piano sonatas, themes from the *Polonia* overture, *WWV* 39, and facsimiles of other early works. Also incorporates the first published edition of Wagner's piano transcription of his own C-major Symphony. Handsomely illustrated with additional documentary facsimiles, as well as portraits of the composer and a good number of musical examples.

Studies of Individual Genres and Works

Compositions for Piano

*   "Works for Piano" = Vol. 19 of *Richard Wagner. Sämtliche Werke*. Described under item 156.

The only study that mentions more than a few of these pieces remains:

803. Breithaupt, Rudolf M. "Richard Wagners Klaviermusik" *Musik* 3–IX (July 1904), pp. 108–34. ML5.M9

Glances at most of Wagner's keyboard works, including his Sonata in B-flat, Polonaise in D for piano four-hands, *WWV* 23b, *Phantasie* in F-sharp, *WWV* 22, A-major Sonata, *WWV* 26, and such shorter pieces as the "Album-Sonata" in A-flat, *WWV* 85, composed in 1853. Numerous musical examples.

Other articles dealing with Wagner's keyboard works are described in alphabetical order by author:

804. Furness, R. S., and Andrew D. Walker. "A Wagner Polonaise." *The Musical Times* 114 (1973), pp. 26–27. ML5.M85

Includes a complete transcription of a "polonaise" sketch Wagner made in 1831, together with a facsimile of its manuscript. No other musical examples.

805. Jahrmärker, Manuela. "Eine Sonata für das Album von Frau M.W. Über-legungen zu Titel und Gattung von Richard Wagners Wesendonck-Sonate." In: *Semantische Inseln—Musikalisches Festland. Für Tibor Kneif zum 65. Geburtstag*, ed. Hanns-Werner Heister et al. Hamburg: Bockel, 1997; pp. 63–74. ISBN 3928770942 ML55.K64 1997

Examines the origins and original 1853 draft of Wagner's "Album-Sonata." Jahrmärker also discusses relationships between that work and the *Siegfried-Idyll* of 1877. Includes five musical examples.

806. Newman, William S. "Wagner's Sonatas." *Studies in Romanticism* 7 (1968), pp. 129–39. PN751.S8

Describes Wagner as a composer of sonatas, especially piano sonatas, in terms of the Sonata in D minor he mentioned having written at the age of sixteen, as well as such later works as the Sonata in A major of 1831, the B-flat major Sonata of 1832, and the "Album-Sonata" (see also item 803), as well as the F-sharp *Phantasie*. Includes two facsimiles: one of the open-ing page of the B-flat Sonata in Breitkopf & Härtel's edition, the other the first page of the "Album-Sonata" as published by B. Schott's Sons in 1878. Anticipates portions of Newman's celebrated *Sonata Since Beethoven* (New York, 1969; revised 1983). Other studies of Wagner's keyboard music are cited in items 1–3, 26, etc.

Compositions for Chamber Ensembles

807. Abraham, Gerald. "Wagner's String Quartet: An Essay in Musical Specu-lation." *The Musical Times* 86 (1945), pp. 233–34. ML5.M85

"Proves" the existence of a sketch for the so-called "Starnberg" Quartet—a work scholars now acknowledge never existed (see item 335, p. 137)—based on a comment by Ernest Newman to the effect "that the 'lullaby' episode beginning at bar 91 [of the *Siegfried-Idyll*] was inserted as an afterthought in 1870" (item 807, p. 233), because one of the themes from the latter work purportedly had been sketched for string quartet in 1864. Includes two musical examples, as well as a diagram devoted to aspects of the musical sources involved.

Some of Wagner's youthful works may have been intended for piano or for instrumental ensemble. One of these, a double fugue (*WWV* 19b) the composer finished around 1831 to 1832, is described in Edgar Istel's "Eine Doppelfuge von der Hand Wagners. Nach dem ungedruckten Original-manuskript mitgeteilt," published in *Die Musik* 11/4 (July 1912), pp. 27–41. Includes two musical examples to demonstrate that Wagner adapted his own work from the C-major Fugue of Bach's "Well-Tempered Clavier," Book I, during his studies with Christian Theodor Weinlig.

Compositions for Orchestra
*   "Orchestral Works" = Vol. 18 of *Richard Wagner. Sämtliche Werke.* Described under item 156.

Surveys of this subject include:

808. Grunsky, Karl. "Wagner als Sinfoniker." *Richard-Wagner-Jahrbuch* 1 (1906), pp. 227–44. ML410.W1A57

    Argues that Wagner's principal work as a symphonist may be found in orchestral portions of his mature music dramas, especially *Tristan*. Grunsky draws comparisons between the *Tristan* score and that of Beethoven's Ninth, one of Wagner's favorite symphonies. Eight musical examples, including a comparatively lengthy one from Hugo Wolf's *Spanisches Liederbuch.*

Wagner's Faust-Ouvertüre, WWV *59, has been the subject of several important studies, including one of book-length:*

809. Voss, Egon. *Richard Wagner. Eine Faust-Ouvertüre.* Meisterwerke der Musik, 31. Munich: Wilhelm Fink, 1982. 41pp. ISBN 3770520041 MT130.W14V67 1982

    Includes information about the origins and an analysis of the musical character and significance of Wagner's overture. Includes twelve musical examples, the last two of which are foldout facsimiles pasted into the end of the volume. Also includes a two-page bibliography.

Other studies of the Ouvertüre *include:*

810. Bülow, Hans von. *Ueber Richard Wagner's Faust-Overture. Eine erläuternde Mittheilung an die Dirigenten, Spieler und Hörer dieses Werkes.* Leipzig: C. F. Kahnt, 1860. 31pp. ML410.W175B9

    Deals with the overture not only in terms of its form, melodies, modulations, and so on, but also of its performance from the perspective of both orchestral musicians and conductors. Bülow writes well; furthermore, he established his reputation in large part as a conductor of Wagner's works, directing the world premiere performances of *Tristan* in 1865 and *Meistersinger* three years later. Lacks musical examples. See also item 977.

811. Sternfeld, Richard. "Die erste Fassung von Wagners Faust-Overtüre." *Die Musik* 15 (1923), pp. 659–64. ML5.M9

Compares an early version with the familiar later one. Sternfeld maintains that Wagner's revisions did not always constitute improvements; he also points out similarities between the work in question, Wagner's *Holländer* overture, and portions of Liszt's *Faust* symphony. Six musical examples.

Another of Wagner's orchestral works to receive scholarly attention is his Siegfried-Idyll, WWV *103, composed to honor the birth of his son Siegfried and, in a famous scene from the annals of nineteenth-century music, rehearsed in secret and performed for his wife Cosima on Christmas morning 1870:*

812. Waltershausen, Hermann W. von. *Das Siegfried-Idyll, oder Die Rückkehr zur Natur.* Munich: Hugo Bruckmann, 1920. 116pp. MT130.W14W2

More than a *Wegweiser* (guide to the music's history and contents), Waltershausen's volume argues that, in this brief and pleasant "fantasy" on themes also employed in the *Ring*, Wagner finally succeeded in freeing himself from Italian, French, and Jewish influences, and discovering his own national—which is also to say, "natural"—identity (p. 106). Contains about a dozen musical examples. Interesting in part, perhaps, to students of Wagner and anti-semitism.

Studies of other Wagner orchestral works include:

813. Istel, Edgar. "Ein unbekanntes Instrumentalwerk Wagners. Auf Grund der handschriftlichen Partitur dargestellt." *Die Musik* 12/3 (May 1913), pp. 152–59. ML5.M9

Describes a twenty-four-page manuscript score of an orchestral movement in E minor, *WWV* 13, composed by Wagner around 1830. Illustrated with ten short musical examples.

814. Mey, Kurt. "Richard Wagners Webertrauermarsch." *Die Musik* 6/2 (1906–1907), pp. 331–36. ML5.M9

Examines the music (*WWV* 73) Wagner composed in 1844 for 75 wind instruments and twenty muffled drums. The work itself, intended as a funeral march for the Weber internment ceremonies in Dresden, is based on two motifs from *Euryanthe*. Includes musical examples.

815. Saffle, Michael. "Wagner's American Escapades: The Centennial March and the American Press." *American Music Teacher* 38/6 (June/July 1989), pp. 20–23. ISSN 0003-0112 (no LC number available)

Outlines the history behind the march (*WWV* 110) Wagner composed for the Philadelphia Centenary Exhibition of 1876, and explains how the press responded to Theodore Thomas's earliest performances of it. Includes quotations from such magazines as *Scribner's* and *Dwight's Journal,* as well as a facsimile of the title page from Joseph Rubinstein's piano arrangement of the work. With regard to *Dwight's Journal,* see item 945; with regard to Theodore Thomas's Wagner performances, see items 48 and 1054.

816. Voss, Egon. "Auch eine Unvollendete: Richard Wagners wiederaufgefundenes Sinfonie-Fragment in E-Dur, WWV 35." *Neue Zeitschrift für Musik* 149/11 (November 1988), pp. 14–18. ML5.M183

Discusses and analyzes a work for which both the composer's original manuscript and fair copy have disappeared. Includes about a dozen mostly hand-copied musical examples taken from this piece and other Wagner compositions. Voss's edition of the work in question was published in 1988 by B. Schott's Sons of Mainz and New York (M1001.W18 E maj. 1988). Another study by Voss, "Wagners fragmentarisches Orchesterwerk in e-moll: die früheste der erhaltenen Kompositionen?" [published in *Die Musikforschung* 23 (1970), pp. 50–54], deals with another fragment, possibly the overture to the *Braut von Messina, WWV* 12, mentioned in *My Life*.

Compositions for Other Instrumental Ensembles

817. *Bläserklang und Blasinstrumente im Schaffen Richard Wagners. Kongreßbericht Seggau/Österreich 1983*, ed. Wolfgang Suppan. Alta Musica, 8. Tutzing: Hans Schneider, 1985. 261pp. ISBN 3795204453 ML410.W131B63 1985

A collection of conference papers devoted to Wagner's writing and scoring for wind instruments, including Rita Fischer-Wildhagen on "Richard Wagner und die Altoboe," Kurt Janetsky on "Richard Wagners Verhältnis zu Hörnern und Hörnisten," and Friend [*sic*] Overton on "Historische Perspektiven und Einflüsse des Wagnerschen Serpert-Pars in 'Rienzi.'" Illustrated with scattered musical examples. Closely related studies include David Whitwell's spiral-bound pamphlet *Wagner on Bands* (Northridge, CA; n.d.), which evaluates such compositions as the *Kaisermarsch, WWV*

104, and "festival song" *Der Tag erscheint, WWV* 68, as well as "authorized arrangements" of other works for wind ensembles.

* "Compositions for the Theater" = Vol. 15 of *Richard Wagner. Sämtliche Werke.* Described under item 156.

Includes works for voices and orchestra.

WAGNER AS CHORAL AND VOCAL COMPOSER

* "Choral Works" and "Songs for Voice and Piano" = Vols. 16–17 of *Richard Wagner. Sämtliche Werke.* Described under item 156.

With the exception of the so-called Wesendonck-Lieder, WWV *91, Wagner's concert works for voice are even less familiar than his instrumental compositions; no survey study of them exists in print. The following articles deal with individual vocal and choral works only:*

818. Kirsch, Winfried. "Richard Wagners Biblische Szene 'Das Liebesmahl der Apostel.' " *Geistliche Musik: Studien zu ihrer Geschichte und Funktion im 18. und 19. Jahrhundert,* ed. Peter Petersen. Hamburger Beiträge für Musikwissenschaft, 8. Laaber: Laaber-Verlag, 1985; pp. 157–84. ISBN 3890070493

Describes the choral composition Wagner wrote for the Dresdener Liedertafel in 1843. Includes six hand-copied musical examples, as well as a diagram of the work's structure (pp. 162–63) and four illustrations, the last including a reproduction of Raphael's *School of Athens,* and a photograph of Dresden's Frauenkirche prior to its destruction in 1945.

819. Mey, Kurt. "Über Richard Wagners Huldigungschor an König Freidrich August II. von Sachsen 1844." *Die Musik* 5–XXI (December 1905), pp. 327–31. ML5.M9

Describes circumstances associated with the composition of this work (*WWV* 71) and reproduces the opening measures of two versions, one by Hösel.

820. Müller-Blattau, Wendelin. "Tout n'est qu'images fugitives: Die französischen Romanzen von Richard Wagner." In: *Festschrift Walter Wiora zum 90. Geburtstag (30. Dezember 1996),* ed. Christoph-Hellmut Mahling and Ruth Seiberts. Tutzing: Hans Schneider, 1997; pp. 322–36. ISBN 3795208904 ML55.W563 1997

Examines six of Wagner's earliest piano-vocal works, not as they have often been examined in the past—as *Nebenprodukte* (by-products) of his work on *Holländer* (p. 336)—but as "romances" in their own right. The origins and stylistic characteristics of these romances—"Attente" (*WWV* 55; see also item 854), "Dors mon enfant" (*WWV* 53), "Extase" (*WWV* 54), "La Tombe dit à la rose" (*WWV* 56), "Mignonne" (*WWV* 57), and "Tout n'est qu'images fugitives" (*WWV* 58)—are described, and two of them— "Dors mon enfant" and "Attente"—are discussed in more detail. Illustrated with musical examples from the last two works and from "Mignonne."

821. Voss, Egon. "Richard Wagner: 'Fünf Lieder nach Gedichten von Mathilde Wesendonck.' " *Neue Zeitschrift für Musik* 144/1 (January 1983), pp. 22–26. ML5.M183

Briefly considers the circumstances behind the composition of Wagner's best-known songs and something of their contents and musical character, especially their stylistic links with portions of *Tristan*. Illustrated with a full-page musical example, as well as a portrait drawing of Mathilde Wesendonk, who wrote the songs' texts, and a silhouette of Wagner cut by Otto Böhler.

WAGNER AS ARRANGER

*   "Arrangements for Piano" = Vol. 20 of *Richard Wagner. Sämtliche Werke.* Described under item 156.

The only survey study devoted to Wagner's arrangements remains:

822. Kleefeld, Wilhelm. "Richard Wagner als Bearbeiter fremder Werke." *Die Musik* 4–X (February–March 1905), pp. 231–49 and 326–37. ML5.M9

Identifies a number of Wagner's lesser-known works, including an arrangement he made in 1848 of Palestrina's *Stabat mater* (*WWV* 79), a piano score of Beethoven's Ninth Symphony (*WWV* 9), and transcriptions of pieces by Gluck, Donizetti, and Spontini. Includes several dozen short musical examples, most of them in footnotes.

Other studies devoted to Wagner as arranger are described below in alphabetical order by author:

823. Einstein, Alfred. "Richard Wagner als Bearbeiter Rossinis." In: Einstein, *Nationale und universale Musik. Neue Essays.* Zurich and Stuttgart: Pan, 1958; pp. 88–90. ML60.E385

Suggests a brief, somewhat hypothetical history for the orchestral arrangement of "Li Marinari" from Rossini's *Soirées musicales* (the arrangement

WWV 47) that probably dates from 1838 and Wagner's sojourn in Riga, if only because of the work's restricted orchestral forces. Includes no musical examples. Published originally in ZIMG [the *Zeitschrift der Internationalen Musikgesellschaft*] 13 (1911–1912), pp. 309–11.

824. Münster, Robert. "Eine 'Serenade' von Richard Wagners: Marginalien zu Johann Karl Eschmann, einem Schweizer Freund von Wagner und Brahms." In: *Studien zur Musikgeschichte: Eine Festschrift für Ludwig Finscher*, ed. Annegrit Laubenthal and Kara Kusan-Windweh. Kassel and New York: Bärenreiter, 1995; pp. 614–21. ISBN 3761812221 ML55.F49 1995

Describes an arrangement for violin and orchestra of "Träume," *WWV* 91B, preserved in a manuscript belonging to the Bayerische Staatsbibliothek, Munich. Includes a two-page facsimile of the manuscript itself, dated Zurich 1857, as well as two additional musical examples and information about Wagner's relationship with Eschmann during the early 1850s. Other studies dealing with Wagner's arrangements of his own vocal works include Reinhard Kapp's " 'Original-Bearbeitung' des Pilgerchors aus Wagner's Tannhäuser 'für den Wiener Männer-Gesang-Verein,' " published in the *Österreichische Musikzeitschrift* 48 (1993), pp. 544–52.

825. Walton, Chris. "Iphigenia Lost and Found: A Newly-discovered Gluck Arrangement by Richard Wagner." *Fontis artes musicae* 45 (1998), pp. 227–36. (no LC number available)

Published copies survive of Wagner's orchestral ending for the overture to Gluck's *Iphigenia en Aulide* (the arrangement *WWV* 77); Walton discusses instead performance directions and other musical details preserved in Wagner's handwriting on copies of the overture made during the early 1850s by Adam Bauer, and owned today by a Zurich musical society. Includes three pages of documentary facsimiles with Wagner's previously unknown corrections and changes.

IX

Performing Wagner:
Studies of Performance Practices,
Productions, and Media Issues

*Scholarly studies dealing with Wagner performance issues are comparatively few,
at least if one considers them separately from performance reviews—there are
tens of thousands of those in print—and studies dealing with Bayreuth and its
Festspielhaus. The latter are dealt with in chapter XIII; this chapter is devoted
exclusively to books and articles devoted to singing, conducting, production and
direction, and media issues.*

*Unless otherwise noted, individual studies are evaluated under each sub-
heading in alphabetical order by author and/or title.*

SURVEY STUDIES

*Item 826 is among the most useful English-language introductions to performing
Wagner's music dramas; the second study, more fulsomely illustrated, may be
better known among German readers:*

826. *Wagner in Performance*, ed. Barry Millington and Stewart Spencer. New
Haven, CT and London: Yale University Press, 1992. x, 214pp. ISBN
0300037180 ML410.W1W12 1992

Incorporates items 849, 947, and 1114, as well as David Breckbill's "Wagner
on Record: Re-evaluating Singing in the Early Years" (pp. 153–67); Clive
Brown's "Performance Practice" survey (pp. 99–119), based largely on comments in Wagner's letters and prose works; Patrick Carnegy's "Designing
Wagner: Deeds of Music Made Visible?" (pp. 48–74); and Desmond Shawe-
Taylor's "Wagner and His Singers" (pp. 15–28), as well as Joseph Horowitz's
essay about "Anton Seidl and America's Wagner Cult" (pp. 168–81). Also
includes a few musical examples; Carnegy's essay is illustrated with

photographs of stage sets, and Breckbill provides more precise discographical information than do many commentators on Wagner recordings. Concludes with endnotes, information about contributors, and an index.

827. Bauer, Ostwald Georg. *Richard Wagner: Die Bühnenwerke von der Uraufführung bis heute*. Frankfurt a.M.: Propyläen, 1965. 288pp. ISBN 3549066589 ML390.H13

A lavishly illustrated, coffee-table-sized volume that describes and depicts the history of and scenes from Wagner's music dramas, beginning with *Die Feen* and concluding with *Parsifal*. Supplemented by photographs, costume sketches, and other pictures—many of them in color—as well as interpolated comments about individual musical passages and performances. Unfortunately, the binding is so weak that the book tends to break even with casual use. Concludes with a brief bibliography (pp. 280–81), an index (pp. 282–87), and information about illustrations.

Two shorter introductions to Wagner performance-practice issues are:

828. Bauer, Oswald. "Performance History: A Brief Survey," trans. Stewart Spencer. In item 2, pp. 502–23.

A history of Wagner's music dramas in performance, beginning with the disaster attending *Das Liebesverbot* in 1836, and concluding with 1970s and 1980s productions at Bayreuth and elsewhere in Germany by the likes of Patrice Chéreau (see items 847–49), Götz Friedrich (see item 851), and Herbert Wernicke. Proceeding roughly in chronological order, Bauer briefly identifies and evaluates the significance of individual "Performances During Wagner's Lifetime" (pp. 502–6), as well as performances presented "From Wagner's Death to the First World War" (pp. 507–11), "Productions during the Weimar Republic and the Third Reich" (pp. 514–19), and "Postwar Productions" (pp. 519–23); he also devotes a section to "Adolphe Appia and Stage Design" (pp. 511–14).

829. Breckbill, David. "Performance Practice." In item 1, pp. 350–59.

Summarizes issues associated with Wagner performance, including orchestration and certain aspects of instrumental style, conducting—among other issues, the author considers reports of Wagner as conductor of his own works—and characteristic practices of Wagnerian singers, as well as "Wagner and the Early Music Movement" (the last pp. 358–59). As Breckbill observes, "authentic" performances of Wagner's works would require such "spontaneity" and "extremes" of expression, and would be so dependent upon "a now unfashionable show of subjectivity," that they could "hardly be achieved in an age where musicians are expected and trained to produce performances of cosmetic perfection" (p. 359). No musical examples.

STUDIES OF INDIVIDUAL PERFORMANCE PRACTICES AND PRACTITIONERS

Conducting and Conductors

830. Breckbill, David. "Conducting." In item 1, pp. 368–74.

Describes approaches to conducting the music dramas adopted by (1) Anton Seidl, (2) such "Bayreuth conductors" as Felix Mottl and Richard Strauss, (3) Hans Richter, (4) "those who favored a fast pace," and (5) "the Mahler/Toscanini legacy of symphonic intentionality" (p. 371). Breckbill also considers post–World War II approaches to Wagner's music, noting that "the prevailing style [during the past fifty years] has come from combining" two of the previously identified styles (p. 372). Unfortunately, references to recorded performances by the likes of Hans Knappertsbusch and Georg Solti lack precise discographical information.

831. Breckbill, David. "Wagner as a Conductor." In item 1, pp. 99–102.

A pocket synopsis of Wagner's own conducting career, his influence as a conductor, and a few of his ideas about music direction in theatrical settings. See also items 186 and 832, among others.

832. *Wagner on Conducting*, trans. Edward Dannreuther. London: William Reeves, 1887; reprinted New York: Dover, 1989. 119pp. ISBN 0486259323 ML410.W1A246 1989

A collection of Wagner's writings about orchestral conducting, illustrated with scattered musical examples. Dannreuther provides four appendices (pp. 109–19) that provide the texts of other Wagner documents, as well as the complete original *Grove's Dictionary* Wagner article published in the first edition of that important reference work.

Singing and Singers

Among the very few surveys of this subject are:

833. Breckbill, David. "Singing." In item 1, pp. 362–68.

A synopsis of approaches, including the two most often adopted by late nineteenth-century artists: "projecting the words" versus "singing the music" (p. 363). Breckbill also considers the influence of Bayreuth on

Wagnerian singers, various geographical styles of singing Wagner—more than a few of them located in Germany—and the legacies of such famous performers as Kirsten Flagstad and her "heavy wobble" (p. 367), Albert Niemann and his "artistic magnetism" (p. 363), and such contemporary artists as Gwyneth Jones and James Morris.

834. Fischer, Jens Malte. " 'Sprechgesang' or Bel Canto: Toward a History of Singing Wagner," trans. Michael Tanner. In item 2, pp. 524–46.

Examines vocal production and performances of Wagner's music dramas. Basing his observations on his own opinions, as well as what he stoutly maintains are issues involving "objective judgments"—the latter include "sovereign command of breath and body," "purity and certainty of intonation," "clarify and balance of vowels and their placement," "balanced timbre in all registers," and so on (see p. 525)—Fischer goes on to consider performances by celebrated Wagnerian vocalists, as well as such historical issues as the development of a "Bayreuth School" as an institution that "began" with the composer's plans for a Munich music conservatory (see item 871) and, especially in detail, the vocal requirements of individual Wagnerian roles for soprano, mezzo-soprano, contralto, baritone, "heroic" tenor (*Heldentenor*), and bass voices. Unfortunately, the only authority Fischer cites is Julius Hey, the author of the three-volume *Deutscher Gesangs-Unterricht* (Mainz, 1884), an important work of German vocal pedagogy, as well as a collection of Wagner reminiscences. No musical examples or precise discographical information. An article by Fischer with virtually the same title appeared in item 1006, pp. 475–90.

Other studies dealing with singers and singing include:

835. Ashbrook, William. "The First Singers of 'Tristan und Isolde.' " *Opera Quarterly* 3/4 (Winter 1985), pp. 11–23. ML1699.O65

Devoted to the 1865 world premiere of Wagner's music drama, as well as plans for earlier performances in Strasbourg, Karlsruhe, and Vienna, and to the roles played both on- and off-stage by Wilhelmine Schröder-Devrient, the Schnorrs, Louise Dustmann-Meyer, and other stars. A good place to begin for anyone interested in nineteenth-century Wagnerian vocal performance practices, and especially Wagner's preferences for certain vocal types.

836. Krech, Hans. "Richard Wagner als Sänger und Sprecher." In: *Festschrift Max Schneider zum achtzigsten Geburtstag*, ed. Walther Vetter. Leipzig: Deutscher Verlag für Musik, 1955; pp. 255–64. ML55.F551

Brings together several dozen of Wagner's observations on vocal quality, diction, and other performance-practice issues. A bit of a mishmash. Unfortunately includes no musical examples.

Orchestral and Instrumental Performance and Performers

837. Sous, Alfred. *Das Bayreuther Festspielorchester—Geschichte, Geschichten und Anekdoten von damals bis heute.* Frankfurt a.M.: Robert Lienau, 1997. 175pp. ISBN 3874841251 ML410.W2S59 1997

Deals with orchestral musicians and music-making at the Festspielhaus from the rehearsals for the 1876 Festival to the 1990s. In addition to historical information about various Bayreuth orchestras and their members, Sous provides a list of all orchestra members from 1872 to 1995 or so (pp. 135–68), as well as a list of conductors (pp. 169–70), some interesting anecdotes about rehearsals and performances, and a variety of illustrations—including a few in color—ranging from a facsimile of Wagner's original design for the Festspielhaus orchestra pit to photographs of famous performers. A full-fledged performance history, with plenty of information about the Nazi era, as well as more politically correct eras and their activities. Also includes a foreword by Wieland Wagner (pp. 6–7). Concludes with an index.

STUDIES DEALING WITH PRODUCTIONS AND PRODUCER-DIRECTORS

Under "staging" and "production" are generally included not only set and costume design, but direction—*which is to say, the artistic supervision of entire productions, series, seasons, and festivals. Many production studies deal with issues of staging, set designs, and so on; more deal with Wagner as his own director or with the accomplishments of other directors.*

General Studies

838. Millington, Barry. "Staging." In item 1, pp. 374–78.

Evaluates Wagner on stage largely in terms of the influence of various directors: Josef Hoffmann's *Ring* for the 1876 Bayreuth Festival, Adolphe Appia's "anti-naturalistic" and "psychologically determined" (p. 375) designs for an incompletely realized Basel *Ring* of the early 1920s, the influence of Wagner's descendents—Siegfried, Wieland, and Wolfgang— at Bayreuth, Joachim Herz's "socially critical Leipzig *Ring*" of the early 1970s (p. 377), and of course Patrice Chéreau's 1980s Bayreuth *Ring* on stage (but not television, where it made a slightly different impression). No illustrations or musical examples.

Other studies of Wagnerian productions and production methods include:

839. Curzon, Henri de. *L'Oeuvre de Richard Wagner à Paris et ses interprètes (1850–1914)*. Paris: Maurice Senart et Cie., c. 1920. 92pp. ML410.W12F67

A brief but well-illustrated and useful survey of Wagner performances in the French capital prior to the beginning of World War I. Includes 24 unpaginated plates comprising 42 especially sharp images of famous Wagnerian singers *en costume*. Also includes tables of performances and performers as well as an index of names.

840. Petzet, Dette, and Michael Petzet. *Die Richard-Wagner-Bühne König Ludwigs II*. Studien zur Kunst des neunzehnten Jahrhunderts, 80. Munich: Prestel, 1970. 840pp. ML410.W11P5

Describes Wagner's plans for a theater of his own: first in Munich, and later in Bayreuth. In additional to historical information and evaluation, the Petzets provide 771 black-and-white illustrations, as well as sixteen tipped-in color plates depicting sketches, architectural diagrams, stage settings, costume designs, and other images associated with those plans. Organized throughout in order of first productions "for Ludwig": thus the volume leads off with the *Holländer* performance of 4 December 1864, followed by productions of *Tristan*, *Lohengrin*, and *Tannhäuser* of 1865 and 1867. Also includes some 100 letters exchanged by Wagner and Lorenz von Düfflipp, Bavarian Court Secretary from 1867 to 1877 (pp. 774–828), as well as a catalog of 291 architectural models, costume sketches, designs for stage sets, and other theatrical artifacts pertaining to actual Wagner productions under Ludwig's sponsorship (pp. 746–74), and two essays: "Die Idee eines Festspielhauses" by Heinrich Habel (pp. 297–316), and "Musik und Musikleben im München Richard Wagners und Ludwigs II." by Martin Geck (pp. 317–28). Indexed.

841. Werckmeister, Johanna. *Bühne und bildende Kunst. Visualisierungskonzeptionen für Musikdramen Richard Wagners seit 1945*. Europäische Hochschulschriften: Kunstgeschichte, 301. Frankfurt a.M. and New York: Peter Lang, 1997. 215pp. ISBN 3631311818 ML410.W13W37 1997

Deals with artistic and social issues associated with important international productions of Wagner's music dramas. Includes twelve illustrations of stage sets associated with such productions, including one designed by David Hockney for a 1987 Los Angeles performance of *Tristan* (pp.

205–16); also includes a list of sources that extends to sub-lists of Wagner performances at Covent Garden, London, the Hamburger Staatstheater, the Paris Opéra, and so on, and productions designed by Ernst Fuchs, Adolf Luther, and Fritz Wotruba, as well as more traditional bibliographic citations (pp. 165–202). Unindexed.

Studies of Productions in Particular Places

Bayreuth Productions: see also items 678–79, 682, 694, 837, and 847–49:

842. Mack, Dietrich. *Der Bayreuther Inszenierungsstil.* Arbeitsgemeinschaft "100 Jahre Bayreuther Festspiele," 9. Munich: Prestel, 1976. 483pp. ISBN 3791300474 ML410.W2B297

Devoted to "Wagner on the Bayreuth stage, 1876–1976." Much of Mack's "authoritative study" (item 1, p. 409) consists of 685 black-and-white photographs of scenes from and details of various productions (pp. 127–480); the rest is mostly taken up with texts relating to the "authentic Bayreuth style" and various subordinate production issues—subdivided, first by music drama (e.g., the *Ring, Parsifal, Tristan,* etc.), then by era (e.g., 1876, 1882–1933, 1951–1958, and so on). Includes observations on the illustrations (p. 46); concludes with an index.

Closely related studies are described below in alphabetical order by author and/or title:

* Baumann, Carl-Friedrich. *Bühnentechnik im Festspielhaus Bayreuth.* Described as item 1123.

* Baumann, Dorothea. "Wagners Festspielhaus. . . ." Described as item 1124. See other studies in chapter XIII as well.

843. Neupert, Käte. "Die Besetzung der Bayreuther Festspiele, 1876–1960." In item 66, Vol. 2, pp. 47–119.

Gives the numbers of performances at each Bayreuth Festival through 1960, together with the names of all Bayreuth soloists (identified by works, roles, and years), conductors, directors, stage designers, chorus masters, costume designers, and so on. Also includes information about Bayreuth performances of Beethoven's Ninth Symphony from 1876 to 1954 (p. 74). Equipped with its own index (pp. 129–42).

Milan Productions

844. *Il caso Wagner al Teatro alla Scala, 1873–1991,* with an essay by Francesco Gellia. Milan: ATR, 1994. 182pp. ML410.W12I8138 1994 (no ISBN available)

A quarto-size volume commemorating Wagner performances at Milan's world-famous opera house, published in conjunction with an exhibit held from December 1994 to January 1995 at the Museo teatrale alla Scala. Includes tables identifying individual productions (pp. 157–79), as well as handsome illustrations, many in color, devoted to stage designs and scenes associated with a host of actual productions (pp. 69–151). Gellia's essay, "Il caso Wagner" (pp. 23–61), reviews the Wagner reception in Italy since the latter decades of the nineteenth century, and is itself illustrated with historic photographs and documentary facsimiles. Contains no bibliography or index, however.

Munich Productions: see item 840.

Paris Productions: see items 839 and 859. See, too, item 72 as well as virtually all the studies of French *Wagnérisme* described in chapter XII of the present research guide.

Studies of Individual Producer-Directors and Stage Designers

Adolphe Appia
845. Appia, Adolphe. *Staging Wagnerian Drama*, trans. Peter Loeffler. Basel and Boston: Birkhäuser, 1982. 94pp. ISBN 3764313633 ML3862.A6613 1982

Describes the director's precepts for Wagner productions at the turn of the last century. A number of other editions also exist: these include *La mise en scène du drame wagnérien* (Paris, 1895) and *Die Musik und die Inszenierung* (Munich, 1899); the latter, according to published bibliographic evidence, was reprinted in Vols. 28–29 of the *Theaterjahrbuch der Schweizerischen Gesellschaft für Theaterkultur* (Bern, 1963). See also R. C. Beacham's article "Adolphe Appia and the Staging of Wagnerian Opera," published in *Opera Quarterly* 1/3 (Fall 1983), pp. 114–39, which considers the influence Appia and Wagner had on each other, and summarizes Appia's career and theatrical writings overall.

Carl Brandt
846. Kaiser, Hermann. *Der Bühnenmeister Carl Brandt und Richard Wagner: Kunst der Szene in Darmstadt und Bayreuth.* Darmstadt: Eduard Roether, 1968. 129pp. ML410.W1K14

Examines the career of the man who helped design and install stage machinery for the first Bayreuth Festival. Most of Kaiser's volume, however, is devoted to pictures of sets and scenes from Brandt's productions, including his work on the 1882 *Parsifal*; a few of these pictures, printed in color, are mounted on colored pages bound into the volume as a whole. Includes a "Brandt family tree" (p. 115); concludes with a short bibliography (pp. 126–27) and an index of names.

Patrice Chéreau

* *Bayreuther Dramaturgie: Der Ring des Nibelungen*, ed. Herbert Barth. Described as item 655.

Includes a chapter on "Die Jahre 1976–1980 von Patrice Cheréaus Ring-Inszenierung," as well as the text of a lengthy interview with the controversial director (pp. 375–402) and a list of contributors (pp. 439–41).

* *Histoire d'un "Ring" . . . Bayreuth 1976–1980*. Described as item 679.

An illustrated history of the Chéreau *Ring* at Bayreuth.

847. Faerber, Uwe. *The Centenary Ring in Bayreuth. A Critical Examination of the New Production of the Tetralogy Which Marked the 100th Anniversary of the Bayreuth Festival*, trans. Stewart Spencer. Berlin: Bote & Bock, 1977. 86pp. ML410.W2F33 (no ISBN available)

A pointedly negative review of Chéreau's production, supplemented by quotations from the books and articles of other critics who attended 1976 Bayreuth *Ring* performances. As Faerber states, the "fascinating spectacle" of Chéreau's production nevertheless "disregarded both the music and its text" (p. 5). No illustrations, bibliography, or index.

848. Bergfeld, Joachim. *Ich wollte Wagner vom Podest holen. Anmerkungen zur Bayreuther Ringinszenierung durch Patrice Chéreau im Jubiläumsjahr der Festspiele 1976*. Typescript 1977. 98pp. (no LC number available)

The texts of two lectures presented to the Rotary Club of Bayreuth on 4 April and 13 June 1977, dealing with the controversial French director's *Ring* productions of 1976. Engaging and comprehensible as well as precise. The Library of Congress owns a microform copy (shelf-number MLCS 84/15323(M)).

849. Nattiez, Jean-Jacques. "Fidelity to Wagner: Reflections on the Centenary 'Ring.' " In item 826, pp. 75–98.

A systematic defense of Chéreau's *Ring*, based in part on the principles of semiotics. One of several similar publications by Nattiez, most of them in French; perhaps the most important of these is *Tétralogies: Wagner, Boulez, Chéreau. Essai sur l'infidélité* (Paris, 1983).

Sergei Eisenstein
850. Burzawa, Ewa. "'Die Walküre' von Sergei Eisenstein: Versuch der Rekon-
struktion." In item 1006, pp. 299–311.

Attempts to "reconstruct" a production of *Walküre* presented at the Bol-
shoi Theater, Moscow, under orders from Josef Stalin and to celebrate the
German-Soviet Nonaggression Pact of 1939; the production itself pre-
miered on 21 November 1940. See also item 1081.

Götz Friedrich
851. *Wagner-Regie. Götz Friedrichs Musiktheater*, ed. Stefan Jaeger. Zurich:
Atlantis, 1983. 240pp. ISBN 3254000803 ML410.W19F65 1983

Reviews individual, comparatively recent Wagner productions by
Friedrich, today *Intendant* (general director) of the Deutsche Oper, Berlin.
Examples include *Tannhäuser* at the 1972 Bayreuth Festival, the complete
Ring at Covent Garden, London, 1974 to 1977, *Meistersinger* in 1977 at
the Royal Opera in Stockholm, and so on. Extensively illustrated with
black-and-white photographs of stage sets, rehearsals, and performances,
as well as with a few facsimiles of playbills and other documents. Includes
a foreword by Hans Meyer, a Friedrich timeline (p. 232), a list of his productions (pp. 232–34), a Wagner timeline (pp. 235–36), and a general
index. Also includes comments on and illustrations of Friedrich's
Tannhäuser and *Lohengrin* television productions and a little information
on film versions of his work.

Gustav Mahler
852. Heuss, Alfred. "Musik und Szene bei Wagner: Ein Beispiel aus "Tristan
und Isolde" und zugleich ein kleiner Beitrag zur Charakteristik Gustav
Mahlers als Regisseur." *Die Musik* 12/2 (1912–1913), pp. 207–13.
ML5.M9

Considers aspects of Wagner's score, including the very beginning of *Tristan*, act I ("Frisch weht der Wind"), in terms of their performance directions or lack thereof, with special regard to Mahler's celebrated Wagner
performances. Includes two musical examples.

Josef Svoboda
853. Burian, Jarka. *Svoboda: Wagner. Josef Svoboda's Scenography for
Richard Wagner's Operas*. Middleton, CT: Wesleyan University Press,
1983. ix, 118pp. ISBN 0819530884 ML410.W19B9 1983

Devoted to Svoboda's highly abstract 1960s and 1970s stage designs for
productions of *Tannhäuser, Tristan, Holländer, Meistersinger*, and the

Ring, many of them presented at Covent Garden, London. Depicts his designs and mechanical devices; photographs of production scenes, many of them in color, are scattered throughout this volume. Also includes a catalog of illustrations (pp. vi–viii) and two appendices: one giving the dimensions of the Covent Garden stage platform; the other listing all of the productions, Wagnerian and non-Wagnerian, mounted by Svoboda during his career (pp. 104–13). Concludes with a one-page bibliography. Reviewed in *Opera Quarterly* 3/2 (Summer 1985), pp. 164–66.

Hans-Jürgen Syberberg: See item 865.

Richard Wagner

A great many studies touch on Wagner's own specifications for and activities on behalf of productions of his works. One example is:

854. Heuss, Alfred. "Zum Thema: Musik und Szene bei Wagner. Im Anschluss an Wagners Aufsatz: Bemerkungen zur Aufführung der Oper 'Der fliegende Holländer.' " *Die Musik* 10/1 (1910–1911), pp. 3–14 and 81–95. ML5.M9

Examines the composer's performance directions and suggestions for *Holländer.* Illustrated with half a dozen musical examples. Additional information about Wagner as artistic director and business manager may be found in Carl Dahlhaus, "Richard Wagner als Manager," published in the American magazine *Art Journal* 1/3 (July–September 1983), pp. 8–11.

855. Srocke, Martina. *Richard Wagner als Regisseur.* Berliner musikwissenschaftliche Arbeiten, 35. Munich and Salzburg: Emil Katzbichler, 1988. 149pp. ISBN 3873970740 ML410.W19S72 1988

Considers Wagner as his own producer-director, with special reference to the Bayreuth Festivals of 1876 and 1882. Concludes with a useful bibliography (pp. 119–24) as well as several appendices, including a complete facsimile of the composer's pamphlet *Anordnung der Proben zu den Aufführungen des Bühnenfestspieles "Der Ring des Nibelungen" in Bayreuth im Jahre 1876* (pp. 126–34) and two indexes.

Wieland Wagner

856. Cheyrezy, Christian. *Essai sur la représentation du drame musical. Wieland Wagner in memoriam.* Paris and Montréal: L'Harmattan, 1998. 250pp. ISBN 273846638–9 ML429.W135C54 1998

Treats Wieland Wagner's career at Bayreuth from a French critical perspective and with a little postmodern wit. Includes an introductory
"prélude" and an afterword ("avant-scène") by Michel Guiomar, as well as
a bibliography (pp. 241–46), a table of illustrations (pp. 247–48), and two
collections of images: a group of production photos placed between pp.
241–42 and a collection of seventeen additional illustrations, some in
color, bound at the very end of the volume.

857. Lust, Claude. *Wieland Wagner et la survie des théâtre lyrique*. Lausanne:
     "La Cite," 1969. 237pp. ML410.W245L9

     Summarizes Wieland Wagner's staging concepts and techniques, illus-
     trated with a number of plates and diagrams and employing scattered
     musical examples to help "place" performers properly on stage. Includes a
     list of Wieland's productions (pp. 219–36); no bibliography or index.

858. Schmid, Viola. *Studien zu Wieland Wagners Inszenierungskonzeption und
     zu seiner Regiepraxis*. Munich: "Dissertationsdruck," 1973. 304pp. (no LC
     number available)

     Devoted to essentially the same subjects covered in item 857. Includes an
     outstanding bibliography (pp. 275–303), but the illustrations Schmid
     refers to are available only at the Institut für Theatergeschichte, University
     of Munich. A photoreproduction typescript; Harvard University's Loeb
     Music Library owns a copy.

Costume and Set-Design Studies

*   *Der Ring des Nibelungen . . . Dekorationsentwürfe von Prof. Max Brück-
      ner in Coburg*. Described as item 683.

859. Gund, Heinz Joachim. *Die Wagner-Bühnenbilder der Pariser Oper von
     1891–1914*. Freiburg i.Br.: photocopied typescript, c. 1980. 212pp. (no LC
     number available)

     Draws upon the collections kept at the Palais Garnier to document stage
     and costume designs employed for productions in Paris at the turn of the
     last century, including 54 sketches, drawings, paintings, and models
     identified in a *Katalog* of their own (pp. 202–12). Supplemented with a
     list of designers—including, among others, Philippe-Marie Chaperan,
     Edouard Desplechin, Marcel Jambon, and Joseph Thierry—as well as
     summaries of their careers, together with references to books and articles
     describing their work (pp. 194–97); also contains a bibliography (pp.
     198–201). Unfortunately unillustrated, although the *Katalog* identifies

images found in 1869 issues of *La Chronique illustré*, as well as in item 839 above.

860. *Hans Thoma's Costume Designs for Richard Wagner's "Ring des Nibelungen,"* with an introduction by Henry Thode. Leipzig: Breitkopf & Härtel, 1897. Not paginated consistently. (no LC number available)

Aside from Thode's essay (pp. 7–11), this volume consists of eighteen full-page, black-and-white plates of designs for several different German productions. A good source of information concerning early *Ring* performances, but rare; Harvard University's Loeb Music Library owns a copy.

* Werckmeister, Johanna. *Bühne und bildende Kunst.* Described as item 841.

861. Zeh, Gisela. *Das Bayreuther Bühnenkostüm.* Munich: Prestel, 1973. 229pp. ISBN 3791300253 ML410.W2Z4

Deals with costumes and costume design for Bayreuth productions between 1876 and 1967. Supplemented (mostly in pp. 123–224) by 401 black-and-white and six tipped-in color illustrations, all painstakingly identified. Concludes with a brief bibliography (pp. 225–26) and an index.

WAGNER AND THE MEDIA

Recording Techniques

862. Culshaw, John. *Ring Resounding: The Recording in Stereo of "Der Ring des Nibelungen."* London: Secker & Warburg, 1967. 284pp. (no LC number available)

An illustrated history of the "Solti *Ring*"; the first complete stereophonic recording of Wagner's tetralogy, sponsored by Decca between 1958 and 1967. Includes a one-page *Ring* timeline covering the years 1848 to 1876 (p. 271), as well as information about performers, discographical details of various "takes," descriptions of recording sessions, and a synopsis of the sessions themselves (the last pp. 273–76). Also includes twenty black-and-white portraits of performers and photographs of recording activities. Concludes with an index.

Film

Most studies of Wagner and the movies concentrate on individual films or film makers. The following is among the few survey studies devoted to this subject:

863. Künzig, Bernd. *Richard Wagner und das Kinematopographische.* Augsburg: Maro, 1990. 51pp. ISBN 3925016678 ML410.W19K97 1990

Evaluates how well Wagner "works" and how "filmable" his music dramas may be. Among other subjects, Künzig considers stage and screen productions by Appia, Francis Ford Coppola, and Luchino Visconti. Unfortunately lacks both illustrations and musical examples.

* Müller, Ulrich. "Wagner in Literature and Film." Described as item 1021.

Refers to films that depicting Wagner and utilize his music in various ways.

Other film studies include:

864. Kolland, Hubert. "Wagner wäre heute Filmmacher." *Wegzeichen: Studien zur Musikwissenschaft,* ed. Jürgen Mainka and Peter Wicke. Berlin: "Verlag Neue Musik," 1985; pp. 117–24. ML55.W32 1985 (no ISBN available)

Speculates that, were he alive today, Wagner would produce films instead of music dramas. Kolland also applies notions of "Montagetechnik" (p. 123) to the *Ring,* and discusses ways of filming *Ring* characters and scenes. No illustrations.

865. Levin, Daniel J. *Richard Wagner, Fritz Lang, and the Nibelungen.* Princeton, NJ: Princeton University Press, 1998. xi, 207pp. ISBN 0691026211 ML410.W11L48 1997

Evaluates Lang's Wagner film, illustrated with twelve stills. Levin draws upon postmodern critical principles to examine such related issues as Nazi-era idolatry of Wagner, aspects of the anti-fascist social comedy *The Nasty Girl*—which opens with a quotation from the *Nibelungenlied*—and so on. Includes a fine bibliography (pp. 189–98); concludes with an index. See also item 672.

    Still other studies of Wagner films by individual directors include Marcia Citron's discussion of Hans-Jürgen Syberberg's *Parsifal* (1982) in *Opera on Screen* (New Haven, CT and London, 2000), especially pp. 141–60. See also item 1166. Finally, see Ken Wlaschin's *Opera on Screen* (Los Angeles, 1997), which identifies and describes films of the various music dramas, as well as such movies as Ken Russell's *Lisztomania* (1975), Francis Ford Coppola's *Apocalypse Now* (1979), the *Wagner* life history starring Richard Burton as the composer (1983), and so on.

X

Wagner as Poet, Prose Writer, and Philosopher

More people know Wagner as a composer than a theorist or poet; fewer still are aware that he was also a music critic, a short-story writer, and something of a philosopher. Furthermore, Wagner powerfully influenced two of Central Europe's most influential thinkers: Friedrich Nietzsche and Adolf Hitler. (One may question the quality of Hitler's "thoughts" but, certainly, not the influence they exerted.) This chapter focuses on studies that deal primarily or exclusively with Wagner's poetry and prose, and the ideas he was associated with during his career.

Unless otherwise noted, studies grouped under individual headings or explanatory observations are described in alphabetical order by author, editor, and/or title.

GENERAL SURVEYS

Among several introductions to Wagner as author and thinker are two book-length surveys in English:

866. Aberbach, Alan David. *The Ideas of Richard Wagner: An Examination and Analysis of His Major Aesthetic, Political, Economic, Social, and Religious Thoughts.* Lanham, MD: University Press of America, 1988. x, 442pp. ISBN 0819168556 ML410.W13A22 1988

Examines "the evolution of Wagner's major ideas as reflection in his prose, poetry, letters, and music-dramas . . . as a manifestation and reflection of several major concerns and themes in mid-19th century European thought and culture" (p. ix). Aberbach quotes extensively from the composer's letters and prose works, but has little to say about broader intellectual and culture issues. Originally published in 1984 (ISBN 0819141453); the 1988 edition includes a "New Addendum: 'The Ring of the Nibelungen,' an Interpretive Guide." Both editions contain brief bibliographies (1988, pp. 433–39); both conclude with three-page indexes.

867. Raphael, Robert. *Richard Wagner.* Twayne's World Authors Series, 77. New York: Twayne, 1969. 153pp. ML410.W1R33

A survey of issues associated with Wagner as author. Raphael discusses not only the librettos for Wagner's operas and music dramas, but a number of his more important prose works and philosophical notions. A bit out-of-date, but still useful. Includes a biographical timeline (pp. 11–12); concludes with a brief bibliography and index.

Other surveys of Wagner's ideas and literary output include:

868. Bermbach, Udo. *Der Wahn des Gesamtkunstwerks. Richard Wagners politisch-ästhetische Utopie.* Frankfurt a.M.: Fischer, 1994. 372pp. ISBN 339612249X ML410.W19B54 1994

Discusses ideas linking Wagner's political and aesthetic speculations, including the notion of a *Gesamtkunstwerk* (total artwork). Equipped with extensive notes identifying primary and secondary sources, as well as a bibliography (pp. 362–72). Studies closely related to Bermbach's especially in terms of their reliance on Wagner's own writings include Ralf Eisinger's dissertation, *Richard Wagner—Idee und Dramaturgie des allegorischen Traumbildes* (Munich, 1987).

869. Friedenreich, Carl Albert. *Richard Wagner. Eine geisteswissenschaftliche Studie über Wesen und Aufgabe seiner Musik,* 2nd ed. Freiburg i.B.: Verlag die Kommenden, 1967. 112pp. ML410.W1F68

A survey of cultural influences on Wagner's instrumental, vocal, and dramatic compositions, including those exerted by Schopenhauer and Nietzsche. Less precise than many scholars might wish. Contains no bibliography or musical examples.

870. Ingenschay-Goch, Dagmar. *Richard Wagners neu erfundener Mythos. Zur Rezeption und Reproduktion des germanischen Mythos in seinen Operntexten.* Abhandlungen zur Kunst-, Musik- und Literaturwissenschaft, 311. Bonn: "Bouvier Verlag Herbert Grundmann," 1982. 187pp. ISBN 3416016459 ML410.W13I5 1982

Evaluates literary and philosophical aspects of Wagner's librettos, especially through comparisons of Wagner's *Ring* poems with portions of the *Nibelungenlied* and works by Ludwig Tieck and Heinrich Heine. Detailed tables help make the author's points clearly and concisely. Concludes with detailed notes (pp. 161–79), a bibliography (pp. 181–85) and an index of names.

Reviewed in *Wagner* 4/2 (April 1983), pp. 51–57, where it is summarized as an attempt "to reconcile some of the deficiencies which recent scholarship has recognized" in structuralist approaches to the *Ring* (item 870, p. 9; translated in the review, p. 54).

871. *Richard Wagner und—die Musikhochschule München, die Philosophie, die Dramaturgie, die Bearbeitung, der Film.* Schriftenreihe der Hochschule für Musik München, 4. Regensburg: Gustav Bosse, 1983. ISBN 3764922680 ML410.W1R547 1983

Includes items 552, 917, and 936, as well as essays dealing with aspects of Hegelian idealism and their influence on the *Ring*, Wagner's representation of nature in *Tristan*, the relationship of film to Wagner's aesthetics, and so on. Published by Munich's leading music school and introduced by Wolfgang Wagner. Concludes with indexes of names and works (compositions, books, and so on), as well as brief biographies of contributors. See item 6 for review information; see also item 834.

Additional studies grapple with Wagner's prose writings as reflections of his political and philosophical attitudes. These include:

872. Nolte, Erich. *Studien zu Richard Wagner's dramatische Fragmenten im Zusammenhange seiner Entwicklung von 1841–1850.* Berlin: Hermann Blanke, ?1917. 98pp. (no LC number available)

Considers Wagner's evolution as author and thinker based primarily on such unfinished prose and poetic theatrical works as *Die Bergwerk zu Falun, Friedrich I, Jesus von Nazareth, Die Sarazenin,* and *Wieland der Schmied.* Musical sketches exist for some of these works, but Nolte's is exclusively a literary study. Includes a brief bibliography (pp. 7–8). With regard to Wagner's *Jesus*, see items 873–74 below.

What appears to be a study along similar lines—Dorothea Ruland's *Künstler und Gesellschaft: Die Libretti und Schriften des jungen Richard Wagners aus germanischer Sicht* (Frankfurt a.M. and New York, 1986)— was unavailable for examination by the author; it received a mixed review in *Wagner* 7/4 (October 1986), pp. 147–48.

Among studies of Wagner as a "thinking writer" are:

873. Dohn, Walter. "Jesus von Nazareth von Richard Wagner." In: Dohn, *Das Jahr 1848 im deutschen Drama und Epos.* Breslauer Beiträge zur Liter-

aturgeschichte, 32. Stuttgart: J. B. Metzler, 1912; pp. 272–86. PT134.H5D6

Included as an appendix to a study of dramatic publications associated with the March revolutions of 1848. Dohn's essay discusses various intellectual influences on Wagner's poem, including that of David Friedrich Strauss's life of Jesus and thematic relationships between the *Jesus* poem and other contemporaneous works by Wagner, including *Wieland der Schmied, Friedrich I,* and early versions of the *Ring* libretto.

874. Grapp, Paul-Gerhard. *Richard Wagners dramatische Entwurf "Jesus von Nazareth." Entstehungsgeschichte und Versuch einer kurzen Würdigung.* Dissertation: University of Marburg, 1920; Marburg a.d.L.: Lehmann & Bernhard, 1920. 93pp. ML410.W19G7

Deals with the prose draft Wagner prepared in 1849 for what might have become a five-act opera or music drama. Grapp especially considers links between Wagner's revolutionary activities and pronouncements, the text of his unfinished *Jesus,* and the ideas of fellow Germans and/or revolutionaries Bruno Bauer, Feuerbach, and David Friedrich Strauss. Musical sketches exist for *Jesus,* but Grapp's volume contains no musical examples.

WAGNER AS POET

Primary Sources

These include but are by no means limited to:

*   Wagner, Richard. *The Ring of the Nibelung*, trans. Andrew Porter. Described as item 163.

    Contains the complete *Ring* poem in both German and English; also includes essays on "Translating the Ring" and "Wagner as Poet." See also items 156–57, 172–74, and 177.

*   Kapp, Julius. *Der junge Wagner: Dichtung, Aufsätze, Entwürfe, 1832–1849.* Described as item 190.

    Also includes prose selections, among them some of the composer's earliest reviews.

Surveys and Critical Studies

Studies of Wagner's poetry, considered primarily or altogether apart from the roles it plays in the composer's music dramas, include two outstanding surveys—

the first more general in contents and approach, the second more concerned with presenting a thesis of its author's own devising:

875. Golther, Wolfgang. *Richard Wagner as Poet*, trans. Jessie Haynes. "Illustrated Cameos of Literature." London: W. Heinemann, 1905. 92pp. ML410.W18G72

Golther introduces the poetry as a whole (pp. 15–25), then turns to the librettos from *Rienzi* to *Parsifal*. Includes a frontispiece portrait of Wagner and fourteen illustrations by Aubrey Beardsley and other artists, as well as a two-page facsimile of the *Tristan* poem in draft form; the Beardsley illustration is printed partially in red, all others in black-and-white. Concludes with a single page of references to other studies, including the author's much more detailed *Sagensgeschichtlichen Grundlagen der Ringdichtung Richard Wagners* (Berlin, 1902; see also item 663).

Originally published under the title *Richard Wagner als Dichter* (Berlin, 1904). An American edition, published in New York in 1907 by McClure, Phillips & Co., is said to exist.

876. Glass, Frank W. *The Fertilizing Seed: Wagner's Concept of the Poetic Intent*. Studies in Musicology, 63. Ann Arbor, MI: UMI Research Press, 1983. xiii, 320pp. ISBN 0835713962 ML410.W19G46 1983

Based on the author's thesis that "the poetic intent . . . inspires the musical response and helps bring it forth as drama" is the foundation upon which *Opera and Drama* is based (p. 15); Glass also discusses which poetry and music work together in the composer's mature music dramas. Illustrated with dozens of lengthy musical examples from *Meistersinger, Parsifal,* and *Tristan*. Includes a summary ("Conclusions," pp. 269–84), as well as extensive notes and a brief bibliography (pp. 313–16); concludes with an index. Reviewed with qualifications in *Notes* 40 (1983–1984), pp. 56–57.

Briefer but useful synopses of the same general subject and issues associated with it include:

877. Black, Michael. "The Literary Background: Poetry, Poetic Drama and Music Drama." In item 31, pp. 60–84.

Introduces literary influences on Wagner's librettos. Black devotes much of his attention to such individuals and schools as Greek tragedy, Shakespeare, Racine, and Calderón; he also mentions Wagner's influence on the poetry and prose of several contemporaries, including Baudelaire and Mallarmé. See also items 576–78.

*   Wapnewski, Peter. "The Operas as Literary Works." Described as item 578.

Considers in order of their conception the stories, literary merits, and ideological implications in the music dramas from *Die Hochzeit* to *Parsifal*.

Older or less comprehensive examinations of Wagner's poetry are described below in alphabetical order by author:

878. Chamberlain, Houston Stewart. *The Wagnerian Drama: An Attempt to Inspire Better Appreciation of Wagner as a Dramatic Poet.* London: John Lane, 1923. viii, 240pp. ML410.W13C54

A attempt to clarify Wagner's poetic-dramatic theories as a whole. Chamberlain also offers brief synopses of the libretti from *Die Feen* to *Parsifal*. Originally published in German as *Das Drama Richard Wagners: Eine Anregung* (Leipzig, 1892; 4th ed., 1910), and reprinted in that form in 1973. No musical examples

879. Gautier, Judith. *Richard Wagner and His Poetical Works from Rienzi to Parsifal.* Boston: A. Williams, 1883. 173pp. ML410.W13G23

Discusses Wagner as a librettist-poet primarily in terms of his mature music dramas, and especially with regard to *Parsifal*, a work that received its world premiere the year Gautier's volume originally appeared in print as *Richard Wagner et son oeuvre poétique depuis Rienzi jusqu'à Parsifal* (Paris, 1882); the French edition includes a single foldout facsimile musical example; both editions include a Wagner frontispiece portrait.

880. Pfordten, Hermann Ludwig von der. *Handlung und Dichtung der Bühnenwerke Richard Wagners: nach ihren Grundlagen in Sage und Geschichte.* Berlin: Trowitzsch, 1893. vi, 394pp. (no LC number available).

A survey of sources, mostly Germanic, for the stories behind Wagner's dramatic poems, and a discussion of his adaptations of them. Illustrated with collections of short musical examples following each principal chapter. Intended, according to the full title page, as an explanation of Wagner's stage works for musical and unmusical readers alike; hence its tertiary title *Erläuterungen der Bühnenwerke Richard Wagners für Musikalische und Unmusikalische.* Uncommon: Harvard's Widener Library owns a copy (shelf-number KD 46900).

NB: The author, born in 1859, should not be confused with Ludwig von der Pfordten (1811–1880)—also known as "Pfo"—who served as Prime Minister of Bavaria from 1864 to 1866 and who, as adviser to Ludwig II, often opposed the composer's plans.

881. Schertz-Parey, Walter. *Richard Wagners Dichtkunst: eine literaturkritische Betrachtung.* Granz: I-A Druck, 1998. 216pp. ISBN 3901149090 (no LC number available)

Considers the literary qualities of Wagner's poetry, based largely on quotations from the librettos. Illustrated with some good-quality photographs, three of them in color, including a frontispiece portrait of the composer; concludes with a brief bibliography. Unindexed.

Among the few critical studies dealing with the language, grammar, and syntax of Wagner's poetic output are:

* Ott, Felix. *Richard Wagners poetisches Wortschatz.* Described as item 96.

A dictionary of words Wagner himself constructed and used in his librettos.

882. Wolzogen, Hans von. *Die Sprache in R. Wagner's Dichtungen,* 2nd ed. Leipzig: Gebruder Senf, 1881. 115pp. ML410.W19W66

Dissects Wagner's grammar, use of conjunctions, cases, word order, and related issues ("Zur grammatischen Stilistik," pp. 47–66), his metaphors, epithets, oxymorons, and "tone" ("Zur künstlicherischen Stilistik," pp. 9–46), and his construction or use of new or unusual words ("Zu Wortbildung und Wortgebrauch," pp. 67–115). Includes a two-page introduction and hundreds of carefully chosen quotations from the librettos. Originally published by Edwin Schloemp (Leipzig, 1875).

WAGNER AS PROSE WRITER

Primary Sources

The most extensive collections of Wagner's books and articles include:

* *Richard Wagner. Gesammelte Schriften und Dichtungen* (10 vols.; 1871–1883); *Richard Wagner: Sämtliche Schriften und Dictungen* (16 vols.; 1912–1914); *Richard Wagners gesammelte Schriften,* ed. Julius Kapp (14 vols.; 1914); and *Richard Wagner's Prose Works,* trans. William Ashton Ellis (8 vols.; 1893–1899). Described as items 172–75.

Together these volumes contain the texts of virtually everything in prose Wagner ever wrote.

Surveys and Critical Studies

No one has dealt in a single study with all *of Wagner's books, essays, and articles, but the books and articles identified below examine much of his work as a prose writer:*

883. Grey, Thomas S. *Wagner's Musical Prose: Texts and Contents*. New Perspectives in Music History and Criticism, 3. Cambridge and New York: Cambridge University Press, 1995. xix, 397pp. ISBN 0521417384 ML410.W19G83 1995

Investigates such subjects as "absolute music," Wagner's relationship to Beethoven, the use of metaphors in *Opera and Drama* (see also item 889 below), the evolution of Wagnerian musical-dramatic form, and so on. Includes a synopsis published on a page of its own before the opening half-title page, as well as a number of musical examples; also includes two appendices—the first containing the text of a lengthy passage from *Opera and Drama* pertaining (pp. 373–75), the second a partial list of Wagner's prose writings (pp. 378–79)—and a bibliography (pp. 380–90). Concludes with an index.

In reviewing this volume for the *Journal of the American Musicological Society* 50 (1997), pp. 217–24, John Daverio suggests Grey's work be read in conjunction with Borchmeyer on Wagner's dramatic theory (item 893), and Kropfinger on Wagner and Beethoven (item 508); Daverio also summarizes Grey's volume as "a study of the principal musical issues broached in Wagner's writings and a sustained attempt to situate these issues in the aesthetic and cultural context of the composer's time" (Daverio, p. 218). Also reviewed in the *Cambridge Opera Journal* 8 (1997), pp. 89–97.

*   Kühnel, Jürgen. "The Prose Writings." Described as item 198.

Identifies and largely summarizes Wagner's books, essays, and reviews in roughly chronological order by date of completion or publication.

884. Westernhagen, Curt von. "Wagner as a Writer," trans. Cedric Williams. In item 31, pp. 341–64

An introduction to Wagner's books and articles on musical and dramatic subjects. In addition to mentioning most of the more familiar publications and saying something about each, Westernhagen points out that seven pages—themselves appended to the end of the original version of the *Ring* poem, published in 1862, and calling for the help of a prince sympathetic to its ultimate production—had "the most far-reaching consequences of any of [Wagner's] writings" (p. 356), in that they brought the composer to the attention of Ludwig II and thus, ultimately, to Bayreuth and much of the celebrity he enjoys to this day.

Other broad-based studies of Wagner's prose deal with certain of its phases and influences:

885. *Die Jugendschriften Richard Wagners*, ed. Paul Bülow. Leipzig: Breitkopf & Härtel, 1917. 124pp. ML410.W18B82

A study of Wagner's earliest writings rather than a collection of them. Drawing upon his dissertation of 1916, Bülow concentrates on the composer's Parisian articles and reviews of 1839 to 1842, his relationship with publisher Maurice Schlesinger, and the literary influences exerted on Wagner by E. T. A. Hoffmann, Friedrich Rochlitz, and Heinrich Zschokke as well as Heine and Tieck. Concludes with a synopsis (pp. 126–29) and an index.

886. Franke, Rainer. *Richard Wagners Zürcher Kunstschriften. Politische und ästhetische Entwürfe auf seinem Weg zum "Ring des Nibelungen."* Hamburger Beiträge zur Musikwissenschaft, 26. Hamburg: Dieter Wagner, 1983. 326pp. ISBN 3921029902 ML410.W13F7 1983

Deals with political and aesthetic aspects of the "revolutionary" prose works Wagner completed and published during his years of exile in Switzerland. Franke also considers ways in which Wagner reacted to Beethoven in his theoretical writings, what he learned from Feuerbach, Schiller, and other of his German predecessors, and ways in which passages from his books and articles anticipate the musical, dramatic, and ideological contents of the *Ring*. Concludes with a bibliography (pp. 319–26) rather than an index. Reproduced for the most part from typescript. See item 6 for review information.

887. Zinnius, Karl Wilhelm. *Die Schriften Richard Wagners in ihrem Verhältnis zur zeitgeschichtlichen Lage*. Heidelberg: Johann Hörning, 1936. 73pp. ML410.W13Z5

Examines Wagner's published prose writings in light of his autobiographical statements and letters, especially in relationship to what he read in the contemporary press. Zinnius's statements should be approached with caution given the date and cultural circumstances of their publication; no Wagner studies appeared in Nazi Germany without "approval" of some kind. Concludes with a one-page bibliography.

WAGNER AS PHILOSOPHER

Primary Sources

Anthologies devoted specifically to Wagner's intellectual, literary, and religious enthusiasms include:

*   *Richard Wagner. Mein Denken*, ed. Martin Gregor-Dellin. Described as item 295.

Documents "what Richard Wagner thought, how he thought, what he thought about, and with what result" (p. ii); includes portions of *The Art-Work of the Future* and *Jewishness in Music*, as well as diary excerpts and passages from the composer's correspondence.

*   Aberbach, Alan David. *The Ideas of Richard Wagner.* Described as item 866.

Includes extensive quotations from the composer's letters and prose works. See also item 90 and a number of other reference works.

Survey Studies

Wagner's philosophical interests ranged from the metaphysics of ancient Greece to contemporary political attitudes concerning vivisection and vegetarianism. These books and articles deal with several or even most of these issues, especially insofar as they are treated in the composer's poetry and prose:

888. Berne, Peter. "Wagners 'hellenistisch-optimistische' Weltanschuung und die philosophische Aussage des 'Ring.' " In: *De editione musices: Festschrift Gerhard Croll zum 65. Geburtstag*, ed. Wolfgang Gratzer and Andrea Lindmayr. Laaber: Laaber Verlag, 1992; pp. 351–375. ISBN 3890072631 ML55.C83D4 1992

Summarizes Wagner's ideas about reality, nature, mankind's place in the world, death, and so on, drawn from the *Ring* as well as such writings as *Jesus von Nazareth* (see items 873–74) and *A Communication To My Friends*. Berne's essay consists of lengthy quotations from primary sources interspersed with linking textual commentary.

889. Kropfinger, Klaus. "Metaphor und Dramastruktur: Bemerkungen zur Sprache in Wagners 'Oper und Drama.' " *Musica* 38 (1984), pp. 422–28. ML5.M71357

An attempt to come to grips with Wagner's often obscure metaphors by examining ways in which he put certain parts of his music dramas together. Kropfinger refers to Nietzsche's metaphorical way of writing philosophy, as well as to *Opera and Drama* and other of the composer's prose works. Also published in Italian and in a slightly different version in item 59.

890. Peterson-Berger, Wilhelm. "The Life Problem in Wagner's Dramas," trans. Hester Coddington. *The Musical Quarterly* 2 (1916), pp. 658–68. ML1.M725

Explores a theme in Wagner's dramas, especially *Tristan*, that the author considers the central, most important, and most "purely human" (p. 660): that of "*love, the superindividual instinct for the preservation of life, appearing as the destroyer of the individual*—in other words: the destruction of life through eroticism, a situation created and enhanced by the biological superiority of fervent beings, by their strength of feeling and spiritual inflammability" (p. 661; italics in the original). To this synopsis Peterson-Berger adds as a telling remark that "the only thing that can be urged against this [theme] as a basis for tragic drama . . . is that its solution is known from the beginning" (p. 661). Extracted from a volume published in Swedish in 1913; no illustrations or musical examples.

* *Re-Reading Wagner*, ed. Reinhold Grimm and Jost Hermand. Described as item 34.

Includes studies of Wagner's opinions on social issues, Wagner and Thomas Mann, and other intellectual and aesthetic subjects.

Wagner, Aesthetics, and Musical-Dramatic Theory

Much of Wagner's philosophical enthusiasm and speculation was concentrated on issues of aesthetics. The best introductions to this subject include:

891. Dahlhaus, Carl. *Wagner's Aesthetics*. Bayreuth; Edition Musica, 1972. 59pp. ML410.W12313 (no ISBN available)

Consists of eight essays, including "On the Term 'Music-Drama'" (pp. 55–59) and "On the Overture" (pp. 31–38). Illustrated with a scattering of musical examples. Originally published in book form as *Wagners Ästhetik* (Bayreuth, 1972), and as a series of articles in 1970 volumes of the *Programmhefte der Bayreuther Festspiele*. Also available in French.

892. Kunze, Stefan. *Der Kunstbegriff Richard Wagners. Voraussetzungen und Folgerungen*. Arbeitsgemeinschaft "100 Jahre Bayreuther Festspiele," 1. Regensburg: Gustav Bosse, 1983. 246pp. ISBN 3764920580 ML410.W13K95 1983

Reviews Wagner's theoretical pronouncements on art, drama, music, and theater, illustrated with two full-page musical examples. Concludes with a bibliography.

Several studies concentrate on theatrical and musical-dramatic issues:

893. Borchmeyer, Dieter. *Richard Wagner: Theory and Theatre*, trans. Stewart
   Spencer. Oxford: Oxford U Press, 1991. xx, 423pp. ISBN 019315322X
   ML410.W13B6913 1991

   Examines theoretical and practical aspects of Wagner as a theatrical com-
   poser, conductor, and producer. Borchmeyer organizes each of his chapters
   around a particular theme, phase of Wagner's career and development, or
   work, such as *The Birth of Tragedy*; the titles of these chapters include "A
   Theatre for the Provinces: Wagner's Plays for Reform and the 'German
   Spirit,' " "The Ideal Audience: The Greeks and 'The Art-Work of the
   Future,' " and " 'Absolute Music' as a Covert or Overt Ideal: Nietzsche,
   Hanslick, and the Aesthetic Outlook of the Later Wagner." Most of the volume, however, consists of a close reading of the librettos from *Die Feen*
   through *Parsifal* (pp. 181–403). Supplemented by a translator's foreword
   (pp. v–vi) and an afterword by the author on Wagner and anti-semitism
   (pp. 404–10); concludes with a short bibliography (pp. 411–14) and two
   indexes.
         Reviewed in *The Musical Times* 134 (1993), p. 177. A review of *Das
   Theater Richard Wagners: Idee—Dichtung—Wirkung* (Stuttgart, 1982),
   the original German version of Borchmeyer's volume, appeared in *Die
   Musikforschung* 40 (1987), pp. 279–84.

*Two studies deal specifically with Wagner's ideas concerning the employment of
various arts in the creation of Gesamtkunstwerke:*

894. Stein, Jack M. *Richard Wagner and the Synthesis of the Arts*. Detroit:
   Wayne State University Press, 1960; reprinted Westport, CT: Greenwood,
   1973. 229pp. ML410.W1S83 1973 (no ISBN available)

   Considers the "musical-dramatic" as an aesthetic construct that incorporates aspects of a number of intellectual and artistic traditions. A guide to
   many of Wagner's mature works and certain of his prose publications,
   including *Opera and Drama* and *The Art-Work of the Future*; also includes
   a chapter on Schopenhauer's influence. As Stein observes, "It was Wagner
   who channeled the two major streams of experimentation, the musical-
   practical on the one hand, and the literary-theoretical on the other, into
   one" (p. 5). Outfitted with a number of scattered musical examples and
   quotations from the composer's librettos; concludes with a bibliography
   (pp. 219–22) and index.

895. Tanner, Michael. "The Total Work of Art." In item 31, pp. 140–224.

Reviews some of Wagner's most controversial and influential notions, including that of the *Gesamtkunstwerk* (i.e., total work of art, or work inclusive of various arts). Prefaced by a vigorous defense of Wagner's music and ideas as independent of his failings as a human being; concludes with references to the composer's influence on D. H. Lawrence.

Other studies take up individual aesthetic arguments associated with Wagner's prose writings and pronouncements:

* Hueffer, Franz. *Richard Wagner and the Music of the Future.* Described as item 312.

Sets out in part to refute the notion that "the works of Wagner . . . are not the emanation of spontaneous production, but have been fashioned after a certain scheme, the result of previous speculation" (p. 5); thus Hueffer contradicts those critics who believed that "the author of [*Opera and Drama*] cannot but produce works of cool deliberation, which . . . must needs lack the life of spontaneous production" (p. 4).

896. McClatchie, Stephen. "The Magic Wand of the Wagnerians: Musik als Ausdruck." *Canadian University Music Review* 13 (1993), pp. 71–92. ML5.C1557

Discusses "music as expression" in terms of Schopenhauer's philosophy, key works of Wagner reception such as Friedrich von Hausegger's *Musik als Ausdruck* (2nd ed., Vienna, 1887), and ways in which that "aesthetic paradigm" (p. 71) was employed in the writings of Hans von Wolzogen and Curt Mey. Includes an abstract (p. 92).

897. Wapnewski, Peter. *Liebestod und Götternot. Zum "Tristan" und zum "Ring des Nibelungen."* Berlin: Wolf Jobst Siedler, 1988. 101pp. ISBN 3886802779 (no LC number available)

Two essays—"Der Ring und sein Kreislauf" (pp. 11–45) and "Rivale Faust: Beobachtungen zu Wagners Goethe-Verständnis" (pp. 51–97)—that touch upon many issues of aesthetics, expression, literary influence, and intellectual history, and that are, as a consequence, difficult to summarize briefly or "place" elsewhere in the present research guide. Includes endnotes for each essay, a short bibliography (pp. 98–99), and several familiar portraits.

Wagner and the Romantic Movement

Closely associated with studies of Wagner and German culture are those devolving upon the composer's relationship to romanticism. This volume concerns itself with the latter issue:

898. James, Burnett. *Wagner and the Romantic Disaster*. New York: Hippocrene, 1983. vi, 202pp. ISBN 0859361063 ML410.W1J3 1983

Grapples with "the impact of Richard Wagner, his theories and his dramas, upon not only the German but the entire European mind and consciousness," as well as the fact that Wagner "achieved his main object, which was to make the unconscious articulate" (unpaginated Introduction). James also considers Wagner's influence on the Nazis, his personal and artistic psychologizing, and the tremendous influence he exerted over his successors—an influence in musical style greater, in fact, than that exerted by "any other composer except Arnold Schoenberg" (unpaginated Introduction). Concludes with a bibliography (pp. 196–99) and a short index.

In a review of James's volume Robert Cumbow stated that "just as he cannot decide whether the decay of German romanticisim into Nazism was inevitable or avoidable, [so] James ultimately cannot decide whether Wagner was culpable or not" [*Opera Quarterly* 2/2 (Summer 1984), p. 186]. Also reviewed rather harshly in *Wagner* 5/2 (April 1984), pp. 58–63.

In addition to items 465, 479, and so on, specialized studies of Wagner and aspects of romanticism include:

899. Edler, Arnfried. "Anmerkungen zur Historizität von Wagners 'Romantischen Opern.' " In: *Traditionen—Neuansätze. Für Anna Amalie Abert (1906–1996)*, ed. Klaus Hortschansky. Tutzing: Hans Schneider, 1997; pp. 203–20. ISBN 3795208785 ML55.A15 1997

Examines issues associated with nineteenth-century German romantic thought, including utopian and other social topics, in *Holländer*, *Tannhäuser*, and *Lohengrin*—issues that Wagner himself attempted to explore in some of his theoretical writings, especially in *A Communication to My Friends*, to put behind him or at least into historical perspective.

900. Fries, Othmar. *Richard Wagner und die deutsche Romantik. Versuch einer Einordnung*. Zurich: Atlantis, 1952. 224pp. ML410.W1F7

A comprehensively documented exploration of Wagner's relationship with German romanticism in most of its guises, from the musical to the theological, philosophical, and cultural. Fries presents Wagner almost exclusively in a positive light. Includes hundreds of endnotes (pp. 197–217); concludes with a bibliography.

901. Siegel, Linda. "Wagner and the Romanticism of E. T. A. Hoffmann." *The Musical Quarterly* 51 (1965), pp. 597–613. ML1.M725

Demonstrates the presence of Hoffmannesque echoes in Wagner's fascination with the occult. Among the works Siegel discusses is *Die Bergwerke zu Falun*, which the composer left unfinished in the early 1840s. Includes a single musical example. A documentary study of *Die Bergwerke* by Jörg Heyne, published in *Musik und Gesellschaft* 31 (1981), pp. 415–18, appeared in conjunction with an exhibition of the manuscripts themselves at the Richard-Wagner-Museum in Graupa outside Dresden.

Wagner and Other Philosophers

Friedrich Nietzsche

To what extent Wagner influenced Nietzsche and vice versa may never be finally determined; certainly the two thinkers were extremely important to one another's philosophical enthusiasms and aversions. Among many fine Wagner-Nietzsche studies, some of them written by professional philosophers, is this discussion of attitudes and influences:

902. Hollinrake, Roger. *Nietzsche, Wagner, and the Philosophy of Pessimism.* Boston and London: Allen & Unwin, 1982. xv, 308pp. ISBN 0049210297 B3317.H56 1982

Devoted in general to Wagner's and Nietzsche's "dependency" as thinkers, and specifically to Wagnerian elements found in *Parsifal* and the *Ring* and taken over by Nietzsche in his *Thus Spake Zarathustra*—the last a work that may have been "planned from the outset" as a reply to Wagner's final music drama [quoted from the review published in *Music & Letters* 65 (1984), pp. 106–7]. Includes quotations from the *Ring* and *Tristan* librettos, *The Birth of Tragedy, The Wagner Case*, and *Ecco Homo*, and portions of the Nietzsche-Wagner correspondence. Also includes extensive footnotes, a timeline spanning November 1868 to February 1883, lists of sources and translations, and a variety of facsimiles, among the last a sketch for "Das andere Tanzlied" in Part III of *Zarathustra,* printed as a frontispiece. Concludes with a useful bibliography,
    Also reviewed in the *Music Review* 43 (1982), pp. 270–71. See, too, Hollinrake's earlier article "Nietzsche, Wagner, and Ernest Newman," published in *Music & Letters* 41 (1960), pp. 245–55.

Other Nietzsche-Wagner philosophical studies include:

903. Hudek, Franz-Peter. *"Die Tyrranei der Musik": Nietzsches Wertung des Wagnerschen Musikdramas.* Epistemata: Würzburger wissenschaftliche Schriften, 64. Würzburg: Königshausen & Neumann, 1989. 214pp. ISBN 3884794221 ML410.W19H8 1989

Traces the evolution of certain Wagnerian arguments about music and their cultural significance from Nietzsche to Adorno. Hudek also provides an excellent bibliography (pp. 204–14).

904. Kalisch, Volker. "Wagner, Nietzsche und die Idee der absoluten Musik." In: *Festschrift Hans Conradin zum 70. Geburtstag*, ed. Kalisch. Publikationen der Schweizerischen Musikforschenden Gesellschaft, Series II, Vol. 33. Bern: Paul Haupt, 1983; pp. 151–61. ISBN 325803236X ML55.C757 1983

Discusses Nietzsche's and Wagner's quite different attitudes toward "absolute" music, a term Wagner himself seems to have invented, as well as of the power of music to project images and of Wagner's own music dramas. Kalisch suggests that disagreements between the two over some of these issues, especially the composer's insistence that Beethoven himself acknowledged the "limits" of instrumental music in the last movement of his Ninth Symphony, may have hastened their falling-out.

The literature on the Wagner-Nietzsche relationship includes more than a few curiosities, one of which is:

905. Diebald, Bernhard. *Der Fall Wagner. Eine Revision.* Frankfurt a.M.: Frankfurter Societäts-Druckerei, 1920. 46pp. (no LC available)

A pamphlet that grew out of a post-World War I report on "decadence" written for the *Frankfurter Zeitung*. Diebald describes the best-known features of the Wagner-Nietzsche controversy; more interesting are his assaults on Wagner for contradictions in his personal life and literary pronouncements, including his attitudes toward the Jews.

Friedrich Schopenhauer
Schopenhauer exerted a tremendous influence on Wagner's thought and his musical-dramatic expression. Perhaps the best discussion in English of the Schopenhauer-Wagner philosophical relationship is:

906. Magee, Bryan. "Schopenhauer and Wagner." Appendix 6 of *The Philosophy of Schopenhauer*. Oxford: Clarendon, 1983; pp. 326–78. ISBN 0198246730 B3148.M27 1983

Maintaining that Wagner was "the only composer of the very front rank who was in any significant sense an intellectual" (p. 326), Magee reflects upon Schopenhauerian elements in the composer's prose works and music-drama librettos, especially those of *Tristan* and the *Ring*. Thus, having observed that Wagner read *The World as Will and Representation* too late for that book to have "brought about any changes in the [*Ring*] text, its influence on the music, and on the synthesis of the music with the drama, was [nevertheless] prodigious" (p. 347). Supplemented by quotations from a variety of works, including Magee's own *Aspects of Wagner* (item 4).[1] Reprinted in *Opera Quarterly* 1 (1983), pp. 50–73; a paperback edition appeared in 1987. See also items 559, 733, 799, and 894.

Other useful surveys include:

907. Barry, Elizabeth Wendell. "What Wagner Found in Schopenhauer's Philosophy." *The Musical Quarterly* 11 (1925), pp. 124–37. ML1.M725

Identifies Wagner's readings in Schopenhauer, proclaimed by Barry "undoubtedly the chief philosophical influence" on Germany's chief music-dramatist (p. 136). Includes discussions of world-weariness in *Parsifal* and theories of love associated with *Tristan*.

908. Hausegger, Friedrich von. *Richard Wagner und Schopenhauer. Eine Darstellung der philosophischen Anschauungen R. Wagners an der Hand seiner Werke.* Leipzig: Edwin Schloemp, 1878. 39pp. ML410.W19H39

A groundbreaking study of Schopenhauer's influence on Wagner's world view. Hausegger includes quotations from the librettos of *Lohengrin, Parsifal*, and several other of the composer's music dramas, but maintains that "nicht mit Argumentum wollen wir der Anschauung des Künstlers das Wort reden. Die überzeugende Kraft seiner Kunst ist hier das einzige . . . Argument" (p. 38). Unindexed.

909. Reinhardt, Hartmut. "Wagner and Schopenhauer," trans. Erika and Martin Swales. In item 2, pp. 287–96.

Includes a summary of Wagner's early encounters with the philosopher's ideas and publications, his influence on Wagner's aesthetic notions, and Schopenhauer-like elements in *Tristan, Meistersinger*, the *Ring*, and *Parsifal*. According to Reinhardt, "Wagner's work cannot be exhausted in terms of Schopenhauer's philosophical tenets, but without this link a number of crucial intentions and connections are simply incomprehensible" (p. 295).

910. Sans, Edouard. *Richard Wagner et la pensée schopenhauerienne.* Paris: C. Klincksieck, 1969. 478pp. ML410.W19S16

Consists mostly of "parallel" passages from Wagner's and Schopenhauer's writings in French translation. Also includes a bibliography (pp. 443–62) and an index of names (pp. 463–66).

Additional Philosophers and Philosophical Constructs

911. Bauer, Jeffrey Peter. *Women and the Changing Concept of Salvation in the Operas of Richard Wagner*. Wort und Musik: Salzburger akademische Beiträge, 20. Anif/Salzburg: Ursula Müller-Speiser, 1994. (vi), 195pp. ISBN 3851450205 ML410.W1B324 1994

A discussion of female figures in Wagner's music dramas, predicated on the thesis that those women bring salvation to men at the cost of their own lives. Bauer also provides lengthy quotations from Wagner's librettos and manifestos. Concludes with a useful bibliography (pp. 187–95). See, too, item 916.

912. Donington, Robert. "The Search for Redemption in Wagner." *The Musical Times* 130 (1989), pp. 20–22. ML5.M85

Summarizes Wagner's fascination with *Erlösung* (redemption), a concept Donington acknowledges is "unlikely to yield to any single interpretation" (p. 20) and which he examines in light of "integration" as perceived from the perspective of archetypal psychology (see item 649). Includes references especially to female and "mother" figures in *Holländer*, *Tannhäuser*, *Tristan*, and *Parsifal*. No musical examples.

913. Hausegger, Friedrich von. "Rousseau als Musiker und das Verhältnis seiner Anschauungen zu denen Richard Wagners." *Die Musik* 1-IV (1901–1902), pp. 1909–17. ML5.M9

Describes relationships between Jean-Jacques Rousseau's musical doctrines and Wagner's own artworks and aesthetic notions, including ideas associated with the common origins of melody and human speech. According to Hausegger, Wagner was "no specialist, but rather a personality" (p. 1909); his thinking was often shaped by whatever he happened to read or think about, not—except, perhaps, in a very few of his prose works—by the systematic application of philosophical principles to particular problems. As Stewart Spencer has observed, "the presence of a book in Wagner's library does not mean [even] that he read it (in some cases the pages of the volume are still uncut)" (item 1, p. 150; parentheses in the original).

914. Maher, Terence J. "Melos and Arete in Richard Wagner's Art and Theory." *Opera Journal* 18/2 (June 1985), pp. 13–29. ML1.O46

Considers the music dramas and prose writings in terms of ancient Greek notions of how music shapes character and social order. Maher quotes Wagner's assertions in *Art and Revolution* "on the subject of modern art in relation to society" in order to demonstrate a "relationship between modern art and society like the one [that] . . . existed between Athenian art and society" (p. 21).

915. Peil, Peter. *Die Krise des neuzeitlichen Menschen im Werk Richard Wagners.* Böhlau Philosophica, 9. Cologne and Vienna: Böhlau, 1990. 505pp. ISBN 3412029904 ML410.W19P34 1990

Considers "modern man" as represented and reflected in Wagner's works and thought, as well as in the writings of Nietzsche and other existentialists, notions of bourgeois consciousness, discussions of justice and other philosophical and cultural concepts, and so on. Concludes with a bibliography.

916. Schwabe, Frieda. *Die Frauengestalten Wagners als Typen des "Ewig Weiblichen."* Munich: F. Bruckmann, c. 1902. 160pp. ML410.W19S38

An early study of Wagner's heroines. Schwabe writes about the notion of the "Eternal Feminine": a phrase taken from the concluding line of Goethe's *Faust*, Part II, and used by Schwabe in conjunction with the notion of salvation through the "woman in all of us" represented by Senta, Elisabeth, Elsa, and Brünnhilde.

917. Seelig, Wolfgang. "Richard Wagners Naturphilosophie. Ihre Grundlagen bei Feuerbach und ihre Weiterführung mit Schopenhauer." In item 871, pp. 21–43.

Documents Wagner's interest in and knowledge of Feuerbach's "philosophy of nature" and those of its principles taken over by Schopenhauer.

918. Wapnewski, Peter. *Der traurige Gott. Richard Wagner in seinen Helden*, 2nd ed. Munich: C. H. Beck, 1978. 319pp. ISBN 3406071333 ML410.W13W2619

A study of Wagner's heroes, among them Wagner himself! Described by John Deathridge as a "richly embroidered" interpretation of the composer's sources (item 152, p. 215). Illustrated with thirteen black-and-white plates depicting the composer himself, Siegfried and Tristan as characters in Wagner's music dramas, and Titian's *Assumption of the Virgin*; also includes several musical facsimiles and other images. Concludes with a bibliography of sources (pp. 309–14) and an index. The first edition appeared in 1978 with the same ISBN.

WAGNER, NATIONALISM, AND GERMAN CULTURE

Wagner attained celebrity during his lifetime and retained it well into the twentieth century in large part because of his association with German culture and its values. At times he argued in favor of revolution; at other times he seemed to preach reaction and defended the status quo; always, however, he defended himself and his art as "authentically" German. This volume summarizes and grapples with most of the German issues and themes in Wagner's life and literary works:

919. Salmi, Hannu. *"Die Herrlichkeit des deutschen Namens . . ." Die schriftstellerische und politische Tätigkeit Richard Wagners als Gestalter nationaler Identität während der staatlichen Vereinigung Deutschlands.* Annales Universitatis Turkuensis B, 196. Turku (Finland): University of Turku, 1993. 320pp. ISBN 9518808996 AS262.T84A3 osa 196

Examines Wagner and Germany, specifically Wagner's writings and thoughts about the German people, national identity, cultural character, and the history of German's unification and consolidation of power under Prussian leadership. Drawing especially upon the ideas of myth and structure associated with Claude Lévi-Strauss, Salmi discusses Wagner's "possible Germany" (p. 39) both as fact and fiction; hence the title of Salmi's epilogue: "My Kingdom is not of this world." Includes chapters or sections on Wagner's relationships with Ludwig II of Bavaria and Otto von Bismarck, and several prose works, including the treatise *German Art and German Politics.* Concludes with a list of sources, including the names and addresses of archives and descriptions of some of their contents (pp. 293–310); a list of Wagner's literary works (pp. 311–15); and an index.

Introductory observations on Wagner's place in nineteenth-century German culture appear in:

920. Gray, Ronald. "The German Intellectual Background." In item 31, pp. 34–59.

Reviews German influences on Wagner's thinking, literary works, and compositions. Gray pays most attention to Schopenhauer and Nietzsche, but he also mentions Goethe, Hegel, and Hölderin as well as Eastern religious influences.

Other studies deal with individual German influences on Wagner's life, art, and thought, especially those associated with German drama:

921. Berendt, Martin. *Schiller-Wagner. Ein Jahrhundert der Entwicklungsgeschichte.* Berlin: Alexander Duncker, 1901. iv, 192pp. PT286.B5

Traces the evolution of German drama from Schiller's *Luther* through his *Friedrich II* to Wagner's *Tannhäuser*, the last proclaimed by Berendt "the culmination of the whole of German dramatic development since Lessing and Goethe" (p. 106). Includes quotations from a number of literary and dramatic sources.

*   Fries, Othmar. *Richard Wagner und die deutsche Romantik.* Described as item 900.

922.   Graves, Marie Haefliger. *Schiller and Wagner: A Study of Their Dramatic Theory and Technique.* Ann Arbor, MI: self-published, 1938. 128pp. PT2494.G7

Compares Wagner, Schiller, and their theories and practices as well as related issues—among them the character and evolution of German dramatic declamation, influences exerted by ancient Greek playwrights and Shakespeare on both Schiller and Wagner, and "the operatic devices of aria, duet, chorus, [and] tableau" in many of Schiller's plays (p. 113). Includes a bibliography (pp. 117–28) and tables of textual and ideological comparisons. Typeset; no publisher is identified.

*   Ingenschay-Goch, Dagmar. *Richard Wagners neu erfundener Mythos.* Described as item 870.

Largely German-nationalist in its orientation and subject matter.

923.   Pinkus, Heinz. *Friedrich Hebbels und Richard Wagners Theorien vom dramatischen Kunstwerk im Zusammenhange mit ihren Weltanschauungen.* Marburg: Konrad Triltsch, 1936. 102pp. PT2296.P5

Examines similarities and differences between Wagner's dramatic theories and those of Hebbel—the latter, author of a Nibelung trilogy Wagner disliked, and a man acquainted with Wagner during the latter's 1862 visit to Vienna. Pinkus also evaluates the influences of Hegel and Schopenhauer on the world views of both dramatists. Concludes with a summary (*Schlußbetrachtung*; pp. 96–100) and a one-page bibliography. Presented as a dissertation at the University of Marburg. Other publications on the Wagner-Hebbels topic exist; see, for instance, Ernst Meinck's *Friedrich Hebbels und Richard Wagners Nibelungen-Trilogien: ein kritischer Beitrag zur Geschichte der neueren Nibelungendichtungen* (Leipzig, 1905).

WAGNER AS POLITICIAN, POLEMICIST, AND REVOLUTIONARY

Wagner's various political involvements and concerns are largely identified and summarized in:

924. Josserand, Frank B. *Richard Wagner: Patriot and Politician.* Washington, D.C.: University Press of America, 1981. xii, 339pp. ISBN 0819114189 ML410.W19J67

A study of the composer's political theories and enthusiasms. Outfitted with a single illustration—a caricature—in the form of a frontispiece, as well as with an extensive bibliography (pp. 311–26) and index (pp. 327–38). Printed from typescript. Useful, but cited in few of the more familiar Wagner bibliographies.

925. Mork, Andrea. *Richard Wagner als politischer Schriftsteller. Weltanschauung und Wirkungsgeschichte.* Frankfurt a.M.: Campus, 1990. 275pp. ISBN 3593343665 ML410.W19M85 1990

Summarizes Wagner's political world view and its influence on later nine-teenth- and twentieth-century European history and culture. Mork also discusses the composer's prose style and Wagnerian aspects of and influences upon Hitler's Germany; chapter 3, for example, is entitled "Der National-sozialismus und Wagner" (pp. 197–237). Concludes with a bibliography (pp. 263–75).

Briefer synopses of these and closely related issues include:

*   Krohn, Rüdiger. "The Revolutionary of 1848–49." Described as item 348.

Summarizes Wagner's thinking about society and revolution, as well as his activities before and during the Dresden uprising.

926. Weber, William. "Opera and Social Reform." In item 1, pp. 153–58.

Considers Wagner's "reforming ideas, the role of nationalism within them, and the concept of regeneration as their intellectual keystone" (p. 153), especially insofar as issues involving opera and social reform are con-cerned. Weber draws his arguments from statements in such works as *Opera and Drama* and *A Communication to My Friends*; he also points out that the rebirth of society became associated near the end of Wagner's life with some of his crankier notions, among them vegetarianism.

927. Weber, William. "Wagner as Polemicist." In item 1, pp. 114–16.

Summarizes Wagner's activities as a proponent of various artistic and social "messages," especially during the early 1850s. Weber refers to *The Art-Work of the Future* and *The Virtuoso and the Artist,* as well as articles in the *Neue Zeitschrift für Musik*—which, after 1852, became largely a forum for debating Wagner's ideas about life, art, and politics.

*Like many of his contemporaries, Wagner was at times interested in the ameliora-
tion of certain problems involving race and class. Among useful introductions to
this area of research is:*

928. Kreckel, Manfred. *Richard Wagner und die französischen Frühsozialisten.
Die Bedeutung der Kunst und des Künstlers für eine neue Gesellschaft.*
Europäische Hochschulschriften III: Geschichte und ihre Hilfswis-
senschaften, 284. Frankfurt a.M.: Peter Lang, 1986. 258pp. ISBN
3820489258 ML410.W19K91 1986

Examines Wagner's relationship to early nineteenth-century socialist
thought in general, and the ideas of Saint-Simon, Proudhon, and the
"Young Germans" in particular. See especially chapter 3: "Richard Wagner und das Kunstwerk der Zukunft" (pp. 165–89), which devolves
directly upon socialist notions and the composer's writings on music
drama. Includes a summary of the volume's principal arguments (pp.
191–96) and extensive notes (pp. 197–240); ends with a bibliography.

Among histories of socialism that at least mention Wagner is Edmund
Wilson's *To the Finland Station: A Study in the Writing and Acting of
History* (New York and London, 1940, and other editions); Wilson refers to
the composer mostly in conjunction with figures like Ferdinand Lassalle
and Bakunin.

Other studies of Wagner's political opinions and pronouncements include:

929. Boucher, Maurice. *The Political Concepts of Richard Wagner*, trans. Marcel
Honoré. New York: M & H Publications, 1950. 222pp. ML410.W1B6412

Considers Wagner's attitudes toward "decadence," "grace," "ideals" (and
idealism), "nationalism," "pessimism," the notion of "German genius," and
so on. Boucher freely confesses that his volume is devoted to analyzing "a
personality much more than a philosophy" (p. 179); he questions whether
post–World War II Germany "will be Wagnerian or Goethean." Includes a
brief bibliography (pp. 209–10); concludes with an index. Originally published in Paris as *Les Idées politiques de Richard Wagner.*

930. Ganzer, Karl Richard. *Richard Wagner der Revolutionär gegen das 19.
Jahrhundert.* Munich: F. Bruckmann, 1934. 191pp. ML410.W1G18

A Nazi-era study of Wagner's revolutionary pronouncements and proclivi-
ties. Includes a one-page bibliography (p. 183) and additional source information in the form of endnotes (pp. 184–90). Unindexed. Presented as a
doctoral dissertation at the University of Munich.

931. Gregor-Dellin, Martin. *Richard Wagner—die Revolution als Oper.* Munich: Carl Hauser, 1973. 112pp. ISBN 3446117873 ML410.W1G73

Consists of eight essays dealing with revolutionary aspects of Wagner's life and thought as reflected and incorporated in his music dramas. Gregor-Dellin pays special attention to the composer's relationship with Nietzsche, the writings of Thomas Mann, and positions adopted by other of his critics. Closely related to some of Gregor-Dellin's other Wagner publications.

932. Harrison, Michael M. "Richard Wagner as a Political Artist." *Programmhefte der Bayreuther Festspiele* III (1984), pp. 17–51. ML410.W2B26

An opinionated examination of political aspects of Wagner's life, thought, and stage works. Harrison argues that Wagner was "the [modern] artist most aware of the social and political dimension of all his creative activities" (p. 17). Includes quotations from and references to the composer's literary and musical creations.

933. Opelt, Franz-Peter. *Richard Wagner—Revolutionär oder Staatsmusikant?* Europäische Hochschulschriften: Musicology, 28. Frankfurt a.M.: Peter Lang, 1987. 267pp. ISBN 3820409440. ML410.W19O85 1987

An evaluation, based largely on Wagner's own writings, of revolutionary and patriotic aspects of his life, compositions, pronouncements, and thoughts. Useful especially insofar as it traces the transformation from the outspoken radical of the early 1850s to the much more politically reactionary artist-statesman of the 1870s. Concludes with a list of primary and secondary sources.

934. Scholz, Dieter David. *Ein deutsches Mißverständnis. Richard Wagner zwischen Barrikade und Walhalla.* Berlin: Parthas, 1997. 381pp. ISBN 3732529138 ML410.W13S275 1997

Discusses the *Ring* as political theater both in Wagner's life and on stage, together with considerations of *Holländer*, *Meistersinger*, and other music dramas. Also includes a cursory discussion of the Liszt-Wagner relationship (pp. 245–58). Aimed at a popular audience, which may account for its largely familiar black-and-white illustrations and its lack of musical examples. Does include a bibliography (pp. 361–73); concludes with an index of names.

WAGNER AS PEDAGOGUE

Studies of Wagner's interest in education and especially in a music school of his own include:

935. Matter, Anne-Marie. *Richard Wagner éducateur. Une méditation péda-gogique sur les rapports de la poésie et de l'education.* Lausanne: Réu-nies, 1959. 229pp. ML410.W1M3M

A typescript dissertation devoted to examining both what Wagner taught society as a whole, and what certain individuals and professions (such as Nietzsche and psychology) learned from him. Includes a discussion of "Wagner et Hitler" (pp. 114–18) and references to Siegfried Wagner's compositions and activities, as well as a brief chronology of Richard Wagner's life (pp. 5–7) and a bibliography (pp. 223–28).

936. Valentin, Erich. "Wagner's 'deutsche Musikschule'—Zur Vorgeschichte der Hochschule für Musik München." In item 871, pp. 11–20.

A "prehistory" of Munich's music conservatory, devolving upon Wagner's "sketch" (*Entwurf*) describing the reorganization of Saxony's National Theater in Dresden (1849), his proposals concerning theaters in Zurich and Vienna, and especially his 1865 *Bericht* (report) to Ludwig II. Valentin's essay appeared in a volume commemorating the conservatory, itself reor-ganized in 1867. For the original edition of the *Bericht*, see item 191.

WAGNER AND OTHER ASPECTS OF KNOWLEDGE AND BELIEF

Religion

Whether Wagner was "religious" in any conventional sense of that term is doubt-ful, but he was unquestionably interested in religious issues. One useful introduc-tion to his spiritual attitudes and opinions is:

937. Aberbach, Alan David. *Richard Wagner's Religious Ideas: A Spiritual Journey.* Lewiston, MA: Edwin Mellen, 1996. 297pp. ISBN 0773487832 ML410.W13A22

Evaluates Wagner's "evolving spiritual journey," one Aberbach claims ulti-mately embraced the composer's "need for a personal and direct relation-ship with God" (from the unpaginated introduction). Raises interesting points in his discussions of the possible influences of Hafiz and Meister Eckhart on the music dramas. Includes bibliographies of primary and sec-ondary sources (pp. 285–94); concludes with an index of names.

Law

Most studies of Wagner and legal issues of various kinds devolve specifically upon the Ring; *see, for instance, items 682–86. The following study deals more broadly with the composer's understanding of "law":*

938. Mattern, Gerhard. *Die große Bedeutung des Rechts in den Bühnendicht-ungen Richard Wagners. Ein Wegweiser zum Verständnis seiner Werke.* Bayreuth: Edition Musica, 1973. 80pp. ML410.W19M377 (no ISBN available)

Identifies references to justice, retribution, and law in works from *Rienzi* to *Parsifal*. A "Bayreuth publication" devoted in part, albeit surreptitiously, to defending Wagner against possible charges of cruelty and injustice in the face of his particular popularity with Nazi leaders. Similar studies exist; see, for instance, Georg Muller, *Der Recht von Richard Wagner* (Berlin, 1914)—the last a pamphlet dealing with issues of "justice" and "law." Another volume which, in spite of its title, deals with moral issues in most of Wagner's music dramas, is Anthony Winterbourne's *Speaking to Our Condition: Moral Frameworks in Wagner's "Ring of the Nibelung"* (Madison, WI and London, 2000: ISBN 0838638473). Like several others, Winterbourne's was received too late to be described separately in the present research guide.

The "Orient"

Several studies have been devoted to Wagner's interest in the Far East and espe-cially Buddhism. The best remains:

939. Suneson, Carl. *Richard Wagner und die indische Geisteswelt.* Leiden and New York: E. J. Brill, 1989. 124pp. ISBN 9004088598 ML410.W19S9514 1988

A two-part discussion of the composer's interest in and knowledge of East-ern lore; the first is devoted to letters and diary entries that reflect his knowl-edge of India's religious and cultural traditions, the second to certain crucial concepts in Indian religion and literature that are reflected in his musical aes-thetics (paraphrased, pp. 2–3). Includes extensive references, especially in footnotes, to primarily and secondary sources; also includes a bibliography (pp. 122–23); concludes with a one-page index of Sanskrit and Pali words relevant to Wagner research. Published originally in Swedish as *Richard Wagner och den indiska tankevärlden* (Stockholm, 1985); as such, reviewed positively in *Wagner* 9/4 (October 1988), pp. 150–52.

Other studies touching specifically on Wagner and Buddhism include:

940. Dauer, Dorothea W. *Richard Wagner's Art in Relation to Buddhist Thought.* Scripta Humanistica Kentuckiensia, 7; 35pp. = Supplement to the *Kentucky Foreign Language Quarterly* 7 (1964), pp. 1–35. ML410.W19D28

Not seen; dismissed by Suneson as "an ambitious undertaking that engenders expectations not altogether fulfilled by its contents" (item 939, p. 2n). Apparently includes bibliographic references.

Notes

1. Magee's subsequent Appendix 7, "Schopenhauer's Influence on Creative Writers" (pp. 379–90), mentions a number of important figures also influenced or believed to have been influenced by Wagner; these include Conrad, Thomas Mann, Proust, Tolstoy, and Zola (see items 1000, 1021, 1025, 1030, and 1041, among others). One wonders whether the *Zeitgeist* that informed *The World as Will and Representation*, not specifically musical or musical-dramatic issues, was really what attracted at least some of these individuals to Wagner. Regarding Tolstoy, see also L. J. Rather, "Tolstoy and Wagner: The Shared Vision," *Opera Quarterly* 1/3 (Fall 1983), pp. 11–24.

XI

Criticizing Wagner:
Wagner's Critics and the Wagner
Reception

Certain of Wagner's critics have dealt with issues that go beyond the superficially biographical or musical-analytical. Furthermore, there exist books and articles devoted primarily or exclusively to reception during and after the composer's lifetime, including studies of criticism in particular nations or among groups of like-minded individuals. Although these last publications cannot finally be separated from studies of the composer's life and his works, they too deserve consideration.

Unless otherwise noted, studies grouped under individual headings or explanatory observations are described in alphabetical order by author, editor, and/or title.

SURVEY STUDIES AND ANTHOLOGIES

Among the best introductions to critical and cultural attitudes toward Wagner and his works are Newman's four-volume biography (item 301), a number of exhibition catalogs, and the following studies:

941. *Richard Wagner 1883–1983: Die Rezeption im 19. und 20. Jahrhundert. Gesammelte Beiträge des Salzburger Symposions*, ed. Ulrich Müller et al. Stuttgarter Arbeiten zur Germanistik, 129. Stuttgart: Hans-Dieter Heinz, 1984. vi, 570pp. ISBN 3880991332 ML410.W13R4 1984

Includes studies devoted to such subjects as the reception of Wagner's works in Eastern European countries (by Ewa Burzawa), Wagner and twentieth-century French literature (by Danielle Buschinger), the influence of Wagner's works and aesthetic pronouncements on dance and ballet (by Sibylle Dahms), Wagner and Ireland (by Raymond Furness), Wagner's music in the literary works of Thomas Mann (by Horst Albert Glaser), Wagner's influence on Schoenberg's music and compositional principles (by Siegfried Mauser), and so on. Includes three production photographs and a few documentary facsimiles, as well as about a dozen plates of miscellaneous illustrations bound between pp. 32–33, but no musical examples. Concludes with an extensive index. See item 6 for review information.

Briefer but nevertheless valuable surveys include:

942. Beckett, Lucy. "Wagner and His Critics." In item 31, pp. 365–88.

A delightful introduction to several important issues in Wagner criticism, including attempts to interpret his musical dramas in terms of his personal life and literary works. Beckett evaluates positions taken by Robert Gutman (item 302), Thomas Mann (see item 981), Ernest Newman (especially item 301), and Friedrich Nietzsche (see item 398), among others. See also Martin Gregor-Dellin's "Wagners Bild in die Literatur" in item 33, pp. 157–61.

943. Large, David. C. "Contemporary Assessments." In item 1, pp. 380–84.

Identifies many of the influential nineteenth-century figures who helped establish Wagner as a "living legend," and quotes briefly from some of their assessments, positive and negative. Among those mentioned by Large are musicians (Liszt, Mahler, Meyerbeer, and Schumann—the last in the pages of the *Neue Zeitschrift*), critics (including Fétis, Hanslick, and James Davison of the London *Times*), and other authorities (Baudelaire, Chamberlain, William Morris, and especially Nietzsche).

*   Taylor, Ronald. "Dealings with Critics." Described as item 378.

Summarizes the "story of a running battle" (p. 126) especially in terms of Wagner's relationships with Ludwig Rellstab and Eduard Hanslick, as well as such events as an 1844 Berlin performance of *Holländer*.

WAGNER CRITICISM IN VARIOUS COUNTRIES

America: see also items 1052–53.

944. McKnight, Mark. "Wagner and the New York Press, 1855–1876." *American Music* 5 (1987), pp. 145–55.

Covers the Wagner reception in two important New York newspapers: the *Times* and *Tribune*. Mostly about Theodore Thomas and his Wagner performances, but McKnight begins with a brief account of Carl Bergmann and the Germania ensemble. Includes a facsimile of a cartoon depicting Thomas conducting a concert in Central Park, as well as source notes.

945. Saloman, Ora Frishberg. "Dwight and Perkins on Wagner: A Controversy Within the American Cultivated Tradition, 1852–1854." In *Music and Civilization: Essays in Honor of Paul Henry Lang*, ed. Edmond Strainchamps and Maria Rika Maniates, with Christopher Hatch. New York: W. W. Norton, 1984; pp. 78–92. ISBN 0393016773 ML55.L213 1984

Devoted more to summarizing John Sullivan Dwight's and Charles Callahan Perkins's attitudes toward German musical and cultural traditions than to examining the observations these critics exchanged in *Dwight's Journal of Music*, one of the most important nineteenth-century American musical periodicals; the articles from *Dwight's Journal* are quoted at length only in pp. 89–91 of Saloman's essay. As that author observes, "Dwight's capacity to support Wagner [during the early 1850s] was limited less by specific musical objections than by a fundamental inability to accommodate Wagner's aesthetic ideas": viz., "the autonomy available to music when it was joined to a text" (p. 91).

NB: Dwight and Perkins are well-known nineteenth-century music critics. Among those less familiar to most Wagnerians is Rush C. Hawkins, whose "The Wagnerian [*sic*] Cult"—published in his own *Corlears Hook in 1820, The Wagner Cult, and Our Manners* (New York, 1904); pp. 43–71—was but one of hundreds of attacks, today most of them justifiably forgotten, launched against Wagner in America, American music critics, and related subjects. Even Hawkins acknowledged, however, that Wagnerian music drama constituted the "greatest art-event" of the nineteenth century (p. 45).

Austria: see also item 1055.

946. Bohe, Walter. *Richard Wagner im Spiegel der Wiener Presse*. Würzburg: Konrad Triltsch, 1933. 122pp. ML410.W12A93

A brief account of the Wagner reception in the Viennese press from the 1840s to the end of the composer's life. Among the critics Bohe discusses are Ludwig Speidel, Eduard Schell, and—of course—Hanslick. Includes lengthy quotations from the *Wiener Zeitung* (1842–1883), the *Morgenpost* (1854–1883), *Das Vaterland* (1860–1883), the *Neue freie Presse* (1865–1883), and other newspapers, as well as from such shorter-lived periodicals as the *Allgemeine Wiener Musikzeitung* (1842–1848), the *Blätter für Musik, Theater und Kunst* (1855–1856), and the *Wiener Zeitschrift* (1842–1848). Also includes the text of the letter Wagner addressed to Hanslick on 1 January 1847 (pp. 23–25), as well as a useful summary (pp. 116–20). Concludes with a two-page list of sources.

947. Glauert, Amanda L. "The Reception of Wagner in Vienna, 1860–1900." In item 826, pp. 120–29.

Discusses performances of his own works that drew Wagner to Vienna in 1860 and 1875, as well as the establishment in 1873 of a Viennese Wagner-Gesellschaft. Glauert also considers the critical positions occupied by the anti-Wagnerian Hanslick and the pro-Wagnerian Josef Schalk, who also supported the causes of Bruckner and Hugo Wolf. See, too, Reinhard Farkas's "Mythos und Moderne: Zur Rezeption des Opernwerks Richard Wagners in Wien," published in *Das Musiktheater um die Jahrhundertwende: Wien-Budapest um 1900,* ed. Farkas (Vienna, 1990), pp. 17–24.

948. Macdonald, Hugh. "Wolf's Adulation of Wagner in the Vienna Press." *Wagner* 7/2 (April 1986), pp. 41–47. ML410.W1A585

A brief examination of the younger composer's attitudes toward "the Master." Macdonald maintains that "of Wolf's writings on Wagner the most obvious feature is the unargued presumption of its [*sic*] greatness" (p. 44). Much of the article is devoted to the Strauss waltzes and their place in both Viennese concert life and the Austrian musical imagination.

949. Tschulik, Norbert. "August Wilhelm Ambros und das Wagner-Problem: Ein Beitrag zur Geschichte der Musikkritik und der Wagner-Rezeption." In: *Studien zur Musikwissenschaft: Beihefte der DTÖ* [Denkmäler der Tonkunst in Österreich], Vol. 29; ed. Othmar Wessely. Tutzing: Hans Schneider, 1978; pp. 155–69. ISBN 379520237X ML55.F13 No. 29

Evaluates the significance of Ambros's critical writings about Wagner from 1872 to 1876 (the latter the year of the critic's death) in Vienna's *Abendpost.* Illustrated with excerpts by Ambros and other critics clearly identified by date and place of publication, printed in italic type, and punctuated with running commentary by Tschulik.

Canada

950. Lefebvre, Marie-Thérèse. "La Musique du Wagner au Québec au tournant du XXe siecle." *Canadian University Music Review* 14 (1994), pp. 60–76. ML5.C1557

A history of Wagner performances in Québec between 1884–1948, together with an evaluation of their cultural impact. Lefebvre employs four tables in order to identify important Wagnerian "events" precisely and highlight their significance; she also provides a facsimile illustration taken from the 1905 *Montréal Star.* Concludes with an abstract (p. 76).

951. Morey, Carl. "The Music of Wagner in Toronto Before 1914." *Canadian University Music Review* 18/2 (1998), pp. 25–37. ML5.C1557

Concerned for the most part with a performance of *Parsifal* presented in the Ontarian capital in 1905, although other works and events are mentioned in passing. Includes an abstract (p. 37), but no illustrations or musical examples.

England

952. Hadow, W. H. *Studies in Modern Music.* 2 vols.; Vol. 1 = *Hector Berlioz, Robert Schumann, Richard Wagner.* London: Seeley & Co., 1893. 335pp. ML390.H13

Incorporates "Richard Wagner and the Reform of the Opera" (pp. 233–326), a lengthy argument on behalf of Hadow's contention that Wagner, especially insofar as his works bodied forth a German "national character" and fulfilled late nineteenth-century Germany's "national aspiration," had thus "clothed [art] with new life [and] . . . taught it to deliver a new message," and that "the echoes of his voice will last, not only in his own work but in that of the days to come" (pp. 325–26). Hadow refers to details of dramatic theory and practice, but provides no musical examples and no visual illustrations beyond a few portraits of the composer. See also item 999.

France

953. *Richard Wagner in Paris: Zwei vergessene Texte von Jules Champfleury and Léon Bloy*, ed. Joachim Schultz. Bamberg: Erich Weiß, 1995. 71pp. ISBN 3928591398 ML410.W12F63 1995X

Reprints in both French and German the texts of Bloy's *Le musicien du silence* and Champfleury's *Richard Wagner.* Includes four pictures as well as a few notes on sources and the text itself; concludes with an afterword by the editor, a brief bibliography, and a page of information about the illustrations. See, too, the translations of Champfleury's *Richard Wagner* and *After the Battle* (1861) prepared by Palomba Paves-Yashinsky and published in *19th Century Music* 13 (1989–1990), pp. 18–27. See also item 1000.

Germany

The most important of all documentary studies devolving upon the German Wagner reception remains:

954. Kirchmeyer, Helmut. *Situationsgeschichte der Musikkritik und das musikalischen Pressewesens in Deutschland dargestellt vom Ausgange des 18. bis zum Beginn des 20. Jahrhunderts.* Studien zur Musikgeschichte des 19. Jahrhunderts, 7. 6 vols. Regensburg: Gustav Bosse, 1967–1990. ML3915.K57

Vol. 1: *Das zeitgenössische Wagner-Bild. Wagner in Dresden.* 846pp.

Vol. 2: *Das zeitgenössische Wagner-Bild. Dokumente 1842–1845.* xxviii pp., 703 cols. + index.

Vol. 3: *Das zeitgenössische Wagner-Bild: Dokumente 1846–1850.* xxix pp., 810 cols. + index and apparatus.

Vols. 6/1–2: *Das zeitgenössische Wagner-Bild: Sechter Band, 1. Halbband Dokumente 1851–1852 IV;* and *Band, 2. Halbband Dokumente 1851V-1852 XII.* Together lxxii pp. + 1,156 cols.

Insofar as Wagner is concerned, in five volumes. Vols. 1–3 comprise Part IV of the *Situationsgeschichte* project; Vol. 6, actually two separate volumes, appeared later. Vol. 1 covers the composer's Dresden years and discusses a wealth of contemporary documents associated with *Rienzi, Holländer,* and *Tannhäuser* published in the *Dresdner Tageblatt,* the *Neue Abend-Zeitung,* and Berlin papers. Vols. 2–3 are documentary anthologies; together they reprint 1,265 items drawn from daily newspapers, magazines like the *Neue Zeitschrift,* and a variety of other sources—among the last are some of Berlioz's reminiscences—as well as illustrations and documentary facsimiles, some of which extend across both columns of text. Vol. 6/1–2 together reprint the texts of another 1,992 documents. In most of these volumes the indexes and other apparatus are paginated separately using upper-case Roman numerals; Vol. 3 also contains a list of typographical errors and a separate index of authors, as well as a short timeline (p. LXXI); in Vols. 6/1–2 the "additional" pages, again identified using upper-case Roman numerals, are split between the beginning of the former and end of the latter fascicles. Musical examples appear in a few articles and extend even to a complete facsimile of Wagner's setting for voice and piano of Victor Hugo's "Attente" (Vol. 2, "cols." 15–18 [2 full pages in all]).

Other studies of value, although somewhat more limited in scope, are:

*   Cicora, Mary A. *"Parsifal" Reception in the "Bayreuther Blätter."* Described as item 788.

955. Großman-Vendrey, Susanna. *Bayreuth in der deutschen Presse. Beiträge zur Rezeptionsgeschichte Richard Wagners und seine Festspiele.* 4 vols. Regensburg: Gustav Bosse, 1977–1983. ML410.W2B296

Possibly the largest collection of primary sources outside editions of Wagner's compositions, letters, and literary works. Its four volumes (the author numbers them "1," "2," "3.1," and "3.2") cover publications dating from (1) 1872–1876 and associated largely with the first Bayreuth Festival; (2) the second Festival of 1882 and the first performance of *Parsifal*; (3) 1883–1906; and (4) 1908–1944. Among Großman-Vendrey's collaborators in this project are Felix Schneider (Vols. 1–2) and Paul Fiebig (Vols. 3–4). See item 6 for review information.

A synopsis of Großman-Vendrey's reception theory, including a diagrammatic representation of its principal features, appears in her "Zur Analyze der Wagnerrezeption in der Tagespresse: Am Beispiel der Bayreuther Festspiele, 1876–1944," published in the *Bericht über den internationalen musikwissenschaftlichen Kongress Berlin 1974*, ed. Hellmut Kühn and Peter Nitsche (Kassel and London, 1980), pp. 509–13. See also Großman-Vendrey, "Wagner. Von der Rezeptionsgeschichte zur Rezeptionsästhetik?" in *Rezeptionsästhetik und Rezeptionsgeschichte in der Musikwissenschaft*, ed. Hermann Danuser and Friedhelm Krummacher (Laaber, 1991), pp. 255–68.

Still other studies of Wagner's reception in German-speaking regions of Europe include:

956. Böhme, Erdman Werner. *Richard Wagners Werk in Pommern; die ersten Aufführungen Wagnerscher Musikdramen in Stettin, Greifswald und Stralsund. Ein musik- und theatergeschichtlicher Beitrag.* Berlin-Halensee: "Im Selbstverlag" (published by the author), 1934; reprinted Wachtberg-Niederbachem: Repro-Nachdruck, 1971. Unpaginated; approximately 28pp long. ML410.W12G43 1971

Devoted mostly to discussions of individual performances and their successes. NB: Since the end of World War II Pomerania has belonged largely to Poland; at the end of Wagner's life it was part of the eastern German Reich.

957. Budde, Elmar. "Der junge Wagner und die Berliner Musikkritik." In: *Festschrift Arno Forchert zum 60. Geburtstag am 29. Dezember 1985*, ed. Gerhard Allroggen and Detlef Altenburg. Kassel and New York: Bärenreiter, 1986; pp. 234–41. ISBN 3761807767 ML55.F657 1986

A perceptive but brief and incompletely documented discussion of German reactions in Berlin to Wagner's early works, specifically the 1844 performance of *Holländer*. Budde cites reviews by Heinrich Dorn, Ludwig Rellstab (the latter in the *Vossische Zeitung*), and other critics, and explains that many journalists disliked the young composer's work because it clashed so harshly with their core perceptions of the classical tradition in music (paraphrased p. 240).

958. Chop, Max. "Richard Wagner im Spiegel des Kritik seiner Zeit." *Richard-Wagner-Jahrbuch* 1 (1906), pp. 61–101. ML410.W1A57

Describes, work by work, the critical reception accorded the operas and music dramas from *Rienzi* to *Parsifal*. Unfortunately, Chop identifies his sources only by critic and/or periodical, sometimes only by periodical and year.

Italy

Again, the most important reception study is a documentary anthology:

959. Jung, Ute. *Die Rezeption der Kunst Richard Wagners in Italien*. Studien zur Musikgeschichte des 19. Jahrhunderts, 35. Regensburg: Gustav Bosse, 1974. 524pp. ISBN 3764920769 ML410.W12I836

A massive collection of documents, interspersed with commentary and devoted to reviews and writings about Wagner in general, as well as performances in Bologna, Florence, Milan, Naples, Rome, Trieste, Turin, Venice, and so on. Organized in four principal sections: the first is devoted to the Wagner reception in various cities (beginning with Bologna and the very first Italian performance of any Wagner work—in this case *Lohengrin*, on 1 November 1871); the second to the influence of Wagner's theories on Italian thought, including Italian reports of the 1876, 1882–1892, and 1894 Bayreuth Festivals; the third Wagner's influence on Italian musical life and thought, including Italian attitudes toward the operas of Gluck, Puccini, Rossini, Verdi, and Weber, as well as Wagner's influence on Gabriele D'Annunzio; and the fourth to libretto translations, the limitations of Italian stages and theatrical machinery, Wagnerian and anti-Wagnerian reactions to the composer's works, and so on. Illustrated with 35 black-and-white documentary facsimiles and other images, as well as a few short musical examples. Includes a bibliography (pp. 459–71); concludes with an index.

See also Großmann-Vendrey, " 'Wagner in Italien': Bemerkungen zur Rezeptionsforschung," published in *Die Musikforschung* 29 (1976), pp. 195–99. Finally, see item 844.

Among other volumes of value is:

960. *Antologia della critica Wagneriana in Italia*, ed. Agostino Ziino. Messina: Peloritana, 1970. 365pp. ML410.W12Z5

A two-part study: the first is devoted to a survey of Italian Wagner criticism from 1871 to the later 1960s (pp. 9–160), the second to representative passages from the writings of mostly twentieth-century critics such as Girolamo Biaggi, D'Annunzio, Luigi Ronga, Alberto Savinio, and Luigi Torchi. Originally published in Vol. 11 of *Analecta Musicologia*.

THE "WAGNER LEGEND"

Few composers have ever received the adulation that was showered on Wagner, especially near the end of his lifetime and shortly afterwards; in Hitler's Germany, too, Wagner was held up as a national icon and treasure. Certain scholars have embraced the "legend" of the composer's greatness; others have attacked it. Studies produced by legend enthusiasts include:

* Abbetmeyer, Theodor. "Wagners Persönlichkeit." Described under item 439.

A hymn of praise to the composer; anything objectionable is kept under wraps.

961. Plüddemann, Martin. *Die Bühnenfestspiele in Bayreuth, ihre Gegner und ihre Zukunft*, 2nd. ed. Leipzig: Gebrüder Senf, 1881. 61pp. ML410.W2P7 1881

Interesting principally for its spirited defense of Wagner—Plüddemann was an acquaintance of the composer and a staunch supporter of Bayreuth—against his "enemies," and especially seven "superstitions" promulgated by them: that Wagner's music dramas (1) ruin the voices of singers and (2) are morally wrong; and that Wagner himself (3) treats artists badly, (4) has turned his back on the classics, (5) is admired only by a clique, (6) is far too arrogant, and (7) writes indecent poetry. Published originally by Carl Jancke's firm (Colberg, 1877).

962. Stefan, Paul. *Die Feinschaft gegen Wagner: Eine geschichtliche und psychologische Untersuchung*. Regensburg: Gustav Bosse, ?1944. 96pp. (no LC number available)

Mostly a discussion of Nietzsche's complex response to Wagner as man and artist; also, however, an evaluation of reasons critics might wish to attack the composer and his works. Stefan's essay itself concludes with a brief bibliography (pp. 83–84); the remaining pages are devoted to advertisements for Bosse's publications. Omitted from item 1019.

963. Wolzogen, Hans von. *Recollections of Richard Wagner*, trans. Agnes and Carnegie Simpson. Bayreuth: C. Giessel, 1894. 103pp. ML410.W1W7

Less a description of personal encounters than a hymn of praise for the man Wolzogen revered and spent much of his life promoting, and a summary of Wagner's ideas and attitudes toward a variety of subjects. Published originally as *Erinnerungen an Richard Wagner* (Vienna, 1891); the firm of Philipp Reclam Jr. issued a paperback edition advertised as "new" and "twice as large" (*Neue, um das doppelte vergrößerte Ausgabe*) as previous versions. See also item 1136.

Denigrators and detractors of the legend have produced:

964. Amerongen, Martin van. *Wagner: A Case History*, trans. Stewart Spencer and Dominick Cakebread. New York: George Braziller, 1984. 169pp. ISBN 0807610917 ML410.W1A59873 1984

Mocks both the composer for his anti-semitism, and Bayreuth for covering up anything and everything unpleasant about him, his music, and his aesthetic, nationalist, and political legacies. Amerongen also notes that his subject "failed miserably" in his search for a type of specifically anti-Jewish music (p. 148), and quips—this is a witty volume—that "Wagner was certainly not a totalitarian composer, since his music is anything but optimistic, in addition to which it is inordinately complex" (p. 149).

Originally published in Dutch as *De buitspreker van God* (Amsterdam, 1983). An English edition of Spencer's and Cakebread's translation (London, 1983) is paginated slightly differently; both editions include a bibliography, discography, and index.

965. Hime, H. W. L. *Wagnerism: A Protest*. London: Kegan Paul, Trench & Co., 1882. 87pp. ML410.W13H36

Attacks the cult of personality that had come to be associated with Wagner's followers and the Bayreuth Festivals of 1876 and 1882, as well as the purported absence of real melody in the mature music dramas, and other aspects of the composer's literary and compositional styles. Contains no specific citations, however.

*   Tappert, Wilhelm. *Richard Wagner im Spiegel der Kritik*. Described as item 97.

A dictionary of offensive terms employed by Wagner's "enemies" during the latter half of the nineteenth century. See also item 1051.

*   Weissmann, Adolf. "Richard Wagner: Constructive and Destructive." Described as item 437.

Attacks Wagner's sincerity, the seductiveness of his music dramas, and so on.

One study documents language employed by supporters and detractors alike during various phases of French history:

966. Fulcher, Jane F. "A Political Barometer of 20th-Century France: Wagner as Jew or Anti-Semite." *The Musical Quarterly* 84 (2000), pp. 41–57. ML1.M725

Demonstrates that the composer was perceived by a variety of modern French figures from d'Indy to the fascists of the 1930s in terms of Jewish stereotypes, seeking alternately to defame Wagner as "Jewish," "feminine," and "modern," or praise him for his anti-semitic sentiments. Includes quotations from less-familiar sources such as Pierre Lasserre's denunciation, published in *L'esprit de la musique française* (Paris, 1917); one of dozens excluded from the present research guide. See also item 1000.

Although Wagner is less often praised today for everything he ever said, wrote, and did, he has also been unfairly criticized by his enemies. This brief but valuable article identifies certain ways in which the composer's reputation has been mishandled:

967. Millington, Barry. "Wagner as Scapegoat." In item 1, pp. 128–29.

A thought-provoking essay. Millington maintains that "all the negative traits associated with Romantic artists in general have been projected on to Wagner and, moreover, have been magnified out of all proportion" (p. 128); he also points out that Wagner is not the only human being to have behaved in a less than perfect manner toward those around him.

WAGNER, MODERNITY, AND LEADING MODERN WAGNER CRITICS

By "modern" (some prefer "modernist") is meant the Weltanschauung *that prevailed among "cultivated" Europeans and Americans between c. 1880–1965. Put it another way: the scientific and philosophical systems devised by Einstein, Freud, and Jean-Paul Sartre, the music of Bartók, Schoenberg, and Richard Strauss, the novels of Joyce, Proust, and Thomas Mann, the paintings of Picasso and Salvador Dalí, and the films of Charlie Chaplin have all been cited as quintessentially "modern." See also item 992.*

Survey Studies

Two works introduce Wagner and modern culture:

968. Bergfeld, Joachim. *Wagners Werk und unsere Zeit*. Berlin: Max Hesse, 1963. 63pp. (no LC number available)

Summarizes Wagner's influence on critics and culture alike. Bergfeld includes chapters on "Wagnerism," the relationship between Beethoven and Wagner in the minds of performers and scholars, and the influence of Wagner on Thomas Mann and Bernard Shaw; he also provides two appendices: one dealing with Friedrich Blume and Helmuth Osthoff, the other reproducing the text of an address delivered by Artur Kutscher at Wagner's grave in 1883. Revised in part from addresses presented at Bayreuth and Tribschen in May 1963 on the occasion of the composer's 150th birthday. Includes a bibliography (pp. 8–11).

969. Lacoue-Labarthe, Philippe. *Musica ficta (Figures of Wagner)*, trans. Felicia McCarren. Stanford, CA: Stanford University Press, 1994. xxiii, 161pp. ISBN 0804723850 ML410.W19L213 1994

Probes Wagner's impact on modern music and thought, especially on Adorno, Baudelaire, Mallarmé, Heidegger, and Nietzsche. Lacoue-Labarthe works from the premise that "no aesthetic practice . . . can declare itself politically innocent" (p. xxii), and that the Wagner reception cannot be separated from political opinions and even from some events. Concludes with detailed notes. Published originally in French in 1991.

Another study deals with Wagner and class issues:

970. Busch, Christiane. "Wagner and Middle-Class Intellectuals. On the History of a Fatal Response: Questions and Corrections." *Bayreuther Festspielprogramme* III (1993), pp. 67–81. ML410.W2B26

Challenges opinions associated not only with the "Old Bayreuth," but an international late-capitalist culture in which "the connection between art and consumption is growing ever closer," and "reception is bound to become an almost insurmountable challenge if it wishes to remain free of tendentiousness" (p. 67). Busch also considers the roles played by Nietzsche and Mann in our own perceptions of Wagner, aspects of Bayrueth Wagner productions, and so on. Supplemented with extensive quotations.

Studies by (and about) Individual Critics

Theodor W[iesengrund] Adorno
971. Adorno, Theodor W. *In Search of Wagner*, trans. Rodney Livingstone. London: NLB, 1991. 159pp. ISBN 0860910377 ML410.W1A5953 1991

A complex argument concerning Wagner's music as a document of nineteenth-century European culture, written during 1937 and 1938 by one of the most influential members of the Frankfurt School. Includes a number of quotations from Wagner's works, especially from librettos previously copywritten by British recording firms. Includes no musical examples, however, and no bibliography; concludes with a three-page index.

Translated from Adorno's *Versuch über Wagner* (Berlin and Frankfurt a.M., 1952 and 1974) and available in other English-language editions. Reviewed in Livingstone's translation in *Music & Letters* 42 (1981), pp. 436–37. An earlier edition was reviewed in *Wagner* 3/1 (January 1982), pp. 28–31. Even more important, perhaps, is Dahlhaus's general review of Adorno as a Wagner critic, published as "Soziologische Dechiffierungen von Musik. Zu Theodor W. Adornos Wagnerkritik" in the *International Review of the Aesthetics and Sociology of Music* 1 (1970), pp. 137–47.

972. Williams, Alastair. "Technology of the Archaic: Wish Images and Phantasmagoria in Wagner." *Cambridge Opera Journal* 9 (1997), pp. 73–87. ISSN 0954–5867 (no LC number available)

Adorno's music-critical prose, "often painful" to read [quoted from Gary Zabel, "Adorno on Music: A Reconsideration," *The Musical Times* 130 (1989), p. 198], is more readily understood even than certain statements of Williams's—among them the following, which summarizes Williams's own argument: "[R]eading Adorno's Wagner through [Walter] Benjamin's appraisal of modernity facilitates a more sanguine interpretation of Wagner's evocation of ur-forms through advanced compositional technology. The rigidity of Adorno's interpretation is further softened by Jacques Derrida's reading of Karl Marx's distinction between use value and exchange value, while, on a broader front, Derrida's attention to the reader also suggests that commodity production need not dominate reception strategies" (p. 73).

Jacques Barzun
Barzun's most influential pronouncements on Wagner appear in the celebrated volume:

973. Barzun, Jacques. *Darwin, Marx, Wagner: Critique of a Heritage*, 2nd. rev. ed. Garden City, NY: Doubleday & Co., 1958. xx, 373pp. CT105.B

Probes especially the authority Darwin, Marx, and Wagner had or claimed to have had as (respectively) "the" scientist, "the" social critic, and "the" artist of the modern world; thus—to paraphrase its author (p. 1)—Barzun's book constitutes an evaluation of the slogans they placed in the mouths of nineteenth- and twentieth-century Europeans and Americans. Barzun also discusses Wagner's friendships with Berlioz and Liszt, the influence of the *Bayreuther Blätter*, Wagnerism in England and its impact on Hardy, Swinburne, and Bernard Shaw, and especially the Nietzsche-Wagner relationship and debate; after Wagner, as Barzun complains, "the 'life of art' became a recognized substitute for life itself" (p. 307). Only the section entitled "The Artistic Revolution" (pp. 219–317) is devoted primarily to Wagner. Reprinted by the University of Chicago Press in 1981.

Responses to Barzun's study, by himself and certain of his contemporaries, include:

974. Barzun, Jacques. "After Wagner: What is Art?" In: *20th-Century Views of Music History*, ed. William Hays. New York: Charles Scribner's Sons, 1972; pp. 321–30. ML55.H29

A lively, highly opinionated essay. Although "forward-looking critics and their readers . . . may say that [Wagner today] is farther away from us than Mozart or Berlioz," Barzun reminds us that performances of the music dramas continue to take place and, especially, that art remains entangled "in previous theorizing and historical justification," a kind of *Schwärmerei* (fanatical attitude) reinforced by the composer's prose works that has become "a more or less explicit assumption" of most twentieth-century critics (pp. 326–27). Includes a few observations about important post-item 973 contributions to the literature.

975. *Darwin, Marx, and Wagner: A Symposium*, ed. Henry L. Plaine. Columbus, OH: Ohio State University Press, 1962. viii, 165pp. CB358.P53 1962

A "reply" to item 973 in the form of a collection of papers presented at a symposium held in October 1959. Includes Joseph Kerman's "Debts Paid and Debts Neglected" (pp. 139–65)—an assessment of Wagner's career and place in musical history—as well as essays on primarily political, social, and biological topics by the likes of Richard Hofstadter and Berthram Leake; Andreas Dorpalen's "Man and His Destiny" (pp. 3–27) contains observations about Wagner and the Nazis. Also includes notes after each essay but no bibliography or index.

Charles Baudelaire

976. Baudelaire, Charles. *Richard Wagner et Tannhäuser à Paris*, ed. Robert Kopp. Paris: Belles Lettres, 1994. xlvi, 143pp. ISBN 2225146011X ML410.W135B38 1994

One of the most influential Wagner pamphlets ever published; Baudelaire virtually launched *Wagnérisme* in nineteenth-century France by himself. Published for the first time both as an article in the *Revue européenne* (Paris; 1 April 1861) and as a pamphlet (Paris: E. Dento, 1861). Reprinted subsequently on many occasions and in more than a few languages— among them Hungarian, as in "Richard Wagner és a Tannhäuser Parizsban," trans. Julia Lenkei, *Muzsika* 43/3 (March 2000). See also items 621, 1032, and 1067.

Hans von Bülow

977. Bülow, Hans von. *Ausgewählte Schriften, 1850–1892*, 2nd enlarged ed. = *Hans von Bülow: Briefe und Schriften*, ed. Marie von Bülow, Vol. III (Leipzig; Breitkopf & Härtel, 1911; comprises two volumes in one). ML422.B9B9

The work of one of the composer's closest friends, most enthusiastic supporters, and former husband of his second wife Cosima. Incorporates Bülow's letters to Wagner (see item 246) as well as a number of articles, among them "Über Richard Wagners Faust-Ouvertüre" of 1856 (incomplete; see item 810), and "Lohengrin' in Bologna" of 1871, as well as a great deal about Berlioz, Liszt, Hiller, and other figures close to or influenced by Wagner during their careers. Scattered musical examples appear throughout both parts of this "two-volume" work. Also includes a list of Bülow's articles omitted from the collection in question (*Ausgewählte Schriften*, Vol. 2, pp. 281–90). See also item 810.

Gabriele D'Annunzio

978. Gabriele D'Annunzio. *Il caso Wagner*, ed. Paolo Sorge. Rome and Bari: Editori Laterza, 1996. 96pp. ISBN 884204962X ML410.W13D38 1996

Comprises "Il caso Wagner" (pp. 45–78) and "La Bestia elettiva" (pp. 79–96) by D'Annunzio himself, as well as an essay by Sorge entitled "D'Annunzio tra Wagner e Nietzsche" (pp. 1–44). The last is interesting insofar as it reevaluates from an Italian perspective the writings of three men associated variously with fascism, the Nazis, and the catastrophes of World War II. No illustrations or other apparatus. See also items 1046–47.

Joseph Kerman

979. Kerman, Joseph. "Opera as Symphonic Poem" = Chapter 7 of *Opera as Drama*. New York: Vintage, 1956; pp. 192–216. ML3858.K4

At its heart an affirmation of the dramatic role played by music in Western opera in general and, in the chapter in question, *Tristan* in particular. In Kerman's words, "Wagner's individual musical style, and only that style, made possible the dramatic achievement of *Tristan und Isolde*" (p. 204). This position, considered suspect by some postmodern critics, has been attacked especially by Carolyn Abbate (see item 481). Kerman's chapter includes two examples from *Tristan* and several quotations from its libretto. See also item 745.

Revised slightly and republished in 1988; reviewed in its revised edition by Ellen Rosand in *19th Century Music* 14 (1990–1991), pp. 75–83, together with item 528 and several other volumes. Several other critics have addressed themselves to "placing" Wagner in music history; see, for instance, Gerald Abraham's *A Hundred Years of Music* (New York, 1938), which includes "Wagner and the Opera" (pp. 91–161) and "After Wagner" chapters. Finally, see item 975 as well as Kerman's recent essays collection, *Write All These Down* (University of California Press, 1994), which contains "Wagner: Thoughts in Season," published decades ago in *Score* magazine.

Franz Liszt

980. Liszt, Franz. *Lohengrin et Tannhäuser de Richard Wagner*, ed. Rainer Kleinertz and Gerhard J. Winkler. Franz Liszt: sämtliche Schriften, 4. Wiesbaden: Breitkopf & Härtel, 1989. xv, 320pp. ISBN 3765102350 ML60.L48615 1989, Bd. 4

A scholarly edition of Liszt's groundbreaking Wagner monograph, published originally in the early 1850s at Weimar, Leipzig, and Paris. Includes the complete texts of both the *Lohengrin* and *Tannhäuser* essays in French and German, as well as scattered illustrations, the musical examples appended to early editions of Liszt's essays, and so on. Also includes extensive endnotes (pp. 276–317), themselves illustrated with a documentary facsimile of the Weimar *Tannhäuser* conductor's score, and a photograph of that city's monument to Herder, as well as a list of abbreviations and *sigla* (pp. xiv–xv); concludes with a bibliography of secondary sources. The *Sämtliche Schriften* is edited as a series by Detlef Altenburg.

Other modern editions of Liszt's essays also exist, including one edited by Jacques Bourgeois (Paris, 1980); among other illustrations, Bourgeois provides a facsimile of the title page to the 1851 Leipzig edition.

Thomas Mann

Most of Mann's observations about Wagner, both positive and negative, may be found in:

981. Mann, Thomas. *Pro and Contra Wagner*, trans. Allen Blunden. Chicago and London: University of Chicago Press, 1985. 229pp. ISBN 0226503348 ML410.W1M253 1985

A collection of writings about the composer who continued alternately to fascinate and repel Mann. Includes the screenplay for a film of *Tristan*, excerpts from *Reflections of an Unpolitical Mann* an essay on "Ibsen and Wagner," and several letters of protest addressed to various officials and functionaries of Hitler's regime—the last predating Mann's own expulsion from Nazi Germany—as well as "The Sorrows and Grandeur of Richard Wagner" and "Richard Wagner and 'Der Ring des Nibelungen' "—all written between 1902 and 1951, and the last two essays among Mann's most important writings. Outfitted with an editorial preface and an introduction by Erich Heller, as well as an index.

Reviewed in this edition in *Wagner* 7/4 (October 1986), pp. 139–46; see also item 1091. Originally published as *Wagner und unsere Zeit*, ed. Erika Mann (Frankfurt a.M.: Fischer, 1963). Blunden's translation was also originally published in 1963 by Faber & Faber, London. Finally, see items 999 and 1047.

Mann's career was linked with important incidents and individuals in German history. Studies of these include:

*   *Cosima Wagner-Liszt: Der Weg zum Wagner-Mythos.* Described as item 1157.

Includes Franz Beidler's correspondence with Mann (pp. 303–59).

982. Vaget, Hans Rudolf. "The Wagner Celebration of 1933 and the "National Excommunication' of Thomas Mann." *Wagner* 16/2 (May 1995), pp. 51–60. ML410.W1A595

Explains that conductor Hans Knappertsbusch may have instigated the attack on Mann in the *Münchener neueste Nachrichten* of April 1933 that followed the author's call for an end to the alliance between Bayreuth and the Nazis; others who sought to punish Mann included Hans Pfitzner and Richard Strauss.

983. Vaget, Hans Rudolf. "Whose Legacy? Thomas Mann, Franz W. Beidler, and Bayreuth." *Wagner* 18/1 (January 1997), pp. 3–19. ML410.W1A595

Traces the history of Mann's growing doubts about Wagner, and especially about Bayreuth's Wagner cult, the author's disavowal of Hitler and the Nazis in 1933, and his disinclination to return to Germany, even after 1945. Vaget also explains that Beidler invited Mann in 1947 to serve as honorary president of the Bayreuth Festival; Mann declined the invitation. Includes several illustrations.

Friedrich Nietzsche

Nietzsche's writings to and about Wagner have already been described; see especially item 398. Other editions specifically of the "Wagner writings" include:

984. Nietzsche, Friedrich. *Richard Wagner in Bayreuth / Der Fall Wagner / Nietzsche contra Wagner.* Stuttgart: Philipp Reclam Jun., 1973. 167pp. ISBN 3150071267 ML410.W13N56

Ostensibly the philosopher's "complete"—and mostly negative—writings on Wagnerian subjects. (The positive writings include *The Birth of Tragedy*, which doesn't deal as directly with Wagnerian issues; and *Thus Spake Zarathustra*, which owes more to Wagner than the text itself admits; regarding the latter, see item 902.) Includes an afterword by Martin Gregor-Dellin.

Other studies evaluate the impact of Wagner's life, thought, and art not only upon Nietzsche, but also upon Thomas Mann:

985. *"Der Fall Wagner": Ursprünge und Folgen von Nietzsches Wagner-Kritik*, ed. Thomas Steiert. Thurnauer Schriften zum Musiktheater, 11. Laaber: Laaber-Verlag, 1991. ISBN 3890072615 ML410.W19F36 1991

A collection of essays addressing the logical semantics of Nietzsche's Wagner criticism, the reception accorded Wagner's and Nietzsche's rather different notions of *Erlösung* (salvation), the response of Second Viennese School composers Alban Berg and Anton von Webern to the Nietzsche-Wagner controversy, and—as the only English contribution—"Saint Offenbach's Post-Modernism," by Allan Janik (pp. 361–81; see also item 993).

986. *Wagner–Nietzsche–Thomas Mann: Festschrift für Eckhard Heftrich*, ed. Heinz Gockel et al. Frankfurt a.M.: Vittorio Klostermann, 1993. (x), 426pp. ISBN 3465026241 PT2625.A44Z9247 1993

Contains four essays of special interest to Wagner scholars: Dieter Borchmeyer's " 'Ein Dreigestirn ewig verbundener Geister.' Wagner, Nietzsche, Thomas Mann und das Konzept einer übernationalen Kultur"; Victor Lange's "Hinweis auf G. B. Shaws 'The Perfect Wagnerite' "; Michael Neumann's "Von den Strahlen der Sonne und dem Zauber der Nacht: Mozart-Wagner-Thomas Mann"; and Ruprecht Wimmer's " 'Ah, ça c'est bien allemand, par exemple!' Richard Wagner in Thomas Manns 'Doktor

Faustus' " (together pp. 1–68). The bulk of the volume is devoted to other topics. Includes an index (pp. 404–10).

George Bernard Shaw

987. Shaw, George Bernard. *The Perfect Wagnerite: A Commentary on Wagner's Ring*. New York: Dover, 1967, xx, 136pp. MT100.W2S5 1967

One of the best-known and most highly opinionated interpretations of Wagner's *Ring*, written by a Fabian socialist as a critique of nineteenth-century capitalism. Originally published in London in 1923, Shaw's *Wagnerite* has gone through many editions; that published by Dover and widely available also includes chapters on nineteenth-century civilization in general, the "Music of the Future," and Bayreuth. Evaluated and criticized by a variety of commentators, including Martin Cooper in "Wagner's 'Ring' as a Political Myth," published in *Ideas and Music* (London: Barrie & Rockliff, 1965), pp. 109–15.

988. *Shaw's Music: The Complete Musical Criticism in Three Volumes*, ed. Dan H. Laurence. 3 vols. New York: Dodd, Mead, 1981. ISBN 0396079679 (set) ML60.S5175 1981

Includes Shaw's many articles on Wagner and Wagnerian performances written between 1876 and 1890 (Vol. 1), 1890 and 1893 (Vol. 2), and 1893 and 1950 (Vol. 3). Thoroughly indexed. Important for every student of Wagner criticism; Shaw is considered by some authorities the finest musical journalist who ever lived. Other, less comprehensive editions include *Shaw on Music: A Selection from the Music Criticism of Bernhard Shaw*, ed. Eric Bentley (New York, 1955; reprinted New York, 1995); and Shaw's own *Music in London, 1890–1894: Criticisms Contributed Week by Week to The World* (London, 1931; reprinted New York, 1973).

A reply of sorts to item 987 appeared shortly after World War I:

989. Steigman, B. M. *The Pertinent Wagnerite*. New York: Thomas Seltzer, 1921. 127pp. (no LC number available)

Shaw asserts that the *Ring* criticizes capitalist civilization and mores; Steigman, writing as an isolationist post-World War I American, asserts that it defends German military and cultural hegemony, even as it illustrates the inevitable results of such "arguments." Also includes comments on *Tristan* and *Parsifal*. A rather odd contribution to the Wagner literature, and possibly of interest to students of the composer's New World reception. Steigman also wrote a biography of the composer, published as *The Unconquerable Tristan* (New York, 1933).

WAGNER, POSTMODERNITY, AND POSTMODERN WAGNER CRITICISM

By "postmodern" is meant the Weltanschauung *that has prevailed among "cultivated" Europeans and Americans since 1965 or so. Put it another way: certain questions of scientific method associated with Thomas Kuhn's books and essays, the critical theories of such different individuals as Jacques Derrida and Camille Paglia, the music of Laurie Anderson and Philip Glass, the writings of Roland Barthes, Jorge Luis Borges, and Thomas Pynchon, the paintings of David Hockney, and the films of Martin Scorsese have all been described as quintessentially "postmodern." See also items 672, 800, 969 and 972.*

Two important works of quite different postmodern musicology deal specifically with Wagner:

990. Abbate, Carolyn. *Unsung Voices: Opera and Musical Narrative in the 19th Century*. Princeton and London: Princeton University Press, 1991. xvi, 288pp. ISBN 0690191404 ML3858.A2 1991

   In the fewest words, a study of the *Ring* in terms of what Wagner included and excluded concerning his various versions, drafts, and final narrative. In the words of review-article author Richard·Tarushkin [*Cambridge Opera Journal* 4 (1992), pp. 187–97]—who describes Abbate as "more than a virtuoso; she is a heroine" (p. 197)—*Unsung Voices* is an "epiphany" that, "by definition, resists parsing and paraphrasing," and one that considers Wagner's works as "not static but phatic (that is, they monitor relationships among composer, characters and listeners—both in the house and on the stage), not detached from the action, but a critical part of the work's 'plastic' unfolding" (p. 187). Abbate draws upon Nattiez's theories of musical semiotics, especially as presented in *Music and Discourse: Toward a Semiology of Music* (Princeton University Press, 1990)—which Abbate herself translated—as well as other theoretical, critical, and factual sources, to reveal a "poststructuralist Brünnhilde," a character who herself proves to be Wagner's "ultimate listener" (review, p. 193). Incorporates musical examples, as well as numerous references to the literature; concludes with a bibliography (pp. 275–82) and index. See also item 995.

991. Nattiez, Jean-Jacques. *Wagner Androgyne: A Study in Interpretation*, trans. Stewart Spencer. Princeton, NJ: Princeton University Press, 1990. xx, 359pp. ISBN 0691091412 ML410.W13N3513 1993

At the heart of this study, as Nattiez himself writes (p. xiii), is a search for unity through perceptions and aspects of androgyny in the composer's life and especially his work. This is not a book about a "gay Wagner," but an attempt to reinterpret the music dramas in terms of mythic elements and the disciplines of structuralism and semiotics. Includes fourteen musical examples, several photographs of performance scenes, and quotations from a variety of sources. Also includes a useful list of Wagner's prose publications (pp. 303–22); extensive notes; a list of sources (pp. 339–51), many of them cited in few other Wagner bibliographies; and an index.

Reviewed with many qualifications, most of them concerning methodology—an obsession with many postmodern critics, especially insofar as issues of "political correctness" are concerned—by Bryan Hyer in the *Journal of the American Musicological Society* 47 (1994), pp. 531–40. Also reviewed by Peter Rabinowitz [*Opera Quarterly* 11/2 (1995), pp. 157–62]—who observes, however, that *Wagner Androgyne* serves "as a concentrated attack on contemporary interpretive techniques, particularly those practices that he gathers under the rubric of 'the hermeneutics of Undecidability,' " and that, as Nattiez puts it, "The author is not dead. He has merely been put to sleep by certain critics" (review, p. 158, quoting from item 991, p. 272).

Other studies devolving upon Wagner and postmodern critical issues include:

* Cicora, Mary A. *Modern Myths and Wagnerian Deconstructions.* Described as item 1012.

Includes "Conclusions: Wagner and Derrida" (pp. 207–10), as well as postmodern arguments of the author's own.

992. Deathridge, John. "Wagner and the Post-Modern." *Cambridge Opera Journal* 4 (1992), pp. 143–61. ISSN 0954–5867 (no LC number available)

Less an attempt to define the boundaries, character, or extent of postmodern Wagner studies than a consideration of Wagner's own contributions to the concept of "modern" in the nineteenth and early twentieth centuries. Among other subjects Deathridge also considers the roles played by Hegel, Baudelaire, the "Young Germany" movement, and Wagner himself in defining the notion of "modernity."

993. Janik, Allan. "Die Postmoderne bei 'Sankt' Offenbach: Neues von die Nietzsche-Wagner-Kontroverse." In: *Die Wiener Schule und das Hakenkreuz: Das Schicksal der Moderne im gesellschaftspolitischen Kontext des 20. Jahrhunderts*, ed. Otto Kolleritsch. Studien zur Wertungs-

forschung, 22. Vienna and Graz: Universal, 1990; pp. 145–55. ISBN 3702401955 ML55.S92 Heft 22

A brief review of the Wagner-Nietzsche relationship and Nietzsche's admiration for Offenbach's music, followed by a more careful evaluation of two articles about these subjects written by Viennese author, editor, publisher, and general eccentric Karl Kraus, and published in his remarkable newspaper *Die Fackel* [Nos. 270/271 (1909), pp. 1–18]. Janik also considers the implications of Offenbach's Jewish origins, and the origins and character of Hitler's regime.

994. Petty, Jonathan Christian. "Hanslick, Wagner, Chomsky: Mapping the Linguistic Parameters of Music." *Journal of the Royal Musical Association* 123 (1998), pp. 39–67. ML28.L8M8

Considers the ideas of all three figures—in Wagner's case (pp. 49–54) largely based on passages in *Opera and Drama*, and on the notion that feeling represents "an awareness of value" (p. 49)—in order to summarize and compare them. Includes lengthy quotations, mostly from non-Wagnerian sources, as well as a diagram.

Finally, much postmodern theorizing is presented in reviews of other studies, themselves often written by or attributed to still other postmodern authors. Among such reviews is:

995. McClatchie, Stephen. "Towards a Post-Modern Wagner." *Wagner* 13/3 (September 1992), pp. 108–21. ML410.W1A585

A review of item 990 that raises many of the issues and procedures associated with that remarkable volume. By no means unique; other extended and often contentious reviews of *Unsung Voices* include Lawrence Kramer's in *19th-Century Music* [15 (1991–1992), pp. 235–39]; and Richard Taruskin's in the *Cambridge Opera Journal* (cited under item 990).

NB: Postmodern criticism is concerned above all in certain musicological circles with "narrative" and hermeneutical exegeses of "narratives." Compare, for example, Cicora's chapter on *Holländer* (item 1012, pp. 25–54) with Arthur Groos's article "Back to the Future: Hermeneutic Fantasies in 'Der fliegende Holländer'," published in *19th Century Music* 19 (1995–1996), pp. 191–211. See also items 969–70.

XII

Wagner and Culture, Past and Present

Like other aspects of Wagner's career and influence, "cultural" issues can be difficult to separate from those involving the origins of individual operas, music dramas, and literary works, as well as criticism. The studies identified and described in this chapter, however, are all devoted primarily or even exclusively to Wagner's interaction with literature, mythology, psychology, and the visual arts, or his interest in the cultural accomplishments of other eras, or with "Wagnerisms" in nineteenth- and twentieth-century Europe and the Americas.

Unless otherwise noted, studies grouped under individual headings or explanatory observations are described in alphabetical order by author, editor, and/or title.

SURVEY STUDIES

Among the best introductions to Wagner's interest in and/or impact on other ages, arts, and national cultures is:

996. *Wagnerism in European Culture and Politics*, ed. David C. Large and William Weber, with Anne Dzamba Sessa. Ithaca, NY and London: Cornell University Press, 1984. 361pp. ISBN 0801416469 ML410.W1W18 1984

A collection of six important essays dealing with national topics—"Wagnerism, Wagnerians, and Italian Identity" by Marion S. Miller; "Wagner and Wagnerian Ideas in Russia" by Bernice Glatzer Rosenthal; "Wagner's Bayreuth Disciples" and "Art and Politics: Wagnerism in France," both by Gerald D. Turbow; "At Wagner's Shrine: British and American Wagnerians" by Sessa; and "Wagner, Wagnerism, and Musical Idealism," by Weber—together with an introduction, information about contributors, and a useful "Conclusion" (pp. 278–300) that summarizes the entire volume's contents. Among the editors' conclusions is that, although having been appropriated as man and artist by a variety of political factions over the years, Wagner and his music are "not by nature proto-fascist" (p. 278). Also includes notes (pp. 301–53) and an index. Reviewed in *Wagner* 7/2 (April 1986), pp. 63–65.

Other surveys of Wagner and cultural issues include:

997. Bertram, Johannes. *Mythos, Symbol, Idee in Richard Wagners Musik-Dramen.* Hamburg: Hamburger Kulturverlag, 1957. 336pp. ML410.W1B47

Devoted mostly to ideas and symbols, not all of them "mythic," associated with or underlying Wagner's librettos. Includes a two-page unpaginated psychological schema of *Parsifal* provided by Wagner's grandson. Also includes extensive quotations as well as a timeline of Wagner's life, works, and correspondence (pp. 321–33); concludes with a bibliography.

998. *Effetto Wagner dalla struttura alla ricezione,* ed. Lia Secci. Perugia: "Edizioni Scientifiche Italiane," 1986. x, 163pp. ML410.W13E25 1986 (no ISBN available)

A collection of essays ranging in subject matter from Walther Dürr on the *Wesendonck-Lieder* to Luigi Quattrocchi on Friedrich Hebbel's *Nibelungen* trilogy, and Isabella Nardi on D'Annunzio's Wagner writings; most of this volume, however, is devoted to issues of cultural history and reception. Includes two indexes, the second of which deals with Wagner's compositions and prose works; Dürr's article also includes several musical examples.

999. *Parole e musica. L'esperienza Wagneriana nella cultura fra romanticismo e decadentismo,* ed. Giuseppe Bevilacqua. Civiltà Veneziana saggi, 35. Florence: Leo S. Olschki, 1986. 227pp. ISBN 8822233972 ML410.W19P27 1986

Devolves upon Wagner's influence on various nations and cultural movements, the Italian Wagner reception among them. Includes item 535 as well as essays on Wagnerism in nineteenth- and twentieth-century England, Belgian Wagnerites and their writings, Wagner and the representation of nineteenth-century subjects in the works of Thomas Mann, Wagner and the Russian Alexander Blok, Wagner and Poland, and so on. Also includes ten plates depicting various individuals and places in Venice; these appear between pp. 144–45 of the text. The proceedings of a conference held in 1983 and sponsored by the Fondazione Giorgia Cini.

1000. *Von Wagner zum Wagnérisme: Musik, Literatur, Kunst, Politik*, ed. Annegret Fauser and Manuela Schwartz. Leipzig: Universitätsverlag, 1999. 642pp. ISBN 3933240697 (no LC number available)

Examines 'Wagnerisms" in late nineteenth- and early twentieth-century France, Germany, and Italy; in other words, a broad-based collection of essays on Wagnerian subjects. Includes Michele Cadot's "Un ardent wagnérien; Joséphin Péladan (1858–1918)" (pp. 475–83), Michael Meyer's "Wagners politische Stellungnahme im deutsch-französischen Krieg" (pp. 87–105), and Matthias Waschek's "Zum 'Wagnérisme' in den bildenden Künsten" (pp. 535–46)—the last unillustrated—as well as essays identified and cross-referenced under other items throughout the present volume. Also includes a scattering of musical examples and reproductions of a handful of caricatures and one or two programs and advertising posters. Some essays in English. Concludes with information about contributors (pp. 623–30) and an index of names. Published as the proceedings of a symposium of "Der Wagnerisme in der französischen Musik und Musikkultur (1861–1914)," held in June 1995 at the Konzerthaus, Berlin.

With regard to Péladan, see Isabelle Cazeaux's article " 'One Does Not Defend the Sun': Péladan and Wagner," published in *Music and Civilization: Essays in Honor of Paul Henry Lang*, ed. Edmond Strainchamps and Maria Rika Maniates (New York, 1984), pp. 93–101.

WAGNER AND THE PAST

Antiquity

By "antiquity" is meant the ancient Mediterranean world, especially Greece. A useful introduction to this subject is:

1001. Müller, Ulrika. "Wagner and Antiquity," trans. Stewart Spencer. In item 2, pp. 227–35.

Describes Wagner's lifelong interest in Greece and Greek drama, including the idea of "festival" in *Art and Revolution* in terms of classical theatrical productions, and "attempts to write in the antique manner"—the last referring to Wagner's plans to compose an *Achilles* and an *Alexander*. For Müller, however, "Wagner's greatest debt to the Greeks . . . and especially to Aeschylus is to be found in the *Ring*" (p. 233). See also item 893.

Other studies of Wagner's interest in the ancient Mediterranean world include:

1002. *Der Geist der Antike bei Richard Wagner*, ed. Gerhard Frommel. Berlin: "Verlag die Runde," 1933. 131pp. ML410.W1A16 1933

An extensive collection of quotations from Wagner's letters and prose works (*in Selbstzeugnissen*, as the title page says), all of them dealing with Greek drama, classical philosophy, Athenian society and politics, and so on. Includes a rather cursory introduction by Frommel as well as a list of sources (pp. 129–30). Not indexed.

*   Ewans, Michael. Wagner and Aeschylus: The "Ring" and the "Oresteia." Described as item 684.

1003. Lloyd-Jones, Hugh. "Wagner." In: Lloyd-Jones, *Blood for the Ghosts: Classical Influences in the 19th and 20th Centuries*. London: Duckworth, 1982; pp. 126–42. ISBN 0715615009 CB204.L59 1982

Concerned with Greek stories of Giants or Titans overthrowing or rebelling against the Gods, and especially with comparisons between such stories and Wagner's *Ring*. Illustrated with a photograph of a calyx krater depicting such a rebellion. Originally published in January 1987 in the *Times Literary Supplement* [London] and reprinted in *Wagner* 11/2 (April 1990), pp. 62–74. A broader discussion by Lloyd-Jones of Wagner's interest in ancient Greece may be found in "Wagner and the Greeks" (item 1, pp. 158–61), which summarizes classical notions and inspirations throughout Wagner's career, from his schooldays in Leipzig to "Promethean" aspects of Brünnhilde.

1004. Schadewaldt, Wolfgang. "Richard Wagner und die Griechen: Drei Bayreuther Vorträge." In: Schadewaldt, *Hellas und Hesperien: Gesammelte Vorträge zur Antike und zur neueren Literatur.* 2 vols.; Vol. 2: "Antike und Gegenwart" (Zurich: Artemis, 1970), pp. 341–405. PA27.S25

Three essays by a prominent classicist and expert on Greek culture and literature: "Richard Wagner und die Griechen" (pp. 343–65), a survey of the composer's knowledge of and involvement with things Greek; "Die Ringdichtung und Aischylos' 'Prometheus' " (pp. 365–86), which considers among other subjects, elements of suffering and defiance of the gods in the *Ring*; and "Nachlese" (pp. 386–405) devoted to additional observations on Wagner and antiquity. Includes a few footnotes.

1005. Braschowanoff [also Wrassiwanopulos-Braschowanoff], Georgi. *Richard Wagner und die Antike. Ein Beitrag zur kunstphilosophischen Waltanschauung Richard Wagners.* Dissertation: University of Erlangen, 1905; Bayreuth: Lorenz Eilwanger, 1905. 94pp. ML410.W19W8

Deals with Wagner's appropriation of ancient Greek ideas, motifs, and aspects of literary style and structure. Braschowanoff mentions Homer, Plato, the *Oresteia*, melody, and ἦθος (i.e., music's ability to move its listeners), as well as relationships between the classical world and the philosophies of Feuerbach and Schopenhauer. Also published in the *Bayreuther Blätter* 29–I, III (1906), pp. 6–67 and 100–113. See also Lada Stantschewa-Braschowanowa's article "Georgi Braschowanoff und seine Dissertation, 'Richard Wagner und die Antike,'" published in the supplement [= item 40] to *Die Musikforschung* 36/4 (October–December 1983); pp. 455–57. Among other interesting facts, that article's author points out that no one knows where and when Braschowanoff died.

The Middle Ages

Among the best discussions of Wagner's interest in "the medieval" is:

1006. *Richard Wagner und sein Mittelalter*, ed. Ursula and Ulrich Müller. Wort und Musik: Salzburger akademische Beiträge, 1. Anif/Salzburg: Ursula Müller-Speiser, 1989. iv, 335pp. ISBN 3851450019 ML410.W11R53 1989

Consists of item 850 as well as twelve other essays by Dieter Borchmeyer, Oswald Panagl, Stewart Spencer, and others, on "medieval" topics ranging from Wagner's unwritten opera *Erec und Enide* to the first complete translation of Wagner's writings into Arabic (by Mustafa Maher in 1987) to—fascinating, if not altogether important—an examination of "medieval" Wagnerian images in book illustrations and comic books! Illustrated with a variety of plates and scattered musical examples. See also item 834.

Briefer summaries of Wagner's medieval enthusiasms include:

1007. Mertens, Volker. "Wagner's Middle Ages," trans. Stewart Spencer. In item 2, pp. 236–68.

Discusses Wagner's transformation of medieval elements in *Tannhäuser*, *Lohengrin*, *Meistersinger*, and *Parsifal*, as well as in his theoretical writings. Mertens maintains that "the classical myths were incapable of satisfying Wagner's desire for originality," at least before they had been "assimilated into Germanic myth" (p. 237); he also acknowledges that "what is missing from Wagner's picture of the Middle Ages is its social aspect" and that even *Meistersinger* "is a backward projection of 19th-century society" (p. 267). Includes only brief quotations.

1008. Spencer, Stewart. "Wagner's Middle Ages." In item 1, pp. 164–67.

Examines Wagner's interest in the Middle Ages, especially in its literature—an interest that "went deeper than the superficialities of medieval local color" (p. 165). Spencer considers elements in the music dramas and prose works derived from the likes of poets Hartmann von Aue and Wolfram von Eschenbach, as well as such contemporary philologists as the Brothers Grimm, Karl Lachmann, and Samuel Lehrs; he also discusses the story of *Tannhäuser*, medieval notions about the "destructive nature of love," and the "incorrigible" perversity of women (p. 176).

Among older or more specialized studies of Wagner and the Middle Ages are:

1009. Golther, Wolfgang. *Zur deutschen Sage und Dichtung. Gesammelte Aufsätze*. Leipzig: Xenien, 1911. 327pp. ML410.W1G66

A collection of essays concerned especially with Germanic sources and versions of stories adapted for Wagner's stage works. Includes discussions of *Holländer* as presented in performances of 1901 and 1902, French and German versions of Wagner's *Tannhäuser* poem, Wagner's relationship to Schiller and Goethe, and the role of music in German classical drama.

1010. Koch, Ernst. *Richard Wagners Bühnenfestspiel "Der Ring des Nibelungen," in seinem Verhältniss zur alten Sage wie zur modernen Nibelungendichtung betrachtet*. Leipzig: C. F. Kahnt, 1875. 93pp. ML410.W15K7

Less a systematic study than a running commentary on the largely "medieval" contents of Wagner's librettos and their relationships to and/or borrowings from other authors. Outfitted with quotations from a variety of sources; Koch's chapter "Die moderne Nibelungendichtung bis auf Wagner" (pp. 25–45) identifies a large number of them. No illustrations, musical examples, or index; in fact, no table of contents.

*   Magee, Elizabeth. *Richard Wagner and the Nibelungs*. Described as item 663.

A careful study of Wagner's readings in and knowledge of medieval literature, especially associated with Dresden prior to 1849.

1011. Müller, Ulrich. "From 'Parsifal' to the Ban on Love: Wagner and the Middle Ages." *Wagner* 7/4 (October 1986), pp. 110–25. ML410.W1A595

Explains what "the medievalism of Wagner's works" looks like to a professional medievalist (p. 122). Documented with notes and supplemented with five production photos. Another version of this article appeared under the title "Vom Parzival zum Liebesverbot: Richard Wagner und das Mitte-lalter" in item 35, pp. 79–103.

WAGNER AND MYTHOLOGY

In addition to his interest in ancient and medieval mythologies, Wagner was him-self a mythmaker; furthermore, certain of his critics have evaluated "mythologi-cal" aspects of his life and thought. Perhaps the best introduction to these subjects is:

1012. Cicora, Mary A. *Modern Myths and Wagnerian Deconstructions: Hermeneutic Approaches to Wagner's Music-Dramas.* Contributions to the Study of Music and Dance, 57. Westport, CT: Greenwood, 2000. viii, 218pp. ISBN 0313305390 ML410.W13C6 2000

Analyzes how Wagner reassembled familiar mythical materials in *Hollän-der, Tannhäuser, Lohengrin, Tristan, Meistersinger,* and *Parsifal.* As Cicora herself explains, "By means of Romantic irony . . . each work . . . deconstructs its mythological or legendary nature, and unravels and disassembles the shreds of raw material that Wagner, in a collage-like way, has pasted together" (p. 3). Includes detailed notes and a bibliography (pp. 211–16), but no index. See also item 666.

Other studies of Wagner and the "mythological" include:

* Bertram, Johannes. *Mythos, Symbol, Idee in Richard Wagners Musik-Dra-men.* Described above as item 997.

1013. Cooke, Deryck. *I Saw the World End: A Study of Wagner's "Ring."* London and New York: Oxford University Press, 1991. 360pp. ISBN 0193153181 ML410.W15C67 1991

Examines mythic images, legendary figures, and modern critical concepts organized around two moments associated with Wagner's story and its sources: the renunciation of love by Alberich and the drawing of the sword Nothung from its tree. Also reevaluates the use of *Leitmotive* in analyses especially of the *Ring*; nevertheless, Cooke's study is centered on myth. Includes 61 musical examples as well as a bibliography (pp. 354–55). Indexed.

Originally published in 1979 and reviewed positively in *19th Century Music* 5 (1981–1982), pp. 247–51, where Cooke's thesis that "the *Ring* must be perceived on progressively deeper levels as it progresses" (review, p. 250) is defended.

1014. Edler, Arnfried. "Mythische und musikalische Struktur bei Wagner." In: *Musik und Dichtung: Neue Forschungsbeiträge: Viktor Pöschl zum 80. Geburtstag*, ed. Michael von Albrecht and Werner Schuberth. Frankfurt a.M. and New York: Peter Lang, 1990; pp. 331–50. ISBN 36331418582 ML3849.M98 1990

Examines Wagner's approach to composing his mature music dramas in terms of Ernst Cassirer's and Claude Lévi-Strauss's ideas about myth and thought patterns. Using the "sleep" motif in the *Ring*, Edler points out structural links between individual *Leitmotive* and mythic deep structures. Includes musical examples.

1015. Hartmann, Otto Julius. *Die geistigen Hintergrunde des Musikdramen Richard Wagners*. Schaffhausen: Novalis, 1976. 182pp. ISBN 3721400283 ML410.W13H17 1976

Refers to a miscellany of critical sources, images, methods, and tools— Homer's imagery, Christian symbolism (including symbols associated with the Grail legend), psychoanalysis, and so on—while exploring the intellectual content of Wagner's librettos from *Holländer* to *Parsifal*. Apparently a revision of Hartmann's doctoral dissertation, *Die Esoterik im Werke Richard Wagners* (Freiburg i.Br., 1960).

1016. Hübner, Kurt. "Wirklichkeit und Unwirklichkeit des Mythos in Richard Wagners Werk." *Jahrbuch des Staatlichen Instituts für Musikforschung Preusischer Kulturbesitz 1983–84* (Berlin, 1987), pp. 59–82. ML5.S74

Employs epistemological methods (i.e., *Wissenschaftstheorie*) to investigate connections involving "reality," the myths presented in Wagner's music dramas, and classical mythology. See also Ludwig Finscher's "Mythos und musikalische Struktur," published in item 670, pp. 27–37, which considers some of the same issues.

1017. Roch, Eckhard. *Psychodrama: Richard Wagner im Symbol*. Stuttgart and Weimar: J. B. Metzler, 1995. 640pp. ISBN 3476012727 ML410.W1R63 1995

Evaluates the world-symbolical legacy reflected in Wagner's works, especially throughout his massive music dramas. Among other symbols, icons, ideas, and myths, Roch discusses the stories of Narcissus, Oedipus, and the Grail legend, images of the Holy Family, notions of dramaturgy presented in Aristotle's *Poetics*, and "ecstasy." Includes a few musical examples as well as 34 black-and-white illustrations, among them a frontispiece photograph of the Regensburg "Walhalla" constructed between 1830 and

1842 by Ludwig I of Bavaria. Concludes with excepts from Wagner's prose works, especially *The Art-Work of the Future*, a bibliography (pp. 631–39), and information about the illustrations.

1018. Wilberg, Petra-Hildegard. *Richard Wagners mythische Welt. Versuch wider den Historismus*. Rombach Wissenschaft: Reihe Musicae, 1. Rombach: Rombach Verlag, 1996. 391pp. ISBN 3793091325 ML410.W13W42 1996X

Examines Wagner's fascination with myth in all its forms, including what the composer read, how mythic elements impacted upon his life and reputation, plans he made to write or compose unfinished or "imaginary" works dealing with both Germanic and non-Germanic mythologies, and so on. Equipped with a bibliography (pp. 355–88) but not an index.

WAGNER AND PSYCHOLOGY

1019. Vetter, Isolde. "Wagner in the History of Psychology," trans. Stewart Spencer. In item 2, pp. 118–55.

Considers, albeit briefly, virtually the entire Wagner "psychological" literature, including psychopathological character and behavior studies, psychobiographies, the writings of Jungian and transpersonal psychologists, issues associated with "ecstasy and eroticisation aroused by Wagner's music," and Wagner's influence on the Nazis. Vetter refers to rare or otherwise obscure sources omitted from the present research guide but cited in her essay by means of *sigla* and identified fully in item 2, pp. 655–80.

Portions of Vetter's work appeared originally in issues of the *Bayreuther Festspielprogramme* of 1990: III, pp. 42–44, 53–56; IV, pp. 51–70; V, pp. 49–54; and VI, pp. 56–58, 67–68; there they also appeared in French and German. See also items 1023 and 1121.

WAGNER IN EUROPEAN AND AMERICAN LITERATURE

General Studies

Most studies of Wagner and literature concentrate on individual authors or works, or on the literary products of particular nations, geographical regions, or linguistic communities. Exceptions include:

1020. Furness, Raymond. *Wagner and Literature*. New York: St. Martin's Press, 1982. xiii, 159pp. ISBN 0312853475 ML410.W13F95 1982

Briefly describes the extent of Wagner's literary influence, in terms of decadence, modernism, myth, parody, and persiflage. Includes a bibliography (pp. 149–54), as well as endnotes appended to each chapter; also includes scattered illustrations (identified on p. vi), among them comic book pages taken from item 105, as well as more familiar images by Aubrey Beardsley and Arthur Rackham. Co-published in Manchester, England, with the Manchester University Press. Reviewed with qualified praise in *Wagner* 3/4 (October 1982), pp. 126–28.

Furness's article "Wagner's Impact on Literature" (item 1, pp. 396–98) addresses more briefly some of the same subjects and works, including: the French Symbolists; Thomas Mann's *Wälsungsblut*; Claude Lévi-Strauss's celebration of Wagner as the "father of the structural analysis of myth" (item 1, p. 398); works by D. H. Lawrence, T. S. Eliot, and James Joyce; and parodies of Wagner in recent literature— among them, Anthony Burgess's *Worm and the Ring*, which depicts "'Albert Rich' in his pursuit of three giggling schoolgirls through the rain" (item 1, p. 398).

1021. Müller, Ulrich. "Wagner in Literature and Film," trans. Stewart Spencer. In item 2, pp. 373–93.

Considers primarily Europe's literary response to Wagner. Beginning with Baudelaire and other French writers, Müller briefly discusses "Wagnerian" novelists, poets, and playwrights of late nineteenth- and twentieth-century Italy, England, Scandinavia (Strindberg in Sweden), the Slavic countries (including Alexander Blok and Leo Tolstoy in Russia), and especially the German-speaking countries (pp. 382–86, including works by Karl Kraus, Heinrich and Thomas Mann, Robert Musil, and Friedrich Nietzsche). Supplemented with a "Postscript (1991)" devoted to developments since the 1986 German edition of item 2; chief among these are the "alternative versions of Wagner's music-dramas" produced on the fringe of the Bayreuth Festival by Uwe Hoppe and the Studiobühne Schützenhaus (p. 392). With regard to Tolstoy, see also item 906n.

Other studies of Wagner and literature "in general" include:

1022. Jacobson, Anna. *Nachklänge Richard Wagners im Roman.* Beiträge zur neueren Literaturgeschichte, Neue Folge, 20. Heidelberg: Carl Winters, 1932. viii, 134pp. ML410.W1J2

Summarizes Wagner's influence on the modern European novel. Jacobson discusses German-language authors—including Max Chop, Hermann Hesse, Paul Heyse, Heinrich Mann, Arthur Schnitzler, and Arnold

Zweig—as well as English and American authors Willa Cather, Somerset Maugham, and George Moore; she also considers novels that depict all or parts of Wagner's life, especially those concerning the composer's relationship with Ludwig II. Includes a bibliography (pp. 130–33) that identifies fictional works by category, then in chronological order of publication.

1023. Koppen, Erwin. *Dekadenter Wagnerismus: Studien zur europäischen Literatur des Fin de siècle.* Komparistische Studien—Beihefte zu "arcadia": Zeitschrift für vergleichende Literaturwissenschaft, 2. Berlin: and New York: de Gruyter, 1973. viii, 386pp. ISBN 3110043882 ML410.W19K75

Considers "decadence" as a phenomenon in its own right, and more especially in terms of Wagner's influence on late nineteenth- and early twentieth-century European literary culture. Koppen grapples with the *Revue Wagnérienne* (item 54), "decadent" sexuality and eroticism as embodied in Beardsley's *Venus and Tannhäuser*, Thomas Mann's *Death in Venice*, and Catulle Mendès's *Zo'har*, the "apocalyptic" character of Mann's *Buddenbrooks*, and *fin-de-siècle* psychological assessments of Wagner as a "degenerate" personality. Includes a valuable bibliography (pp. 341–74); concludes with an index. Reviewed by Reinhold Brinkmann in *Die Musikforschung* 29 (1976), pp. 343–45.

Studies of Wagner and Individual National Literatures

American Literature: see also item 1027.
1024. Briggs, Harald E. *Richard Wagner and American Music-Literary Activity from 1850 to 1920.* Dissertation: Indiana University, 1989. viii, 365pp. ML410.W12U5 1989a

Examines the contents of three important turn-of-the-century American magazines—*Century, Cosmopolitan,* and *Harper's*—and their Wagnerian contents. Unfortunately, due to poor photoreproduction of Briggs's typescript, some of the facsimiles he refers to are almost illegible. Outfitted with a bibliography but no index.

British Literature: see also items 754 and 1045.
Wagner's influence on British writers was greater than often acknowledged. Useful surveys of that influence, which extended to a few British artists and illustrators, include:

1025. DiGaetani, John. *Richard Wagner and the Modern British Novel*. Rutherford, NJ: Fairleigh Dickinson University Press, 1978. 179pp. ISBN 083861955X PR888.W34D5

Deals primarily with on Joseph Conrad, Forster, Joyce, Lawrence, and Virginia Woolf. DiGaetani addresses Wagnerian allusions in the novels of all five authors and possible influence on their forms of fictional organization. Includes a bibliography of primary and secondary sources (pp. 164–75); concludes with an index.

1026. Moser, Max. *Richard Wagner in der englischen Literatur des XIX. Jahrhunderts*. "Schweizer anglistische Arbeiten" [unnumbered]. Bern: A. Francke, 1938. 118pp. ML410.W12G76

Considers Wagnerian aspects of fiction, poetry, plays, and other artworks by Beardsley, William Morris, John Payne, the Rossettis, Bernard Shaw, Algernon Charles Swinburne, and especially Alfred, Lord Tennyson. Includes quotations from a variety of primary sources; concludes with a brief bibliography.

Other studies concentrate on individual writers or schools:

T. S. Eliot
1027. Martin, Stoddard. *Wagner to "The Waste Land": A Study of the Relationship of Wagner to English Literature*. London: Macmillan, 1982. x, 277pp. ISBN 0333289986 PR486.W34M37

Comments on Wagnerian elements in the American-born poet's works, as well as those of the French Symbolists, Joyce, Lawrence, Shaw, Swinburne, Arthur Symons, Oscar Wilde, and William Butler Yeats. Martin quotes extensively from works by these and other authors and even includes one or two scattered musical examples depicting various *Leitmotive*. Also includes detailed notes (pp. 242–66) and an index.

William Shakespeare
1028. Inwood, Margaret. *The Influence of Shakespeare on Richard Wagner*. Studies in History and Interpretation of Music, 64. Lewiston, NY: Edwin Mellen, 2000. xx, 213pp. ISBN 0773477748 ML410.W19I59 1999

Treats Shakespeare as one of the most important influences on Wagner's theoretical writings and music dramas. Inwood's most interesting chapter traces "The Use of Motifs by Shakespeare and Wagner" (pp. 55–122). Includes 20 motivic musical examples as well as quotations from the texts of such different plays as *Henry IV, King Lear, Measure for Measure, Per-*

icles, and *A Winter's Tale,* the librettos for *Das Liebesverbot, Lohengrin, Rheingold, Siegfried,* and *Tristan,* and a variety of the composer's prose works, including his essay on Liszt's symphonic Poems. Concludes with a synopsis (pp. 199–203), a list of primary and secondary sources (pp. 205–208), and an index.

1029. Istel, Edgar. "Wagner and Shakespeare," trans. Theodore Baker. *The Musical Quarterly* 8 (1922), pp. 495–509. ML1.M725

Almost entirely taken up with a discussion of textual similarities and differences between Shakespeare's *Measure for Measure* and the libretto of Wagner's *Liebesverbot.* On the other hand, Istel reminds us that the youthful Wagner dreamed of combining the talents of the English playwright with those of Beethoven to create an entirely new kind of music drama, and that Shakespeare was "of the greatest importance for the totality of [Wagner's] artistic view of life" (p. 507). Includes three short musical examples.

French Literature
Among the best and broadest introductions to this subject are the following volumes:

1030. Hartman, Edward. *French Literary Wagnerism.* New York: Garland, 1988. xii, 131pp. ISBN 0824074890 PQ295.W33H37 1988

Explores French responses to Wagner's art and theories, including those of such "anticipators" of *Wagnérisme* as Honoré de Balzac, Gérard de Nerval, and George Sand, as well as those of such early supporters as Judith Gautier, Villiers d'Isle-Adam, and Edouard Schuré. Hartman also considers Wagnerian elements in works by Huysmans, Proust, and Zola, and in symbolist poetry. Concludes with a list of contributors to the *Revue Wagnérienne* (item 54) and a collection of sonnets written by lesser-known French Wagnerian poets. Also contains a useful bibliography (pp. 121–27); concludes with an index.

1031. Jäckel, Kurt. *Richard Wagner in der französischen Literatur.* Romantische Reihe, 3. 2 vols. Breslau: Priebatsch, 1931–1932. ML410.W12F74

A wide-ranging survey of Wagner's influence not only on French poetry and prose, but on painters and the whole of the symbolist movement. Vol. 1 discusses Stéphane Mallarmé, Paul Verlaine, Paul Valéry, and other symbolistes; Vol. 2 takes up Catulle Mendès (pp. 24–40; see also item 1037), Marcel Proust (pp. 209–42), André Suarès, and so on. Illustrated in Vol. 1

with black-and-white reproductions of Rédon's *Brünnhilde*, Fantin-Latour's *L'evocation d'Erda*, and—as a frontispiece—Renoir's portrait of the composer. Each volume separately indexed.

Charles Baudelaire

1032. Miner, Margaret. *Resonant Gaps: Between Baudelaire & Wagner*. Athens and London: University of Georgia Press, 1995. x, 254pp. ISBN 0820317098 ML80.B35M5 1995

Examines Baudelaire's essay of 1861 (item 976). In two appendices Miner also provides its complete text (pp. 167–96; see also item 976), as well as a piano reduction of the Prelude to *Lohengrin* (pp. 197–201). Concludes with a useful bibliography (pp. 239–47) and an index. Based on the author's Yale University doctoral dissertation, *Between Music and Letters: Baudelaire's "Richard Wagner et 'Tannhäuser' à Paris"* (Ann Arbor, MI, 1990); this microfilm publication also includes a bibliography (pp. 181–86).

Less comprehensive but nevertheless useful is:

1033. Jackson, John E. "Baudelaire and Wagner, or The Meeting of Two Modern Minds." *Programmhefte der Bayreuther Festspiele* VII (1991), pp. 36–50. ML410.W2B26

Explains that Baudelaire not only was one of Wagner's "greatest and earliest admirers" and the author of an essay on *Tannhäuser* in its 1861 Paris production (p. 36), but also shared with the composer a "conception of death which, far from viewing it as a wellspring of anxiety, transformed it instead into an object of longing" (p. 37). Includes quotations from Baudelaire's poetry and prose, as well as the *Holländer* libretto. Also available in French and German in the same volume.

Paul Claudel

1034. Claudel, Paul. *Richard Wagner. Rêverie d'un poëte français*, ed. Michel Malicet. Centre de recherches de littérature française (XIXe et XXe siècles), 1. Paris: "Les Belles-Lettres," 1970. 179pp. ML410.W205C6

A critical edition of the controversial poet's 895-line Wagnerian poem, originally published in 1927 and also reprinted in July 1934 in the *Revue de Paris*. Massively documented: the endnotes alone fill pp. 85–176.

Additional information about Wagner's influence on Claudel's poetry and political notions may be found in:

1035. Bancroft, David. "Claudel on Wagner." *Music & Letters* 50 (1969), pp. 439–52. ML5.M64

Examines especially Claudel's opposition to Wagner during the later 1930s, a reaction that extended to the poet "as a critic, as an aesthete, and even as a Catholic" (p. 439). Includes quotations in French from the collected edition of Claudel's works, including his essay *Le Poison wagnérien.*

Stéphane Mallarmé

1036. Zimmermann, Michael. *"Träumerei eines französischen Dichters": Stéphane Mallarmé und Richard Wagner.* Berliner musikwissenschaftliche Arbeiten, 20. Munich and Salzburg: Emil Katzbichler, 1981. 171pp. ISBN 3873970600 ML80.M15Z54

Deals with "decadence" in France near the end of the nineteenth century, and especially with Mallarmé's advocacy of Wagner's music and artistic influence. Zimmermann provides several diagrams as well as facsimiles both from the first volume of the *Revue Wagnérienne* published in Paris in 1885 and 1886 (*Revue*, pp. 195–200; Zimmermann, pp. 111–16), and from Mallarmé's *Divagtions*, published in Paris in 1897 (Mallarmé, pp. 141–50; Zimmermann, pp. 117–26). Equipped with source citations in the form of footnotes. Unindexed.

Joseph Winkel's *Mallarmé-Wagner-Wagnerismus* (Buckeburg, 1935) also reviews Mallarmé's life, and contributions to the *Revue Wagnérienne,* as well as *L'après-midi d'un Faune,* and *Un Coup de dés* in light of Wagner's influence.

Catulle Mendès

1037. Festerling, Wilhelm. *Catulle Mendèz' Beziehungen zu Richard Wagner.* Greifswald: Julius Abel, 1913. 139pp. (no LC number available)

Reviews Mendèz's career, discusses his personal and professional relationships with Wagner, and evaluates Wagnerian (or "Parnassian") elements in Mendèz's own poetry, as well as his biography of Wagner and the essays Mendèz published in a variety of periodicals, including the *Revue Wagnérienne* he helped found in 1885. Includes a brief but useful bibliography (pp. 5–7) as well as extensive quotations from Mendez's works. A published dissertation.

Jean-Paul Sartre

1038. Keefe, Simon P., and Terry Keefe. "Sartre's Wagner." *The Musical Times* 137/1846 (December 1996), pp. 9–11. ML5.M85

Deals with Sartre's short story "Une défaite," concerning Wagner, his wife Cosima, and Friedrich Nietzsche. Wagner becomes "Richard Organte" in the story and is described in quite negative terms, perhaps—as the Keefes suggest—because Sartre was reminded of similarities between the composer and Sartre's maternal grandfather, Charles Schweitzer.

Emile Zola

1039. Fantin-Epstein, Marie-Bernadette. "Richard Wagner—Emile Zola: Analogies et correspondences." *Les cahiers de littératures: Textes, images, musique,* ed. Andrée Mansau and Louis Cabanès. Toulouse: Université de Toulouse II, 1992. ISSN 0563–9751 (no LC number available)

Describes Zola's place among French Wagnerians, and discusses Wagnerian elements in his *La faute de l'Abbé Mouret* and *La curée,* Zola's libretto for Alfred Bruneau's opera *Messidor;* also considers analogies between that work and *Rheingold.* Includes several musical examples. NB: each issue of the *Cahiers* is sometimes cataloged by subtitle.

German Literature
Again, most studies concentrate on individual authors and their works. Exceptions include these two useful book-length surveys:

1040. Galli, Hans. *Richard Wagner und die deutsche Klassik.* Bern and Leipzig: Paul Haupt, 1936. 94pp. ML410.W19G3

Examines Wagner's relationship with Schiller and Goethe rather than German classical music. Also considers what Wagner learned from Schiller's and Goethe's plays, Wagner and "classical" treatments of German myths, links between Goethe's *Faust* and Wagner's *Faust* overture, and so on. Includes a short bibliography (pp. 7–8). With regard to Faust, see Joachim Müller's "Richard Wagner über Goethes Faust" in Müller's *Neue Goethe-Studien* (Halle a.d.S., 1969), pp. 225–233.

1041. Park, Rosemary. *Das Bild von Richard Wagners Tristan und Isolde in der deutschen Literatur.* Deutsche Arbeiten der Universität Köln, 9. Jena: Eugen Diederich, 1935. 141pp. ML410.W14P23

A study especially of the influence exerted by Wagner's *Tristan* on the "Tristans" of Herwegh and Thomas Mann, as well as on the novels and non-fiction of Paul Henze, Nietzsche, Franz Werfel, and Bernard Shaw. Park also provides information about the origins of Wagner's music drama and its early reception. Handsomely printed in *Fraktur.* Concludes with a useful bibliography.

Berthold Brecht

1042. Brown, Hilda Meldrum. *Leitmotiv and Drama: Wagner, Brecht, and the Limits of "Epic" Theater.* Oxford: Clarendon, 1991. 217pp. ISBN 0198162278 PT2603.R397Z58113 1991

Primarily of interest to Wagner scholars for its chapter "Leitmotiv and Commentary in Richard Wagner's Theory of Drama" (pp. 25–67), and for its three "select bibliographies" (pp. 206–11), the second of which— "Wagner, "Gesamtkunstwerk,' Leitmotiv" (pp. 207–09)—identifies a few sources not mentioned in the present research guide. Indexed. NB: Brown means something rather different and much more literary by "Leitmotiv" than do most students of Wagner's music dramas. Furthermore, Brown never addresses head-on whether Wagner did influence Brecht.

Thomas Mann

1043. Emig, Christine. *Arbeit am Inzest: Richard Wagner und Thomas Mann.* Heidelberger Beiträge zur deutschen Literatur, 1. Frankfurt a.M. and New York: Peter Lang, 1998. 284pp. ISBN 3631327331 PT2625.A44Z552 1998X

Explores incestuous situations in Mann's *Felix Krull, Königliche Hochheit,* and other novellas, and in certain aspects of Wagner's music dramas, especially the Wotan-Brünnhilde relationship in the *Ring.* Emig also refers to the story of Oedipus, the old Germanic sagas, the *Nibelungenlied,* Freud's psychoanalytic writings, and other sources Wagner and/or Mann drew upon or knew of. Illustrated with several diagrams, among them a table of dates associated with the origins of the various *Ring* dramas (p. 283); also includes an excellent bibliography (pp. 263–81). An earlier version of this study was defended in 1996 as a doctoral dissertation at the University of Heidelberg. See also items 981–83.

1044. Gregor-Dellin, Martin. *Wagner und kein Ende. Richard Wagner im Spiegel von Thomas Manns Prosawerk: eine Studie.* Bayreuth: Edition Musica, 1958. 70pp. PT2625.A44Z575

A pamphlet-length review of Mann's several responses to Wagner's influence; these include *Buddenbrooks* as well as the novellas *Tristan* and *Wälsungenblut.* With regard to the last of these works, see also Nachum Schoffman, "Mann's 'Wälsungenblut' and Wagner's 'Walküre,' " in *The Music Review* 55 (1994), pp. 293–310. See item 38.

Irish Literature

1045. Martin, Timothy. *Joyce and Wagner: A Study of Influence.* Cambridge and London: Cambridge University Press, 1991. xviii, 287pp. ISBN 0521394872 PR6019.O9Z7268 1991

An outstanding reconsideration of a writer who, like his nineteenth-century predecessor, "exploit[s] the resources of myth, emphasize[s] sexual themes, pursue[s] 'totality' of form and subject matter, and represent[s] the

'modern' or 'revolutionary' in art" (p. xi). Martin tackles Joyce's relationship to literary Wagnerism; the figure of the Wandering Jew especially in
Ulysses; and the theme of redemption in *Tannhäuser*, *Tristan*, *Exiles*,
Finnegan's Wake, and other works. Includes a list of *sigla* (pp. xvii–xviii)
as well as an appendix identifying, line by line, hundreds of direct or indirect allusions in Joyce's literary works to Wagner's life and music dramas
from *Holländer* to *Parsifal* (pp. 185–221). Also contains copious endnotes
(pp. 222–58), and a list of primary and secondary sources (pp. 259–77).
Concludes with an index. See also item 941.

Italian Literature

*Studies of this subject deal largely with a few figures, especially Gabriele
D'Annunzio:*

1046. Donati-Pettèni, G. *D'Annunzio e Wagner*. Florence: Felice le Monnier,
      1923. xii, 156pp. PQ4804.D6

   Concerned in part with Wagner's influence on the Italian "warrior-poet,"
   which Donati-Pettèni discusses in an essay that shares the same title as his
   volume (pp. 19–87). Concludes with a bibliography limited to editions of
   D'Annunzio's works (pp. 141–56), and a one-page index.

1047. Schaffman, Nachum. "D'Annunzio and Mann: Antithetical Wagnerisms."
      Journal of Musicology 11/4 (Fall 1993), pp. 499–524. ML1.J693

   Examines figures the author considers in terms of their fascist (D'Annunzio) and anti-fascist (Mann) approaches to Wagner, an individual they both
   respected and learned from. As Schaffman explains, "D'Annunzio
   embraces Wagner's mythical conceptions as consummations of personal,
   esthetic, and national ideals. Mann, on the other hand, perceives the peril
   in Wagner's seductiveness" (p. 499). Accompanied by three musical examples, all from *Tristan*; concludes with a table comparing passages found in
   Wagner's *Tristan* libretto, Mann's *Tristan* novella, and D'Annunzio's *Tri-
   onfo della Morte*.

WAGNER AND "WAGNERISMS"

Survey Studies

*There have been many "Wagnerisms"—which is to say, many movements
that have, in whatever ways or for whatever reasons, self-consciously embraced Wagner as idol or inspiration. Among the few surveys of these movements is:*

1048. *Les Symbolistes et Richard Wagner* = Die Symbolisten und Richard Wagner, ed. Wolfgang Storch and Josef Mackert. Berlin: Hentrich, 1991. 216pp. + "Beiheft" (51pp.). ISBN 3894680083 ML410.W19S98 1991

The proceedings and "program notes" associated with four events: conferences in Berlin and Brussels held during Fall 1991, a complete performance of the *Ring* presented at the Théâtre de la monnaie, Brussels, and a "Filmprogramm Richard Wagner" sponsored by the Goethe-Institut, Berlin. The principal volume ("Les Symbolistes") contains the conference proceedings, as well as a timeline covering the years 1839 to 1917 (pp. 197–200), a catalog of artworks reproduced or discussed in the volume itself (pp. 201–10), and information about contributors; the supplement ("Die Symbolisten"), separately bound and inserted into the larger volume, consists of German translations of well-known Wagnerian essays by Pierre Boulez, William Morris, Susan Sontag, and so on. Illustrated throughout with high-quality reproductions of paintings, drawings, etchings, and woodblock prints, many in color. Also contains a few musical examples.

Briefer surveys of "Wagnerisms" include:

1049. Koppen, Erwin. "Wagnerism as Concept and Phenomenon," trans. Erika and Martin Swales. In item 2, pp. 343–53.

Explains that late nineteenth-century national Wagnerisms, all of them based on "predominantly, if not exclusively, *extramusical*" forms of reception and influence, involved the "worship . . . of particular spiritual, literary, and other currents and conceptions" in the composer's life and work, as well as on "certain programs and ideologies" projected more or less plausibly onto Wagner's legacy (p. 343; italics in the original). Koppen devotes much of his attention to Baudelaire's ground-breaking *Tannhäuser* essay, as well as magazines such as the *Revue wagnérienne* and *The Meister* (item 55), links between Wagner and the Symbolist movement in literature, "decadence," Shaw's arguments in *The Perfect Wagnerite* (item 987), and so on.

1050. Large, David G. "Posthumous Reputation and Influences." In item 1, pp. 384–89.

Begins with "Wagnerism" as an international phenomenon, then goes on to discuss various later nineteenth- and earlier twentieth-century Wagnerian movements in France, Great Britain, Italy, Russia, and Germany herself. Large refers in passing to such "fan magazines" as the *Cronaca Wagneriana, The Meister*, and the *Revue Wagnérienne,* as well as the less familiar *Mir iskoustva* (*World of Art*) associated with Sergei Diaghilev's

Ballet Russes. Large also mentions Wilhelm II, the "Bayreuth Circle," and Hitler, as well as Prussian generals who, during the First World War, named "German military positions on the front after Wotan, Siegfried, Brünnhilde, and Hunding" (p. 389).

A somewhat more specialized study concentrates on reactions to Wagner near the end of World War I:

1051. Mornald, Jean. *Le cas Wagner. Le musique pendant la guerre.* Paris: Georges Crès et Cie, 1920. 281pp. (no LC number available)

Includes "Le cas Wagner" (pp. 3–28), "Arguments Wagnerphobes" (pp. 136–51), and "Wagner en Italie" (pp. 213–23), which comprise at most half of Mornald's volume. Concludes with an appendix reproducing the letters about Wagner addressed to the editors of French newspapers between 1915 and 1916 (pp. 246–62), and with an index of names (pp. 263–79). Of particular relevance to the Wagner reception in post–World War I Europe in general, and within France in particular.

Wagnerisms in Various Nations and Parts of Europe

America

1052. Horowitz, Joseph. *Wagner Nights: An American History.* Berkeley and London: University of California Press, 1994. xiv, 389pp. ISBN 0520083946 ML410.W13H7 1994

Discusses Wagner performances and their reception in the United States between the American Civil War and the beginning of World War I. Horowitz pays special attention to the role played by Anton Seidl as conductor and Wagnerian, as well as to ways Wagnerism impacted upon certain groups of listeners, especially "respectable" women. Illustrations include eighteen pictures of Seidl and other turn-of-the-century Wagner performers, documentary facsimiles, and other images. Supplemented by endnotes (pp. 353–76); concludes with an index. See also item 815 as well as Michael Saffle's " 'Parsifal' Performances in America, 1886–1903: Changing Taste and the Popular Press," published in *Opera and the Golden West: The Past, Present, and Future of Opera in the U.S.A.,* ed. John L. DiGaetani and Josef P. Sirefman (Madison, WI, London, and Toronto, 1994), pp. 161–68.

Less comprehensive but also useful is:

1053. Horowitz, Joseph. "Finding a 'Real Self': American Women and the Wagner Cult of the Late 19th Century." *The Musical Quarterly* 78 (1994), pp. 189–205. ML1.M725

Examines the influence Wagner and his heroines, including Elisabeth and Senta, had on such individuals as Willa Cather, Mabel Dodge Luhan, and Ella Wheeler Wilcox. To these and other women, Horowitz maintains, Wagner's female characters served as "models of exalted purity" (p. 198). Includes lengthy quotations as well as three illustrations, the last a facsimile of the 1889 Brighton Beach program cover for concerts conducted by Seidl. Much of this material also appears in item 1052.

Among several dozen books and articles dealing with the American Wagner reception (many of them antiquated and/or difficult to obtain) is this readily available essay:

1054. Peretti, Burton W. "Democratic Leitmotivs in the American Reception of Wagner." *19th Century Music* 13 (1989–1990), pp. 28–38. ML1N77

Covers some of the same ground as items 1052–53 above, although Peretti also points out that, after 1890 or so, Americans were less likely to associate Wagner with "democratization." Includes a cartoon ridiculing "Parsifalitis" published originally in December 1903 in the *New York Times*.

Austria

1055. McGrath, William. *Wagnerism in Austria: The Regeneration of Culture Through the Spirit of Music*. Dissertation: University of California, Berkeley, 1965. 311pp. (no LC number available)

Not seen; summarized in *Dissertation Abstracts International* 26/12 (June 1966), pp. 7284–85. According to this source, McGrath's work deals primarily with a group of liberal students known as the "Pernerstorfer Circle"—its members included Victor Adler, Gustav Mahler and, briefly, Hugo Wolf, as well as Engelbert Pernerstorfer himself—who, during the last decades of the nineteenth century, evolved "a philosophical alternative to the liberal outlook," and one in which "Wagnerianism played a crucial role." McGrath's dissertation is often cited in bibliographies, but his volume *Dionysian Art and Populist Politics in Austria* (Yale University Press, 1974) is better known; unhappily, it received a disparaging review from Thomas Bauman in *19th Century Music* 4 (1980–1981), pp. 77–79.

Belgium: see "Flanders."

Bohemia (formerly part of Czechoslovakia; today part of the Czech Republic)

1056. Vyslouzil, Jiří. "On Prague's 'Wagnerians' and Czech 'Wagnerism.'" *Programmhefte der Bayreuther Festspiele* I (1993), pp. 59–71. ML410.W2B26

Briefly identifies positive and negative aspects of Czech "Wagnerianism"—a word the author prefers to "Wagnerism" because the former adheres better to the principles of Czech word construction—mostly in the last half of the nineteenth century. Among other figures, Vysloužil discusses the impact of Wagner's music on that of Antonín Dvořák. Available in French and German. See also item 550.

Brazil

1057. Chaves, Edgard de Brito, Jr. *Wagner e o Brasil (Rio de Janeiro)*. Rio de Janeiro: Emebê, 1976. xi, 64pp. ML410.W12B72 (no ISBN available)

Not seen: cited in the Library of Congress on-line catalog, but unavailable for examination when the present author visited the library's music division in person. In Portuguese.

Catalonia: see "Spain"

Czechoslovakia / Czech Republic: see "Bohemia"

England

1058. Sessa, Anne Dzamba. *Richard Wagner and the English*. Rutherford, WI: Fairleigh Dickinson University Press; and London: Associated University Presses, 1979. 191pp. ISBN 0838620558 ML410.W12E5

Describes England's Wagner reception from the mid-Victorian era to 1914. Sessa evaluates the significance of David Irvine's Wagner studies, including *"Parsifal" and Wagner's Christianity* and Ernest Newman's review of that work (pp. 79–85); she also touches on the ideas and publications of Shaw, Ellis, Newman, and other important English Wagnerians. Illustrated with a frontispiece facsimile of a cover from an issue of *The Meister*. Includes extensive notes (pp. 150–71) and a bibliography (pp. 172–85); concludes with an index. Reviewed with qualifications—and together with items 31, 303, and 654—by John Deathridge in *19th Century Music* 5 (1981–1982), pp. 81–89.

Among a dozen or more specialized studies devoted to particular aspects of Wagner's reception in England is:

1059. Blissett, William. "Ernest Newman and English Wagnerism." *Music & Letters* 40 (1959), pp. 311–23. ML5.M64

Considers Shaw's and Irvine's opinions, then turns to Ernest Newman and his publications. Blissett quotes extensively from Newman on programmatic and "absolute" compositions, but provides no bibliographic citations.

Flanders

1060. Wauters, Karel. *Wagner en Vlaanderen, 1844–1914. Cultuurhistorische Studie*. Ghent: "Secretariaat van de Koninklijke Academie voor Nederlandse Taal- en Letterkunde," 1983. 539pp. ML410.W13W29 1983 (no ISBN available)

A thoroughly documented examination of Wagner publications, performances, and influences in the European Lowlands prior to the outbreak of World War I. Illustrated with a few documentary facsimiles and outfitted with a superb bibliography of English, French, German, and Italian sources, as well as articles and essays in a variety of Flemish-language publications (pp. 506–26; described as item 78). Among the individuals and publications discussed are singers Emiel Blauwaert and Ernst van Dyck; authors and commentators Pol de Mont, Albrecht Rodenbach, Edgar Tinel, Omer Wattez; Alfred Hegenscheidt's *Wagner-sonnetten*; and a host of newspapers and their critics.

Other studies of Wagner and Europe's Lowlands include Michele Isaac's "Reception et expansion de l'oeuvre de Richard Wagner à Liège, 1855–1914," published in the *Revue de la Société Liègeoise de Musicologie* No. 10 (1998), pp. 5–35.

France

In no other country, not even Germany, did Wagner exert a more powerful influence on late nineteenth-century culture than in France. Among several useful introductions to Wagnérisme *and French culture is:*

1061. Guichard, Léon. *Le Musique et les letters en France au temps du Wagnérisme*. Université de Grenoble: Publications de la Faculté des Lettres et Sciences Humaines, 29. Paris: Presses Univérsitaires de France, 1963. 354pp. ML270.G853

Devoted to late nineteenth- and early twentieth-century France, especially French literature. Guichard discusses Wagner's visits to Paris, his influence on Baudelaire, and Wagnerian elements in the works of Dujardin, Schuré, Verlaine, and Zola. Includes lists of French Wagner premiere performances (pp. 246–49) and "principaux texts français inspirés par les oeuvres de Richard Wagner" (pp. 249–56), as well as a brief catalog of etchings, lithographs, and other illustrations (*tableaux*) on Wagnerian subjects by the likes of Gustave Doré, Fantin-Latour, de Groux, and Odilon

Redon (pp. 256–58). Also includes notes (pp. 259–322), a bibliography (pp. 325–46), and an index of names.

Other survey studies include:

1062. Beaufils, Marcel. *Wagner et le wagnérisme*. Paris: Editions Montaigne, 1946. 380pp. ML410.W1B25

Describes the Wagner reception in France, mostly between the 1840s and the 1870s, and largely in terms of Mallarmé; includes additional comments about later French composers such as Debussy. A few hand-copied musical examples are scattered through the text, but Beaufils's study lacks other kinds of illustrations, a bibliography, or an index.

1063. Lassere, Pierre. "Wagner, the Poet" and "Wagner, the Musician." In: Lassere, *The Spirit of French Music*, trans. Denis Turner. London: Kegan Paul, Trench, Trübner & Co., 1921; pp. 148–85 and 186–218. ML270.4.L28T9

Post–World War I observations on French culture's debt to one of Germany's most nationalistic composers. Lasserre identifies what he considers Wagner's "gross and glaring" musical-dramatic methods, among them *Leitmotive*; he also asserts that Wagner "administered a salutary shock" to mid- and late-nineteenth-century France, and "brought comfort and support" to such musicians as Eduard Lalo, Jules Massenet, Camille Saint-Saëns, and César Franck (pp. 214–15). No illustrations or musical examples.

　　Co-published in New York City with E. P. Dutton & Co. Published originally under the title *L'Esprit de la musique française* (Paris, 1917).

1064. *Wagner et la France* = *La Revue musicale*, "Numéro spécial" (1 October 1923); reprinted New York: Da Capo, 1977. 192pp. ISBN 0306708892 ML410.W12F747

A collection of articles, published as a special issue of one of France's most important music magazines. Includes items 269 and 366 as well as composer Paul Dukas on "L'influence Wagnérienne," "Les premiers Amis français de Wagner" by Maxime Leroy, "Richard Wagner et l'opéra français du début du XIXe siècle" by André Schaeffer, an all-too-brief comment on "Wagner et Renoir," by Henry Prunières, and so on. Also includes scattered musical examples and illustrations. Paginated separately from other 1923 *Revue* issues. See also item 63.

Several anthologies have also been devoted to French Wagnerism:

1065. Henry, Ruth, and Walter Mönch. *Richard Wagner und Frankreich.* Bayreuth: Edition Musica, 1977. 68pp. ML410.W131H46 (no ISBN available)

Consists of two essays—Henry's "Was Tristan French? Variations and Constants in the French View of Wagner," and Mönch's "Wagner: A German Cosmopolitan: The Importance of His Experiences in Paris"—translated and printed in French and German, as well as English. Originally published together in the Bayreuth *Festspielprogramme* for 1976.

1066. Linden, Brigitte. "Umdeutung und Neubeginn durch Richard Wagners 'Tristan und Isolde,' " and "Die Rezeptions der Tristanoper zur Zeit des französischen Wagnerismus (1880–1910)." Both in Linden, *Die Rezeption des Tristanstoffs in Frankreich vom Ende des 18. bis zum Beginn des 20. Jahrhunderts.* Europäische Handschulschriften, 134. Frankfurt a.M.: Peter Lang, 1988; pp. 91–104, 105–37. ISBN 3631406835 PQ283.L56 1988

Examines the influence of Wagner's *Tristan* on the imagination of later nineteenth-century French poets, philosophers, and artistes, including Baudelaire, Claudel, Mendès, and so on. Concludes with a bibliography of primary and secondary sources (pp. 169–84).

1067. *Richard Wagner et "Tannhäuser" à Paris / Charles Baudelaire; suivi de texts sur Richard Wagner par Nerval, Gautier et Champfleur,* ed. Robert Kopp. Paris: Les Belles Lettres, 1994. xlvi, 143pp. ISBN 225146011X ML410.W135B38 1994

Consists of an essay by Kopp (pp. ix–xlvi), as well as the complete text of Baudelaire's *Richard Wagner et "Tannhäuser" à Paris* (pp. 1–71; see also item 976) and excerpts from Nerval's *Les fêtes de Weimar. Le "Prométhée,"* and *Lohengrin*; Gautier's *Sur "Tannhäuser";* and Champfleury's *Richard Wagner* (see item 952). Concludes with notes that double as a list of sources.

1068. Woolley, Lawrence Grange. *Richard Wagner et le symbolisme français. Les rapports principaux entre le Wagnérisme et l'évolution de l'idée symboliste.* Paris: "Les Presses universitaires de France," 1931. 179pp. (no LC number available)

Considers Wagner's influence on Verlaine, Valéry, Mallarmé, and other symbolist poets, as well as the movement as a whole. Includes a bibliography (pp. 163–74) and index (pp. 175–77). Presented as a doctoral dissertation at the Sorbonne.

Germany

This volume serves as an introduction to many aspects of this complex and controversial subject:

1069. Zelinsky, Hartmut. *Sieg oder Untergang: Sieg und Untergang. Kaiser Wilhelm II., die Werk-Idee Richard Wagners und die "Weltkampf."* Munich: Keyser, 1990. 112pp. ISBN 3874052028 DD228.2.Z45 1990

Draws connections and traces influences among Wagner, Nietzsche, Emperor Wilhelm II, Adolf Stoecker, Hitler, and a host of other figures. Zelinsky calls attention to fascist culture in pre–World War II Europe and events that preceded the beginning of that conflict, but concentrates on the years 1888 to 1913. Illustrated with portraits, political cartoons and caricatures, and a facsimile of the emperor's sketch for a German Wagner memorial. Also includes notes (pp. 92–111) and a table identifying illustrations (p. 112).

Older, quite different surveys of the German-cultural Wagner reception also exist. See, for instance, items 105, 107, 113-14, and so on, as well as:

1070. Wirth, Moritz. *Bismarck, Wagner, Rodbertus: drei deutsche Meister. Betrachtungen über ihr Wirken und die Zukunft ihrer Werke*, 2nd ed. Leipzig: Oswald Mutze, 1885. 395pp. (no LC number available)

A detailed critique of later nineteenth-century pro-German political activities and sentiments. Wirth devotes at least as much attention to Wagner as to Otto von Bismarck and Karl Johann Rodbertus, the latter an economist, socialist, and author. Wirth also discusses classical, romantic, and revolutionary aspects of Wagner's music and its relationship to works by Beethoven, Gluck, Haydn, and especially Mozart and his *Magic Flute* (see items 793–94), Wagner's personal and professional relationships with Bismarck, and the composer's continuing influence and "victory" over German opera.

Originally published in 1883. Uncommon in American collections; Harvard's Widener Library owns a copy (shelf-number GerL 11760.9.5); the Library of Congress owns a microform copy. Closely related studies include Werner Wolf's "Richard Wagners Verhältnis zu Schopenhauer, Ludwig II. und Bismarck," published in the *Beiträge zur Musikwissenschaft* 24 (1982), pp. 202–16.

Among studies that focus on Wagner and the culture of German fascism are:

*   Hanisch, Ernst. "The Political Influence and Appropriation of Wagner." Described as item 1138.

Discusses German nationalism of the 1870s, events leading up to and away from the First World War, and Wagner as Nazi hero.

1071. Kolland, Hubert. "Wagner-Rezeption im deutschen Faschismus." *Beiträge zur Musikwissenschaft* 28 (1986), pp. 62–72. ML5.B352

A neo-Marxist analysis of Wagner's *Jewishness in Music,* and especially of its reception as part of the class struggle. According to Kolland, Wagner's anti-semitism became part of his "populist" revolutionary image; at the same time his acceptance as a "German" composer led to "state" performances of his music dramas, although his real significance as an artist was misunderstood or ignored by his contemporaries.

Hundreds of books and articles devoted to Hitler and the Nazis refer to Wagner, but these two survey studies described concentrate on that subject, as well as Wagner's impact on German culture:

1072. Köhler, Joachim. *Wagners Hitler: Der Prophet und sein Vollstrecker.* Munich: Karl Blessing, 1997. 505pp. ISBN 3896670166 DD247.H5K596 1997X

Examines Wagner's influence on the German dictator's life, thought, and pronouncements from the 1920s to Hitler's death in 1945. Supplemented by a large amount of documentation, including detailed notes (pp. 420–82), a bibliography (pp. 483–98), and an index. Unfortunately unillustrated. Recently published in English as *Wagner's Hitler: The Prophet and His Disciple,* trans. Ronald Taylor (Malden, MA, 2000); and reviewed as such enthusiastically in *Wagner* 21/3 (November 2000), pp. 184–90.

1073. Matter, Jean. *Wagner et Hitler. Essai.* Lausanne: "L'Age d'Homme," 1977. 183pp. ML410.W1M272 (no ISBN available)

Concerned with Wagner, Hitler, Nietzsche, Pierre Boulez, *Parsifal,* and other interrelated topics. Matter also describes the contributions made by Houston Stewart Chamberlain, the composer's son-in-law (see items 13, 256, and so on), and Winifred Wagner, his daughter-in-law (see item 1166), to the pan-German and anti-semitic movements of the early twentieth century. Includes a short bibliography (pp. 179–81). Finally, see item 532.

Older and somewhat more limited in scope is:

1074. Jacobs, Robert L. "Wagner's Influence on Hitler." *Music & Letters* 22 (1941), pp. 81–83. ML5.M64

Did Wagner actually shape Hitler's thinking? Jacobs examines passages from *Mein Kampf* and concludes that, although the composer's "Aryanism, his anti-Semitism, [and] his vegetarianism" were incidental in the German dictator's ideology, a *"dramatic* motive" may have underlain much of Hitler's thinking and career (p. 81; italics in the original).

German Wagnerians weren't always solemn. The following study is devoted to comic and sarcastic aspects of the German Wagner reception:

1075. Schneider, Andrea. *Die parodierten Musikdramen Richard Wagners. Geschichte und Dokumentation Wagnerscher Opernparodien im deutschsprachigen Raum von der Mitte des 19. Jahrhunderts bis zum Ende des ersten Weltkrieges.* Wort und Musik: Salzburger akademische Beiträge, 27. Anif bei Salzburg: Müller-Speiser, 1996. 522pp. (no ISBN or LC number available)

A fascinating study of Wagner parodies produced on German stages prior to 1914. Illustrated with facsimiles of documents and periodical pages (pp. 481–522), as well as caricatures and other likenesses of the composer. Among the dozens of works discussed by Schneider are Johann Hestroys's *Lohengrin* parody of 1859, a *Tristan* parody by Julius Stettenheim published in the *Berliner Wespen,* and Richard Huch's *Fliegende Holländer: eine groteske Komödie* produced in Munich in 1911. Outfitted with a bibliography (pp. 444–75) and an index of names. See also items 131–33 and 299.

Italy
1076. Florimo, Francesco. *Riccardo Wagner ed i Wagneristi.* Ancona: A. Gustavo Morelli, 1883. 117pp. ML410.W12183 1883

A review of the Italian Wagner reception during the 1870s and early 1880s, written by an author of monographs on Bellini and the Naples Conservatory who also corresponded with Hans von Bülow, Verdi, and Cosima Wagner; included in this volume are letters from all of them (pp. 98–113). Also includes as its only illustration a two-page, four-sided foldout facsimile of a letter of Wagner's written in French and dated 22 August 1880. No bibliography or index. Not to be confused with a much shorter work of the same title, also written by Florimo and published in 1876 by G. de Angelis of Naples (ML410.W12183).

1077. Ipser, Karl. *Richard Wagner in Italien.* Salzburg: "Das Bergland Buch," 1951. 240pp. ML410.W12I8352

A fulsome account of Wagner's visits to Italy, Italian productions of his works, the Wagner reception among various Italian composers, authors, publishers, and so on. Includes a timeline of events (pp. 211–32) as well as a second, somewhat scantier timeline devoted to events in European history during the composer's lifetime (pp. 233–38). Ipser's observations are enlivened by 88 illustrations, including photographs of places in Italy and documentary facsimiles.

1078. Panizzardi, Mario. *Wagner in Italia*. 2 vols. Milan: Carisch & Jänischen, 1914, 1923. ML410.W12P2 1922

A two-part survey of Wagner's activities in and relationship with Italy as a whole. Vol. 1 deals primarily with biographical issues and includes 36 illustrations, including a portrait of a gondolier who once carried the composer across the Venetian lagoon. Vol. 2 deals primarily with musical matters and the Italian Wagner reception; it contains a few documentary facsimiles, but no musical examples per se. Indexed (Vol. 2, pp. 289–308). See also items 122 and 844.

1079. *Wagner in Italia*, ed. Giorgia Manera and Giuseppe Pugliese. Venice: Marsilio Editori, 1982. 217pp. ML410.W12I88 1982 (no ISBN available)

Almost entirely devoted to reception issues of the late nineteenth and early twentieth centuries. Includes essays on performances in Italy, and especially in Venice, together with a detailed compendium of information—dates and places of production, conductors' names, casts, stage-designers' names, and so on—for Italy in general between 1871 and 1982, and especially for the Teatro La Fenice, Venice, from 1874 to 1981. Also includes essays on Wagner's influence on modern Italian literature and musical culture. Includes a few facsimiles of posters and other illustrations.

Netherlands: see "Flanders"

Poland

1080. Musioł, Karol. *Wagner und Polen / Wagner a Polska*. Bayreuth: Mühl'scher Universitätsverlag, 1980. 111pp. ISBN 3921733219 ML410.W12P6M

Includes chapters on Wagner's interest in the Polish crisis of 1830 and 1831, his influence on Polish music and musicians, his observations about Chopin, celebrated Polish Wagner singers, Wagner performances and publications in Poland, and—especially useful—a bibliography of Polish Wagner studies published between 1859 and 1980 (pp. 103–10). All chapters are printed both in German (pp. 9–53) and Polish (pp. 55–98). Illustrated with some thirty black-and-white portraits, photographs, and documentary facsimiles, as well as with a few musical examples. See also Musioł's article "Richard Wagner und Polen," published in the *Beiträge zur Musikwissenschaft* 6 (1964), pp. 53–65; as well as item 534.

Russia

1081. Bartlett, Rosamund. *Wagner and Russia*. Cambridge and New York: Cambridge University Press, 1995. xx, 405pp. ISBN 0521440718 ML410.W13B195 1995

Examines the Wagner reception in Russia between 1841 and 1890, especially the first *Ring* performances in Russia. Bartlett then turns to "Wagner and Russian Modernism" between 1890 and 1917, and evaluates the role of the periodical *Russkaya muzykal'naya gazeta*, as well as Wagnerian influences on such Russian symbolists as Alexander Blok and Vyacheslav Ivanov; finally she takes up "Wagner and Soviet Russia" and such related subjects as Eisenstein's production of *Walküre* (see item 850) and Wagner's influence on Soviet literature prior to the outbreak of World War II. Includes 32 portraits, photographs, caricatures, and the like, as well as ten color plates mostly devoted to stage sets and costume designs by Ivan Fedotov, Alexander Khvostenko-Khvostov, and Georgy Yakulov for *Rienzi*, *Lohengrin*, *Rheingold*, and other music dramas. Also includes a bibliography (pp. 372–400); concludes with an index. Reviewed at length in the *Cambridge Opera Journal* 8 (1996), pp. 83–92; and more briefly, but extremely positively, in *Notes* 54 (1997–1998), pp. 920–21.

Spain

Among the few studies dealing with Wagner's influence on Castile (i.e., central Spain) is:

1082. Borrell, Félix, *El Wagnerismo en Madrid*; and Valentín de Arín, *Biografía de Ricardo Wagner*. Both Madrid: Imprenta Ducazcal, 1912. 62pp. (no LC number available)

The texts of two lectures delivered before the Asociación Wagneriana de Madrid in May 1911. Of the two, Borrell's "Wagnerismo" (pp. 5–40) remains useful for its synopsis of the Spanish Wagner reception prior to the outbreak of World War I. In Spanish. Harvard's Loeb Music Library owns a copy of this pamphlet.

Perhaps the best introduction to Wagner and Catalonia (i.e., eastern Spain) is:

1083. *Wagner i Catalunya. Antologia de textos I gràfics sobre la influència wagneriana a la nostra cultura*. Barcelona: Edicions del Cotal, 1983. 281pp. ISBN 8473100603 ML410.W12S7 1983

A Catalan "reader," complete with some delightful early twentieth-century newspaper cartoons. Also includes an essay by Francesc Pujols on "Wagner I Gaudi," another by Joon-Josep Tharratson on Salvador Dalí's designs for a surrealist production of *Tannhäuser*, newspaper reviews of Wagner performances, and so on. Illustrated with pictures of Catalan Wagner performers, photographs of buildings by Antoni Gaudi, and caricatures. Concludes with a specialized bibliography that concentrates on Wagner publications in Catalan.

Other, more specialized studies—some dealing with Catalonian culture, some with the culture of Castile—include:

1084. Coleman, Alexander. "Calderón/Schopenhauer/Wagner: The Story of a Misunderstanding." *The Musical Quarterly* 69 (1983), pp. 227–43. ML1.M725

Devoted in large part to Wagner's rather ambivalent interest in the Spanish playwright's work. For Coleman "Calderón was always lurking in Wagner's imagination" (p. 243); comments and misunderstandings about the playwright surface, for example, in Cosima's diaries and elsewhere in the Wagner literature; furthermore, Parsifal as a Wagnerian character may have been influenced by the *autos sacra neutales* tradition of seventeenth-century Spain. No musical examples. See also item 751.

1085. Janés I Nadal, Alfonsina. *L'obra de Richard Wagner a Barcelona.* Barcelona: Fundacio Salvador Vives Casajuana, 1983. 406pp. ISBN 842320216X ML1747.8.B18J3 1983

Assesses Wagner's influence on Catalan music and poetry. Illustrated with five pages of plates, including facsimiles of pages from published Catalan Wagner scores, as well as with scattered caricatures and cartoons reproduced from Catalan magazines and newspapers. Includes information about every Wagner performance presented at the Gran Teatre del Liceu from 1951 to 1983 (pp. 281–343); also includes a useful bibliography (pp. 345–55) and an index of names (pp. 357–98).

Not to be confused with the author's sixteen-page dissertation of the same title (University of Barcelona, 1976); the latter includes a list of Wagner scores published in Madrid and other cities between 1905 and 1915 (pp. 10–13).

WAGNER AND THE VISUAL ARTS

The articles described touch on late nineteenth- and early twentieth-century European pictorial reactions to Wagner:

1086. Descharnes, Robert. "Dalí and Wagner." *Programmhefte der Bayreuther Festspiele* VI (1989), pp. 46–48. ML410.W2B26

Describes the surrealist painter's interest in Wagner and his works. Includes a translation of Dalí's "Geological Foundations of the Venusberg" (pp. 47–48)—an essay, written in 1939, that acknowledges the artist's paranoid-critical and dream-photographic methods in its assertions that "the first demand that music makes is that you do not touch it but listen to it half in a dream with your eyes fully closed, gazing inwards rather than outwards," and that Wagner himself is "an actual mountain of mythological images and hallucinations" (p. 47). Unfortunately not illustrated.

1087. Huckvale, David. "Kitsch and Curiosities: Wagner Illustrations, 1890–1920." *Wagner* 13/1 (January 1992), pp. 3–11. ML410.W1A595

Considers Wagner's influence on the *fin-de-siècle* visual imagination. Includes good-quality black-and-white reproductions of pictures by John Bryant Shaw, Franz Stassen, Hans Thoma, and several other artists. Huckvale also discusses the influence of Stassen's work on Hitler-era German propaganda posters.

1088. Jempson, Janet. "Aubrey Beardsley and the 'Ring.' " *Wagner* 17/1 (January 1996), pp. 65–77. ML410.W1A595

A useful summary of the interest this "decadent" artist showed in Wagner's music dramas. Includes a photograph of Beardsley taken in 1894, as well as ten handsome reproductions of his celebrated illustrations.

1089. Jempson, Janet. "Henri Fantin-Latour and Wagner." *Wagner* 18/1 (January 1997), pp. 20–31. ML410.W1A595

Includes five reproductions of Fantin-Latour's Wagner lithographs, as well as a survey of his involvement with the composer's world and works during the 1880s and 1890s. See also Marc Edo Tralbaut's *Richard Wagner im Blickwinkel fünf grosser Maler: Henri Fantin-Latour, Paul Cézanne, Odilon Redon, Auguste Renoir, Vincent van Gogh* (Dortmund 1969) for information about Fantin-Latour's Wagner illustrations and those of other artists.

1090. Boehn, Max von. "Die Nibelungen in der Kunst." In item 300, pp. 1–138.

A "visual history" of the *Nibelungenlied* and its influence on a variety of artists—all of them "German" and most of them active during the nineteenth century, although a few fifteenth-century illuminated manuscript scenes are also figured and mentioned—including Arnold Böcklin, Max Brückner, Peter Cornelius, Franz Staffen, and especially Julius Schnorr von Carolsfeld. Also includes depictions and discussions of sculpture and artistic reproductions of real-life scenes from individual productions, as well as paintings, drawings, engravings, and book illustrations. Otherwise undocumented.

Additional studies of this subject also exist. See, for instance, Ulrich Schulte-Wulwer, *Das Nibelungenlied in der deutschen Kunst des 19. und 20. Jahrhunderts* (Giessen, 1980); and especially Hermann Hendrich, *Der Ring des Nibelungen in Bildern* (Leipzig, c. 1909). The latter contains an essay by Wolfgang Golther.

WAGNER AND ANTI-SEMITISM

That Wagner condemned "Jewishness" among musicians and in musical compositions is today all but universally acknowledged; that his anti-semitic bias extended to certain individuals and figures in his music dramas continues to be debated.

In the following pages and unless otherwise noted, studies grouped under individual headings or explanatory observations are arranged in alphabetical order by author, editor, and/or title.

General Studies

The place to begin any inquiry into Wagner and anti-semitism is with Wagner's own anti-Jewish pronouncements. See items 204–05, 211–12 (Cosima's diaries), and especially:

* Wagner, Richard. *Judaism in Music (Das Judenthum in der Musik).* Described as item 193.

 Among Wagner's most hotly debated and frequently criticized prose works. Editions of this pamphlet, which appeared in print originally in 1850 and again, with amendations, in 1869, include those published in *Wagner* 9/1 (January 1988), pp. 20–33. The original German text was reprinted by Insel-Verlag (Frankfurt a.M. 2000; ISBN 3458343172). Portions of this, among the most often reprinted of Wagner's tracts, also appear in items 105–07 as well as collected editions (items 172–95), in item 188, and so on.

Perhaps the best study, especially in English, of Wagner's racial biases remains:

1091. Katz, Jacob. *The Darker Side of Genius: Richard Wagner's Anti-Semitism.* The Tauber Institute for the Study of European Jewry Series, 5. Hanover, NH: University Press of New England, 1986. xii, 158pp. ISBN 0874513685 ML410.W19K3313 1986

Traces the evolution of anti-semitism in Wagner's life, writings, and relationships from his growing distrust of Meyerbeer to the anti-Jewish utterances recorded in Cosima Wagner's diaries (item 211). Katz also evaluates *Jewishness in Music* from a variety of perspectives and discusses the reception that greeted both its 1850 and 1869 editions; he grounds his study of Wagner's shifting attitudes in widespread nineteenth-century German anti-semitic biases, including those of Bruno Bauer and Karl Marx. Katz's conclusion that "Wagner's attitude to Jews and Judaism was not a uniform phenomenon, but went through various phrases in the course of time" (p. 120) is well documented; his denial that there are signs of anti-semitism in Beckmesser (*Meistersinger*) and Kundry (*Parsifal*) have been disputed. Supplemented by a two-page timeline (pp. xi–xii), endnotes, and a list of "Additional Readings" that includes most of the sources cited in the notes (pp. 153–54). Concludes with an index. See also items 104, 106–7, and 773.

> Reviewed by John Deathridge in *Wagner* 8/3 (July 1987; see item 152); and, with item 980, by Leon Botstein in *19th Century Music* 11 (1987–1988), pp. 92–104.

Other excellent, albeit mostly more harshly argued evaluations of Wagner and the Jews include:

*   Eger, Manfred. *Wagner und die Juden. Fakten und Hintergründe.* Described as item 106.

An exhibition catalog that includes the entire German text of *Jewishness in Music* and a variety of other materials.

1092. Rose, Paul Lawrence. *Wagner: Race and Revolution.* New Haven, CT: Yale University Press, 1992. x, 246pp. ISBN 0300051824 ML410.W19R75 1992

A spirited attack on Wagner as racist. Among other things, Rose attempts to demonstrate that anti-semitism permeates Wagner's mature music dramas, *Tristan und Isolde* among them. Rose's comments on this last topic have been denied by prominent Wagnerians, including Thomas Grey in his review for the *Cambridge Opera Journal* [6 (1994), pp. 181–87]. For Grey, Rose merely reasserts claims made by previous scholars that anti-semitism permeated every aspect of Wagner's life and work. Barry Millington, on the other hand, not only accepts Rose's premise but has built arguments of his own that support it (see item 773). A more enthusiastic review of Rose's work appeared in *Wagner* 16/1 (January 1995), pp. 46–48.

1093. Stein, Leon. *The Racial Thinking of Richard Wagner.* New York: Philosophical Library, 1950. xiv, 252pp. ML410.W19S83

Examines both Wagner's glorification of pan-Germanism and his anti-semitic notions. Stein asserts that the composer's racial theories, rather than his contributions to music and *belles lettres*, influenced modern political history; he also discredits Wagner's prejudices against Mendelssohn and rejects suggestions that Wagner's music be ignored because its composer was biased. Published soon after World War II ended, Stein's volume represents a groundbreaking exploration of this challenging subject. Includes a bibliography (pp. 242–47) as well as a few illustrations; concludes with an index.

Other studies concentrate more on the historical significance and influence of Wagner's anti-semitism:

* Kolland, Hubert. "Wagner-Rezeption im deutschen Faschismus." Described as item 1071.

1094. Rose, Paul Lawrence. *German Question/Jewish Question: Revolutionary Antisemitism from Kant to Wagner.* Princeton, NJ and New York: Princeton University Press, 1992. xviii, 397pp. ISBN 0691008906 DS146.G4R64 1992

A study of Wagner vis-à-vis the traditions of German revolutionary philosophy, beginning with Kant and Hegel. Rose argues primarily that Wagner's anti-semitism cannot be regarded as peripheral to his overall development as author and even as music-dramatist. Published in a somewhat different version in 1990 under the title *Revolutionary Antisemitism in Germany from Kant to Wagner* (ISBN 0691031444). See also Rose's article "The Noble Anti-Semitism of Richard Wagner" in the *Historical Journal* 25 (1981), pp. 751–63, which deals with many of the same issues.

1095. Weiner, Marc A. *Richard Wagner and the Anti-Semitic Imagination.* Lincoln, NE, and London: University of Nebraska Press, 1995. xvi, 439pp. ISBN 0803247753 ML410.W19W23 1995

A postmodern study of Wagner's hatred of the Jews. Weiner extends his arguments to include "the body" (eyes, smells, feet, and such "degenerate" sexual practices as masturbation), and ways in which the composer's prejudices are "inscribed" on the figures in his dramatic productions. Supplemented by a substantial bibliography of variegated sources (pp. 393–421), as well as copious notes (pp. 355–91), scattered musical examples, photographs of Nietzsche and several stage sets, and facsimiles of a few caricatures—including, in the last category, Gustave Doré's *Heldentenöre.*

Reviewed perceptively by Grey in the *Cambridge Opera Journal* 8 (1996), pp. 185–97. Weiner's volume was printed in 1997 with a new postscript but the same ISBN.

There also exist a number of pamphlets and broadsides, many of them published during the nineteenth and early twentieth centuries, devoted to Wagner's racial prejudices. Among these are three little-known volumes:

1096. "Dr. C . . ." *Unmusikalische Noten zu Richard Wagner's "Judenthum in der Musik."* Munich: Neuburger & Kolb, 1869. 15pp. ML410.W18U4

One of several contemporary responses to the 1869 republication of *Jewishness in Music*; others are cited in Katz's notes (item 1091 above, pp. 135–51), but this one is not. The author argues against the age-old notion that Judaism and Christianity are incompatible by asking rhetorically, "Who was he, this great Christ, the Nazarene? A Jew! At what source had he imbibed [*erforscht und gefunden*] the truth? At the fountainhead [*Muttersbrust*] of Jewish wisdom . . . and understanding. And who were his apostles, the pupils of this astonishing master—who were Paul, Mark, and those who heard the glorious Sermon on the Mount? Jews, Jews all!" (translated from p. 5).

1097. Ganzer, Karl Richard. *Richard Wagner und das Judentum.* Hamburg 1938. 36pp. ML410.W1A1925

Probably a synopsis, from the perspective of doctrinaire Nazis, of Wagner's anti-semitism. Not seen, but Katz cites Ganzer as one of several authors who argued that the composer's relationships with Schlesinger in Paris were in part responsible for his anti-semitic feelings (see item 1091, p. 137). The Judaica Division of Harvard University's Widener Library owns a copy that was unavailable for examination by the present author; according to Library of Congress officials, their copy is "lost." No publisher is identified in either library's catalog.

1098. Grunsky, Hans. *Richard Wagner und die Jüden.* "Deutschlands fürende Männer und das Judentum," 2. Munich 1919. 96pp. (no LC number available)

A defense of the Jews? Possibly, but the name "Hans Alfred Grunsky" also appears on the title page of a pamphlet published in Berlin in 1937 entitled *Seele und Staat: die psychologischen Grundlagen des nationalsozialis-*

tischen Siegs über den bürgerlichen und bolschewitischen Menschen. Grunsky's 1919 pamphlet appears to be rare: the Judaica Division of Harvard University's Widener Library owns a copy, but it was unavailable for examination. Again, no publisher is given.

At least two "readers" devoted to Wagner and Jewish issues have appeared in print:

1099. *Richard Wagner. Wie antisemitisch darf ein Künstler sein?*, 2nd ed. Musik-Konzepte, 5. Munich: "text+kritik," 1981. 112pp. ISBN 3921402670

Includes several editorials, a transcript of Thomas Mann's letter to the editor of *Common Sense* (1940), Peter Viereck's essay "Hitler und Richard Wagner: Zur Genese des Nationalsozialismus" (1939), and a new essay by Zelinsky entitled "Der 'feuerkur' des Richard Wagner" (pp. 79–112), in which the author alleges Wagner consciously worked anti-semitism messages and figures into several of his music dramas. An influential publication. Appeared originally in 1978 without Zelinsky's contribution.

1100. *Who's Afraid of Richard Wagner? Aspects of a Controversial Personality*, ed. Rina Litoyen and Hezy Shelah Keter. Jerusalem 1984. 349pp. (no ISBN or LC number available)

Seen but not read. Reviewed at length and on the whole positively in *Wagner* 6/1 (January 1985), pp. 38–40. According to this review, Litoyen's and Keter's volume includes a translation of item 30 and extracts from celebrated Wagner works by Baudelaire, Mann, and Bernard Shaw, as well as several essays dealing with the composer's anti-semitism and a complete translation into Hebrew of *Jewishness in Music*. Most interesting, perhaps, is an article entitled "Who's Afraid of Richard Wagner?" that examines anti-Wagnerian sentiments in contemporary Israel "and tries to show that both the supporters and the opponents of the ban [on performing Wagner in public] are wrong" (review, p. 39). In Hebrew throughout. No publisher given; at least the review lists none.

Several articles also summarize Wagner's anti-semitic attitudes and pronouncements:

1101. Borchmeyer, Dieter. "The Question of Anti-Semitism," trans. Stewart Spencer. In item 2, pp. 166–85.

Acknowledges that *Jewishness in Music* stands "at the crossroads of traditional and modern anti-Semitism" (p. 169), and proclaims its "underlying inhumanity" (p. 170). Borchmeyer describes Wagner's personal fascination with various 1870s and 1880s anti-semitic movements, including the

Berlin Movement begun by Adolf Stöcker; he also evaluates the significance both of anti-semitic observations recorded in such variegated (and occasionally unreliable) sources as *My Life* (item 204) and Cosima's diaries; finally, he suggests the music dramas contain anti-semitic characters and messages. Also published as "Richard Wagner and Anti-Semitism" in *Wagner* 6/1 (January 1985), pp. 1–18.

1102. Millington, Barry. "Wagner and the Jews." In item 1, pp. 161–64.

Summarizes Wagner's intense anti-semitism, based especially on events associated with the publication of both versions of *Jewishness in Music* and the influence of Count Gobineau's racial theories on Wagner during the last years of the composer's life. Millington does his best in a very few pages to consider Wagner's attitudes as characteristic of his time and personal circumstances. See also Iris Gillespie's summary article "Wagner and Racism," published in *Wagner* 4/3 (June 1983), pp. 79–87.

1103. Millington, Barry. "Wagner Washes Whiter . . . Barry Millington Responds to His Critics" *The Musical Times* 137/1846 (December 1996), pp. 5–8. ML5.M85.

A polemical reply to those who have disagreed with him. Millington, for example, "corrects" Borchmeyer by suggesting that Wagner's use of anti-semitic characters such as Alberich, Beckmesser, and Mime was more instinctive than part of a plan to propagate racist and nationalist views. Useful especially for its synopses of anti-semitism studies omitted from the present volume. Reprinted in *Wagner* 18/2 (May 1997), pp. 83–90.

Specialized Studies

These books and articles deal with particular aspects of Wagner as anti-semite and his relationship with certain Jews and anti-Jews:

1104. Bermbach, Udo. "The Aesthetic Motive in Wagner's Anti-Semitism: 'Jewishness in Music' in the Context of the 'Zürcher Kunstschriften,' " trans. Claudia R. Kalay. *Wagner* 21/1 (January 2000), pp. 3–22. ML410.W1A595

Evaluations of Wagner's bias in terms of its evolution, from his earliest "revolutionary" writings to those of his later years. Bermbach explains that, for Wagner, "anti-semitism" meant, among other things, holding the fort against artistic sterility. Originally presented as a lecture at a Bayreuth conference devoted to "Wagner and the Jews" in August 1998.

1105. Eugène, Eric. *Wagner et Gobineau. Existe-t-il un racisme wagnérien?* Paris: "le cherche midi éditeur," 1998. 255pp. ISBN 2862745561 ML410.W1E86 1998

A detailed examination, supplemented by quotations from the works of both the celebrated composer and the infamous Count. Includes discussions of Wagner's borrowings from Gobineau, as well as both men's ideas about racial purity, Christian redemption, and other themes associated in Gobineau's mind with anti-semitism. Concludes with a bibliography (pp. 237–43) and index.

1106. Kreis, Rudolf. *Nietzsche, Wagner, und die Jüden.* Würzburg: Königshaus & Neumann, 1995. 227pp. ISBN 382601071X ML410.W19K915 1995

Attacks Wagner as a bigot and describes the influence of anti-semitism in his life and works. One focus of Kreis's polemic is *Parsifal* and its purportedly "Christian" character. Includes a foreword by Gottfried Wagner, the staunchest foe of anti-semitism among Wagner's direct descendents, and a polemicist honored by the Israeli government.

* Matter, Jean. *Wagner et Hitler. Essai.* Described as item 1073.

Among other subjects, Matter deals with contributions made by Chamberlain and Winifred Wagner to early twentieth-century pan-German and anti-semitic movements (see also items 1072 and 1074).

1107. *Meyerbeer, Wagner: eine Begegnung*, ed. Gunhild Oberzaucher-Schüller, Marion Linhardt, and Thomas Steiert. Vienna: Böhlau, 1998. 305pp. ISBN 320598983X ML390.M512 1998

Covers a variety of "Jewish-musical" topics. In addition to discussions of Wagner's attitudes toward Meyerbeer, this volume includes Erhard Busek's "Der jüdische Künstler des 19. Jahrhunderts in der Gesellschaft" (pp. 9–17); Manuela Jahrmärker's "Wagners Aufsatz 'Das Judenthum in der Musik' im Spiegel zeitgenössischer Reaktionen" (pp. 120–41); and Oberzaucher-Schüller's "Chez Schlesinger" (pp. 101–19), an account of Wagner's relationship with his Parisian publisher Maurice Schlesinger. Also includes an extensive collection of documents (pp. 142–296)—letters, newspaper squibs, diary entries, and so on—all of them related to the Wagner-Meyerbeer controversy; the documents themselves, which span the years 1834–1892, incorporate the complete *Jewishness in Music* text of 1850 (pp. 238–58), as well as comments by Eduard Hanslick on the centenary of Meyerbeer's birth (pp. 295–96). Incorporates endnotes for each article and an index of names but no bibliography or musical examples.

1108. Werner, Eric. "Jews Around Richard and Cosima Wagner." *The Musical Quarterly* 71 (1985), pp.172–99. ML1.M725

Deals with Wagner and such individuals as Hermann Levi and Joseph Rubinstein, Drawing upon Cosima's correspondence with her daughter Daniela (see item 1151) and holograph letters preserved in the Bayerische Staatsbibliothek, Werner describes the Wagners as patronizing, back-stabbing racists and snobs, as well as opportunistic "befrienders" of those Jews useful to their causes. Includes a full-page facsimile from a letter Cosima addressed to Levi, as well as the text of a poem (in both English and German) Wagner wrote on the death of Karl Tausig. Regarding Levi, see item 797.

1109. Werner, Eric. "Mendelssohn—Wagner. Eine alte Kontroverse in neuer Sicht." In: *Musicae scientiae collectanea. Festschrift Karl Gustav Fellerer zum siebzigsten Geburtstag am 7. Juli 1972*, ed. Heinrich Hüschen. Cologne: Arno Volk, 1973; pp. 640–58. ISBN 3872520393 ML55.F35 1972

Reevaluates Wagner's opinion of Mendelssohn as composer *and* Jew, the impact of Hegel on Mendelssohn's aesthetics, and of anti-semitism on his musical reputation, Mendelssohn and National Socialism, and related issues. Werner includes the text of a letter written by Carl Gördeler on 5 February 1937 protesting the destruction by the Nazis of the Mendelssohn monument in Leipzig (pp. 641–42); he also refers his readers to new documents pertaining to the Mendelssohn reception and owned by the New York Public Library, the Library of Congress, and the Bodleian Library, Oxford.

Finally, publications devoted to Wagner and the Jews include a few studies difficult to classify. Among the most interesting of these is:

1110. Mass, Lawrence D. *Confessions of a Jewish Wagnerite: Being Gay and Jewish in America*. London: Cassell, 1994. xvii, 268pp. ISBN 0304331104 HQ76.3.U5M37 1994

An autobiography devoted to grappling with "unconscious anti-semitism," AIDS, and Wagner's life and music. Symptomatic of postmodern approaches to Wagner and his many cultural influences. Introduced by Gottfried Wagner (pp. xiii–xvii). Unfortunately includes neither notes, bibliography, nor index.

XIII

After Wagner:
Bayreuth, the Festivals, and Wagner's Descendents

BAYREUTH AND THE WAGNER FESTIVALS

Among the most important of Wagner's legacies are the Festival Theater he built in Bayreuth and the performances that have taken place there with comparatively few interruptions since the mid-1870s. Closely associated not only with the composer but with the festivals in particular are Wagner's successors; these—especially his wife Cosima, son Siegfried and grandsons Wolfgang and Wieland—made Bayreuth one of Germany's most influential cultural capitals. This chapter identifies and describes some of the books and articles devoted to Bayreuth, its Festivals, and the Wagner family following the composer's death in 1883.

Unless otherwise noted, studies grouped under individual headings or explanatory observations are arranged alphabetically by author, editor, and/or title.

General Studies

Among surveys of Bayreuth as a monument both to individual artistic dreams and nineteenth-century German musical theater are the following books and articles:

1111. Skelton, Geoffrey. *Wagner at Bayreuth: Experiment and Tradition*, rev. ed. London and New York: White Lion Publishers, 1976. 251pp. ISBN 0856170682 ML410.W2535 1976

Introduces readers to how and especially *why* Bayreuth came into existence: to present the *Ring* and *Parsifal* to the world in the finest possible surroundings. Skelton also discusses Bayreuth productions designed by Adolphe Appia, Max Brückner, Josef Hoffmann, Paul von Joukowsky, and Wieland and Wolfgang Wagner. Illustrated with a number of well-chosen portraits, family photographs, stage designs, and sets; concludes with a brief bibliography and index.

Reviewed enthusiastically by Robert Bailey in *Notes* 24 (1967–1968), pp. 266–67. Reprinted in 1983; originally published (New York and London, 1965) in a slightly shorter edition and with a few full-color illustrations. Some editions include a foreword by Wieland Wagner. See also Skelton's "Idea of Bayreuth" (item 31, pp. 389–411).

1112. Mayer, Hans. *Richard Wagner in Bayreuth, 1876–1976*, trans. Jack Zipes. New York: Rizzoli, 1976. 248pp. ISBN 3763090185 ML420.W2M25

One of the best surveys in English of the Bayreuth phenomenon. Considers in chronological order the plans for both the Festival theater, Haus Wahnfried, the 1876 and 1882 Festivals, and the "reigns" of Cosima, Siegfried, Winifred, Wieland, and Wolfgang Wagner. Includes photographs of rehearsals and performances taken by Jaroslav Schneider, as well as a few other illustrations; also includes a "prelude" taken from Nietzsche's writings; concludes with an index. Published in German with the same title (ISBN 3763090185). Reviewed with items 211, 1119, and Winfried Schüler's *Der Bayreuther Kreis* (Münster, 1971) by David Large in "Art, Ideology, and Politics at Bayreuth, 1876–1976," *Journal of the History of Ideas* 39 (1978), pp. 149–56.

1113. Spotts, Fredric. *Bayreuth: A History of the Wagner Festival*. New Haven and London: Yale University Press, 1994. x, 334pp. ISBN 0300057776 ML410.W2S6 1990

Reviews the origins of Wagner's Theater and the performances held in it. Illustrated with portraits of Wagner and his family, as well as other illustrations and documentary facsimiles; also includes information about Wagner's descendents as well as a bibliography (pp. 315–22) and an index. Reviewed with qualified approval in the *Cambridge Opera Journal* 7 (1995), pp. 277–84.

1114. Vogt, Matthias Theodor. "Taking the Waters at Bayreuth." In item 826, pp. 130–52.

A witty postmodern description of Bayreuth as *Kurort* (bath or spa), based in part on Wagner's own words, as well as mythological allusions and a more careful study of how Festival visitors have been expected to behave during their pilgrimages to the Holy City. Vogt describes Bayreuth's Wagnerian festivities as "cultic rituals" (see pp. 131–33), and "the composer's festival ideal . . . [as] bound up with the ideology of hydropathic cures"

(p. 130). Illustrated with several amusing images of nineteenth-century resorts.

Other, mostly briefer surveys of the Bayreuth phenomenon include:

1115. Large, David C. "The Bayreuth Legacy." In item 1, pp. 389–92.

In addition to reviewing the origins of the Festival and saying something about the "Circle" that surrounded Cosima after her husband's death and influenced German culture for decades, Large comments on Wagner's briefly-considered plans to emigrate to the United States and establish a "New World Bayreuth" in Minnesota (p. 390), reactionary tendencies in Bayreuth productions during the "reign" of the composer's son Siegfried, and the "refreshingly heretical" character of productions endorsed after World War II by grandsons Wieland and Wolfgang (p. 392).

1116. Spencer, Stewart. "Bayreuth and the Idea of a Festival Theater." In item 1, pp. 167–70.

Traces Wagner's longing to see his works produced in ideal circumstances, beginning with remarks he made in 1850 to Benedikt Kietz about a performance of *Siegfrieds Tod*, and ending with the erection of the Festspielhaus and the Festivals of 1876. Spencer also refers briefly to the Patrons' Certificates that helped pay for the theater's construction, and to Wagner's disappointment after the first production of the complete *Ring*—a disappointment brought on by thoughts of racial degeneration and of a "pristine Germanic Paradise which could never be regained" (p. 170).

Still other broad-based discussions of Bayreuth, Wagner's family, and the Festivals include:

1117. Bronnenmeyer, Walter. *Richard Wagner—Bürger in Bayreuth. Wechselspiel von Allianz und Mesalliance*. Bayreuth: Ellwanger, 1983. 200pp. ML410.W2B74 1983 (no ISBN available)

Describes Wagner's relationship with Bayreuth, the Festival, and its impact upon those institutions, told largely in the form of illustrations: portraits (a few in color), photographs of places and productions, maps of the city and environs, documentary facsimiles, and so on. Includes neither extensive quotations from primary sources, bibliography, nor index.

1118. Bude, Nicola, and Manfred Bockelmann. *Unsterblicher Wagner—lebendiges Bayreuth. Eine Hommage*. Bayreuth: Hestia, 1983. 272pp. ISBN 3777002534 ML410.W2B78 1983

A picture book published in conjunction with the centenary of Wagner's death. The bulk of the volume consists of scenes from everyday life, some in color: photographs of Festival guests, events, meals, performers, and performances, as well as historical portraits, documentary facsimiles, and the like.

1119. Karbaum, Michael. *Studien zur Geschichte der Bayreuther Festspiele (1876–1976)*. Arbeitsgemeinschaft "100 Jahre Bayreuther Festspiele," 3. Regensburg: Gustav Bosse, 1976. 106 + 158pp. ISBN 3764920602 ML410.W2K28

Comprised of two parts: a discussion of Wagner's theater and its productions and activities from the beginnings to the "new Bayreuth" (106pp.), and a collection of texts and excerpts associated with the same topics (158pp.). The documentary section concludes with a two-page bibliography.

1120. Schreiber, Hermann, and Guido Mangold. *Werkstatt Bayreuth*. Munich and Hamburg: Albrecht Knaus, 1986. 236pp. ISBN 381352292X ML410.W2S38 1986

Mostly an account of rehearsals and performances associated with Wolfgang Wagner's Bayreuth "workshop" and productions, although Schreiber and Mangold also touch on the history of the Festspielhaus, pre-Wolfgang productions, etc. Illustrated with numerous production photos, some in color. Concludes with biographies and photo portraits of important modern Bayreuth performers, Manfred Jung—to name but one example—among them.

Two additional studies might be considered eccentric and/or ephemeral by many scholars:

1121. Meinertz, J. *Richard Wagner und Bayreuth. Zur Psychologie des Schaffens und des Erlebens von Wagners Werken*. Berlin and Wunsiedel: Max Hesse, 1961. 48pp. (no LC number available)

Evaluates Wagner's need for a Festspielhaus, and the influence of that need on his works and career. Meinertz also reviews opinions about Bayreuth and the Wagnerian music dramas expressed by the likes of Thomas Mann, Friedrich Nietzsche, Heinrich Wölfflin, and others. Includes neither bibliography nor index.

1122. *Bayreuth: 1876–1976*, 2nd ed. No publication data! 84pp. (no ISBN or LC numbers available)

Resembles an American high-school yearbook, in that it consists primarily of photographs, many in color, of 1970s Bayreuth personnel—administrators, members of the office staff, orchestral musicians, dancers, and so on (pp. 55–83). Also includes portraits and photos of late nineteenth- and early twentieth-century performers, a number of production pictures, and a few documentary facsimiles. Skips over 1933 to 1945 as if they never existed. Printed in oblong format. Apparently rare in American collections; Harvard University's Loeb Music Library owns a copy, however (shelf-number Mus. 5662.93).

The Festspielhaus and Haus Wahnfried

Several studies of Wagner's theater and Bayreuth home also deal with architectural, biographical, cultural, and musical-dramatic issues:

1123. Baumann, Carl-Friedrich. *Bühnentechnik im Festspielhaus Bayreuth.* Munich: Prestel, 1980. 328pp. ISBN 3791304933 ML410.W2B256 1980

Considers Bayreuth's stage equipment and machinery, which runs the gamut from architectural aesthetics to details of fire prevention. Baumann draws upon a wide variety of sources, including the information found in fourteen tables and some 159 photographs, to explain precisely how Wagner and his successors have made individual productions possible. Includes a bibliography (pp. 319–22) and catalog of the illustrations themselves (pp. 323–25); concludes with an index of individuals and manufacturing firms.

1124. Baumann, Dorothea. "Wagners Festspielhaus—eine akustisch-architektonisches Wagnis mit Überraschungen." in: *Festschrift Hans Conradin. Zum 70. Geburtstag,* ed. Volker Kalisch et al. Bern and Stuttgart: Paul Haupt, 1983; pp. 123–150. ISBN 325803236X ML55.C757 1983

Devoted to Wagner's search for the perfect theater, presented in terms of the buildings he planned or dreamed of: Munich's Cuvilliéstheater, Altes Residenz-Theater, and Nationaltheater; Gottfried Semper's plan for a Wagner theater in Munich; and the Bayreuth Festspielhaus designed by Otto Brückwald to Wagner's specifications. Illustrated with fourteen diagrams—some architectural, some depicting how sound produced by singers "carries"—as well as charts of Bayreuth's covered orchestra pit and seating arrangement, and photographs of most of the buildings mentioned above. The "surprises" (*Überraschungen*) in the title refer both to Wagner's innovations and ways the Festspielhaus actually works.

1125. Habel, Heinrich. *Festspielhaus und Wahfried. Geplante und aufgeführte Bauten Richard Wagners.* Munich: Prestel, 1985. 685pp. ISBN 3791303864 (no LC number available)

An architectural history of the buildings Wagner intended to build, as well as those that were actually built. Illustrated with hundreds of photographs, diagrams, and plans depicting the theater as well as Wahnfried, the Wagner family home since the 1870s. Includes a catalog of the plans themselves (pp. 651–74); concludes with a bibliography (pp. 675–77) and index.

1126. Kraft, Zdenko von. "Wahnfried and the Festival Theatre," trans. Cedric Williams. In item 31, pp. 412–32.

A "Bayreuth survey" that also includes a few paragraphs about the Festivals of the late nineteenth and earlier twentieth centuries. Kraft concludes with item 108: an appendix, "The Wahnfried Archive" (item 31, pp. 429–32), devoted to documents preserved in Wagner's home from his death to 1973, and the establishment of the Richard-Wagner-Stiftung.

The Bayreuth Wagner Festivals, 1876–2000

Festivals held during Wagner's Lifetime (1876–1882): see also items 837 and 842.
Discussions of the earliest festivals and especially of their economic and political underpinnings include:

1127. Veltzke, Veit. *Vom Patron zum Paladin. Wagnervereinigungen im Kaiserreich von der Reichsgründung bis zur Jahrhundertwende.* Bochumer historische Studien: Neuere Geschichte, 5. Bochum: N. Brockmeyer, 1987. 434pp. ISBN 3883395994 ML410.W12G84 1987

A fascinating account of the *Patronatvereine*, Wagner societies (or branches) initially established during the 1870s, mostly to raise funds to support the construction of the Festival Theater; active as well between 1877 and 1882. Veltzke also examines other German Wagner organizations. Includes notes and a bibliography (pp. 413–32). Offset-printed from justified typescript; no illustrations or musical examples. Additional information about the *Patronatvereine* may be found in Hans von Wolzogen's pamphlet *Grundlage und Aufgabe des Allgemeinen Patronatvereines zur Pflege und Erhaltung der Bühnenfestspiele zu Bayreuth* (Chemnitz, 1877; ML410.W2W8).

1128. Large, David C. "The Political Background of the Foundation of the Bayreuth Festival, 1876." *Central European History* 11 (1978), pp. 162–72. D901.C34

Concerned mostly with the reasons behind Bismarck's refusal to offer Wagner any real help during the 1870s, although Large also discusses the Society of Patrons and its "serious flaws as a tool for raising money" (p. 167), as well as the 1876 Festival that "failed to engage the whole German nation . . . at the box office" (p. 172). A useful summary that draws upon few new documentary sources. See also Large's review article "Art, Ideology and Politics at Bayreuth, 1876–1976," published in the *Journal of the History of Ideas* 39 (1978), pp. 149–56.

Studies of the Festivals that predated Wagner's death in February 1883 include:

1129. Engel, Gustav (Eduard). *Das Bühnenfestspiel in Bayreuth. Kritische Studien.* Berlin: A. C. Challier & Co., 1876. 83pp. (no LC number available)

Contains essays about and reviews of the first Bayreuth Festival, the Festspielhaus, Wagner's music, and so on. Originally published in the form of supplements to Berlin's *Vossische Zeitung* (13–30 August 1876), then one of Germany's most important daily papers.

1130. Hassard, John R. G. *Richard Wagner at Bayreuth / The Ring of the Nibelungs: A Description of its First Performance in August, 1876.* New York: Francis Hart & Co., 1877. 57pp. (no LC number available)

Detailed reports on the Festival, its artistic activities and merits, the distinguished visitors who attended it, and so on. Includes cast lists and other worthwhile information, but contains no illustrations or scholarly apparatus. Hassard's account first appeared serially in the *New York Tribune*.

1131. "La Mara" [pseud. of Marie Lipsius]. *Das Bühnenfestspiel in Bayreuth.* Leipzig: Schmidt & Günther, 1877. 47pp. (no LC number available)

An eyewitness account by one of nineteenth-century Germany's first and foremost female musicologists. La Mara devotes most of her attention to the music of the *Ring* and illustrates her observations with scattered musical examples. Rare in American archives: the only copy the present author has been able to consult is available on microfilm at Harvard's Loeb Music Library (shelf-number Isham 3710.369.24.3, No. 2); the some library also owns print copies of the two pamphlets described above as items 1129–30.

*   Plüddemann, Martin. *Die Bühnenfestspiele in Bayreuth, ihre Gegner und ihre Zukunft.* Described as item 901.

Defends Wagner against critical attacks associated with and launched during the 1876 Festival.

Festivals held prior to World War I (1876–1914)
Two studies deal exclusively with Festival visitors and their impressions:

1132. *Bayreuth, The Early Years: An Account of the Early Decades of the Wagner Festival as Seen by the Celebrated Visitors and Participants,* ed. Robert Hartford. London and New York: Cambridge University Press, 1980. 284pp. ISBN 0521238226 ML410.W2B265 1980

Includes observations garnered from the writings of visitors to and performers at Bayreuth between 1876 and 1914, among them Walter Crane, J. W. Davison (see item 278), Gabriel Fauré, Edvard Grieg, Lill Lehmann, Angelo Neumann (see item 287), Romain Rolland, Camille Saint-Saëns, Igor Stravinsky, Mark Twain, and Sir Henry Wood. A preliminary essay ("Richard Wagner and the Idea of the Festival," pp. 15–43) provides historical context. Illustrated with images of the Festspielhaus auditorium and orchestra pit, the swimming apparatus used to support the Rhinemaidens in 1876, and drawings of Wagner taking part in Festival rehearsals. Also includes several appendices and a list of sources (pp. 275–78); concludes with several indexes.

1133. Habermann, Sylvia. *Der Auftritt des Publikums: Bayreuth und seine Festspielgäste im Kaiserreich, 1876 bis 1914.* Bayreuth: "Druckhaus Bayreuth," 1991. 48pp. ML410.W2H313 1991 (no ISBN available)

A "who's who" of early Bayreuth Festival guests, illustrated with photographs of them and the places they visited, as well as facsimiles of newspaper articles and advertisements, playbills, and so on. Habermann's volume served as the catalog of an exhibition held in Bayreuth during the summer of 1991.

More than a few Festival guidebooks were also printed prior to 1914:

1134. Bahr-Mildenburg, Anna, and Hermann Bahr. *Bayreuth,* 4th ed. Leipzig: Rowohlt, 1912. 114pp. ML410.W2B2

A cursory history of the Festspielhaus and the performances associated with it, from Cosima to the "present time," together with comments on the construction and character of Haus Wahnfried, and raising monies to sponsor the Festivals of 1876 and 1882. No bibliography or index. Earlier editions identify only Anna Bahr-Mildenburg as author.

1135. *Bayreuth. Ein Wegweiser durch die Stadt und Umgebung unter besonderer Berücksichtigung der Bühnenfestspiele. Zugleich eine kurze Chronik von Bayreuth*, 4th enlarged ed. Bayreuth: Carl Giessel, 1889. 130pp. (no LC number available)

A high-quality tourist brochure, probably purchased primarily by Festival visitors. Includes 26 pages of additional information (numbered i–xxvi at the end of the volume) concerning the Festivals of 1876 and 1882 to 1883, including the names of all ticket holders. Also includes color-highlighted fold-out maps of Bayreuth, a seating diagram of the Festspielhaus, and a few other illustrations; among the last is a frontispiece portrait of Luitpold, then Bavaria's Prince-Regent and "Protector of the Bayreuth Bühnenfestspiel." Uncommon; Harvard's Loeb Music Library owns a copy (shelf-number Mus. 5662.450).

1136. Redesdale (Lord). *Bayreuth in 1912*. London: Ballentyne, 1912. 44pp. (no LC number available)

An unintentionally amusing sketch of Bayreuth and its musical treasures, written by a British peer who acknowledges Wagner as a socially acceptable "gentleman" (unlike the ill-educated and tasteless Mozart!), and praises him for his classical erudition and "indomitable courage" (pp. 22–23). Uncommon; the University of Toronto Music Library owns a copy.

1137. Wolzogen, Hans von. *Bayreuth*, 3rd ed. Leipzig: C. F. W. Siegel, n.d. 81pp. (no LC number available)

A guide to the Festival rather than the town, written by a leading Wagnerian of his day and published in cooperation with the magazine *Die Musik*. Includes 21 full-page illustrations (several of them foldouts), among them a frontispiece of the Wagner bust by Lorenz Gedon. Not to be confused with Wolzogen's *Wagneriana* (Leipzig, 1888); see item 45.

Festivals held between World War I and the collapse of Hitler's Germany (1914–1945)
Among the few publications to deal specifically and more or less exclusively with the Festivals of the 1920s, 1930s, and early 1940s is:

1138. Hanisch, Ernst. "The Political Influence and Appropriation of Wagner," trans. Paul Knight. In item 2, pp. 186–201.

Explains that, although Wagner "cannot be reduced to Hitler's idiosyncratic view of him" (p. 186), the composer as well as his milieu and
legacy—German nationalism of the 1870s, the cataclysmic events leading
up to and away from the First World War, and the Nazis' embracing of
Wagner as one of their cultural heroes—helped make the composer synonymous in many minds with the atrocities of the Third Reich, even as
"Bayreuth helped [Hitler] ideologically by making him respectable in the
eyes of the bourgeoisie" (p. 200). See also Hanisch's essay "Ein Wagnerianer Namens Adolf Hitler" (in item 35, pp. 65–76).

*   Wagner, Friedelind, with Page Cooper. *Heritage of Fire*. Described below
         as item 1174.

A first-hand account of Hitler's Bayreuth, written by one of the composer's granddaughters. Also available in English under the title *The Royal
Family of Bayreuth*.

Festivals held since 1945: see also items 847–49

*The literature concerning Bayreuth after World War II is considerable. Among
general introductions to the "new Bayreuth" is:*

1139. Herzfeld, Friedrich. *Das neue Bayreuth*. Berlin: Rembrandt, 1960. 63pp.
      ML410.W2H36

A pocketbook discussion of Wieland Wagner's Bayreuth Festivals, beginning in 1951. Illustrated with a scattering of poorly printed black-and-
white portraits and photographs; also equipped with a list of Wagner
recordings (pp. 62–63). No musical examples, bibliography, or index.

Other descriptions of post-World War II Bayreuth and its Festivals include:

1140. *Bayreuth-Brevier. Ein Führer für den Festspielgast*, ed. Volker Gondrom.
      Bayreuth: Niehrenheim, 1970. 149pp. ML410.W2G62

A guidebook-*cum*-essay collection devoted to Bayreuth as a city, the Wagner Festival as a local institution, and Franken as a region (i.e., northern
Bavaria, where Bayreuth is located), as well as information about 1970s
hotels, restaurants, bars, and other "important" local addresses. Includes
an essay by Erich Rappl commemorating twenty years of the "new" or
"post-World War II Bayreuth" and comments by Curt von Westernhagen.
Also includes scattered illustrations of the town, various rehearsals and
productions, and a map of the city. Information about the authors appears
on the last page of the volume.

1141. Müller, Marieluise. *Bayreuth ist anders. Festspielgespräche.* Bayreuth: Ellwanger, 1994. 160pp. ISBN 3925361197 (no LC number available)

Describes and evaluates Bayreuth from 1967 to 1994 in brief comments provided by conductors, singers, orchestral performers, office staff, Festival visitors, town residents, and a variety of other individuals; nevertheless, more a description of the city and its Festival as phenomena than a performance study. Some contributors are famous, Patrice Chéreau and Wolfgang Wagner among them; others are not. Illustrated with photos of the contributors themselves. No bibliography or index.

1142. Wagner, Nike. "Bayreuth—?" (trans. Detlev Rotweiler). *The Musical Quarterly* 78 (1994), pp. 159–70. ML1.M725

Calls for a reinvigoration of the "Bayreuth monoculture," so long dependent on churning out productions of the master's works, often without serious reconsideration of the works themselves. A thoughtful essay by a great-granddaughter of the composer who also published a book entitled *Wagner Theater* (Frankfurt a.M., 1998). Includes two photographs.

WAGNER'S FAMILY AND DESCENDENTS: FROM 1883 TO THE PRESENT

General Studies

The following volumes are but two of dozens that deal mostly with the Wagner family and its relationship to the Bayreuth Festivals:

1143. Wagner, Nike. *The Wagners: The Dramas of a Musical Dynasty,* trans. Ewald Osers and Michael Downes. Princeton, NJ: Princeton University Press, 1998. xvi, 327pp. ISBN 069108811XML410.W13W11213 1998

A lively introduction to the Wagner family as a whole, as well as an evaluation of Wagner's ideas and works "in theory" and "on stage." Includes a gathering of black-and-white portrait photographs and a few documentary facsimiles bound between pp. 140–41; also includes a family tree (pp. xviii–xix) and scattered quotations from a variety of sources. No footnotes, endnotes, or bibliography, however. Indexed.

1144. Wagner, Wolf Siegfried. *The Wagner Family Albums: Bayreuth 1876–1976,* trans. Susanne Flatauer. London: Thames & Hudson, 1976. 160pp. ISBN 0500011538 ML410.W192G413

An iconography of value for students of Wagner's marriage, children, and musical influences. Includes hundreds of black-and-white portraits and photographs of Cosima, Friedelind, Gertrud, Isolde, Siegfried, Wieland, Winifred, and Wolfgang Wagner, as well as information about other family members, Festspielhaus management history, Hitler's visits to Bayreuth, and the impact of two world wars on Wagner's reputation. Concludes with a one-page bibliography.

A more compact introduction to the Wagner family and the Bayreuth Festivals is:

1145. Eger, Manfred. "The Bayreuth Festival and the Wagner Family," trans. Stewart Spencer. In item 2, pp. 485–501.

Describes Wagner's lifelong quest for perfect musical-dramatic production circumstances, culminating in his choice of Bayreuth, construction of the Festival Theater, and the roles played by various family members in maintaining and/or altering the character of Festival activities and productions. Eger does not pause to mention the names and dates of many celebrated Bayreuth events.

Studies of Individual Wagner Family Members

At least half a dozen Wagners have played major roles—acknowledged through publications of their own, or evaluated in the books and articles written by others—in keeping the composer's memory, and especially his Festival, alive in Bayreuth. Studies of the Wagners are dealt with below first by generation, then by individual family member, and finally in alphabetical order by author and/or title:

Cosima [*née Liszt, later von Bülow*] **Wagner:** Wife of Richard Wagner and Mother (by him) of Siegfried, Isolde, and Eva
Stories of Cosima's life include this useful volume:

1146. Marek, George R. *Cosima Wagner.* New York: Harper & Row, 1981. xii, 291pp. ISBN 006012704X ML410.W133M4

A straightforward biography, illustrated with nine photographs and family portraits—among the latter, Friedrich Preller's drawing of Cosima at eighteen. Includes a list of Bayreuth performances "under Cosima's direction" given between 1886 and 1906 (p. 279) as well as a bibliography (pp. 281–84) and index.

NB: Many Wagnerians interest themselves only in Cosima's "later" life (or *zweites Leben*; see item 1150), although some 200 pages of Marek's volume are devoted to the years prior to Wagner's death. Nevertheless, studies of her girlhood and young adulthood also exist; see items

1147–49 below, for instance, as well as Alice Hunt Sokoloff's *Cosima Wagner, Extraordinary Daughter of Franz Liszt* (New York, 1969). Sokoloff's monograph was reviewed by Robert Donington in *Notes* 27 (1970–1971), p. 270.

Other general studies of Cosima as individual and Bayreuth as institution include:

1147. Giroud, Françoise. *Cosima la sublime.* Paris: Fayard/Plon, 1996. 282pp. ISBN 2213595321 ML429.W133G57 1996X

A popular biography, supplemented by a collection of often-reproduced portraits and photographs as well as a brief bibliography (pp. 281–82). No index.

1148. Millenkovich-Morold, Max. *Cosima Wagner. Ein Lebensbild.* Leipzig: Philipp Reclam jun., 1937. 489pp. ML410.W11C633

Published when the Third Reich was at the height of its "glory." Illustrated with a variety of portraits, photographs, and documentary facsimiles, none of them very interesting. Includes a brief bibliography (pp. 479–81); concludes with an index.

1149. Moulin-Eckart, Richard du. *Cosima Wagner: Ein Lebens- und Charakterbild.* Munich and Berlin: Drei Masken, 1929. x, 1,024pp. ML410.W11C62

Examines Cosima's life as a whole. Includes discussions of her relationships with her father, Liszt, and her mother, the Comtesse Marie d'Agoult; more of the volume, however, is taken up with Cosima's marriages—first to Hans von Bülow, then to Wagner—as well as observations on the activities of her children and grandchildren. Illustrated with 22 plates of portraits, places, and documentary facsimiles; among the last is a reproduction of the original title/dedication page for the *Siegfried-Idyll.* Indexed. Also translated into English by Catherine Alison Phillips as *Cosima Wagner,* 2 vols. (New York, 1930).

Collections of Cosima's massive correspondence include this anthology:

1150. *Cosima Wagner: Das zweite Leben. Briefe und Aufzeichnungen, 1883–1930,* ed. Dietrich Mack. Munich and Zurich: Piper, 1980. 897pp. ISBN 3492024726 ML429.W133A4 1980

A massive collection of documents, most of them dating from the last decades of the nineteenth century and a great many of them letters Cosima exchanged with a variety of individuals. Mack also provides an introduction, a timeline (pp. 27–30), genealogical information about Cosima's antecedents and descendents, and notes associated with the documents themselves (pp. 767–872); concludes with an index.

Other collections of Cosima's letters are described below in alphabetical order by sole or primary recipient (if a Wagner family member, by first name):

1151. *Cosima Wagners Briefe an ihre Tochter Daniela von Bülow, 1866–1885, nebst fünf Briefen Richard Wagners,* ed. Max von Waldberg. Stuttgart and Berlin: J. G. Cotta, 1933. xx, 376pp. ML410.W11C5

Includes the texts of 192 letters from Cosima to her daughter Daniela, as well as five letters Richard Wagner addressed to the same young woman. Includes an introduction (pp. v–xx) and four illustrations: a frontispiece portrait of Cosima; a photograph of Cosima with Daniela, taken in 1865; and two letter facsimiles, bound as foldouts. No bibliography; concludes with an index.

1152. *Cosima Wagner und Houston Stewart Chamberlain im Briefwechsel, 1888–1908,* ed. Paul Pretzsch; 2nd ed. Leipzig: Philipp Reclam jun., 1934. 714pp. ML410.W11C53

Reproduces the texts of hundreds of letters exchanged by the composer's widow and his apostle: the Englishman who preached "German" doctrines involving race and the Jews (note the date of publication above) in dozens of his own books and articles. Illustrated with seventeen portraits and documentary facsimiles, including a photograph of Chamberlain reproduced as a frontispiece. Outfitted with an introduction by the editor (pp. 7–13) and a fine index.

1153. *Briefe. Eine erstaunliche Korrespondenz. Cosima Wagner und Ludwig II. von Bayern,* ed. Martha and Horst Heinrich Schad. Bergisch Gladbach: Gustav Lübbe, 1996. 576pp. ISBN 3785708319 ML429.W133A4 1996

Presents the complete texts, never previously published, of 228 letters addressed by Cosima to the Bavarian king between 1865 and 1885. Includes an introductory essay by the editors entitled "Ludwig-Richard-Cosima" (pp. 7–25), as well as a concordance of the letters themselves (pp. 557–63) and a bibliography (pp. 564–69); concludes with an index. Illustrated with a facsimile of Cosima's handwriting that serves as a frontispiece.

1154. *Cosima Wagner: Briefe an Ludwig Schemann,* ed. Bertha Schemann. Regensburg: Gustav Bosse, 1937. 84pp. ML410.W11C54

Includes the texts of 42 letters addressed by Cosima between 1877 and 1902 to Schemann, a financial supporter of the Festival in its early years, and later a disciple of the prominent racist Count Joseph Gobineau. Illustrated with a black-and-white frontispiece portrait of Cosima and a fold-out facsimile, printed on blue paper and devoted to the first letter in the collection, dated 27 September 1877. No bibliography or index.

1155. *Cosima Wagner—Richard Strauss: Ein Briefwechsel*, ed. Franz Trenner and Gabriele Strauss. Veröffentlichungen der Richard-Strauss-Gesellschaft München, 2. Tutzing: Hans Schneider, 1978. 312pp. ISBN 3795202582 ML410.W11C555

Comprises several collections of letters—chief among them 177 of Cosima's letters to Strauss, dated 1889 to 1906 (pp. 1–258), and twenty of Siegfried Wagner's letters to the same composer, dated 1890 to 1928 (pp. 259–82). Concludes with an index of names. Published in a series underwritten by the Richard Strauss Society of Munich.

Other documentary anthologies devoted largely to Cosima's activities on behalf of the Wagner legend and family fortunes include:

1156. *Besuch bei Cosima: Eine Begegnung mit dem alten Bayreuth. Mit einem Fund der Briefe Cosima Wagners*, ed. Vladimir Karbusicky. Hamburg: von Bockel, 1997. 78pp. ISBN 3928770969 ML429.W133B47 1997X

A glimpse of "Old Bayreuth" in the form of quotations from Cosima's correspondence and diary entries outfitted with linking text. Karbusicky provides facsimiles of a number of documents, including one of a letter Cosima addressed to the singer Bertha Lauterer; he also provides a few pictures and photos of Wagnerian places. No bibliography or index.

1157. *Cosima Wagner-Liszt: Der Weg zum Wagner-Mythos. Ausgewählte Schriften des ersten Wagner-Enkels und sein unveröffentlichter Briefwechsel mit Thomas Mann*, ed. Franz W. Beidler. Bielefeld: Pendragon, 1997. 427pp. ISBN 3923306865 ML410.W11B45 1997

Reminiscences of Haus Wahnfried and the Bayreuth circle by Franz Beidler (1901–1981), son of Isolde Beidler *neé* "von Bülow," because—although Isolde was, in fact, the oldest daughter of Richard and Cosima Wagner, she was known by the surname of Cosima's first husband, from whom Cosima was not yet divorced when her daughter was born. Beidler's memories make up much of the volume, but Franz W. Beidler—the older Beidler's son and Wagner's great-grandson—also includes, as editor, excerpts from his father's literary works, the texts of letters the older

Beidler exchanged with Mann (pp. 303–59), as well as an afterword by
Dieter Borchmeyer (pp. 361–424) and a list of previous publications
where portions of the letters included in this volume appeared in print (pp.
425–26). Includes scattered photographs of Wagner family members, as
well as notes for some chapters and sections, but no bibliography or index.

1158. Prod'homme, J. G. "Correspondence of Cosima Wagner with Victor
Wilder," trans. Theodore Baker. *The Musical Quarterly* 8 (1922), pp.
44–52. ML1.M725

Reproduces and describes several of Cosima's letters, all of them dating
from 1885, to a French translator of Wagner's librettos. No illustrations or
musical examples.

Siegfried Wagner: Son of Richard and Cosima Wagner

*Wagner's only son and heir to the Bayreuth legacy was a composer in his own
right, as well as an accomplished operatic director and manager. Useful summaries of his character and activities in these capacities include:*

1159. Pachl, Peter P. *Siegfried Wagner: Genie im Schatten*. Munich: Nyphen-
burger, 1988. 544pp. ISBN 3485005762 ML410.W24P2 1988

Examines the career and compositions of a talented son who nevertheless
stands today in the shadow of his even more talented father. Pachl
describes Siegfried Wagner's personal and professional activities; he also
provides a timeline (pp. 449–55), a discography of recorded works (pp.
334–36), a bibliography (pp. 525–33), and a guide to *Der Bärenhäuter*, the
younger Wagner's best-known opera (pp. 457–524), itself illustrated with
production photos; the volume as a whole contains some 154 mostly
black-and-white illustrations: family portraits, a few documentary facsimiles, and even a horoscope! (p. 10). Concludes with an index.

Other studies of Siegfried Wagner's life and musical career include:

1160. Glasenapp, Carl Friedrich. *Siegfried Wagner und seine Kunst*. Leipzig:
Breitkopf & Härtel, 1911. 423pp. (no LC number available)

A collection of essays, most of them devoted to individual dramatic compositions. Worth looking at today, if only for its handsome page designs,
Fraktur typeface, and beautiful woodcut illustrations by Franz Staffen. A
few musical motives appear as chapter headings. No bibliography; concludes with a general index. A pamphlet-length publication of Glasenapp's, entitled merely *Siegfried Wagner* (Berlin, 1906), appeared as Vol.
15 of the "Das Theater" series.

1161. Kraft, Zdenko von. *Der Sohn: Siegfried Wagners Leben und Umwelt.* Graz and Stuttgart: Leopold Stocker, 1969. 344pp. ML410.W24K7

A straightforward biography rather than musical study. Kraft mentions his subject's compositions but concerns himself more with the Bayreuth Festival as part of Siegfried Wagner's intellectual and spiritual "environment." Illustrated with a variety of portraits, photographs, caricatures, and documentary facsimiles; among the last is a frontispiece reproducing in color a diploma and medal, dated 22 May 1913 (the centenary of Richard Wagner's birth), conferring honorary Bayreuth citizenship upon the composer's "son." Also includes a brief foreword by Winifred Wagner, Siegfried's wife (p. 5), and an appendix concerning Bayreuth Festival activities from 1931 to 1944 (pp. 299–336). No bibliography; concludes with an index. Draws upon Siegfried Wagner's own reminiscences, published as *Erinnerungen* (Stuttgart, 1923).

1162. Schmitz, Eugen. "Siegfried Wagner." *Die Musik* 8/3 (1908–1909), pp. 21–34. ML5.M9

When this article appeared in print Siegfried Wagner had already assumed responsibility for the annual Bayreuth Festivals. Useful especially for comments on some of his earlier compositions. Includes nine musical examples.

The most complete discussion of Siegfried Wagner's compositions remains:

1163. Pachl, Peter P. *Siegfried Wagners musik-dramatische Schaffen.* Tutzing: Hans Schneider, 1979. ix, 195pp. ISBN 3795202485 ML410.W24P3

Identifies and discusses the subject's music dramas, among them *Herzog Wildsang*, *Der Kobold*, and *Schwarzschwanenreich*. Pachl illustrates his explanations with 63 musical examples; he also provides 194 visual images—among them a color frontispiece that reproduces a portrait of Siegfried Wagner painted by his son Wieland, a number of facsimiles, family portraits, and photos of stage sets. Concludes with a bibliography (pp. 171–79) and index.

Other, more specialized compositional studies include:

1164. Daube, Otto. *Siegfried Wagner und das Märchenoper.* Leipzig: Deutscher Theater-Verlag, 1936. 139pp. ML410.W24D3

Devoted for the most part to an evaluation of the "fairy-tale operas," especially *Der Bärenhäuter* and *An allem ist Hütchen schuld*, in terms of their subjects, musical style and content, texts, and certain romantic elements manifest in them. Daube also devotes one chapter to his subject's life and activities. Illustrated with a scattering of family photos, production designs, and documentary facsimiles; also contains several dozen musical examples.

1165. Gunter-Kornagel, Luise. *Siegfried Wagners Opernschaffen. Zwischen Mythos, Mystik und Realität.* Wolfratshausen: J. L. G. Grimm, 1995. 465pp. ISBN 3980269523 ML410.W1G82 1995

A study of works in performance. Gunther-Kornagel provides color facsimiles of set and costume designs rather than photographs of recent performances; black-and-white portraits and other visual images are also scattered throughout her volume, and a photograph of Siegfried himself is reproduced as a frontispiece. Also includes a timeline spanning 1869 to 1930 (pp. 19–25), a bibliography (pp. 455–63), and a list of the composer's works (p. 464). No musical examples, however. See also Gunter-Kornagel's *Weltbild in Siegfried Wagners Opern* (Karlsruhe, 1998), which includes an impressive collection of color illustrations entitled "Die Opern in Bildern" (pp. 545–634) and a bibliography (pp. 527–38).

Winifred [Klindworth] Wagner: Daughter-in-law of Richard Wagner and wife of Siegfried Wagner

1166. Schertz-Parey, Walter. *Winifred Wagner: ein Leben für Bayreuth.* Graz and Stuttgart: Leopold Stocker, 1999. 312pp. ISBN 3702008586 ML429.W136S34 1999

A biography that conceals even as it reveals; Nazi issues are examined rather perfunctorily, and Schertz-Parey does everything possible to flatter Winifred Wagner, his subject. Includes interesting interview material as well as observations about film director Hans-Jürgen Syverberg and several of his Wagner projects. Also includes a variety of scattered black and white Wagner family portraits and photographs as well as two useful family trees ("the Wagners," pp. 306–7; and "the Klindworths," pp. 308–9); concludes with a cursory bibliography rather than an index.

NB: Ernst Hanisch has pointed out that Winifred Wagner helped bring "Bayreuth and national socialism together, as Hitler appreciatively noted" (item 1138 above, p. 200), and that she became one of the Führer's "show women," with whom he was *per du*—on intimate terms insofar as German forms of address are concerned. See also Nike Wagner's article " 'To Us He Was the Führer': On Winifred Wagner," published in *Wagner* 21/2 (July 2000), pp. 75–86.

Wieland Wagner: Grandson of Richard Wagner and son of Siegfried and Winifred Wagner

Although not a composer of consequence, Wieland Wagner is nevertheless better known today than his father Siegfried; his fame devolves especially upon his revolutionary Wagner productions and his role in restoring life and health to the Bayreuth Festival after World War II. Accounts of his life and activities include:

1167. Skelton, Geoffrey. *Wieland Wagner: The Positive Skeptic*. London: Victor Gollancz, 1971. 222pp. ISBN 0575007095 ML420.W135S6

A study especially of the director, emphasizing especially his Bayreuth productions. Includes a large number of illustrations, most of them photos of stage sets, as well as a frontispiece portrait of Wieland; also includes a scattering of short musical examples and a facsimile of a letter Wieland addressed in 1944 to Kurt Overhoff of the Salzburg Mozarteum, Overhoff being an important influence on Wieland's career as a whole. Outfitted with a list of Wieland's productions at a variety of theaters, 1936 to 1966 (pp. 203–14), and a bibliography (pp. 215–16). Indexed.

* Lust, Claude. *Wieland Wagner et la survie des théâtre lyrique*. Described as item 857.

Describes Wieland Wagner's staging concepts and techniques. Also includes a list of Wieland's productions.

1168. Panofsky, Walter. *Wieland Wagner*. Bremen: Carl Schünemann, 1964. 104pp. ML410.W245P3

Mostly a black-and-white picture book devoted to Wieland Wagner's Bayreuth productions from 1951 to 1962. Includes a catalog of the productions themselves (pp. 99–104) as well as an introductory essay; concludes with an index.

1169. Wessling, Berndt W. *Wieland Wagner der Enkel: eine Biographie*. Cologne-Rodenkirchen: P. J. Tonger, 1997. 445pp. ISBN 3920950283 ML429.W135W47 1997

A full-fledged biography of "Uncle Wieland," illustrated with a variety of portraits, family photographs, and other images—including a few caricatures. Wessling does his best to appear impartial and confronts most of the links between the Wagner family and the Nazis. Includes a brief bibliography (pp. 434–35), as well as a more extensive index.

Gertrud [Reissinger] Wagner: Wife of Grandson Wieland Wagner

1170. Schostack, Renate. *Hinter Wahnfrieds Mauern: Gertrud Wagner—ein Leben.* Hamburg: Hoffmann & Campe, 1998. 448pp. ISBN 3455035350 ML429.W135S36 1998

A straightforward life story of the director's wife and helpmate. Illustrated with a few photographs and outfitted with a brief bibliography (pp. 442–43) and an index.

Wolfgang Wagner: Grandson of Richard Wagner and son of Siegfried and Winifred Wagner

Also familiar to opera-goers as a director and manager of the Bayreuth Festivals after brother Wieland's death in 1966 is Wolfgang Wagner. Among publications about him is his own account of his life and activities:

1171. *Acts: The Autobiography of Wolfgang Wagner,* trans. John Brownjohn. London: Weidenfeld & Nicholson, 1994. xii, 324pp. ISBN 0297813498 ML420.W137A3 1994

The self-told life story of one of the twentieth-century's foremost operatic producers and impresarios. Illustrated with sixteen plates of portraits and photographs. Also includes three appendices: the first identifies the 321 performances of Richard Wagner's music dramas presented at Bayreuth during Wolfgang Wagner's management of that theater (p. 282); the second presents cast lists for each of those performances (pp. 283–311); and the third reproduces the text of Siegfried and Winifred Wagner's last will and testament, dated 8 March 1929 (pp. 312–13). Concludes with a useful index.

Other books devoted to Wolfgang Wagner include:

1172. *Mit ihm: Musiktheatergeschichte. Wolfgang Wagner zum 75. Geburtstag: eine Ausstellung,* ed. Marion Linhardt. Tutzing: Hans Schneider, 1994. 223pp. ISBN 379520805X ML429.W137M58 1994

A collection of essays by Dieter Borchmeyer, Pierre Boulez, Walter Jens, and other Wagnerians that doubled as the catalog of an exhibition held in Eichstätt, Germany, in October 1994, and in Bayreuth the following January. Includes documentary appendices (pp. 187–222), among them complete cast lists for all Bayreuth performances from 1953 to 1994; also contains a photograph of Wolfgang Wagner as a frontispiece.

1173. *Wolfgang Wagner zum 50. Geburtstag.* Bayreuth: Edition Musica, 1969. Unpaginated. ML55.W15W6

A collection of essays organized and apparently edited by the Festspielhaus staff. Includes contributions by Jim Ford ("Wotan's Ring"), Paul-André Gaillard, and Martin Gregor-Dellin. Illustrated with a variety of production photographs and a handful of other images, including three caricatures of Wolfgang himself drawn in 1954, 1957, and 1968. No bibliography or index.

Franz W. Beidler: grandson of Cosima Wagner and son of Franz Beidler and Isolde von Bülow [Wagner]

* *Cosima Wagner-Liszt: Der Weg zum Wagner-Mythos.* Described as item 1157.

A collection of reminiscences and other documents. See also item 983.

Friedelind Wagner: Granddaughter of Richard Wagner and daughter of Siegfried and Winifred Wagner

1174. Wagner, Friedelind, with Page Cooper. *Heritage of Fire: The Story of Richard Wagner's Granddaughter.* London: Eyre & Spottiswoode, 1948. x, 203pp. DD247.W3A3 1948

Personal, family, and Bayreuth reminiscences that cast a great deal of light on Hitler's relationship with the Wagner family. Friedelind Wagner herself fled the Third Reich, was temporarily imprisoned in England, and was released thanks to the intervention of Arturo Toscanini. Illustrated with some half-dozen family photographs, including a frontispiece picture taken in 1941 of Friedelind and Toscanini as well as familiar images of Haus Wahnfried and the Festspielhaus. Also includes a family tree (p. 2). Unindexed

Published for the first time in America in a slightly different version (New York, 1948); reprinted in that version by Greenwood in 1974 (ISBN 0837175739). Originally published in German as *Nacht über Bayreuth* (Bern, 1946). Also available in French.

Nike Wagner: Great-granddaughter of Richard Wagner and daughter of Wieland and Friedelind Wagner

See items 1142–1143.

Gottfried Wagner: Great-grandson of Richard Wagner and son of Wolfgang and Ellen [Drexel] Wagner

1175. Wagner, Gottfried. *He Who Does Not Howl With the Wolf. The Wagner Legacy: An Autobiography*, trans. Della Couling. London: Sanctuary, 1997. 335pp. ISBN 1860742289 ML429.W134A3 1997

A self-told life story full of observations about Wagner's musical and cultural legacy, especially his anti-semitism, as well as the Wagner cult promulgated by leaders of the Third Reich and attempts to cover up Bayreuth's involvement in Hitler's Germany. Among the most outspoken "enemies" of the Bayreuth conservatives, Gottfried Wagner has been applauded in Israel for his outspoken denunciations of his great-uncle's attitudes toward the Jews. Illustrated with three groups of portraits, caricatures, family photos—some of them quite recent—and other pictures. Includes a preface by Rabbi Julia Neuberger (pp. 11–13), an introduction by Ralph Giordano (pp. 15–26), and a few notes (pp. 325–28) as well as an index.

Originally published as *Wer nicht mit dem Wolf heult. Autobiographische Aufzeichnungen eines Wagner-Urenkels*, 2nd ed. (Cologne 1997; ISBN 3462026224). Recently revised and published in English as *The Wagner Legacy: An Antobiography*, trans. Couling (London, 2000). Another English-language edition, published under the title *Twilight of the Wagners: The Unveiling of a Family's Legacy*, also translated by Couling, appeared in the United States in 1999. At the time the present research guide went to press, the author had not been able to compare these editions with one another.

Index of Authors, Editors, and Translators

Authors, editors, and translators are identified by item numbers or, in the case of **bold italic** numerals, by page numbers in chapter I. Authors, editors, and translators of items merely mentioned in observations or annotations are identified by item numbers in parentheses. A very few items are identified by footnotes attached to item and/or page numbers. Thus "Abbate, Carolyn, *6*" for a reference to page 6 in chapter I; "Abbate, Carolyn, 481" for a reference to the author of that item; "Abbate, Carolyn, (619)" for reference to a publication discussed in the annotation to the item in parentheses; and so on.